# TWO ALONE,
# TWO TOGETHER

*Also edited by Sonia Gandhi*

FREEDOM'S DAUGHTER:
  *Letters between Indira Gandhi and Jawaharlal Nehru 1922–39*

# TWO ALONE, TWO TOGETHER

## LETTERS BETWEEN INDIRA GANDHI AND JAWAHARLAL NEHRU

### 1940-1964

❧

*Edited by*
Sonia Gandhi

Hodder & Stoughton
LONDON SYDNEY AUCKLAND

**British Library Cataloguing in Publication Data**

Two alone, two together: Letters between Indira
Gandhi and Jawaharlal Nehru, 1940–64.
I. Gandhi, Sonia
954.04092

ISBN 0-340-50287-8

First published in Great Britain 1992

Published by Hodder and Stoughton,
a division of Hodder and Stoughton Ltd,
Mill Road, Dunton Green, Sevenoaks, Kent TN13 2YA.
Editorial Office: 47 Bedford Square, London WC1B 3DP.

Photoset by Rowland Phototypesetting Ltd,
Bury St Edmunds, Suffolk.

Printed in Great Britain by
St Edmundsbury Press Ltd, Bury St Edmunds, Suffolk

To Rajiv

# CONTENTS

Preface                                                                    xi

The Language of the Letters                                               xiii

Family Trees                                                               xiv

The Political Setting of the Early 1940s                                  xvii

Jawaharlal Nehru, Indira Gandhi and their Kinship Circle                  xix

Political Circle                                                          xxv

Circle of Friends                                                        xxxi

Journeys Undertaken by Jawaharlal Nehru
and Indira Gandhi between 1941 and 1963                                  xxxv

PART I: HOMECOMING (1940–1942)                                             I

PART II: PRISON WALLS (1942–1945)                                        145

PART III: TOWARDS FREEDOM (1945–1946)                                    509

PART IV: IN THE PRIME MINISTER'S HOUSE (1947–1962)                       545

Postscript                                                               675

Index                                                                    677

# ILLUSTRATIONS

between pages 314 and 315

Feroze and Indira on their way to India, 1941
Jawaharlal Nehru, Vijaya Lakshmi Pandit and Indira Nehru, 1942
The marriage of Feroze and Indira, 1942
With Rajiv, born 1944
With Sanjay, born 1946
Nehru with Indira, Feroze and Rajiv, 1945
Indira with Jawaharlal and a refugee girl, 1948
Teen Murti House, New Delhi
Children presenting flowers to Nehru on his birthday, 1953
Nehru, Indira and Feroze with Liaquat Ali Khan and Raana Begum, 1950
With Chou En-lai, 1954
With N. A. Bulganin, 1955
With Jammu and Kashmir folk dancers
With Clement Attlee, 1953
With Harry S. Truman, 1949
With John F. Kennedy and Jacqueline Kennedy, 1961
With Nigerian leaders, 1962
With a group of visitors at Teen Murti House
Feroze and Indira Gandhi
At an A.I.C.C. session, Madurai, 1961
At Bhubaneswar, 1964
The body of Jawaharlal Nehru lying in state

All the illustrations appear through the kind offices of the Indira Gandhi Memorial Trust, New Delhi.

# ACKNOWLEDGEMENTS

The poem 'I sit alone' by Walter de la Mare is quoted by kind permission of The Society of Authors; 'Mrs Reece Laughs' by Martin Armstrong is included by permission of Secker and Warburg; and 'Epitaph' by permission of HarperCollins Publishers. The poem 'In Memory of Shelley Wang' is quoted by kind permission of the author John Hewitt.

# PREFACE

This volume of the letters exchanged between Indira Gandhi and Jawaharlal Nehru covers the years 1940 to 1964.

As I had suggested in my Introduction to the earlier volume, Indira Nehru's stay in Oxford as a young scholar in the late 1930s witnessed an extraordinary maturing of her mind. She acquired, in this period, a substantial interest in world affairs, particularly as they impinged upon the liberation of India and the struggle between democracy and fascism. A brief spell of illness, which obliged her to recuperate in a sanatorium in Switzerland, deepened her introspection. The onset of the Second World War compelled her to return to India.

By the early 1940s Indira Gandhi had grown into an individual of depth and poise. In her marriage to Feroze Gandhi in August 1942, and in motherhood afterwards, she found emotional enrichment and fulfilment. She recorded in meticulous detail for her father each tender moment of motherhood, as she watched the flowering of a young life. The correspondence between Indira Gandhi and Jawaharlal Nehru when both were in prison is particularly poignant. They were lonely persons. Yet their minds were endowed with a rich interior landscape. Father and daughter shared a passion for books on a wide range of subjects. Above all, they loved the beauty of nature. One can see in Indira Gandhi's letters the making of the future crusader for ecological conservation. In this, as in other respects, she was so much ahead of her times.

The turn of events in 1946 brought Indira Gandhi and Jawaharlal Nehru to Delhi. Jawaharlal Nehru was now drawn into high political office and, from August 1947, he shaped the political destiny of India as Prime Minister. Since father and daughter lived under the same roof, the exchange of correspondence between them became infrequent. However, the notes which Indira Gandhi now addressed to Jawaharlal Nehru when she travelled to different parts of India, or overseas, show her in the role of a political activist. She always wanted to be near the scene of action, and she brought a penetrating intellect to bear on a variety of issues. She also acted as the eyes and ears of her father.

The 1950s served as a rewarding apprenticeship to power for Indira Gandhi. Yet her involvement in politics did not impoverish the richness of her inner life. As her letters written during these years show, even when she dwelt upon politics the personal ties which bound father and daughter together were reflected, again and again, in a chance phrase or a stray reference. Such a fusion of the public and the private worlds confers on these letters a distinctive quality. Indeed, the correspondence bears witness not only to the depth of the relationship between father and daughter but also to shared political and moral values. Jawaharlal Nehru had already made his mark on history; Indira Gandhi was destined to do so before long.

# The Language of the Letters

Jawaharlal Nehru and Indira Gandhi wrote to each other in English except when Indira was a young child. All the letters in this collection are in English unless otherwise indicated. At home, the Nehrus spoke Hindi with a liberal sprinkling of Urdu. But, like most Indians who have had the benefit of higher education, they were fluent in English and corresponded in English – except for Swarup Rani and Kamala Nehru.

The Nehrus were prolific letter-writers, Jawaharlal particularly. Letters with biographical and historical interest have been included in this book. Those of a routine nature have been deleted. Within the letters, to save space, passing references to relations and minor events have been omitted. It could be said that over three-quarters of the correspondence between father and daughter is included in the selection. The style of indicating dates and the spelling of names have been standardised as far as possible.

*Note about Names*
It is customary in Hindi and in other Indian languages to add the suffix -ji (sometimes written as -jee) to personal names, especially to the given names; it denotes respect or affection, as the case may be. In the case of men, the word 'Bhai' (which means 'brother') is often used (e.g. Madan Bhai). With women, the suffix commonly used is 'behn' or 'ben' in the North; or 'bai' in the South. Discrepancies in the form of names arise from the use of Hindi adaptations of Sanskrit names (e.g. Shri Shridhara Nehru, the original Sanskrit form, becoming Shri Shridhar, the Hindi version dropping the final 'a'). This practice has been given further currency due to westernisation. Another example of this is found in the suffix -pur (from the Sanskrit *pura*, town) anglicised to -pore, as in Alipore.

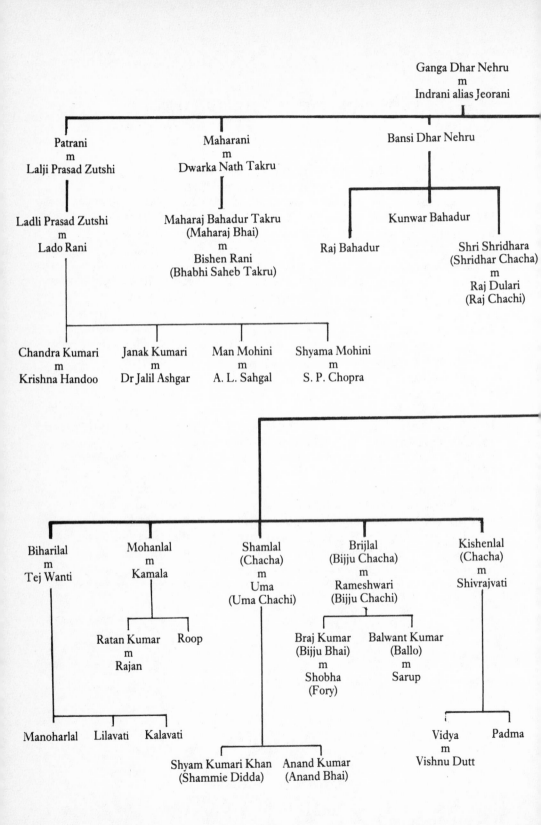

# NEHRU FAMILY

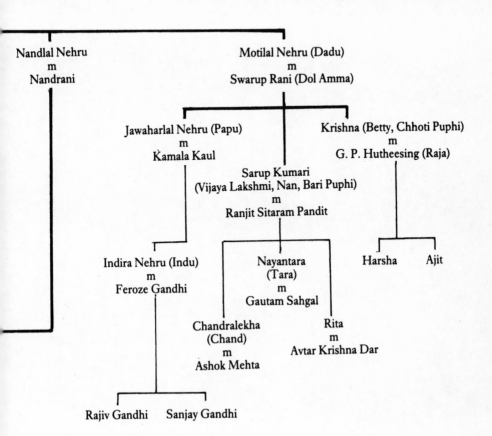

## KAUL FAMILY

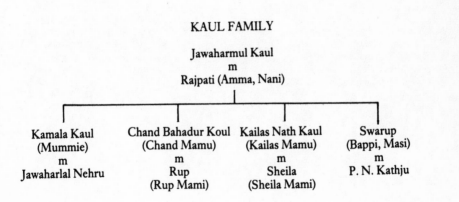

# THE POLITICAL SETTING OF THE EARLY 1940S

The year 1940 was a turbulent and eventful one in Indian politics. When the British Government declared India to be a belligerent in the war which had broken out between Great Britain and Nazi Germany in September 1939, the leaders of the Indian National Congress viewed such a declaration as unjustified, since the people of India, whom they represented, had not been consulted before the declaration of war. Indeed, the various Congress Governments which had been constituted in the Provinces of British India in 1937 resigned as a protest against the British move.

Among the leaders of the Congress, Mahatma Gandhi, Jawaharlal Nehru, Sardar Patel and Maulana Azad, to mention only a few, there was a feeling that the people of India were unequivocally opposed to the unilateral action of the British Government, and they would therefore seek to give expression to their resentment in an anti-imperialist struggle. Consequently, at the annual session of the Congress in Ramgarh in March 1940, a resolution was adopted, at the initiative of Jawaharlal Nehru, urging the British Government to commit itself to conferring independence upon India after the war, and also to constituting a Provincial Government with the participation of the nationalist leadership. A free India, it was pointed out, would readily join hands with the British in fighting Nazi Germany. Thereafter, there were several rounds of consultations between the Congress leaders and the British Government, as a result of which the Viceroy, Lord Linlithgow, issued a statement on 8th August, 1940, holding out: 1) that his Executive Council would be expanded to include nationalist leaders, who would also be invited to serve on a War Advisory Council; and 2) that the British Government would refrain from vesting governmental authority over India in the hands of a party which did not enjoy the confidence of all sections of Indian society.

The leaders of the Congress considered the Viceroy's statement wholly unsatisfactory. Indeed, the statement constituted an open invitation to the minorities to obstruct the attainment of independence by India. As a result of this, a decision was taken to initiate a movement of individual *satyagraha* in September 1940. This decision was taken as an interim measure, since the adoption of a mass *satyagraha* called for a period of intensive preparation before the signal for popular assault on the British Raj could be given. As we shall see, such a popular movement was actually initiated in August 1942, in the shape of the famous 'Quit India' Movement.

Indira Gandhi was a little over twenty-two in January 1940. She had last been with her father when she was in India between November 1938 and April 1939.

# Jawaharlal Nehru, Indira Gandhi and their Kinship Circle

Ganga Dhar Nehru: grandfather of Jawaharlal Nehru, he was a police officer in Delhi, from where he fled in 1857.

Motilal Nehru: father of Jawaharlal Nehru, Vijaya Lakshmi Pandit and Krishna Hutheesing. Prominent lawyer in Allahabad. Bought the house Anand Bhawan, Allahabad, in 1900. President of the sessions of the Indian National Congress in 1919 and 1928. Leader of the Swaraj Party in the Central Legislative Assembly. Indira called him Dadu, the Kashmiri variant of Dada, meaning grandfather.

Swarup Rani Nehru: mother of Jawaharlal Nehru. Indira as a young child called her Dol Amma because she used to give her sweets from a *doli*, or a cabinet, with doors of wire-mesh used for storing food (Amma = mother).

Kamala Nehru, née Kaul: married Jawaharlal Nehru in 1916. Gave birth to Indira in 1917. Active in the national movement. Suffered from a pulmonary ailment and died in 1936 at Lausanne.

Bibi Amma: widowed sister of Swarup Rani Nehru, who lived with the Nehrus in Anand Bhawan.

Feroze Gandhi: political activist from Allahabad. Studied at the London School of Economics. Married Indira in 1942. Member of the Constituent Assembly. Elected to the House of the People of the Indian Parliament in 1952 and 1957. Died in 1960 at the age of forty-eight.

Motilal Atal: great grandfather of Kamala Nehru. He was Prime Minister of Jaipur.

Rajpati Kaul (Amma or Nani): mother of Kamala Nehru, she was actively involved in the freedom movement and was imprisoned more than once.

Chand Bahadur Koul: brother of Kamala Nehru. He served in the State Bank of India.

Rup Koul: wife of Chand Bahadur Koul.

Ashok, Chitra, Om and Hari: children of Chand Bahadur and Rup Koul.

Kailas Nath Kaul: brother of Kamala Nehru. Indira refers to him as Mamu (maternal uncle). A botanist, he was Director of the National Botanical Garden and Vice-Chancellor of the Chandrashekhar Azad Agricultural University.

Sheila Kaul: wife of Kailas Nath Kaul. She was Minister of State for Education and Culture (1980–4) and is a General Secretary of the Indian National Congress.

Gautam Kaul: son of Kailas Nath and Sheila Kaul. Senior Officer in the Indian Police Service.

Swarup Kathju, née Kaul (Bappi): younger sister of Kamala Nehru.

P. N. Kathju: husband of Swarup Kathju (Bappi).

Naresh Kathju: son of P. N. and Swarup Kathju.

Madan Atal: cousin of Kamala Nehru. A physician, he accompanied Kamala Nehru to Europe during her last illness. He went to Spain in 1937 on a medical mission and led the medical mission sent by the Indian National Congress to China in 1938.

Brijlal Nehru (Bijju or Bijji Chacha): a nephew of Motilal Nehru, he grew up in Anand Bhawan and rose to be a senior official of the Indian Finance Department.

Rameshwari Nehru (Bijju or Bijji Chachi): wife of Brijlal Nehru. Active in politics, she was one of the founders of the All-India Women's Conference.

Balwant Kumar Nehru: referred to as Ballo, younger son of Brijlal and Rameshwari Nehru. Engineer and business executive. Currently Secretary of the Jawaharlal Nehru Memorial Fund.

Braj Kumar Nehru: referred to as Bijju, son of Brijlal and Rameshwari Nehru. A member of the Indian Civil Service, he was Indian Ambassador to the United States, 1961–8, Indian High Commissioner in London, 1973–7. Later he was Governor of Assam and of Jammu and Kashmir.

Shobha Nehru, also called Fory: Hungarian-born wife of Braj Kumar Nehru.

Vijaya Lakshmi Pandit, née Sarup Nehru: sister of Jawaharlal Nehru, born 1900. Called Nan, shortened form of Nanni or young girl. Married Ranjit S. Pandit. Indira Gandhi refers to her as Bari Puphi or Senior Aunt. Was Minister in the United Provinces. After independence, represented India in London, Moscow and Washington. President of the United Nations General Assembly. Governor of Maharashtra, 1962–4. Member of the Indian Parliament, 1964–8.

RANJIT SITARAM PANDIT: husband of Vijaya Lakshmi Pandit. Participated in the freedom movement. Imprisoned along with Jawaharlal Nehru.

CHANDRALEKHA MEHTA, NÉE PANDIT: eldest of Vijaya Lakshmi Pandit's three daughters. Referred to as Chand by Indira Gandhi.

NAYANTARA SAHGAL, NÉE PANDIT: second daughter of Vijaya Lakshmi Pandit. Author and novelist. Referred to as Tara.

RITA DAR, NÉE PANDIT: youngest daughter of Vijaya Lakshmi Pandit. Married to Avtar Krishna Dar of the Indian Foreign Service.

KRISHNA HUTHEESING, NÉE NEHRU: sister of Jawaharlal Nehru. Born 1907. Died 1967. Called Betty, the Anglicised form of Beti or daughter. Indira Gandhi refers to her as Chhoti Puphi or Junior Aunt.

G. P. HUTHEESING: husband of Krishna Hutheesing and known in the family as Raja. A member of the Socialist Party.

HARSHA HUTHEESING: son of Krishna and G. P. Hutheesing.

AJIT HUTHEESING: son of Krishna and G. P. Hutheesing. His wife is Amrita.

SHRI SHRIDHARA NEHRU: a cousin of Jawaharlal Nehru. Mathematician and civil servant. Indira Gandhi refers to him as Shridhar Chacha.

RAJ DULARI NEHRU: wife of Shri Shridhara Nehru. Indira Gandhi refers to her as Raj Chachi.

RATAN KUMAR NEHRU: a second cousin of Indira Gandhi. Was a member of the Indian Civil Service. Retired as head of the Foreign Office.

RAJAN NEHRU: wife of Ratan Kumar Nehru; a social worker.

SHAMLAL NEHRU: a cousin of Jawaharlal Nehru; journalist and politician.

UMA NEHRU: wife of Shamlal Nehru; active in nationalist politics.

ANAND KUMAR NEHRU: a cousin of Indira Gandhi.

SHYAM KUMARI KHAN: a niece of Jawaharlal Nehru. Active in politics and social work. Indira Gandhi called her Shammie Didda (Didda = elder sister).

LADLI PRASAD ZUTSHI: an uncle of Indira Gandhi; a lawyer.

CHANDRA KUMARI HANDOO, NÉE ZUTSHI: a cousin of Indira Gandhi.

KRISHNA HANDOO: husband of Chandra Kumari. Retired as Managing Director of State Bank.

JANAK KUMARI: a cousin of Indira Gandhi; an educationist and a nationalist. Married to Dr Jalil Ashgar.

SHYAMA MOHINI CHOPRA, NÉE ZUTSHI: a cousin of Indira Gandhi; participated in political activities.

MAN MOHINI SAHGAL, NÉE ZUTSHI: a cousin of Indira Gandhi. Indira Gandhi called her Manno Didda.

KALAVATI MADAN, NÉE NEHRU: a niece of Jawaharlal Nehru. Indira Gandhi called her Kala Didda.

VIDYAVATI DUTT, NÉE NEHRU: a niece of Jawaharlal Nehru.

PADMA SETH, NÉE NEHRU: a second cousin of Indira Gandhi.

KANWARLAL KATHJU (Nikku): a cousin of Jawaharlal Nehru.

MAHARAJ BAHADUR TAKRU: a cousin of Jawaharlal Nehru.

BISHEN RANI TAKRU: wife of Maharaj Bahadur Takru; Jawaharlal Nehru refers to her as Bhabhi Saheb Takru (Bhabhi = sister-in-law).

JANKI NATH SHURGA: husband of Jawaharlal Nehru's cousin Brij Mohan Rani.

SHIVRAJVATI NEHRU (Shona Chachi): wife of Kishenlal Nehru, who was a cousin of Jawaharlal Nehru.

MOTI KATHJU: a cousin of Jawaharlal Nehru. He worked for the *Pioneer*, Lucknow, before joining the Indian Army. He was a member of Wingate's expedition and was killed in May 1943 in a Japanese ambush in Burma.

ANAND BHAWAN: Motilal Nehru bought a large house which stood in groves measuring more than ten acres in 1900. It had been built some years earlier by a Judge of the Allahabad High Court. Motilal remodelled it to suit his needs and named it Anand Bhawan (Anand means joy or bliss and Bhawan means abode). In the late 1920s, Motilal built a smaller house on the same grounds, on which also he conferred the name Anand Bhawan, giving away the original house to the nation. The 'old' house, which was renamed Swaraj Bhawan (or Freedom House), was the headquarters of the Congress until India attained independence.

# POLITICAL CIRCLE

ABDULLAH, SHEIKH (1905–82): nationalist leader of Kashmir; spearheaded a democratic and secular movement against the Maharaja and suffered imprisonment; Prime Minister, Jammu & Kashmir, 1948–53, 1975–82.

AMRIT KAUR (1889–1964): disciple of Mahatma Gandhi, participated in the freedom struggle; Minister for Health, 1947–57.

ANSARI, M. A. (1880–1936): prominent physician; nationalist Muslim; President, Muslim League in 1920; actively participated in the Khilafat and non-cooperation movements; President, Indian National Congress in 1927.

AZAD, MAULANA ABUL KALAM (1888–1958): scholar, theologian, journalist and nationalist; entered politics and started the Urdu weeklies *Al-Hilal* and *Al-Balagh*; came into close contact with Mahatma Gandhi during the non-cooperation movement; President, Indian National Congress, 1923 and 1940–6; served as Education Minister, 1947–58.

BAJAJ, JAMNALAL (1889–1942): businessman and philanthropist who participated in India's struggle for freedom; took keen interest in Mahatma Gandhi's constructive work.

BOSE, SUBHAS CHANDRA (1897–1945): was selected for the Indian Civil Service in 1920 and resigned in 1921; joined the freedom struggle in 1921 and suffered imprisonment on many occasions; elected to the Bengal Legislative Council; President, Bengal Congress Committee for several years; President, Indian National Congress, 1938, re-elected, 1939; founded the Forward Bloc, 1939; escaped to Europe during the Second World War; organised the Indian National Army; died in a plane crash in 1945.

CHAMAN LALL, DIWAN (1892–1973): Labour leader and politician; Barrister; member, Indian Legislative Assembly, 1923–30, 1945–6, Punjab Legislative Assembly, 1937–45, Constituent Assembly, 1946–8; Ambassador to Turkey, 1948–9; member, Rajya Sabha, 1952–67.

CHATTOPADHYAYA, KAMALADEVI (1903–88): political activist, social worker and author connected with the theatre and handicrafts movements in India; associate of Mahatma Gandhi and Jawaharlal

Nehru; Secretary, All India Women's Conference; one of the founders of Congress Socialist Party, presided over its Meerut session, 1936; member, Congress Working Committee, 1946.

DESAI, MORARJI (1896): eminent politician; Chief Minister of Bombay, 1952–6; Union Minister of Commerce, 1956–8, and Finance, 1958–63; Prime Minister of India, 1977–9.

DOULATRAM, JAIRAMDAS (1892–1979): lawyer who participated in the national movement; General Secretary, Indian National Congress, 1931–4; Minister of Food and Agriculture, Government of India, 1948–50; Governor of Assam, 1950–6.

GUPTA, C. B. (1902–80): Congress leader from U.P.; participated in the freedom struggle and suffered imprisonment; held various ministerial portfolios in the U.P. Government, was also its Chief Minister, 1960–3, 1969–70.

HAKSAR, P. N. (1913): civil servant and intellectual; Secretary, Prime Minister's Secretariat, 1967–71; Principal Secretary to Prime Minister, 1971–3.

HUSAIN, DR ZAKIR (1897–1969): educationist; Vice-Chancellor of Jamia Millia Islamia, Delhi, 1926–48, and of Aligarh Muslim University, 1948–56; Governor of Bihar, 1957–62; Vice-President of India, 1962–7, and President, 1967–9.

JINNAH, MOHAMED ALI (1876–1948): barrister of Bombay; President of the Muslim League, 1916, 1920 and from 1934 till his death; a nationalist who later agitated for and presided over the creation of Pakistan.

KAMARAJ, K. (1903–75): Congress leader from Madras; Chief Minister of Madras, 1954–63; President, Indian National Congress, 1963–7.

KATJU, KAILASH NATH (1887–1968): Advocate of the Allahabad High Court; took part in India's freedom movement; member, Constituent Assembly, 1946–7; Governor of Orissa, 1947–8 and of West Bengal, 1948–51; Union Minister for Law, Home Affairs and Defence, 1952–7; Chief Minister of Madhya Pradesh, 1957–62.

KHAN, ABDUL GHAFFAR (1890–1988): Congress leader of the North-West Frontier Province, popularly known as Frontier Gandhi; before 1947 suffered imprisonment for his participation in the nationalist struggle; was later arrested by the Pakistan Government and held in prison for many years; awarded Bharat Ratna, 1987.

KHAN SAHEB, DR (1883–1958): brother of Khan Abdul Ghaffar Khan and a friend of Jawaharlal Nehru during his student days in London; Premier, N.W.F.P., 1937–9 and 1945–7; Chief Minister, West Pakistan, 1955–7.

KIDWAI, RAFI AHMED (1894–1954): Congress leader from U.P.; member, Indian Legislative Assembly, 1926–9; member, Congress Working Committee, 1947–51; Union Minister for Food and Agriculture, 1952–4.

KRIPALANI, J. B. (1888–1982): General Secretary of the Congress, 1934–46 and President, 1946; later resigned from the Congress; Chairman of the Praja Socialist Party and member, Lok Sabha, 1952–7, 1957–62 and 1963–70.

KRIPALANI, SUCHETA (1908–74): active in the national movement; member, Lok Sabha, 1952–60, 1967–70; Chief Minister of U.P., 1962–7.

MAHMUD, DR SYED (1889–1971): a noted barrister of Patna High Court; gave up practice to join the freedom struggle; Minister of Education and Development, Bihar, 1937–9; Minister of Development and Transport, Bihar, 1946–52; Union Minister of State for External Affairs, 1954–7.

MALAVIYA, KAPILDEV (1894–1944): nephew of Madan Mohan Malaviya. He was a leading criminal lawyer of Allahabad; gave up practice to join the non-cooperation movement in 1921 and suffered imprisonment; Chairman, Allahabad Municipal Board, 1925.

MALAVIYA, KESHAV DEV (1904–81): Congress leader from U.P.; joined the freedom struggle and courted jail several times; member, U.P. Legislative Assembly, 1946–51; Deputy Minister in the Union Government, 1954–7; Union Minister for Mines and Oil, 1957–63 and 1973–7.

MALAVIYA, PANDIT MADAN MOHAN (1861–1946): educationist and nationalist; President, Indian National Congress in 1909 and 1918; member of the Imperial Legislative Council; member, Swaraj Party and later organised the Nationalist Party; Founder of the Benares Hindu University.

MEHTA, JIVRAJ (1887–1978): physician and nationalist; Chief Minister, Gujarat, 1960–3; Indian High Commissioner, U.K., 1963–6; member, Lok Sabha, 1971–6.

MENON, K. P. S. (1898–1982): civil servant and diplomat; Ambassador to China, 1947; Foreign Secretary, 1948–52; Ambassador to the Soviet Union, 1952–61.

MENON, V. K. KRISHNA (1896–1974): Secretary of the India League in London, 1929–47; High Commissioner in London, 1947–52; member, Indian delegation to the United Nations, 1952–62; Minister without Portfolio, 1956–7, and for Defence, 1957–62.

MENON, V. P. (1894–1966): civil servant; Reforms Commissioner, 1942–7; Secretary to the Government of India, Ministry of States, 1947–51; member, Finance Commission, 1951–2.

NAIDU, SAROJINI (1879–1949): poetess and nationalist; President, Indian National Congress in 1925; attended the second Round Table Conference in 1931; Governor, U.P., 1947–9.

PANT, GOVIND BALLABH (1887–1961): Advocate and leader of the Swaraj Party in U.P. Council, 1923–30; suffered many terms of imprisonment; Premier, U.P., 1937–9 and Chief Minister, U.P., 1946–55; Home Minister, Government of India, 1955–61.

PATEL, SARDAR VALLABHBHAI (1875–1950): lawyer who became associated with Gandhi in 1918 and participated in the nationalist struggle; organised no-tax compaign in Bardoli, 1928, and thereafter came to be known as the Sardar (leader); President, Gujarat Congress Committee for many years; President, Indian National Congress in 1931; member, Interim Government, 1946–7; Deputy Prime Minister and Minister for Home, States, Information and Broadcasting, 1947–50.

PRASAD, RAJENDRA (1884–1963): lawyer who joined Mahatma Gandhi in 1917 and participated in the non-cooperation movement; President, Indian National Congress, 1934, 1939 and 1946–7; Minister, Food and Agriculture, Government of India, 1946–8; President, Constituent Assembly, 1946–50; President of India, 1950–62.

ROY, BIDHAN CHANDRA (1882–1962): physician and nationalist; elected to the Bengal Legislative Council in 1923; President, All India Medical Council, 1939–45; Chief Minister, West Bengal, 1948–62.

SHASTRI, LAL BAHADUR (1904–66): Congress leader from U.P.; Union Minister for Railways, 1952–6, for Communication, 1957–8, for Commerce and Industry, 1958–61, for Home Affairs, 1961–3; Prime Minister, June 1964–January 1966.

SINGH, DINESH (1925): Raja of Kalakankar, U.P.; member, Lok Sabha, 1957–77; Union Minister for Commerce, 1967–9, for External Affairs, 1969–70, for Industrial Development and Internal Trade, 1970–1.

TAGORE, RABINDRANATH (1861–1941): poet, novelist, essayist and dramatist; recipient of the Nobel Prize for literature in 1913; was deeply involved in the social and political regeneration of India; founded the Visva-Bharati University of Santiniketan in West Bengal.

JAWAHARLAL NEHRU AND FELLOW PRISONERS IN AHMADNAGAR FORT: Jawaharlal Nehru served his longest term in prison from 9th August, 1942 to 15th June, 1945, a period of 1040 days, in Ahmadnagar Fort. During this period, he was incarcerated with eleven other members of the Congress Working Committee, which had passed the famous Resolution of 8th August, 1942, asking the British to 'Quit India'. The names of these leaders are as follows:

1. Asaf Ali
2. Azad, Abul Kalam
3. Deo, Shankarrao
4. Deva, Narendra
5. Ghosh, Prafulla Chandra
6. Kripalani, J. B.
7. Mahmud, Syed
8. Mahtab, Harekrushna
9. Pant, Govind Ballabh
10. Patel, Vallabhbhai
11. Sitaramayya, Pattabhi

Till March 1945, all these leaders were incarcerated in Ahmadnagar Fort. Thereafter, they were transferred to various prisons in the provinces to which they belonged. Jawaharlal Nehru was moved first to Naini Prison, then to Bareilly and finally to Almora, from where he was released on 15th June, 1945.

# Circle of Friends

ALI, ASAF (1888–1953): a Congressman and barrister of Delhi; actively associated with the freedom struggle; first Indian Ambassador to Washington, 1947–8; Governor of Orissa, 1948–52; Ambassador to Switzerland, 1952–3.

ALI NÉE GANGULI, ARUNA ASAF (1906): prominent socialist leader; married to Asaf Ali; took part in the Quit India Movement, 1942; Mayor of Delhi, 1958–60.

BAKER, BEATRICE MAY: Principal of Badminton School, where Indira Gandhi spent some time in 1936–7.

BANERJI NÉE GANGULI, PURNIMA (Nora): a political activist of Allahabad who was a friend of the Nehrus. She was the younger sister of Aruna Asaf Ali.

BEY, FOUAD SELIM: friend of Jawaharlal Nehru from Cairo (Egypt).

BHANDARI, P. C.: physician who was associated with the India League, London; friend of the Nehru family.

BOSE, NANDALAL (1883–1966): distinguished artist on the faculty of Visva-Bharati; Padma Vibhushan, 1955.

CAPTAIN, GOSHIBEN: granddaughter of Dadabhai Naoroji, a founder of the Indian National Congress.

CAPTAIN, PERIN (1888–1958): granddaughter of Dadabhai Naoroji; took part in the freedom struggle and suffered imprisonment on several occasions.

CHAKRAVARTY, AMIYA (1901–86): taught philosophy at Visva-Bharati and at various universities in U.S.A. and Australia; Secretary to Tagore; joined Mahatma Gandhi in peace marches during communal disturbances, 1946–8.

CHANDA, ANIL KUMAR (1906–76): Secretary to Rabindranath Tagore (1933–41); member, Lok Sabha, 1952–62 and 1967–70; Deputy Minister, Ministry of External Affairs, 1952–7, and Minister, Works and Housing, 1957–62.

DARBYSHIRE, HELEN: Principal of Somerville College, Oxford, when Indira Gandhi was a student there.

DESAI, MAHADEV (1892–1942): Secretary to Mahatma Gandhi,

1917–42; participated in the freedom struggle; died a prisoner in the Aga Khan's Palace, Poona, in 1942.

DEVA, NARENDRA (1889–1956): popularly known as Acharya (or 'The Scholar') Narendra Deva; eminent socialist and scholar; participated in the freedom struggle; one of the founders of the Congress Socialist Party; associated with Kashi Vidyapith; was also Vice-Chancellor of Lucknow and Benares Hindu Universities.

GANDHI, SHANTA: classmate and friend of Indira Gandhi. Later taught in the National School of Drama.

GEISSLER, LOUISE: German national who helped Indians during the pre-Hitler period.

GRANT-DUFF, SHEILA: journalist friend of the Nehrus.

GURTU, RAM NARAIN (1901): a barrister of Allahabad, Judge of the Allahabad High Court (1951–61); at present Adviser, Jawaharlal Nehru Memorial Fund, Anand Bhawan. A close friend of the Nehrus.

HARI: valet to Motilal Nehru; after his death attached himself to Jawaharlal Nehru; elected to the U.P. Legislative Assembly, 1937; died in 1961.

HARRISON, AGATHA (1885–1954): friend of Mahatma Gandhi and of the Nehru family, she was a Quaker who worked for India's freedom.

HEMMERLIN, L.: Principal of L'Ecole Nouvelle, Bex, Switzerland, which Indira Gandhi attended in 1926; she was again under Mlle Hemmerlin's care in 1935–6.

KARAN SINGH, DR (1931): son of Maharaja Hari Singh of Kashmir; Regent of Jammu and Kashmir, 1949–52, and Sadr-i-Riyasat, or Governor, 1952–65; Union Minister for Tourism and Civil Aviation, 1967–73, for Health and Family Planning, 1973–7; Indian Ambassador to the United States, 1989.

KATIAL, C. L. (1898–1978): practising physician in London, 1927–43; Director-General, Employees' State Insurance Corporation of India, 1948–53.

KAUL, T. N. (1913): author and diplomat; Ambassador to Iran, 1958–60, to U.S.S.R. and Mongolia, 1962–6, and to U.S.A., 1973–6; Secretary, Ministry of External Affairs, 1966–8; Foreign Secretary, 1968–72.

KRIPALANI, KRISHNA RAMCHAND (1907): scholar and author who taught

taught at Visva-Bharati; Secretary, Sahitya Akademi, 1954–71; Padma Bhushan, 1969; nominated member of Rajya Sabha in 1974.

LASKI, HAROLD J. (1893–1950): Professor of Political Science at the London School of Economics, 1926–50; active in the socialist movement and Chairman, Labour Party, 1945–6.

MEHTA, KRISHNA (1913): a friend of the Nehru family; engaged in the rehabilitation of refugee women and children in Jammu and Kashmir, 1948; member, Lok Sabha, 1957–62.

MIRABEN (MADELEINE SLADE) (1892–1982): disciple of Mahatma Gandhi; she lived at Sabarmati Ashram for many years and participated in the freedom struggle.

MORIN, LOUISE (1883–1970): French journalist and friend of India who was in charge of the French unit of the All-India Radio, 1952–65.

NAHAS PASHA (Mustafa Nahas Pasha) (1876–1965): Egyptian statesman and leader of Wafd Party.

NAIDU, LEILAMANI (1903–59): daughter of Sarojini Naidu; served in the Indian Foreign Service, 1948–58.

NAIDU, PADMAJA (1900–75): daughter of Sarojini Naidu; Governor of West Bengal, 1956–66. She was called Bebee by kinsmen and close friends.

NAMBIAR, A. C. N. (Nanu) (1896–1986): worked for Indian freedom in Europe and lived in exile in Germany till 1947; Indian Ambassador to the Federal Republic of Germany, 1955–8.

NAOROJI, JAL: grandson of Dadabhai Naoroji and close friend of the Nehru family; died 1938.

NAOROJI, KHURSHEDBEN (1894–1966): granddaughter of Dadabhai Naoroji; was associated with Gandhian institutions.

SAMANT, DR VATSALA: Medical Superintendent of the Kamala Nehru Hospital, Allahabad, 1942–72; a friend of Indira Gandhi.

SAPRU, TEJ BAHADUR (1875–1949): eminent jurist and liberal leader from Allahabad; Law Member of Viceroy's Council, 1920–3.

SARABHAI FAMILY: the Sarabhais are a notable family of Gujarat, prominent in industry and in culture. Ambalal Sarabhai, a mill-owner of Ahmedabad, his wife, Saralaben, and his sister, Ansuyaben, came under Mahatma Gandhi's influence. Among Ambalal's children, Mridula Sarabhai was prominent in politics and social work.

Vikram, a scientist, rose to be chairman of the Atomic Energy Commission. Bharati was a poet and writer. Leena founded a school which undertook educational experiments. Suhrid was another brother who died young. Vikram's wife Mrinalini is one of the country's foremost dancers.

SARAN, RAGHUNANDAN (1900–53): a Congressman of Delhi; was Director of *National Herald.* A close friend of the Nehru family.

SARAN, RAKSHA: wife of Raghunandan; social worker.

SHERWANI, TASADDUQ AHMAD KHAN (1885–1935): barrister-at-law; practised at Aligarh; arrested during the non-cooperation movement, 1921; President, U.P. Provincial Congress Committee, 1930; member, Congress Working Committee; member, Indian Legislative Assembly, 1926–30, re-elected to the Assembly in 1934.

SRI PRAKASA (1890–1971): contemporary of Jawaharlal Nehru at Cambridge; Secretary, U.P. Provincial Congress Committee, 1928–34; Secretary of the Congress 1927 and 1931; after 1947 served as Indian High Commissioner in Pakistan; Union Minister; Governor of Assam, Madras and Maharashtra.

THOMPSON, EDWARD (1886–1946): author and friend of Jawaharlal Nehru; supported the cause of Indian freedom.

TYABJI, BADR-UD-DIN (1907): diplomat and friend of Jawaharlal Nehru. He was Commonwealth Secretary in the Ministry of External Affairs, 1952–3 and Ambassador to Indonesia, 1954–6, to Iran, 1956–8, to West Germany, 1958–60. He was also Vice-Chancellor, Aligarh Muslim University, 1962–5.

UPADHYAYA, S. D. (1899–1984): served as personal secretary to Motilal Nehru, 1923–31, and to Jawaharlal Nehru, 1931–46; imprisoned several times; member, Lok Sabha, 1952–67 and Rajya Sabha, 1967–70.

THE VAKILS: Jehangir Jivaji Vakil and his wife Coonverbai; J. J. Vakil was teacher at Santiniketan; they opened the Pupils' Own School at Poona which was influenced by Tagore; Indira Gandhi was admitted to the Pupils' Own School in May 1931.

YUNUS, MOHAMMAD (1916): a friend of the Nehru family; joined Indian Foreign Service after independence; served as Head of Missions at Jogjakarta, Ankara, Baghdad, Madrid, San Francisco and Algiers; Chairman, Trade Fair Authority of India, 1980–9; currently member of the Upper House in the Indian Parliament.

# Journeys Undertaken by Jawaharlal Nehru and Indira Gandhi between 1941 and 1963

1.   Indira Gandhi returned to India from Europe with Feroze Gandhi in April 1941. Jawaharlal Nehru was in prison at this time. Indira spent the summer months of 1941 in the hill resort of Mussoorie. Jawaharlal was released from prison in December 1941.

2.   Indira married Feroze Gandhi in March 1942. She and her husband accompanied Jawaharlal Nehru to Bombay to attend the special session of the All India Congress Committee where the famous Quit India Resolution was passed on 8th August. On her return to Allahabad, Indira was fully drawn into the anti-British agitation and was arrested on 10th September, 1942, while addressing a public meeting. Feroze was also arrested the same day.

3.   After her release from prison in May 1943, Indira spent some time at Bombay with her aunt, Krishna Hutheesing. She returned to Allahabad at the end of August.

4.   In the month of March 1944, Indira Gandhi travelled to Bombay where she planned to stay with Krishna Hutheesing till her confinement. She also visited Matheran, Poona and Mahabaleswar during this period. Rajiv was born on 20th August, 1944, in Bombay. Mother and child returned to Allahabad in October 1944.

5.   In May 1945, Indira Gandhi went to Kashmir with Rajiv. She returned to Allahabad in June to meet Jawaharlal Nehru on his release from prison. She went back to Srinagar, and Jawaharlal proceeded to Simla for the Simla Conference.

6.   After his release, Jawaharlal Nehru was drawn into political consultations which led to the formation of an Interim Government. During the summer of 1946, Indira spent some time at Almora and then moved to New Delhi, where Sanjay, her second son, was born on 14th December, 1946. During this year Jawaharlal Nehru travelled to Malaya in March and to Egypt in December.

7.   On 15th August, 1947, India became independent and Jawaharlal Nehru was sworn in as Prime Minister. Indira Gandhi had already started living under the same roof as her father and she was present on this momentous occasion.

8.   Jawaharlal Nehru went to London in October 1948 and then again

in April 1949 to attend the Commonwealth Prime Ministers' Conference. Towards the end of 1949, Indira Gandhi visited London and the
United States with her father.

9. In January 1950 Indira accompanied her father to Sri Lanka where
he was to attend the Commonwealth Foreign Ministers' Conference.
She and her father visited Pakistan in April 1950.

10. Indira spent the summer of 1951 in Kashmir with Rajiv and Sanjay. The winter of 1951–2 witnessed hectic political activity due to the
forthcoming General Election. Indira was fully drawn into the election
campaign and toured the country extensively.

11. In May 1953 Indira attended the coronation ceremony of Queen
Elizabeth in London with her father. She made her first visit to U.S.S.R.
in June–July 1953. She visited U.S.S.R. again in the company of her
father in the summer of 1955. In February 1955 and in the third week
of June 1956 Jawaharlal Nehru went to London for the Commonwealth
Prime Ministers' Conference. Indira and her two sons accompanied
him. She also accompanied him to U.S.A. and Canada in December
1956.

12. In June 1957 Jawaharlal Nehru went on a four-week tour of foreign
countries. The Commonwealth Prime Ministers' Conference formed
part of this tour. Indira visited Japan for the first time in October 1957
with her father. In July 1958 she travelled to London. She was again
with her father on his first official visit to Bhutan in the second week of
September 1958.

13. In February 1959 Indira Gandhi was elected President of the
Indian National Congress and had to travel widely across the country
in that capacity. She visited Afghanistan and Iran with Jawaharlal Nehru
in September 1959.

14. Jawaharlal Nehru travelled to London in May 1960 to attend the
Commonwealth Prime Ministers' Conference. Indira Gandhi went to
New York in the second week of May and was there for about a week.
She joined Jawaharlal Nehru at Istanbul (Turkey), where they spent a
couple of days. They visited Lebanon and Syria on their way back to
India. In September Jawaharlal was in New York at the U.N. In October
1960 Indira was in Mexico, going to New York the following month to
receive the Howland Memorial Prize of Yale University for Distinguished Achievement from the President of Yale University. She also
unveiled a portrait of Elihu Yale. From New York she went to Paris.
She was elected a member of the Executive Board of UNESCO. She
also paid a short visit to Germany in December 1960.

15.   In March 1961 Jawaharlal Nehru was in London. Indira Gandhi travelled to Europe in May 1961 to attend the meeting of the Executive Board of UNESCO in Paris. She was accompanied by Rajiv. In August 1961 she was sent as Nehru's emissary to East Africa, Kenya, Uganda, Tanzania and Rhodesia. In the first week of September, Jawaharlal Nehru proceeded to Belgrade for the Non-Aligned Conference and returned to India through Moscow.

16.   Indira Gandhi visited U.S.A. in March–April 1962. Later in September she accompanied Jawaharlal Nehru to London for the Commonwealth Prime Ministers' Conference. In October 1962, in the wake of the Chinese invasion, she visited Tezpur in Assam, the military and civil headquarters of the North-East Frontier Agency.

17.   Indira visited London and New York in March–April 1963. She spent the summer in Srinagar with her son Sanjay. Towards the end of the year, she visited many African countries – Tanzania, Rhodesia, Zambia, Ethiopia and Kenya – on a goodwill mission.

# PART I

# Homecoming
## (1940–1942)

1.

Les Frênes,<br>
Leysin,<br>
Switzerland,[1]<br>
2nd January, 1940

Darling Papu,

Your letter of the 20th[2] came this morning. About the telegrams, I hear there was quite a dispute between Krishna,[3] Bhandari[4] & Agatha[5] as to who should send the cable about my departure – I don't know what was ultimately decided.

Dr Rollier[6] has his own system of breathing & other exercises and, as I am under his care, I think it is best to stick to his methods. He is very firmly of the opinion that breathing exercises should not be undertaken until much later. I am to start with leg exercises. At the beginning of next week, I shall begin lying in the 'position ventrale' – only a few minutes to start with – on my tummy with pillows supporting the chest and the head held high.

I was weighed today: 38 kgs – that is just under 84 lbs – I ought, for my height, to be at least 110 lbs!

Dr Schmidt, one of the Frênes doctors, was quite excited the other day. His sister who lives in America sends him, more or less regularly, *Life*. In the issue of Dec. 11th was an article 'Nehru of India' by John[7] & Frances Gunther.[8] It is, with some additions & alterations, taken out of *Inside Asia*. It had several pictures of the family too. Since then Mrs Nanavati has circulated it right round the clinic.

4th January

I don't seem to be able to write these days, or indeed do anything else. Tomorrow it will be exactly three weeks since I arrived, and still I am just where I began. No one expects miracles but I must say it is very discouraging – the more I stay in bed the weaker I feel and the less I want

---

1. Indira Nehru was in a sanatorium in Switzerland in January 1940 owing to a bout of ill-health.

2. Letter not published.

3. V. K. Krishna Menon: radical nationalist who promoted the cause of Indian freedom in Great Britain. He was very close to the Nehrus.

4. Dr P. C. Bhandari: Indian doctor practising in England who was often consulted by Indira.

5. Agatha Harrison: British Quaker activist who supported the national movement in India. She was close to Mahatma Gandhi and Jawaharlal Nehru.

6. Dr Auguste Rollier: Swiss physician.

7. John Gunther: American journalist and writer.

8. Frances Gunther: American journalist, wife of John Gunther.

to do anything. The days are most frightfully monotonous, especially as there is no one to talk to – the patients are allowed to pay visits to one another in the evenings, but they all have their families with them. Mrs Nanavati was a great help – she used to come for ten minutes in the morning and again in the evening. But now they have gone to a clinic above Montreux to consult a Dr Jacquot (I don't know how to spell his name). They hoped to be back in a fortnight but weren't sure if they'd be able to.

I better get this posted now or else it will never go.

Much Love,
Indu

P.S.
It is quite hot today – I found it too hot to stay on the balcony.

---

2.

Anand Bhawan,
Allahabad,
5th January, 1940

Darling Indu,
Your letter from Leysin dated 22nd Dec.[1] reached me on Jan 2nd when I returned to Allahabad. It had come here a day or two earlier. So that it took a little over a week – much less time than letters from England to India. This is comforting.

I am glad you like Leysin and Dr Rollier. From what you write about him, he must be an attractive and competent person. I shall now eagerly look forward to the transformation of Indira Nehru into a Diana.

I was in Amritsar a few days ago to attend a Scout *melá*[2] and I had a narrow shave in an accident which might have been serious. Punjab crowds are astonishingly overwhelming and indisciplined. They are full of affection and enthusiasm but will not observe any discipline, which is surprising as the Punjab is supposed to be a military province. I had gone to Amritsar after nearly three years and the Scout *melá* there was attractive. There were nearly 7000 Scouts from all India gathered there – both boys and girls – looking quite smart. Amritsar decided to observe holiday and all the shops were closed for the day. Men and women poured into the Scout area. They were made to line up outside a huge field which was kept free for parade and various exercises. Everything

1. Refers to letter No.319 in *Freedom's Daughter: Letters Between Indira Gandhi and Jawaharlal Nehru, 1929–39*, edited by Sonia Gandhi.
2. Fair.

seemed to be well organised and there were barricades and eight rows of Scouts to keep the crowds back. I arrived and went into the centre of the field and suddenly the crowd rushed, broke all barriers, swept aside the Scouts and filled the field. Over a hundred thousand men and women, shouting slogans, full of enthusiasm, surrounded me. It was impossible to move them away and the programme for the day could not be started. I decided to get on horseback and move about the surging crowds. A fine, big, spirited horse was produced. It was wholly unsuitable as it was unused to crowds. It shied continually and reared up on his hind legs. Suddenly there was a rush by the crowd and the horse grew frightened and reared up so much that it lost its balance and fell back. For a fraction of a second I saw myself being crushed by the huge weight of the beast. Visions of being a cripple for life rose before me. It was surprising what a lot of images passed before my mind during that tiny fraction of a second. Meanwhile instinct and old habit functioned and I just managed to extricate myself as the horse fell to the ground. Then he rolled a little and my foot was pressed by his body – not much, otherwise it would have been crushed. The stirrup where the foot had been an instant before was all buckled up. I got up with some pain in the foot but otherwise sound and immediately mounted the horse again – to show off, I suppose, but partly also because walking was a little painful. The foot has almost recovered since then.

I went to Lahore for a day also and addressed a vast meeting there. Again an absence of discipline and bad management. Whenever I go to Lahore I stay with Iftikhar-ud-Din[1] (an Oxford man) and meet many Muslim young men and women. It is surprising how Muslim young women of the upper middle classes are taking to socialism, or at any rate think they are. There is friction in many a home because of this. But this theoretical approval of socialism does not come in the way of the joys of life, which in Lahore consists of the most inane and unsupportable round of parties and dances.

Do you remember Sappho, the Great Dane babe at Betty's[2] place in Bombay? The babe grew and grew and was about a year and a half old last month. We were all tremendously fond of her and I looked forward to seeing her and playing about with her whenever I went to Bombay. Raja[3] doted on her. Harsha and Ajit[4] took all manner of

1. Mian Iftikharuddin: eminent Punjab politician, member of Punjab Legislative Assembly and President of Punjab Provincial Congress Committee; he left Congress in 1945 and joined the Muslim League, and was for some time Minister for Rehabilitation in Punjab, Pakistan. Later he formed the National Party along with Abdul Ghaffar Khan.

2. Krishna Hutheesing (née Nehru): sister of Jawaharlal Nehru.

3. G. P. Hutheesing (Raja): Krishna Hutheesing's husband.

4. Harsha Hutheesing and Ajit Hutheesing: the two sons of Krishna and G. P. Hutheesing.

liberties with her. Suddenly the poor thing developed rabies and died within two days. Betty and Raja were heartbroken. Just at this time Nan,[1] Chand,[2] Tara[3] & Rita[4] were also there. So everybody in Betty's family & Nan's have since had to take daily injections of some anti-rabies serum. Sappho had not bitten anybody but she was always licking and sometimes scratching peoples' hands. This has been a real tragedy. I don't think I could keep a dog. They die too soon.

I enclose rather a good picture of Nandita[5] which I took a couple of months ago. This is just to show you how I am progressing in the art of photography. She is leaning out of the window in my room; in the background is the door leading to your room.

Love,

Your loving,

Papu

Did I tell you that I have stopped the sending of *Herald*[6] clippings to you by airmail. The full *Herald* will now go to Leysin by the Ocean route.

---

3.                                                Anand Bhawan,
                                                       Allahabad,
                                          16th January, 1940

Darling Indu,
I have not written to you for about ten days. For nearly all this time I have been touring intensively in some of our north-western districts of the U.P. [United Provinces] – Aligarh, Bulandshahr, Meerut, Muzaffarnagar, Saharanpur, Moradabad. It was a tour after the old style, going from town to town and village to village, addressing huge gatherings, being stopped at numerous wayside places by peasant groups. The day's work began early and went far into the night, sometimes till after two a.m. I was tired out and could not summon enough energy to write letters there. So I could not write to you. I returned yesterday and got

1. Vijaya Lakshmi Pandit (née Nehru): sister of Jawaharlal Nehru, married to Ranjit Pandit.
2. Chandralekha Mehta (née Pandit): the Pandits' eldest daughter.
3. Nayantara Sahgal (née Pandit): the Pandits' second daughter.
4. Rita Dar (née Pandit): the Pandits' youngest daughter.
5. Nandita Kripalani: granddaughter of Rabindranath Tagore, wife of Krishna Kripalani.
6. *National Herald*: an English daily which commenced publication in 1938 from Lucknow. Jawaharlal Nehru was associated with it.

your letter of the 2nd January. [1] I wanted to write to you immediately but a stream of visitors kept me occupied and I went to bed early to recover somewhat from the fatigue of the tour.

Such tours are of course tiring. But they are invigorating also, at any rate I find them so. Our peasant masses depress me with their poverty but their enthusiasm is catching. More and more I feel in tune with them rather than with the listless and argumentative folk of the cities. I have even begun to appreciate just a wee bit the peasant's attachment to the soil. The good earth has something solid, substantial and permanent about it, which is comforting in these days when everything else seems to be fleeting. Wars may rage and decimate humanity, but the seasons follow each other in regular succession, and the flowers bloom, and the soil produces food, and the fields look peaceful and gay. I felt the call of the good earth and the joy of seeing things grow out of this soil.

The districts I visited are relatively prosperous and compare very favourably with our eastern districts like Gorakhpur and Ballia where the poverty is extreme and the multitudes that gather are semi-naked. This poverty is oppressive and tragic, especially in these winter months when there is no covering except a cotton sheet. But in our northern districts, as in the Punjab, standards are a little higher and people are properly clothed. Many of the peasants who came had fat *razais* [2] with them to wrap themselves in. They were healthier looking. Often they came on their bullock-carts from many miles around, bringing their wives and children with them. Hundreds of these bullock-carts used to surround our meetings, giving the place the look of an encampment or fair.

The Jats [3] are strong in these areas. They are perhaps more passionately attached to the soil than any other group. Hefty, weather-beaten and healthy looking, they are almost parts of the country landscape. Always when I go to these rural areas, I am pleasantly surprised by the handsome types of humanity that I see. There are ever so many attractive-looking young women and the children are very bonny. In spite of my heavy programmes, I manage to spend a few minutes at almost every meeting with the children. I get [a] large number of garlands and I take these to the children and distribute them. Sometimes there is a petty riot as the children gather round me, each one demanding a garland. But unfortunately there are never enough to go round.

On my way back I spent a few hours at Lucknow and a deputation

1. Refers to letter No. 1.
2. Quilts.
3. A tribe of land-owning peasants situated in North-West India.

from the Uday Shankar Company,[1] which was performing there, [was] waiting on me and invited me to attend. I was glad of the chance and I went to see them perform. I liked the show but I must confess that I am less impressed by it than I used to be. There was a new item or rather series of items – the Rhythm of Life. This is an ambitious theme. The conception is good and the execution of parts was also not bad. I enclose a part of the programme dealing with this.

I can quite understand how boring it must be for you to keep in bed most of the time. But I suppose that after the initial months you will gradually be getting up more and more. Lying in bed makes one weaker and more listless but it is meant to give rest to the lungs so that they might get strong. In other words, the rest of your body is for the moment being ignored to some extent for the sake of concentrating on the lungs, pleura, etc. Having got a strong foundation to build upon, more emphasis can be laid on general development. To hurry the initial process might lead to lack of results later. I am sure, however, that progress will be rapid as soon as you move about. In the past the lungs & pleura not being quite as they should be, it was difficult to build anything substantial on them. I am a sinner in this respect for, being impatient and being myself tough in body, I am inclined to push others too far. I do not therefore trust my own judgement in such matters. As Rollier told you, your lung capacity is small and this has to be increased. This will be done by breathing exercises when the time comes. But before you start such exercises the lungs should have rested and must be fit. Do not worry therefore about a few days' or even weeks' delay. What is important is to lay a firm and lasting foundation for health. You are in very good hands and I am content that you are being well cared for.

Of course you will have to follow Dr Rollier's advice regarding breathing exercises and practise his own system. The directions I sent you were for Dr Rollier to see. As a matter of fact Birju Bhai's[2] note shows how a normal breath should be taken. There is nothing complicated about it although the description is long. I have been taking these breathing exercises, off and on, for many years. They revive me when I am tired.

Your weight is not likely to go up much in bed. It is only the first month in bed that pushes up the weight and you were in bed at Brentford[3] for a long time. When you are up and about, the weight will soar up.

1. Uday Shankar Company: Uday Shankar pioneered the revival of classical dance forms in India, and combined them with elements of modern choreography. He founded a company to promote his art.

2. Brijlal Nehru: cousin of Jawaharlal Nehru, a civil servant.

3. Indira Gandhi spent some months in Brentford Hospital, Middlesex, before moving to the sanatorium in Switzerland.

I have not had much illness myself and have not been tied up to bed for long. But I have lived for long periods in isolation, confined to a small space, so I have sufficient experience of this kind of thing. The only way to keep normal and sane in prison is to live in the mind, intellectually, as well as manually with some handicraft. One must find mental and physical equilibrium in oneself and then it does not matter. Indeed I think this is excellent training for one and it helps one greatly in life afterwards. Modern conditions are very upsetting as they provide excitements and sensations in quick succession and prevent an equilibrium from developing. Hence the great value of restful and uneventful periods. Do not worry or feel discouraged. That is not like you. I wonder if you have taken to some definite work, both mental & manual. Anything of this kind regularly done is very helpful.

My foot has not yet recovered from the slight injury received at Amritsar. It would have recovered soon enough if I had given it even three days' rest. But I have [been] continuously touring about, often running and pushing about in crowds. We age. I cannot judge about myself but I am often surprised to see others around me showing signs of age. Nan's hair is almost all grey now. Betty is very matronly.

In about ten days' time the All-India Women's Conference is meeting in Allahabad. There is a great deal of running about because of it and the women of Allahabad are quite excited. The arrangements are on a big scale. Anand Bhawan will be invaded by many guests.

I am going to Wardha tomorrow for a Working Committee meeting. The amount of time one spends on these long journeys!

Love,<br>
Your loving,<br>
Papu

4.

Anand Bhawan,<br>
Allahabad,<br>
23rd January, 1940

Darling,

This morning I returned from Wardha. I feel somewhat out of place here for the moment. The All India Women's Conference is filling the picture and our house will be, and partly is already, full of the distinguished delegates. The president, Mrs Hamid Ali [1] (plus husband),

---

1. Begum Shareefah Hamid Ali: prominent social reformer; wife of A. Hamid Ali, civil servant.

Rani Rajwade,[1] Amrit Kaur,[2] Sarojini Naidu,[3] Padmaja,[4] Papi,[5] Mridula[6] and possibly some others will be staying here. The conference camp is in Durbhanga Castle and over a hundred delegates will put up there. There is tremendous bustle and activity and women getting excited and shouting at each other. A week of this.

The Gunthers have sent me a lovely book – *The Last Flower* by James Thurber.[7] I almost felt like ordering a copy for you as you are sure to enjoy it. But in these war days it is difficult to send books. In one of the recent numbers of *Life* some of Thurber's pictures and text are reproduced. I am enclosing these two pages. They will give you some idea of the book.

What do you do for books? I suppose you brought a supply with you and then Mlle Hemmerlin[8] sent you some. It is easier for you to make direct arrangements with booksellers in England than for me to do so. I thought of ordering the American *Life* & *Time* for you but again I thought it was easier for you to get them if you want them. Are you getting the *National Herald*? This should go weekly by ordinary post.

Today I received the number of *Life* containing Gunther's article on 'Nehru of India' and the close-up picture, about which you wrote to me.[9] I wonder where they got the big picture from?

Suddenly I have begun to feel as if I had nothing special to do – [the] kind of feeling I have had when I have gone out of India. Curious things are happening in India and all over the world and all manner of doubts fill me. I do not like playing the spectator's role and yet there is no other obvious job to be done. Of course there is plenty of work of various kinds but it all seems so ineffectual. Perhaps it is the desire to see you that makes me so restless. But any way, there is no escape for me for the present and in the near future.

I hope that your progress continues. After your long rest, the changes

1. Rani G. Laxmibai Rajwade: chairman of the sub-committee on women's rights, National Planning Committee of the All India Congress Committee, 1938.
2. Rajkumari Amrit Kaur: member of the princely family of Kapurthala and a disciple of Mahatma Gandhi.
3. Sarojini Naidu: nationalist leader and poet.
4. Padmaja Naidu (Bebee): daughter of Sarojini Naidu, active in politics and in social service. Governor of West Bengal 1956–66 and Chairman, Indian Red Cross, 1971–2.
5. Leilamani Naidu: younger daughter of Sarojini Naidu; served in the Indian Foreign Service, 1948–58.
6. Mridula Sarabhai: member of the Sarabhai family of Ahmedabad, who was active in the freedom struggle.
7. James Grover Thurber: American humorist and cartoonist.
8. L. Hemmerlin: Principal of L'Ecole Nouvelle, Bex, Switzerland, which Indira Gandhi attended in 1926 and 1935–6.
9. Refers to letter No. 1.

and exercises will probably have to be slow, but so long as they are sure, it is all to the good. I am quite sure that as soon as you are up and about, you will go ahead fast. Do not worry about the slowness at first. You have to lay some foundations and nature is usually very slow and does not easily forgive lapses. I understand that Rollier does not believe in medicine much. He leaves much to nature, to sunlight and a careful regime.

The Memorial Hospital[1] building is growing up rapidly here. The Governor came to see it last week and then expressed a desire to come to Anand Bhawan next door. He came and spent some time here. I was in Wardha then. His visit created quite a sensation and all manner of foolish and unwarranted conclusions were drawn.

Chand, Tara & Rita are here and I like to play about with them. They are jolly kids.

Can I send something to you – magazines or anything else which will keep you in touch with India and things Indian?

Love,
Your loving,
Papu

---

5.

Anand Bhawan,
Allahabad,
4th February, 1940

Darling Indu,

The shouting and the rushing about has ended and the women who had gathered in Allahabad for the All India Women's Conference have gone home to their various provinces. Anand Bhawan is quiet again. During these ten days of guests and bustle, my own daily programme was much upset, although I had next to nothing to do with the Conference. But many friends and old acquaintances had come and I had to meet them, and then there were busloads of women invading Anand Bhawan to see it and examine its chief exhibit. They were all very nice and all that and it was pleasant to meet many of them whom I had known off and on for long years, but I felt very lonely and somewhat depressed throughout this week or so. My thoughts were continually going to you and the desire to see you held me.

For two days I went to Benares to meet a Chinese Buddhist mission that is touring India. We gave them a good welcome there and there was a great procession and a huge meeting. We celebrated the day as

---

1. The Kamala Nehru Memorial Hospital.

Ashoka Day. I went to Sarnath[1] again though I had no time to wander about as I should have liked to have done. Two hours were spent in a laborious conversation with the mission and especially its leader, the Rev. Abbot Tai Hsu. Laborious, because all conversations through an interpreter are heavy and tiring. The old Abbot – but he was far from old looking – was delightful and had the face of a cherub. The more I see of the Chinese the more I like them.

There is a chance of the Women's Conference sending a small delegation to China, if the Chinese Govt are agreeable.

Crowds of women who came here, both those I knew and those I did not know, asked me to send their love to you.

Today is what is called Literacy Day in the U.P. This was started last year by the Congress Govt and it has met with fair success. Today was its anniversary and from early morning school children have been shouting slogans vigorously – 'down with illiteracy' etc (in Hindi of course). It is quite exciting to see these children and grown-ups seize hold of illiterate workers and others and try to teach them to read and write.

Tonight I am going to Lucknow for two days – then to Bombay. Up and down I travel to attend various committee meetings or other functions and I try to deal with them as well as I can. But my mind is elsewhere and my heart still further away. Doubts creep into my mind if all this is worthwhile or not. Still I go on as most of us do. For the last year or two I have avoided engagements and only those I cannot refuse have been accepted – responsibilities I have undertaken must be discharged. These responsibilities grow in spite of me and the coils of fate bind me. Not that I have any desire to shirk them but the future is so uncertain that the urge to activity lessens. Activity to what end? I wish often enough that I could retire for a while in some remote far-away place where I could read and write and there is no engagement, no visitors, no letters, no newspapers – preferably somewhere near to you so that your presence and company might fill the emptiness within me. Sometimes a foolish desire to be ill and to lie in bed – but the illness should not be serious! – comes to me. How pleasant it must be, I think, to laze and not be forced to do this and that when the mind is unwilling and rebellious.

Do you get the *National Herald* now? It will bring you news, stale but still news, for you of India. I often think what I can send you from here that might interest you. But there is little I can send and in wartime

1. Sarnath: a few kilometres from Benares, Sarnath is a sacred spot and place of pilgrimage for Buddhists, where Gautama Buddha (563–483 BC), the founder of Buddhism, preached his first sermon after attaining Enlightenment. The Emperor Ashoka had been an upholder of Buddhist values.

parcels to neutral countries are a nuisance. Still if you think of anything, let me know . . .

I am sorry to find in your last letter [1] a note of depression at having to remain confined to your bedroom, and chiefly to bed, for all this long period. This is tiring business, no doubt, and yet what do a few weeks matter when one is planning for a life of health and activity? You will make rapid enough progress soon. This very unusual cold must have come in the way. If the Thames was frozen over and there was 25° and 30° of frost in London, what must it have been at Leysin? What was your minimum temperature there? Here the winter has been unusually mild and the last week of January was just like English summer weather. Already there is the breath of spring in the air and soon *Vasanta Panchami* [2] will be upon us. The seasons follow one another, and the trees bloom and the flowers come out, while we poor mortals get entangled in our problems and war with each other and destroy what careful labour has built up.

Do you know anything about Efy Aristarchi? [3]

Love,
Your loving,
Papu

---

6. 

Anand Bhawan,
Allahabad,
7th February, 1940

Darling,

. . . Sheikh Abdullah of Kashmir [4] is staying with us. I like him. He presses me to fulfil my old promise to go to Kashmir. How I wish I could. It is twenty-four years since I was there. But I have no heart to go just by myself.

There is a young Kashmiri girl here freshly come from Kashmir. Her husband works in Swaraj Bhawan. [5] She feels so homesick already and talks of the almond-blossoms that must be coming out in all their beauty at this time in Kashmir. Spring must be creeping in there after the hard

1. Refers to letter No. 1.
2. *Vasanta Panchami*: a festival marking the coming of spring.
3. F. E. Aristarchi: Greek princess, a disciple of Mahatma Gandhi.
4. Sheikh Abdullah: nationalist leader of Kashmir, later its Chief Minister.
5. Swaraj Bhawan: Freedom House, Congress headquarters till Independence.

winter and the air will be full of fragrance and life will renew itself.
Here in Allahabad we approach the hot summer.

Love,<br>
Your loving,<br>
Papu

---

7.                                                      Les Frênes,
                                                            Leysin,
                                                      Switzerland,
                                          9th February, 1940

Darlingest Papu,
What great joy your letters bring to me! They are something to look
forward to, something that not only breaks the monotony, but brings a
sort of light to the days. To the gloom and darkness of my mind each
letter is rather like the single flower of Thurber's parable – a messenger
of hope, an assurance that something is there, even in the midst of this
darkness, on which one can build anew. And then they bring you close,
so close to me, as though the vast Indian Ocean were only a pond, and
all the lands between just stepping stones.

What is it that has so depressed me? I don't really know. It is not just
the lying in bed, nor even the being so lonely, or this truly wintry
weather. For winter, shorn of its glistening silvery mantle of snow, can
be truly dreary: roads wallowing in mud; trees so desolate and naked
without their foliage; grass all yellow, pressed to the ground, dead;
and the sky so endlessly grey, but worst of all the thick mists that so
often rise up from the valley, clothing everything in obscurity. Most
of all, it is, I expect, this complete inactivity – physical as well as mental.
For, as you know, I was not allowed any books or even magazines
out of England. Nor can they be posted out here unless the book is a
new one and is sent by a bookseller who is in possession of an export
licence.

Dr Roche of Montana has been a true friend although I have never
met him. He attended your meeting at the Civil Liberties Union in
London last year, or wherever it was. Every week he sends me regularly,
or at least as regularly as he himself gets them, the *Tribune, New Statesman & Nation, Reynolds News* and any other English paper that has come
his way and he thinks might interest me. From Geneva, from friends of
Agatha's, come the *Reader's Digest* and the *Manchester Guardian* weekly
and once some novels. Mlle Hemmerlin has also sent me books but
hers are mostly very old ones, and not the sort of old ones which have
a lasting interest.

From Mlle H., I have now procured the new edition of *Glimpses*.[1] In London, I was one of the very few Indians that I know of who did not receive a complimentary copy. I meant to buy one before going on to Oxford but just then I fell ill. So this is really the first proper look I have had at it – earlier I had a brief glimpse at Agatha's copy. Mlle H. happened to mention to me, when she came up here, that she has received a copy – so I asked her to lend it [to] me for a while. And now I am reading it right from the beginning. It will give a sort of continuity to my reading, for I find that reading a lot of newspapers & short stories one after the other is most unsatisfactory. If I have to stay in bed much longer, I am thinking of taking lessons in German. My vocabulary in that language is quite big but most ungrammatical.

Mr Griffiths, the Church of England chaplain in Leysin, visits and circulates magazines among all the English-speaking – by which he means British & American subjects – patients. He comes once a week and occasionally his wife drops in for a short chat. They are quite nice. They bring me old issues of *Time* sometimes but more usually *Punch* or English society magazines such as the *Tatler*. I have also made the acquaintance of rather a nice French girl who is in one of the smaller clinics. The other day she brought with her a young doctor who was rather interesting. He was in Spain during the war and came to the R.U.P.[2] meeting in Paris with Pasionaria[3] straight from Spain.

That article – 'Nehru of India' – in *Life* has now appeared in a condensed form in this month's *Reader's Digest*.

Since I have been in Leysin the only Indian news, apart from your letters, that I have had is through the *Harijan*[4] that the Nanavatis get. Neither the cuttings nor the daily *National Herald* have so far arrived.

I do hope your foot is much better. I wish you'd take more care of these things, they are not always as harmless and small as they may apparently seem.

As for me, there doesn't seem to be outward progress – of course I know nothing of the condition of the lungs except that the pain on the left side is persistent. Dr Rollier now wants to put something there (I forget the name) which pulls the blood and hence lessens the pain. Dr Rollier had said that as soon as I had gained one kilogram since arrival he would let me get up a bit. This morning I was weighed and find that

1. The letters Jawaharlal Nehru wrote to Indira from prison, between 1930 and 1933, were later published as *Glimpses of World History* (Allahabad, 2 volumes, 1934).
2. R.U.P.: The Republican Union Party, formed in Spain in 1934 by a group of Radicals and led by Diego Martinez Barrio.
3. La Pasionaria (Dolores Ibarruri): leader of the Communist Party in Spain, attained fame during the Spanish Civil War.
4. *Harijan*: an English weekly started by Mahatma Gandhi in 1933.

I have lost the 400 grams I gained last fortnight. So my weight now is 38 kgs i.e. 83.6 lbs. So there's nothing more to be done but lie back and wait!

Nearly every week there is a new discovery that will in course of time change our way of living. And because one never hears of the years of research and trial and failure that have gone before it, it seems rather like the waving of a fairy's wand. At the moment I am especially excited about the stroboscope and Nylon. You have probably heard of them. The stroboscope is known as the 'lamp that freezes motion'. Through its rays you can not only see each drop in a waterfall suspended in the air but also you can make it move backwards & upwards! Which means that no movement on earth is now too fast to be photographed and hence studied in all its details. Fascinating, isn't it? Meanwhile Nylon is already on the market. It is a material made from water, air & coal – in a word, 'ersatz' at its best. It is elastic, strong, transparent or opaque and never loses its shape unless heated above boiling point. It can be made into anything from tooth brush bristle to women's sheer stockings. The more it's pulled about the stronger it gets. And already stockings, dresses & underwear are being made of Nylon. Furthermore, it is cheap and lasting and beautiful to look upon. Hence it is thought that it presents a very serious rival to silk and [thus] to Japan's trade.

By the way, since last writing to you I have three letters from you. Of these, the one dated Jan. 16th [1] arrived first. Then on the 3rd Feb. came the other two, dated 5th Jan. [2] & 23rd Jan. [3] respectively together! So you see how very irregular is the post.

Even as I have been writing, the dirty muddy little village of Leysin has been transformed into a fairy land Christmas card. For it has been snowing, oh, so hard. Everything is all white & beautiful again and still it snows.

With all my very best love, darling, and special thoughts too.
Indu

8.                                              Lucknow,
                                    15th February, 1940

Darling Indu,
In the last six or seven days I have tried daily and I have tried hard to write to you. But my day ended long after midnight and sleep and

---

1. Refers to letter No. 3.
2. Refers to letter No. 2.
3. Refers to letter No. 4.

tiredness overcame me. I could have written of course but I want to write to you when I am fresh and some element of repose comes with my writing. Haste peeps out of a letter and is not pleasing. I fear I have not chosen a good day or night after all, for it is just midnight and I must get up very early.

I have been in Bombay for five days – all manner of odd committees, chiefly the Planning Committee, and the States Peoples' Conference, and some new developments about China. Bombay always interests me, perhaps [because] there are so many friends there. But it is very exhausting and I looked forward to my long journey to Lucknow. I took a rather slow train which took thirty-four hours, two full nights and a day, and I managed to put in nineteen hours' sleep during this period. I made up for arrears, but I have immediately started overdrawing again.

In Bombay a young man named Agarwala, who has recently returned from England, gave me a large number of coloured photographs of you, which he said Feroze[1] had asked him to bring to me. These pictures are very good but they are tiny. I suppose they should be seen through some kind of a magic lantern.

I have informed Bachhraj[2] to send you £50 by the end of this month. I shall await further news from you about finances before sending more remittances. I have very little idea of how you stand.

Just before I left Allahabad for Bombay, we had this *Amavas*[3] day of the *Magh melá*[4] and, as usual, vast crowds of pilgrims visited Anand Bhawan. They were all over the place and life became difficult for the day. But it was very exhilarating to see them and note their enthusiasm. Later in Bombay I saw different sights – crowds at meetings of course but what struck me most was an enormous long procession of cars going to the racecourse. It was an unending affair and I sensed more than I had ever done before the strength of the Bombay bourgeoisie.

I am here for the new elections of the P.C.C.[5] There is vast excitement and canvassing going on.

Love,
Papu

---

1. Feroze Gandhi: a young political worker of Allahabad, who assisted Kamala Nehru in her political activities. He married Indira Nehru in 1942.

2. Bachhraj & Co.: banking firm owned by Jamnalal Bajaj, a businessman and nationalist leader; served as bankers to Jawaharlal Nehru.

3. The dark night preceding the new moon.

4. Magh is the eleventh month of the Indian calendar. It is spread over January and February. A big fair (*melá*) is held every year during Magh at the Sangam, or the confluence of the rivers Ganga, Jumna and the mythical Saraswati, in Allahabad.

5. P.C.C.: Provincial Congress Committee.

9.                                             Les Frênes,
Leysin,
Switzerland
17th February, 1940

Darling Papu,
Your last letter – of Feb. 4th [1] – took only eight days to arrive. A record for these days.

I am feeling much better these last days – mentally, that is. That dreadful depression has lifted somewhat – maybe as a result of reading the *Glimpses*! I read a bit everyday while doing my 'position ventrale'. Physically there is no visible change. In my case Prof. Rollier seems to have changed his mind about helping the 'process of nature'. He was rather alarmed about my losing weight and asked me to take cod liver oil as well as

*'Phytine', qui forme la partie essentielle du principe phosphoré existant dans toutes les céréales et légumineuses, et constitue l'aliment phosphoré le plus concentré et le plus assimilable que l'on connaisse. D'après sa teneur en phosphore, 1 gramme de Phytine correspond à 500g de farine de froment ou 600g de pommes de terre.* [2]

Thus runs the little leaflet. I take a gram of it each day. I do not know if it is my imagination, but I have an idea that since I have started taking Phytine my appetite has improved slightly.

I am afraid this pen is misbehaving disgracefully. The one you passed on to me in Allahabad has not been very trustworthy. The one I have been writing with all these days is a cheap & unknown make. I picked it up – the pen, I mean – in a train when I came to Switzerland last summer. Someone left it behind. The conductor, to whom I offered it, refused to take it – so I kept it!

*18th February*
It's been snowing for days and still the soft white flakes flutter down endlessly. Already on my balcony there is a good three-inch layer. But it is not very cold. Isn't it strange how all one's remarks are comparative? When in India one says it is hot, the temperature is at least 112° F. But now in Leysin, when I write to you & say that it is quite hot, the

1. Refers to letter No. 5.
2. 'Phytine', which is the main element of phosphoric content found in all cereals and pulses. This is the best-known phosphorus-based food in its most concentrated and digestible form. Its phosphorus content makes 1 gramme of Phytine equivalent to 500 grammes of wheat flour or 600 grammes of potatoes.

temperature at the most is $-6°$ C. The coldest here, so far, has been $-22°$ C. And as soon as the temperature rises to $-16°$ C one thinks it is much warmer! When it is really cold, you have but to throw a handful of water on the ground or the window for it to freeze immediately into a most intricate and lovely design of hundreds of ice particles.

A letter dated the 25th January has just come from Chhoti Puphi.[1] She doesn't seem to know my address, for she sent it to Agatha. Will you please let her know? I shall write of course but I don't know how soon. I find it so difficult to write letters. Until three thirty p.m. the room is too cold to write in. At about three thirty or three forty-five the window is closed – then, by the time I have had tea and tidied myself, people start drifting in and out – Mrs Nanavati and some of the other patients who have now started getting up in the afternoons. Sometimes I go into their rooms in my bed! But always there is this pain, sometimes more, sometimes less, gnawing away at my side. Twice I have had the 'jam jar' treatment (the real name, I believe, is 'ventouses'), but it doesn't seem to make the slightest difference. Besides about what can one write to people – they have their own little troubles and are not really interested in anybody else's.

Two lots of the *National Herald* have arrived.

Two months in Leysin. Four and a half months in bed. When I first arrived here, Prof. Rollier himself suggested the time limit of three months at Les Frênes as being the time required to set me up on my feet strongly. I suppose the three months have been extended – by how much, I do not know. If only I could see or feel, or that at least the doctor could see, any improvement – then staying in bed or anything else would not matter. If – if.

The way they squeeze money out of you in this country is nothing short of scandalous. Those little things that most patients need at one time or another but in such minute quantities that in no other country would a hospital dream of charging for them cost money. And not only cost money but most exorbitant prices. For instance one teaspoon liquid paraffin costs one Swiss franc! The same price as a pot of tea! My weekly bill comes to an average of 180 Frs.

Meanwhile Mrs Stinnes,[2] who has taken a cottage in Celerina, invites me to stay with her as soon as I am able to. Mr Stinnes had extended this invitation while I was still in London. To him I said I would think about it but to Agatha I expressed the opinion that I should not like to owe anything to people like the Stinnes. This was meant for her alone but apparently she passed it on to Mr S., who suggested to

1. Junior Aunt: Krishna Hutheesing (Betty).
2. Mrs Stinnes: an American friend of Indira Gandhi.

her, that his wife & he had been thinking of having an English girl stay with them to talk English with the children, and having me with them would have the same end.

My writing seems to get worse and worse. At the moment I am in the 'position ventrale', which is not conducive to a good hand.

In three days there is 'La vente Rolliers', [1] a charity sale for the poorer patients. Madame Rollier has been to see us all & given us a pile of embroidery to do for it. And so these last days I have not done much else.

Don't be depressed, darling – I think it transfers itself to me. And do, do look after yourself.

Much love,
Your
Indu

10.

Anand Bhawan,
Allahabad
22nd February, 1940

My darling,
Your last letter of Feb. 9th [2] has put me out somewhat. It cannot be too cheerful of course resting all the time, and this terrible cold which you have been having must be depressing. But to suffer from lack of books and papers is something that never struck me. I know well how I would feel if I had to do without them. I could bear almost anything but that. Even then I could write if paper was not denied me but, much as I want to write, it would bore me after a while if there was no other activity or diversion. I never thought that there would be much difficulty in getting books from England, and it seemed rather absurd for me to send books from here, unless they were published here. Ever since I got your letter three days ago I have been trying to find books from the library which I might send you. There were many of course and yet it was not easy to pick and choose. Then I went to Kitabistan. [3] There was not much to choose. They complained that books were not coming in. Still I picked up a few odd books and these were sent to you by parcel post today. I hope they reach you. One never knows what happens to letters and parcels during these war days.

I enclose a list of the books sent. I have not read several of them

1. 'The Rollier Charity Sale'.
2. Refers to letter No. 7.
3. Kitabistan: a publishing house in Allahabad.

but they seemed interesting, especially the Dragon Book on Chinese literature. Capek[1] is always worth reading. The *Oxford Book of English Verse* is a very good collection. Kropotkin's[2] book is an old classic – perhaps heavy reading but still often extraordinarily interesting. I have added Arnold's[3] two little books: *The Light of Asia* and *The Song Celestial*, both of which Kitabistan have recently brought out in a new Indian edition.

It must be pretty bad for you if you have to fall back on *Glimpses of History*! Somebody would have to give me a prize if he wanted me to read it again. It was bad enough to revise it. I refused to read the proofs.

I am asking Agatha to arrange to send you some books and papers and am sending her £5 for this purpose. Will you indicate to her what you would like to have?

I am also arranging to have the *Harijan* and the *Hindu Illustrated Weekly* sent to you regularly. They are not very exciting but they will at least keep you in touch with events here to some extent. That is if they reach you. Evidently the *Herald* is not reaching you. For the moment I can think of nothing else that I can do in this respect. If I have a brainwave I shall act up to it.

Has not Dr Rollier suggested some hand-work for you? I thought that was a part of his treatment and a very good part too. I almost felt like sending you a *takli*.[4] I have been spinning off and on recently, that is when I am in Allahabad, and I find it very soothing. You can knit as you did in England. Or play about with cardboard. I hear children in the Basic Schools here make delightful boxes and other things out of cardboard. It is a fascinating pastime.

But I do hope that by the time this reaches you, you will be moving about a little more. Spring will be nearing then and the breath of it will invigorate you. You will grow stronger and stronger and push out all traces of weakness from your body. I wish I could transfer some might from my body to yours. I have been growing disgustingly plump. Perhaps I exaggerate, but the tendency is there and I am worried about it. Indian clothes, both *dhoti*[5] and pyjamas, adjust themselves to any size of waist and one does not notice changes in its size. When I went to China in August last, I put on European clothes and I discovered immediately that all was not well. The other day in Bombay I weighed myself and I

1. Karel Capek: Czech journalist, playwright and writer.
2. Peter Alexeivich Kropotkin: Russian geographer, revolutionary and social philosopher.
3. Sir Edwin Arnold: English poet and journalist; *The Light of Asia* was a poem on the life and teachings of Buddha.
4. Spindle.
5. A long piece of cloth tied round the waist and wrapped around each of the legs.

was horrified to find that I had gone up to 143 pounds. This was 3 lbs more than I have ever been. It is true that I was well-clad at the time and was wearing a heavy *sherwani*.[1] Still! Another weighing machine a fortnight later gave me 135 pounds as my weight, which was much more satisfactory. Probably both the machines were wrong. Anyway I have had a fright and after a long gap, I have taken to some kind of physical exercises again when I am in Allahabad. I feel a little better for them, or at any rate I hold myself better and that makes a difference.

My foot is ninety-five per cent right now. It is curious how these little ailments hang on. In Bombay I took electric treatment for it and this did me good.

I have seen again and again the technicolor photos of you that Feroze sent me. They are very fine and I love looking at them. But they are so tiny and I do not know how they can be enlarged. I have lost all, or nearly all, interest in my Contax camera. It lies unheeded. I wish you had taken it with you. Anyway it will reach you some time or other and will then be of some use.

Makkhi Atal's[2] marriage with Ganga Raina is coming off here in two or three days and there are numerous parties and feasts. The world may go bang but an Indian marriage must take place in the old style, with all the usual waste. I never feel more out of place than at these feasts and indeed I hardly ever go there. But on this occasion I must put in an appearance once at least, lest all manner of wrong political inferences might be drawn.

I have been reading a new book – Van Passen's[3] *Days of Our Years* which Alex Fraser[4] sent me for the New Year. It is a press correspondent's account of his life & adventures and is very interesting and worth reading. You might ask Agatha to have it sent to you. Why did you not get a copy of *Glimpses*? This is absurd. It was not necessary for me to mention this to Krishna. He ought to have known. But as a matter of fact I sent him a list of persons to whom complimentary copies should be sent and your name topped the list. I did not give an address as I did not know where you might be when the book came out. Please ask Krishna to have a copy sent to you or to Mlle Hemmerlin.

In reading any serious book (I am not referring to *Glimpses*) it would be a good thing if you took copious notes. This slows down the pace of reading and allows time to think and absorb the book. Otherwise the

1. A long coat with buttoned-up collar.
2. Jai Kumar Atal: served in the Indian Foreign Service; married Ganga Raina, the granddaughter of Raja Narendranath Raina, a distinguished civil servant of Lahore, whose daughter, Rameshwari, was married to Brijlal Nehru.
3. Pierre Van Passen: Dutch-born journalist and author living in U.S.
4. Alexander Campbell Fraser: Scottish philosopher.

book leaves only a fleeting impression and too many fleeting impressions, one after the other, create confusion. I always remember that Erasmus (or some other big scholar of the Middle Ages) had a library of only fifty or sixty volumes. And yet he was one of the wisest and most learned of men.

I suppose Louise Morin[1] could send you interesting reading matter if you suggested it to her.

You complain of some pain on the left side of the lungs. Of course it is for the doctor to say what this is. But from some slight personal experience I would say that this is nothing to worry about. Pleurisy is an extraordinarily sticky thing and sometimes adhesions and thickenings are formed which pain. Do you know that even now, and quite frequently, I get a pain due to some ancient pleurisy? Whenever I am at all low in health, I get this pain – or when I am tired. And yet my general health is A1. It was this slight hangover from old pleurisy that induced me to allow myself to put on a little weight as a kind of insurance. But unfortunately weight attaches itself at the wrong place!

I am vastly interested in your account of the stroboscope and of Nylon. I know nothing about them but your account of them is exciting. All our day-to-day politics seem so silly and childish when such discoveries are made, which might change human life so much. I wish you could send me some more information about these two – that is if you can easily do so.

It is almost a year now, or at least ten months, since I saw you. It seems an age, and I long to have a glimpse of you again. Every little while, whether I am at work or in a crowd, my mind wanders away and centres itself round you, and the desire to be near you almost overwhelms me. You are lonely at Leysin. There is also a loneliness in the midst of crowds. If there is no other way, I might not be able to restrain myself from packing up a suitcase and taking a plane to Europe!

But meanwhile there is the Congress coming at Ramgarh in Chhota Nagpur – a lovely spot, I am told, nestling at the foot of the hills. It is far from cities and the like. After the Congress, no one knows what will happen. How helpless we all are in the hands of vast forces! We shout and imagine that we are doing great things and yet we are prisoners of these forces and of destiny. Big things apart, which may come unheralded and drag us in their wake, I am tied up especially after the Congress with the National Planning Committee. This is going to be heavy labour. I hope however to finish with it by early July.

---

1. Louise Morin: French journalist who was later to be in charge of the French unit of the All India Radio. She was a friend of the Nehrus.

And now to other work. So goodbye for the present, *carissima mia*, [1] and may it be well with you.

Love,
Papu

*ENCL.*

*List of Books*

1. *Literature and Society* – David Daiches
2. *The Mother* – Karel Capek
3. *Week-End Caravan* – S. Hillelson
4. *Ding Dong Bell* – Walter De La Mare
5. *The Oxford Book of English Verse 1250–1918* – Sir Arthur Quiller-Couch
6. *The Dragon Book* – E. D. Edwards
7. *The Light of Asia* – Sir Edwin Arnold
8. *The Song Celestial* – Sir Edwin Arnold
9. *Ur of the Chaldees* – Sir Leonard Woolley, Pelican Books
10. *Mutual Aid* – Prince Peter Kropotkin, Pelican Books

---

11.

Anand Bhawan,
Allahabad,
27th February, 1940

My darling one,
Tonight, in an hour's time, I go to Patna and I had decided to send you a brief letter before I left. Not that there was anything special to write about. But it is pleasing to write to you and I did not know how I would fare at Patna with the Working Committee there. I went to a tea party (one of the Makkhi Atal wedding ones) and on returning found your letter of Feb. 18th [2] waiting for me and I looked at your handwriting with joy. By the same *dak* [3] came a letter from Krishna from London dated 25th January by air. While your letter took nine days, Krishna's took over a month. Partly the delay is no doubt due to our friend the censor who must take a very special interest in Krishna's letters, for they are political. Indeed some of his letters do not reach me at all. Your letters being personal fare better.

I am happy to learn that you were feeling better and that cod liver oil

---

1. My dearest.
2. Refers to letter No. 9.
3. Mail.

and phytine, *qui forme la partie essentielle du principe phosphoré,* [1] etc., are doing you good. I am sure that with the coming of somewhat milder weather you will gain in appetite and weight. I do not suppose you will ever be a heavy weight or will have to indulge in Hay diet [2] or something else in order to slim. You are not made that way. But your weight should be at least 100 pounds. It will be that presently when you move about.

You complain of your pen. I am myself feeling very sad at present for I have just lost my favourite one. I guard nothing so jealously as my fountainpens, especially those that I like. As a matter of fact I lose them seldom. But at this afternoon's tea party I was giving autographs and something unusual happened to it. It has disappeared.

I am not depressed, *Cara mia,* although the world, as well as my own particular world, goes all awry. I have become completely *behaya.* [3] If you want to know what depression is you should read Krishna's letters to me. He works himself up terribly and, bad as the world is, imagines all manner of things which are worse. And then, with many apologies, he gives me a lot of good advice, not knowing how I would take it all. I like him of course to give the good advice. It helps. But I wish he would not get so excited. It is not good for him. His nerves have never been his strong point.

About the Stinnes, there is no hurry for you to decide. We shall see later and if you feel like it, you can go there for a while.

Tara has just come in and sends you her love.

The Atal-Raina wedding has taken place with all pomp and circumstance. It was the first Kashmiri wedding I attended since my own! Puphi's wedding in 1921 was not a full-blooded Kashmiri one and apart from that I have attended no other similar function. Chhoti Puphi's was a simple registration ceremony. I was glad I went as this enabled me to see the new generation. Children whom I knew long ago were grown-up boys and girls and young women. The picture in my mind had remained static and it was surprising for me to discover how they had grown. They looked an attractive crowd. Ganga looked very pretty in her wedding dress but exactly like a doll.

Cheers! Upadhyaya [4] has discovered my pen. So all is well. You will notice the change in the writing.

My mind goes back to a year ago. Were we not at Almora then? And one day I broke off a cactus cone or bundle of leaves, and here it is

1. Which forms the essential part of phosphorus.
2. Hay diet: fashionable diet regime in the 1930s.
3. Shameless.
4. S. D. Upadhyaya: personal secretary to Motilal Nehru and later to Jawaharlal Nehru.

lying in front of me now, all dried up. But I keep it and often handle it for it reminds me of Almora and you.

The Congress is coming. Last year I was busy writing a series of articles – *Where are We?* I have not been writing much lately but possibly I might burst out suddenly with a series. My mind is full of it but I am not sure of other factors. The Working Committee might give a push to my mind. Meanwhile I have been trying to clear up my odd commitments so far as I can and I have done a good bit of work during the last few days. All my A letters have been disposed of – all my foreign letters (they are becoming voluminous) – but the fat B lot still remain. I have gone through vast numbers of odd papers and destroyed them or filed them. Indeed my room has undergone a spring cleaning and I have even rearranged my books. I started doing this rather casually one evening after dinner and went on and on till two thirty a.m. At that attractive and witching hour the floor of my room was full of books and papers lying in complete disorder! The next day was devoted to arranging them.

If I could get a clear week more I would tie up many of the loose strings in my activities and have a clean slate for intensive work in future. I like this feeling of a clean slate. My mind feels relieved and in a mood to go ahead. Life's burdens seem less.

I must go now. A hurried dinner and then to the station.

All my love,<br>Papu

I gave Betty your address.

------

12.                                                       Anand Bhawan,<br>
               Allahabad,<br>
         2nd March, 1940

Darling Indu,
I have come back from Patna. The Working Committee passed only one resolution for the Congress. I enclose a copy of this.[1] Presumably the Congress will adopt this and finish its work soon. But one never knows. You will see that events are marching, even in India, and we are likely to get more and more caught in their coils.

In Patna I stayed with Mahmud.[2] His sons have grown so much that

1. The resolution, subsequently adopted at the annual session of the Congress at Ramgarh, urges the British Government to commit itself to conferring independence upon India after the war, and also constituting a Provincial Government with the participation of the nationalist leadership.
2. Dr Syed Mahmud: barrister and nationalist who held high office after 1947.

it is difficult to recognise them. One of them, aged fourteen, is already two or three inches taller than I am!

Apart from political work, I visited a very interesting private collection in Patna. It was surprising to find a Marwari businessman developing into an art collector. He lives in a lovely house by the riverside and he has gathered together many fascinating articles, especially a fine collection of old Chinese jade. There are good examples of old Sèvres and Gobelins. A part of the dinner service of Marie Antoinette, a writing cabinet of Henry II, King of France, very beautiful Arabic, Persian manuscripts, old German statuettes, shawls, a piece of old Dacca muslin ten yards weighing 7¼ tolas [1] – just imagine the gossamer fineness of it! And so many other things which I had hardly time to see. He has also built a small but very delightful guest-house overlooking the river Ganga.

After a few days I shall have to return to Behar for the Congress which is being held at Ramgarh in Chhota Nagpur. This . . . [place] is hilly and beautiful. So I have decided to take two days off and motor slowly through Chhota Nagpur just before the Congress. Mahmud is fixing up the car and we start from Patna on the 13th morning reaching Ramgarh on the 15th morning. Probably we shall be in Ramgarh for a week.

You are always in my thoughts and I imagine you growing stronger and stronger – a real Diana.

Love,
Papu

---

13.                                                   Les Frênes,

Leysin,
Switzerland,
3rd March, 1940

Papu, you great darling!

How very thoughtful of you to send all those books! As a matter of fact I ought to have exerted myself in that direction long ago but most books are so expensive and at this distance I found it difficult to choose the ones I wished to buy. However, about a week and a half ago, I did order some books from Blackwell's in Oxford (I have an account with them):

> Laski's *The Danger of Being a Gentleman*
> Vera Brittain's *Testament of Friendship*
> D. N. Pritt's *Must the War Spread?* a Penguin Special

---

1. Tola: a unit of weight. One tola is equal to ten grams.

Gallocha's *The Chosen Few* – a pamphlet
T. S. Eliot, *Waste Land & other poems*
Stephen Spender, *Poems*

both these last in a new half-a-crown edition called the Sesame Series. So far I have not heard from Blackwell's. Thanks so much for your lot. I do hope they arrive safely, all of them, and soon. Have Kitabistan got an exit permit? And, in case the books are not allowed out of the country, I hope they will be returned to you & not kept by the censor!

The *National Herald* now arrives fairly regularly. I think Agatha had better hang on to the £5 for the moment, for I don't think I shall order any more books from England just yet.

Two of your letters, dated the 15th[1] & 22nd Feb.,[2] arrived together last evening. And with them also, one from Chhoti Puphi dated the 18th.

I am so glad you liked the colour pictures. As a matter of fact I had them taken specially for you. The original intention was to have them printed in England – the things you have now are the negatives – and to send you the prints. But this is rather an expensive process: 4 sh per copy! And also, I did not care for the results, the colours came out rather crude & unnatural. The best way to see them is either through an ordinary projector, in which case you have to have a screen as well, by the way. I wonder if the old Pathé projector that used to lie about in Anand Bhawan will do. I suppose not. The other way is through a special gadget which I looked at in Lucerne. In Switzerland it costs 50 francs – at the present rate of exchange, nearly £3. Do you think it is worth buying? If so, I'll ask the local photographer to procure one.

I thought two of the pictures particularly beautiful. They were taken from a bedroom window in Burgenstock at about eight thirty a.m. with an exposure of half an hour, and show the Lake of Lucerne & the lights of Lucerne town.

I have two lots of hand-work going at the same time but I don't get along very fast nowadays almost all the morning & afternoon I have to lie on my tummy, resting on my elbows. In this position I find it difficult to do anything but read – though now I am practising writing letters as well. Between four & four thirty p.m. I get up – since this last fortnight. I go for a short walk, walking very very slowly for about fifteen to thirty minutes, & then sit either with the Nanavatis next door or in the lounge downstairs until six p.m.

Since I have been getting up, I have gained 700 grams: just over 1½

1. Refers to letter No. 8.
2. Refers to letter No. 10.

lbs. Total gain since arrival two and a half months ago equals 2 2/5 lbs! I know that the pain does not mean anything but there is no way of relieving it except perhaps by taking drugs & to this both the doctor & I am averse, and when it is present I find it impossible to concentrate on anything. I have been having rather bad nights probably due to the warmth – for I drink glass upon glass of water all night. Or maybe, the getting up tired me too much. Yesterday when Dr Rollier came I asked him about how long I should have to stay on at Les Frênes, since my three months would be up on the 15th. *'Encore quelques mois'* – some more months still – was the reply, whatever that may mean! So that's that.

I miss you so much and long to see you and to be near you. But even when all these wretched months here are over, I shall have to stay in the mountains in India for about two years. There is no such thing as a comfortable hotel in India, except in the big cities, and I know of no one who could come & set up house for me for that long period. Last year we saw how very difficult & complicated it was to stay up in Almora even for one and a half months. Puphi was eager to be back home in Bombay & there was all the trouble over the servants. Mrs Nanavati here suggests that I go and stay with them, for she has to keep Mr Nanavati in the hills too. But her idea of mountains are Devlali, or at most, Mahableshwar. Dr Bhandari thinks I ought to stay in Kashmir during the whole period, not once descending into the plains. The only person I can think of who is more or less free is Nani[1] and I could hardly expect her to go for walks with me. Can you suggest something? Even if the *'quelques mois'* means four months – that takes us to July. I should then like to go to England just to collect my belongings & then sail towards the end of August.

Meanwhile, as you say, there is the Congress. Perhaps this letter will reach you at Ramgarh! And after that no one knows what is going to happen. And in May you are going to Kashmir. So we are both tied up by such very different things.

Nylon is just a small part in this new artificial world which the chemists are bringing into being. And what great strides they have taken these last twenty years. At the end of the Great War, as Dr Stine of the Du Pont Co. points out, 'sheep, plants, & worms supplied the fibers for our textiles. Bone, hides, tusks, horn, the saps and barks of trees, the excretions of insects & animal life and countless other products as ancient as commerce filled motor trucks & freight cars and the holds of ships, just as they made up the burdens of caravans in the days of Marco

1. Rajpati Kaul: (Amma or Nani): Kamala Nehru's mother, Indira's grandmother.

Polo. [1] We were building and designing better homes, but of the same materials – stones, brick and wood – of which homes had been made for thousands of years. We were wearing the same clothing that our grandfathers wore, merely cut to a new style & woven by machine instead of by hand.' In India this is where we still stand. But in Europe & America things have been changing slowly but very surely. And this is not in spite of wars but because of them, and foreign trade, embargoes, tariffs and even occasional scarcity of and lack of uniformity of raw materials. And now, every few days, in newspapers we read of yet another 'miracle' from this or that great chemical laboratory – 'wool' from milk; alcohol, rubber and false teeth from gas; liquorice from old tree stumps – or a new way to poison grasshoppers. I am afraid, all that I know about Nylon is that it is made from coal, air & water into a fine silky thread, more elastic than silk. When hardened and formed it also makes bristles, going now into millions of toothbrushes. Man has been imitating nature and yet you cannot call these things that he has produced mere imitation, for they are not only quite different articles even in their chemical compositions, but in many ways superior to the natural product. Thus we can now make true daylight and by using a compound of iodine & quinine in coating a glass take away the glare from it, even from bright sunshine! 'Polaroid' is the name of this new material. It is just a film of tiny needle-shaped crystals containing iodine and quinine, all lying parallel and fixed between two sheets of glass or transparent plastic. One can look through several thicknesses of a Polaroid sheet if they are on top of the other, or in a roll. But if a corner of the sheet is turned up, the parallel slots are crossed and no light may pass through & Polaroid becomes completely opaque. Polaroid is used in spectacles, reading lamps, camera filters, etc – also for motor car headlights, in which case it helps considerably in making night driving safer.

Yet another example of man outwitting – or rather, improving on – nature is glass. Nature made obsidian, or glass, in volcanoes. It was in chunks. Now man spins it; from a common glass marble he can unwind a ninety-mile filament, finer than spiderweb; or he can twist it and make it as strong as piano wire.

Insects may eat ordinary sawed boards. But man can now stop this waste. He can take trees or old stumps, digest them, recover the fibre, and rearrange it to make his own boards that cannot split or stain or rot.

No less wonderful is 'Lucite', a new addition to the plastic family.

1. Marco Polo (1254–1324): Italian traveller; journeyed to China, Sumatra, India and Persia; captured by the Genoese and imprisoned for a year at Genoa (1298), where he dictated to a fellow prisoner the story of his travels, published under the title of *The Book of Marco Polo*.

Through Lucite, light flows like water in a pipe, it is even carried around a bend! Lucite instruments are mostly used in surgery & dentistry, to illuminate body and oral cavities without the risk of burning the patient, for the light coming through the rod is quite cold!

I must stop or I'll go on and on, for the story of the chemical industries is not the least fascinating and wonderful amongst all the marvels of this world of ours.

The Nanavatis are leaving tomorrow morning. They sail from Genoa on the 8th.

Heaps & heaps of love,
Indu

P.S.
Published in America is a small book of photographs taken with a stroboscope. They are said to be remarkably lovely. I shall try & get one for you.

---

14.

Les Frênes,
Leysin,
Switzerland,
9th March, 1940

Darling Papu,
I have just been reading – in the *National Herald* – your article on Russia & the Finnish war. Also the use that is being made, in England, of your statements on the subject. You seemed to be shocked equally by the Russo-German Pact and the war on Finland. And yet, doesn't the responsibility of both rest heavily on these eight years of British foreign policy? At Munich, England and France proved definitely on which side they stood. Russia's policy of collective security having failed, she retired into her pre-Litvinov [1] isolation and her chief preoccupation was bound to be how to keep herself out of the impending European war. (Hence the advance into the Baltic.) The Russo-German Pact was certainly not a change of front, since Germany primarily asked no more of Russia than that this isolation should continue. And the pact has not made any difference to the Soviet Union's condemnation of Nazism and Imperialism – viz Molotov's [2] speech in November, or the Manifesto of the

1. Makim Makimovich Litvinov: Soviet statesman and diplomat; as Foreign Minister, 1930–9 he was in favour of a joint front with the democratic countries in the 1930s; Soviet Ambassador to U.S., 1941–3.
2. Vaycheslav Mikhailovich Molotov: Soviet statesman and politician; Prime Minister, 1930–41, and Foreign Minister, 1939–49, 1953–6.

Communist International on the present war. As to Finland, you agree that the Soviet Union's demands were justified. Why, then, did the war come as such a shock to you? Did you expect the Soviet Union, after her demands had been rejected at the instigation of the Allies, to sit back & say no more about it until the whole war should be directed against her? For such was – is still – the intention of the Allies, as the British press is at no pains to conceal.

A recent *Times* leader reminded the British public of the 'deep gratitude' they owed to Baron Mannerheim [1] for occupying Russia in a way that was very convenient to the Allies since it hindered Russia in sending supplies to Germany. Almost the day on which war broke out in Finland, the National Govt – in the words of its Prime Minister – 'decided to permit the release & immediate delivery to Finland . . . of a number of fighter aircraft of which the Finnish Govt stood in urgent need, and they intend similarly to release other material . . .' This when Britain was herself involved in a war. Compare these words with those Chamberlain spoke a year ago on the subject of sending arms to Republican Spain. 'So far as this country is concerned the effect of allowing the Government of Spain to purchase arms would be very little because we ourselves obviously want all the armaments that are in our possession for our own protection.' Was this because, as Lady Ironside [2] remarked at a certain house party I remember, 'But Franco is such a gentleman'? And so, of course, is Baron Mannerheim. There was a time when the Finnish Social Democrats & Communists held a majority in the Finnish Diet. [3] A hastily organised army by Mannerheim proved inadequate so Germany sent an army of 12,000. And with its aid the counter-revolution emerged the victor and promptly proceeded to slaughter, as even the *Encyclopaedia Britannica* will acknowledge, 15,000 Communists of whom over 4500 were women & children, 'to maintain order'. Who says that Finland has forgotten that appalling White Terror? And even von der Goltz, [4] the general in charge of the German Army, admits in his memoirs 'that the "Red" Finnish revolution was not accompanied by any terror or atrocities'.

1. Baron Karl Gustav Emil von Mannerheim: a conservative Finnish soldier and statesman who led Finnish resistance to the Bolsheviks in 1918 and subsequently conducted the defence of Finland in 1944–6. President of Finland, 1944–6.

2. Lady Ironside: wife of William Edmund Ironside, Chief of Britain's Imperial General Staff, 1939–40.

3. After the declaration of Finnish independence in 1918 revolutionaries seized Helsinki and the large industrial towns of southern Finland. The right-wing government organised a counter-attack under the leadership of Count Mannerheim. With German help his White Army suppressed the rebellion, which was followed by trials in which harsh sentences were passed.

4. Rudiger von der Goltz: German general in the First World War.

This is the 'democracy' the world imperialism is aiding against the country who was practically alone at the League of Nations in upholding the one method of banishing war from the world. And the Liberals and the Labourites go on glibly talking about 'the freedom of the press' & and the 'freedom of speech', even as in their own countries and all around them, Communists and socialists are being hounded down into concentration camps. As late as 1933, Sir Walter Citrine [1] now so loud upon the side of the great 'Finnish democracy', called Finland a dictatorship at a Trades Union Congress. All this talk of poor Finland makes me sick. Just because a country is small in size, do the crimes of its Government lessen also and does its repression & totalitarianism likewise become softer & more bearable to its people & the people of the world?

Today I am feeling better again after rather a bad few days, when I was ordered back to bed! I got up today & went out for a wee walk. It was cold but perfectly beautifully clear & sunny. This last week has been bitterly cold with lots of snow.

While I was in my bath, which I'm allowed to have only once a week! – this evening, came a phone call from Mlle Hemmerlin. She wants to have lunch here tomorrow.

By the way, I had a letter from Nanu [2] the other day. He sounds very dejected. He's not got much work & though he does not say so, I gather that he is lacking in funds. He says he has written to you several times but has not had any reply.

Do excuse this perfectly appalling paper. I went & bought it this evening. It was all they had at the shop.

In an old issue of *Life* I have discovered some 'stroboscopic' photographs. I shall try & send them to you in my next letter soon.

Darling, don't bother about my fits of depression. They come & go and don't really matter one bit.

With lots & lots of love,
Your
Indu

---

1. Sir Walter Citrine: General Secretary of the T.U.C., 1925–46; he led a British Trade Union delegation to Moscow in October, 1941.

2. A. C. N. Nambiar (Nanu): a journalist, active in the struggle for freedom who was a close friend of the Nehrus. Mr Nambiar was in Europe at this juncture and was caught up in the turmoil of the Second World War.

15.                                                      Anand Bhawan,
                                                             Allahabad,
                                                        11th March, 1940

Darling,
Your letter of the 20th February[1] has just come. It does not make
cheerful reading. I long to help you or to do something for you but I
feel so helpless. Not only are you far from me, with a major war coming
in the way, but otherwise too I am hardly capable of even advising. Only
you can judge or your doctors or others whom you can consult. I wish
I could take the burden somewhat from you but I have lost faith in
myself in many ways. I am writing to Bhandari and I hope you will also
keep in touch with him.

      Thinking about you so often, it has struck me how little we have been
together during these years, especially since 1930. You were a babe in
arms when I became entangled in non-cooperation and the like and for
some years I saw you irregularly. Then we were together in Geneva for
some months before you went to Chesières. From 1930 onwards I was
often in prison and you were first at the Poona school and then at
Santiniketan. Later Switzerland, Bristol, Oxford, etc. You came to India
in 1937 and I went to Europe in 1938. Again you came to India for a
few months but even here you were mostly at Almora. It is almost a year
since you went.

      Off and on we have met but my mind has been full of you and has
formed a thousand pictures which keep me company. Long ago when
you were at Mussoorie and I was in Allahabad, I tried to fill the gap
created by your absence by writing to you those letters which came out
later as a little book. I continued this practice because it soothed me
and pleased me and supplied something that I lacked. I seldom thought
of writing books, I was thinking of you. But books resulted.

      During all these years of separation and thinking of you, you came
very close to me, or rather the image I made of you became almost part
of me. But then that was a creature of my thought. You were far away.

      I moved about in crowds, my days filled with incessant activity. To
save myself from being submerged in these crowds I lived my own life
of the mind, where I had myself for companion and those pictures of
my dear ones which were largely my own creation. The crowds gave
something to me of value but they took a lot out of me. Gradually I
came to realise that while perhaps I understood crowds a little, I did
not understand individuals. Probably this deficiency, which distressed
me, was innate in me and had little to do with the crowds or my activity.

      1. Letter not traceable.

Only that activity covered and hid it from my eyes. I realised with something of a shock how little one person really knows another, and how often those that are nearest and dearest to us are almost as strangers to us. I had read this somewhere in French poetry and hardly realised its significance. This knowledge, with all its disturbing consequences, came to me. I wondered if this was a general rule or at least a common occurrence, or was it peculiar to a few? Meanwhile life passed on, leaving many an impress upon me. The crowd ceased to fascinate me as it used to, and I found how utterly alone I was. I had learnt much in the passage of years, but I had failed in the hard test of life. I had proved incompetent and life is hard on the incompetents. Large numbers of people, men and women, came to me or wrote to me for advice about their own personal problems. Because of my political notoriety, they took me to be an expert in matters beyond my ken. The success that had apparently come to me and made me known to large numbers covered a failure in much that counts in the life of the individual.

Public and private life act and react on each other, and this sense of failure has pursued me in almost all I do. With this lack of faith in myself, how can I advise anyone? What right have I to interfere in another's life? I have not made my own a brilliant success and all my good intentions, or so I imagined they were, have not prevented me often from making a mess of things. In my pride I thought that I could do great things, but life has humbled me and shown me the error of my thought.

So, my darling, I am a poor kind of person to seek advice from. Everything that I can possibly give you is yours for the asking, but do not seek advice from me for my mind is disturbed and lacks clarity. Even this letter, I suppose, is a jumble of ill-assorted ideas which will possibly confuse and worry you. I am sorry. But it represents a fraction of my mind.

I had written to you that I intended going by car to Ramgarh from Patna. I do not like motoring much, but I wanted to get away from myself – if that is ever possible – and visit Nalanda and Gaya and especially the thick jungles of Chhota Nagpur. A jungle, I thought, would certainly bring relief. Now all that is off and I am staying on in Allahabad till the last moment, that is the 14th night. This is at the bidding of Maulana Abul Kalam Azad,[1] our new President. He has written his presidential address in Urdu and he wants me to translate it into English. I am no good at this job and have never done any translation work – except from Latin in school. The whole address even has not

---

1. A leader of the struggle for freedom in India, he was President of the Ramgarh session of the Indian National Congress, 1940.

reached me yet. It is coming in driblets. Yesterday I spent about eight hours over it, wrestling with Maulana's graceful and flowery Urdu. I had taken the precaution to have a draft translation made first by some others. I merely revised and yet this was a terribly fatiguing affair.

Maulana is a curious type, very attractive. He reminds me very forcibly of eighteenth-century Rationalists and French Encyclopaedists. [1] That does not mean that he is reactionary but he is out of touch with many modern developments. Most people who might even consider themselves advanced and talk the jargon of the day, are really quite medieval in outlook. Maulana has got a mind like a razor which cuts through a fog of vague ideas – only it functions in the atmosphere of eighteenth- & early nineteenth-century Europe. It is always a pleasant surprise to realise that a person whose education has been entirely a religious one, and who is steeped in Muslim religious lore should be so rational and keen-minded. If he had had the chance to learn well one or more European languages and had thus come more in contact with modern thought, he would have been a very remarkable person. Even now he tries to grapple with these problems and succeeds more than many others.

You might have heard that one of the Imperial Airway liners disappeared somewhere *en route* to Europe from India. This was carrying mails and it appears that these mails included a £50 remittance to your bank. I think I wrote to you about this. It is not certain yet whether this remittance order has been lost or not. Anyway I have asked Bachhraj to send you another £50 immediately.

I have sent you during the last week or two some new pictures of mine. This is not to flood you with my pictures or to add to your luggage. They were recently taken and I thought they might interest you. You can pass them on to others. One of them was taken in my room. I was sitting at my writing table, as I am doing now. So much of my life is spent at this table that this picture is characteristic.

All my love to you, my dear one,

Your loving

Papu

---

1. Encyclopaedists: the collaborators in the 35-volume Encyclopaedia published under the direction of Diderot and d'Alembert between 1751 and 1776. Contributors included Voltaire, Montesquieu, J. J. Rousseau and other brilliant writers and embodied the philosophical spirit of the eighteenth century, its attempt to give a rational explanation of the universe being marked by a love of truth and contempt for superstition.

16.                                                    Les Frênes,
                                                            Leysin,
                                                       Switzerland,
                                                   12th March, 1940

Darling Papu,
Your two letters – of Feb. 27th,[1] March 2nd[2] arrived together last evening, also the Working Committee resolutions.

And well may Krishna be depressed. There is cause enough. In the B.B.C. news last evening we learnt of Chamberlain's announcement in the House that Great Britain & France will help Finland to their utmost capacity.[3] I do not think this announcement came as a surprise to anybody. How could Chamberlain who has so far been goading on Finland, now allow her to accept the Russian terms, as obviously she was prepared to do. To say that Finland would be giving up her independence is ridiculous. What about Estonia & Latvia, who are certainly not regretting their treaties with Russia, since the Soviet Union has in no way interfered with their internal affairs, but has, in return, brought them more trade & therefore prosperity? 'We are not going to war with Russia – yet,' says Mr Chamberlain which shows that Russia is not the only country who has learned & adopted something from German methods, as the press has been shrieking out at us these last weeks. Chamberlain has been just as apt & more willing a pupil. This bland acceptance of the German and Italian kind of 'non-intervention' being advocated – can hardly be followed without the clearest risk of retaliation by Russia. And this, presumably, is what the British Government wants. And not only the Government, but the Hugh Daltons[4] of the world. Mr Attlee[5] has, so far, remained discreetly silent. So the war with Russia that England has been wanting, & preparing for, these many months is upon us and once England is in, India will be automatically in and there will be yet another occasion for all the Maharajahs to show their loyalty and generosity and abhorrence of 'aggression & inhumanity'! Well may we be depressed – this is a fight that we have long expected, and now that it has come we are ill-prepared to face it. The National Govt. is not fighting against one Mr Stalin's aggression but

1. Refers to letter No. 11.
2. Refers to letter No. 12.
3. On 11th March Chamberlain announced that the Allies would respond to Finnish appeals for help against the Russian invasion but peace was signed in Moscow on 12th March and hostilities between Russia and Finland ceased on 13th March. The Finns handed Hangö to the Russians on 22nd March.
4. Hugh Dalton: Labour politician, Minister of Economic Warfare, 1940–2.
5. Clement Attlee was at this time Leader of the Opposition.

against the liberties and rights and the restricted semblance of power for which the lower classes have sacrificed and struggled and in spite of many defeats, advanced step by step, not today nor yesterday but through hundreds of years.

When I am feeling particularly fed up, there come to my mind, the last words of Mayakovski: [1]

> Futile to pass in review
> the sorrows
> the misfortunes
> and mutual wrongs,
> Be Happy!

I sent you a cutting from the *Manchester Guardian*.

I am glad you have decided on that motor trip. It will refresh you before the strain of the Congress Session. I suppose it is very hot this time of the year round about Nagpur. I am ashamed not to have seen more of India but I do not suppose I shall ever be able to travel much, being so allergic to heat. Even here, though I prefer the milder weather to the severe cold now prevailing, whenever the sun comes out & is strong and hot, I droop like a faded flower. In any case, the sun is supposed, even by sun-enthusiasts such as Professor Rollier, to be bad for weak lungs. So I am allowed to sunbathe only below the hips and that for not more than half an hour continuously and two hours altogether.

Mlle Hemmerlin came to lunch on Sunday and stayed through the 'Silence', for tea. She had to catch the 4.20 train back to Aigle. She brought some books – French ones – and the first snowdrops of the year. It is already spring in Bex and Aigle. The snow is all melted and the flowers are hesitatingly pushing through the layer of autumn leaves. The train route from Aigle to Leysin is, I hear, covered on both sides by masses of hepatica.

By the way, in those 'Agfa-colour' pictures, did you notice the flowers? They are so small that it is difficult to photograph them except in a close-up. But in one or two pictures, I believe, you can see marsh marigolds and gentians. Surely, all these flowers exist in Kashmir? They ought even to be in Almora, if climate is anything to go by. And yet one never hears of them, nor are they used in designs for wood carving & embroidery as the lotus & rose & iris are in Kashmir. I wonder why? Is it because, in India as so often in the hotter countries, most flowers are

---

1. Vladimir Vladimirovich Mayakovski: Russian poet and playwright, identified with the futurist school. He committed suicide in 1930.

so big and bright and gaudy that these small, delicate and modest heralds of spring are passed by unnoticed?

I suppose the Ramgarh Congress will mean a family reunion, or isn't Chhoti Puphi coming with Rajabhai? She writes to me, 'To me it seems rather futile staying on in Switzerland' and 'I hear from a friend that Leysin is not a very [pleasant?] place'. What does she imagine I am doing here? I can't think – perhaps going the round of parties, such as form the social life of the 'elect' in India.

I am sending this – as I do all my letters to you – to Allahabad, since I do not know when it will reach India & where you will be at that moment.

Lots of love – darling Papu,
Your
Indu

17.
Ramgarh,
19th March, 1940

Darling,
Your letter of the 3rd March [1] did reach me at Ramgarh. I got it with a huge bundle of letters from Allahabad this afternoon and picked it out and read it hurriedly. I had to go out just then and I carried it in my pocket intending to read it more carefully at leisure. Soon after I had to go to the opening session of the Congress and there many adventures befell all of us. It was a magnificent sight. An enormous arena, well filled with colourful people, with artistic gates leading into it. At the back were low hills and a small river gurgled at their foot. Dark clouds covered the sky. They were threatening, for if they brought rain the open air session became difficult. But the threat apart, it was a perfect setting. The whole audience was sitting in an enormous natural bowl. Delegates and visitors were streaming in. The volunteers, both boys and girls, were patches of colour. Most of us, members of the Working Committee, arrived about twenty minutes before the time fixed for the beginning of the session. We waited for the President and Bapu [2] to arrive for the formal presidential procession. Two bands were in readiness. And then it began to rain. Not merely to rain but to pour in torrents. Within a few seconds the scene changed. A few visitors left hurriedly but the vast numbers remained. But suddenly the people almost disappeared from view. There was a sea of bamboo mattresses

1. Refers to letter No. 13.
2. Mahatma Gandhi.

to be seen and many umbrellas. In order to protect themselves from the fierce onslaught of the pouring rain, the people picked up the mattresses they were sitting on and crept underneath them. I went about from place to place, getting thoroughly soaked in the process, and was delighted to find how cheerful almost everyone was. The women were specially in difficulties because of their saris. But it was a jolly crowd. The rain continued. Soon the bottom of the huge bowl, where the dais was situated, was a lake, two or three feet deep. Yet people stood in it. The President arrived. Bapu did not come. In spite of the rain the President insisted on starting the session. Unfortunately the loudspeakers failed just then, for their engines were completely under water. Still we began formally and after a few words of welcome from the Chairman of the Reception Committee, the President spoke for a while and then I proposed formally the one and only resolution for the Congress. This was seconded formally and thus the session was adjourned till tomorrow.

We waded back through lakes of water. It was surprising how well everybody took these untoward occurrences. They were singing and shouting slogans. And so we marched to our respective camps – a good distance. Here we found that most of our goods & chattels had got wet. The roofs were leaking all over the place. We shifted as best we could. It was vastly entertaining to see the leaders of the Congress sitting perched up in odd corners trying to escape the rain.

It struck me that if conditions were so bad in this 'Leaders' Camp' how much worse they must be in the delegates' camps. So I went for a tour of these and especially visited some of our guests from abroad. Everywhere I found jolly groups almost enjoying their discomforts. I felt quite exhilarated by the experience and sensed the strong bond that united us all in a common endeavour. An American girl, who was my guest, was much impressed by this attitude of the crowds and by their good humour in spite of acute discomfort.

Many of us spent the whole evening in fixing up people, providing extra blankets, and in putting on extra mats on some of our roofs. And thus at last, late at night, we retired. That was not such an easy matter for it was difficult to escape the rain dripping from the roof. Here I have been sitting writing to you, trying to dodge these raindrops, not very successfully.

I am tired now but I wanted to write to you. We do not know what will happen tomorrow but anyhow the Congress will meet and get through its business. The one resolution means a lot. It opens out a whole vista of possibilities and conflicts. It seems inevitable that these should come, and not distantly. Fate or destiny or whatever it is drives us on.

I shall write to you more later. But I want to say how happy I am to learn of your progress. This is rather slow but I am not very worried about that. It must be sure and the pace quickens as you get along. When you come to India there will be no difficulty in your staying in the hills. Certainly not the housekeeping difficulty.

All my love,
Your loving
Papu

---

18.

Les Frênes,
Leysin,
Switzerland,
22nd March, 1940

Darling,

> The Sunne shone
> Upon my bed with bright bemes,
> With many glad gilden stremes,
> And eke the welkin was so faire.
> Blew, bright, clere was the air.

Years ago I read this, or may be even learnt it by heart, at school. And all of a sudden, as I was doing my 'Plut-ventre' out on the balcony, it came back to me this morning. It's Chaucer, isn't it?

But your letters dated February 7th [1] and March 11th [2] arrived together on the 21st March!! One of them taking a whole month and a half and the other, ten days.

And you are so sad that it took all the blue, clear brightness out of my sky. It filled me with a great sadness, and above all, with a great longing to be with you. It is little enough that I can do for you, but if my mere presence can be of any comfort to you, it is only right that I should be with you. And I do so want to be. Here we are, miles away from each other, both so lonely, and needing each other so. It would help both of us tremendously if we could see each other even occasionally. There is no point in my staying here . . .

Here are the facts of Leysin as I see them & as I more or less presented them to Bhandari. There is no doubt that I am better now than when I arrived over three months ago – but not much. I look slightly better, I breathe much better. In weight I have gained 3 lbs, my

1. Refers to letter No. 6.
2. Refers to letter No. 15.

present weight being 85½ lbs. Just about a month ago I started getting up in the afternoons – starting with fifteen minutes and now for two and a half hours, during which I go for a short walk. On the other hand, that perpetual fatigue I used to feel is still a faithful companion, my appetite is not improving and I eat very little with great effort, and I don't sleep at all well. Most afternoons I am usually too tired to want to get up but, since remaining in bed does not seem to help matters, I do get up all the same. When I first arrived here Prof. Rollier said I need only stay here three months. This period came to an end on March 15th and the Prof. said a further three or four months were essential. Last Sunday Lady Maharaj Singh[1] came to lunch with me & collared the Professor for a talk about me. You have probably heard from her already – she said she would write you a detailed account of my condition & her talk with the Prof. She was much impressed with how much better I was looking, but that is hardly a criterion to judge since the last time she saw me was in November when I still had my pleurisy and was running a temperature. Anyway, the Professor told her that I should stay at Les Frênes for a year more, i.e. until spring 1941. And apparently he seemed to take it for granted that I would do so! This news has upset me considerably.

Personally I'd like to leave as soon as possible. I'm not saying that Leysin hasn't done me any good or that these three months have been wasted. These months here have rested me somewhat and have given me a good start, the kind of which I could not possibly have got had I gone to India direct from hospital. They have given me also a definite idea of Dr Rollier's method of treatment and what routine I should follow and how to regulate it. And this is of great importance. If I had had this experience last year, my stay in Almora would not have been as aimless and fruitless as it turned out to be. But, having given me this direction, there is nothing more Leysin can do for me. There is nothing in the routine to be followed which could not be done equally well in any other place, provided the air is good & the temperature not too high.

Dr Rollier would probably argue that it would do me no good to leave Leysin just when I was beginning to make some progress and that, in the process, I would lose what little I have gained. This is obviously for the doctors to decide and I cannot resist their decision.

But it does seem to me that I would lose weight whenever I left Leysin, whether it be now or three months hence or a year hence.

1. Lady Maharaj Singh: wife of Sir Maharaj Singh of the princely family of Kapur-thala State. He was a brother of Rajkumari Amrit Kaur, close associate of Mahatma Gandhi.

Everybody does when he leaves the mountain for the plain. Also I think my fatigue and insomnia are due mostly to the state of my nerves. I have always been 'a bundle of nerves', as they say. But never have I been in such a state of perpetual nervous agitation as I seem to be here. With the amount of nervous energy I use up every second, it is no wonder I can't gain any weight.

I have a very strong – almost overpowering – desire to go to India. It obsesses me. Most of the time I would probably be more alone than I am here but perhaps you would be able to visit me now and then, which, of course, is infinitely better than not seeing you at all. With a good and intelligent *ayah*, I feel I would get along better than if I stayed on here, for I would have more mental calm. One of the difficulties is that before sailing I should have to go to England to collect my belongings – I have next to no clothes here: just night pyjamas & one skirt & one sari! – and take them with me, since I know of no one who would be able to pack them either to my satisfaction or my convenience as well as bring them out to me. This is a tiring job but it need not take long.

But, of course, all this is as yet just a castle in Spain. I must do whatever the doctors advise. I do hope they will let me come.

The books I ordered from Blackwell's have arrived. Almost at the same time came a further instalment from Mlle Hemmerlin. So I have been quite occupied. From my lot I have read *The Testament of Friendship* – it is the story of Winifred Holtby, who was rather a wonderful person.[1] At Somerville she had been very popular and I met several people who knew her well. I have just finished reading Stefan Zweig's *Les Heures Etoilées de l'Humanité*, and have now begun Zweig's biography of Tolstoy in French.[2]

Somewhere in this letter I have mentioned Lady Maharaj Singh. She came to Leysin on Sunday. Rather nice of her, don't you think? – arrived about twelve noon, had lunch with me & stayed until four fifteen p.m. In between she walked the length and breadth of Leysin in search of a fruit shop that might be open on a Sunday. She found one eventually and bought me a basketful of fresh fruit. From Montana she brought a large armful of forsythia – those bright golden sprays, that are almost the first spring shrubs to bloom – I do love it. Almora, I remember, was full of it last winter and I used to gather them for Mrs Brewster,[3] who

1. Winifred Holtby (1898–1935): novelist and essayist, educated at Somerville College. Director of *Time and Tide*, her best-known novel is *South Riding*. She shared a house with Vera Brittain, who wrote *Testament of Friendship*.
2. Stefan Zweig (1881–1942): Austrian author.
3. Achsah Barlow Brewster: wife of Earl H. Brewster. They were American artists who visited India twice and lived in Almora for some time.

loved them too. By the way – how is she? And are they still in Almora? Lady M.S.'s son is in Montana, you know. Last year they suddenly discovered that he had an acute stage of tuberculosis, with both lungs infected. And now in May he hopes to be back in Oxford. I gathered from her talk that some day soon he was going to address a long discourse on his political views to you!

On Tuesday came Dr Hilary Roche, the Montana doctor I wrote to you about. I liked him. He is Australian. He knows well & likes Mrs Henderson, a great favourite of mine at Somerville. From his wife he brought me a pot of lovely sweet-smelling hyacinths, so that now my room is all a-bloom with spring and fragrant with lovely scents. I do love flowers and colour.

Yesterday I went to tea with rather an eccentric Irishwoman. Her father was a general in India twenty years ago. She's been ill since the age of six but is practically all right now. She has given me some books on Irish poetry to read.

From all this you will think that I meet a lot of people & have quite a social life! But this week has been exceptional. Most days I just go for my little lonely walk & then back to the little gossiping group of Les Frênes patients whose main topics of conversation are: food & the strangers who pass by on the road below. Sometimes we play cards & that passes the time . . .

It will be April when you get this & May by the time I get your reply. Suppose I left here in June, which is the best month in England – that would mean six months altogether in Leysin. A fortnight in England (eight days to pack & eight days to rest) & then sail for India where the rains would have begun by that time.

Lots of love, darling mine,
Indu

---

19.

Anand Bhawan,
Allahabad,
23rd March, 1940

Darling Indu,

Yesterday we came back to Allahabad from Ramgarh via Gaya. I found to my joy three envelopes, with your familiar handwriting, waiting for me here. I picked these out of a bundle of letters and read them. I was very tired. The Congress is always an exhausting affair and the rain and storm this time had made it even more so. Then our journey back was not a simple affair. So ever since my return I have been slowly recovering from the fatigue and by tomorrow morning I hope to be normal.

I wrote to you from Ramgarh[1] just after the deluge of rain which washed away the *pandal*[2] and much else. Even as I wrote that letter, water dripped all round me and sometimes on me and on the notepaper. The next morning it continued to rain with occasional lucid intervals. It was impossible to hold the Congress in the normal way and ultimately a hurried session was held in the open. Fortunately we had only one resolution to get through. So ended the shortest session on record and everyone began to pack up and go. Indeed we had to as it was very difficult to stay on. The water supply was failing as the pumping wells had disappeared under the flood water. In spite of all this the Congress session was an exhilarating affair and most people who attended it enjoyed the novel experience. The only resolution passed was the one I have already sent you.

I could not get proper accommodation in the train for Allahabad as vast numbers of people were departing that day. The small station was a mass of human beings huddled up together. So we decided to go to Gaya and spend a day there. We did so and visited the Bodh Gaya temple and for a while forgot the India of today and lived in the brave old days when Gautama flourished. In the afternoon we motored seventy-five miles to the excavations of Nalanda, the old university where our friend Hiuen Tsang[3] studied for fourteen years and became a Master of the Law. I was surprised to find how big this place was. It had been planned on a vast scale, or rather it had grown with the years, for the university flourished for 800 years.

From Nalanda we went to Rajgir, or Rajgriha as it used to be called in the old days when the Chinese pilgrim Fa Hien[4] came and described it. There are hot springs here which, they say, contain radium. But India has a habit of giving everything a religious significance and these springs became a place for pilgrimage with the attendant *pandas*[5] exploiting the pilgrims. Many people came for cures but there was nothing like the development one sees in Europe wherever such springs exist. We bathed in these springs and the water was delightfully refreshing. It was just hot enough to be comfortably borne. Probably some enterprising syndicate will develop the place within the next few years and bottle the water for sale.

1. Refers to letter No. 17.
2. Marquee.
3. Hiuen Tsang (AD 600–664): Buddhist monk, scholar and traveller of Chinese origin, who came to India during the reign of the Emperor Harshavardhana in the seventh century, and stayed for more than a decade. His account of what he saw and observed during his stay in India throws valuable light on the country during this period.
4. Fa Hien (AD 399–414): a Buddhist priest from China; author and traveller; journeyed overland to India and spent about ten years there during the reign of Chandragupta II (AD 376–415); wrote an account of his travels, and translated Buddhist texts.
5. Priests.

And then back to Gaya, stopping *en route* at Pawapuri, a great place of Jain pilgrimage, where Mahavira[1] died or, as they say, attained *maha nirvana*. Here, in the middle of a beautiful lotus-covered lake, stands a lovely temple. It is lovely from a distance, not so from near by, for our worthy Jain millionaires have lavished money on it and succeeded in converting it into a cross between a gorgeous lavatory and a seaside pier with the most blatant electric posts and marble everywhere. They love marble.

Back in Gaya at nine p.m., dinner, and then two meetings. To bed after midnight for less than three hours, for our train left at three thirty a.m.

All this was tiring but I enjoyed it, as I always enjoy my new discoveries of India. I am always discovering something new in this wonderful land and the hold of India grows upon me. Long ago – do you remember it? – when we were travelling in the air-conditioned coach in Malaya towards Penang, I sat down to write an essay on the Discovery of India. I wrote only a few lines then though my mind was full of ideas. That unfinished sheet is still with me. I suppose I shall write on the subject one day, for it grows upon me.[2]

Thank you for the cuttings from *Life* about the stroboscopic pictures. As a matter of fact I get *Life* regularly, or irregularly since the war, but I seldom see it or look through it with care.

In Ramgarh there was not much of a family reunion although Nan & Ranjit[3] & Betty were there. Raja could not come as he was busy with the Planning Committee. I was so busy that I hardly had time for any members of the family, and Betty was busy in her own way. She has a large and very miscellaneous circle of acquaintance which is a source of some surprise to me occasionally. Whenever I stay with her in Bombay I meet many new people and I have a succession of dinners, etc, to which I am not used.

In one of your letters[4] you say that when you leave Switzerland, you will return to India after a brief visit to England to gather your belongings. Also that Bhandari wants you to spend two years without a break in Kashmir. You seem to be thinking already of the difficulties of housekeeping in Kashmir or the hills. I do not myself see why you should spend the winter in the hills or in Kashmir, but if you want to do so there will be no difficulty about it. Remember that India is a very friendly place, especially for us, and wherever you might go you will find friends who want to help. Housekeeping on a small scale offers no difficulty. I

1. Mahavira (599–527 BC): founder of the Jain sect in India.
2. This refers to a brief manuscript which Jawaharlal later developed into a book. See p. 526 n. 1.
3. Ranjit Pandit: husband of Vijaya Lakshmi Pandit, a fine scholar of Sanskrit. He was later to be imprisoned along with Jawaharlal Nehru in Dehra Dun Jail.
4. Refers to letter No. 13.

have lived in Anand Bhawan all by myself for months and the cook has done what he liked about housekeeping. I have never even asked him anything about it. It may be that I could have saved a little money otherwise. But it was not worthwhile and I wanted peace.

A crowd of Burmese have descended upon us tonight. They are of the Dobama Thakin party, a kind of young socialists, whom you might perhaps remember. They came to Ramgarh. I expected five of them here but nine turned up, to the discomfiture of the cook, Hari[1] and others. It was dinnertime and there was not enough room at the table. So we had a stand-up dinner and the food was just sufficient. Enough beds were found with some difficulty. All these nine are crowded up in the big guest room, but most of them are sleeping on the verandah. Your room was unoccupied but I do not like other people taking possession of it, though sometimes I have to put up with this. So many people come to see me and often put up with us. Your room remains as you left it. I have often shifted books and other things in my room, but yours remains unchanged. I prefer it so.

Tonight is the *Holi*[2] night and tomorrow is the festival.

Here is a little poem which might interest you. It is by A. E. Housman:[3]

> Yonder see the morning blink:
>     The sun is up, and up must I,
> To wash and dress and eat and drink
>     And look at things and talk and think
> And work, and God knows why.
>
> Oh often have I washed and dressed
>     And what's to show for all my pain?
> Let me lie abed and rest:
>     Ten thousand times I've done my best
> And all's to do again.

Love,
Your loving,
Papu

---

1. Hari: valet to Motilal Nehru; after his death attached himself to Jawaharlal Nehru.
2. A spring festival marked by revelry and the throwing of coloured water and powder on each other by the participants.
3. Alfred Edward Housman (1859–1936): English classical scholar and poet; Professor of Latin, University College, London, 1892–1911, and Cambridge, 1911–36.

20.                                              Anand Bhawan,
                                                      Allahabad,
                                                  7th April, 1940

Darling Indu,
I have been spending some days in a camp on the other side of the
Jumna. The camp routine occupied every minute of the day and sometimes a bit of the night also and it was almost impossible to write there.
To add to this, all manner of people came to Allahabad to see me and
they were important enough for me to find time somehow for them. To
begin with there was a crowd of Burmese, and then came the Ceylonese,
all of them stopping at our house. An American couple turned up and
a Chinese young man on his way from England to China. Most important of all was the Congress President, Maulana Azad, who chose this
very time to visit Allahabad. I was hard put to it to fit in all these
engagements with our camp routine and the process was an exhausting
one. During the whole of yesterday I tried to recover from it and I feel
better today.

Your letter of the 22nd March [1] reached me in just a week's time,
on the 29th March. I could not reply to it properly then but I dictated
something hurriedly to Upadhyaya. I hope you received that typewritten
letter.

As you say yourself, the doctors will have the last word. So I wrote
immediately to Jivraj Mehta [2] and Bhandari and told them how you felt
about it, for your own viewpoint is the most important consideration. I
suggested to them also that they might write directly to Rollier. I have
not heard from them in reply yet, and indeed I could not within this
brief period. But I know, more or less, what they will say. Jivraj is very
keen that you should let good alone and give every opportunity to yourself to eliminate all disorders from your system. That is fundamentally
a sound proposition. It would be folly to do anything which would undo
the good already done. His inclination will therefore be to ask you to
stay on in Leysin for the whole of the summer and to return to India in
the early winter. Bhandari will think likewise but will be more amenable
to a variation or to a somewhat shorter stay. But both would press you
to stay as long as you can manage it. If Rollier falls in with our wishes,
then, of course, it would be much simpler. I think we had better leave
it at that for the present.

Need I say what I feel about it? I want so much to see you and touch

1. Refers to letter No. 18.
2. Dr Jivraj N. Mehta: renowned doctor and nationalist worker; served as Indian
High Commissioner in the United Kingdom after 1947.

you and hear you, but I am not fool enough to allow my wishes to interfere with your treatment. We absolutely must build on a firm foundation this time, and if we have to err, we must err on the safe side. You know well enough that weak lungs or pleura take a devil of time to strengthen. They will not be hurried and attempts at speed often mean greater delay. So we must accept this position. After all, howsoever much this might inconvenience us, two or three months this way or that do not make a vital difference. Oxford is out of the question now, and you have more or less decided to return to India. The sooner you come the better, certainly, but that sooner must not be at the cost of your health.

I suggest that you should now wait for the advice of your doctors. Meanwhile you should settle down till June at least. If you like, and if Rollier allows it, you can go for a change to La Pelouse [1] for a week or so. But you come back to Leysin. I suppose it is possible for you, if you so choose, to move from Clinique Frênes to some other clinique in Leysin, under Rollier of course. The latter might be cheaper. But this is not desirable if it interferes with your treatment or otherwise inconveniences you. This is entirely for you to judge.

Some weeks ago Krishna Menon wrote to me suggesting that as you were lonely Betty might go and join you. I doubt if it will be desirable or feasible for Betty to go. She does not feel happy anywhere out of her particular set in Bombay or away from her children. If she comes to Allahabad, she feels bored. Leysin will not amuse her at all. She has fixed up going to Mussoorie this summer in company with some of her Bombay friends. I think therefore that it will not be right to press her to go. This will be a costly business also. And then as there is some chance of your returning before very long, this will be pointless.

I have been thinking however that it will be well worthwhile to find a suitable companion for yourself. This is not an easy matter but it can be done. Are you in touch with Lu or Eva? [2] Could either of them join you for a while (you paying their expenses, etc, of course) or could they suggest someone?

Subject to what the doctors say, I think it would be a good idea for you to go to England sometime in June and spend a fortnight there. You could pack up and send all your heavy luggage and such as you do not require direct from London to Bombay. Keep the rest with you. I suggest then that you should go back to Switzerland for another few weeks' rest, say a month. You may go back to Leysin, or to Montana where

1. Indira attended Mlle Hemmerlin's school, L'Ecole Nouvelle at La Pelouse in Bex, 1926–7, and again in 1935–6.
2. Louise Geissler and Eva Geissler: the Geissler sisters were friends of Indira Gandhi.

you have your friend Dr H. Roche. It will be a good thing for you to refresh yourself by this stay in Suisse on the eve of your departure for India. This will also give you and the doctors an opportunity to observe how you have reacted to travelling and a fortnight in England.

You can then travel to India direct from Switzerland by the Italian Lloyd Triestino from Genoa or Venice. This line will be more suitable than P & O. I presume you would not care to come by air. It is difficult to get accommodation and I doubt if the sudden changes due to too rapid travelling will be good for you.

According to this programme you should be back in India about the end of August. It is not a very good time climatically, but it is not too bad. If another month or so in Suisse makes a difference to your health, I would not hesitate to stay on. Early October is a much better time to reach India. I have told you what I think about it. But my opinion should count least. It is the doctors' opinion and yours that count.

Do not bother yourself about my programme or what becomes of me. It is absurd to trouble oneself about matters outside our control. I have not the ghost of an idea of what is likely to happen to me. Everything changes rapidly nowadays and I am not prophet enough to peep into the future. It is clear that I am not going to leave India. The rest is unclear. In one of your letters you mentioned that I would be going to Kashmir in May. I had casually said so but nothing is decided. The idea of going to Kashmir obsesses me – it is so long since I have been there and I do so want to have a look at it. Even if I go, it will be for a few days only, possibly a week, just to satisfy my thirst for a sight of its beauty. Meanwhile, I shall be going to Wardha on the 14th and from there on the 19th probably to Bombay for the National Planning Committee. I expect to remain in Bombay for a fortnight. Then Allahabad and to whatever place calls to me . . .

It was a delightful and worthwhile experience for us middle-aged folk, feeble of limb and short of breath, and some actually unwell, to try to live the strenuous life of a volunteer camp. We were drilled and made to do exercises and sentry duty, and spinning of course, and first aid, games, etc, etc. Up in the morning at five thirty – lights out, in theory at nine thirty p.m. It was all very ridiculous for us to behave like boy scouts, but there was a deeper and a psychological aspect for, by doing so, we raised the idea of volunteering. All of us were just ordinary volunteers taking training – no officer class or the like. Apart from actual drill which we had morning and evening, and a route march, and camp fires at night, the games were very popular. After more than thirty years I seized hold of a cricket bat again. After eighteen years I played volley-ball, and played it rather well. Volley-ball became the favourite game, and fiercely contested matches were played.

I am afraid I could not do my full duty owing to important visitors barging in. Nevertheless I did a bit of sentry work in the middle of the night, and I liked it.

Ranjit was the only really qualified man amongst us as he has spent two or three years in a cavalry regiment. Unfortunately he could not stand the strain and got a bad heart attack.

We lived on the other side of the Jumna and I made friends with her and became her ardent admirer. What a lovely river she is and how she used to change her colour and her mood as the day progressed. In the early dawn she was a sight of rare beauty and even the ugly waterworks building on the other side caught the spell and seemed almost like a moated castle.

At night we had camp fires and folk songs – delightful village songs sung in the village way. Some of the villagers from the surrounding villages trooped in and joined. But I must stop now. I have written enough.

Have you heard that Charlie Andrews [1] – Uncle Charlie – died two days ago in a Calcutta nursing home? He had been ill for a long time and had been operated upon several times. His death has distressed me greatly. I do not know that I have ever come across a more lovable or more generous-hearted man. In these days of hatred and passion and conflict, it is good to remember this man who was so childlike, so foolish sometimes, and yet so utterly devoid of hatred or ill-will against anyone, and so full of love and goodwill. If there is such a thing as Godliness, he had it. It is very sad to think that he is no more.

I fear Gurudeva [2] cannot last very long. He grows weaker and weaker as his eightieth birthday approaches. Charlie's death must have been a terrible blow to him. India changes. The old guard fade away. The old lamps go out and it is not clear what the new ones are like.

Love,
Your loving,
Papu

---

1. Charles F. Andrews: Cambridge missionary who supported the nationalist movement in India. He was a close friend of Mahatma Gandhi and Jawaharlal Nehru.
2. Rabindranath Tagore.

21.                                        Anand Bhawan,
                                              Allahabad,
                                         8th April, 1940

Darling Indu,
Yesterday I sent you a long letter.[1] Today is *Nauroz*[2] and so I feel I
must send you my good wishes for the New Year. Our old customs fade
out and sometimes this is a pity. No one brings the *thali*[3] in the mornings. Indeed one almost forgets that *Nauroz* has come. Usually I am
alone in the house and Hari reminds me and produces new clothes for
the occasion.

But *Nauroz* is a good day to remember and celebrate. And so I send
you my love on this our New Year's Day.
                               Your loving,
                                  Papu

---

22.                                          Les Frênes,
                                                Leysin,
                                           Switzerland,
                                         13th April, 1940

Darling Papu,
I do not think I have written to you for some time. I have been tired
and absent-minded. Even my brief outings used to exhaust me, so that
I was unable to sleep. So, about a fortnight ago, I decided to stay in
bed and, to everybody's amazement, just slept and slept, soundly and
dreamlessly, for twelve solid hours a day – ten at night and two in the
afternoon! Now I have my fill of sleep and Professor said I may get up
again and go out too, if the weather permitted. But the weather does
not permit – it is bitterly cold with fog and sleet, or alternatively quite
wintry snow. I may go out when the snow is dry, but not otherwise . . .

Your book on *China, Spain & the War* arrived a couple of days ago.
But of the packet of books you ordered Kitabistan to send sometime
ago, there is no news. I do hope they are not lost.

I have been reading, in the *Reader's Digest*, a condensation from the

---

1. Refers to letter No. 20.
2. The various religions and regions of India have their own New Year Day. *Nauroz*
(also *Navroz*, *Nawroz* and *Naoroz*) is the New Year Day of the Kashmiris. The exchange
of gifts is a common practice during such festivals.
3. Refers to the custom of the lady of the house taking a *thali*, or a silver plate full
of ritual offerings, to each member of the household on *Nauroz* day.

book *Flowering Earth* by D. C. Peattie.[1] I am sure it would fascinate you, as it did me. It is the story of green life – the plant kingdom – upon the earth. Is it not wonderful, the oneness of life? It is ever a source of marvel to me how intrinsically the fates of all living things are bound together and how dependent on one another they are. It makes one humble and awed and proud all at once to feel that fundamentally this life which keeps us breathing is the same as the life in Psilophyton, which was no more than the 'dim beginning of an idea for a plant' – 350,000,000 years ago. Or maybe we could go back yet another half a billion years & more to the very earliest form of life – the iron bacteria! Humble to feel how very minute and negligible one is in the midst of all this grandeur, and proud to know that being so small, one is yet not insignificant, that one is an organic part of this great Wonder, that one does contribute to making this world what it is, in spite of everything, more marvellous and beautiful than even our tiny brains can grasp. And one's mind, D. H. Lawrence says, 'has no existence by itself, it is only the glitter of the sun on the surface of the waters'. He goes on to say: 'So that my individualism is really an illusion. I am part of the great whole, and I can never escape. But I *can* deny my connections, break them, and become a fragment. Then I am wretched.' Again,

what we want is . . . to reestablish the living organic connections with the cosmos, the sun and earth, with mankind and nation and family. But how? How, when all our sense of values has gone crooked, when life is dominated not by the living organic connection but by the false inorganic connections, not by the sun and earth but by money and the like – How?

My love to you, darling mine,
Indu

---

23.                               Bombay,
20th April, 1940

Darling,
This is a funny, topsy-turvy world. Here I am in Bombay intent on planning, planning of industry, of agriculture, of social life, of everything; thinking or trying to think of an ordered sane world, a new order as they call it. And way across the seas war rages and spreads and casts its shadow on us here. Even Bombay, far from the war zone, has semi-

---

1. D. C. Peattie: American botanist and writer.

darkened streets. I read and write and answer letters normally but civil disobedience looms ahead and I do not know when this normality will be suddenly interrupted. I have long accustomed and trained myself to occupy myself with the work of the moment and not to think of the troubles and difficulties ahead. Yet the mind wanders and it is not easy to hold it in leash. And now vague rumours come of the possibility of the war spreading and, it may even be, of coming nearer to you. Even if Switzerland escapes, it may well become isolated or difficult of access and communication. The Mediterranean may become a closed sea and the normal routes between Europe and India barred. What of you then, my dear?

I think of you so often. Suddenly, in the middle of a conversation, you intervene and your picture takes possession of my mind and I lose the thread of the talk. Or I may be reading a book or writing on a sheet of paper and the page or the sheet is blotted out as my mind travels to you. I comfort myself that you are marching on the road to health, and though the pace be slower than one wishes, the march is steady and sure. It is better to hold on to this job and get it done well. But then the tragic drama of this war forces itself on my attention and I wonder what new complications it might bring.

In Bombay it is the season of the Alphonso mangoes and that again reminds me of you and I think of your liking for them. But the crop is poor this year.

I came here yesterday after spending four days in Wardha. I have a long stay here to look forward to. But Bombay wearies me in spite of the large circle of acquaintance that I have here. I am in no mood for meeting large numbers of people and, here in Betty's flat, there are always people coming to meals and at other times. They are nice people and I like many of them. But my mind is elsewhere and it is a strain to fit in. My work suffers.

So tomorrow I am going to Andheri – Psyche's [1] house – and possibly I might move to Juhu later. This will mean coming to Bombay daily but I shall have my mornings and evenings free.

It is long since I heard from you – or is this just my imagination? Perhaps your letter has reached Allahabad.

Love,
Your loving,
Papu

---

1. Goshiben Captain (Psyche): granddaughter of Dadabhai Naoroji, who was a pioneering leader of the national movement in India.

24.

Les Frênes,
Leysin,
Switzerland,
20th April, 1940

Darling Papu,

Last evening's Radio Rome news announced that Bapu had declared Civil Disobedience. I can't help being glad. All success to you. Here is my body, so far from India & you, but the rest of me is quite near you and my mind is full of you every moment.

Prof. Rollier has written to Dr Bhandari – I do not know if a copy of that letter has been sent to Dr Mehta. I was shown the letter & have made a copy of it. The English is doubtful but I have copied it just as it was written. I have, however, made some small corrections because otherwise the meaning was not quite clear – these are in pencil. I enclose the copy.

I am anxious that it should reach you as soon as possible, so will not write further.

This last month I have not gained any weight.

The packet of books from India has at last arrived – thanks so much.

Lots of love, darling mine,
Your
Indu

25.

Andheri,
25th April, 1940

Darling Indu,

It is long since I heard from you, nearly three weeks I think. But in these days of war, letters have a way of coming in bunches after long gaps. I suppose they accumulate in the Censor's office and when he or she has leisure, they are passed.

In my last letter [1] I wrote to you that the new international developments had made me wonder if it would be possible for you to stay on in Switzerland, even if you wanted to. I wrote to Bhandari about it, for it is as well to be prepared for all eventualities. Then I decided to cable to him. His reply came yesterday that he was going to Leysin himself to fix up arrangements. I am glad he is going to you. He mentioned in his cable that in any event Leysin was about as safe a place as any and it was always possible to go to France from there as the French frontier

1. Refers to letter No. 23.

was not far. Which of course is true. This was a reason why I was inclined towards Leysin when you were considering where to go to in Switzerland. Anyway I hope everything will be fixed up provisionally in case of need. To worry about what might happen is foolish but one must always be prepared for it. That gives peace of mind. You know, of course, that Mademoiselle Hemmerlin will gladly help you in case of need.

Rollier has sent a long report to Jivraj Mehta about you. It is a good report full of scientific words which I do not wholly understand.

I have been in Andheri for four or five days and it is very pleasant here, far better than Bombay. The chief advantage is the quiet. I try not to go [to] Bombay, though I do not always succeed, and sometimes people come to see me here. This house (it is Psyche's) is well situated and has a pleasant garden. It is a very old-fashioned house and the furniture belongs to some antique age. Everything is heavily carved and the rooms are overfull of these massive articles. I do not fancy this style. It is depressing and uncomfortable. But this is a minor point. The house is delightful and Psyche sees to it that I have a quiet and restful time. She herself lives in Bombay but comes here sometimes in the afternoons.

We overlook the Juhu aerodrome and the noise of planes flying about is constantly with us, in the daytime at least. At night the red lights of the aerodrome peep through the palm trees.

This evening I went for a walk. I wanted to go to Juhu and I managed to reach there before it got dark. But the way back was more difficult as it was quite dark and I lost my way. Ultimately I took a bus to Santa Cruz (the busman refused to charge fares) and from there a taxi brought me. How helpless I get when I venture out by myself. I am so used to not going anywhere or to being accompanied by someone, that by myself I get lost. Today was my first experience of a bus ride in Bombay. And even a taxi I hardly ever take as there is some other car available. Usually I do not have any money with me. Without Upadhyaya I get into difficulties about posting letters, as I do not have stamps! So you see to what a helpless state I have reduced myself.

I had a glimpse of the Vakils [1] yesterday. They have gone off to Kashmir for the holidays.

Yesterday I met Sir Malcolm Darling, [2] a Punjab civilian who is

1. Jehangir Jivaji Vakil and his wife Coonverbai; they ran the Pupils' Own School at Poona (and later in Bombay). Indira Nehru studied in this school from 1931 to 1934.
2. Sir Malcolm Darling: member of the Indian Civil Service and author of books on rural development.

retiring and is taking up some job in the B.B.C. He asked me if you could give talks on the microphone for the B.B.C.

Raja, Betty and the children are coming here tomorrow. Day after tomorrow I am going to Miraj for a day to visit an old acquaintance who is lying very ill there. I have not seen him for years but I remember how he came to me twenty years ago after having non-cooperated from school or college. He has begged me to see him and I do not know how to refuse. The journey is a long and tiring one and this visit will interfere with my work.

I met Mrs Bhagwandin Dube here. She is a terribly lonely person with more money than she wants and a villa in Cannes which is totally useless to her.

My love to you, my dear,
Your loving,
Papu

*26th April, 1940*

Last night I wrote to you and I gave my letter to be posted this morning. Soon after your letter of April 13th, [1] forwarded from Allahabad and Sakina Mansion, reached me. I found that my letter had not been posted, so I am adding this postscript.

It is no good my writing to you about your programme as I have already discussed this matter fully in previous letters and now that Bhandari is going over to see you, he and you should fix it up . . .

I do hope Louise Morin will visit you and spend a few days with you. If she comes, I wish you would treat her as your guest. Her visit will be good for you and good for her. Jean-Jacques's [2] departure for the front must have been a blow to her. I am writing to her also.

I am sorry to learn that the books I sent you have not reached you yet. I suppose one is helpless in the matter and enquiries are pretty useless. The Post Office here will say they have sent them, the P.O. at Leysin will say they have not received them. It is in between that they disappear or are held up. The books, as you know, were entirely innocent from the political or war point of view. They dealt with poetry, etc. You might however write a note and enquire from the Leysin post office. I think they were sent in two, possibly three, parcels, all registered.

Your account of D. C. Peattie's book, *Flowering Earth*, is fascinating. I must try to get the book. Science, in all its manifold aspects, is almost

1. Refers to letter No. 22.
2. Jean-Jacques: son of Louise Morin, he worked in the International Labour Organisation.

a new adventure for your mind, but I have been thrilled by it for long years. Remember that at one time, long long ago, I studied chemistry and physics and geology and botany, and even took my degree in them. Science has given more faith and confidence and peace of mind than almost anything. Without it I would have been rudderless. For me it has taken the place of religion. But Science must be allied to life – to the earth – to flowers and trees and mountains and rivers, and human beings. Otherwise it is lifeless – 'A little primrose by the brim, a yellow primrose was to him, and it was nothing more.'

As you are so interested in biology and the early forms of life, I wish you could see them under the microscope.

Harsha and Ajit have just turned up and it is not possible to continue writing.

Love,<br>Papu

---

26.                                                                  Andheri,
                                                              1st May, 1940

Darling Indu,
Today it was announced that the Mediterranean route is closed and ships are coming via the Cape. And so the barriers grow and this tight little world, which flying and the rest of it had made so small and accessible, again expands. The wasteland spreads and we live our lives cut off from each other or at least with fewer contacts. And you go further away from me in the physical plane. I suppose these processes will continue and develop and our days will progressively grow darker in the blackout which envelops the world.

I wonder how long letters will go by air from India to Europe. I wonder when this note will reach you. However that might be, I shall continue writing till it is certain that the letters cannot get through. And then also we shall find some means of communication.

All manner of people are asking me continually, why do you not cable to Indu to come back immediately. It is curious how generous people are with their advice. Anyway I hope Bhandari will have reached you by this time and he will help you to fix your programme for all eventualities. Whatever you decide in consultation with him will be best for you . . .

The Planning Committee started today. We are having long sittings, both morning and afternoon, every day. It is not easy now to stay on in

Andheri as it takes too long to go to Bombay from here. So tomorrow I move to Bombay.

I saw *Snow White* for the first time here and liked it.

It is warm here but the sea breeze is pleasant.

All my love to you, darling

Your loving,

Papu

---

27.

Les Frênes,
Leysin,
Switzerland,
10th May, 1940

Darling Papu,

This is just a hurried line to reassure you – though I'm sure this letter will be hopelessly out of date by the time it reaches you. [1] Don't worry about me, darling. Even if the worst comes to the worst, as far as Switzerland is concerned, Leysin will be quite safe. This morning two frontier towns were bombarded – but they say it was a mistake. The Swiss, however, are not taking any chances and have ordered general mobilisation.

The war has come right on top of England now – bombing in France, fighting in Belgium & Holland. The next step is England. There is one thing to be said for the Nazi Government – it's been damned thorough on every one of its frontiers. I hope the aid to Belgium & Holland will be prompter & more efficient than that offered Norway . . . [2]

My thoughts are with you.

Lots of love,

Indu

---

1. Germany invaded Holland, Belgium and Luxembourg on 10th May, the same day on which Winston Churchill replaced Neville Chamberlain as Prime Minister.

2. The British landings at Narvik started six days after Germany invaded Norway (9th April).

28.                                                                    Andheri,
                                                              10th May, 1940

Darling Indu,
For the last week or more I have been wanting to write to you daily but
this Planning Committee exhausts me and by the end of the day I am
hardly in a fit condition to do anything. We sit daily from nine in the
morning to six in the evening with an interval for lunch. At night I have
to do some hours' work to prepare for the next day. All this is hard
concentrated work which takes a great deal out of one. I had moved to
Bombay from Andheri and I stayed there for a week. Yesterday, however, I fled from Bombay and came back to Andheri in order to escape
visits from well-meaning friends and also to have more restful nights. I
spend an extra hour coming & going daily but the night makes up for
it and is much pleasanter here.

Anyway our work will end soon or rather will be forcibly ended. There
is yet mountains of it but all members are tired and want to go away, so
per force we must adjourn. Probably we shall wind up for the present
on the 14th and I may go on the same day or the 15th. I want to go to
Wardha for a day to have a talk with Bapu. Strange developments are
taking place all over the world and I want to know how Bapu is reacting
to them. Then Allahabad and Lucknow.

A reason for my delaying writing to you was an expectation of a cable
from Bhandari. This came in due course from Leysin sent by you and
Bhandari. As you have come to this decision after full discussion with
Bhandari, the matter must rest there and we must all reconcile ourselves
to it. It is best that you should give first place to a complete recovery to
health, even though that means a few months more. That is obviously
the first essential and having come to this decision, one need not worry
about it further.

And yet, Europe is becoming such a cauldron that it is a superhuman
feat not to worry. There is no certainty, no security about anything
or any person. Still, I suppose Leysin is about as quiet a place as
you could find anywhere in Europe and I do not see why anyone
should intrude on this quiet dullness of Leysin. Anyway it is no good
being oppressed by the future. The present is troublesome enough;
when the future comes we shall face that also, whatever it might
be.

Today brought the news of the German invasion of Holland, Belgium,
etc. Bombay is naturally excited and so I suppose is a good part of the
world. Events are moving rapidly. The old world seems to be passing.
What will the new one be like? . . .

Some time back – about two months or more – I sent you two or three new photographs of mine. I wonder if they reached you. I now enclose a curious snapshot taken here by a friend. There was a mistake in developing and the film cracked – hence the curious effect.

Betty is going with her children to Mussoorie tomorrow.

Love,
Your loving,
Papu

29. Les Frênes,
Leysin,
Switzerland,
16th May, 1940

Darling Papu,
This is a very hurried line. I have your cable.

Here are my plans. I am staying on in Leysin unless and until Switzerland is involved in the war. When this happens I am told that all 'foreigners' will have to leave. So I shall go to England. There is no other course open. Switzerland will not become a belligerent unless Italy does, I think. So going to Italy will be quite out of the question, especially as the Italian maritime service to the East will stop. Don't worry, darling, there is no danger or difficulty in all this. I am getting in touch with the British Consul to find out what he suggests & also to make arrangements about getting a transit visa through France, should the need arise.

The only thing that I was a little worried about was money. I have none here & haven't paid my bills here for a month. The money is of course in London & I have sent for it but heaven alone knows when it will arrive. Anyway, I was quite frank about it with Miss Rollier, who is the matron here, and she assured me that Prof. would lend me enough to see me through to England & from there I could pay my bills, etc. So that is settled. Only this morning an American – Mrs Schellens – had to leave at literally a night's notice. Last night at eleven she had a phone [call] from the American Consul in Italy who is a friend of her husband's, telling her to take the first train from Leysin – she left at eight a.m.

If I have to leave, it is no use sending numerous telegrams asking for advice. I shall merely inform you & London that I am arriving in England. Further plans can be discussed there. I may be able to get a boat coming to India – via the Cape, of course.

Don't get agitated or worried about me, darling. I shall be perfectly all right. A crisis is the one time when I do keep my head. Besides there isn't really anyone to give advice. Bhandari is a dear but he hasn't an original idea in his head. Every time one asks him anything he cables to you, or refers me to Ahuja or somebody else.

Much love darling – look after yourself.

Indu

---

30.                                                    Anand Bhawan,
                                                           Allahabad,
                                                    23rd May, 1940

Darling,

The world we knew seems to disintegrate and dissolve and to give place to something new. My mind is restless and sometimes distressed, and at all times it tries to peer into the future, but it does so in vain. But whatever may happen to the world, you are there, and I hope it is well with you. It is curious to think of you in the quiet restful valley of the Rhone, surrounded, as it were, with the clash and butchery of war. How helpless we all seem. And yet in the aggregate we are not perhaps so helpless, if we only knew how and what to do. Possibly some day we will.

Do my letters reach you, I wonder. But I shall continue to write and hope that some of my letters at least will manage to reach you . . .

You have decided to stay on in Switzerland but one can never be sure what new developments might compel us to do. Still I hope you will stick on to Leysin & Suisse for as long as you can.

I have had an interesting guest today. He is a distinguished Chinese who is on his way back from Tibet to China – they have to go via Darjeeling. He went to represent the Chinese Government at the installation of the new Dalai Lama – a lad aged four or five. This new Dalai Lama has been recently chosen because he is supposed to show signs of his predecessor. One of the strong points in his favour was that he never laughs or smiles. He sits gravely through the various ceremonies and behaves in a lordly manner to all who approach him. But, I was told, he grew very tired one day after two or three hours of prayers and ceremonies.

I am off to Lahore & Peshawar and then Kashmir, just for five days. It is rather absurd to go to Kashmir for this short period, but if I do not seize this opportunity I might have to wait for a long time again. I have waited long enough. I want to freshen the picture I have in mind. It will help me in the days to come.

And now to bed. I am frightfully sleepy and it is two a.m. The Chinese occupied me for the whole day and so I had to work in the night.

Love,
Papu

————————

31.

Rampur,
Jhelum Valley,
Kashmir,
29th May, 1940

Darling Indu,

I am at last in Kashmir and I feel a little excited and moved about it. Probably I would be still more excited if I was not oppressed by the rapid developments of the war situation. These are disturbing in many ways but, apart from this, there is always a possibility that I might be called back at any moment. It was on this understanding that I came.

I spent two days in Peshawar. I was the guest of my young Pathan friend about whom I wrote to you once – Mohammad Yunus [1] – who stayed with us in Allahabad. I told you that he had forty-three brothers and sisters, many of them half-brothers, etc. All these having one father. There were eight mothers or rather eight wives successively, though sometimes overlapping. Yunus was the youngest of the family and he was born when his father was eighty-nine years old. The old man was hale and hearty to the end and died partly through an accident when he was ninety-nine. The family mansion was in the heart of the city of Peshawar, a big house of the old style, as solid as a fortress. The mother-tongue of the family was, in a way, Persian and conversation was carried on alternately in Persian, Pushtu, Hindustani and sometimes in English.

It is really astonishing how much a Pathan can eat, and remember that he does not waste time and energy over vegetables and rice and the like. He concentrates on solid chunks of meat, rich pulao and thick very wholesome bread. The bread is as big as a *thali* [2] and an inch thick. A day of this food in the extreme heat of Peshawar upset me and I have been gradually recovering since then.

We left Peshawar yesterday – Abdul Ghaffar Khan [3] was with me. We stopped at Attock where the Indus meets another river and had a

---

1. Mohammad Yunus: friend of the Nehrus, he joined the Indian Foreign Service after 1947 and has held important diplomatic assignments. Later he became Chairman of the Trade Authority of India and a member of Rajya Sabha (Upper House of Indian Parliament).

2. Metal platter.

3. Khan Abdul Ghaffar Khan: Pathan leader who was a close associate of Mahatma Gandhi.

dip in the cold water of the Indus. There we passed within ten miles of Taxila and I was sorely tempted to go there. But our programme was heavy and I resisted the temptation. We spent the night in Abbottabad. This morning we started from Abbottabad and followed the road to Kashmir, joining the Jhelum Valley route at Domel. My mind was continually going back to the autumn of 1916, nearly twenty-four years, when I had gone by this very road out of Kashmir with Dadu,[1] Mummie[2] & others. There were numerous halts as people had gathered to welcome us all along the route. We have now stopped here at Rampur for the night. Srinagar is only fifty miles away and it was not difficult to reach it today. But the people there insist on my reaching there in the afternoon, so that they can have a river procession. I understand that this is going to be a big affair.

I shall spend only two days in Srinagar and then go to various places, including Kausarnag and Pahalgam. It will be a hurried four-day tour. If I could extend this by another four or five days I could go along the Liddar valley and on to Sonemarg, which is a magnificent spot. But I dare not do it. Probably I shall be back in Allahabad on 9th June. I shall return via the Banihal Pass to Jammu.

As usual my visit is full of meetings and interviews and I shall hardly have even a few hours to myself. Still I find Kashmir exhilarating and I have a sense of coming back to my own – it is curious how race memories persist, or perhaps it is all imagination.

Love,<br>
Your loving,<br>
Papu

---

32.                                        Srinagar,
                                      3rd June, 1940

Indu darling,

Two of your letters have reached me here. I am not worrying, my dear. I am not of the worrying kind. The only worry one feels is when one has to make a decision. When that is done one faces the consequences with a measure of composure . . .

It is difficult to write about a situation which changes from day to day. But as far as I can gather, it is neither easy nor desirable for you to go to England. You will find it difficult to get away from there or get a passage.

I have had a wonderful time here in Kashmir during these four days

---

1. Motilal Nehru: father of Jawaharlal Nehru.
2. Kamala Nehru: mother of Indira Gandhi.

that I have been here. Kashmir is surpassingly lovely and, when you add to that the gift of a people's love, the result is apt to be intoxicating. I shall not write to you much now, I am too rushed. I am going to Pahalgam and from there to the Kolahoi glacier. I shall be back in five days and then I return via Jammu and the Banihal Pass. My future programme is:

| | |
|---|---|
| Allahabad | 13th to 17th June |
| Wardha | 17th to 19th June |
| Bombay | 20th to end of June |

All my love,
Your loving,
Papu

---

33.

Anand Bhawan,
Allahabad,
16th June, 1940

Indu darling,
Will this letter reach you, and if so how and when? I do not know. But I take the risk in the hope that ultimately it will get to you. All round little Switzerland are belligerent Powers now and war rages. For the present, I suppose, all idea of your leaving Switzerland for another country is out of the question. There appears to be no feasible way. But events are taking place with astonishing speed and the future may be [less] certain. Anyway I know that you can look after yourself, especially when crisis comes, and I do not worry.

I have paid my brief visit to Kashmir and I am exhilarated by it. What an enchanting land with an air that vitalises! Taken as a whole I am convinced that it is superior to Switzerland and, I would say, healthier. I am sure that a stay there in the higher valleys would be of enormous benefit to you. I wish I myself could go there for two months every year – one month trekking towards Ladakh or Baltistan or the various glaciers and upper valleys, and one month's rest and intensive reading and writing also in a higher valley. That would be an ideal life. But ideals are difficult to realise!

I wrote to you from Srinagar.[1] During my brief stay I went to the Kolahoi glacier via Pahalgam. I loved this trip and came back thoroughly tanned. Indeed my skin – such as was exposed – is peeling off.

---

1. Refers to letter No. 32.

I am going to Wardha today for a Working Committee meeting and from there to Bombay for the National Planning Committee. I shall be back in Allahabad early in July . . .

I think of you almost continuously. There are so many enquiries about you. The world changes – an epoch is over. Let us keep cool and steady and not allow ourselves to be bowled over by any change. If you have news of Louise and Jean-Jacques let me have it.

All my love,

Your loving,<br>Papu

---

34.                    [Cable]                    Leysin,
                                                  [22nd June, 1940]

Nehru
Anand Bhawan
Allahabad
Postal communication impossible don't worry am alright don't write stop newspapers love.

[Indu]

---

35.                    [Cable]                    Leysin,
                                                  22nd July, 1940

Nehru
Anand Bhawan
Allahabad
Am well Xray satisfactory weight stationary postal communication re-established am writing much love.

[Indu]

---

36.                                              Les Frênes,
                                                 Leysin,
                                                 Switzerland,
                                                 23rd July, 1940

Darling Papu,
A couple of days ago the post office informed us that we could again write to England and India. Yesterday I wired [1] to you and I am writing

1. Refers to letter No. 35.

all my letters as soon as possible just in case communications break down again. As a matter of fact, I had just got hold of Sherwood Eddy's [1] address and was meaning to write to you through America. It would have taken rather long but that was better than nothing.

These weeks, so completely cut off from the rest of the world, have been dreadful. Three letters which I had written to you [2] – two before and one after the fall of Paris [3] – were returned to me from Chiasso, the Italy frontier. For a fortnight, the entire mail of the 'clinique' were returned letters. The day the Germans marched into Paris, I had two great surprises – a letter from Efy Aristarchi from Zurich and a telephone call from Louise Morin from Lausanne. I had been worried and anxious about her and Nanu and all the other people who, I knew, were still in Paris, so it was a relief to have her news. Nanu, Bannerjee and others managed to get on the last train to leave Paris – they had no idea where it was going, probably in the direction of Bordeaux. That left Louise Morin quite friendless and rather frightened in her little flat with no means of getting out of Paris except on foot. Just then the Swiss Government sent a special train to repatriate Swiss subjects living in Paris. Perhaps for the first time, Louise was glad to have a Swiss passport (her husband was Swiss, you know). She managed to squeeze into the train, which was packed more tightly than a tin of sardines – to the extent of four people standing in the WC! – and arrived in Lausanne. She was anxious to get to Dieulefit as soon as possible but it was not so easy, for Dieulefit was in the '*Zone des armées*'. Mme Morin came over to Leysin for the weekend and on Tuesday left for France on a train – the train service having been suspended on this Monday.

Dr Bhandari and I had decided that if there were a question of the communications being cut, I should return to England. But of course things moved so fast that before you could take in just what was happening, it was too late and you could not move out of Switzerland in any direction.

Meanwhile, Nanu has managed to reach Montpellier (unoccupied territory). He is utterly miserable, for he hasn't any money and so far none can be sent to France from outside. The French Govt, moreover, have decreed that no foreigner shall leave his present habitation.

The Franco-German armistice had an immediate effect on the Swiss radio and newspapers. You cannot imagine how poisonous is the atmosphere here nowadays. At 'Frênes' there are two Spaniards who fought for Franco, two Frenchmen who were clamouring for a military dictator-

---

1. Sherwood Eddy: American writer.
2. Letters not traceable.
3. Paris fell on Friday, 14th June, 1940.

ship even before Pétain[1] formed his government & asked for armistice terms. The *famille* Rollier is loud in its praises of imperialism – British and French. As a result I just can't open my mouth on any subject. At one moment I thought I could not bear it and, when I heard that it was, after all, possible to get to London via Portugal, I decided to risk it. This service has come into being only since about ten days. One goes by bus from Geneva to Barcelona and then by air to London via Lisbon. The trip takes nearly four days and costs about 800 Swiss francs. Terribly expensive! I would have gone too, but I have such a horror of falling ill again that I felt that whatever happens I didn't think I could risk that. So here I am still.

Everyone is forever reminding me of the safety and security of Leysin. I suppose it's a great deal to be thankful for. But I don't want safety just for myself – I want to share the bombs and everything. I don't believe anybody who has not actually experienced bombardments and trials of refugees and the sound of cannons can ever imagine what it's like. I hate war as much as anyone, and much more than most, but while there is one on, I want to know what it is like – all the horror and beastliness of it.

On the 15th July I was X-rayed again – the result was very satisfactory. In weight, since June the 1st, I have put on about ½ lb – 250 grams!

Most days we have a heavy damp mist and it pours with rain. We have not even had a week of sunshine this summer. When the sun does show itself, it is so hot that we are bound to have a thunderstorm in the evening. But I love storms and the flash of lightning and rainbows, don't you?

My thoughts have been with you so much all these days when no letters came. I am hoping to hear from you soon. Do give me all your news.

My love to you,

Your loving
Indu

---

37.                                                              Bombay,
                                                       1st August, 1940

Darling,
On my return from Kashmir, I wrote half a dozen articles on Kashmir.

---

1. Henri Philippe Pétain: French political and military leader. After the fall of Paris in the Second World War, he headed the Vichy Government that collaborated with Nazi Germany.

I enclose the first of these. It might interest you as it gives my emotional reactions to the long deferred visit. Possibly I imagined much that I write about. But the visit had a powerful effect upon me. Even physically it made me feel fitter and everyone remarked on this. Actually, to my disgust, I put on two pounds in weight, in spite of the strenuous life I lived there. And yet my waist measurement lessened by an inch or two! Which shows what a healthy animal I am.

On my way back from Poona I paid a visit to the little state of Aundh. I wrote to you once about this. This tiny state has become a group of village republics, partly because the Raja is a go-ahead person, partly because of the influence of his son, recently returned from Oxford. It was an interesting visit, though Aundh is too small a place for any effective experiment. Kirloskarwadi and Oglewadi are in Aundh and we visited both of these industrial concerns. At Oglewadi I was reminded that some years back you had gone there, probably with the Vakils.

The Raja of Aundh[1] is a delightful and extraordinary person. He is about seventy-three but considers himself, and is in many ways, a young man. He is famous for his *surya namaskars*, the old form of exercise, in the form of salutation to the sun. Every schoolboy & girl in the state does these *namaskars* and the Raja himself does a hundred of them every morning, in addition to a brisk run up and down a hill. His energy is extraordinary. He remarked casually to me that in another twenty years' time, perhaps he might begin to grow old and not be able to run up & down a hill! For thirty years or more he has done these *namaskars* without a day's break and during all this period he has not had a day's illness or even a cold.

This letter must end now as I have to go out. This evening I go to Allahabad. I shall have to come back here within a month for the Planning Committee.

All my love, darling.

Your loving,<br>Papu

---

38.                                              Cawnpore,<br>
11th August, 1940

Darling,
The situation here is developing rapidly and this has kept me busy and

---

1. Bhavanrao Shrinivasrao alias Balasaheb Pant (1868–1951): Raja of Aundh; liberal ruler of a small princely state who adopted a federal constitution for his principality. His son Apa B. Pant later represented India as a diplomat in many countries.

moving. We have had a meeting of the A.I.C.C. [All India Congress Committee] in Poona. I spent some days in Allahabad – about a week – and I tried to clear up various arrears of work and to tie up loose ends. One must keep ready for emergencies. One matter which was worrying me, I tried to dispose of, though not very satisfactorily I fear. This was the writing of an additional chapter for the American edition of my *Autobiography*. This book has been considerably abridged in America and I have not been able to see the abridgements. I had promised to write a final chapter giving a survey of the last five years, since I finished my book. This was a hard job. I did it at express speed, writing about 8000 or 9000 words in a little over a day. Inevitably the writing is hurried and does not fit in with the leisurely narrative of the book. It was difficult also to compress the events of the past five years within these limits. And then there is the censor. The thought of him cramps one's style.

In Allahabad a major occurrence has been Lado Bhabhi's [1] efforts at fasting. For reasons of health, she decided to go in for a long fast. She did well for a week and then there was a sudden upset inside her and her condition became rather serious. She is slowly recovering now. I think however that the fast will do her good, and she will be better for it.

Today I came here for various functions, especially to see the Congress volunteers. It is unusual for me to tour in this way now. I have not the time nor the inclination. A certain Government of India order about volunteering, however, produced a curious situation and this visit of mine to Cawnpore today became an all-India event. There was a procession, a march past and speech by me to a huge crowd of about 50,000. For an hour during the procession I stood at the back of the car. Then I stood saluting while nearly 1000 volunteers marched past, and then I held forth for an hour and forty minutes! How long-winded I have become! But I seem to have so much to say, my mind is full and I want to share it. Anyway I am tired now . . .

I go to Lucknow from here – then to Benares – Allahabad – Wardha for the Working Committee. This is tiring business. Perhaps I shall have real rest soon.

Bappi [2] is ill in Lucknow and Amma [3] is with her. I shall see them.
Love,

Your loving,
Papu

---

1. Lado Ranri Zutshi: wife of Ladli Prasad Zutshi, a cousin of Jawaharlal Nehru. ('Bhabhi' means sister-in-law).
2. Swarup Kathju (Bappi): Kamala Nehru's younger sister.
3. Refers to Rajpati Kaul, Kamala Nehru's mother.

39.                                               Wardha,
                                      20th August, 1940

Darling Indu,
Over a month ago I had your cable that you were writing to me.[1] But
no letter has come yet. I must not be impatient.

I have come here to Wardha for a meeting of the Congress Working
Committee. I think I wrote to you that I was going to Bombay from here
for the Planning Committee. All that seems to be in a melting pot now
and everything is uncertain. The situation in the U.P. [United Provinces]
is particularly difficult and I feel I cannot keep away.[2] Anyway the next
fortnight at the most will decide many things.

Quite a long time ago a letter came for you in French from 'Catherine'
from a place called 'Olli Viller'. Evidently Catherine was with you at La
Pelouse. I am not enclosing this as I do not know if it will reach you . . .

I do not quite know what to write to you. My mind today is somewhat
agitated and all manner of thoughts tumble over one another. It is a
queer world we live in. I shall write to you more later, when I have the
chance.

Meanwhile, may it be well with you, my dear.
                                      Love,
                                      Papu

---

40.                                          Les Frênes,
                                             Leysin,
                                       Switzerland,
                                      20th August, 1940

Darling Papu,
How long it is since I have any news of you!

Indeed the only news of India that has managed to leak through to
Leysin was contained in a tiny paragraph in *The Irish Weekly Times,* or
some such paper, stating that Bapu was opposed to Civil Disobedience
and his opinion would surely prevail, although you with a small following
did not agree with him.[3]

Need I say how much my thoughts have been with you all these

1. Refers to letter No. 35.
2. At this time a large number of Congressmen were offering individual *satyagraha*
and were arrested thereafter.
3. This news item is obviously incorrect. Both Mahatma Gandhi and Jawaharlal
Nehru were in favour of offering Civil Disobedience to the British after adequate
preparation.

difficult months – specially difficult for India. My body has been here wrapped in blankets & sheets but I have sometimes wondered how by sheer force of thinking, I were not really with you.

I have written two letters[1] to you since my cable.[2] I do not know when, if ever, they will reach you. Yesterday we heard on the wireless that a boat would leave Lisbon for India on Sept. 4th. So I am sending this.

Darling, I am simply asking for news about you.

As for me there isn't any great change. I am feeling considerably stronger but my weight remains the same. At the beginning of next month – September – I am hoping to go to Bex.

I won't write any more as I'm told the shorter the letters the quicker they pass through the censor. Besides I don't like writing letters which get lost.

All my love, darling one, and my thoughts.

Your
Indu

---

41.                                          Wardha,
                                   12th October, 1940

Darling,

Your letters do not come to me and presumably my letters do not reach you. Yet I continue to write to you from time to time in the hope that perhaps, some time or other, the letter might reach you. It is a curious and depressing world we live in when we can neither meet nor communicate with those we love. When will I see you again, I wonder. Will it be months or years? I do not know, just as I do not know anything about the future that is unfolding so painfully for all of us. This process ages one and most of us grow older faster than the years warrant. It does not matter much for those who are already, like me, past the half century mark. But it does matter for the young who have their lives before them.

A letter that came recently to me brought joy to me. It was from Louise Morin. How it came from France to me I do not know. Perhaps it got through in the early days of the changes. I was glad to have news of her. But what pleased me especially was her account of the visit she paid to you at Leysin. She gave me a very satisfactory account of how you looked and how healthy you seemed to be.

I am here in Wardha for the usual Working Committee meetings.

1. One of the letters referred to is letter No. 36, the other is not traceable.
2. Refers to letter No. 35.

The strain of uncertainty about the future is bad. No one knows how many morrows we have to face in the normal way and the feeling of voyaging through strange lands grips me. There seem to be no resting places on the way – one must move on and on. I have no objections to movement – I like it to be rapid. But to move blindfolded, as it were, is not so pleasant.

And yet, I often wonder, do not most of us go through life rather like sleepwalkers, unaware of what is happening all around us. A slow awakening comes to some, and others do not awaken at all. Perhaps the Somnambulists are not so unfortunate. They escape the horror and tragedy – but who would willingly be a sleepwalker?

I write foolishly to you, words and phrases which may have some significance and yet which may be just words. Suddenly I felt like writing to you, but there was little to write about. I can't write about the odd happenings here for they would be stale and flat by the time this letter reached you. Still it is good to write and to think of you in a far corner of the world.

Madan Atal[1] seems to be obsessed with the notion that you should join a Swiss University. I wrote to you about this previously. Your health is the primary consideration and then you will do as you think best. We are all going through the university of life and that is the hardest of all.

Love,

Your loving,<br>Papu

---

42. 

Anand Bhawan,<br>Allahabad,<br>25th October, 1940

Darling,

At last, after long waiting, a letter[2] from you has just, or almost just reached me. Was it four months ago when I got your last letter? It took full three months for this to come. I was in Lucknow when it came in a bundle containing about twenty or more letters. I looked at it and handled it carefully and was in no hurry to open it. I had waited so long for it – why hurry? I wanted to read it at leisure when I was alone. So I opened and read the other letters and later retired to my room with the message from you.

Three months for a letter to come! My mind goes back to the old

---

1. Madan Atal: cousin of Kamala Nehru, a physician.
2. Refers to letter No. 36.

days when mails went to Europe via the Cape in slow-moving vessels. Are we going back in this as in other matters? Or is this going back only to spring forward with greater speed and energy? I wonder. I cannot quite believe that the world will go back, even though much of what is called modern civilisation lies in ruins.

I thought of you a great deal as I read that letter and all day as I carried it about with me. Not that the inducement of a letter was required. You are seldom out of my mind and sometimes I have a feeling that you are very near me. The door between your room and mine is always open and I walk in and out of it frequently for no apparent reason. Your room is as it was. I do not like to have changes made or even an alteration of the furniture. In my own room you look at me from every side. You will be amused to learn how many pictures of you I have round about me. Yesterday I counted them up. There were twenty-six of them – all different ones of course – in my sitting room and dressing room! From babyhood upwards you sprawl or sit or stand and the past comes up before me and becomes more real than the present.

I have had many reports of the fall of Paris and France. Suhrawardy[1] – do you remember him? – was in Paris when the Germans came and he gave us a vivid account. Then the letter from Louise Morin after her return from Switzerland. For sheer tragedy and drama the sudden collapse of France would be hard to beat. It made people realise suddenly that the old world we knew was cracking up. It was the end of an era. And yet, I suppose, most people in India, both Indians and English, still fail to appreciate what is happening. They stick to the old ruts and close their minds in sheer self-defence. But the ostrich does not save himself by hiding his head.

What a world we live in! It is a nightmare. And yet even the most sensitive grow used to its daily horrors. I read about the bombing of London and then remember that Chungking has had this kind of thing for years – and still carries on. I do not suppose any city has had this experience for such a length of time. I do not know how people feel when they are bombed. I did not feel the slightest bit nervous as I watched the bombing of Barcelona and Chungking.[2] I was fascinated by the sight. Indeed I resented being pushed into a dug-out.

I sent you a cable [the] day before yesterday. I suggested in this that you might visit other parts of Switzerland for a change. This was not

1. H. S. Suhrawardy: leader of the Muslim League in Bengal. He was Chief Minister of Bengal, 1946–7, and later Prime Minister of Pakistan, 1956–7.
2. Jawaharlal Nehru visited Barcelona in June 1938, during the Civil War, and Chungking in August 1939. China had been at war with Japan since 1937 and Chungking, which became the centre of government during the hostilities, was severely damaged by intensive Japanese bombing.

only because of what you wrote about the oppressive atmosphere at Les Frênes. Movement and changing scenery divert the mind and give it some rest. That is very necessary in these days of stress and strain. Unfortunately you cannot come out of Switzerland or, at any rate, [not] without great difficulty. Perhaps it is as well at least for another three months. It would have served little purpose for you to have gone to England. You would not have been able to do anything worthwhile and you might well have experienced a hitch in your progress to complete health. And then you would have had to be looked after by others. Of course there should be no question of our avoiding the risks or dangers of bombing or anything else. We might as well know the world we live in by personal experience. I think it would be a good thing if many people in India had that experience. Perhaps they will, some time or other.

But one must face risk in the course of doing something worthwhile. Otherwise this becomes just a gesture and a foolhardy one at that. We have a long road to travel and I have no doubt that there will be plenty of dangers for all of us. Let us get our minds and bodies in fit condition.

I do not suppose it is very necessary for you to remain at Leysin all the time. The climate and other benefits of Leysin could be obtained at many places in Suisse. So it might be worthwhile to visit other places. The visit to Bex must have been a pleasant change, though Bex is a dull enough place.

I am glad you met Nanu. I wish I could help him. But I cannot get into touch with him. The last time I wrote to him many months ago my letter did not reach him. And it contained a cheque.

You ask for news. What news am I to give you? There is plenty of course but then there is also an army of censors to get through. We also have a perpetual crisis and this is an exhausting affair. But we seem to be on the eve of big events. Indeed they have begun already.

For the rest, life goes on. Betty is coming here tomorrow with her children for a few days. I am at present quite alone in the house. I have just returned from a very heavy tour.

If at any time in the future you are able to return to India, it would perhaps be better to come via America and China.

Within a month you will have your birthday. This letter will reach you long afterwards, if it reaches you. And that makes me wonder if my letters are reaching you at all.

Send my love to Nanu, if you can reach him, and lots of it to you, my darling one.

Your loving
Papu

43.                                                    District Jail,
                                                       Gorakhpur,
                                                 5th November, 1940

Darling Indu,
Again I am writing to you from prison after many years. When was it
last that I did so? Over five years ago and then also you were in Europe.
The five years have gone with all their shocks and changes and I revert
to my normal routine. It was difficult enough to write to you during
these past five months and I yet do not know if any of these letters of
mine have reached you across the warring armies. Now fresh obstacles
arise. But I shall continue to write to you, while I may and, perhaps
months hence, some of my letters may overcome these many impediments and reach your hands.

I came here with the new moon and it is five days old now. The
slender crescent has put on more substance and nightly it grows fuller.
I was arrested the day after *Diwali* and brought here from Allahabad.
The next day after my arrival was *Id*, the great Muslim festival ending
the *Ramzan* fast. So in feasting and rejoicing I came here, or was brought
here. My trial lasted two days and today I was sentenced. There were
three counts on three speeches I had delivered a month ago in Gorakhpur district and on each charge I was sentenced to a year and four
months rigorous imprisonment, each sentence to run consecutively, that
is four years in all. That is the biggest sentence I have so far had in my
longish experience, but then I suppose this was only proper as I grow
in years and presumably in importance.

Four years seems a long time to look forward to. And yet in this world
of shock and change, it makes little difference what period is fixed for
a sentence. For my part I might as well be here as elsewhere. For the
last five days my tired mind and body have been clamouring for rest and
I have slept more than I have done for many months. The mind has not
been so restful. It is a wayward creature and not easy to control. Soon,
I suppose, it will get into tune with my surroundings.

Cables were sent to you, I understand, informing you of my arrest
and sentence. I hope you received them. I do not know where you are
– at Bex or Leysin or elsewhere. Leysin, I suppose, is the safest address
and so I address you there. But it would ease my mind to have news of
you for your last cable came six weeks ago.

Betty came to Allahabad with the children on the 27th October for a
few days, just over *Diwali*. But suddenly I was summoned to Wardha
by Bapu and I left on the 28th. I spent a day in Wardha or rather at
Sevagram, where Bapu lives, and returned to Allahabad, catching the
mail from Bombay at Jubbalpur. At Chheoki on the night of the 31st

October I was arrested and taken by car to the Superintendent of Police's house in Allahabad. A fair number of people had gathered at Allahabad station, not expecting of course that I would be arrested at Chheoki. Upadhyaya went on and told them.

That night I was sent by car from Allahabad to Gorakhpur. The distance is not as much as I thought it was, but it was a long enough journey – 175 miles with a river to cross on a ferry. Our car was a bad one and gave trouble. All night we motored and I was so tired that even the discomforts and petty accidents on the way could not keep me awake for long. We reached the Ghaghra river at a quarter to five in the morning. The stars were still out but there was the smell of the dawn in the air as we crossed that placid river. And then forty miles to Gorakhpur.

Nan and Betty and an American girl, who was staying at Anand Bhawan at the time, Kay Stimson,[1] came for my trial to Gorakhpur. So also Madan Bhai.

And now the preliminaries are over, the formality of the trial gone through and sentence duly pronounced. All that remains is for me to settle down – to my books, to spinning and to such other activities as come my way. Yet it takes a little time to adjust the mind, and I have a feeling that as I grow older my mind becomes more complex. Often I look at it, as far as I can objectively, and fail to understand it. I do not know where I shall be kept – in Gorakhpur or elsewhere. It really does not matter much to me. Interviews are very pleasant in jail but there are no particular interviews that I hanker after. Worthwhile persons have work to do outside and I do not want my interviews to come in the way.

My trial, within the jail premises, was a curious *Alice in Wonderland* affair. Of course it was all formal and proper and the legal formalities were gone through. But an air of utter unreality hung over it and somehow it was difficult to take it seriously. It was a new experience for the American girl and she could not quite take it in. Was it seriously meant, she said? And yet it must be so for a sentence and prison will follow. But it was not my trial that had this curious unreal look. India is so unreal today – a Mickey Mouse affair or Snow White. Or perhaps the world itself is behaving like that. What a mad lot of people we all are in this mad world!

And now about you, my darling one. My arrest and sentence must not make the least bit of difference to what you intend doing. Do not worry in the slightest. I have deliberately chosen my path, well knowing the consequences, and have trained myself to it. Age creeps upon me but I am young enough still in mind and body and hardened to most occurrences. It would distress me greatly if I felt that the odd things that happen to me upset any

1. Kay Stimson: wife of Robert Stimson who was Editor of *The Times of India*, Bombay at this juncture.

plans that you may make for yourself. I cannot help you much in the making of these plans and indeed this is not necessary. You are well enough I hope now and will be quite fit soon. To a large extent circumstances and world happenings control our lives today. You are tied up in Switzerland and cannot easily get away. The barriers that confine me are much narrower. We shall put up with these temporary impediments and mishaps without being affected by them too much. Anyway, my life is on the wane, though it may take an unconscionable time about it. Yours is to come. Each generation has to solve its own problems, and that perhaps applies far more today, in this fast changing world, than ever before. For a passing generation to impose itself on a new one is bad. Yet we are always doing it, consciously sometimes, unconsciously most of the time. I have no doubt that I do it. And yet I do not want to and I would like you to help me in this. Do not therefore consider me, or what you may think are my wishes in anything, as a burden and an obstacle in your way. I have almost ceased to have any wishes about others, individually considered, though I have these wishes for large impersonal objects. I have learnt from experience that I am not wise enough to advise others. I find difficulty in deciding many questions for myself; how can I decide for others, even though they are dear to me?

In the solitude of prison I shall think of you a great deal. I shall sit here wrapped up in my thoughts and you will be a constant companion bringing joy and solace to me. So I shall not be really lonely, and the years or months that I pass here will perhaps bring peace to my mind. I shall make friends again with the stars and watch the moon wax and wane, and see the pageant of the world, with all its beauty and horror, as an onlooker from a distant place or a different world. I have worked hard during most of my life but I have worked as I wanted to, and life, in spite of many hard knocks, has been gracious to me. I suppose I have hard work still to do. There are no ways of escape from it. But at present I feel somewhat weary in mind. When I feel this way I seek refuge in poetry and the classics. What is wisdom, asks Euripides,

> What then is Wisdom? What of man's endeavour?
> To stand from fear set free, to breathe and wait,
> To hold a hand uplifted over Hate.
> And shall not Loveliness be loved for ever?

Do I not betray my age and generation in what I write, and in my quotations?

The safest address for you to write to me will continue to be Anand Bhawan, though I do not know what will happen to Anand Bhawan in the months to come.

If you are in touch with Louise and Nanu send them my love. If it is possible for you to help Nanu in any way, I wish you would do so. For months I have been worried about him not knowing what to do. You will remember that when you want money cable directly to Bachhraj.

All my love, *carissima*, and may it be well with you.

Your loving,
Papu

44.

La Pelouse,
Bex,
Switzerland,
7th November, 1940

Darling Papu,

I do hope this will reach you sometime. My thoughts are constantly with you but how I long for some more material and substantial contact!

Your letters [1] written in Kashmir arrived last week. I was glad to get them just then – glad that you were able at last to go to Kashmir and refresh your mind and body with the mountain you love so much. And now you will have this memory to keep you company in dark moments. Are you in Naini, I wonder?

La Pelouse and the surrounding mountainsides are incredibly beautiful – such rich gold and bronze and wine-red tints. And on the peaks, a sprinkling of snow. If only one could compress all this – like perfume in a bottle – and send it to you. But 'We cannot cage the minute within its nets of gold.' [2]

Do you know that since the middle of September I have been making efforts to get out of this country? I did not let you know for I did not wish you to be worried unnecessarily before anything was definitely decided. I consulted Rollier of course – he thinks I ought to spend the winter in Leysin. I also saw another doctor here just to have his opinion, which was that my chest is quite quite clear. There followed the usual lectures about prudence and caution and rest. Bhandari and Agatha sent numerous lengthy radiograms (does such a word exist?). Letters from England take two to six weeks or more and one can say so little in a cable. All this took a lot of time. And all the while I was getting more and more agitated lest the Spanish or the French frontier be closed. Well, the frontiers are still open, though the Spanish one less so. For ten days ago the Spanish Government brought into force a new law: all visas, transit or otherwise, can only be granted in Madrid.

1. Refers to letters Nos 31 and 32.
2. From 'Sunlight in the Garden' by Louis MacNeice.

How complicated life is! I just cannot imagine the bliss of being able to pass from one country to another as one goes from one town to another – no passports, no identification papers, no visas. Did such days really exist? Anyway now they belong to history.

To come to India I must go to England. To go to England I must pass through France, Spain and Portugal. The Portuguese visa is unavailable unless one produces one's ticket as proof of one's intention of leaving Portugal immediately. The Spanish Consulate will not even think of a visa until you show them your Portuguese one. Then you take your Spanish visa to the French Consulate!

I spent some days in Geneva. I have now my air ticket to England and my Portuguese visa. Nothing else to do but wait – wait . . . wait . . . The Spanish Consulate says cheerfully that the visa may take three weeks or six weeks or months.

So I sit alone and admire the autumn tints. Was it Mussolini, or his son Bruno, who said that . . . [1] 'completed' the beauty of nature? We have even that 'perfection' here.

From ten p.m. until seven in the morning we have a complete black-out. Foodstuffs have of course been rationed for sometime except milk and a few other things. Prices are going up almost every few hours. Since last week there is absolute prohibition for the selling of any kind of clothing or cloth, shoes, wool, cotton, silk, all rubber goods, soap and a whole host of other things. Eventually ration cards will be issued for these commodities – eventually; the Lord knows when. Such is life in a neutral country!

Do you know in Geneva, on my way to see a friend of Agatha's, I was surprised to notice at a tram stop, a façade, vaguely familiar. On peering I saw the number clearly – 46. It was our flat in the Boulevard des Tranchees. I remembered so well the open space in front – even the wire netting had not changed. [2]

Meanwhile, to pass the time I am learning Spanish – I want to be able to *'se débrouiller'* [3] if, as has happened to several people, I get held up in Spain.

Much love, darling one,

Indu

---

1. Deleted by censors: letters written or received in prison had to pass through official censors. Any deletion is hereafter indicated in a footnote 'Deleted by censors'.

2. The Nehrus stayed in Geneva in 1926 while Kamala Nehru underwent medical treatment and Indira attended L'Ecole Nouvelle at Bex.

3. To manage.

45.            [Cable]            District Jail,
Gorakhpur,
12th November, 1940

DLT Nehru,
Chez Hemmerlin,
Pelouse,
Bex (Switzerland)

Darling your cable fourth[1] don't upset your programme because my convictions keep me informed your movements love.

           Nehru

---

46.            District Jail,
Dehra Dun,
18th November, 1940

Darling Indu,

I wrote to you about two weeks ago from Gorakhpur on the day my sentence was passed.[2] A few days later I received the cable you sent to Puphi at Allahabad. The idea of your coming back to India and of my seeing you fills me with joy. Still I cabled to you not to upset your own programme because of my conviction. You have now been in Switzerland for nearly a year and that is a long enough time. At the most, even in normal times, you might have spent some of the winter months there, say till March, and then left the place. Winter is good in Suisse. But there are other factors also and I can well understand your anxiety to leave the place. I suppose that even if you tried your utmost, it would take you a month or two to get away. Indeed I am not at all sure that you will succeed even then.

The only possible route seems to be for you to go via Marseille to Barcelona and Lisbon, chiefly by air, and then also by air to London. You wrote about this once to me. Whether that route is open now I do not know. Even after you reach London the problem of returning to India is not solved. I am told that there is a long list of persons, including children, waiting to be sent to India. It takes months to get a passage on a convoy. I do not know how far it is possible for you to return to India without going to London, that is from Lisbon directly via the

---

1. Cable not traceable.
2. Refers to letter No. 43.

Cape. You must have all these factors in mind and will be able to decide for yourself.

Bear in mind that the good you have derived from your stay in Switzerland is not jeopardised. I want to see you healthy and strong and it is better to curb one's impatience for a while if thereby one can lay the foundations of sound health. All of us, including you of course, will have to bear heavy burdens in this mad world and the fitter we are for them, the better.

Personally, even from the health point of view, I think India has numerous ideal spots to recuperate, if that is necessary. That depends so much on the individual's liking and on what might be termed psychological reactions. If I was ill, of which there appears to be not the least chance, even a short stay in the higher valleys of Kashmir would fill me with energy and vitality.

It is quite impossible for any of us to forecast the future. Anything may happen in the world at large or in India. All we can do is to face our job and do it as well as we can and to remain tranquil in spite of shock and disaster. We of this generation are fated to have these shocks in over-abundant measure and to carry this terrible burden of war and conflict and sorrow whether we like it or not. Perhaps the next generation, your generation, may have a better and happier time. That hope keeps us going. But you overlap with the passing generation and cannot escape its burdens. We grow old mentally with amazing rapidity when we come up with these stark and cruel realities of life. Perhaps we grow wiser also, though there is little wisdom in evidence anywhere.

I quite agree with you that it is not good enough for any man or woman to sit at ease, doing nothing, while millions have to risk everything they possess from day to day. Life is something much more than a round of eating and sleeping and amusing oneself. Indeed, as someone has said, one can enjoy life properly only after resolving not to count the cost. I am not of the calculating variety, neither are you, and I would not like you to be one. We must face the risks and perils of the adventure of life. If I was an Englishman, I would not leave England now whatever happened, and in spite of bombing and everything else. Being an Indian, my job lies in India and I would not leave India now even if I could.

Let us therefore not be frightened of perils, real or imaginary – the real ones are bad enough, but to be frightened of them is far worse. But to face danger calmly and courageously is one thing: to be foolhardy and melodramatic about it is quite another thing. It is folly. Therefore one avoids needless risk and danger. You will do so I hope.

I wrote to you in my last letter[1] that with the passing of years I have grown more and more reluctant to force my advice on others about matters involving personal decisions. I am free enough with my advice on larger questions involving the mass. That is my job in life and I cannot escape it. But individual decisions must be taken by oneself. In this rapidly changing world, where we are forced to learn from the shock of events, the gap between two generations is apt to grow wider in the sense of understanding each other. I have tried hard to understand the new generation and perhaps I have not wholly failed. But this very attempt has taught me not to impose myself.

I write this letter to you well knowing that the chances are that it will not reach you. It will be lost somewhere in the 'fog of war'. But it may reach you sometime or other and in any event it gives me pleasure in writing it. So why deny myself that escape from myself in thinking of you and imagining you to be beside me and listening to me?

Long before this letter reaches you, if it reaches you at all, you will have come to your decisions and possibly made your arrangements for your future programme. I can be of little help from here. But fortunately you have plenty of friends across the seas to help you.

Two nights ago I was suddenly informed in Gorakhpur Jail that I was being transferred to Dehra Dun. Soon after I left and by a devious and complicated route, partly by train and partly by motor car, I reached here last night. I travelled in comfort by train, in a small saloon, but as a *purdanashin*[2] with all the shutters and blinds up, lest an evil eye might fall upon me.

I am back again in my old place in Dehra which I left over six years ago – in August 1934 I think it was. What a six years they have been!

Tomorrow is your birthday, my darling one. At Bex it will pass off rather quietly, but you will be in the minds of numerous people who care for you, and you will haunt me even more than you usually do. I sent you a cable today. I wonder if it will reach you in time.

Chand & Tara & Rita are at Mussoorie near by. Chand is finishing her school career and probably Tara and Rita will not go back to Woodstock. They will be going down to Allahabad soon and perhaps I might see them. By the time they reach Allahabad it is quite possible that there will only be Upadhyaya to welcome them. Nan and Ranjit may have gone to safer quarters.

I had a letter from Nanu the other day. Will you write to him that I was happy to receive it? He tells me that he is in touch with you. Give him my love.

1. Refers to letter No. 43.
2. A veiled woman.

I had a cable also from Louise. This was in answer to one I sent her. And so, *au revoir, cara mia*, and may it be well with you.
Love,

Your loving,<br>Papu

This letter will be forwarded to you by Puphi from Allahabad. I am sending it as an enclosure to her.

---

47.                    [Cable]                    Geneve,
25th November, 1940

Nehru,
District Jail,
Dehra Dun

Leaving Switzerland twenty seventh Lisbon England whence hope to come India via Cape Don't worry Darling much love,

Indu Nehru

---

48.                    Casa de Sao Mamede,
159 Rua da Escola,
Politecnica,
Lisboa,
14th December, 1940

Darling Papu,
Two letters of yours – both written in August[1] have followed me here.

It was a fortnight yesterday since my arrival in Lisbon. The date of departure is still one big question mark. I have an aeroplane ticket but I have put my name down on the boat list as well – I shall leave by whichever service offers me a passage first. Of course the air service takes some hours and the boat at least a month to reach England. But I think one month on the journey is better than being stuck on in Lisbon indefinitely. Feroze has managed to get me priority for the plane. But as there are at least sixty other names before mine on the priority list, most people think it is quite hopeless waiting for a seat.

I left Geneva at seven a.m. on the 27th November by bus. On the

---

1. Jawaharlal Nehru wrote three letters to Indira in the month of August. These were dated 1st, 11th and the 20th. Here she may be referring to any two of these letters.

bus were Dr & Mrs Ceresole (he is the brother of Pierre Ceresole, whom you surely know). We spent four hours at the Franco-Swiss frontier. At first we were in a thick mist and the ground was covered with frost. Quite suddenly we emerged from the mist and beheld a most magnificent range of snow-topped mountains rising out [of] a sea of white foam like clouds. The scenery all along was rather glorious. I like the rugged wildness of the Haute Savoie. The only outward signs of the war that we saw were a few blown-up bridges, the complete absence of sugar and the undrinkable concoction which is called '*café national*'. Of course there is a lack of many many things, but this it was difficult for a passing traveller to notice. All the towns we passed were very gloomy and quite deserted. We lunched at Gorian and dined and slept at Nîmes. We left Nîmes next morning at six thirty and saw the most superb sunrise of my life. We were driving along the sea and I was looking out at the calmness of the Mediterranean when I saw the tiniest drop of blood on the horizon. For a moment I couldn't think what it was. And then it rose and grew bigger and bigger. It was a perfect poem, this ball of the very essence of red reflected in the sea. It was just so majestic and splendid, one did not wonder that he was called a God and worshipped.

For this second day we had been told to bring our own provisions. And we ate our sandwiches and hard-boiled eggs for breakfast at Sète and again for lunch at Le Perthus, the French frontier. Between Le Perthus & La Junquera, Spanish frontier, we spent nearly five hours in a howling gale. Everybody caught a cold. Up till here the journey had not been at all bad. But at this frontier we had to change buses, for the Spanish Govt doesn't allow any foreign bus to enter their territory. The road to Barcelona was like a village road in India, full of holes and bumps and oh so dusty. Moreover we were packed like sardines. We were glad to see the glimmering hill of lights that was Barcelona. How different it was when you were there! I fell completely in love with Barcelona and the Spaniards – especially the women. Barcelona is beautiful but sad, sad to the point of pain. Such misery on every face! Apart from anything else there is so little food, no butter, no sugar, inedible bread. About the only thing one saw in abundance were flowers, masses and masses of them. There was one other thing in equal abundance – portraits of Franco[1] and of José Antonio,[2] whoever he is or was. Also posters about the victory. I was sorry to leave. But my seat was reserved on the next morning's plane to Lisbon. From the air, Spain looked like an enormous patchwork quilt, the browns, deep greens,

1. Francisco Franco (1892–1975): Spanish military leader and dictator.
2. José Antonio Primo de Rivera (1903–36): founder of the Falange, the Spanish Fascist Party.

beiges blending together exquisitely. At four thirty p.m., Portuguese time, we landed at Cintra aerodrome. Police, passport, customs all over again. This was the beginning of trouble for me. After one look at my passport photograph the police officer said that it was not me, and therefore the passport could not be mine! I just kept mum – after all what can one say? Then he wanted to see my ticket and I found that I had lost it – trust me to choose just this journey to lose my ticket for the first time in all my travels! Anyway after a most unpleasant half-hour at the police I was allowed to leave. Cooks of Geneva had wired for a room reservation a whole week ago but on arrival I found there was no reservation for me. The next two hours were spent in going from one hotel to another in search of a bed. At half past eight we arrived at a poky little hotel where there was a double room vacant for just one night. I took it, dumped my luggage and then went out in search of a Mrs Moreton, whose address had been given [to] me in Geneva. Mrs Moreton is [the] Swiss widow of an English person – she has lived all her life in Lisboa. She is one of those persons brimming over with undiluted goodness.

The next morning – the 30th – I found that a room had been reserved for me in Estoril, a resort some miles from Lisbon. So I moved there. Estoril is terribly like Juhu, only full of enormous hotels. My own hotel was altogether too luxurious and expensive & besides it was a nuisance being so far from Lisbon – forty-five mins by train. However I was forced to stay in bed for at least a couple of days for by this time my cold had taken on enormous proportions, I had a bad cough and my voice had taken a holiday. On the 3rd I went up to Lisbon & with Mrs Moreton as guide began a second hunt for a room. The next day I moved to this pension, and have been here since.

I have got a brand new passport. My old one had no place left in it for an exit visa.

Nothing that I was told about Lisbon seems to be true. They said in Geneva that Portugal was very cheap, that the shops were wonderful, the best in Europe, for they still had American and English goods, the weather was very good. I find that everything is very expensive – much more so than in Switzerland. For instance a letter telegram to England cost 3.90 frs in Suisse. Here it costs the equivalent of 14 Swiss francs. After the gloom of France & the misery of Spain, the shops did indeed look rather dazzling but on closer view one finds nothing one wants and the quality of the goods is poor. As for the weather, it has so far behaved itself but apparently this is the first winter when it has not poured.

The Portuguese are very poor and very dirty. A lot of women & children are barefooted and there are many beggars. People spit all over the place – there is a terrific amount of shoutings and many hawkers singing out their wares from house to house. It is almost like being in India. This is the first time I have seen custard-apples in Europe. The milk is watery and unappetising – water has to be boiled. Portuguese meals swim in oil. Compared to other commodities food is cheap – and ample too, though a shortage of butter is being felt.

Lisbon is swarming with foreigners, mostly refugees trying to get away to the Americas. Whichever office one goes to one is practically trampled under foot.

In most of the offices, people understand 'um po' of French but otherwise the language difficulty is another complication in a complicated situation. Written Portuguese is like Spanish and very easy – but when spoken it sounds like Czech, only worse. I find it impossible to understand a word – for instance when a Portuguese says 'Lisboa' all one hears is 'shbo'.

Some days ago I bought the *News Chronicle* of the 6th Dec – the first English paper I've seen for nearly a year. It gave me the news of Puphi's arrest and also of some kind of 'truce' that the moderates were trying to negotiate. Apart from this no news of India.

This morning came a cable from Agatha, 'Have received money from your father.' Thank you so much. But I think I have already quite enough – I believe I cabled to this effect to Puphi when I told her of my intended departure.

I have left with Wagons-lits Cook, Rue Mont-Blanc, Geneva, just over 4000 Swiss francs. This is in my name (old passport No. 7757-C). They assured me that I could draw the whole or part of this amount anywhere in the world – that is at any branch of Cooks after cabling to the Geneva office. So I left the money, just in case I needed it on my journey to India, when taking money out of England would be difficult. I am telling you this so that you may claim this money just in case (this is highly improbable, but still) anything should happen to me. There is no point in making a present of it to Cooks. The above sum – 4000 S.frs – is part of 618900 S.frs which were transferred to Cooks from my account No. 11774 at the Banque Cantonale Vaudoise, Lausanne. The cheque from the bank was sent on the 22nd Nov., 1940 (Reference No. A 11774).

I wrote to you from Bex and enclosed the letter with a note to Puphi. But perhaps this will reach you first. In Bex I was told that the letter had to go through England & that there was no air service to India. This I am sending via America – by the clipper to New York.

I hope it is not too cold in Dehra and that you are at least keeping well. The enforced rest should be good for you, at least in the beginning. My thoughts are with you always and I long to see you. There is so much more than high walls between us. When will I reach India, when will I be able to see you? And meanwhile, I have no idea what is happening, how things are shaping themselves.

From everybody who has ever met you in Switzerland & France, I bring you greetings. Nanu is in Montpellier – he hasn't a sou. I sent him 500 Swiss frs. I had hoped he would leave the country but it isn't as easy as it sounds; so he is trying to make the best of it – he will probably take up some course at the University there. Louise Morin is with Jean-Jacques in Lyon. Jean-Jacques's incurable cheerfulness has given way to pessimism. And who can blame him? What cheerless prospect for the youth of France! They want so much to help their country and they are so afraid of helping to build up something of which they cannot be proud. How heartrendingly tragic is the position of France! J. and many of his comrades tried to take the journey that I am taking but there are endless obstacles to that and they had to give up the idea.

From Switzerland – good wishes from Mlle Hemmerlin and many people in Geneva. I have left a suitcase and some books in Bex.

You must be tired of my chattering. How hard it is to write when one has to think of censors all the time! What can one say that will not evoke their displeasure?

So shall I say – *Au revoir* – darling one. And may we meet soon!

My wishes for the coming New Year and all all my love to you.

Your<br>Indu

Will 1941 bring some hope for this poor old, sick world of ours? Or is it too ill to get well?

P.S.
I enclose a snapshot of myself taken in Sept. just before I left Leysin.

---

49.                    [Cable]                    London,
2nd January, 1941

Nehru,
District Jail,
Dehra Dun,
India

Arrived last night well Plans uncertain.
[Indu]

50.

District Jail,
Dehra Dun,
10th January, 1941

Darling Indu,

So you are in London now. Long before your cable [1] came – for cables take time nowadays, especially to reach in prison – I learnt of your arrival in London from the newspapers. Another cable came from Bhandari later informing me that he had found you in excellent condition. I am very happy to learn this. I am glad you have got out of dismal and depressing Leysin. I did not want to press you to leave the place so long as you felt that your health might improve there. But on general principles I am entirely opposed to very long stays in sanatoria, unless there is no choice left in the matter.

Now that you are fit you can fix your future programme as you choose, taking just a little care to remain fit and not overtax your strength and health. Long before this reaches you – it may not reach you at all – you will have decided upon your programme. Perhaps you may have left England. Anyway you are in the best position to decide.

What a changed London you must have found! Changed not merely in outward appearance but in so many other ways. It is a symbol of the titanic changes that are convulsing the world. London has had a bad time, like so many other cities in various countries. And yet perhaps no city has suffered more during the past years than Chungking. Some time back I had a letter from Madame Chiang Kai-shek. [2] She said in this:

If you were to visit Chungking now you would not recognise it. Square miles of the most prosperous business districts have now become shambles, and so far as the eye can see nothing but debris and ruins stretch out in all directions. All of us who are still sound in limb have worked and toiled incessantly for the relief of the tens of thousands of homeless refugees deprived of every means of livelihood through the insensate destruction of human lives and property with the most calculated cruelty ever conceived by man.

Such is our world today. Something much more vital than buildings has gone to pieces. It will not be pieced together after the old pattern

1. Refers to letter No. 49.
2. Madame Chiang Kai-shek: educated in the U.S.A., she married General Chiang Kai-shek in 1927 and accompanied her husband on many of his military campaigns. She did much relief work among orphans and refugees and received the highest military and civil decorations of the National Government of China.

again, whatever happens. Meanwhile we as individuals feel rather lost, at least the older generation do, lost most of all in a spiritual sense. Out of that feeling of loss one forgets oneself and then finds oneself perhaps in a vast movement where individuals count for little. And yet through this impersonal finding of ourselves, the individual also recovers.

I have been reading a book about China – Lin Yu-tang's [1] new novel of Chinese life – *Moment in Peking*. It is a tremendously long book and rather unlike a modern novel. And yet it is worth reading and I hope you will get hold of it. China is very different from India and yet there is so much in common. Both have been passing through a tremendous period of transition in their inner lives and this transition has suddenly to face a world change. I have been drawn more and more towards China and admire her culture greatly.

Betty and Raja and Janak [2] came to interview me yesterday. Betty and Raja have gone back to Bombay and my interviews are not likely to be regular in future. There are not many people available whom I am anxious to interview. I should like to see Amma and perhaps she will come next fortnight or later. Amma is anxious about Kailas, [3] having had no news of him for a while. I have sent her Bhandari's address.

Anand Bhawan has fewer occupants now that Chand has joined college in Lucknow. There is Tara and Rita. For the present Padmaja is there for a few days. She will be leaving next week. I am sending this letter through her. (The letter is going direct.)

I understand that Lindsay Drummond is bringing a collection of my writings and calling it *The Unity of India*. Please ask Krishna to have complimentary copies sent on my behalf to various friends of ours. You can make a list. Copies should be sent to Bapu and Gurudev. Also to Madame Chiang Kai-shek (Chungking) and Madame Sun Yat-sen [4] (27 Grampion Road, Kowloon, Hong Kong) and to the Chinese Ambassador in London. To Agatha, Edward Thompson [5] and Carl Heath. [6] You can add to this list in England & India. Also to Mrs Frances Gunther, 300 Central Park West, New York City. Mrs Gunther has written to invite you to America and says she will look after you.

1. Lin Yu-tang: Chinese author and philologist, who stayed at Anand Bhawan on his visit to Allahabad in March 1944.

2. Janak Zutshi: a cousin of Indira Gandhi who was an educationist and a nationalist.

3. Kailas Nath Kaul: Kamala Nehru's brother. He was a botanist.

4. Madame Sun Yat-sen: wife of the President of the Chinese Republic. She later became a Vice-President of the People's Republic of China.

5. Edward Thompson: missionary and writer who supported the cause of Indian freedom. He was a friend of Jawaharlal Nehru.

6. Carl Heath: President of the Conciliation Group, created in 1931, on the initiative of Mahatma Gandhi, during his visit to London. This Group mediated between British and Indian leaders.

It has been cold here, not nearly so cold as you must be having. But in just three weeks on February 1st *Vasanta* begins and that means a change to spring.

All my love to you my darling one.

Your loving,

Papu

I have no account at any bank in London now. You might continue your account at Lloyds and ask Krishna to deposit any royalties received for me in your account.

---

51.

District Jail,
Dehra Dun,
31st January, 1941

Darling Indu,

For more than three weeks I had received no news of you and though it is not my habit to worry, I decided to cable to Agatha. I sent the cable to her as I was not quite sure where you might be. And even if I cabled to you it would be care of Agatha. Your answer[1] to this cable came yesterday and I was happy to get it. It gives no indication whatever of when you are likely to get a passage. This, I suppose, is a mystery which is not revealed till the last moment.

Day before yesterday I received your letter from Lisbon dated 14th December.[2] It took just a month and a half to travel round the world *via* New York, Manila, China, etc. Perhaps a good part of this time was taken up by the various censors reading your letter. What a crowd of these not very lovable individuals must have pored over it from Portugal to India! It would be interesting to make a list. In India alone it has to pass, I think, four scrutinies, three of these being in Dehra Dun. It is not an easy matter to get excited about letter writing under these circumstances. Anyway I have no occasion for excitement as letters for me or from me are rare indeed.

I looked long at the envelope which contained your letter. Your hand-writing on an envelope had not come to me for some months. (The letter you sent from Bex has not reached me yet.) Like a treasure which has come my way unexpectedly and out of which I wish to take full delight before examining it, I gazed long at the envelope. It seemed to me that your handwriting was not quite the same as it used to be. It was

---

1. Letter not traceable.
2. Refers to letter No. 48.

yours of course and yet it made me imagine that someone was trying to copy it. Handwriting of course changes and develops and there was nothing surprising about a slight change which seemed to have crept in yours. But then, I wondered, does this indicate some change in you also? We all change as the days and years roll by and I am myself conscious of very definite changes in my own make-up. As I look back I seem to see a procession of different personalities merging with each other and yet each with its own distinctive features. Whether the changes are for the good or not I do not know. Or perhaps it is not so much a change of personality that takes place as the emergence of different aspects of the same personality. We are, each one of us, a group of different individuals, all tied up together with no hope of release, and sometimes they quarrel amongst themselves and we feel the tension and the pain.

So, I wondered, during these two years since we met, how have you progressed and changed in this changing and moving world. I looked at the snapshot you have sent me. It is a good one and I like it. But it did not help me in my enquiry.

I have read your letter several times and, as I read it, travelled with you from Geneva to Lisbon. We stayed at Barcelona for a while but the thought of that lovely city produces a catch in my throat and a pain in my heart. And then your adventures in Lisbon. Anyway you are out of all that and facing fresh adventures.

Three weeks ago I tried to send brief letters to Agatha and Edward Thompson but I was not successful. The rules regarding correspondence that are being enforced this time are different and stricter than on previous occasions. You are an exception and I am allowed to write to you and to receive your letters when they come – there are not too many of them! – but otherwise I am rather cut off from the world. It does not matter. It is a change for me to which I am rapidly adapting myself. The change is big enough for, as you know, my normal existence is overfull with correspondence. I grope about in a very jungle of letters and make mighty, and seldom wholly successful, efforts to cope with it. And now to receive practically no letters and to write once a fortnight will no doubt do my soul good.

I am glad you sent some money to Nanu. I wish I could help him more. For years past I have been trying to induce him to come to India for a change at least and to make himself fitter for his work. But he is or was extraordinarily in certain ruts and cannot pull himself out till fate gives him a kick. Send him my love if you can get through to him. Louise Morin and Jean-Jacques also. It will cheer them up if they get messages of love and friendship from outside.

I was amused to read your testamentary dispositions of the money you had deposited at Cooks. You must have got the money in London and you will no doubt make good use of it. No more will be sent to you. But I am glad I had that £70 sent to Agatha for you. If you do not require it, you can pass it on to others who might stand in greater need of it – there is Kailas, Krishna, Feroze or Nanu, or anyone else. During these days of abnormality and uncertainty all manner of difficulties arise and grip one and so many of our friends may stand in need of a little help.

I wish you would send me a brief cable at least every two weeks just to say how you are getting on. Any message from you cheers me and seems to lessen the distance between us.

I am having odd interviews from time to time – usually even beyond the normal fortnight. I am not particularly keen on them. Last week Bijju[1] & Fory[2] motored up from Delhi to pay us a visit. Next week probably Chandra[3] and Sri Handoo[4] will turn up. They are being transferred to Burma again and want to say goodbye to me. I should have liked to see Amma but she is busy looking after Bappi in Agra.

The Memorial Hospital in Allahabad is practically ready now and the question has arisen as to whether there should be a formal and big opening ceremony by Bapu. I was not very keen on it under the circumstances but Jivraj Mehta is anxious to have it. Jivraj has taken enormous trouble over this hospital and his wishes carry weight. Perhaps Bapu may agree to come over next month for the opening ceremony. The hospital is an attractive and efficient looking building. Some time or other, I suppose, Anand Bhawan will become an annexe of it, perhaps for little children. That will be for you to consider and decide.

The flowers in our barrack are slowly appearing. In another few weeks' time they should be in full bloom. The cold weather is still with us but its last stage has come. Tomorrow is *Vasanta Panchami*, the day which heralds the coming of spring. Usually it is remarkable how the season changes after this day, though perhaps in Dehra Dun the change may be slower. For me this day is an anniversary which I can never forget.[5]

The little barrack we live in is a very ancient affair. I am told it was built nearly a hundred years ago. The roof has been pronounced unreliable and so we are being shifted to a little tent in our small courtyard while the roof is repaired or changed.

1. Braj Kumar Nehru (Bijju): cousin of Jawaharlal Nehru.
2. Shobha Nehru (Fory): wife of Braj Kumar Nehru.
3. Chandra Kumari: a cousin of Indira Gandhi; daughter of Ladli Prasad Zutshi (see Kinship Circle); married Krishna Handoo.
4. Krishna Handoo: husband of Chandra Kumari; retired as Managing Director, State Bank.
5. Jawaharlal Nehru was married on *Vasanta Panchami* day in 1916.

Give my love to Agatha and Krishna and Feroze and Kailas and all our other friends.

Ranjit sends you his love. He is busy with his translation work from Sanskrit – an old play written 1300 years ago dealing with Chanakya's [1] time. Extraordinarily interesting some of these plays are. I wish I knew Sanskrit and could read them in the original.

My love to you, my darling one, and all good wishes.

Your loving,<br>Papu

---

52.                                                     *City of Paris*,
                                                        22nd March, 1941

Darling Papu,

I cabled [2] to you from the last port of call. At the next port, I shall cable to Puphi in Bombay – she will probably inform you.

There is practically nothing that one is allowed to say in letters from sea.

I do hope you have not been anxious about me, because really we have been having the most astounding luck. A palmist told me long ago in India that all sorts of divine powers were protecting my lifeline!!

I have been keeping fairly well. Just before leaving London, I caught a cold, started the usual high temperature and was scared stiff that the old trouble had started again. I was staying with Bhandari at the time, and one day he even detected the fluid. But my resistance had improved so tremendously that within forty-eight hours it was absorbed, & completely disappeared.

This is the longest sea voyage I have ever been on and I must say I do not fancy it at all – specially under war conditions. It was a great relief to hear that we were going to call at a port. We did not stay long and were not allowed to land. But it was good to look at the brownness of the earth and the greenness of the trees after the eternal blue of the Atlantic. I was longing to go ashore and feel land with my naked toes. (How well I can understand the joy and relief felt by Columbus and his men when they sighted land!) However we had to be content with watching it from a distance and buying lots of fruit, which was being sold by men in canoes. I bought dozens of lovely green bananas and mangoes and oranges, and devoured them with the zeal of one who has

---

1. Chanakya: also called Kautilya or Vishnugupta: Hindu statesman and philosopher who lived in the fourth century B.C.
2. Cable not published.

not tasted food for many months. The food we get on board is most monotonous and inedible.

We crossed the Equator a few days ago. There was the usual 'Crossing the Line' ceremony. It is completely mad. One person dresses up as King Neptune & holds court on the ship. Whereupon all persons crossing the line for the first time were tried and sentenced to being ducked & white-washed and what not!

These last days it has been most frightfully hot. Blackout restrictions were very strict and after sunset it was quite impossible to sit in the lounge or anywhere inside, because [it was] so stuffy and close. One had to sit on deck, out in the pitch darkness.

I bought Lin Yu-tang's *Moment in Peking* in London but have not started reading it yet. Somehow I don't feel in the mood for reading. Have you heard of Zoshchenko?[1] He is one of the leading humorists of the Soviet Union. Translations of his short stories appear quite often in magazines like *Lilliput*. Now for the first time some of them have been collected in book form. They are really lovely – and very very funny.

By the way, I received three letters from you just before I left London. I do not know what arrangement you have with regard to interviews. I hope I shall be able to see you immediately or at least soon after my arrival in India. Chhoti Puphi will let me know.

We have a most peculiar mixture of people on this ship. Fortunately I already knew some of them in London, otherwise I would have been bored stiff the whole voyage.

Mamu was well when I left London. I suppose you know that Mami is expecting a baby.[2] I believe it is expected towards the end of March. They both want to return to India and hope to be able to do so by June or July. Mamu is quite fed up of living in England but he likes his work very much & is apparently doing very well in it. It is some sort of research in tropical plants.

All your friends in England sent you their best regards. I forwarded your instructions about your new book to Krishna. He had told me that somebody would bring the proofs to the station for me to bring to you. But nobody came. Krishna himself was out of town.

*Au revoir* darling and very much love.

Indu

---

1. Mikhail Zoshchenko: Russian writer and humorist.
2. *Mami* is maternal aunt and *mamu* is maternal uncle. The reference is to Kailas Nath Kaul and Sheila Kaul, the maternal uncle and aunt, respectively, of Indira Gandhi.

53.                        [Cable]                        Bombay,
                                              17th April, 1941

Jawaharlal Nehru,
Central Prison,
Lucknow

Arrived safely much love writing.

                              Indu

_____

54.                                     Anand Bhawan,
                                           Allahabad,
                                        1st May, 1941

Darling Papu,
I was hoping to be able to come and see you this Sunday. But the heat
is getting me down completely – and the journey to Dehra is long &
very tiring.

   Puphi is not taking Pupha's interview until later on next week so I am
sending Madan Bhai & Feroze to see you on Sunday. Madan Bhai wants
to talk to you about my future treatment and programme.

   On further consideration, I have not mentioned our talk to Puphi as
I think it is unnecessary to do so – at least at this stage. I am writing to
Madan Bhai & he will explain the position to you.

   Anna[1] and the children are leaving on the 3rd for Khali. Puphi is
staying on here for a few days to supervise some typing work. Nothing
has yet been settled about my own departure. I have started taking the
injections.

   With much love,

                              Indu

_____

55.                                     District Jail,
                                          Dehra Dun,
                                        3rd May, 1941

Darling Indu,
I am writing this note before seeing Madan. Presumably he is coming
tomorrow morning. There was some difficulty about the interview as it
came only a week after the last. Not realising the consequences, I wrote

---

   1. Anna Ornsholt: governess of the daughters of Vijaya Lakshmi Pandit.

a letter about the Urdu translation of *Glimpses* two days ago and this was sent off. The publication of this book was hung up because of some references to me. Having written a letter, I could not, in the ordinary course, have an interview within a fortnight. As a matter of fact I had written a letter after two and a half months. It is all rather vague and the rules as applied to me are not clear. Anyway it is well to remember the restrictions on letters and interviews. In a very special case, the Superintendent will probably give special permission. But as far as possible, I should like to avoid this as it might mean references to higher quarters. Probably, however, I shall continue to receive letters sent to me. There is some delay before these are formally delivered to me as they have to go for censoring to the District Magistrate, who is often in Mussoorie. I have been shown your letter of the 1st May[1] but it will not be formally delivered to me for two or three days more.

The Superintendent told me this morning that he had allowed the interview with Madan as he was coming as your medical adviser but he had not allowed it to Feroze as there was no special reason for this.

The weather is getting hotter and hotter – this is the worst time of the year and it will last for nearly two months. It will be a great trial for you to take long journeys during this weather and a risky business. I do not propose any letters for the present in order to keep interviews open. But do not take this journey to Dehra Dun and back without special reason.

Puphi, when she comes, will ask for an interview with Ranjit. That is due and she can have it when she chooses. I shall meet her incidentally as it were, as interviews have to take place in our yard.

You will decide as you think best in consultation with Madan Bhai and others [what you should now do]. I can hardly be of help to you from here. In drawing up your programme, it is best to proceed on lines which do not appear as odd to other people, especially those connected with us in various ways. Unfortunately all of us attract a great deal of public attention and our movements are chronicled in the press. This attention is a friendly and an affectionate one but it creates difficulties. Then there are those, like Ladli Chacha,[2] who have been good enough to help us in family matters for the last ten years or more, ever since Dadu died. All these people have to be treated in a friendly way and made to feel that they are not being ignored or not consulted about matters on which they are usually consulted.

Life is rather a complicated business, as no doubt you will realise as you grow older. To me, personally, there are few complications left and

1. Refers to letter No. 54.
2. Ladli Prasad Zutshi: uncle of Indira Gandhi.

I run a more or less straight course. But for me other lives, and notably yours, have inevitably great interest, to put it mildly. They impinge one upon the other. But even so, the burden of decision will rest with you. That would have been so if I was out of prison and with you. It is even more so when I am in prison and thus disabled from action or capacity to help. Age is sometimes just a passage of years with no other distinguishing feature; sometimes it is record of worthwhile experiences which may lead, it may be, occasionally to glimpses of wisdom, or an understanding of the extraordinary thing that is life and human relations on this planet. That wisdom in its fullness comes to very very few; even in part it does not come to many. It is something deeper than the facile formulae with which we often seek to confine it. And because it is deeper, it cannot be easily passed on to others who have not experienced it in their own lives and minds. And so again and again that experience has to be gone through and often the price we pay in such experience is great.

In politics, I am a little weary of those – and they are so many – who without taking the trouble to understand the intricacies of a complicated problem, seek to solve it out of hand. We are always announcing answers to questions which we have not even framed. If that is so in politics, it is even more in life itself, with its amazing diversity and complexity. As I grow older and experience upon experience piles up with me, I am appalled at my own smallness in this mighty scheme of things. Perhaps that is the effect of age. Youth is fortunately free from this disability.

I write all this because circumstances have put you on the threshold of life and at every turn you will have to face a question mark. By your answers to these questions your future will be moulded, and often those answers will not be entirely pleasant ones. Distress and suffering consume the world today. Nobody can avoid them. But integrity of mind and action can be ours, whatever happens. And if we are fortunate enough to possess this, then it does not much matter what else we lack.

This note or letter sounds perilously like sermonising – it is not meant so. It is only an attempt to express some odd thoughts that came into my mind as I was thinking of you. I talk too much and write too much – I grow garrulous with age. But the period when as a father it was my function to guide you in many ways has ended, because you have grown up and because of other things. And I wonder so often if during these past years I guided you aright or failed to do what I should have done. Anyway that period of life for you and for me is past history. The moving finger has written and moved on. And now you face another period and the burden of that is much more on you.

I have written above about Ladli Chacha. Of course I do not mean that he should be taken into every confidence. What I mean is that he should not be made to feel that he was being ignored.

As for telling Puphi or not – as you have decided for the present not to consult her on the subject, I shall do likewise, and await the development of events.

I want my old razor (Gillette type). There are two old ones in my bathroom in Anand Bhawan. Someone might bring them here – Puphi when she comes next.

Love,
Papu

56.

District Jail,
Dehra Dun,
4th May, 1941

Darling Indu,
I have had a long talk with Madan Bhai and he will no doubt tell you all about it. Though there is not much to tell. I have already told you that under the circumstances you should decide about your programme. I cannot be of much help anyway. Madan seems to think that Solan will be a suitable place for you for two months or so and after that, when the rains are well set, you will be fit enough to go elsewhere – to Allahabad or Kashmir or where you like. If you agree with this, certainly go to Solan. Madan Bhai will be there to advise you. You can decide later what to do afterwards. Even when the rains come the weather in Allahabad is very close and depressing and you will not improve under it. Perhaps it may be desirable and worthwhile then – sometime in July or so – to go to Kashmir for a couple of months. That will tune you up and you can return to Allahabad about the end of September, just when the autumn is beginning and the nights at least are cool.

On your way to Solan you can pay me a visit, also on your way down. My next interview is due on Sunday or any day afterwards. I shall take no other interview and shall not write any letters which might come in the way of an interview. But you can write to me.

These jail interviews, even when the authorities are lenient (and this is not likely to be repeated on the same scale), are very unsatisfactory, welcome as they are. I do not know how to unlock the doors of my mind and heart, which burst with things to say. Nor do you, I fancy, for you have found it even more difficult to do so even outside jail. And then in my long moments of silent thought I wonder often if words are so important after all. They help of course but only slightly and when the doors of understanding have been unlocked. Otherwise they are valueless – just hot air. Having used an abundance of words all my life, I grow more and more to distrust them. Something that is vital escapes them. I wonder sometimes if my love for you has been so wanting in something as to prevent those doors from opening. I seek to find the error, to purge the fault. Meanwhile we grow older and time passes and events happen – and I draw into my own shell.

In the quiet of Solan, or wherever you may be, you will also do a lot of thinking. Try to think out things for yourself and build your thoughts on an integral and integrated mind. There is nothing so important as integrity of thought which is not swept away by momentary gusts or rumour or hearsay. If we can keep that hard gem-like flame of mental integrity, our actions are coloured by it and we grow in the process. Else we remain petty, inconsequential and unimportant in any real analysis. We live in times of chaos or of approaching chaos. It may be years before any ordered living comes back to us. There is no chance of my coming out of prison for a long time, and I do not want to. I should like to develop more peace and strength of mind and more charity than I possess. Perhaps the Bodhisatva will help!

You might write to Birju Chacha that you will not be going to Kashmir just yet. Tell him that we have received the seeds, & saplings he has had sent to us and we are tending them carefully.

Love,
Papu

Some foreign papers are being returned. *Nation* has a review of my book. This might be taken out. Ask Upadhyaya to keep them separately. *Time* had one. I enclose another.

––––––––––––––– ––––––––

57.                                                District Jail,
                                                   Dehra Dun,
                                              15th May, 1941

Indu,
Why have I suddenly begun writing to you – and today of all days? This letter is not meant to be sent to you in the ordinary course and I do not know when you will see it. I do not know when you will come to interview me again. Yet the writing of this has suddenly become an imperative need, an urge I cannot resist, even if I would, and indeed I have no desire to do so. I hope you will see it some time.

Letters from prison, with all manner of evilly inclined folk and knaves and fools running their eyes through them and, often enough, blue-pencilling or blacking out passages. How can one write a real, intimate letter under these circumstances? For months I have hardly written a letter from here, except for one or two semi-business communications. I was annoyed at the Govt's attitude, irritated at parts of my letters – innocent enough I thought, they were – being blacked out. And so in sheer perversity I did not write just when Govt relaxed the rule for me and allowed me to write frequent letters. Probably I would still have written to you but you were out of reach and expected every moment to leave England for India.

And yet this business of censorship is no new thing, although jail and C.D. [Civil Disobedience] aggravate it tenfold. During the last twenty years, ever since the first C.D. movement or even earlier, I have always had the idea at the back of my mind that my letters might be read by censors and the like. Even during the slack periods, politically speaking, some kind of censorship always continued. Possibly all our letters were not censored, but some always were, and I could never write as freely and frankly as I wanted to. My political life and methods were such that there was little secrecy about them, though inevitably there were things I did not want to shout from the house-tops. But when it came to personal matters it was a different story. Not that there were any great secrets of mine which I wished to hide from the public gaze. But no one likes to undress his mind and soul in public. So, always, through all these long years, whenever I took pen in hand to write a letter, subconsciously I kept a check on myself, feeling that strangers would see that letter. I could write with a certain measure of clarity and even my restraint of language gave some evidence of the mind and thought behind. But that could only be a fleeting glimpse and sometimes an irritating one, for there was a suspicion of a veil hiding much.

Perhaps even before these iron bars of the censorship enveloped us and made me retire a little more into my shell, I had developed a measure of restraint in expression and behaviour. That too, I am inclined to think, was a way of self-protection against a fear I always had of being swept away by too much sentiment. You will be surprised to find me accusing myself of sentiment, for I show precious little of it and [am] much more of a hard-boiled egg, now at any rate. Yet, I fear, this hardness is only at the surface and underneath lies a sea of sentiment which has often frightened me. A lifetime of disciplined living and deliberate training of the mind and body to make them efficient instruments for the purpose I had in view, has thrown a hard shell over this turbulent mass and on the whole I feel fairly sure of myself. This has given me a certain degree of self-confidence and usually a crisis or difficulty makes me clearer-headed and calmer. Yet on occasions the shell bursts to my great discomfiture.

Apart from this fear of my own tendency to wallow in sentiment, there was another reason which induced me to fortify my shell – that mighty Maginot Line which could after all be so easily turned. I realised that any slackening on my part produced far-reaching reactions in others, and I was alarmed at the consequences. I could not live up to them and indeed I had no intention of doing so. Thus I caused needless pain to others and I blamed myself for this. And so again I retired into my shell and peeped out of it.

What is Papu driving at? you will say. Why all these patches of early autobiography? Well, I really do not know myself. My mind cooped up for months past is just bursting and if, by some miracle, I could transfer all those ideas and thoughts to paper suddenly, a fat volume might materialise! The ideas are not methodically arranged as they would have to be if I tried to write a book, and they just tumble over each other and the poor pen cannot possibly keep pace with them. But I am not writing a book and I do not just see myself writing a book for some considerable time. I toyed with this writing idea for weeks and months: I almost sat down to it, but I could not begin and it grows harder to do so as time goes by.

Why so? Because I cannot write superficially, unless I am writing a political or non-personal article, and even then it is frightfully difficult for a person who is an active politician. He may not say everything he wants to say, he may not discuss frankly his own colleagues or his opponents, for he has to think of a hundred consequences. Every word spoken or written has to be weighed, consciously or subconsciously. How cribbed and confined and imprisoned we are by these iron bars of the spirit!

If this is so about political matters, how much more difficult it is about personal matters. Can anyone ever be really frank about oneself, one's own emotions and mental struggles, one's urges and desires and those half-conscious imaginings which float, dreamlike, through the mind?

My *Autobiography* is, I think, about as frank and truthful a document, both politically and personally, as I could make it. Probably it compares favourably with others of its kind in this respect. I poured out myself in it at a time when I was going through much agony of soul. And yet, in spite of all this pouring out, all the restraints and inhibitions were there, and I suppressed much that filled my mind and heart. To that extent I was untruthful. Especially this was so in the last few chapters dealing with my personal life. It was impossible for me to lay bare my heart before anybody, much less before the world at large.

But these last six years since the *Autobiography* was written have had a powerful effect upon me. I have suffered greatly, experienced many hard knocks in my personal, as well as my political life, saw some of my ideals become airy nothings and some of my dearest personal relations fade away. I have survived all this, hardened, matured, call it what you will. I am now just one and fifty years old. Somehow my body keeps healthy and fit in spite of everything, in spite of the hardest use of it, in spite even of a growing tiredness with it. But I feel as if I was hundreds of years old in mind and the weight of these centuries lies heavily upon me. If this is the beginning of wisdom, then I am on the threshold of Saraswati's [1] haven. But I would barter this wisdom and experience, so dearly bought, for the lighthearted unwisdom of my younger days.

How can I write about these six years with any frankness and throw my naked soul before the public? And if I miss out everything that really mattered to me, what remains that is worthwhile? These six or seven years are bound up in my inner life with Kamala and you. Of course even before this period both of you played a major part in my personal and inner life. But one takes many things for granted in one's younger days; even our struggles have a passing quality. Apart from this, in the twenties I was totally abnormal. I had a flame-like quality, a fire within me which burned and consumed me and drove me relentlessly forward; it made me almost oblivious of all other matters, even of intimate personal relations. I was in fact wholly unfit as a close companion of anyone except in that one sphere of thought and action which had enslaved me. Gradually I woke up to other matters. I realised then, and I realise now even more, what an impossible person I must have been to get on with. My very good qualities, which made me an efficient instrument for political action, became defects in the domestic field. Yet I found, to my infinite joy, that those I cared for above all else had gladly and willingly tolerated me and put up with my vagaries. As my awakening proceeded, I yearned above all else for those closer human contacts of the spirit with those I loved with all my heart. Unfortunately long and trying periods of jail came, year after year, and normal life and contacts were denied. It was in those days of the early thirties that I wrote those hundreds of letters to you which came out subsequently as *Glimpses*. That was one attempt of mine somehow to quench a little the insatiable thirst that consumed me.

Dadu was dead. He had meant a great deal to me: I was infinitely proud of him and of the traditions of our family which he had set up – the traditions of great ability, great courage, great perseverance, great sacrifice, all directed to the service of India. That tradition it was my ambition to keep alive in so far as I could.

But father was dead. Dol Amma [2] was there, frail, ailing, enveloping me with the overwhelming love of a mother for her son. I was very fond

1. The goddess of learning.
2. Swarup Rani Nehru (Dol Amma): mother of Jawaharlal Nehru.

of her but she could take no part in the life I was living. I was anxious
to give her peace and comfort during her few remaining years. There
were my sisters, both of whom were so much younger than me that my
relation to them was partly paternal and partly brotherly. One of them
had married and was, what is called, settled in life. She had lived since
her marriage chiefly in Calcutta, Rajkot and other places and had lately
taken a house with her family in Allahabad. Although I was very fond
of her, she had largely gone out of my life and lived her own life. The
younger sister was with us. The difference in our ages was so great that
I had looked upon her more as a child than as a sister. Soon after she
married and went away. My family life revolved and centred round two
persons – Mummie and you. The others, however much I liked them,
lived their own lives apart from ours, though there were of course
contacts.

Ever since father's death I felt the burden of a new responsibility: I
was the head of the family and as such must look after, in a sense, my
sisters and make them feel that nothing had changed in their old home.

But I cannot go on and on with this past history – certainly not now
when the lights are going out. I had not intended to write all this but it
is strange how the pen becomes almost an independent entity when one
writes and sometimes does just what it likes.

*May 16*

Last night, when I sat down to write, I was trying to explain why the
urge to write to you suddenly took possession of me. And instead of
doing this in a straight fashion, I wandered into the past and began to
lose myself in its mazes. It is an unfortunate way I have with you – as
if I was talking casually and inconsequentially. I go on and on and do
not give you much time to put in a word.

What I was driving at was the extraordinary difficulty of my writing
about these past six years in a book. I dared not do it and expose all my
inmost feelings and torments to others. Not that there was any great
secrecy about them, but some things are private and sacred because of
that, especially when others are concerned. I am not a secretive person
but there are limits even for me. There is much that I could tell you for
you have the right to know. But even to you I could not say everything.
It would hurt me and it might hurt you.

So a feeling of suppression grew upon me. In jail this is always so
and I try to find a way of escape in hard work, a regular routine, spinning,
reading etc. In the past writing, doing creative work, has helped me
tremendously. This avenue seemed to be closed this time. I looked
forward to your coming back: you filled my mind and this thought of

you, tinged with anxiety about your health and journey, kept me more or less calm in spite of occasional worry.

You arrived – you came to see me. That was an event for me. It was an event for many others. It was extraordinary how odd people were interested in this. Everyone in jail was somewhat excited about it. English police officials and others who saw me on business spoke about it with some enthusiasm. I felt how both you and I represent something more than our individual selves. We become symbols in the minds of countless people.

You arrived and I was happy. But soon a cloud fell on my happiness for I realised that you were not as well as I had hoped and that there were troubles ahead of you. My training held, however, and immediately I grappled with the new problem and gave you advice as to what you might do. You accepted it for the moment and, though I had a dull feeling inside me about your health, I felt that we were going to face the situation in the most effective manner. To take the best possible action when a difficulty confronts one itself brings relief to the mind. It is always inaction and doubt and uncertainty that crush one.

You went away. Then Madan came and I learnt that on further consideration you had decided to follow a different course. I was sorry that partly at least you had not followed my advice but I tried to convince myself that the other course might be equally suitable. Anyway Madan told me he had made arrangements at Solan and everything was practically fixed up. So nothing more seemed to be necessary. Still I did not quite like this development; it preyed upon my mind. Life is a complicated business and is always playing us tricks. I have, in much hardship and pain, learned to understand her a little, very little, and to proceed warily where it is concerned. Each act has a hundred consequences and those who would step with assurance have to keep all these in view. No one can possibly expect you to think of all these consequences and possibilities. You have not the experience. Even Madan, a dear friend and valuable counsellor though he is, is very inexperienced in the byways of life, or even on its highways. I am quite sure that if I had the chance and the time to explain to you and Madan why I advised as I did, you would have agreed with me unhesitatingly from your own point of view, not mine. Indeed I gave the advice from your point of view.

In spite of this disappointment I accepted the new arrangements. When I heard later, however, that the Solan visit had fallen through and that no arrangement was visible, then suddenly I was completely upset. Very casually enquiries were being made in Mussoorie for hours and even there it was not easy to get ... [information]. What was this casualness and inefficiency, I thought, when every day counted and the heat was at its worst? This was not the way to do things and if the beginning was casual what about developments later? It seemed to me clear that Madan by himself would find great difficulty in fixing things up. I grew almost ill with anxiety and could do nothing but pace up and down like a caged animal, fretting at my inability to help you. It was absurd my not being able to help my own daughter when she required this help most. A word or a whisper from me and thousands all over the country would gladly do everything in their power for you. Yet things had taken such a shape that I could do little and had left everything to Madan. The whole thing was fantastic, absurd in its folly. Fancy everything being hung up because you had nowhere to go to!

So I raged for two days and life became a terrible burden. I could do no work, could not even spin which soothes me. I could sleep with difficulty and would suddenly sit up in the middle of the night unable to control or direct the ideas that battered my mind. Yesterday morning I got up about four a.m. and decided to write to Madan. I sent him this letter. This relieved me somewhat, for at any rate I had taken some step.

But still my mind was ill at ease. I longed to meet you and talk to you. The desire to do so almost overwhelmed me. Yet I could not even write for an official jail letter was no good.

In the evening it struck me suddenly that I could write to you fully and frankly, even though my letter might not be sent to you. Later perhaps you might see it. This was just a subterfuge, a trick, and yet, would you believe it? My mind calmed down immediately. I grasped at this way out. Just then Ranjit & I went out for our short stroll in the evening. It had been cloudy & stormy during the day but the evening had cleared up and the outline of the hills stood out sharp and clear. It struck me how equally rapidly the stormy weather of my mind had subsided because of this new idea and I had felt calmer and more at peace.

We came back to our barrack and I was eager to begin to write to you. Ranjit spoke to me. I could hardly follow his words for my mind was with you. I must have behaved oddly. There were interruptions. At last I sat down to write to you. And this was the beginning last night. . . .
[incomplete]

58.                            St Clair Cottage,
Mussoorie,
22nd May, [1941]

Darling Papu,
We have just arrived. Pushkarnathbhai[1] was waiting for us at King's
Craig. We reached St Clair Cottage to find the curtains up & vases of
flowers and everything – just as if people had been living in it for weeks.

The cottage is tiny: two very small bedrooms with lilliputian bathrooms, one dining room & one drawing room. I am thinking of acquiring
the drawing room as a bedroom for myself – the dining room can serve
for sitting room as well. That will leave the two bedrooms for Madanbhai
& Upadhyaya. When anyone else comes up, Madanbhai can share with
Upadhyaya. We shall be short of bathrooms but I expect we shall manage
all right.

Here is a plan of St Clair Cottage – St Clair itself is occupied by
some Nawab or the other. It is some distance away & I don't think we
shall run across one another.

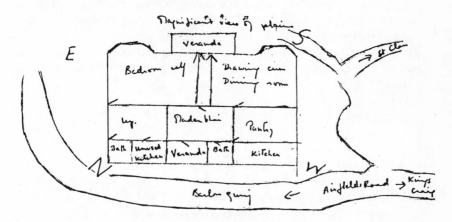

I am afraid this is all out of perspective but it will give some idea. All
the rooms have lots of windows and are, I am told, sunny and airy. The
view is lovely. And of course it is delightfully cool.

Darling – please don't worry. Everything will be all right. I was quite
shocked to see how you had changed since I saw you last. You mustn't
let these things get you down. I manage to keep the right side up in
spite of everything.

In some of your letters you have talked of joy and fulfilment. I have

---

1. Pushkar Nath Tankha: political and social activist who was a friend of the Nehrus.

found mine. I have a serene happiness surging up from within, that no one and nothing can mar or take away from me. All troubles – illness and discomfort and disputes – just seem to sail away on the surface without really touching me. Most people spend their lives waiting for happiness but the cup always seems to be just a little beyond their reach and they have not the courage to stretch their arms to grasp it. I took it in my two hands and drank deep into it – and it entered into every nerve and tissue of my mind and body, and bathed me in its rich warm calmness. I have this now and forever. Happiness is undefinable – how can my feeble attempts at description suffice when the great writers of the world have not succeeded? But I hope I have been able to convey at least one small part of what I feel.

I am glad to be alone. I was thinking of asking some friends to come up when Madanbhai goes away but I think I would rather be quite alone. I get on remarkably well with myself, which is a good thing. I forgot to bring the gramophone – or rather left it behind for lack of records. But I think I shall send for it & start buying a few good records one by one. I am starving for good music, especially Beethoven. It is a pity you have not made friends with him. He is the very essence of poetry, and he fits in to every mood – but I am always attempting the impossible; first I try to define Happiness and now, Beethoven's music!

I love you a lot and I am worried about you just as much as you are about me. So keep your sunny side up & look a lot better when I see you next.

Much love,

Indu

P.S.
The nearest phone is at King's Craig – the car terminus. I shall make arrangements for the receiving & sending of messages from there through Ram Saran's agent.

---

59.
District Jail,<br>Dehra Dun,<br>26th May, 1941

Darling Indu,
I am very glad you are (more or less) comfortably established in your little cottage. This does appear to be rather small but even that might be an advantage. One can make a small place cosier. It is pretty dismal to live by oneself in a large place.

It is a comfort to know that you are not far from me and that news of you can reach me quickly. But I am sure that the first thing you should attend to is your rest and treatment. All this long journeying, ever since you left Switzerland many months ago, must have been exhausting and one can take no risks with your health. So rest a lot even if this is a trifle boring. Indeed for the next month or so I would not recommend even an interview with me here. I would love to see you of course as often as possible, but this business of running up and down between Mussoorie and Dehra Dun must interfere with rest and treatment. So till the end of June at least, stick to Mussoorie. We shall see afterwards about future interviews. As for your treatment you should carry on what has been recommended to you and there is Madan Bhai always there to consult. It is not necessary to refer matters to me. Madan Bhai and you can always decide any matter that arises.

I am very fond of Beethoven, but my life has been spent far from the cultivation of the graces and pleasures which sometimes accompany it. I suppose I must not complain, for I have got a great deal out of it in my own way. Happiness is rather a fleeting thing, a sense of fulfilment is perhaps more abiding. The world changes and I grow old fashioned already. All of us claim certain rights – individual, national, etc – and quite rightly so. But in the old days I was taught that rights carried obligations and duties with them, and I have got rather entangled in this sense of obligation and duty. Even so, life has been very generous to me, and even the knocks and kicks it has given me have had their lessons and have perhaps benefited me.

But I was writing about music. Get the gramophone and records by all means. It struck me that a radio might be useful. So with the help of some friends I have tried to make arrangements for a radio to be sent to you. I hope it will get there and function properly.

About money you will remember to draw as much as you require from Allahabad. You can also, if need arises, get it from Bachhraj in Bombay (from my account, not yours).

Within a fortnight, I think, or possibly three weeks, the monsoon will reach the little hill on which is perched Mussoorie. There is a tremendous deal of rain during the first month especially. So be prepared for it.

That reminds me, I had asked Upadhyaya to bring my raincoat. He did not do so. Do not worry about it now.

Did Upadhyaya order the books I wanted? I forget to ask him. I sent the list with Puphi. They were chiefly Plato's and the Greek plays translated by Gilbert Murray.

Another book I have been wanting for a long time (and asking Upadhyaya for it) has been *Kavita Kaumudi* Part I. We had it in the library but it has disappeared. So a new copy can be obtained. It is published and sold in Allahabad.

Keep cheerful and well and grow strong.

All my love,

Your loving,
Papu

---

60.                                            St Clair Cottage,
Mussoorie,
28th May, 1941

Darling Papu,

Your letter[1] came just as I had written the above address.

Madanbhai is away and Upadhyaya has gone to the bazaar, so I am all on my own. I do not go out at all. In fact I lie down most of the time. I am feeling rather tired & it is very hot – Dehra Dun must be roasting. My right arm is rather painful because of the injections – which, by the way, are now over.

Why did you bother about a radio? It is sweet of you. But we are spending so much already & these little things add up tremendously. Anyway the radio has not yet arrived.

I am sorry you did not get the things you asked for. I personally was quite unaware that you had asked for them. Upadhyaya says he was not told either. I am writing to Allahabad. Sunder[2] probably knows where the raincoat is and can easily send it by post. About the books also, I knew nothing, otherwise it would have been very easy for me to bring them. I nearly brought one or two of the Greek ones for myself. I am sure some arrangement can be made for them to be sent even if Puphi is out of town.

Puphi's programme seems to be vague. She was to have gone to Bombay on the 27th. But I see in the Hindi *Hindustan* that she had a slight temperature & has decided not to go, but is proceeding to Khali in a day or so. I cannot find this news in the *Hindustan Times* or the *Herald*, so I do not know how far it is true.

I have brought a most odd collection of books with me. Among them: Africa Danes' *Living Philosophies, Uncle Tom's Children*, Ernst Toller's *Letters from Prison* & *I was a German*, Carl Crow's *I speak for the Chinese*, Ralph Fose's *This was their Youth*. And two or three others.

The most attractive things in the whole house are a couple of

---

1. Refers to letter No. 59.
2. Sunder: domestic servant at Anand Bhawan.

postcard-size reproductions of two paintings of Franz Marc.[1] Have you seen any of his work, I wonder? The *Red Horses*, which is in Chhoti Puphi's sitting room, is one of his. His pictures are rather like Roy Campbell's[2] poetry, splashed with bright colours, brimming over with vitality and strength. So alive. And very decorative.

I enclose a picture in words – Mrs Reece Laughs by Armstrong. It doesn't pretend to be great poetry or a thing of beauty. But as a picture, isn't it perfect? It always amuses me when I am not feeling too bright. And doesn't it remind you of Ammaji Thussu[3] and so many other similar women! I had a landlady like that once – a Dutchwoman.

I do hope I shall be able to come and see you soon – I can't say when.

Nora[4] is up in Mussoorie. I haven't met her or anyone else, for I have told Upadhyaya not to encourage any visitors. I find talking more tiring than anything else. Upadhyaya tells me that the town is frightfully crowded – especially with overdressed women.

Lots and lots of love.

Your
Indu

Mrs Reece Laughs

Laughter, with us, is no great undertaking,
A sudden wave that breaks and dies in breaking.
Laughter, with Mrs Reece, is much less simple:
It germinates, it spreads, dimple by dimple,
From small beginnings, things of easy girth,
To formidable redundancies of mirth.
Clusters of subterranean chuckles rise
And presently the circles of her eyes
Close into slits, and all the woman heaves
As a great elm with all its mound of leaves
Wallows before the storm. From hidden sources
A mustering of blind volcanic forces
Takes her and shakes her till she sobs and gapes.
Then all that load of bottled mirth escapes
In one wild crow, a lifting of huge hands
And creaking stays, and visage that expands
In scarlet ridge and furrow. Thence collapse,

1. Franz Marc (1880–1916): German painter; known especially for his paintings of animals.
2. Roy Campbell: British poet.
3. One of the senior ladies of the Thussu family. Swarup Rani Nehru, Indira's grandmother, came from this family.
4. Purnima Banerji (Nora): a friend of the Nehrus; active in the national movement.

A hanging head, a feeble hand that flaps
An apron-end to stir an air and waft
A steaming face. And Mrs Reece has laughed.

Martin Armstrong

61.                                                           [Mussoorie],
2nd June, 1941

Darling,

I am in the throes of remorse and regret – as usual, when it is too late to remedy what has or, as in this case, has not been done. I am writing this because I believe one should always admit one's mistakes even though it be too late to remedy them.

How simple, practical and obvious was your advice! It was only my blind prejudice which prevented me from following it. Truly it is feeble-minded to let oneself be so influenced by prejudice. What I am bitterly regretting now is not the consequence to myself. I am amazed at my selfishness. I should have lumped my feelings and thought a little of your feelings. I seem to hurt you on purpose. I do not know what will be the result of this Calcutta visit.[1] To you it has already brought endless worry. Worry that I could so easily have prevented. Is it any use saying forgive me?

I can only hope and pray that this worry will soon be at an end. I can only hope and pray that this will be a lesson for me to be less stubborn. For this episode only proves how much I need you – how utterly lost I am without you. I have been so arrogant and stupid. I tried to sail out on my own before I knew the rudiments of managing a boat. I deserve to sink. And yet that would cause you so much pain.

'"Take what you want – Take it, and pay for it" said God' – so runs an old Spanish proverb. But why, oh why, must others pay too?

In some of your letters you say that you do not wish to impose yourself or your advice. Perhaps it is my own attitude that has made you feel this way. For that I am sincerely sorry. Far from being an imposition, your advice is the strongest prop on which I can lean – for my own legs are pretty shaky. And I can only explain my former attitude in one way – that I did not realise how necessary this prop was to me until it was proved to me that my legs would give way without it.

And so the erring child asks for forgiveness, and asks too that you believe her when she says that she loves you ... *Tous les jours je t'aime*

---

1. The proposed Calcutta visit was for a medical consultation.

*davantage, aujourd'hui plus qu'hier et bien moins que demain.*[1] For each day I discover something in you which moves me profoundly and makes you more precious and infinitely dearer. I seem to be just beginning to have a glimpse at the beauty and the richness in you. In the past you were rather an [un]approachable being, always so immersed in work and, for all your love of fun, I was rather scared of you – you seemed so high up. One feels so inferior when you are about and I suppose that unconsciously one resents it.

  With very much love,

                              Indu

———————————

62.                                           District Jail,
                                              Dehra Dun,
                                              4th June, 1941

Darling,

I hope your journey was not too bad and that you reached Calcutta fit and well. But Calcutta itself must be hot and close. Perhaps a week or so will not matter and then you can rest and recuperate in Mussoorie. My thoughts will be with you and I hope you or Madan will send me a brief letter to say how you are getting on and when you expect to be back. Now that you have gone to Calcutta, it is as well to take full advantage of your visit and have yourself thoroughly overhauled by the doctors and take full directions about the future.

  If your previous X-rays are required I think it might be better for Upadhyaya to run up himself to Allahabad and get them. This will be preferable to someone else bringing them from Allahabad. The cost will be the same. Ask Dr Roy[2] if he wants them.

  Give my love to Dr Roy and tell him that though fortunately I do not stand in need of doctors, it is a comfort to know that such wise and clever doctors as he is exist!

  I have got plenty of books with me to carry on for weeks and weeks, and besides I am just flirting with the idea to begin writing! But still the old failing asserts itself and the desire to see new and worthwhile books. So I am giving on a separate sheet a list of books which should be handed over to Upadhyaya. He might go round the bookshops in Calcutta, beginning with the Book Company, to find out if any of these are available. I doubt if you can get them there, as they are mostly new

1. . . . With every passing day I love you more & more, today more than yesterday and much less than tomorrow.

2. Dr Bidhan Chandra Roy: physician and Congress leader, later Chief Minister of Bengal.

American publications. Still, he can try. Some of the books have probably been published in England also. These books could not be obtained in Bombay.

All my love to you, my dear, and may you grow strong and healthy.

Remember to get a good light mackintosh for yourself in Calcutta. Ask Dr Roy for the address of the Indian firm. If you cannot get a good ready-made one, get some strong Assam silk (preferably double-thread) and have a mac made out of this.

Your loving,<br>Papu

63.                                                                District Jail,
                                                                   Dehra Dun,
                                                                   9th June, 1941

Darling Indu,

I have just received a note from Madan to say that you are under some treatment and that Dr Roy has not come back from Shillong yet. I hope he will come back soon. Meanwhile it is as well that his associates and assistants should prepare the ground for him so that he might have all the data.

Madan says that you are not likely to return before the 21st as Bidhan will want to keep you under observation for some days. A few days this way or that do not matter, though Calcutta is hardly a desirable place to stay in at this time of the year. But now that you have gone all the way to Calcutta you might as well do the job thoroughly. Dr Roy's advice must have first place. I have great faith not only in his ability as a doctor but also his sound commonsense and thoroughness. He and Jivraj Mehta are the two persons I think of whenever I have to worry about medical matters. They are stolid and careful and can be relied upon. So, while I am sorry that your programme was messed up a bit and you had to rush down from here, I am glad that Bidhan Roy is looking after you and I hope you will follow his advice and directions.

Fortunately the monsoon has started early and this must have lowered the temperature of Calcutta. It is pleasant here and there is some rain almost daily. In Mussoorie, I am told, it has been dismal owing to too much rain.

I have received my raincoat from Allahabad – also some books! Murray's translation of the Greek plays. Please remember to get a raincoat for yourself in Calcutta. All you have to do is to choose some stuff, preferably thick Assam silk, well-woven, and leave your measurements. It can then follow you, if it is not ready by the time you leave.

Mridula has just wired to say that her visit to Lucknow has been postponed to 24th. So she will come here before or after that date.

All my love,

Your loving,
Papu

---

64.                                     District Jail,
Dehra Dun,
12th June, 1941

Darling Indu,

I wonder when you will come back this way. I suppose you will stay on in Calcutta for another week at least as Dr Roy wants to keep you under observation. On your way up to Mussoorie you will of course come to see me. I am taking no other interviews, except for Mridula's and that is likely to be about the 26th.

Here it rains every day, though not too much so far. Considerately it clears up for a while in the mornings and evenings to allow us to walk up and down a little. The rain soon runs off or is absorbed by the soil which is stony. I like the rain unless there is too much of it. I suppose by mid-July I shall begin to get tired of it.

Just outside our barrack wall there is a little channel for canal water to pass through to the field. Right through the summer this channel was used once or twice a fortnight and the water pouring down it, and gurgling as it went, made a merry noise. Especially at night, it was pleasant to hear this sound of running water. Now the rains fill this channel and we have this sound more frequently, though often it cannot be heard on account of the beating rain. Yet it is a pleasant and soothing noise when it comes through.

> A noise like of a hidden brook
> In the leafy month of June,
> That to the sleeping woods all night
> Singeth a quiet tune . . .

I suppose in prison one's ears grow sharper and many other senses, which lie dormant during an active life outside, waken up and so open out a new world of sensation, just as a blind man becomes far more sensitive in other ways. Birds and insects and of course flowers become real companions whose acquaintance we renew from day to day. A creeper is a fascinating thing. Have you ever watched its sensitive feelers – how full of life they are! – creeping on and on and holding on to twig or string or wall? In Sanskrit poetry women are always likened to creepers! Bengali names of girls are full of Lata's. [1]

Good friends in Dehra Dun have been sending us fruit – luscious, delicious fruit grown here on the foothills or from other places. Grapes, locally grown, plums, pineapples (not grown here!), *langras* and *dasehris* [2] just beginning and fine apples. Yesterday we had a pleasant surprise when a basket of lovely cherries all the way from Kashmir came our way. They were not the choicest variety as these are too thin-skinned and delicate to travel. Still they were very good and very welcome and they made me think of Kashmir, where, just a year ago, I used to eat them in large quantities. So you see we have compensations in jail!

I am beginning to think again of doing some writing work. For the moment I am just playing about with the idea, revolving it in my mind, sometimes pushing it away, and then allowing it to come nearer. I know that once I give in to it, it will obsess me and my pen will become a tyrant ordering me about and interfering with my programme and other activities.

American reviews of my book have had curious reactions on me. Pleasant of course. It is so delightful to be praised and I swell up with satisfaction. And yet all this talk about style and lucidity rather frightens me. I wrote previously without thinking of style. I had to say something and I said it as simply and effectively as possible. Now I cannot forget that I have to keep up to a certain style and standard and this continuing reminder is a nuisance.

What is this much-praised style of mine, I begin to think? A certain simplicity and a certain lucidity in short sentences, partly due to clear thinking and having something to say. But partly also, I think, to a certain rhythm and a love of the sound of words. I hate an ill-balanced sentence. It jars. Why this rhythm? I do not know. It is not just an external thing, an ear for it or an eye to balance it. It has to do ultimately with a mental rhythm, or perhaps something even deeper than that. During these past twenty years or so, while you have been growing up, slowly this sense of rhythm in life has grown within me as ideas and action fitted in, or at least approached each other. It is a soothing and comforting experience and it helps greatly in the tug-of-war of life. The shouting and cursing become unimportant and rather silly, and much of the vulgarity that surrounds us lessens in significance and effect.

It is curious how the manner of writing (even more than the manner of speaking) betrays a person. The style is the man, they say. In old China they judged people for high appointment from the style of an

1. *Lata* in Sanskrit means a 'creeper'.
2. Refers to special varieties of mangoes.

essay. Perhaps that is going too far, but there is a lot in it. When outside prison I get a large number of letters from strangers and I have developed a habit of drawing a mental picture of the writer from the few sentences he may have written. Sometimes just one sentence, a few words, give me an ultimate glimpse and I feel drawn to the person.

How my letters taper down to absurd topics! But, as I said, when I take pen in hand, it is the tyrant pen that is master and it goes its self-appointed way. And yet what I have written is not so absurd after all. More and more I have come to think that what is important in a person is not what he says or proclaims but what he is and does. There is something after all about these ancient civilisations, like India and China: thousands of years of a cultural continuity which has sunk deep into the racial consciousness. Even the poverty-stricken peasant in China and India has some impress of that on his face and in his manner.

I should like you to ask Dr Roy about breathing exercises. Can you do them regularly? Personally I am a great believer in them, not only for bodily health but to some extent for mental health also. These exercises bring rhythm (I am at it again!) to the breathing and through it to the whole bodily system. They create the background and environment for composure and mental calm. Look at a person in a temper or one who is agitated. He breathes heavily and shortly. It is a little difficult to conceive of a person who breathes deeply and regularly becoming easily agitated! So I would like you to try these exercises and hold on to them.

I must desist now and stand up to my pen. So my love to you.

Your loving

Papu

I wonder if you can borrow or buy any books by Admiral Mahan[1] who wrote long ago about sea power. He is an American whose books became classics. There are a number of books by him:

> *The Question of Sea Power*
> *The Problem of Asia*
> *American Interest in International Problems*, etc, etc

I should particularly like to have *The Problem of Asia*. Possibly some of these books can be obtained from a library in Calcutta. If so you can bring one or two and I shall return them later. Please ask Dr Roy if he can help.

---

1. Alfred Thayer Mahan (1840–1914): American naval historian and military theoretician.

65.
Indira Nehru,
c/o Dr B. C. Roy,
36, Wellington Street,
Calcutta,
16th June, 1941

Darling Papu,
I have five letters from you – three from Dehra Dun, [1] quite recent and normal, and two others which decided to do some travelling on their own. They were written in October, [2] and have since been gallivanting all over Europe – from Allahabad to Leysin, to Bex, to Lisbon and thence London. And from there admonished by dear old Agatha, and packed off home to Allahabad again. Nor did they rest until they had paid a brief visit to Mussoorie and then came to Calcutta. But at last they have reached the end of their wanderings. I have a letter from Agatha, too – dated April 1st – but she says nothing about herself, or London, or anything. Have you any English mail? Krishna ought to have written about the book.

Talking of Krishna, just before I left London, I had a letter from you asking me to keep my account with Lloyds open, so that Krishna could deposit the royalties, etc, that came from the sale of *The Unity of India*, into my account as you had already closed your own. I wrote to Krishna to inform him of this. He was out of town, so I also informed Bee Batlivala, [3] who seems to be second-in-command at the office. I have quite a lot of money at the bank there – it was not possible to bring it over with me, but I was told that there would not be any difficulty in sending for it after my arrival in India. So, if you think it is all right, I shall leave about £20 – just enough to keep the account open – & send for the rest.

Bidhan is still away – I think he is arriving tomorrow evening. He has been with a patient of his, who is very very ill, so it was not possible for him to come away earlier. Meanwhile I am feeling much much better. I shall ask Bidhan about the breathing exercises, though I do not think it is necessary. I can do them. Do you know – when I left Leysin, Rollier said that it was very rarely he had seen anyone breathe as 'perfectly' as I did! These last months I have let that slip, I am afraid, but I have no doubt it will soon come back with a little practice. It did not seem worthwhile to breathe in the fog of London, or the dust of Allahabad – one must have fresh clean air.

1. Refers to letters Nos 62, 63 and 64.
2. Refers to letters Nos 41 and 42.
3. Mrs Mansell née Bee Batlivala: contemporary of Indira Gandhi; she practised law in London for some time.

Upadhyaya has gone to Allahabad. There has been a new arrival in his family. I do not know whether it's a boy or a girl, but guess it must be the latter because of the lack of enthusiasm. Anyway, he was keen to go home for a while and as he was doing absolutely nothing here, I thought he might as well go. He will meet us at Lucknow on our way back to Mussoorie.

I have given him the list of books that you sent me. None of the new American publications are available here. The translation of the Upanishads has been ordered. I hope Upadhyaya will find the other books you asked for, in the library. If you want anything else from Allahabad, please let me know – or, if you can, write direct to Upadhyaya.

I shall ask Bidhan about Admiral Mahan's books.

The monsoon has started in right earnest. Outside, trees and leaves are bright in a varnish of rain. Big, beautifully-shaped drops, round and perfect as pearls, balance themselves on the tips of petals of flowers and blades of grass. It's rather lovely – and, what is far more important in this country, delightfully cool. One needs a blanket at night, and sometimes a light shawl is not *de trop*[1] in the day time. But there can be too much of good things. The continuous tip-tip-tip of the rain can be very irritating. Here, in Calcutta, it doesn't rain, it pours and how it pours. For five days it hasn't stopped for a minute. My *chappals*[2] have got mildewed and disgusting. And that awful clammy dampness!

Which reminds me: some time before the war began, I wrote to Louise Morin saying that 'I felt in my bones' that such & such a thing would happen. Madame was up in arms at once, as she usually is at anything 'English'. She wrote back: 'How curious and typically English that expression is! I suppose the English climate is so damp that everything enters into the bones & the system!'

I have been given a horrid bitter tonic. It contains all sorts of essentials – iron phosphates, calcium phosphates & what nots. Who was it that said, 'The drive to take medicine is perhaps the greatest feature which distinguishes man from animals'? And can it possibly be true? It must be, or else the doctors would surely make some effort to make these nasty concoctions more appetising. And then there are countless true stories like that of the Negro woman, who, when asked how she felt, said, 'I'se poorly, thank Gawd. And how's you?' This welcome of illness is no doubt due to the fact that the poor folks had no rest & no holidays during their dreary existence.

And talking of Negroes, here is a delightful story about praying. A

1. Too much.
2. Leather thongs, exclusively used in India.

little Negro boy was competing in a race. He kept dropping behind and his chances seemed slim; then suddenly his lips began to move with great regularity, his legs picked up speed, and he won the race. Asked later what he was whispering to himself, he said he was talking to the Lord, saying over and over: 'Lawd, you pick 'em up, and I'll put 'em down. You pick 'em up, and I'll put 'em down.' Isn't it sweet?

Darling, I've been spending a frightful amount of money here – doctors, medicines and so on. Just before coming I had sent for some from my own account with Bachhraj but it has proved to be quite insufficient. Madan Bhai has sent for some of his own, saying that I could pay him later. But perhaps it is better to square accounts here. Madan Bhai thinks we will need about Rs. 1100. It sounds prodigious, I know. I am quite dazed myself at the cost of things. I think I had better send for this amount from my own account. What do you advise? I sent for a statement of accounts some time ago but I am afraid I did not understand at all what they wrote back. However, I am sure I must have enough for all that is needed now. I shall await your reply before doing anything, just in case you are writing yourself about it, I think it is better to send for a couple of hundred extra – for later on – Mussoorie and so forth.

Much love,

Indu

---

66.                                                District Jail,
                                                   Dehra Dun,
                                              29th June, 1941

Darling Indu,
It was a joy to see you [the] day before yesterday after three and a half weeks. The interview ended all too soon. I want to make up for all your long absences from me. There is so much I want to ask you, to tell you, to discuss with you. Not argument and debate – the less we have of that the better. I have enough of it in my life outside and I am weary of it. But just a calm consideration of all the odd little & big things that surround us and make life so rich and yet sometimes so distressing. Today in the world it is distressing enough. Fate in many ways has been kind to us. Yet in some ways it has been most unkind, and its greatest unkindness to me has been the enforced separation it has brought repeatedly between you and me. All these long years in prison with only an occasional interview thrown in, and then your years in Europe. Now again I have to wait for each coming interview. I am looking forward to your next visit already. Suit yourself about the date. Probably round

about the 9th July, as you suggested, would be suitable. Remember to avoid Sundays for interviews. They are busy days in jail. I have no news of Mridula.

Some little time after you left us [the] day before yesterday we sat in our little yard as the evening glided into the night. I searched the skies (it was rather misty) for the new moon and discovered it bashfully peeping through a veil of mist. It was not very new as it must have been three days old; but it was lovely enough and so arch! You know of course that your pet name, Indu, means the moon – I told you this when you were almost a baby. I have always been fascinated by the new moon. Lately it has become somehow connected with my imprisonment, for I was arrested on the first day of the moon. And so whenever I see the new moon it means another month gone by, another month begun. Possibly not exactly as the calendar goes, but it is good enough for me, and it is far pleasanter to judge the flight of time by the waxing and waning of the moon.

I am writing today to Dr Zakir Husain [1] of the Jamia Millia of Delhi to send you some elementary books in Urdu. I am also asking him to send some books to me. The account for all this will be sent to you.

Apart from Urdu and Hindi, it might be worthwhile for you to start on a voyage of discovery of India. For many years now I have been travelling in these oceans of time and space. I have seen a great deal of the physical aspect of this country of ours and met thousands, and indeed millions, of its varied people. It is a fascinating journey, not so much in just sightseeing but in its mental aspect, when the past and present get strangely mixed together and the future flits about like an insubstantial shadow, or some image seen in a dream. The real journey is of course of the mind; without that there is little significance in wandering about physically. It is because the mind is full of pictures and ideas and aspects of India that even the bare stones – and so much more our mountains and great rivers, and old monuments and ruins, and snatches of old song and ballad, and the way people look and smile, and the queer and significant phrases and metaphors they use – whisper of the past and the present and of the unending thread that unites them and leads us all on to the future. When I have the chance – and alas! it is not too often – I like to leave my mind fallow and receive all these impressions. So I try to understand and discover India, and some glimpses of her come to me, tantalise me and vanish away.

The real voyage of discovery cannot be confined to books. And yet books are essential for they tell us of the past – of history, of culture, of

1. Dr Zakir Husain: eminent educationist; Vice-President of India, 1962–7, and President, 1967–9.

the way people lived, thought, acted. So why not dip into this treasure and try to understand what our forefathers were?

There are many books which I could suggest to you, though unfortunately good books about India or Indian history and culture have yet to be written. But we cannot wait for them. We must profit by what we have got. Indeed there are far more books now on the subject than there were when I was a boy. I remember well still the excitement with which I saw and read Vincent Smith's *Early History of India*. I was very young then and did not understand all I read. But this book suddenly opened out vast vistas before me and India's past, which had been a blank in my mind, became filled with great deeds. That book of Vincent Smith's, though far from good (no English I.C.S. [Indian Civil Service] man can write a really good book about India) was the first of its kind and it created, not only in me but in others, a new outlook and a certain pride in our past. That book is still a standard book though it is out of date because of recent discoveries. For instance, it does not mention Mohenjo Daro.[1] Still it is worth reading and you might get it. Our old copy at Anand Bhawan disappeared long ago and so a new copy had better be purchased. It is worth having and keeping.

Havell's *History of Aryan Rule in India* is not very good history (official historians dislike Havell intensely) but it is a good book, imaginative, understanding and based on the artistic record of India. Havell was an artist. There are many other books I could tell you of but they must wait. One book worth reading for the British period is Thompson & Garrett's *Rise & Fulfilment of British Rule in India*. (Thompson is our old friend of Boars Hill.) This is a hefty tome but light reading. We might as well know something of this sorry record of British rule which we want to displace. The book is in Anand Bhawan.

It would also be worthwhile for you to go to our oldest history book – the *Rajatarangini*[2] which Ranjit translated in prison. This book is a big one. Many parts of it are dull reading, some parts are very interesting. As a whole it is a *tour de force* of Kalhana, the author. Ranjit's translation has many appendices which are important.

Have you read Kalidas's *Shakuntala*?[3] or the *Mrichhakatika*?[4] The

---

1. An ancient site of the Indus Civilisation dating to the second millennium BC.

2. *Rajatarangini* (River of Kings): a poem in Sanskrit by Kalhana, narrating the history of Kashmir up to the twelfth century.

3. *Shakuntala*: a drama in Sanskrit by Kalidasa, the classical Sanskrit poet and dramatist.

4. *Mrichchakatika* (or the toy cart): a drama in Sanskrit by King Shudraka, written in the first or second century AD.

play Ranjit has been recently translating – the *Mudrarakshasa*[1] – should be read also. Perhaps he will be able to let you have a spare typed copy when you come next. It is peculiarly interesting just at present as it deals with politics and war and spying and fifth column activity etc – all over 2000 years ago!

Apart from Ancient Greece, India was the only country which developed a regular drama, which was performed in the old days. No other country has anything comparable to these two.

I have received three big bottles of excellent honey from Psyche. You should take at least one of them away when you come next.

Write to Amma (Nani) some time. When you do so send her my love.
Love,

Your<br>Papu

67.
District Jail,<br>Dehra Dun,<br>28th July, 1941

Darling Indu,

I have had another letter from Betty. It appears that they have decided to go to Kashmir. To begin with they are going to Poona for some days. They expect – subject to Harsha's condition – to spend about ten days in Poona and to pass Dehra Dun during the second week of August. I am writing to her that she can fix her programme according to her convenience and come here any day that suits her.

As you know I am having an interview tomorrow with Amrit Kaur. Nandan[2] and his wife Raksha[3] are also coming. The next interview, as fixed, will be on August 12th with Mridula & co.

I have had no news from you since we met last. I hope you are keeping well and putting on weight. At last we have had some rain here. Our plants were badly in need of it. I suppose you are having a good deal of rain also.

During the past few months I have read many books on mountaineering in India – almost always among the Garhwal mountains. This has been fascinating reading. I was surprised and pleased to find that there is complete agreement among those Englishmen & Americans who have

---

1. *Mudrarakshasa* (The Signet of the Minister): a drama in Sanskrit by Vishakadatta, dating back to the eleventh or twelfth century AD.
2. Raghunandan Saran: a prominent Congressman of Delhi; was Director of *National Herald*.
3. Raksha Saran: wife of Raghunandan Saran.

taken part in these expeditions that Garhwal has the most beautiful mountains and valleys in the world. The men who give this opinion were widely travelled and knew what they were talking about. This really applies to the higher regions of Garhwal and not to the dusty and rather bare valleys and hillsides below. In these upper regions there is an extraordinary and enchanting mixture of magnificent snow peaks, thick forests and valleys carpeted with lovely flowers. Indeed of one such valley, appropriately named the Valley of Flowers, it is said that it has no rival anywhere.

I have been to Garhwal only once for a few days. It is not easily accessible as even roads are lacking, except bridle paths for pilgrims. I only visited some of the towns in the lower regions. I had a glimpse, however, of the whole vast area and beyond from the air. For we took a plane from Hardwar and flew right over Badrinath till we seemed almost to collide against the huge snow wall of the mountain barrier which separates India from Tibet. That flight lasted a few hours only – there and back – and I carried away vivid impressions which endure. Two impressions especially: the snowy range, with its mighty peaks, majestic and fiercely beautiful, and the silver thread of the Alaknanda river, winding its way deep down below through the mountains. The Alaknanda, as perhaps you know, is one of the principal source streams of the Ganga.

You and I, in our respective abodes, are on the verge of Garhwal. I can see the Garhwal foothills from here and a longish walk will take you to the district boundary. The knowledge of this surpassing beauty, so near us and yet so far from this warring world, so peaceful and unperturbed by human folly, excites me. Those strange people who were our ancestors in the long ago felt the wonder of these mountains and valleys and, with the unerring instinct of genius, yoked this sense of awe and wonder to man's old yearning for something higher than life's daily toil and conflicts offered, something with the impress of the eternal upon it. And so for two thousand years or more, innumerable pilgrim souls have marched through these valleys and mountains to Badrinath and Kedarnath and Gangotri, from where the baby Ganga emerges, so tiny and frolicsome, but to grow and grow in her long wandering till she becomes the noble river that sweeps by Prayag and Kashi and beyond.

Shall I ever go wandering again in these mountains, and pierce the forest and climb the snows and feel the thrill of the precipice and the deep gorge? And then lie in deep content on a thick carpet of mountain flowers and gaze on the fiery splendour of the peaks as they catch the rays of the setting sun? Shall I sit by the side of the youthful and turbulent Ganga in her mountain home and watch her throw her head in a swirl of icy spray in pride and defiance, or creep round lovingly some favoured rock and take it into her embrace? And then rush down joyously over the boulders and hurl herself with a mighty shout over some great precipice? I have known her so long as a sedate lady, seemingly calm but, for all that, the fire is in her veins even then, the fiery vitality of youth and the spirit of adventure, and this breaks out from time to time when her peaceful waters seem angry and tumble over each other and spread out over vast areas.

I love the rivers of India and I should like to explore them from end to end, and to go back deep into the dawn of history and watch the processions of men and women, of cultures and civilisations, going down the broad streams of these rivers. The Indus, the Brahmaputra, the Ganga, and also that very lovable river of ours – the Jamuna.

Heigh ho! How many things I would like to do, how much there is to see, how many places to go to! What wonderful dreams we can fashion out of the past and out of the unknown future that is still to be! Men come and men go but man's dreaming and quest go on, and when failing hands can no longer hold the torch, others, more vigorous and straight, take hold of it, and they in their turn pass it on to yet others still.

How I begin musing when I write to you.

Love,

Your loving
Papu

———————————————

68.

District Jail,
Dehra Dun,
30th July, 1941

Darling Indu,

Your note and the bundle of Urdu books. What a bunch! I have not seen them separately yet but the number itself was impressive. Curiously enough Raghunandan Saran yesterday also brought a number of Urdu books for me. So now I have a respectable Urdu library – quite enough, I imagine, to last me for the rest of my term!

I am sending you a basket of fruit – chiefly apples from Amrit Kaur's garden in Simla, which she brought yesterday. Also some foreign newspapers and Arthur Koestler's new book: *Darkness at Noon*! I liked this book. It is amazingly well written (although it is a translation).

About our next interview – my dear, I would like to see you every day. But that would be sheer extravagance even if it was feasible, and it would mean far too much trouble and fatigue for you. I think we might have these interviews roughly once a fortnight, unless there is some special need for an interview in between or you wish to see me. Suit your convenience. In jail almost all days are alike. It is already twelve days since you came. Perhaps some day towards the end of the first week in August, say round about the 6th & 7th, might suit. But this is for you to decide and to let me know.

I have had no further news from Betty. My interview with Mridula & Nandan on August 12th holds. Perhaps Puphi (Nan) might come on that day also. As for Upadhyaya coming to meet Mridula, it will hardly be necessary if others are accompanying her. I do not know her programme – where she goes to from here.

Love,

Your loving,<br>Papu

69.                                                        District Jail,
                                                           Dehra Dun,
                                                 10th September, 1941

Darling Indu,

I have not had any news of you for a long time, except what Puphi told me on her way down. I hope you are flourishing and that Raja has got over his finger trouble.

I am sending you some magazines & foreign papers.

I do not know where Upadhyaya is now. I was told that he was going for some days to his home in the mountains. You did not think it necessary for him to return to Mussoorie, but he has nothing special to do in Allahabad, and he might be of some use to me here. So I suggested that he should come back. Of course he can go to Allahabad for a few days if he wants to.

I want some more *punis* (cotton slivers) for my spinning. I shall exhaust my present supply in about ten days. If Upadhyaya is about you can tell him to arrange for this. Or if he is not there, you might write yourself to The Manager, Maganwadi, Wardha, and ask him to send me direct by post 2 pounds of good slivers of the best quality of cotton obtainable.

I should also like some cigarettes to be sent to me within a few days.

Love,

Your loving,<br>Papu

You need not bother about the *punis* or the cigarettes as I have conveyed this message to Upadhyaya.

70. St Clair Cottage,
Mussoorie,
12th September [1941]

Dearest Papu,

Your letter & the magazines arrived last evening. I was surprised to hear
that you had not had my letter or one that Puphi wrote to you.

This is a hurried note. Nani wants to come on the 21st or 22nd. She
wants to know when she can interview you. Are your interviews fixed
up for this month? And if so, can she come with me? Shall I wait for
her or come by myself soon?

Please let me know.

The weather is misbehaving disgracefully but we are all keeping well.

Love to you,

Indu

---

71. District Jail,
Dehra Dun,
17th September, 1941

Darling,

I hope you are flourishing and profiting by the drier weather. The real
good weather in Mussoorie will begin soon. I hope also that Raja is
quite well now. I had a letter from Betty about ten days ago to say that
he was very much better.

Upadhyaya passed this way. I think that he should come back to
Mussoorie after he has spent some days in the bosom of his family. I
told him so. He might be useful to me here.

I sent you through Ram Saran a fat packet of foreign papers. I hope
it reached you.

For the past two years it has been my practice to buy some *khadi
hundies*[1] during Gandhi Jayanti[2] and distribute these – some to
Upadhyaya, some to the servants. I think this might be kept up. I am
therefore enclosing a cheque for Rs. 100. Buy the *hundies* in Allahabad
preferably but it does not matter much where you get them. You can
send the cheque direct to the Khadi Bhandar, Allahabad, and ask for
the *hundies* – or send it to Upadhyaya if he is in Allahabad. You will
have to endorse the cheque.

The *hundies* should be distributed in this way:

1. Coupons for buying cloth.
2. Gandhi Jayanti: Mahatma Gandhi's birthday.

| | |
|---|---|
| Upadhyaya | – 30/- |
| Bhola | – 10/- |
| Hari | – 10/- I suppose he will soon be out |
| Other servants | – 50/- division as you like |

But remember that my favourite is Lakchamania, who is the oldest member of our household.

I have got a copy at last of *The Unity of India*. It was sent by a friend who purchased it in Delhi. I like the get-up of the book. Krishna has taken a lot of trouble over it. I have not heard from him at all. You must have seen his long letter – and the Edward Thompson correspondence in the *New Statesman*.

Love,

Your loving,<br>
Papu

---

72.                                           District Jail,<br>
Dehra Dun,<br>
18th September, 1941

Darling Indu,

Your letter of the 12th[1] has only just reached me. Last night I wrote to you and I suppose my letter was posted today.[2] As far as I can remember I have not received any letter from you, other than the one that has now come, since our last interview. I had a brief note from Puphi some time ago.

About Nani's interview, I cannot answer your questions without referring to the Superintendent and this will mean a day's delay. But I think that anyhow it will be possible for her to see me on *Sept 22*. I am already having an interview on that day, or at any rate, I am expecting one. Three persons have been asked to come then from three distant parts of India: K. T. Shah[3] from Bombay, Dr Mahmud from Chapra, and Dr Subbaroyan[4] (Mohan Kumaramangalam's[5] father) from Madras.

1. Refers to letter No. 70.
2. Refers to letter No. 71.
3. K. T. Shah: Professor of Economics, Bombay University.
4. Dr P. Subbaroyan: barrister and political leader of Tamil Nadu.
5. Surendra Mohan Kumaramangalam: contemporary of Indira Gandhi in Great Britain, prominent in student politics. He was later a leading member of the Indian Government.

I have had no answer from Dr Subbaroyan and so I am not expecting him. Mahmud too is slightly doubtful, though he is likely to come. At the most therefore I shall have two persons to interview me and Nani can come on that day if it is convenient to her. She need not come with the others or try to find out when they are coming. If she is in Dehra Dun she can come straight to the jail.

If she cannot come on the 22nd then a fresh date will have to be fixed in consultation with the Superintendent. I have no other normal interview this month. You can of course come when you choose but I do not know if she can accompany you. I shall enquire and let you know. Meanwhile if she can come on the 22nd, let her come.

As for your interview, owing to the delay in my getting your letter, it is difficult for you to come here before the 21st. That will be just about the time when Nani will be coming up. I should not like you to come on the 22nd as there will be others here on that day. For the rest fix any day that suits you.

Love,

Your loving,<br>Papu

---

73.

Wardha,<br>16th March, 1942 [1]

Indu darling,

Maulana has just sent me a pair of pearl bracelets (I suppose that is the right name) for you. They are not frightfully expensive I suppose but still such gifts, especially from the Maulana, are a little embarrassing.

Kamalnayan [2] says he will be coming to the wedding. [3] I do not know yet if Savitri will accompany him – probably not. Om is not here – she is in Naini Tal. I think you should send her a card (No. 1). Her address is given below.

Please have a No. 3 (Party card) sent to Raghupati Sahai of the University. He is a lecturer, I think in the English Dept. He is an old colleague of mine who drifted away and became rather useless. He is a bit of an Urdu poet with the poetic name of *Firaq*.

Also I think No. 3 invitation should be sent to Mr & Mrs Bhagwat Dayal – also of the University – & Kayastha Pathshala. I had, rather

1. Jawaharlal Nehru was released from prison about ten weeks after he wrote letter No. 72. Since he and Indira were together at Anand Bhawan, there is a six-month break in the correspondence.
2. Kamalnayan Bajaj: son of Jamnalal Bajaj (see Political Circle).
3. The reference is to Indira's wedding – 26th March, 1942.

deliberately, left his name out when we were trying to limit the lists. But now that many other names have been included, I think he might be added also.

Om is Uma – her present address is:

> Mrs Raj Narayan Agarwal
> The Mahal
> Krishnapuri
> Naini Tal

The invitations had better be sent to Mr & Mrs.

It is definitely warmer here than in Allahabad though this night was pleasant.

Love,

> Your loving,
> Papu

---

74.                                            New Delhi,
                                          7th April, 1942

Darling,

I have had no news from you, except for your telegram[1] since I came here. I hope you are well and the growing heat of Allahabad does not trouble you too much. I expected to get away from here by tomorrow night but now I am not certain. We tussle daily with problems and they take new turns and put on new shapes. And so we go on from day to day and meanwhile war has reached India.[2] Possibly I might get away from here by the 9th or 10th but I am not at all sure of what will happen. I am a little worried about you. Why should you hang up or postpone your programme because of me?

Madame Chiang wrote to me that she wanted to send you as a wedding gift something she had valued in her girlhood. I do not know what this is but she was trying to get it from some odd place.

The other day I met Shuaib Qureshi[3] here and he expressed his sorrow at not having been invited to your marriage. I am sorry I missed him out. I remember his sending a telegram of congratulations. I would like you

1. Telegram not traceable.
2. After the fall of Burma in March 1942 the Japanese armies stood on the Indian frontier.
3. Shuaib Qureshi: son-in-law of Maulana Mohamed Ali; journalist and politician; moved to Pakistan after partition; was later Ambassador of Pakistan to U.S.S.R., 1949–52, and High Commissioner in India 1952–3.

to write to him and thank him for his good wishes. His address is: The Hon'ble Mr Shuaib Qureshi, Minister, Bhopal, C.I. And now to work.

Love,

Your loving,
Papu

You might also write a few lines to Sir Stafford Cripps[1] to thank him for the good wishes he sent you through me. You will remember the letters he wrote. His address is: 3, Queen Victoria Road, New Delhi.

---

75.                                5 Fort Road,[2]
Allahabad,
9th April, [1942]

Darling Papu,

I have not written all these days because we did not know when you'd be back. Now it seems to be pretty definite that you will have to stay on in Delhi for a while.

Your letter of the 7th[3] has just arrived. I am sending off the letter as you suggested.

About Kashmir nothing is definite yet. There is an increasing likelihood of all transport being dislocated as soon as the Japanese strike at any of the important junctions. I don't like the idea of being cut off in far-off Kashmir. Bijju Bhai has written to somebody that tonga transport will not be available this year as no arrangements have yet been made. And if anything is to happen in Allahabad I want to be here. I don't really feel like going away at all. This is no time for anybody to take a holiday – can't I stay and do something? I'm so tired of being at a loose end.

I had hoped that if I went to Kashmir you could come up for a week or so – but now that that possibility is remote I should prefer to be somewhere where I can have a glimpse of you, occasionally at least.

Much love,

Indu

P.S. I am bearing the heat very well.

---

1. Sir Stafford Cripps: socialist politician who was head of a mission to India in 1942 for constitutional talks with Indian leaders.

2. As already indicated Indira and Feroze were married on 26th March, 1942. After their marriage they set up house (the Tagore Town house) at 5 Fort Road, now known as Jawaharlal Nehru Road.

3. Refers to letter No. 74.

76.                                        36, Wellington Street,
                                                      Calcutta,
                                             18th April, 1942
                                             nearing midnight

Darling Indu,
The first day here is over and I am glad you did not come with me. It is heavy work and there would be little fun or amusement for you in it. Tomorrow is a heavier day with no gap at all from seven a.m. to eleven p.m. Day after tomorrow (20th) I leave at noon for Gauhati. I spend nearly four days in Assam visiting Tezpur, Dimapur, etc. But my safest address during these four days will be Gauhati. I return to Calcutta on the 25th afternoon and leave the same night for Allahabad where I reach on the 26th morning by the Calcutta-Delhi mail.

     Bidhan Roy is not here. He is in Shillong but he might return day after tomorrow just after I have gone.
                                             Love,
                                             Papu

---

77.                                         5 Fort Road,
                                                 Allahabad,
                                            21st April, 1942

Darling Papu,
Your letter[1] has just come. It always makes me happy to have a letter from you but I do wish you would take more care of yourself. Is it absolutely necessary to have such a heavy programme?

     Bebee[2] was here this evening, the rest of the family having deserted her. Puphi and Pupha are out of town – Puphi has gone to Benares and Pupha to Bombay. Chand had taken the children to Guzders to suck ice-creams.

     There are several telegrams for you – including one from Jankibai[3] urging you, begging you to have the A.I.C.C.[4] in Wardha and one from Anita Blaine,[5] which looks much more like a pamphlet than a cable.

     1. Refers to letter No. 76.
     2. Padmaja Naidu (Bebee): see Circle of Friends.
     3. Jankibai Bajaj: wife of Jamnalal Bajaj; was active in the freedom movement; later joined the Bhoodan (or land gift) movement of Vinoba Bhave.
     4. A.I.C.C.: All India Congress Committee.
     5. Anita Blaine (1866–1945): American philanthropist; founder, School of Education, University of Chicago.

Also a letter from Bapu. I am not quite sure if there is time to send them to Gauhati, so we are sending them to Calcutta – it would be awful if the letter went astray.

The work on the construction of the *pandals* [1] is proceeding fast. The house is according to the *Leader*, 'humming with activity'. Kripalaniji [2] arrived this morning.

Last evening I went to see the Cripps film. You have come out very well in it . . .

Much love,<br>Indu

———————————

78.       New Delhi,
5th/6th May, 1942

Indu darling,

I have not written to you since I came here. Only a telegram to which you sent a reply. [3] There has been heavy and exhausting work and complete uncertainty about my stay or the future. I stay on from day to day. As I see it now, I am likely to be here till Wednesday night or possibly Thursday night.

On my return to Allahabad I doubt if I can stay there for more than a couple of days for events in Bengal call me. I might even go to Assam.

I am worried about your staying on in Allahabad and delaying your departure for Kashmir. It depends of course on how you feel but it is best not to take risks.

Events are marching fast and are likely to overwhelm us within a few weeks. I must be in the thick of them for that is my job. But there is no reason why you should upset your holiday.

Raja is going to Bombay this morning (6th).

Love,<br>Papu

———————————

1. Marquee: it was being set up for a meeting of the All India Congress Committee.
2. J. B. Kripalani: a leader of the struggle for freedom. He was General Secretary of the Congress from 1934 to 1946, and President, 1946.
3. Letter not traceable.

79.                                        The White House,
                                                Murree,
                                           25th May, 1942

Darling Papu,
I do hope you had a good journey and that Allahabad is not too
unpleasant.

We had a fairly busy time in Lahore after you left – but I enjoyed
myself. Yunus, with the help of Nawabzada Saheb, made most efficient
arrangements for our journey. We had a first class coupé, very clean
and cool (for water was sprayed on the roof). We reached Pindi at seven
forty-five a.m. and were met by the Sardar. After a quick bath & breakfast we drove here in a spacious and very posh Plymouth, arriving just in
time for lunch. It is very pleasant here. We leave for Srinagar tomorrow
morning.

This is the house of the Sardar's brother. Everybody seems rather
surprised that we should be going to Kashmir before the Maharajas
have arrived! That is their mentality.

Very much love,
                                                Indu

────────────────────

80.                                              Wardha,
                                           27th May, 1942

Darling Indu,
I came in direct from Delhi. I felt that I must see Bapu as soon as
possible even though for a short while. I am only here for a day and am
going direct to Lucknow tomorrow morning. I shall be in Lucknow from
the 29th to the 31st night and then in Allahabad for two or three days.
After that I return to Wardha, probably with the Maulana, and stay here
for a few days. From Delhi I sent my heavy luggage direct to Allahabad.

The journey was hot and the change from Kulu marked. I feel quite
fit. Last evening I weighed myself here and found that I was 6 lbs less
than I was at Nagpur. Partly this was due to absence of clothes.

In Delhi I met Louis Fischer (the man who was in Russia for many
years as *Nation's* correspondent). I shall probably see more of him.

At Delhi also I learnt of Ballo's [1] return from a somewhat odd source.
A certain Colonel or Captain Schuiter rolled up at Rajan's [2] place on
a motor bicycle and informed me that he had flown over with my

1. Balwant Kumar Nehru: son of Jawaharlal Nehru's first cousin, Brijlal Nehru.
2. Rajan Nehru: wife of Jawaharlal Nehru's nephew Ratan Kumar Nehru.

nephew. He added that Lady Willingdon[1] had sent me her love! Also that he was a Harrow man. He was a tall, Haw-Haw type of a person.

I hope you had a good journey and are comfortably housed in Srinagar. Do not hurry back to the plains. It is better to get the full benefit of the change. On your way back, if it is possible, you might visit the Frontier Province and spend a day or two with Dr Khan Sahib[2] in Peshawar. You should of course see Abdul Ghaffar Khan also but I am more anxious about Khan Sahib. As you know, he had a difficult time recently and has been surrounded by hostility. Every manifestation of friendship and affection will be good for him.

Give my love to Ballo and remember me to Sheikh Abdullah.

Love,

Your loving,<br>Papu

81. 18 Gupkar Road,<br>Srinagar,<br>30th May, 1942

Darling Papu,

I see from the papers that you are in Wardha.

We are having a lovely time – the Sheikh is planning a trip to the Kolahoi and lots of other places that I have not seen. We do not yet know whether we shall be able to go. The weather is not behaving as well as it generally does at this time of the year. This house has a marvellous situation – gorgeous view.

Much love,

Indu

82. 18 Gupkar Road,<br>Srinagar,<br>3rd June, 1942

Darling Papu,

Your letter[3] from Wardha. Srinagar is perfectly lovely and we are

1. Lady Willingdon: wife of Lord Willingdon, the Viceroy and Governor-General of India, 1931–6.

2. Dr Khan Sahib: brother of Abdul Ghaffar Khan (see Political Circle) and a friend of Jawaharlal during his student days in London; Prime Minister, North-West Frontier Province, 1937–9 and 1945–7; Chief Minister, West Pakistan, 1955–7.

3. Refers to letter No. 80.

having a glorious time. Fortunately it has stopped raining – it's quite warm, really – and we are able to have more frequent glimpses of the magnificent semi-circle of snow-covered ranges right in front of our house. I don't think I have ever had such a view from a house. You would love it. We miss you so much.

We have had one or two meals at Bijju Chacha's and also a tea party. Nikku Bhai[1] also gave a small tea party for us yesterday.

Our major excitement at the moment is a movie camera we are thinking of buying.

We are leaving Srinagar on Saturday the 6th for Pahalgam. Sheikh Abdullah has planned a trip to the Kolahoi for us. I don't quite know the details of it. I expect we shall follow your route, more or less – except for Sonemarg, where I am very keen on spending a few days.

I don't know what address to give you as we shall not be in any place for more than a couple of days or so.

Sheikh Saheb is going with us & also the Vakils, who are already in Pahalgam. It is rather difficult to make plans as we see very little of Sheikh Saheb.[2] He is very busy these days with the problems of food rationing and food control.

It must be very hot in the plains. I hope you are looking after yourself. What shape is this new movement[3] going to take, I wonder.

Much love,

Indu

---

83.

Anand Bhawan,
Allahabad,
5th June, 1942

Darling Indu,

Your note[4] from Murree has reached me.

I have been here just four days. Tomorrow morning I am going again to Wardha. Possibly from there to Bombay. I expect to be away for eight or nine days. It is very hot here but I rather like it – only I feel pretty limp.

Keep me informed of how and where you are.

Nan came here for a day and then went off to the Women's Camp at Surat.

1. Kanwarlal Kathju (Nikku): a cousin of Jawaharlal Nehru.
2. Refers to Sheikh Abdullah, the distinguished leader of Kashmir.
3. Refers to the preliminary discussions leading to the famous 'Quit India' movement of August 1942.
4. Refers to letter No. 79.

I have just had a long and agitated cable from Krishna Menon.

Love,
Papu

---

84.                                                                Sevagram,
                                                            9th June, 1942

Darling Indu,

I was happy to receive your little note [1] from Srinagar and to know that you liked the house. Srinagar is not a bad place early in June.

Excursions to Kolahoi sound very attractive but do not overdo this kind of thing. They are tiring and I am not sure that it is good for you to invite fatigue. If later you feel quite fit and rested then you may take an excursion in easy stages. The Kolahoi trip is not a long one and except the last stage is not tiring. But the last stage over rocks and boulders right up to the glacier is definitely exhausting.

I imagine an interesting trip from Pahalgam would be to the Lake (I forget the name – is it Shesh nag?) two stages on the way to Amarnath. This lake, I am told, is very lovely.

But do rest a lot.

I have been here two days and Maulana is due here tonight. Probably we shall stay here another four days and then I propose to go to Bombay for three days. I expect to be back in Allahabad on the 16th or 17th.

Things are warming up, especially in our province. So anything might happen in the future. It really does not much matter what happens. You must not cut short your stay in Kashmir because of happenings here.

Love to you & Feroze,
                                                          Your loving
                                                          Papu

Have you got the two numbers of *Reader's Digest* which I took to Kulu? If so I would like you to send them by post to Pandit Govind Ballabh Pant, [2] Tallital, Nainital, U.P.

---

1. Refers to letter No. 81.
2. Govind Ballabh Pant: distinguished nationalist from the United Provinces (now the State of Uttar Pradesh); active in the struggle for freedom, later Chief Minister of U.P., 1946–55, and Home Minister in the Central Government, 1955–61.

85.                                              Pahalgam,
                                              11th June, 1942

Darling Papu,
Your letter[1] from Allahabad arrived yesterday. How hot it must be
there and in Wardha! Here it is very delightful. The Vakils are here and
also Sheikh Saheb, who is being very sweet. This afternoon we are all
leaving for Anar *en route* to the Kolahoi. The weather is fine so we hope
it will be a good trip. I am leaving Hari behind, as he is not keen to go
and also I do not think he would stand the height or the cold.
   Going to the Kolahoi means no post, no newspaper for at least four
days. We hope to return to Srinagar on the 16th.
   Pandit Shyamlal, fat and jovial, is also accompanying us.
   Much love,
                           Indu

_____

86.                       [Cable]                    Srinagar,
                                              [17th June, 1942]

Nehru,
Anand Bhawan,
Allahabad

Back from Kolahoi brown as chocolate fit.
   Happy love
                           Indu

_____

87.                                            Mohanmarg,
                                              5th July, 1942

Darling Papu,
Do forgive me for not writing for such ages. When one has nothing to
do one seems to get all the lazier. And then, I am so full of the joy of
discovering Kashmir. I just had not realised it was so very beautiful.
   On our return from Kolahoi we went straight to Srinagar without
stopping even at Pahalgam. As the Ramlals'[2] house was still empty, I
took the Vakils there with me. They, the Vakils, could not make up their

   1. Refers to letter No. 83.
   2. Dewan Ramlal: brother of Dewan Chamanlal, who was a parliamentarian and a
friend of the Nehrus.

minds about staying on in Kashmir and for a while we decided that we would all go to Bombay. I was very keen on going to the Konsa Nag – it is supposed to be one of the most beautiful lakes in the world. But unfortunately the road was blocked by an avalanche, so the trip was cancelled. Soon afterwards the Vakils left for Bombay and Sheikh Saheb took us to Gulmarg. I agree with you about Gulmarg – I don't like it one bit, but Sheikh Saheb was very keen on our staying with his family for a few days. We spent four days there – Yunus was with us. Then we came to Srinagar and spent three days on a houseboat. Three glorious moonlit nights.

On to Mohanmarg – King of Margs. Truly if there is a heaven it must be this. There is nothing in Switzerland to compare with these flower-filled slopes, the sweet-scented breezes. Maybe there are other things besides running water that pour over the soul the anodyne of forgetfulness and peace. I wish I could stay on here longer. But we have tied up our plans with Yunus and so tomorrow we proceed to Sonemarg.

By the way, Steen lives here for six months in the year – for the last forty-six years! He came to see us. How old he is!

Feroze & I are thinking of returning to Allahabad on the 15th. Until then we shall remain in Sonemarg. Sheikh Saheb keeps on saying that we should remain until September but Feroze thinks it is high time he went back.

Vidya[1] is here with us.

How you would love it here – yesterday we got up at five to see the sunrise on Nanga Parbat. It will be a rude shock to find ourselves, one hot and sticky day, in the ugliness of Allahabad.

Since I cannot bottle the beauty of Mohanmarg, I am sending you two little flowers as a token – forget-me-not and edelweiss. They both grow in abundance along with anemone, buttercups, Dutch slippers and a host of other so-called Alpine flowers. There are some wild animals as well but the only one we have seen is the marmot, which is like a giant rat. Rather sweet and soft.

Feroze has taken some films. I hope they will come out well. We have not seen them ourselves yet.

Sheikh Saheb is being very kind to us & I am afraid we have wasted a lot of his time.

What will happen to Rita's schooling if she joins Uday Shankar's troupe?

Nani is rather annoyed that we have not been to Nowshera yet – I don't quite know how to fit it in. It must be frightfully hot there. On my

---

1. Vidya Dutt (née Nehru): a niece of Jawaharlal Nehru.

return I shall also have to go to Agra where she is with Masi[1] and to Bombay to see Feroze's Aunt.

By the way, did you know that Mamu[2] was not keeping at all well? He has appendicitis.

Feroze sends his love & Yunus his salaam.

Much love,

Indu

P.S.

Address in Sonemarg c/o Postmaster.

Your letter from Allahabad reached me yesterday.

I enclose a letter on birch-bark from Sheikh Saheb.

Indu

---

88.                                  Wardha,
8th July, 1942

Darling Indu,

Asaf Ali[3] has given me some news of you and Feroze – I am glad you are having a really good time and are keeping fit. Do not hurry to come back. The rains have put an end to the heat here but it is obviously infinitely pleasanter in Kashmir.

Badshah Khan is here. He has again reminded me that he will expect you at his home in Utmanzai on your way back.

I do not know if you & Feroze have had the time or the opportunity to meet many Kashmiri Pandits in Srinagar or elsewhere. It is worthwhile your trying to get into touch with them, especially their womenfolk . . .

My stay here is still uncertain. Bapu has grown very weak and gets tired soon.

Love,

Your loving,
Papu

---

1. Refers to Swarup (Bappi) Kathju, sister of Kamala Nehru ('Masi' means maternal aunt).

2. C. B. Koul: uncle of Indira Gandhi.

3. Asaf Ali: a Congressman of Delhi; was later Indian Ambassador to the United States and Governor of Orissa.

*[1942 was a momentous year for India and for the Nehrus. Within the country there was a massive growth of sentiment for liberation from British rule. In response to this, Congress leaders, including Jawaharlal Nehru, who was accompanied by Indira and her husband, Feroze, assembled in Bombay and on 8th August adopted a resolution – popularly known as the Quit India Resolution – asking the British to hand over India to her people. Jawaharlal Nehru was arrested on 9th August and imprisoned in Ahmadnagar Fort. The entire country was shaken by an anti-British upsurge for the next few months, which was controlled by the British Government through repression.]*

---

89. Anand Bhawan,<br>Allahabad,<br>4th September, 1942

Darling Papu,

It is good news indeed that I may write to you and, it may be, receive letters from you. And though there will be little news in the letters, they will be most welcome. Something is better than nothing. And it is good to see a loved and familiar hand even though it cannot convey any message. What a strange life it is – my mind is full of news that I want to give to you, news that I know you must be most eager to have, and yet it cannot be. What may we talk about but the weather?

The weather is indeed wonderful, perhaps out of kindness to me, for this is my first summer in the plains for many many years. It is delightfully cool and fresh for it rains a lot. Indeed just now it is pouring away. However, when the rain stops it gets stuffy and hot.

There are four of us staying here now. Tara, Rita, their new Chinese governess, Mrs Chew, and I. Chand is with her mother. Puphi had thought of having the two girls sent to Bombay but since Mrs Chew has arrived they are going to stay on here. Miss Owen [1] is here these days. I sent for her to stay with the girls before we had heard of Mrs Chew. She (Miss Owen) will probably go away in a few days. Mrs Chew is a refugee from Singapore. She has been sent to Allahabad by Pupha. She is thirty-one years old and rather nice. The girls seem to like her. There was great excitement at lunch today. Remembering how thrilled Mr Woo was when we produced chopsticks, I had them brought out for Mrs Chew.

---

1. A governess.

Because of the military,[1] we have got several new restaurants and even the oldest & most decrepit are doing good business. Among the new is a Chinese restaurant and a place which calls itself the 'Broadway Blues'. They both look pretty dismal from outside. I don't think anything will ever look 'gay' in Allahabad – leastways not until we have the sort of parties we used to long ago in Anand Bhawan. But absence of gaiety does not indicate absence of excitement. No Sirree, as the Americans would say, we are not bored. Far far from it. In fact I have been forced to dose myself with a thing called Bellargal, which is supposed to calm one's inside, as a counter-measure.

Don't worry about us folks outside, darling. We can look after ourselves and a lot more besides. And just now we are having a grand time, the sort of time you would like us to have. So stay cheerful as we all are.

Actually, at the moment there is a blot on our horizon. You must remember how poor little Tangle was not looking too bright before we went to Bombay. Latterly he just got worse & worse until suddenly he started having the most awfully painful fits. He would give piteous cries and writhe in agony. The vet tried all sorts of things but in the end we had to have him destroyed. We all miss him awfully, the house is so quiet without him.

Johnnie Walker[2] is still going strong. He is less vicious now and doesn't greet every arrival & departure with his awful trumpeting. He has acquired a rather distant companion in the shape of a peacock who is also living in the garden. They do not seem to care much for each other's company, or it may be they have both got used to solitude.

Everybody here sends you heaps & heaps of love and a tight hug from
Your loving<br>Indu

---

90.                                              Anand Bhawan,
                                                    Allahabad,
                                              9th September, 1942

Darling Papu,

Why still no news of you? Puphi has had a letter from Rajabhai and Bebee from her mother.[3] Bebee writes every two days asking after you

---

1. The reference is to soldiers posted in India during the war.
2. A pet dog.
3. Raja Hutheesing and Sarojini Naidu (Bebee's mother) were imprisoned, as was Jawaharlal Nehru, during the 'Quit India' movement. The former two were able to communicate with their relatives. Jawaharlal Nehru refused to accept the conditions of censorship (see letter No. 91) and could not communicate for some time.

and, of course, I have no more news than she. Did you get my letter?

The latest addition to the menage is a monkey! I am afraid he is most unwelcome. He has been coming for the last three days making a thorough nuisance of himself. This afternoon he locked himself in the kitchen and ate up all our vegetables, so that it is extremely doubtful whether we will have any dinner! I think he must be somebody's pet, for he is very well-fed and has a lovely silky coat.

The rains are still continuing. The nights are quite chilly, even the days are nice & cool.

Mrs Chew, the new Chinese governess, seems to be getting on well. Whenever she goes out she is the centre of attraction, because of her Chinese dresses.

Darling, I hope you are looking after yourself, as far as possible in the circumstances. Don't worry about all of us. We are well.

Very much love,

Indu

PART II

# Prison Walls
## (1942–1945)

*[Indira and her husband, Feroze, were fully drawn into the tumultuous events of 1942. On their return to Allahabad from Bombay, after the passing of the Quit India Resolution, they organised the anti-British agitation in Allahabad. On 10th September Feroze was arrested for convening a public meeting and Indira was arrested while addressing it. Both were taken to Naini Prison, but were lodged in different sections, unable to communicate with each other. Later Feroze was moved to Faizabad Jail. Indira shared prison life with Vijaya Lakshmi Pandit, Chandralekha Mehta, Purnima Banerjee (Nora) and Vimla Varma, and was released on 13th May, 1943. Feroze was released from Faizabad Jail on 8th July, 1943 on grounds of ill health.]*

91.                                     Somewhere in India,
                                  but not at Anand Bhawan,
                                             Allahabad,
                                  18th September, 1942

Darling Indu,
It is now a month and nine days since I said goodbye to you and came here and for the first time I am writing a letter. About three weeks ago we were told that we could write letters subject to a number of restrictions and limitations. Yet I have not written all this time to anyone, much as I would have liked to write to you. But being somewhat perverse by nature I did not take kindly to these restrictions and I postponed writing till I felt in a better mood for it. I thought I had better wait till I received a letter. The tortuous procedure of sending letters meant delay and was no incentive to writing. I was confirmed in my reluctance when I found how long it took for other people's letters to reach their destinations, if they reached them at all. I wondered afresh at the amazing dilatoriness and inefficiency of the governmental machinery of this country.

On the 4th September I received a letter from Betty – my first letter here. Also some clothes and books. Much later came the suitcase, containing clothes and books, which you had sent from Allahabad. And then on the 15th September came your letter of the 4th[1] – an absurdly long interval of time between despatch and receipt. The desire to write to you grew and grew within me and has now overcome my reluctance to face these irritating delays and incompetence. So here is the letter which will go off from here today. When you will receive it, or whether you will receive it at all, is another matter.

I was very happy to get your letter and to know that you were well and flourishing. Yet I was not anxious about you for I knew well that

---

1. Refers to letter No. 89.

you could and would look after yourself and face cheerfully whatever happened. Nevertheless to be assured of all this was very pleasing and I felt lighter in mind and body.

As for myself, there is little to say. You know that I can manage to fit in almost anywhere and keep my body and mind in active condition. One of my numerous failings is that I expect others to do so also and when they do not keep up to the mark, I become a nuisance to them. I have tried hard to overcome this weakness but the passing of years does not seem to make much difference. Here I have Mahmud especially to look after, with all his ailments, and I am not sure whether he enjoys all my ministrations and good advice which he receives in great abundance. So also others in a lesser degree.

I was very sorry to learn of poor Tangle's death. Yet it had to be as he was old and feeble. Rita must have felt this most.

I have enough clothes and other necessaries for the time being. Possibly I might require a blanket or two or one or two other things with the coming of winter. I am writing to Betty about them and she will, I suppose, communicate with Upadhyaya or Hari or whoever is available. Even if these articles do not reach me, it will not make much difference. I can carry on without them.

As for books, of course, they are always welcome. When I came here I had three with me: Plato's *Republic*, Marcel Proust's *A la recherche du temps perdu* (2 vols) and Lin Yu-tang's *With Love and Irony* – an odd mixture. I read through Plato again in a leisurely way, allowing myself to absorb him as far as I could and adding to my admiration for him. Proust seemed to belong to some other and far-away world, or like faint memories of a vanishing age. And yet he wrote these books after I had left Cambridge. How this world of ours has changed and is changing!

There were some other books with my companions and I read them perforce because there were none better available. Then came a few odd books sent by Betty and later your little collection. So I have carried on. I have tried to purchase through Government a fairly large number of books but this is a frightfully slow process. I ordered them three or four weeks ago. I still live in hope and expectation. Perhaps in the course of another few weeks or months, they might turn up.

Betty wrote to me that new books were difficult to get. As a matter of fact I am not keen on new books, unless they are very special ones. Most of these new books are just trash in spite of their attractive bindings and publishers' blurbs. When I look at the books I have purchased during the last dozen years or more, there are exceedingly few which are at all worthwhile. In prison I go back almost automatically to good old classical literature. And so the books I have recently ordered are very largely taken from Everyman's Library – partly because that is the only list I had.

I wonder what is happening to such foreign papers as manage to reach Anand Bhawan. I do not want them to be forwarded to me. I would much rather that they went to you and Nan.

Maulana is an extraordinarily interesting companion. The more I know him, and I have known him now for over twenty-one years, the more I find in him. I wish I could profit more by this enforced companionship. Meanwhile, I am having a peep into Urdu poetry. He tells me, or rather writes for me, a verse or two daily.

There is one small matter which has been in my mind for some time. I presume market prices have risen and are rising from day to day. This must affect our servants greatly. They were being given some kind of extra allowance but in view of the rise in prices, this cannot go far. I want them to be treated fairly and generously in this matter. It is better to err on the side of generosity. I am writing to Betty about this matter so that she can communicate with Ladli Bhai.

I was glad to learn from your letter that a Chinese governess had been engaged for the girls. The Chinese are good at this job and, besides, I like all contacts with the Chinese people.

How does one spend one's time in prison, the ignorant wonder? There is reading and writing of course. But apart from this there are innumerable other activities which are fascinating. I remember spending long hours in Dehra Dun watching ants and wasps and various insects. It was not a cold-blooded scientific survey but a human, friendly companionship, and I grew quite fond of them. Here, on a very ordinary patch of wild grass and dried-up ground within our prison yard with a few pebbles lying about, we have discovered an amazing collection of fine stones of all manner of colours. Asaf Ali is particularly expert at this game. We are building up almost a museum of these.

And then there is the sky and frequently the rainbow spans it. Although we live in a kind of Plato's cave, yet we have this sky over our yard and a lovely sky it is with fleecy and colourful clouds in the daytime, and, now, brilliant starlit nights. What a fascinating world this is if only we kept our eyes and ears open.

As is my habit in prison, I get up very early, even before the dawn. I make up for this short night of sleep by sleeping a little in the afternoon. Yesterday I was tired and fell off into a deep sleep for an hour or so. I had an odd dream, one of the oddest I have ever had. Some time, perhaps, I might tell you about it, if I remember about it then. It was dramatic with a climax developing step by step till I grew faint with excitement and then, at the very moment of the last and final climax, there was a sudden anti-climax. All the accumulated strain vanished and I felt a little limp. And I laughed. Just then I woke up!

There is some new-fangled time abroad we are told, a trick to save daylight. We see no reason to abide by it and so we carry on with the old time.

I am a little anxious about Mehr Taj.[1] I hope all is well with her.

I do not know where you are, but wherever you may be I hope it is well with you, my dear. Keep bright and fit, for there is much to be done and we have to be in perfect condition to do it. Send my love to Feroze. Perhaps you are with Nan and Chand. If so give my love to them.

And so, *au revoir, carissima*, and all my love.

[Your loving,]
Papu

Do not worry if you do not hear from me frequently or regularly.
Later: I have just received through Betty your note of the 9th[2] written just on the eve of your departure. Good to see your handwriting again.

Love,
Papu

---

92.                         From the Unmentionable Place!
                            15th October, 1942

Darling Indu,
It is nearly a month now since I heard from you or wrote to you. During this month I have had no news of you or Puphi or Chand. I did not write to you again as I was waiting for your answer. I was not quite sure about my letter reaching you – there were so many high walls to be crossed, so many hurdles to be overcome, so many pigeonholes which might engulf it. So I waited. Normally, I have learnt from the past nine weeks' experience, it takes about ten days for a letter to get through, and that is long enough in all conscience. I do not worry about you for I know you will look after yourself and keep cheerful and well. But there is occasionally a feeling of emptiness and some news, some lines written in your handwriting, fills this and I feel better.

So I am not waiting any longer and am writing to you today for the act of writing itself gives a little satisfaction. If you can write from time

---

1. Mehr Taj: daughter of Khan Abdul Ghaffar Khan.
2. Refers to letter No. 90.

to time, I shall be happy. Perhaps, through you, I might have some news of Feroze also.

Round about Allahabad it must be cool now and the nights must be very pleasant. Here it is still warm, though there has been a slight change for the better during the last two days. After the rains stopped it became very hot – September and early October were hotter than August. Perhaps by the end of the month it will be pleasant and cool. But I must say we have little to complain of the climate. It is dry and healthy.

What do you do? How do you occupy yourself? There is nothing like taking to gardening. Even apart from the beauty that flowers give to our surroundings, the joy of tending them and seeing them grow and bloom from day to day is a fascinating business. I love to play about with the soft warm earth. I think there is a certain psychic satisfaction about the earth, and we, who have cut ourselves away from it, miss this very essential thing; if I read or write all day, there is something that I lack, and this contact with the earth goes some way to supply it – not wholly of course, for the human personality requires many things.

So I hope you will take to gardening. It does not matter much whether you do it well or badly, whether you arrange the flowers in the right order or not. It is the act of doing it that matters and one learns more from this than from books. I suppose you can easily get flower seeds. Even Anand Bhawan could provide you with some. But it is better to get good ones if these are available. Sweet peas are, I think, the most suitable flowers for one in jail. They appeal equally to the sight and the sense of smell. But there is no reason to confine oneself to a few varieties. Get good tools. It is pleasant to use a clean good tool. You should not dig. But there are many other operations that you could do.

For the last month or more we have been thinking of growing flowers here. The soil is none too good, being stony, but that can be remedied with labour. We have been trying to get seeds – so far without success. But we live in hopes. Meanwhile, I have been doing a fair amount of digging and that is good in itself. I feel pleasantly weary afterwards and a sense of well-being fills me. I was a little afraid that I might not be able to dig as my right arm has grown strangely weak during the past year and even a hard game of badminton was a painful affair. I discovered this in Dehra Dun and I think I told you about it then.

But, strange to say, digging, though a much heavier task, did not affect the forearm that way. It was the turning and twisting of badminton that gave twinges of pain. So I have dug regularly for many days and played about with the earth. In addition, I have been carrying on with some other moderate exercises, the *shirshasana*,[1] etc, and of course

1. Refers to Yogic exercises.

breathing. Quite a good deal of time is taken up by these various activities, but then one has time here.

I played a little badminton here. I did not take to it much partly because of my forearm and partly because, to begin with, I was too good for the others. I have now practically given it up.

As for books, I wade through them. I had tried to get a large assortment of them but relatively few came. Perhaps more may follow. I have enough for some time and then others here have their own lots. So it does not really matter. A large number of books round about one gives one a homely feeling and it is pleasant to choose from them and dip into odd books. With a limited number one is bound down and sometimes one has to read books which normally one would not go near.

I have just finished reading Hogben's *Science for the Citizen* – a huge tome of nearly 1100 pages, with Horrabin's illustrations. It is an amazing performance, this book, and though sometimes it is heavy reading and the mathematical formulae are none too easy, on the whole it is an astonishingly good book. I am surprised that I should have kept away from it for these five years or so since it has been out. Though perhaps I would not have had the time to read it outside, I am anxious now to read Hogben's other book – *Mathematics for the Millions* – but I cannot get it.

I suppose you know both these books though you may not have read them. Try to get them if you can and read them at leisure, skipping over the technical and more difficult parts. Chand might try reading them also.

Another fat tome that I am reading now, but a very different one, is an ancient Chinese novel,[1] written at various times several centuries ago. I have Pearl Buck's translation and it runs to 1279 pages! It is interesting, giving a picture of Chinese life and custom and as a tale it is seldom dull.

I am trying to get some more books on science in order to qualify myself to some extent at least for the presidentship of the All India Science Congress which holds its next session at Lucknow next January! Not that there is the slightest chance of my presiding over it.

This was an ideal opportunity for me to improve my Urdu. I have been trying hard to get some Urdu books from Bombay – so far without success. Meanwhile, Maulana writes down for me an Urdu couplet or two every other day out of the vast stores accumulated in his mind. Thus I am getting an insight into Urdu poetry. He has an astonishing memory and his information on a variety of subjects is encyclopaedic. He is

1. *All Men Are Brothers*, translation of the Chinese classic *Shui hu Chuan* by Shih Nai-an.

conversant enough with many trends of modern thought, reads masses of books, and yet he is essentially the eighteenth-century rationalist – the type that especially flourished in France just before the Revolution there, like Diderot,[1] etc, who were called the Encyclopaedists. He is soaked in the lore of the Middle Ages and especially of the Arab world and Western Asia and India during Muslim times. He has Plato and Aristotle at his fingertips and is perfectly at home at Cordoba[2] of Arab Spain. He is full of intimate anecdotes of kings and scholars of the past. It seems such a pity that with such vast learning and a very unusually keen mind and a powerful style, he should have written so little, when third-rate people are continually producing tenth-rate books. Do you know that when he was barely fifteen he was delivering lectures in logic and philosophy to learned audiences!

I write on – but I must take pity on the various bright persons who will have to read through all this – all the Sherlock Holmeses and the Watsons, chiefly the latter – and whose eagle eyes are ever in search of *lèse majesté*[3] against the British imperial fabric. Poor eyes – how dull they must grow at this unattractive work. But if I write too much, they might roll themselves in wrath and wreak vengeance on this letter, consigning it to some dusty pigeonhole. So I must restrain myself for otherwise I would write on and on to you and thus carry myself in fancy to some other place where you are near me and I can turn to you and see you and touch you and talk to you.

Keep well and cheerful, my dear, and make the best of this period. It does us all good if we only know how to pick out that good.

My love to you,

Your loving,
Papu

93.                             [Ahmadnagar Fort Prison,]
5th March, 1943

Darling Indu,

What an age it is since I wrote to you or had a letter from you! Ever since you were a tiny tot and learnt laboriously to spell out your letters and write a fantastic hand, I do not think there has ever been such a lengthy period without my writing to you. Whether I was in prison or you were thousands of miles away, I continued to write from time to

1. Denis Diderot (1713–1784): French encyclopaedist and philosopher.
2. During the Omayyad period (756–1031), Cordoba was a centre of Muslim and Jewish cultures and a seat of learning.
3. Treason.

time. Not so this time. Need I say how I have missed this? Two brief letters[1] came from you in mid-September and they gladdened me. I wrote in reply. Long afterwards I learnt that my letters did not reach you as no letters were allowed to détenus in the U.P.,[2] nor were they allowed to write. So that was that and I adjusted myself accordingly.

More than two months ago I read in some newspaper that you were now allowed to write. I do not put much faith in newspaper items of this kind, still there was no reason why it should not be true and I looked forward to a letter from you. None came. Then Betty wrote to me that the U.P. Govt, or someone on their behalf, had informed her officially that you could write letters. That was definite enough. Yet no letter came. I cannot make out what the position is. Whatever it is, I shall of course accept it and adjust myself to it, as one must, but not to know worries me. I am writing now hardly a proper letter, but more to find out if this reaches you, and whether it is worthwhile my writing to you. It is not much good my doing so if my letters do not reach you.

I understand you are in Naini and I am addressing this letter there, though of course it will go through the Bombay Govt and, for ought I know, through the U.P. Govt also. So far as we are concerned, we may not say where we are – that is supposed to be a dead secret, though everybody seems to know about it! So when you write to me you should address your letter c/o The Secretary to the Government of Bombay, Home Department (Political), Bombay. That I think, is the correct form, brackets and all.

Towards the end of November I received a message about you through various provincial Govts as usual. This was to the effect that you had been examined by the Civil Surgeon of Allahabad and that though your health was indifferent, there had been no marked deterioration since your arrest and detention. That was not a pleasing message and it did not cheer me up. Yet I knew that you would look after yourself wherever you might be, and would adapt yourself to your new surroundings. So I had to be content with that. Naini Prison is not a health resort at any time of the year. The female part of it is peculiarly disagreeable and it is no easy matter to put up with it. As summer approaches I find it more and more difficult not to worry about your health.

We have been here now for nearly seven months. At the end of August we were informed that we could write to certain near relatives and receive letters from them. This list of possible relatives was small enough

1. Refers to letters Nos 89 and 90.
2. Indira Gandhi was imprisoned in the Naini Central Jail, U.P., from 11th September, 1942 to 13th May, 1943.

but, so far as I was concerned, it vanished away almost to nothing, for I could not even write to you or Nan as both of you were not allowed to receive letters. The only person who remained was Betty and Betty has therefore been my window to the outside world during these months. I have written to her from time to time, not very frequently – usually once in three weeks or so. Occasionally I have written to Tara also though I was not quite sure whether a niece came in that list of approved relatives. However she seems to have got my letters. I have written to no one else. I am told that I can write two letters a week and receive four letters a week. As a matter of fact I have not even written two letters a month so far.

Early in November I was anxious to send you something for your birthday. This was not an easy matter. I tried to pick out half a dozen or more books from booksellers' catalogues. I was informed later that only one or two of them were available and these had been sent to you. Did you receive them? I do not even remember now which ones they were.

As for books, I am thinking of sending you a fat packet of them soon. It will go of course through the Bombay Govt. and I hope it reaches you. Some of them are from Anand Bhawan, others are newly purchased or sent to me by Betty. It is not a very choice selection but you may find some of interest. Nan and Chand, who I believe are with you, may like some of them. If you people can send any on to Ranjit & Feroze, you might do so. When you finish with any of these books you can get them sent to Anand Bhawan. I suppose this is possible.

As for me, I am as usual fit and healthy. I am minus one more tooth which gave me trouble and which I had pulled out here. My waistline has improved by a suitable reduction in weight!

But I am anxious to have news of you and of Nan and Chand. Also of Feroze and Ranjit, if you can give it. Tell me all about yourself. I have always believed that this jail-going, though troublesome enough and sometimes a difficult burden to carry, is good for one's education and mental development, provided one can lead the proper life. This is your first experience and you have had six months of it. I do hope you have been able to adjust yourself to it and have tried to profit even from its tremendous inconveniences and utter boredom. We begin to see life in a new perspective and new values take the place of old ones.

For my part, I am a great believer in some manual occupation in prison and so I devoted a great deal of time to gardening. There has been no expert like Ranjit with us and so we have floundered aimlessly and made many foolish mistakes. But I have dug deep and played about with the soft earth and watched the little seedlings appear and then blossom forth into a fantasy of colour. We have succeeded in converting a bare and uninviting stretch of ground with something which may be very poor from an expert gardener's point of view but is nevertheless a great relief and pleasure to us. And the amount of time and labour it has taken up! I wish you could interest yourself in gardening. I managed to get from Pocha's in Poona some dicky little garden tools.

How callous and beautiful is nature and how it carries on in its old way regardless of human woe and suffering! I have just been reading about the Greeks – I have read through all these extant tragedies and comedies – and I came across a pregnant passage. Athens had destroyed Melos utterly – unoffending, innocent Melos – and not a man or woman or child was left there to tell the tale. But soon other people came to live in that island, and once more there was corn in her little valleys and men sat in her city market place drinking the sweet wine from her hill-sides.

> Where bled her children hangs the loaded sheaf.
> Forgetful is green earth: the Gods alone
> Remember everlastingly: they strike
> Remorselessly, and ever like for like.
> By their great memories the Gods are known.

But the gods seem to have had their day and have sunk into everlasting sleep, and man, as H. G. Wells tells us, has yet to develop into *Homo Sapiens*. He is brute still and his brutish qualities are only too evident. But while war goes on with all its horror and desolation and misery, nature carries on unheeding and unconcerned.

I have a habit of forgetting where I am, and forgetting even the course of events. Sometimes I would think of Mummie and want to tell her something. Sometimes you would seem to be quite near me.

Betty sent me an electric shaver, which was very welcome as blades are scarce. I rather liked this gadget and the thought came to me that I might get one for Feroze and one for Ranjit. Then I realised that this was not easy and I could hardly reach them. And anyway they would not have electric current where they were.

Soon you will have your wedding anniversary and the first year of your wedded life will be over – most of it spent in Naini Prison! Perhaps this experience has much good in it if we know how to extract it. Life is a curious business after all, and it seems to grow curiouser. To be thrown on oneself and out of the ordinary rut of life gives us a deeper understanding and makes our lives richer and more worthwhile. It is worthwhile, anyway, to break away occasionally from the amazing triviality and utter futility of what most people call life.

I would have written to you sooner but the last three weeks or more have been abnormal and all manner of possibilities have loomed ahead and cast their shadow on us. Now that Bapu's fast[1] is successfully accomplished a weight is off my mind and I can write.

I have written a longer letter than I had intended. How could I help it when I am writing to you after seven months? My mind goes back to that early morning of August 9th when I parted from you and left you standing while the car carried me away to our unknown destination. And yet all of us are continually journeying to unknown destinations and few give thought to it!

Give my love to Nan and Chand. I hope both are well and keep good cheer. I hope Feroze and Ranjit are also well.

My love to you, my dear,
Your loving,
Papu

If it is possible for you, try to get my two letters addressed to you in September last.[2] They should be in Anand Bhawan.

---

94.                                Ahmadnagar Fort Prison,
                                        12th March, 1943

Darling Indu,

Just a week ago tonight I wrote a letter[3] to you and in this letter I promised to send you a number of books. This parcel of books has gone off today, at any rate so far as I am concerned. It is going, in the first instance, to the Bombay Government, which is our one and only window for communications, and then, if the fates so will it, it will reach you.

I enclose a list of the books. It is an odd list and a very odd collection of books. They have not been selected for your especial benefit. They are just some of the books that have come my way here and which I no longer require. Some of them will not interest you at all. Others ought to. I intended sending a few more but at the last moment some of my companions developed a passion for reading them, and so they remained. Possibly I might send you another, and a smaller, packet later on after some weeks when I know that this lot has reached you.

Lin Yu-tang's new novel – *A Leaf in the Storm*[4] – is good, though

1. Mahatma Gandhi undertook a twenty-one-day fast from 10th February to 3rd March, 1943 in protest against the Government's accusation that he was responsible for the disturbances and violence in the country after 9th August, 1942.
2. Possibly refers to letters Nos 91 and 92.
3. Refers to letter No. 93.
4. It tells the story of China in wartime.

not quite so brilliant as the one that preceded it (*Moment in Peking*). *All Men Are Brothers* is an ancient Chinese novel which takes some reading – it is nearly 1200 pages! I waded through about 1000 pages and then began to droop. Still, it is interesting in many ways and gives an insight into Chinese life and manners.

The complete collection of Greek plays is a treasure. Personally I like the so-called tragedies far better than the comedies. It is a pity that Gilbert Murray's translations are not always given. They are usually the best. Then there is Plato's *Republic*, a book for all time, if one can get into its spirit.

*Science for the Citizen* is, I am afraid, heavy reading often and sometimes the mathematics and formulae will be beyond you. Still it is an extraordinarily good book and very much worth reading and reading carefully. The best approach to it is to skip the difficult and technical passages and try to get the general hang of the progress and development of science, and even more so the spirit that lies behind science. It would be a good thing if you and Chand read it, or parts of it.

Homer Lea's *The Day of the Saxon* [1] is an extraordinary book by a very extraordinary man. It is well worth reading. So also, for entirely different reasons, are Voltaire's *Charles XII* [2] and Benjamin Franklin's *Autobiography*. [3]

The four little volumes of *U.S.S.R. Speaks for Itself* [4] are fascinating.

I have added a small book of poems by Edward Thompson – his latest, which he sent me as a Christmas present. It reached me here. It pleased me to get it.

So much for the books I am sending you – I have done a fair amount of reading since I came here, and yet it has not been nearly as much as I expected it to be. Often the mood to read is absent and I look with some distaste on rows and rows of books. But the mood passes and I go back to them. Kripalani manages to get a goodly number of them, sent by Sucheta. [5] These are usually of a lighter quality than mine.

Much of my time has been taken up by Urdu. I suppose I have made progress, yet it is extraordinarily slow work. For months past I have been

---

1. In this book the American soldier and author, Homer Lea (1876–1912), warns of conflict between the East and the West.
2. *History of Charles XII*. It gives an account of the wars fought by Charles XII, King of Sweden (1697–1718) with Poland and Russia.
3. Benjamin Franklin (1706–1790), the American patriot and scientist, wrote his autobiography in the form of a letter to his son.
4. They give an account of Russian achievement.
5. Sucheta Kripalani: active in the national movement; was a member of Lok Sabha, 1952–60, 1967–70, and Chief Minister of U.P., 1962–7. Married to J. B. Kripalani (see Political Circle).

reading a very fat tome about Akbar[1] and his times. I had read previously a good deal about him, of course from English books. This new approach from an Urdu angle, full of details, has thrown a great deal of fresh light on him. What a fascinating man he was!

And so the days pass by, and it grows warmer, and I often wonder if I am growing any the wiser for all this miscellaneous reading and the musing that inevitably accompanies it. Wiser or not, there is no doubt that I grow older, as all of us do unfortunately. Some can afford to, others are less cheerful about it.

Is it well with you, my dear? This world is none too agreeable a place for the sensitive and the thin-skinned. And yet it is better that way than to be insensitive and thick-skinned. Inevitably we harden with the impact of life; we are fortunate if that hardening is on the surface only and not of the mind and heart. For if it probes deeper, it is not well with us. Life plays strange tricks and we must not allow it to overcome us in any way. It is friendly to those who meet its challenge with straight eyes and a stout heart, and out of the very experience that it burdens us with, arises a deeper knowledge and appreciation of its significance.

My love to you and Nan and Chand.

Your loving,
Papu

Enclosure: List of books, etc.

*List of books and old magazines*
*sent by Jawaharlal Nehru to Indira Nehru Gandhi*

1. *The Complete Greek Drama* – 2 volumes
2. Hogben: *Science for the Citizen*
3. Lin Yu-tang: *With Love and Irony*
4. Do: *A Leaf in the Storm*
5. Upton Sinclair: *Between Two Worlds*
6. Edward Dahlberg: *Do These Bones Live*
7. Guenon: *East & West*
8. G. Dahlberg: *Race, Reason & Rubbish*
9. Bentwich: *Wanderer Between Two Worlds*
10. Homer Lea: *The Day of the Saxon*
11. Sohrab: *Broken Silence*
12. Postgate: *Those Foreigners*
13. Scanlon: *Very Foreign Affairs*

---

1. Akbar (1542–1605): Moghul Emperor of India. An enlightened ruler, he promoted religious toleration and banned *Sati*.

14. *All Men Are Brothers*
15. Bunyan: *The Pilgrim's Progress*
16. Douglas Reed: *All Our Tomorrows*
17. Aeschylus: *Lyrical Dramas*
18. Virgil's *Aeneid*
19. Swift: *Gulliver's Travels*
20. Do: *The Journal to Stella*
21. Voltaire: *History of Charles XII*
22. *Autobiography* of Benvenuto Cellini
23. Bjornson: *Three Comedies*
24. Do: *Three Dramas*
25. Neab: *The Fall of Constantinople*
26. E. Thompson: *The New Recessional & Other Poems*
27. *The U.S.S.R. Speaks for Itself* – 4 volumes
28. Moraes: *The Story of India*
29. Epstein: *Let There Be Sculpture*
30. C. Haldane: *Russian Newsreel*
31. H. G. Wells: *You Can't Be too Careful*
32. W. Steed: *That Bad Man*
33. Leach: *Reveille in Washington*
34. Benjamin Franklin: *Autobiography*
35. Holmes: *The Autocrat of the Breakfast Table*
36. Priestley: *Out of the People*
37. Plato: *The Republic*

*41 Volumes in all*

---

95.                                     Naini Central Prison,
                                                Allahabad,
                                        25th March, 1943


Darling, darling Papu,
At last your letter [1] has come – almost three weeks after it was written. But what is three weeks after a silence of seven months? All these months I have been waiting and waiting and was finally giving up all hope of hearing from you. And all the time, miles away, you were waiting too. You behind one set of walls and I behind another. Is it funny or is it sad? I don't really know. Soon I shall have to say with Beaumarchais's [2] Figaro: *'Je me presse de rire de tout, de peur d'être obligé*

1. Refers to letter No. 93.
2. Beaumarchais, title assumed by Pierre Augustin Caron (1732–99), French dramatist. Figaro is the hero in Beaumarchais's *Barber of Seville* and *The Marriage of Figaro*.

*d'en pleurer.'*[1] However, the fault is neither yours nor mine. Your information is quite correct. I cannot write to you of my own accord but I may reply to any letter of yours delivered to me. I told Feroze to ask his sister to write to Chhoti Puphi to let you know. It's hardly surprising that there should be a mistake!

By now you may have heard from Puphi too. She is out on parole since the 9th and isn't coming back until 5th April. I hope she has written to you.

There is a strong rumour that Chand may be released. Prisoners may come and prisoners may go but we seem to go on for ever! In the Female Ward (ghastly name) our numbers are dwindling fast. Many have served their sentence and been released, convicted prisoners with longer sentences are transferred to other jails. We are missing some of them, especially those with children. For three months we had the most adorable baby – aged four to seven months. It was fascinating to watch her grow under our very eyes, making new noises, learning some new trick each day. While she was here I took her almost completely under my wing. She flourished on the schedule we drew up for her – sunbath, massage, orange juice, etc. Though this afforded much amusement to her mother and the other women, who thought it a huge joke that such a fuss should be made over a mere baby – and a girl-child at that! I didn't realise what a lot of time I had spent on wee Sarala until suddenly it was time for her to go. She had come in dirty & miserably thin with a bad cold and a dazed look. She left, pink & round, purring with comfort & sheer content and with a mischievous twinkle in her eye. There's only one 'political' baby left now – Sardar Saheb's sister-in-law's adopted daughter: a veritable miniature Gama![2]

Feroze was transferred to Fyzabad about a couple of weeks ago. Before that we were allowed a brief interview once a fortnight. Puphi and Chand also had fortnightly interviews with Pupha. Feroze of course, being sentenced, could have the usual outside interviews. He was also allowed letters and wrote to you once, but the letter was returned to the jail by the Allahabad District Magistrate or somebody. Pupha had his old foot trouble when he was arrested but I believe he is all right now. Just before leaving for Fyzabad, Feroze had something the matter with one foot. It got swollen to a tremendous size and he was in excruciating pain for a few days. You can surely guess at the efficiency or, rather, the lack of it that prevails here in these matters as well as in all others.

Just now we are all planning ways and means of dealing with the fast

---

1. 'I make haste to laugh at everything for fear of being obliged to cry.'
2. Famous wrestler, Ghulam Mohammad, who became a household name in India, famed for his sturdiness.

approaching summer. The only practical suggestion I can think of is to keep our heads wrapped up in wet towels like the Sevagramites.[1] It isn't hot enough for that, yet, unless we go out in the sun. Actually the worst part of the day is locking-up time. It is still light and just beginning to get pleasant enough to sit out when we are herded into our hot, mosquito-infested barrack. After all these months I have still not got used to reading by lantern light, and anyway it is much too hot to sit near a lantern, so I go to bed very early. There is nothing to stay up for. Outside the moon may be up – 'the lovely moon lifting slowly her white brow among bronze cloud-waves . . . her soft light falling lightly on roof and poplar and pine'. But we cannot see her. Only rarely are Orion or the Pleiades or Cassiopeia vaguely discernible before we have between us and the stars, ugly iron bars and the red tiles of our roof. We may, later on, be allowed to sleep out.

Don't worry about me, darling. What was it Gurudev said, 'Pray not for the stilling of thy pain but for the heart to conquer it'. Through no fault of mine I have been equipped with a frail body, which has always been a great nuisance. But in spite of it – or is it because of it? – my inside is steadily getting tougher. And I think I can honestly 'thank whatever Gods may be for my unconquerable soul'. Of all the things that old Hebert[2] of Harley Street once (how long ago it now seems) said were absolutely necessary to me I have here only one: rest. But I am determined to make it take the place of all the others and more. Summer is not going to get me down.

Pupha has as usual managed to have a lovely garden and he sometimes sends us flowers. He gave some seeds to Chand, so we had some pots – petunias, cornflower, sweet sultans, poppies, nasturtiums, sweet peas and pinks. Also morning glory. Neither of us are green-fingered but it was a brave show while it lasted – the morning glory is still flourishing and the poppies but not much else. We had also a vegetable plot – about two square yards – peas, radishes, turnips, *chanbut*[3] -lettuce and *dhania*.[4] When these went to seed we had another one of tomatoes. The fruit is still green but looking sweet.

The ground here is awfully stony. In spite of the trees it has the black and bare aspect of a desert. We have only three large shady trees. Or rather had, for one of them, a stately gnarled old neem, fell with a tremendous thud the other day. It looked so strong and one would have thought it would last for ever. Its roots had all been eaten away by the

1. Inmates of Mahatma Gandhi's ashram at Sevagram.
2. Dr Hebert, a Harley Street specialist, was consulted by Indira in May and August 1939.
3. A small plant of gram.
4. Coriander.

white ants and it was rotten to the core. There was majesty in its every branch even as it lay prostrate, but almost immediately it was chopped up for firewood and removed. Only a stump now remains. Remember –

> The potent bear whose hug
> Was feared by all, is now a rug.

After the fall, Chand and another girl wanted to climb up on to the trunk, but the convicts were simply terrified and refused to allow them, saying that the evil spirits dwelling in the tree would get into their bodies!

It is really a most interesting psychological study watching these people, their superstitions and beliefs. And most interesting of all is the effect of these beliefs on their actions and their daily lives. Here one is thrown into close enough contact with village women for them to unveil their thoughts. It would take years of living and working in a village for its womenfolk to be so friendly and so unsuspicious of a stranger.

I am in what is called an association barrack – that is we do not have separate cells. Each of us has tried to have a corner to herself so as to ensure at least a minimum of privacy. It is strange – here we are all together and yet each one a world to herself, separate and aloof. So many people about and yet one is alone. More alone than if one had been in solitary confinement. I even feel I am developing the awkwardness that comes of being companionless.

> Alone . . . The word is life endured and known.
> It is the stillness where our spirits walk
> And all but inmost faith is overthrown.

The second lot of books you mention have not arrived. Of the first, two came – *Wild is the River* by Louis Bromfield,[1] and a *Told to the children* edition of Don Quixote. Puphi & I couldn't believe you had sent them. I cannot imagine your reading Bromfield, to say nothing of liking him. And why should you send an abridged edition of Quixote when you know I have the complete one and even large chunks of the original Spanish?

I haven't been reading anything special – there isn't anyone to send books. Had I known that I would be here for such a long time I might have made some arrangements. I have read a lot of old books – classical and otherwise, Balzac, Rousseau and so on – that one is always meaning

---

1. Louis Bromfield (1896–1956): American novelist and playwright whose works include *Night in Bombay*.

to read but somehow keeps on postponing. Two new novels I liked. Phyllis Bottome's *London Pride*, the story of a little Cockney boy's courage during the blitz. How well she writes! The second is Lin Yu-tang's *A Leaf in the Storm*, which is the sequel to *Moment in Peking*. Have you, I wonder, come across *An Anthology of Modern Verse* compiled by A. Methuen. It is quite an old one – first appeared in 1921. But it has taken me all these years to discover it. It is one of the richest anthologies of its kind that I have ever seen, and Robert Lynd has written a perfectly delightful introduction to it. Another lovely book I've read here is Van Loon's *Acts of Mankind*. I have sent for that fat tome – *The Science of Life*, do you remember, you sent it to me in Santiniketan? Its size is rather terrifying and not too easy to cope with in the rushing hither and thither that constitutes our daily life outside. Later I think I might re-read *War and Peace*. Interesting too, though long and wordy, is Upton Sinclair's *The Dragon's Teeth*, a very vivid and realistic portrayal of Europe just before the war. An altogether different kind of book which we all enjoyed was Verrier Elwin's detective story about the clouds, *A Cloud that's Dragonish*. Very fresh and light reading.

Rita, I hear, has acquired a new dog – a terrier. It's called 'Spring Breeze' and came to her by air from Calcutta!

I seem to be ambling on and on. This is what comes of being 'alone' – when one starts talking one doesn't know where to stop. Write soon. Write often. Tell me about yourself. How is your arm? The one that was worrying you in Dehra. I hope it doesn't pain or trouble you any more, and that you are looking after it and the rest of yourself too.

Lots and lots of love to you,

Indu

96. Ahmadnagar Fort Prison,
26th March, 1943

Indu Darling,
This is the third letter I am writing to you this month. The two previous ones were dated 5th and 12th March.[1] I mention this so that you and I might know if my letters are reaching you. Previously I had written to you on September 18th[2] (the first letter I wrote from this place) and on October 15th,[3] but both these did not reach you.

1. Refers to letters Nos 93 and 94.
2. Refers to letter No. 91.
3. Refers to letter No. 92.

Some light has been thrown on the mystery of our correspondence – indirectly of course – but I am still by no means sure what the fate of my letters is. Something about it appeared in a newspaper and last week I received a letter from Betty in which she quoted a few lines from a message she had from Nan. Nan explained that while I could write to you and to her, neither of you could take the initiative in the matter. But you could answer my letters! This is all very complicated and my poor mind took some time to grasp the situation. However, I have written to you already and so have done my job.

It is an odd arrangement, but everything is pretty odd nowadays. What amazes me is the fact that the U.P. Government, or whoever is responsible for this business, should have taken no steps whatever to inform me of it, for unless I knew and took action, no one else could take the initiative. It was not much good your knowing for you could not write to me unless I wrote to you previously. Even now I have had no formal or official intimation and if Nan had not succeeded in sending me a message through Betty, I would have remained in the dark. I cannot rely on newspaper reports as they have misled me in the past and led me to believe during these last three months that you could and were going to write to me.

Even now I am by no means certain. This assurance will only come to me when I get a letter from you. Betty tells me that Nan wrote to me nearly three weeks ago – soon after coming out for her brief period. This letter of hers has not reached me so far.

So now if you want to send a message to our house in Allahabad or elsewhere, the way is simple and clear. I write to you so that you can send an answer; then you write to me and your letter passes through various governments and censors and possibly reaches me ultimately. Then I convey your message to Betty, and lastly Betty writes to Allahabad! With luck all this may be done well within two months. We must learn from these swift and efficient ways of doing business.

Anyway if there are any books or anything else which you require and have no other means of getting, you can adopt this course and let me know. I shall try to set this intricate machinery in action. Possibly Chand may require some particular books. It is not very easy to get the books one wants. Few new books seem to come and of the old books, the Bombay booksellers seem to avoid the decent ones – possibly there is little market for them.

I might mention that I sent you a case full of odd books on March 12th.

Normally I shall keep writing to you once a week. Occasionally I might write to Nan or Chand. In any case someone of you three ought to get a letter from me every week. If it is not forthcoming or is delayed, the fault lies elsewhere. Last week I did not write to you but wrote to Nan instead at Anand Bhawan.

Having said so much about the procedure of writing, I suppose I had better come to the substance of the letter. And yet there is not much substance in a letter from one prison to another, unless one takes to analysing and recording states of mind – an alarming undertaking! There is little else that happens within prison walls, short of physical illness. Many succumb to this illness, but that change & variety does not come my way and I have no intention of allowing it to do so.

In a sense I have had a novel experience this time. Previously I was kept alone or with one companion. Now we are a round dozen and many of them very interesting companions. The brightest of companions is apt to pall on one in the inescapable intimacy of prison. Still, this is a definite advantage. Sometimes, especially in the evenings, some of us emerge out of our shells and talk on all manner of subjects: the development of the war situation, international affairs, national happenings, politics, religion, science, philosophy, ethics, art, economics, linguistics, literature, cooking, gardening, India old & new, China, Europe, America, the ancient civilisations, the future & so on and so forth – anything to take us out of ourselves and give us the feeling of activity – mental if not physical.

You may be surprised to learn how many languages are represented in our group, nearly all of them in a scholarly way. Of classical languages: Sanskrit, Pali, Arabic and Persian. Of modern Indian languages: Hindi and Urdu, Gujrati & Marathi, Bengali & Oriya, Tamil and Telugu, and Sindhi – also a little Punjabi. Then of course English, and a smattering of French and German. A formidable list, yet we are no dwellers in Babel. In a sense, it is an ideal opportunity to learn some of these languages and some of us are pegging away at them. But life is too short for this business, especially at our respective ages. For my part Urdu is all I have taken up so far. But I nourish a secret hankering to read *Shakuntala*[1] in the original Sanskrit with Narendra Deva,[2] and to learn a little modern Persian from the Maulana, an ideal teacher, except that he is too erudite. Meanwhile, the Maulana, out of the vast stores accumulated in his mind, throws out a few Urdu verses at me every few days, and sometimes even an Arabic or Persian couplet, which I transcribe painfully. Thus I have collected some hundreds. But I have a feeble memory.

1. *Shakuntala*: a well-known Sanskrit drama by the classical poet and playwright Kalidas.
2. Narendra Deva: eminent socialist and scholar; participated in the freedom movement; associated with Kashi Vidyapith; was also Vice-Chancellor of Lucknow and Benares Hindu Universities.

And I read of course – a miscellaneous assortment of books, old & new. Just at present one of the books I am entangled in is Lewis Carroll's collected works. They bring back memories of my childhood to me and I love reading his stories & verses. I have a fine edition – Nonesuch Press. It had a lovely cover but that, alas, is no more. Poor Alice had a new adventure when she travelled to this unknown part of the world. She came with a mixed retinue of books, clothes, cigarettes and oddments, including bottles of delicious honey which Psyche sometimes sends. The honey was really quite separate but some wise person in the Bombay Secretariat forced the honey bottles into the suitcase. And when the case was opened I saw a ghastly sight – the very horror of it fascinated me. There was honey, honey everywhere, flowing, sticking, oozing out all over the place. Alice was swimming in it. Well, having survived the first shock, we began our work of salvage. But Alice bears traces of it to this day, and the cover is no more, and in spite of all the wiping and drying & sunning, ants smell their way to her. I think I shall send this book to you in my next lot next month. That is if the first lot has reached you –

You will be sorry to learn that Yunus is very ill and has grown even thinner than he was. It is T.B., so Betty writes. He is at present in detention in Abbottabad. I am very worried about him. He is one of the most likeable persons I have come across.

I understand from a message sent by Amma (through Betty) that Kailas and Sheila are flourishing in London –

It is warming up here. So it must be in Naini.

Keep well and cheerful, my dear. My love to you.

Your loving,<br>Papu

---

97.                           Ahmadnagar Fort Prison
2nd April, 1943

Indu Darling,

This is letter No. 4, new series. No. 1 was sent on March 5th, [1] that is nearly a month ago. An answer to this is due. I await it daily.

The day after I wrote to you last week [2] I received Nan's letter from Anand Bhawan. Tell her of this and also that I shall write to her next week. I presume she will be with you again by the time you receive this letter. This week I am writing to Betty, apart from this letter to you. I

1. Refers to letter No. 93.
2. Refers to letter No. 96.

have fixed upon Friday evenings for writing and I propose to write two letters every week, one of these being to you. On Saturday morning I hand these letters to the emblem of authority here and I understand that they are sent off, under registered cover, the same day. Presumably they are delivered at the Bombay Secretariat on Monday. After that what happens to them and how long they take in reaching you I do not know. They should not take more than ten days at most from the time of my writing.

Nan's letter gave some news of your health – how you were unwell for about six weeks after your arrest and had a rise in temperature but that later you recovered. I understand now why it was necessary for the Civil Surgeon of Allahabad to examine you in Naini. His message, sent to me through Government, bears a special meaning now. It said that your health was indifferent on the whole but that there had been no marked deterioration since your arrest and detention. Considering that when arrested you were running a temperature and were unwell, this was not saying much. However, I am glad you kept well during the winter. The test will be during the next three months. This will be your first full summer in the plains since – when? I really do not remember but it was years and years ago, somewhere in the middle Twenties, I imagine, when you were about three feet or less in height. It will be a change after the Swiss winters and Kashmir last year.

Personally I think this fear of the heat is, partly at least, psychological. One can largely ignore it if one sets about it the right way. It is not possible wholly to forget it or not to be affected by it. Still, I hope you will face the heat intelligently and feel a little friendly to it, as I have more or less succeeded in doing.

We are getting on here – it is over 100°F in the shade and the midday hot wind reminds us a little of the *loo*[1] . . .

What has happened to your little house in Tagore Town? I hope you have given it up and are not holding on to it. That was hardly worthwhile. And where is your furniture and your marvellous radio? Safe and properly looked after, I hope.

That reminds me that we have now got a gramophone here! Of course Sucheta is responsible for sending it to Kripalani. It came a few days ago with a fair selection of records – nothing very highbrow. Then a dozen records of European music and two dozen Indian ones. I wished there might have been some Beethoven records. And then I thought how good it would be if you could have your gramophone & Beethoven.

Nan writes that Feroze tried to send me a letter but did not succeed. Why this failure I do not know for the ways of the U.P. Govt are peculiar.

---

1. Hot winds that blow across the Indian plains in summer.

Feroze, on his side, is allowed to write and I am told that a son-in-law is on the favoured list of those I can correspond with. What is Feroze's sentence?

I learn from Betty that Yunus is better now and rejoicing in the coming of spring in Abbottabad or at least he was when he wrote to her.

Buddhi, [1] so Nan wrote, has become expert at making Chinese dishes under the guidance of Mrs Chew. This is tantalising, but I shall hold my soul in patience. Do you know those lines, to be sung or recited with slow solemnity, after the well-known air, and with a proper mixture of pathos and romance? I do not remember them myself very well but here is an attempt to reproduce some of them:

> There is a boarding house, far far away,
> Where they give ham and eggs,
> Three times a day.
> Oh! how the boarders yell
> When they hear the dinner bell
> Three times a day!

And so on. Of course we do not have ham and eggs here – we have the local substitute – and, need I say, we do not yell. We are much too polite and restrained.

The subject of food reminds me that you should have plenty of fruit. Whether you get it or not I do not know. Allahabad is poor in fruit at this time of the year. So I am asking Betty to arrange with a fruiterer in Bombay to send you a weekly parcel to Naini C.P.

Who are your companions? I have just seen in the papers that Chand has been released – I sent her a letter last week to Naini. This will miss her now – I hope you are not alone now, for Nan also will not be back for another three days. Is Nora with you?

I was glad to learn that you can have a fortnightly interview with Feroze.

I am collecting more books to send you.

All my love to you, darling,

Your loving,<br>Papu

———————————

1. Buddhilal was cook in Anand Bhawan.

98.                                                          Naini Central Prison,
                                                                          Allahabad,
                                                                    6th April, 1943

Darling One,
I did not reply to your letter of the 12th March [1] immediately for I was
waiting for the books to arrive. However, there are no signs of them yet,
and meanwhile your letter of the 26th [2] came last evening – on our
'Naoroz'. So I am not waiting any longer. Your first two letters [3]
delivered to me took almost three weeks to reach me but this last one
has come in ten days – a considerable improvement.

Meanwhile Chand has been released. Now we are only three of us in
our barrack. It's like the old old song 'Ten Little Nigger Boys'!

> Four little Indian girls sat down to tea
> One was released & then there were three.

Nora keeps on harping on the idea that eventually there will be only
one left – herself. By the way, she sends you her regards.

I am looking forward to the books & I do so hope they will come soon
and all of them. Some of them – a very few – I have already got
here. Among them: Franklin's *Autobiography*, Plato's *Republic*, Benvenuto
Cellini's *Autobiography*. The autobiographies are in the Jail Library
which also contains – *The Confessions of an English Opium Eater, Memoirs
of Madame Pompadour, Confessions of Rousseau & of St. Augustine*. The
Jail Library has some good books – I read John Stuart Mill's *Essay on
Liberty* here and also *The Autocrat of the Breakfast Table* – but usually they
are extremely difficult to get hold of. *All Men Are Brothers* is a book that
I have long wanted to peep into. Hasn't it been translated by Lin
Yu-tang? A long time ago Mamu gave me *Mathematics for the Millions*
and as far as I remember you did not approve of it then. Have you got
that too?

I have been reading quite a lot of French books – the ones Mademoiselle Hemmerlin sent me in 1932! One or two novels were good.

It's getting quite hot now, only the mornings and the part of
the evening spent outside the barrack are bearable. But as far as
reading or any other work is concerned, even the mornings are not
much use . . . [4]

Often we have visitors in the night. Bartholomew Bat is the one I

1. Refers to letter No. 94.
2. Refers to letter No. 96.
3. Refers to letters Nos 93 and 94.
4. Deleted by censors.

dislike most. In the days when Knights were bold, they used to give names to their swords. Following that charming custom, I have given names to all the animals and insects, & lots of other things besides, which come here. Among our nightly visitors are, Minto & Morley Musk-rat (their predecessor Montague was killed by Mehitabel, the cat) and Marmaduke, who is the husband of Mehitabel. Marmaduke is an errant coward and is most unbeautiful, though he has a marked resemblance to Mr Gladstone. He only comes at night. On the other hand, Mehitabel is very pretty and is our constant companion as also are her kittens Kanhaiya, Moti and Parvati.

I am feeling quite worried about Yunus. Is he still in detention? Just before Feroze left he told me that he thought Yunus had been released. Fortunately Abbottabad has a better climate than most places in India except in the rainy months. What happened to the much-talked-about book? During the A.I.C.C. Yunus wrote to say that it would soon be out. If Yunus is in detention he may be able to write to me – that is if he is well enough to write. All accent is on the word 'may'. For nobody seems to know anything for a definite fact. However, we have been led to believe that if any prisoner or détenu outside the U.P., wrote to a détenu in the U.P. and the Government saw fit to deliver the letter, the U.P. détenu would be allowed to reply. Will you mention this to Chhoti Puphi (I think she is in Allahabad now). If it were possible I should like to have news direct.

Last year I sent for good old Otto and tried to do some German on my own. But the key to the German is nowhere to be found and as there was no one to correct my exercises there was not much point in continuing with them, so I gradually dropped off. I read a bit now and then, and have memorised some poetry.

And speaking of poetry – why can't I share the Maulana's treasures with you? If in each letter you wrote out a couplet or verse, either in Urdu or Hindi, I should soon have a little collection of the most delectable. Nora & I have been trying to get hold of Ghalib [1] but without success. We are both very keen on Urdu but there is no one to teach us, and the books we have (mostly children's tales) are not interesting enough for solitary plodding. However, now that I have dropped German I shall devote some time each day to reading them, just to get more used to the script. Unfortunately my vocabulary is very feeble. I sent for your Hindi-Urdu Dictionary but it was not found.

Since Puphi has left, I have had to learn to cook – actually I learnt watching her. But now I have to manage on my own. I rather like it,

1. Asadullah Khan Ghalib (1797–1869): Urdu poet.

though I don't think I'm interested enough in food to ever make a good cook. Besides, raw vegetables are so much more appetising than cooked ones. If it weren't for the trouble to other people I think I would have taken to a raw diet ages ago! What do you have in the way of food? Do you all eat together? And can you order whatever you like? Before my arrest Mrs Naidu wrote to Bebee to say that she was having good food and as many hot baths as she wanted!

By the way, have you any news of Bebee? Let me know.

Trying out a new exercise, I sprained my right shoulder and it has been behaving very badly indeed. Even writing has become a painful job. It is slightly better now. How is your arm?

Much much love,
Indu

99.                                                    Ahmadnagar Fort Prison,
                                                       9th April, 1943

Darling Indu,
This is letter No. 5. I am still looking forward to your letter which has taken an unconscionable time in coming. I am sure the fault is not yours. The tortuous methods which are applied to our correspondence, and possibly a lack of care, lead to amazing delays. It takes Mahmud quite a month sometimes to get a letter from his wife in Chapra. She is ill and he is naturally anxious but he has to put up with this.

I would have begun to doubt about my own letters reaching you. But some days ago I was informed officially (through a communication sent from the Bombay Secretariat) that my letters and a parcel of books had been forwarded to you. The first letter was apparently sent to the U.P. Government, the others direct to Naini Prison. So I suppose they reached you ultimately.

Fortunately I had another letter from Nan from Anand Bhawan and in this she gave me an account of your life in Naini. I was happy to read this and to find that you had adapted yourself to this new existence with energy and with humour. The odd names that you and Chand had given to almost everything within your reach were amusing and I laughed at several of them. It is surprising how much amusement we can extract from the dullest environment and from the most unpromising material, if only we know how to set about it. Evidently you know this art, and because of this you are favoured of the gods. Nothing is more foolish than to put on a long and tragic face at happenings we do not like – yet most of us do it, I am afraid, from time to time. The world is too tragic for us also to be tragic. But there is another side to the world also, which smiles and laughs and is ever playing tricks with us. Even prison walls cannot keep this out wholly.

Nan writes that you were all greatly intrigued when you received two books purporting to come from me – a child's edition of *Don Quixote* and a novel by Louis Bromfield. I thought you would be. It happened this way. Early in November the desire to send you something for your birthday caught hold of me. I did not know what to send and how to send it from here. Books were indicated, but how to get them? I happened to have a new catalogue of the New Book Co. of Taraporevalas of Bombay. There were a number of new books mentioned in it. Some of these were by good authors, some others were obscure but something about their names or authorship attracted me – I made a list of about ten books, adding *Don Quixote* for good weight or measure. I felt that *Don Q.* might be interesting reading in prison. Of course I did not mean a child's edition of it. This list was sent subsequently to the Bombay Govt with the request that they might arrange to purchase and send these books to you on my behalf. Long afterwards I was informed that they could only get two of them and that these had been sent to you. Presumably they were sent to the U.P. Govt first so that all the formalities and mysteries might be preserved.

Today I am arranging to send you a few more books. They are:

1. *A New Anthology of Modern Poetry*
2. Ferdinand Czermin: *Europe Going, Going, Gone!*
3. Virginia Woolf: *Between the Acts*
4. Lewis Carroll: *Complete Works*
5. Thomas Reveille: *The Spoil of Europe*
6. A pocket diary for 1943
7. *Saur Roznamcha* or Hindi diary for *Samvat* 2000

For most people following the *Samvat* era,[1] the New Year began four days ago with the new moon. But some reformers want to make the months conform to the solar pattern more and they have fixed April 14th as the first day of the year. The *Saur Roznamcha* I am sending you

1. *Samvat* era: Birthdays and other events in India are celebrated on the basis of either the Christian era (reckoned by the Gregorian Calendar) or the *Samvat* era or other traditional eras. To convert a date in the *Samvat* era into a date in the Christian era fifty-seven years have to be deducted.

The Gregorian Calendar is a solar calendar based on the relative positions of the sun and earth, whereas the *Samvat* Calendar is based on the relative positions of the sun, the earth and the moon. As a result, events computed on the basis of the *Samvat* Calendar fall on different dates of the Gregorian Calendar. The Nehrus generally observed the *Samvat* Calendar in their household so far as birthdays, etc, were concerned, but Jawaharlal Nehru apparently preferred the Gregorian Calendar.

begins on April 14th. Curiously enough this is *Rama Naumi* day, the anniversary, according to the *Samvat*, of your wedding. [1] Among Kashmiris, of course, *Naoroz* (which is a big day for them) takes place according to the lunar reckoning. It was on April 5th last – how did you observe it? Nan wrote that you there welcomed in the New Year (January 1st) in proper style.

The coming of a New Year always affects us, or most of us, as if we were really turning over a new leaf. What then of a new century and, even more so, a new millennium (in the mathematical sense)? You will remember how in the past this has led to great excitement. The end of the first 1000 years after Christ led to Peter the Hermit [2] and widespread hysteria and the Crusades. Most people in Christendom thought that the world was ending. A thousand years after the Hegira [3] also made people imagine that the old world was ending and a 'new order' was going to begin. Akbar tried to give a push to this by his *Din-e-Ilahi* [4] but the world did not change very much.

Now for years past people have dreamed and imagined and prophesied that *Samvat* 2000 was the critical year in human history. Well, there is enough of crisis all over the place to justify that prediction at least! But what will come out of it is more than the stoutest of prophets can say. Always the human mind, consciously or subconsciously, yearns for a change for the better and builds up castles in the air of a better world to come – usually as if by a miracle. But miracles only seem to occur in old books. A New Year! Yet every day is a new beginning for us, every moment the old world dies and something new takes its place. How many dead selves we have, each one of us, about us, round which cluster innumerable memories! We seem to be continually dying and being continually reborn. Every moment that is past is dead and we who lived it are dead with it; every moment that is yet to come is a mystery and we look with hope towards it.

And so may it be well with you in this new *Samvat* year and the new century and the new millennium, and as the mystery of the future unfolds itself in the brief living present, may it ever bring fulfilment to your being.

1. In 1943, the anniversary of Indira's wedding according to the *Samvat* Calendar fell on 14th April, the *Rama Naumi* day (the birthday of Lord Rama, the semi-divine hero of Hindu mythology). Indira Gandhi got married on 26th March, 1942, according to the Gregorian Calendar.

2. Peter the Hermit (1050–1115): ascetic and preacher who played a prominent part in the launching of the First Crusade.

3. Hegira: the flight of Mohammed from Mecca, AD 622.

4. A religious circle created by the Emperor Akbar which drew in its fold Hindu and Muslim notables from his court.

Today we have completed eight months, and you just seven months, for we had a month's start of you. And the summer months, long and hot, steal over us, to give place later to the miracle of the rains. So the cycle of nature goes round, heedless apparently of what happens to that insignificant animal, man, who presumes so much and yet is so beast-like still. Yet he has something big, something worthwhile in him and perhaps, perhaps . . .

I am glad you have been spending some time over Sanskrit and Hindi. Sanskrit is really wonderful – I wish I knew it well. But I am past learning it now – I am stupid at languages. Yet it is something even to be able to read Kalidas or Bhavabhuti[1] with some understanding.

I have asked Betty to arrange with a fruiterer in Bombay to send you a weekly parcel of fruit – I hope this reaches you in good condition.

Nan writes that Feroze has been transferred to Fyzabad. That is a pity for in Naini you could sometimes see him.

My *Glimpses of World History* came out in an American edition last year. A copy of it managed to reach me here. It is exactly like the English edition, even the cover. It is amusing to learn that many persons who had previously not cared to read it, thinking it a child's book, are now, in prison, reading it and finding out how mistaken they were. Mahmud is so enamoured of it that he wants to read its thousand pages again and again. Pantji is sufficiently impressed, and so, Betty writes, is Raja in Yeravada Prison.

As I was writing this letter news came of the death of Maulana's wife. In a sense we had been partly prepared for bad news. Still hardly anyone here expected this sudden end. She had not been well for some time but only two months ago she was well enough to plan to go to the hills. Some sudden change pulled her down. It is a great shock to all of us, and you can well imagine what it is for the Maulana – I have come to know him very intimately during these months here. I knew well how full of learning he was, how wise in counsel. I have found him to be also a very brave and gallant gentleman, a finished product of the culture that, in these disturbed days, unhappily pertains to few – I am greatly exercised. I wish I could do something for him. But what can I do? I hardly dare go to him.

I am writing separately to Nan. I shall send this letter to Anand Bhawan as her parole has been extended, but it is just possible that she may miss my letter.

You must feel a little lonely since Chand left you. I do not yet know who your other companions are except that Nora is with you. A little

1. Bhavabhuti: celebrated Sanskrit dramatist who flourished in the eighth century AD.

dose of more or less solitary living is not bad for one, provided one can adapt oneself to it. In a sense you have had experience of it in sanatoria in Switzerland. But what a comparison I make! Naini Prison and a Swiss sanatorium at Leysin.

I have been reading Bernard Shaw's plays again. Twice I have read them previously and seen some of them on the stage. And now for the third time I am going through the lot. It is surprising how much there is in them. What a wise man he is, full of the deepest understanding of life, which often he covers with his levity and over-smartness. Few writers provoke me to thought so much as he does. I am sorry when I think that I am never likely to meet him. He is eighty-seven years old now – I once saw him at Cambridge when I was an undergraduate there. Not again. [1]

Love,<br>
Your loving,<br>
Papu

100.                                        Naini Central Prison,
                                                       Allahabad,
                                            12th April, 1943

Darling Papu,

Your letter of the 2nd April [2] was handed to me just before lock-up. I was surprised to hear that you have not received even my first letter yet. I have written two: one on 25th March [3] and the other on 6th April. [4] Official news of the parcel of books you are sending has come to the Superintendent in the form of a list of the books and intimation that they will come by railway parcel.

As soon as the key turned in the lock, I hastened with pen and paper and lantern to write to you. Then I thought that I had better prepare dinner first. The eggs were just cooking and I was balancing on my haunches over the stove, when a tremendous gust of dust burst in upon us and 'turned me and near inurned' me. The next five minutes were spent in a mad rush retrieving flying paper, sheets, dusters, etc, and trying to save the other things from the onslaught of dust. For the most important things – ourselves – there was neither opportunity nor means: the only thing possible, which I did, was to wrap my sari well over my head and to flatten myself against the wall, thus hoping that the main

1. In fact Jawaharlal Nehru and George Bernard Shaw were to meet in 1949.
2. Refers to letter No. 97.
3. Refers to letter No. 95.
4. Refers to letter No. 98.

gusts would sweep past me. However, the dust is cleverer than to be taken in by such a simple ruse. Nora, in the meantime, was feeling in a gay mood and in between coughing and choking was singing *mausam salona hai!*[1] It is the refrain of a record we have here. Whether her singing had the desired effect on the Heavens, I don't know, but at this stage came the welcome drip, drip of enormous raindrops and the downpour started in real earnest. I emerged from my corner to sniff at the lovely fresh smell that the rain alone can draw forth from out of the parched earth. How funny everybody looked, eyebrows and eyelashes white with dust!

Now, after a meal of *oeufs à la poussière,*[2] which I do not recommend to anyone, I am sitting down to write. Peace reigns again in our barrack. As I sit by the dim lantern, the kitten Parvati curled up in a snowy ball at my feet, a soft cool breeze is blowing in with incredible caressing messages from the lightning and thunder and rain, and the beauty of the storm-tossed night outside – the night which my complexion was supposed to resemble. Remember the Paris journal: *brune comme une nuit d'été?*[3]

We have a gramophone too – it has been lent to us. We keep it for brief periods, then return it, then send for it again. The records are not up to much – only three nice ones, which we play over and over again. One of them is a song that Kanta of Lahore sang at several of the parties there. Yes, I miss a lot of things but nothing as much as Beethoven and Bach. That is because Beethoven could have brought the snow-covered mountains and green green pastures with rivulets rushing across them right here in our bleak yard.

I was glad to hear that Yunus is better. I hope he uses this opportunity for a thorough rest which will take him a long way towards complete recovery.

The house has not been given up yet. At first I did not know how long I would be here, and so decided to keep it on. I heard that after my arrest, Upadhyaya rented half of it to somebody. The other half is now occupied by Mrs Varma.[4] After Varmaji's arrest she had to give up her house, so as mine was lying vacant I thought it would save her a lot of bother to stay there while looking round for something else. Now that I seem to be staying on here almost indefinitely, something had better be done about it, but it is difficult, for I have no means of contacting my sister-in-law or anybody who could see to the whole thing.

Do you have Indian food? And which variety of it? We get fixed ration:

1. The weather is fine.
2. After a 'dusty' meal of eggs.
3. Golden like a summer's night.
4. The wife of a Congressman who was a friend of Indira and Feroze Gandhi.

so much *ata* [1] & so much rice, and so on. Quantitatively there is enough & more than enough. But as you know it is no good to me at all. On alternate days I exchange the whole of my flour and rice for a loaf of bread. Apart from these fixed rations I am allowed, as an 'A' class prisoner, three as extra. Out of this I get two eggs, which, with some milk, constitute my dinner. Chand has a great repertoire of these ghastly songs about eggs and toothbrushes and so on, which she used to sing, changing the words slightly to suit our circumstances better.

In our rations we get two oranges on five days of the week. I am also allowed to get fruit from home. So there is plenty at the moment. I even had a taste of *cheekoos* [2] when Chhoti Puphi came to Allahabad. Don't send any more just yet. May be as the summer goes on and there is a dearth of fruit, some may be sent from Bombay.

I think your letter to Chand has been sent on to her to Anand Bhawan.

I have been reading so much and so fast this last week that my head is in quite a whirl. What an awful habit it is always to want to do something. We laugh at the 'oldest inhabitant' who said: Sometimes I sit and think and sometimes I just sit. And yet it is no mean achievement – how many of us city dwellers could sit quietly of an evening and relax not only one's body but one's mind as well? But no, even when the body is resting the mind goes racing on thinking, thinking to no purpose. Outside at least thoughts can be diverted or translated into action but here they can only go round and round, can only lead to frustration. One can't do nothing all the time – though I feel the oldest inhabitant is justified even in that, for has he not passed the major part of his life (a longer life than most's) in hard gruelling work in the daytime, boister-ous fun in the evenings with no time for thoughts – idle or otherwise? The true value of inaction and relaxation is only when it comes in the midst of action and activity. 'Let my doing nothing when I have nothing to do become untroubled in its depth of peace like the evening in the seashore when the sea is silent.' Gurudev has something to say about everything and he says it so simply and clearly and beautifully.

And while we are on the subject of quotations, I must give you another one. I have just read a lovely article in *New Writing* called 'Metamor-phosis of the Snow' by André Chamson. [3] He describes an excursion on skis. So vivid it was, I could all but feel the cold air through my hair and sharpness of the newly fallen snow cutting into my features. I thought I must share this with Papu. So here it is only a small portion, naturally.

1. Flour.
2. Sapodilla.
3. André Chamson: French novelist and essayist.

I am deaf and oblivious to all, as when earlier I struggled up the slope.
But now, it is no longer my efforts which have swept me clear of
thought, it is whistling joy, the dizzy flight of a stone hurled endlessly
into the abyss, its whole nature transformed by the sole fact of its
speed. All consciousness has vanished in my wild concentration on
the motion that sweeps me on; and, as always, when keyed up to this
point, there is a strong feeling of pleasure.

How correctly and minutely he has caught the spirit of skiing!

Alas – we are far from snow and skiing. But we can and do have rain
and Lord, how beautiful it is. Is this weather usual at this time of the
year? Or will it ruin the crops and especially the wee little mangoes just
out? Ever since I wrote my last letter, we have been having rain off and
on and it has been quite cool especially in the nights.

You give no news of your arm, so I hope it has not been troubling
you. Look after yourself.

Much much love, darling one,

Indu

P.S.                                                              *13th April*
The books have at last arrived. They are all there, plus one which you
do not mention – Virgil's *Aeneid*. Shall write more about them in my
next letter.

Love,

Indu

---

101.                                              Ahmadnagar Fort Prison,
                                                     16th April, 1943

Darling Indu,
At last a letter [1] from you. It was so exciting to have it after this long
waiting for it. It came three days ago, just twenty days after you wrote
it. Today I had a letter from Chand also from Anand Bhawan and she
gave me some further news of your life together – and about the baby!
This is my letter No. 6.

What shall I write to you, my dear? Of course I can write about a host
of things. Reading your letter again I realise what a powerful effect jail
has on our mental make-ups. It makes us grow up mentally and gives
us a different, and perhaps a truer, perspective on life and the world.
Partly because we are thrown on our own mental resources much more

1. Refers to letter No. 95.

than elsewhere, partly because of new experiences, new companions, so different from those we are used to. All of us are apt to live and move in our own little grooves, imagining that one's own particular rut is an epitome of the world. It is curious that jail life, which is a terrible narrowing of the world of experience and sensation, often gives us deeper experiences and sensations. It depends on the individual and his or her capacity to receive and profit by these new experiences and thus to grow in mind. Some do not and cannot profit by them and are even injured mentally and, of course, physically. Others develop a richer life, a deeper understanding, a more human outlook and a poise which gives a tone to their whole existence. For my part, I have no doubt that I have managed to profit by my visits to jail. The very lack of things in jail, the absence of normal family and social life, the long hours alone, the want of the most ordinary amenities we are so used to and take for granted, give a value and significance to them and we enjoy them all the more when we have the chance. Prison is the true home of that dreadful thing ennui, and yet, oddly enough, it teaches us to triumph over it. And so we grow more vital, more aware of the manifold variety of life and even, in a sense, younger in mind. That is, in a sense, a contradiction, for the mind grows older too in prison, or at best more mature. But then life is full of such contradictions. Immaturity is not really youth; it is more like childhood.

Being your father, my mind inevitably goes back to a similar period of my own growth. I took a mighty long time in growing – perhaps I am not quite grown-up yet? Or, more correctly, I am grown-up in part only; the rest of me is still struggling to find out and understand. I was amazingly non-grown-up even in my middle twenties and even afterwards the process was slow. Possibly that is why I am still younger in mind and body than almost all my contemporaries. I imagine you are more grown-up now than I was when I was your age. That is easily understandable for you have lived through a far more turbulent period of history than I had done then. My life till then had been quiet and peaceful and almost uneventful – the events were piling up for later years.

It was about the time of your birth, or soon after, that these events started on their mad career. Almost you were a child of a turbulent world. I do not know what memories of these early days you carry about you. But whether you remember them or not, they must have influenced you and subconsciously they must cling to you. You wrote to me once about the old days in Anand Bhawan. But you have no real experience of those old days, for the great change came in our lives when you were a babe in arms. It is difficult for the younger generations to picture to themselves that world which vanished, it seems now, so long ago. They have lived all their young lives transitionally, and we have all become travellers and wayfarers marching on and on, sometimes footsore and weary, but without resting place or haven. Yet, for those who can adapt themselves to this continuous journeying, there is no regret and they would not have it otherwise. A return to the dull and uneventful past is unthinkable.

I have few regrets. But there is one that in your childhood and early girlhood I saw so little of you.

Your inside is tough of course, I know that. I want that outside of yours also to grow tough. It is a nuisance otherwise. I am sure that you will succeed in strengthening your body. It requires will and intelligence. Do you know that Dadu was considered to be a weakly infant and the family had a bad record then of disease and early death. Everybody thought that Dadu would follow this bad example. But, because of this, even in his early boyhood he made up his mind to be strong physically and he took all the care he could. He succeeded. I was also an ailing infant and child and I did not turn the corner till my boyhood. But I did turn the corner and I have since been an unusual example of good health and vitality. This did not happen of itself. I worked to that end.

So I am sure you will get over your physical weakness and your frail body will grow strong and fit. This will take time and require attention. These summer months in Naini, or wherever you might be put, will be a trial for you, for this will be almost your first experience of a summer in the plains. It is unfortunate that this first experience should be in the unwholesome surroundings of Naini Prison. Yet it does not matter and you may be even the better for the experience.

I remember how frightened I used to be of the sun in the early twenties. But somehow I forgot about it when, during the hottest part of the year, I went wandering (without even a sun hat) through the villages. I returned heavily tanned but fit. I then tried another experiment. I used to have an office in Hewett Road then. I decided not to use a fan and I sat there working through the hottest part of the day – and Hewett Road can be hot. I perspired profusely, in fact I had a regular bath of it. My chief trouble was how to write when I was dripping all over and my hand was wet and clammy. But I kept fit and a feeling of triumph came over me. I realised that I was not a slave to the weather or to a climate. I could bear both extreme heat and cold without any great disturbance of my body or mind or temper.

Now I am not suggesting that you should try to indulge in these pranks. Your case is different and should be treated differently. You know well enough how to take yourself in hand. But a time will surely come when you will be as tough in body as I have been and am.

Having to sleep inside a mosquito-infested barrack in this weather is an imposition which only a peculiar type of mind can evolve. How well I know that experience! Not here, but I have had enough of it previously. Perhaps some change has been made since April began. I hope so. I often think of what Bernard Shaw once wrote – that every judge and magistrate and jail official, should, as a matter of course and training, be made to live for a while as an ordinary prisoner. He must know exactly how it feels to undergo the sentences he imposes. A famous governor of the Sing Sing Prison in New York actually did this and lived for some months as an ordinary convict in his own prison. He became a great reformer of the prison system! Of course no such person can ever undergo the mental agony and have the sense of utter helplessness which a convict has. But even so the physical experience is worthwhile.

I am glad you retire early for the night. Do not read by the wretched light of a hurricane lantern. When I was in Naini I used to go to bed at eight thirty p.m. and get up before four in the morning. About lighting, why do you not use candles? They are much better than the dirty & smoky lanterns.

Presumably you have Flit or something like it for the mosquitoes – keep some lemon grass oil (citronella) also.

You have taken me to task for that book of Louis Bromfield's. So did Nan. I am quite overwhelmed. So I had better confess that I know nothing of the person and, so far as I can remember, have never read a book of his.

Do you do any breathing exercises? I hope you do – gently of course without exerting yourself in any way.

'Female Ward' is an absurd and offensive name. Two years ago Aruna,[1] who was then in the Lahore Female Prison or Ward, agitated about this and she succeeded in getting the name changed to 'Women's Prison'.

Our garden is shrinking daily and drying up. Still there are a good number of flowers still out because of the trouble we take over them. They are my 'babies' here and I tend them daily and water them properly. It is surprising how the petunias, hollyhocks, pansies and phloxes have survived. A new generation of zinnias is coming out, so also morning glories and tuberose and some kind of a lily. Coleus (the fancy leaves) is also flourishing and caladium is trying to grow. We hope to have a kind of jasmine-*motiya* soon. With the coming of the rains, we shall spread out more. Our soil here is also excessively stony and we had to dig hard and deep before we could plant anything. We sometimes

1. Aruna Asaf Ali: prominent nationalist leader, 'heroine' of the 1942 struggle; Mayor of Delhi, 1958.

come across remains of old buildings, and once a bit of a wall with a lovely lotus flower carved on it.

I shall ask Betty to arrange to send you Pocha's *Garden Guide* and his small set of garden tools. The book is not up to much. Still, it may help.

I do not remember having seen Methuen's *Anthology of Modern Verse*. I have just been reading Aurobindo Ghose's *Essays on the Gita*. What fine English prose he writes and his amazing lucidity. He writes quite tolerable verse also, with an occasional line of good poetry. His background of Greek, Latin & Sanskrit has been excellent training.

You will be amused to learn that Nandita, who is in Rajshahi Jail, is threatening to become plump. Sucheta writes that she is worried as this will interfere with her dancing.

My arm has given me some trouble since I came here but it is very much better now. Occasionally when I play badminton I have a twinge of pain. Otherwise it functions normally. I thought at first that badminton caused the pain and so I gave it up. This did no good. So I started again. I think what has done it good is the daily carrying of bucketfuls of water for the plants and flowers!

Do you have any badminton or any other game? I suppose there are not too many people with you who can join up in this. Nora is with you – give her my love. Who else is with you?

We are just fixing up with Narendra Deva to read the *Kadambari*[1] with him. This is a big book and I doubt if we shall ever go through it. It is a laborious process. Still it is rather fascinating to read this ancient romance in Sanskrit – probably one of the earliest novel-like books in the world.

I read the other day a review of a book – a collection of writings, chiefly poems, by women in Sanskrit – *Women Writers in Sanskrit*. It is all old stuff of course. Four volumes have already come out and two more are due.

It is surprising what a mass of literature in Sanskrit we possess and how little we know about it. In spite of enormous destructions and loss, and the fact that a large number of manuscripts are buried in religious institutions and have not so far been properly traced, there are at present about 60,000 manuscripts, big and small, properly catalogued! Only a small proportion of these have so far been printed. What a lot of work we have to do when we have the chance!

The night is far advanced and it is amazingly quiet and peaceful. Everybody is asleep, excepting me. The new moon of the new *Samvat*, eleven days old, is casting its radiance on everything and seems so unconcerned, as if nothing was the matter with this mad world of

1. *Kadambari*: a novel by Banabhatta, who lived in the court of Harsha (*c.* 606–647).

unhappy and warring mortals. Yet behind this apparent peace there is trouble all over the world.

Everybody here sends you his love – more especially Pantji, Mahmud, Kripalani and Asaf Ali. The Maulana is bearing up wonderfully but the shock of his wife's death has been a hard one and he shows it.

I have written enough. The Censors will probably say much more than enough. So let us give them some peace now and a respite from their heavy toils.

My love to you, darling one,
Your loving,
Papu

---

102.                                          Naini Central Prison,
                                                        Allahabad,
                                                  19th April, 1943

Darling Papu,
Your letter No. 5 dated the 9th[1] of this month was given to me last evening. It explains why your first letter took three weeks to arrive and the others only twelve days. Also why my letters are taking so long in reaching you. This is reply No. 4. I missed one letter and so shall always be one number less than yours.

The postscript in my last letter[2] will have told you that the books have arrived correct and all intact. Some of them had got rather wet and almost all of them had some sticky substance all over the covers. And countless ants because of it. Our other companion – Vimala Verma – helped me to clean and dry them. Perhaps you are puzzling over my writing that there was one extra and unaccounted for book. I was wrong – I might have known you were too methodical to make such a mistake. Bjornson[3] and Lin Yu-tang have already gone to Pupha who asked for them. I am in the midst of *Between Two Worlds*. How long-winded it is! I have read and liked its sequel – *Dragon's Teeth* – but this one I am not finding so interesting.

I also have been re-reading old G.B.S.[4] The smaller plays at the end I read for the first time in jail, as also *Back to Methuselah* (strange to think I had overlooked it for so long). I enjoyed it immensely and I am afraid made a perfect nuisance of myself to Puphi & Chand by

1. Refers to letter No. 99.
2. Refers to letter No. 100.
3. B. Bjornson (1832–1910): Norwegian poet, dramatist, novelist, and political leader.
4. George Bernard Shaw.

insisting on reading out aloud large chunks of it to them. A long time ago you took me to see *Saint Joan* as a treat for my tenth birthday. The memory of it has grown rather vague and I do not even remember whether it was in London, or in Paris, in French. Since then I have seen only two other Shaw plays on the stage: *Candida* and *The Doctor's Dilemma*. Both brilliantly acted.

The fruit also came the day I wrote to you – April 12th. I forgot to mention it in my P.S. It was a delight to see the *Alphonsoes*.[1] All afternoon I was lying close to the fruit-basket and the smell was so reminiscent of the good things of life outside jail. I could hardly bear to cut them up and eat them. Really I find it difficult to understand how anyone cannot like mangoes. The Maulana doesn't, does he? Some of the fruit I sent to Pupha.

Have you ever heard of Begam Samroo? She lived in the eighteenth century and a person called Brajendranath Banerji wrote a biography of her years ago. I saw it advertised at the back of a book on ancient India. Apparently the Begam was a wonderful woman: 'A Kashmiri girl who from abject poverty and obscurity rose to the command of an European-drilled brigade, the sovereignty of a territory as large as two English counties, and the honoured position of a shield to the Delhi Imperial Family, and died in the fullness of her years in the odour of sanctity as the honoured ally of the English rulers and a saint of the Roman Catholic Church.' This book is said to be the first attempt to write her biography on the basis of a critical study of all the available historical materials in print or MS – in English, Persian, Marathi and French – besides the mass of old state papers in the Imperial Records Office, Calcutta.

The night I wrote my last letter[2] to you, I had a most lovely dream. I was walking on a broad path – deep deep brown it was and probably wet and cool without being at all muddy. I had a feeling that it was suspended in the air although there was nothing to show it positively. And in a perfect circle all around – far away as if there was no obstacle to prevent me seeing the whole horizon at the same time – there was a chain of mountains. All sorts of mountains: high towering into the sky besides smaller ones, ragged and smooth, snow-covered and bare. And on a single peak in front of me there was a dazzlingly beautiful light. It seemed like a spotlight from above although the sky was pitch dark, neither sun, nor moon, nor stars. It was awe-inspiring. I was looking at it and walking on and on when the road became narrow and covered with deep snow like a mountain pass. I woke up feeling exhilarated and fresh, as if I had been to the Mont Blanc or the Matterhorn at least.

1. A variety of mangoes.
2. Refers to letter No. 100.

I am glad to see that you are sending the *Roz Nāmchā*.[1] I have been wanting to get hold of it but had forgotten the address in Benares. In spite of not having any sort of Indian calendar, we have been doing very well in the way of finding out when the various high days and holidays fall. And we have celebrated nearly all that we could reasonably do. On *Vasanta Panchami* day, we wore Vasanti saris[2] – on Holi we had grand fun too – but now the awful jail colour refuses to part with our clothes! On *Nauroz*, I wore a new sari and was gay all on my ownsome! For Chand's birthday we gave her a party – it wasn't half as pretentious as it sounds. We had sweet *bhattā*[3] and *kachālu*[4] and one other thing. The invitation ran as follows: 'To express their thankfulness at the successful termination of Bapuji's fast and on the happy occasion of Chandralekha's nineteenth birthday, her "fellow-martyrs" of 1943 and the years to come, invite her to tea'!

Whenever I am bored or depressed and tired of all the books I follow Lin Yu-tang's advice and open a dictionary. It is really interesting and sometimes quite exciting. I have two here. *The Pocket Oxford* & your *Twentieth Century*. It's fun to compare them. How do you pronounce 'What'? I had always left out the 'h' & Chand kept it in. I felt I must be wrong and looked it up to make sure. The Oxford says 'wot' and the other says 'hwat'. 'Wench' according to the *Twentieth Century* is pronounced 'wensh'!

Permission to sleep out has been granted to the 'A' class which means about three of us and four or five people in the male side. As far as I am concerned, this does not make much difference. I was already allowed out on medical grounds but I did not take advantage of this. How frightful to be out in the very sight of a barrackful of people who are locked up! The position remains unchanged, for there are three women who will still be locked in our yard.

I was very sorry to hear about Maulana's wife. Nothing one can say is really adequate on such an occasion. And especially so when one does not know the person. She was very beautiful, Mrs Naidu always used to tell us.

The summer is behaving quite reasonably and it isn't very hot. We have been allowed a fan in the afternoons. Towards morning one actually needs a sheet!

In all your letters there is no mention of your arm. I am anxious about it. Do write & let me know.

Puphi has just arrived and says there is talk of our being transferred

1. Literally 'account of the day's events' (Persian).
2. Yellow saris.
3. Sweet rice, served in Kashmiri families on auspicious occasions.
4. A variety of edible root.

– I do hope not. One gets used to people and their ways and adjusts
one's daily life accordingly. Then to be moved to a new environment
means uprooting all these habits and forming new ones. All this takes
time and is enervating. And then what companions will there be? Really
I'm feeling quite upset.

Much love,
Indu

103.                                  Naini Central Prison,

Allahabad,
25th April, 1943

Darling Papu,
Your letter No. 6 dated April 16th[1] came last evening. I was glad to
hear that you have at last received my first letter – by now perhaps the
second has also arrived.

Puphi is back with a lot of books. So for the moment I have abandoned
your lot. I am now reading Verrier Elwin's[2] *Leaves from a Jungle* and
*You Can't Be Too Careful*. What a very disagreeable person is Edward
Albert Tewler! You must have read Elwin's book. We could do with his
Pandu Baba right here – he's the Gond magician, you know. The most
popular subject for discussion among the convict women is still *tutka*,
which means a sort of bewitching, or rather bewitchment, if such a word
exists. If one has a pain anywhere it is because someone else has
given you her own pain or else because she wishes you ill for some
reason. So naturally how can mere medicine cure it? No explanation is
any good.

Have you heard that the letter you wrote Chand was heavily censored
– Puphi was telling me. And talking of Censors: all the books you sent
were disfigured since the name of your abode has been struck out most
thoroughly and unaesthetically. Why all this secret and mystery – since
we have all known for a long time just where you are – does it lend zest
to an otherwise tiresome game?

Did Chand tell you that I wanted to adopt the baby Sarala? If I had
been out, I surely would have done, for the mother was willing enough.
It was really a darling baby and after her release the mother wrote to
say that baby was missing our care so much that she had lost weight and
begun to cry a lot. Mother-love in India consists mostly of stuffing food

---

1. Refers to letter No. 101.
2. Verrier Elwin: British anthropologist sympathetic to nationalist aspirations in
India.

down their offspring's throat, all at the wrong time too. They have no
baby-talk or any kind of demonstrative love that the wee one can understand or appreciate. I was reading in an American magazine that now
they have even intelligence tests for tiny ones under six months old!
Anyone can avail himself of these but they are especially meant for
babies that have been put up for adoption, so that the foster parents
may know the child's personality characteristics such as sensitivity,
resourcefulness, muscle coordination and whether the baby is of normal
intelligence. They can even gauge the baby's response to colour and
sound thus determining what sort of parents would be most suitable for
the infant. The tests are apparently easy and the test toys – rattles,
coloured tubes, etc – look simple enough but they are considered so
highly scientific that their sale is restricted to professional child-
psychoanalysts. All these things are a long way off from India but I do
wish we could have at least the ordinary type of nursery, where mothers
could be taught the most essential things about baby-care. It is a shame
how quite bright children are suppressed or at least not given the incentive necessary for their full development. Wee Sarala is a case in point.
She was a really intelligent baby, quick and willing to learn and understand. In her home she will soon lose her alertness and will grow up
into just such a bovine creature as her mother. Maybe when the hospital
grows bigger and has more funds it will be possible to open some such
section.

Whatever difference stone walls and iron bars may make to the human
soul, let us be thankful that they offer no obstacle to the vegetable
kingdom, which follows the cycle of the seasons, year in and year out,
come war or peace. We have a peepul in our yard, a tree which, had it
depended upon human praise and approbation, would have withered
away long since. However it ignored our derision and went on its lordly
way. And now that *phagun*[1] is come again, the few remaining shreds
of last year's garment, yellow with age, are being shed off and its bare
limbs are being clothed in glorious sunset pink. It looks as if a deep
blush were spreading along the branches which gives it rather a coy
look. Amazingly beautiful it is. But spring doesn't last long and soon
summer will transform this flimsy pinky garment into the thicker and
more serviceable green one. In your *Twentieth Century Dictionary* I found
pressed a couple of these tiny new pink leaves. Over the walls we have
glimpses of the tops of some mahua trees – a balm for sore eyes.

Beautiful things attract other beautiful things. Our solitary peepul
provides our only opportunity of watching birds, other than the ever-
present sparrows, babblers, crows, pigeons and parrots which are

1. Spring.

numerous and extremely rowdy. Unfortunately the peepul is in such a spot that by the time one hears the call of a bird and rushes round one can just see it disappearing into the sky. In this way I failed to identify a most peculiar specimen. It happened in the evening. It was singing on a warbling, whistling note. It took me quite a while to locate the sound as coming out of the peepul (this is a feat, the sound being thrown back and forth by the high walls). Just as I got under the trees, the bird gave an extra loud whistle and away he flew. All I saw was a bit of beige, a bright tail in two dazzling shades of blue, a long dull red curved beak. Can you tell us what it is? The only birds that have come often and long enough to be properly examined and classified are the king crow, bulbul (is it quite the same as the nightingale!), woodpecker and the wagtail, extremely elegant in black, grey and white.

Our tomatoes are flourishing – so round and red but diminutive in size. Every time I look at them I think of Agatha and the trouble she used to take over her tomato window-box in the back yard – how proud she was of it. Shridhar Chacha [1] had to inspect it of course, when I once took him over for tea and he surrounded it with the inevitable wire netting but no change, miraculous or otherwise, was forthcoming.

Mehitabel the cat is getting increasingly vicious and quite adept at catching and devouring pigeons and sparrows. She has recently produced some more kittens. It is difficult to tell the exact number as they are all hidden away in a dark corner which no human is allowed to approach. The latest family to join us is the Cuthbert centipedes. Several of its members have been found in our yard.

I seem to be making up in sleep for all the late nights I have ever kept. Not only do I retire at nine thirty or ten but I don't get up until six forty-five or seven especially as the nights are so disturbed. And in between if it's hot I have a short fifteen-minutes' snooze in the daytime!

Dame Rumour has it that all 'A' classers are going to be transferred – Pupha and the men to Bareilly. We women will probably go to a cooler place. Shona Chachi [2] is all on her lonesome in Lucknow. Do you know Atkinson's verse on rumour?

> Actual evidence I have none
> But my aunt's charwoman's sister's son
> Heard a maid in Downing Street
> Say to a policeman on his beat
> That she had a brother who had a friend

1. Shri Shridhara Nehru: cousin of Jawaharlal, married to Raj Dulari.
2. Shivrajvati Nehru: wife of Indira Gandhi's uncle, Kishenlal Nehru ('Chachi' means aunt).

Who knew when the war was going to end.

The only really effective armour against mosquitoes are mosquito-nets. These we have acquired. Around lock-up time all the mosquitoes gather in the far end of the barrack, probably debating their strategy for the night. They produce such a variety of sound as to put to shame even S. K. Niazi – remember the zoological and ornithological linguist?

Puphi wants me to tell you that Hari's pay has been increased and the dearness allowance of the other servants has also been raised, as you desired.

I hear that Feroze received a letter from the I.G. [Inspector-General] of Prisons sometime ago, saying that I was in perfect health and had gained 12 lbs! Where the I.G. got this extraordinary information I cannot tell. Actually I have gained 3 lbs. I wonder if you got a similar communication. I am still 5 lbs. below my normal outside weight which used to be 100 lbs.

Lots & lots of love,
Indu

---

104.                                           Naini Central Prison,
                                                      Allahabad,
                                                  1st May, 1943

Darling Papu,
The censors do not seem to have objected to either Ghalib or Taba Tabai[1] for they have both arrived intact and your letter[2] has come in the usual week.

I am told that the second parcel of books has arrived in a damaged condition and has been lying at the station for two weeks or more. Apparently no one has yet been sent to fetch it.

Today is May Day. A host of memories come crowding into my mind. I unfold my wings and go flying away over the walls into the May days of the past. Mammoth gatherings in Hyde Park and Trafalgar Square. Processions and banner-waving. The shouting and the singing: 'Then Comrades come rally!' The enthusiasm of it! Gayer though hardly less noisy: the folk-dancing. Have you ever seen any? It's great fun and very good exercise, since every muscle from the head to the toe comes into use. I owe my discovery and appreciation of it largely to Miss Baker,[3]

1. Haider Ali Nazm Taba Tabai: Urdu poet.
2. Letter not published.
3. Miss B. M. Baker: Headmistress of Badminton School.

who made the whole school learn it because of her disapproval of ball-room dancing. And last, though certainly not least, the charming custom in France of giving bunches of lilies-of-the-valley to one's friends. When I was lying all forlorn in Leysin, Jean-Jacques and other friends sent parcels of these – my favourite flowers – and they arrived fresh and fragrant, on the eve of the fall of France, followed closely by Madame Morin lugging the suitcases which contained all that she could retrieve from her Paris flat.

Yippee, as Chand would have said. Good news has just come through. Security prisoners in the U.P. will henceforth be allowed (1) a daily newspaper – at last. (2) To write and to receive one letter, not exceeding 500 words, every month. These five hundred must include lists of clothes, books and any other articles required. Also 'gardening as a hobby may be allowed, where convenient'! This rule will probably replace the old vague one about communication with prisoners of other provinces. To be on the safe side, tell Yunus (if you have already mentioned this to Puphi) not to write, as it may interfere with my monthly letter. If I am also allowed the monthly letter, I propose sending the May letter to Feroze to settle about the house and other matters. The June letter to Nani who, I hear, is terribly worried, poor darling. July is a long way off to decide yet. It feels awfully like being back in school and having the monthly tests – write an essay on 'Jail life' in 500 words!

There are many hitches in Chand and Tara's obtaining all the signatures and statements necessary for Government sanction for going to America. Many people are helping – you will no doubt get a fuller version from Betty who is, so to speak, in the thick of it. The latest development will amuse you. Puphi hears from Shiva Rao[1] that a whole heap of new rules and regulations have cropped up. If you want to go out of India for your studies, you must first try to go to England, to Oxford, Cambridge or London. This when English parents are doing their very best to send their own children out of the country! However, if that is not possible, then Australia. Third choice is Canada. Furthermore, the Education Commissioner must be assured that on your return you are going to put your newly acquired knowledge at the service of your country – India!!! Isn't it too absurd for words. The girls will be very disappointed if the whole idea has to be abandoned. They are already so Americanised by Woodstock[2] that they will easily fit in Wellesley or any other American college. America now is probably a better place than it has ever been, for some of the best elements of

---

1. B. Shiva Rao: prominent journalist who was a member of the Indian Parliament during 1952–60.

2. A school in Mussoorie under American management.

European talent have gathered there. Going to America will of course take them further away from India – mentally, I mean. And is that a good thing just now? – situated as we are. At this time every Indian outside the country must be longing to get back – that is if he has an ounce of patriotism, the true variety. When Chand was released you wrote that we must be missing her. Do you know, except for the first evening we just felt she had never been here? This was because she was not happy here. Perhaps it sounds ridiculous to talk of happiness in jail, but at the moment I cannot think of a more appropriate word. I am happy because I am sure that I have done the right thing. 'Mourn not your captive comrades . . . but rather mourn the apathetic throng . . . who knows the world's great anguish and its wrong, and dare not speak.'[1] Also I am intensely interested and curious about this world of ours and its inhabitants and I have so trained myself that as the years go by I am less and less dependent on exterior forms of amusement and entertainment . . .

Vimala was released on the 30th, so now all three of us in our barrack are 'A' class. Nora and I also decided to sleep out – Puphi had been doing so since her return. It is really wonderful to be outside the hateful barrack and to sleep, as the French so picturesquely say, *à la belle étoile.*[2] I am sorry to say I have forgotten what little astrology I used to know and find it difficult to distinguish even some of the better known stars. But it is thrilling to wake up at night and see the Great Bear sprawling comfortingly and protectively overhead.

It is getting really hot now, so that the fan sends out burning gusts of air and we cannot yet decide whether it is better to have the fan or not to have it.

Please give my love & regards to your companions.

Much love,
Indu

---

1. Mourn not the dead
      But rather mourn the apathetic throng
   The cowed and the meek
      Who see the world's great anguish and its wrong
   And dare not speak.

                                        (Ralph Chaplin, 1867–1961)
   In quoting this poem, Indira has deliberately altered the first line, changing 'the dead' to 'your captive comrades'. This makes the quotation even more relevant to the situation in the India of 1943, when there were tens of thousands of freedom fighters in prison.
2. Under the open sky.

105.                                  Ahmadnagar Fort Prison,
                                         7th–8th May, 1943

Darling,

This is my letter No. 8. I did not write to you last week as I wanted to write to the two Puphis. You must have seen my letter to Nan.

Two days ago I received your letter dated April 12th/13th – No. 3.[1] It took a longer time than usual in coming – twenty-three days. I learnt from it that you had just then received the case of books I had sent you. Since then I have sent you two small packets of books, and yesterday I sent yet another – the fourth. I have decided to send you small parcels of books as these can go by post and thus save time and trouble to everybody.

Yesterday's parcel contained:

1. Voltaire: *The Best of All Possible Worlds*
2. Chiang Yee: *The Men of the Burma Road*
3. Peter Abrahams: *Dark Testament*
4. Plato: *Five Dialogues*
5. Chekhov: *Plays and Stories*
6. *The Upakhyan-mala*
7. Two Reports & 4 Bulletins of the Commission to Study Organization of Peace.
8. Four copies of the *Reader's Digest* – last year's numbers

No. 7 above were sent to me by your friend Stinnes from New York and they managed to reach me after a devious journey.

Your description of the storm in Naini reminded me of some stormy weather we have recently had here – even more so of some terrific storms we had in Bareilly Central Prison. How well I remember that envelope of dust which wrapped itself round everybody and everything. There was no escape from it as there are no doors in the prison barracks which can be closed – only bars; how cheerful they are! At night the effect was even more disconcerting.

Probably it is much hotter now in Naini than it was when you wrote. The Allahabad temperature now is said to be 109°F. Here we have not so far gone beyond 105°F or so. Even that is disagreeable enough and the nights are close and stuffy. I sleep in the open with a mosquito-net and I keep fanning myself with a small hand-fan. What it must be like inside a barrack at night in the shadow of high walls is a thought that is very far from pleasant.

1. Refers to letter No. 100.

I was a little surprised to learn of your food. There used to be fixed rations at Naini of two kinds and a choice was possible. One consisted of rice, *dal, ata, ghee,* [1] etc, the other of loaf of bread, butter, etc. I used to take the latter as it suited me. Obviously it would suit you also. Or it may be possible for one of you to take one kind of ration and someone else to take the other. I hope at any rate you have plenty of fresh vegetables.

As for fruit, I have arranged for a weekly parcel to be sent to you from Bombay and this will, I hope, continue. There is no point in stopping it for a while.

If you want me to arrange to have sent any message about your Tagore Town house to your sister-in-law I could perhaps manage it through Chhoti Puphi. It is a very complicated and roundabout way of doing things but for the present there is no help for it. Perhaps it is hardly worthwhile worrying about the house and it might well continue as it is. If Mrs Verma is staying there, nothing should be done to inconvenience her, and indeed we should go out of our way to help her. Whenever you go out, and perhaps you may be out long before I emerge, I should like you to stay in Anand Bhawan.

A few days ago I was informed by the Bombay Govt that a book previously ordered by me, called *Virginia Woolf,* had been forwarded to you. I was surprised. The only time I asked for books to be sent to you was six months back, for your birthday. That was when you got those two odd books which surprised you. I suppose this is a left-over from that order. Presumably the book is Forster's *Life of Virginia Woolf.* It should be good.

What has happened to that fine mare which Nawabzada gave you in Lahore?

You ask me about my arm – I think I have already written to you about it. I tried various massages, ointments, I gave it long rest from any kind of exercises – but the pain continued. Then I decided to deal with it in a different manner – through regulated exercise. I think the carrying of pailfuls of water was especially good for it as this stretched the muscles. Anyway it is far better now than it has been at any time during the last two years or more. It is almost quite well – only occasionally when I give a somewhat violent twist, does it pain me.

I have had a curious experience in connection with this arm. There is electric current here and Mahmud was given some simple electric treatment here for some pain. It was suggested that I might also indulge in this for my arm. Being always agreeable to having new sensations &

---

1. *dal*: pulse; *ata*: flour; *ghee*: clarified butter.

experiences I readily agreed – not that this electric business was very novel. So a mild current was passed through my arm for a few minutes. No obvious results. Next time, a few days later, a stiffer and a larger dose was proposed. While this was being given, and the force of the current increased, I was asked: Can you bear it? An odd question, or at any rate oddly put. I can bear a good bit in the way of pain and if it is for my good, I saw no reason to object. So I bore it without a whisper. When it was all over and my arm was unwrapped, it was discovered that my skin and some tissues had been burnt up to some extent. It was entirely my fault for quietly submitting to this ordeal without pointing out that something untoward was happening. Anyway it took about three weeks for this burn to heal and I have got a biggish mark on my forearm which I am likely to carry to the end of my days. It is as well to have a permanent souvenir of this place.

A week ago Beatrice Webb[1] died at her country house where you and I visited her five years ago. Her age was stated to be eighty-five. I thought she was even older. What a magnificent woman she was! Bernard Shaw said about her on her eightieth birthday, or thereabouts, that he was amazed that such a woman 'should survive in apparently undiminished vigour after eighty years among fools and savages who will rise to nothing but ecstasies of murder'. That compliment or observation could well be passed on to G.B.S. himself, for he has managed to survive for an even longer period, and is yet full of vigour and mental alertness. He is eighty-seven now.

How well I remember that visit of ours to Sydney & Beatrice Webb. Sydney was definitely the weaker of the two and I would have thought that he would not survive his wife. (I suppose he is still alive – I am not sure.) The walk across country we had with this lady of eighty and the light springy step she had! But what was really amazing was the up-to-dateness and mental alertness she displayed. It was a privilege to meet her and I shall long cherish her memory. You have a visible token of that visit – the book she gave you.

In my last letter[2] I gave you an account of how I spent my day – a regular timetable was outlined. Such timetables seldom last and anyway this one went to pieces very soon after. The Urdu and Hindi lessons were suspended because Mahmud was not well, the reading of the *Kadambari* came to a sudden end because Narendra Deva was not well. So my so-called Easter holidays have been unduly prolonged for unfortunate reasons.

1. Beatrice Webb (1858–1943): prominent British socialist. She and her husband Sydney Webb were both active in various radical causes.
2. Letter not published.

However, Maulana carries on with his astonishing punctuality. There is a story about Kant, the German philosopher, that for twenty or thirty years he used to go out punctually at five p.m. for his walk and all his neighbours and many others corrected their watches and clocks as soon as they saw him. So, whenever Maulana is to be seen slowly walking in the direction of the place where we feed, one can say definitely that it is thirty seconds to the time fixed for the meal.

A few days ago I read in a newspaper some extracts from a review in the *American Current History* of my book *Glimpses of World History* which has recently appeared in the U.S. The review was very friendly and eulogistic and, as an author, I felt very puffed up. He said that it was a better survey of world history than H. G. Wells's *Outline*. I have not seen any other reviews yet. It was just ten years ago, in Dehra Jail, that I was writing it, and I seldom thought of publication then – mostly I thought of you.

Hogben's *Mathematics for the Millions* is, from all accounts, a very good book. I have been trying to get it myself. If you have got it, read it. I do not remember what I told you about it five years ago or more – probably I made some inane remark, not knowing the book.

Some time back I sent you flower seeds grown in our little garden here. Use them in the rains, or some of them at least.

Here are two verses by Ghalib:

ے آدمی بجاے خود ایک محشر خیال

(غالب)     ہم انجمن سمجھتے ہیں خلوت ہی کیوں نہ ہو

The same in Hindi:

है आदमी बजाए ख़ुद एक महशरे ख़याल ।
हम मंजुमन समझते हैं ख़लवत ही क्यों न हो ॥ [1]

महशर means a crowd – ख़लवत is being alone, solitary रोज़-ए-महशर is Judgment Day – presumably because the biggest crowd will be seen there.

ناکردہ گناہوں کی بھی حسرت کی ملے داد

(غالب)     یا رب اگر ان کردہ گناہوں کی سزا ہے

The same in Hindi:

---

1. Ghalib: Man is himself
      a tumultuous world of thought:
   A company all around me I feel
      even if I am all alone!

नाकर्दा गुनाहों की भी हसरत की मिले दाद।
यारब ! अगर इन कर्दा गुनाहों की सज़ा है ॥  ¹

The first couplet tells us that man is not just a simple individual but a crowd of thoughts and ideas. Even when he is by himself, he is a kind of meeting or debating society all inside himself! The idea is well put.

The second is famous & often quoted. If we are to be punished for the sins we have committed, at least we should be praised for our yearning for the sins we have not committed.

Have you any news of Feroze?

Your loving,<br>Papu

Later

8/5. I have just received two letters from you together – dated 19th & 25th April.² I feel happy to have this feast. Betty writes that she has sent two *khadi*³ saris for you together with some meant for Nan. *Khadi* is very difficult to get nowadays.

---

106.                  Ahmadnagar Fort Prison,<br>14th May, 1943

Darling,

This is letter No. 9. Last week, after I had finished my letter⁴ to you and was on the point of sending it off, I received three letters in a batch, two from you⁵ and one from Betty. This was the biggest mail I had received for a long long time – well, nine months to be accurate. It was quite exciting and the normal serenity of mind, which I have developed here, was disturbed, pleasantly of course. Always I seem to be getting your letter immediately after writing mine to you. It struck me that I had better change the day of letter-writing and make it Monday. But on second thoughts I have, for the present, decided to stick to the old day.

Yesterday came yet another letter from you – your No. 6 dated May

---

1. Ghalib: If punishment there needs must be
         for the sins committed,
     Some appreciation, O my Lord,
         for the sins in thought left undone!
2. Refers to letters Nos 102 and 103.
3. Hand spun and hand woven cloth made popular by Gandhi during the freedom struggle.
4. Refers to letter No. 105.
5. Refers to letters Nos 102 and 103.

1st. [1] Also one from Puphi (Nan). Please tell her I have received it. (It is dated May 3rd.)

I am glad you and other détenus in the U.P. can write letters now, even though it be once a month and not exceeding 500 words. For my part, I have arrived at a stage – is it age or increasing wisdom? – when I can adjust myself mentally and bodily to any set of circumstances that for the moment control my existence. Nevertheless letters and interviews make a very great difference to people in prison . . . [2]

One brief letter a month is not very much and you will naturally want to write to Feroze and others. If you so prefer, you need not write to Nani. I shall write to her next week and give her news of you. I have not written to her so far, since I came here, because in the list of relatives to whom we were allowed to write mother-in-law was not mentioned. But now I understand that a mother-in-law is considered permissible. I am not sure but I shall take my chance.

As for Yunus, you are quite right and the difficulty applies to him in an equal degree. He can only write once a month.

About Chand & Tara going to America, the wheels have been set in motion but whether ultimately they can go or not, I do not know. There appear to be all manner of difficulties. Perhaps they can overcome them. If not, they will have to adjust themselves differently. I liked the idea of their going, especially Chand's. I did so more for impersonal reasons than for personal ones. I think I have grown to think impersonally more & more. Taking everything into consideration – the pros and cons – I came to the conclusion that the pros had it. But apart from my own personal or impersonal views, the fact that Chand was anxious to go was quite enough for me. I would hate to thwart a child and come in her way. Individuals, even & perhaps more so young ones, are terribly delicate & sensitive, and I have neither the knowledge nor the confidence in myself to force my will on another in regard to his or her personal life and development. I have to be particularly careful and to check myself because I am of an aggressive nature and am always trying, consciously or unconsciously, to 'improve' others. I do this in the mass, and I suppose I shall continue to do so. But when it comes to an individual I have become more restrained.

I was amused to learn of the considerable blackouts in my letter to Chand. What on earth could I write to Chand that was capable of rubbing up the authorities the wrong way? I have not the least idea. I wish the censors would inform us of the rules or principles that they are meant to apply. Perhaps that might help a little.

1. Refers to letter No. 104.
2. Deleted by censors.

When I sent you my first lot of books I took the trouble myself to black out any reference to our place of detention, as I knew this might cause trouble and delay. I did so neatly and clearly. Evidently this was not considered sufficient and fresh layers of blacking were applied. It is oddly diverting to realise what pains are taken to keep our place of detention a secret, when everybody who is at all interested has known of this from the very beginning . . . [1]

Did you see that Amery [2] is developing a heavy kind of humour? Asked in the House of Commons whether members of Parliament could write to me through Govt he answered: Yes, provided they were members of my family and wrote only on domestic matters!

For long now I have been hearing about your possible transfer. But a good part of the summer is over and the rainy season is approaching. There is not much point in a transfer after the summer is almost over. I hope you and the others will be taken elsewhere soon. You say you do not like the idea because you are used to your present environment. That always happens and it is astonishing how conservative human nature is and how suspicious of change. I have had that feeling so often when I was transferred from one jail to another. I was sorry to leave my companions and to have to change my way of living. But soon I got used to the new place and to new companions. The power of adaptation we have!

I have had no communication from the I.G. or anyone else about your weight. You are the first person to tell me of it. I wish you would keep me informed of it. How did you manage to gain 12 lbs in the I.G.'s imagination?

Yes, I remember well taking you (when you were under ten) to see *Saint Joan* in Paris. I have an idea that we have seen the original English version also.

Upton Sinclair is very long-winded. You started at the wrong end of his trilogy by reading *Dragon's Teeth* first. I have gone through all the three volumes. One of the reasons, perhaps, why you found *Dragon's Teeth* more interesting was that it dealt with a period you knew and so you were interested. The others are just before your time, and the world before we gained mental awareness of it is apt to be dull and uninteresting.

I have not read Verrier Elwin's new book.

You mention the peepul tree in your yard. We have only one tree here – a neem, but little shoots of the peepul are continually coming out at odd places – how irrepressible they are! I have watched the

1. Deleted by censors.
2. Leopold Amery (1873–1955): Secretary of State for India, 1940–5.

unfolding of a new peepul leaf and been charmed and fascinated by it. The peepul, I suppose, might well be considered the typical tree of India. Of course there is the chenar in all its magnificence, but it is of Kashmir only; and the deodar in all its stately glory, but again it is confined to the mountains, and the neem, and the lovely areca, and so on. But the peepul is the Tree of India – and it is fixed so for ever by the Buddha legend. [1]

What of the flowers? Obviously the lotus is the Flower of India. Equally obviously the mango is the Fruit of India. I am not sure about the animals – is there any really typical animal?

You give me a vague description of a new bird you saw and want me to name it from here! This faith in my extensive knowledge is very touching but it has no justification. But surely you have a kind of an expert on birds with you. Nora fancies herself that way and sent me a book on Indian birds when I was in Dehra Jail.

I remember once in Almora Jail catching sight of a new and lovely bird. I was excited and, having no one else to refer to, I asked a minor jail official if he knew anything about the birds there. 'Well, yes,' he said. 'I know the crow!' I am not quite so bad but my bird-love is strictly limited. Do you remember when we were stopping with Horace Alexander [2] in Birmingham or near it, how full his house was of books on birds and ornithology? These books seemed to be in every room, the hall, the landing, etc.

It has suddenly struck me that you should keep some money in your jail account for emergencies – probably you have some and you can always draw upon your bank. But then I cannot quite get rid of my habit of being a fussy old father. So I am trying to send you Rs.50/-. It will take many weeks to reach you, if past experience is any guide.

Begam Samroo – yes, most of us have heard about her though very few know much. I have read a magazine article about her and, in the course of my wanderings, I have passed Sardhana, near Meerut, which used to be her headquarters. There is, I am told (I did not see it myself), a fine Catholic Church built by her with a lovely statue of the Virgin Mary. Also a picture of the Begam, when she was young, and she was good to look at. In Delhi there are still houses which are called Begam Samroo's houses and in one of these, or in a gallery, there is another picture of hers, when she was old.

On receiving your letter I went to Maulana and asked him, for he is

1. The reference is to the Buddha attaining Enlightenment while reflecting under a peepul tree at Bodh Gaya (528 BC).
2. Horace Alexander: taught at Woodbrooke Quaker College, Birmingham; sympathised with the Indian struggle for freedom; was in close touch with Mahatma Gandhi and other leaders of the freedom movement.

a treasure-house of all such old stories and happenings. He told me something and gave me a book he happened to have here. This is *The History of the Reign of Shah Alum* by W. Francklin, Captain in the Hon'ble East India Company's service, published in London in 1798. Francklin was the Begam's contemporary, more or less, and was her guest for a fortnight at Sardhana. He was much impressed by her. He says that she belonged to an impoverished family of a Moghul nobleman. She married Samroo, a German adventurer in command of a body of trained troops, including foreign soldiers. (Samroo is an odd name for a German – probably it was a new name.) She became a Christian after her marriage. Samroo apparently died soon after marriage, in 1778. He had been given a large *jagir*[1] round about Sardhana and in addition to his own battalions was given command of a body of Moghul horse. He became a kind of feudatory chief under the Moghal king at Delhi.

On Samroo's death, the Begam became possessed of this principality and also functioned as the leader of the armed forces. She was a good administrator and a good captain of the forces. She built a fort and arsenals & foundries for cannon. Sardhana prospered & remained peaceful while chaos often ravaged the surrounding areas. She was loyal to the Delhi king and on several occasions saved him from destruction and collapse in battle by her personal initiative & bravery. The king gave her the title of Zebu-nnisa – the 'ornament of her sex'.

Later she got into trouble: she married for a second time and this resulted in a revolt of her troops. She married one of her European officers, again said to be a German adventurer (though his name is given as Vaissaux). She was imprisoned by a step-son. Her new husband committed suicide. Some months or a year later, however, she gained possession of her *jagir* again and remained there till a ripe old age.

This, in brief, is her story as Francklin gives it. He is enthusiastic about her:

> We embrace this opportunity of paying a tribute deservedly due to the spirit, activity, and talents of this noble lady. Endowed by nature with masculine intrepidity, assisted by a judgment and foresight clear and comprehensive, Begam Samroo, during the various revolutions above detailed, was enabled to preserve her country unmolested, and her authority unimpaired.

I had not heard that she was a Kashmiri – she might well have been. Anyway she was an outstanding and interesting woman and I should like to know more about her.

1. Estate.

In Francklin's book I found two or three other instances of women playing a notable part in battle and administration. Referring to another woman he says, 'The Begam herself, who, with a gallantry and spirit not uncommon among the females of Hindustan, was accustomed to be present in action, was slain by a cannon ball.'

About this time also there was the famous Ahalya Bai of Indore. [1]

Another passage from Francklin might interest you: referring to the quashing of a rebellion, he says that the king set all the womenfolk of the rebels at liberty, 'It being an inviolable maxim throughout Hindustan, and in general most religiously observed, to respect the honour of the harem.' (Harem meaning all the women of the household, whatever their rank or condition.)

Here are two couplets from Ghalib. They are in simple language and the ideas finely put.

زندگی اپنی جب اس طرح سے گزری غالب
(غالب)    ہم بھی کیا یاد کریں گے کہ خدا رکھتے تھے

The same in Hindi:

ज़िंदगी अपनी जब इस तरह से गुज़री ग़ालिब—
हम भी क्या याद करेंगे के ख़ुदा रखते थे ! [2]

ان کے دیکھے سے جو آجاتی ہے منہ پر رونق
(غالب)    وہ سمجھتے ہیں کہ بیمار کا حال اچھا ہے

In Hindi:

उनके देखे से जो आ जाती है मुंह पर रौनक ।
वह समझते हैं के बीमार का हाल अच्छा है ॥ [3]

Last evening, a little after sunset, I saw a curious sight. The eight- or nine-day moon looked quite green. I had never seen it so. Fed up, I suppose with the goings-on in this world.

---

1. Ahalya Bai (1735–95): the ruler of Holkar State with its capital at Indore.
2. Ghalib: If life be so as we have had,
        How adoringly shall we e'er say:
        'We too had Gracious God with us!'
3. Ghalib: With just a glance of hers at me
        A cheerful face I show;
        But it makes her think
        The love-sick is so much better now!

I have exceeded all bounds in this letter – I fear it is much more than 500 words! So my apologies to the censors.

Your loving,<br>
Papu

---

107.                             Anand Bhawan,

Allahabad,<br>
22nd May, 1943

Darling Papu,

This is going to be a short short letter, for two reasons. Firstly I don't think I shall have much time. Secondly I have hurt the index finger of my right hand, so that it is an effort to hold on to the pen.

Your letter of the 7th/8th[1] reached me here, while we were having a brief interlude between jail-goings. You must have read of our release and of the order[2] served upon us. These last days have been full of indecision, Samant[3] advising me to go to Khali, I not feeling like it, and so on. Dr Samant's point was my health. The heat is simply terrific. On top of that, going in and out of the house, I have caught a bad cold and my temperature has been going up to 101°. However it is nothing to worry about and will very soon be all right. But at the moment my head is feeling so heavy and stupid.

Our letters to the District Magistrate have gone off, informing him that we cannot comply with the terms contained in the order. So now it is just a matter of waiting for the police lorry. The police, I hear, have already been to Anand Bhawan twice in our absence. Puphi was in Lucknow consulting her doctor and I went to Fyzabad to interview Feroze. I returned yesterday afternoon and Puphi arrived this morning.

I am sending *Virginia Woolf* to Chhoti Puphi who will forward it to you.

I was very worried to hear about your arm. Do be more careful.

I can't find Hogben's book on Mathematics anywhere.

Both the radio and newspapers are full of eulogies of Moti,[4] who,

---

1. Refers to letter No. 105.

2. Indira Gandhi and Vijaya Lakshmi Pandit were released from Naini Prison on 14th May, 1943 and an order was served upon them to go to Khali, the estate of Ranjit Pandit near Almora, and live there in internment.

3. Dr Vatsala Samant: a friend of the family who was Medical Superintendent of the Kamala Nehru Hospital, Allahabad, 1942–72.

4. Moti Kathju: a cousin of Jawaharlal, he worked for the *Pioneer*, Lucknow, before joining the Indian Army. He was killed in action in Burma in May 1943.

poor chap, is reported to have been killed on the bank of the Chindwari. I believe he was very brave & liked the army life too.

Khali must be very pretty just now and full of flowers, but as the popular Bombay Talkies song goes:

*unka phoolon se rishta hi kya,*
*jinki kismet hai kanton ke beech pali re.* [1]

Feroze was looking pulled down. He is being kept apart from every-body else . . .[2]

Masi & Mausa[3] have left Agra after twenty-three years. Mausa has now got a job in Jaipur. Nani is with Mamu in Lahore. I hear she has been having a lot of trouble with her eyes. She had an operation which didn't turn out too well.

Darling, I shall stop now. If we are not arrested I shall continue later.

Tons of love,
Indu

---

108.                                Ahmadnagar Fort Prison,
                                        23rd May, 1943

Darling,
This is my letter No. 10. It is being written two days later than usual. I have been in a quandary and have not escaped from it yet. Where are you likely to be and to what address must I send my letters?

The very day my last letter[4] went off to you I saw in the newspapers that you and Puphi had been released from Naini and later some kind of an order had been served upon you both calling upon you to proceed to Khali and live there under the surveillance of the District Magistrate. I wondered immediately what the outcome of this would be. I was by no means sure of the developments and so I decided to wait for further news before I wrote to you again.

Yesterday I received a letter from Puphi from Naini Prison dated May 9th. This was mainly concerned with Chand's & Tara's going to America. There were a few lines, however, to say, that you too had been informed of coming events – that you were going to be released and served with an externment or internment order – whatever it is – to live

---

1. A rough translation of this song would be: Those hapless individuals whose destiny is nurtured in thorns/What have they to do with flowers?
2. Deleted by censors.
3. Swarup (Bappi) and P. N. Kathju: aunt and uncle of Indira Gandhi.
4. Refers to letter No. 106.

at Khali. She added that both of you felt that you could not obey an externment order. It was up to the Government to send you wherever they thought fit.

In spite of this you were both released and the order was apparently served. So what has happened and where are you now? I was inclined to wait till I heard from you but now I have decided to write. It is foolish waiting. Probably you are in Anand Bhawan. If not, I suppose some arrangements have been made for the forwarding of letters.

Your departure from Naini must have left Nora all by herself. Or has she been sent elsewhere?

I suppose Chand and Tara have sailed, though I do not know. I had a letter from Chand a week ago to say that they had been told to keep ready to leave at a moment's notice.

If you happen to be in Anand Bhawan could you send me Shridharani's [1] *My India, My America* (or some such silly title). It must be in my room. It is a fattish book. Also one or two books by Dewey, [2] the American professor & philosopher – also in my room.

The monsoon is still some way off but we have had some rain – the *chhoti barsāt* [3] I suppose. This has brought down the temperature and I am again busy with my gardening. This will keep me well occupied for two or three weeks. Did you get some small gardening tools from Pocha's?

I wonder if you can trace the two letters I wrote to you in September and October last. Not that there is anything important or worthwhile in them but I am interested in their fate.

Here are two more Urdu couplets. The first is by Mir. [4] The second by Ghalib.

الٹی ہوگئیں سب تدبیریں کچھ نہ دوا نے کام کیا

(میر)      دیکھا اس بیماری دل نے آخر کام تمام کیا

In Hindi:

उल्टी पढ़ गईं सब तदबीरें, कुछ न दवा ने काम किया ।

देखा इस बीमारी-ए-दिल ने आख़िर काम तमाम किया ॥[5]

---

1. Krishnalal Shridharani: journalist and author; Congressman; resided in the United States, 1934–47; returned to India after independence.
2. John Dewey (1859–1952): American philosopher and educationist.
3. The pre-monsoon showers.
4. Mir Taqi Mir (1774–1810): Urdu poet.
5. Mir:    All the measures and plans have proven false;
           No medicine did me good;
           See, this disease of the heart,
           At length, put an end to me!

رنج سے خوگر ہوا انسان تو مٹ جاتا ہے رنج

مشکلیں اتنی پڑیں مجھ پر کہ آساں ہو گئیں     (غالب)

In Hindi:

रंज से ख़ुगर हो इनसां, तो मिट जाता है रंज ।

मुश्किलें इतनी पड़ीं मुझ पर के आसां हो गईं ॥[1]

ख़ुगर होना means to get accustomed to something. आदी हो जाना . Taba
Tabai is short in both places – तब तबई –

Your question about the pronunciation of 'what' put me on enquiry
and I was a little surprised at the result. I find I say 'wot' in normal
casual conversation. But if I am reading out something rather slowly or
saying something with deliberation, I am inclined to say 'hwat'. So, in a
way, I please both the schools of pronunciation. But my general tendency
is all for 'wot'.

I read yesterday about Moti Kathju's death somewhere in the jungles
of Burma. Having survived the African campaign for nearly two years,
he was to meet his end in a skirmish against the Japanese.

You grow philosophical in your letters and introspective. Perhaps it
is inevitable and circumstances force us to be so. Yet do not grow up
too soon! I took a long time over the business. Anyway it is definitely
an advantage to be intensely interested and curious about the world and
its inhabitants – that is not introspection. But most of the inhabitants
are a lousy lot! I am interested in humanity, both in the mass and in
individuals, but have often found relief from the burden of too much
humanity in turning to animals and plants and the like.

I am immersed at present in a careful reading of the 1200 pages
of Beatrice & Sydney Webb's *Soviet Communism*. It is an astonishing
and a wonderful book. Somebody walked away with my old copy
long ago. So I am reading Puphi's copy and – tell her – marking it
profusely.

I am writing today to Amma also. I do not quite know where to
address her. Pyare Kathju[2] is I believe now the Director of Industries
in Jaipur State. Chand used to be in Lahore, presumably in the Imperial
Bank there. She intended going to Lahore. So I shall send my letter

---

1. Ghalib:   Pain afflicts no more
           when it comes to be a part of life;
           So many vicissitudes of fortune I have seen
           that easy they come on me!
2. Pyarelal Kathju: uncle of Indira Gandhi.

there. She was to have had an eye operation a month or two ago. I do not know the result of it. You had better write to her also.

Love,

Your loving,
Papu

---

109.                                    Ahmadnagar Fort Prison,
                                           28th May, 1943

Darling,

This is my letter to you No. 11. It is just fifteen days today since I received the last letter from you and that was dated May 1st – May Day.[1] During this fortnight much seems to have happened of which I have received the vaguest information. Indeed I know nothing except what the newspapers have given, and that is little enough. More than ever I have waited for your letter.

The papers say you are in hospital and are suffering from influenza. Influenza is usually a trivial affair but not for you and I hate this idea of your having to go to hospital again. You have already spent long months and years in hospitals and sanatoria and I had hoped that you had rid yourself of them for good. Of course it is not the hospital that upsets me. It was as well that you went there for you will be better looked after there than at home. But the idea of your not being well distresses me. Perhaps it is not so surprising after nine months of the 'Female Barrack' in Naini Jail.

And now news comes that Puphi has gone back to Naini. All roads, so far as we are concerned, lead there, and that is our journey's end! I suppose you would have been there also for a second time but for the fact that you are actually in hospital. Perhaps a little later you will also be escorted there. Well, well – it is well.

So again I live in uncertainty about you and what the immediate future will bring. The calm and monotony of jail life is broken into by these incursions of uncertainty and anxiety. I wonder often why this kind of thing happens to me rather than to others. I am strong and tough and can bear a good deal. But that others who are not so strong of body should have to put up with such burdens is an unpleasant thought for me. And yet after all it is the mind that counts and that overcomes the weakness of the body. And I am happy to know that wherever you might be, in hospital or jail, your mind will be at peace and you will be able to find in its recesses a measure of contentment. And you can dream,

1. Refers to letter No. 104.

as you have been doing, of wonderful snow-covered mountains, rose-coloured and radiant in the light of the morning sun.

Allahabad seems to be particularly hot at present and for another month it will continue to be so. Here some rain has brought the temperature down a little. In anticipation of the coming monsoon I am busying myself with the garden. This occupation keeps my hands and mind busy when sometimes it is a little difficult to concentrate on reading. Apart from this, I believe it satisfies some inner craving for work and activity. So I am filling up wooden boxes and pots with seeds and treating them as nurseries for the little seedlings to grow up. Some of them shot up with amazing rapidity, others linger and take their time. Within two or three weeks I shall begin transplanting these seedlings and putting them in beds.

Betty writes that Raja is ill and is also in hospital. There appears to be a possibility of an operation for gallbladder or some such thing. He has lost in weight a great deal and he could ill afford to do so. Poor Betty is naturally upset. So many people seem to be ill, and often seriously so.

I wonder if you have received all the packets of books I sent you to Naini. In all I sent four parcels, including the first big one. The fifth one has been ready for dispatch but I do not quite know where to send it. So I shall hold on to it for some days. Besides, you are not likely to require it in hospital and you can draw upon books from Anand Bhawan.

I give you two more couplets from Ghalib. The first one has a certain appropriateness. It is really in the Sufi tradition [1] and deals with the inner meaning of life.

هم وہاں میں جہاں سے ہم کو بھی

(غالب)      کچھ ہماری خبر نہیں آتی

In Hindi:

हम वहां हैं जहां से हम को भी ।

कुछ हमारी ख़बर नहीं आती ॥ [2]

چلتا ہوں تھوڑی دور ہر اک تیز رو کے ساتھ

(غالب)      پہچانتا نہیں ہوں ابھی راہبر کو میں

In Hindi:

1. Islamic reformist and mystical movement of late tenth and early eleventh centuries.
2. Ghalib:    We are there
               Where of ourselves
               Even we do not know!

चलता हूं थोड़ी देर हर एक तेज़ रौ के साथ ।
पहचान्ता नहीं हूं अभी राहबर को मैं ।।[1]

**तेज़ रौ** – means literally 'fast goer'
**राहबर** – one who shows the way – the leader

I shall hold on to this letter till tomorrow morning. Perhaps a letter from you might come then.

*29th May*

No letter has come and so this goes off –
   All my love,
               Your loving,
                Papu

---

110.
                                  Anand Bhawan,
                                    Allahabad,
                            29th May, 1943

Darling Papu,
Your letter No. 10[2] has just come.

First of all I must reassure you about my health – I hope the newspaper headlines about my flu have not worried you. (By the way, what newspapers do you get?) I remember writing a somewhat incoherent letter[3] to you some time ago but I haven't the foggiest notion what I wrote. Before we were released, it was so hot in jail and I was feeling very low and running a temperature. Coming to Anand Bhawan from the Female Ward was like suddenly being landed at Mussoorie after a stay near the Equator. I caught a cold at once. Colds are a great nuisance at any time but in the middle of summer it becomes almost impossible to deal with them. When the temperature is over 110° in the shade it takes all one's will power and more not to sit under the fan, not to drink iced water. And I am afraid I did not exercise all my will power. Then I went to Fyzabad to interview Feroze. The heat, the dust, the crowded compartment, the fatigue of the journey made my temperature rise alarmingly. I started to cough. All this was helped considerably by the fact that the

1. Ghalib:  With every traveller moving fast
              A little distance I do go;
              Who is to be the real guide
              I cannot yet say!
2. Refers to letter No. 108.
3. Refers to letter No. 107.

people with whom I stayed in Fyzabad kept their house very cold! However by the time I got back home I was feeling like nothing on earth – as only influenza can make you feel. Dr Samant said that I must gargle & have my throat painted and swallow some ghastly concoction every hour or so. And as this was rather difficult to manage by myself, she decided to take me to the hospital. It is really remarkable what difference a hospital does make. I think I stayed there four days – Doctor wanted to keep me a little longer, for though my temperature is down I still have a nasty cough, but it is so hot there, I decided to come away.

Puphi was rearrested while I was in hospital. Now I am just waiting to be whisked back to good old Naini. The police have been to consult Samant! I shudder to think of the heat in our barrack. I hear the rains have started in Bombay. Hari swears that it ought to rain here in a couple of weeks. But most people say that the rains will be delayed this year.

Poor Dr Samant is so very fed up with the weather. She hasn't yet got used to the heat and in the winter she freezes!

Hari sends his *salaams*. [1] He still hasn't got his land and so is rushing about frantically but I am afraid nobody listens to him. Just before we came out of N.C.P. Hari married off his son, daughter & brother's son. This entailed further quarrels with the Hospital since he was determined to have the awful tin-tinny band that is usual on such occasions. Khaliq [2] also asked to be remembered to you. He brought his daughter here the other day. She has grown up into a smart & perky young lady in Rita's *salwars*! [3] Poor Lakchamania [4] is getting older and weaker and there is nothing one can do about it. Her granddaughter Champi, attractive young thing, has got T.B. I have arranged milk for her. Old Jessie still comes to see us with offers of cooking Madrasi meals.

Keshav's [5] wife came to see me. She says that Keshav had typhoid very badly – now he is cured of that but is having heart trouble. Medical aid is most incompetent and slack. News about other people is not good either. Poor old Rafi [6] is, I hear, having a very bad time. He is in Bareilly with Pupha.

Motibhai's death was tragic. So much of his life he had wasted just lounging about and when he does at last decide to do something it ends

1. Salutations.
2. A chauffeur in Anand Bhawan.
3. A kind of trousers.
4. Mother of a sweeper in Anand Bhawan.
5. Keshav Dev Malaviya: Congress leader from U.P., Secretary of Allahabad City Congress Committee and General Secretary, U.P. Provincial Congress Committee; was later Union Minister for Mines and Oil, 1957–63.
6. Rafi Ahmed Kidwai: nationalist Muslim leader from U.P.; active in the struggle for freedom; was later Union Minister for Food and Agriculture, 1952–4.

like this. Chhoti Puphi is very cut up, for they were the greatest of friends. I hear his family are so absorbed in their film-star daughter that they cannot give thought to anything else.

Yes, the gardening tools have arrived, also quantities of seeds. I shall consult Datadin[1] as to when they should be sown.

Chand & Tara sailed on the 15th, two days after our release. On the eve of their departure they spoke to Puphi on the phone. Rita is still in Bombay. She is now staying with Chhoti Puphi. Mrs Chew has, from all accounts, turned out to be most unsatisfactory. She is still with Rita. Puphi is trying to make other arrangements.

At the end of a long search I found Shridharani's *My India, My America* in Puphi's room. The books by Dewey I cannot find anywhere. I shall have the book sent to Chhoti Puphi. I have already sent the pamphlet on Virginia Woolf.

Yes, I have seen your letters of September & October.[2]

Thanks for the Ghalib. Nora & I enjoy him. All the while – one week – that Puphi & I were both out, Nora was alone. The Govt are not going to the bother of sending anybody to a cooler place, no matter what the state of their health.

Nani has written to me. She wanted to come and see me but with all this uncertainty it was not worthwhile sending for her. She has been having great trouble with her eyes. Mamu has had his teeth out – so writes Lado Chachi[3] from Lahore. Shama,[4] as you may have heard, has married a S. P. Chopra, chartered accountant. His father is Director of Industries in Kashmir. They were married in a terrific hurry and rushed off to Kulu for a fortnight. They are due back on the 30th. Lado Chachi will give an At Home on the 2nd, then come back. Manno Didda[5] is now in Bombay.

All our subscriptions to American magazines seem to have given out all together. What nice letters they send to remind one of the fact! Could you write, or rather ask Chhoti Puphi to write, to your publisher in New York to subscribe to *Fortune* for Feroze, and *Asia*, for me – also *Reader's Digest*? All this time I have been getting *Asia* as a Christmas present but I don't think it is being renewed this year. These magazines go a long way towards brightening up life in jail.

1. A gardener in Anand Bhawan.
2. Refers to letters Nos 91 and 92.
3. Lado Rani Zutshi: wife of Indira Gandhi's uncle Ladli Prasad Zutshi (see Kinship Circle).
4. Shyama Chopra née Zutshi: daughter of Ladli Prasad and Lado Rani Zutshi. A cousin of Indira Gandhi.
5. Man Mohini Sahgal née Zutshi: daughter of Ladli Prasad and Lado Rani Zutshi and a cousin of Indira Gandhi. Indira called her Manno Didda ('Didda' means 'elder sister').

As soon as I knew we would have to go back to jail, I sent for the barber and had all my hair chopped off. Now it is almost as short as a boy's – what is called in America the service bob. It is so much cooler and easier to manage. Everybody prophesied that I would look ghastly, but I decided on comfort and coolness at all costs of looks. Actually it has not turned out at all bad. The barber who came to cut my hair was not our usual one but his son, who seems to have led an adventurous life. He has been a ship's barber & was torpedoed some time ago. Before that he had a shop in Glasgow. How is your burn?

Looking for your books, I came across the old Mah-jong set you bought in Paris ages ago. I wish I could take it to jail – it would help pass the time. But I wonder if it would be popular with Puphi and Nora – both of whom do not like learning new games.

Did you read Louis Fischer's San Francisco speech? [1] *The Hindustan Times* printed nearly the whole of it. It was very good indeed. What a dearth of news there is!

Along with *My India, My America,* I shall send you *London Pride* if I can find it anywhere.

Very much love,<br>Indu

---

III.                                                      Anand Bhawan,
                                                              Allahabad,
                                                    30th/31st May, 1943

Darling Papu,
Your letter No. 9 came this morning. This was dated May 14th. [2] Yesterday I had already received and replied to a later letter – No. 10, dated the 23rd. [3] No. 10 probably came quicker as it was addressed to Anand Bhawan. No. 9 first went to the jail, then to the District Magistrate, who sent it to the Kamala Nehru Memorial Hospital. This is my ninth letter to you. I am replying immediately as it is so much easier to

1. Louis Fischer was an American journalist and author, who had spent some time in India and was very sympathetic to the nationalist cause. He knew Mahatma Gandhi, Jawaharlal Nehru and some other leaders personally. In the speech under reference, delivered by Fischer at the Town Hall in San Francisco on 23rd February, 1943, he spoke of the reasons which had compelled the nationalist leaders of India to initiate a movement against the British Government in 1942. As Fischer observed in his lecture, the Indian leaders were fully determined to fight against Fascism, provided their country was granted freedom in the first instance. The speech was reproduced in *The Hindustan Times* of 22nd May, 1943.

2. Refers to letter No. 106.

3. Refers to letter No. 108.

write from home than it is in jail and I may be arrested any time. And since you are allowed to receive four letters a week I do not suppose there will be any difficulty in its being delivered to you.

Just as I was finishing my letter[1] to you yesterday, we had a terrific dust-storm. In anticipation of it, Bansi had already tightly closed all doors, windows and ventilators, so that I was hardly aware of the storm – when it came or how long it lasted. Afterwards there was a cool breeze and in the night a few drops of rain. This morning was delightful – just the weather for a long walk. However this is quite the wrong time for rain and we shall have to pay for this brief moment of coolness in the form of even greater heat in the days to come. The temperature is now 117°. It can't rise very much more, can it? I am sure the jail barracks temperature is at least a couple of degrees higher. You see the high walls seem to reflect back the heat, at the same time as they are preventing fresher, cooler air from penetrating inside.

This is your first letter to me which is considerably blacked-out: nearly a page where you are discussing letters and interviews in prison, your line where you say, presumably, something about your place of detention & a sentence about sending me money.

About this money. Up till the 1st of May we were not allowed to deposit any. The permission for this came along with the order about letters and newspapers. The Naini people are not keen on our depositing what they call 'large' sums. Moreover jail accounts are vague and unsatisfactory. Puphi & I each had Rs. 10/-, out of which Puphi spent twelve annas and I brought home the whole sum intact! So if you have not already made arrangements – as that portion of your letter is blacked out I cannot tell – please do not do so. If I do happen to run short of money, more can always be deposited through Ladli Chacha.

I was interested in Begam Samroo's story.

Darling, shall I tell you a secret? I think I'm getting old! Proof? An almost complete change of taste. You know how I have always adored mangoes. I now find to my horror that I really relish only the Alphonso! There is also a growing fondness for food – or do you think this is merely the result of not having a decent meal for eight months? One always has taken the good things of life for granted, especially the day-to-day things such as food, comfortable furniture, good service.

Talking of service, now that the car is gone, Khaliq is blossoming into an indoor servant. He is acting as bearer these days, as Lala has toothache and Sunder and Tulsi are with Rita in Bombay. All the servants send you their *salaam*. I consulted Datadin about the seeds. He

---

1. Refers to letter No. 110.

says only the zinnia & balsam & cosmos should be sown at the beginning of the rainy reason. All the others are winter flowers.

Living in jail one forgets how green and beautiful even dusty old Allahabad can be. The day we were released, it was quite a shock to see the colourful Gulmohars,[1] the abundance of trees, the curve of the Jumna. I was so overcome that I shed a few tears through sheer excitement!

I sleep out on the lawn here, in front of Puphi's bedroom. It was such a relief not to have the major portion of the sky hidden behind the roofs of barracks and the high walls. I sat down with *Stars Shown to the Children* but am sorry to say that even with the diagram in front of me I could not spot very many! On a dark starry night, have you ever seen shadows cast by the light of the stars? It does happen sometimes.

Do you sleep out?

The mystery of the I.G.'s letter to Feroze has been solved to some extent. Apparently Feroze himself wrote to the I.G. asking news of my health as he was not allowed to communicate with me direct. I did not write to you about my weight, as the jail machine is most unreliable and sometimes a slight movement of the foot would make a difference of six or seven pounds! The weighments are most irregular. They are supposed to be taken every fortnight but actually the machine only comes once in two months or even longer. Then all the gaps on one's ticket are filled in at random. Apart from making me gain 12 lbs instead of the less sensational but more accurate 3 lbs, the I.G. has been going about telling people that I was keeping better health in jail than even in Switzerland! Who gave him reports of my health in Switzerland, I don't know.

Hardly anybody I know is in Allahabad now. The day I was going to Fyzabad I met Pyarelal Banerji[2] at the station going off to Mussoorie – the day I returned I saw Kala Didda[3] complete with family and Shrinarainji in the train for Lahore *en route* to Kashmir.

Do you know that Shona Chachi is all on her lonesome in Lucknow jail? Kishen Chacha[4] has not been keeping at all well – he is now in Kashmir. Vidya is on the *Pioneer's* staff.

I hear that it was largely due to Hariji's – Hridaynath Kunzru's[5] – efforts that U.P. détenus were at last allowed the newspaper and monthly letter. He is now somewhere in the middle East.

1. Gulmohars: trees with brilliant red flowers.
2. Pyarelal Banerji: father-in-law of Purnima Banerji (Nora).
3. Kalavati Madan née Nehru: a cousin of Indira Gandhi.
4. Kishenlal Nehru: uncle of Indira Gandhi ('Chacha' means uncle).
5. Hriday Nath Kunzru: President of the Servants of India Society. Later, a member of Rajya Sabha, or the Upper House of the Indian Parliament, for two terms.

*31st May*

Do you remember the baby Sarala, about whom both Chand and I have written copiously to you? Her mother brought her to see me the other day. My worst fears with regard to her have proved true. She was no longer the bonny baby who left jail, but had shrunk, in these four months, back to her former skinny smallness, instead of getting rounder and fatter as all babies should. She didn't even look intelligent as she used to do. I was really most disappointed. I am arranging for the mother to go to school since she is anxious to do so, though I think it would be more to the point if she were to learn to look after her children.

I am staying these days in the room just below mine as it is cooler than upstairs. As I write I can see through the open door three fat owls sitting all in a row on the neem outside.

Somebody's pet monkey has escaped & come into our garden. For a couple of days it made a perfect nuisance of itself, breaking the *surahis*,[1] going off with any glasses or other vessels left lying about and was up to all sorts of tricks. Then Kishori caught it and is keeping it as a pet – the poor thing is tied with a bit of string. Poor old Johnnie Walker is not going so strong. He hurt his leg & it went septic – it is still not well and he hobbles along on one leg and is not very chirpy. He hardly ever comes out in the front now but spends his time behind the kitchen or near the servants' quarters. The peacock has disappeared.

Lots & lots of love,
Indu

---

112. Ahmadnagar Fort Prison,<br>1st June, 1943

Darling One,

Your letter of May 22nd/23rd[2] reached me yesterday. Also a later letter from Puphi who gave me some more news. In spite of all my tall talk and long practice in keeping cool and collected in untoward circumstances, I have felt worried and distressed about your health. It is aggravating not to be able to get frequent and rapid news of you – to have to wait for a fortnight or so for stale reports. I watch the figures for temperature in various places in the papers. My eye runs down to Allahabad and steadily, and sometimes with an amazing jump, the figure mounts up. 112, 113 – bad enough and, for you, most difficult to bear – and then a jump to 117°F! That is beyond the limit even for Allahabad

---

1. Narrow-necked earthen flagons used for storing water in summer.
2. Refers to letter No. 107.

– I do not remember a higher temperature than 116 at the most there. And the rains there are still far off – it is a good test for you.

I am sending a few more books to you – as follows:

1. Adams: *The Epic of America*
2. Zimmern: *The Greek Commonwealth*
3. Sinclair Lewis: *Main Street*
4. *Modern Plays* (Everyman's Library)
5. *Sculpture Inspired by Kalidasa*

*The Epic of America* is a good book and worth reading if you are in the proper mood. It is the best short survey of America during the past 200 years or so. Zimmern may not interest you unless the subject appeals to you. For my part I am more and more interested in tracing similarities and contacts between ancient India and ancient Greece. This book does not go far in this direction except unconsciously, for India is not in the picture at all, but all manner of traditions, habits & customs crop up which remind one of India.

You must have read all, or nearly all, the plays given in Everyman's selection. Possibly you have seen some. Yet they are good and you might care to re-read some of them.

During this month of May that is just over I thought often of the Kulu Valley where you and I went a year ago. It was a cooling and refreshing thought. Somehow the Himalayas have always a soothing effect on me – even the thought of them helps. That is not merely because I love mountains and glaciers and the deodar and so many other things that are there, but also because of their calm imperturbability which smiles at my own fitful nature. They remain, howsoever excited we may get. They are always there to welcome us whenever we can find our way to them. They represent to me the old strength and the spirit of India, rather remote but ever-present, enduring. I suppose one day you and I will go there again, not for a few days or a week but for an unhurried wandering, away from the burden of this world for a while . . .

I am sorry you found Feroze none too well when you saw him. Some lines in your letter [1] have been blacked out. I suppose they referred to Feroze.

I have something to do with illness here – not my own, for I flourish, but other people's – a fair part of my time is being spent in looking after them, though I am not a good nurse.

---

1. Refers to letter No. 107.

This is my letter No. 12 to you –

Love to you, my dear,<br>
Your loving,<br>
Papu

I understand that the Government of Bombay, in search of a better and pleasanter climate, has shifted to Poona. So letters addressed to me had better be sent now c/o The Secretary to Government, Home Department, Poona. This will probably save delay.

---

113.                                                 20, Carmichael Road,

Bombay,<br>
18th June, 1943

Darling Papu,

Here I am quite close to you, comparatively speaking. But the walls in between are just as high, so that being near or far doesn't make any difference at all.

I left Allahabad on Tuesday. Vatsala Samant has taken a month's holiday – her sister is getting married and her mother and brother were also in Allahabad, so we all travelled together. Hari came too to fetch Rita. Rita and Hari left last night. Travelling is a terrific business these days. The trains are so crowded. However the journey was quite pleasant.

Puphi has just shown me your letter to her. Darling, I think you people are being quite insulting about my health! All this concern merely proves that you don't believe me. I have been ill in the past but I am determined *not* to be ill any more – minor troubles such as flu & appendicitis are naturally not counted in this. I just keep on repeating this but nobody listens to me. I lost some weight because of the flu but am now back to my jail winter weight of 96 lbs. I enclose a typewritten report by Samant.

To set your mind at rest, as you especially ask for a doctor's report, I got examined by Dr Bharucha, and have had an X-ray taken. The full report will be sent to you when it is ready.

Psyche proposes that we should go to Panchgani but that if it pours beyond bearing we should come down to Poona which, I hear, is perfectly delightful these days.

Rajabhai is better and has gained 2 lbs.

Yesterday Puphi took me to a film called *The Moon is Down*. It's about the Nazi occupation of a Norwegian village. Much of it has been censored – you can guess why. It is a good film.

It is only on arrival in Bombay that I finally got away from the shadow of Naini. Smart-clothed people, radios and telephones and cars – how can one associate anything here with Naini? But in the midst of it I think of those who are still there and I can't really enjoy anything. If this is the state of affairs so soon after being released, in a couple of weeks more, being out will become unbearable. As you have perhaps noticed, my mind works in its own peculiar way, so I rarely find anyone who will sympathise or understand.

In Allahabad, I found in a corner of Puphi's room a pile of foreign papers unopened. They are very old but perhaps you have not seen them so I am sending them along. By the way Chhoti Puphi & I have both been getting our *Asia* more or less regularly. I think the reason you don't get a copy is that you, in spite of being a contributing editor, are expected to subscribe. My copy was a Christmas present from an American friend. The subscription ended with 1942.

Sometime in October or November of last year in the days when I was not allowed any letters at all, I was surprised when one letter was handed to me. It was from this same American friend – written in April '42 and posted in Switzerland! It was on the strength of this letter that I wrote to the Government of the U.P. asking whether I could not receive your letters.

I saw Feroze last Sunday. He was well but his foot is still giving him trouble. I have letters from Prabha [1] who is in Bhagalpur with Bul, [2] and Madan Bhai who is in Lucknow. They don't say much.

Last August Tendulkar [3] took some snaps of Puphi and me in *salwar*. I believe they came out quite well. This time he came again and took some more snaps. He is going to send me copies of them all. I should like to send them to you – are you allowed to have photographs? Have you seen his book – *30 Months in Russia?* . . .

Bharati's [4] book is well got up. I haven't recd. it yet.

Just as I was leaving Anand Bhawan I received your parcel of books – the one containing Voltaire's *The Best of All Possible Worlds* and all the reports and bulletins of the Commission for Peace or whatever it is. No signs of the money yet.

Manno Didda is in Bombay and has asked Ladli Chacha to spend

1. Prabhavati Devi: wife of Jayaprakash Narayan, the distinguished Sarvodaya leader. She was deeply influenced by Mahatma Gandhi and active in the freedom struggle. She was also a close friend of Kamala Nehru.

2. Khurshedben Naoroji (Bul): a disciple of Mahatma Gandhi and a friend of the Nehrus. She was a granddaughter of Dadabhai Naoroji.

3. D. G. Tendulkar: political worker and author; well-known for his monumental biography of Mahatma Gandhi.

4. Bharati Sarabhai: a member of the Sarabhai family of Gujarat, who was a poet and writer.

his holidays with her, so he might be coming over. He hadn't made up his mind when I left.

Lots of love, darling,

Your loving,<br>
Indu

---

114.                                                       

20 Carmichael Road,<br>
Bombay,<br>
21st June, 1943

Darling Papu,

Actually I am writing from Auntie's.[1] I came to visit her and am now marooned because of the rain – the local trains are not running! Psyche sometimes motors up to Bombay so I rang her up but Mac[2] has had a heart-attack so she is staying at home. So now there is nothing to be done except sit around. I was feeling most annoyed until the bright idea of writing to you struck me.

I have been examined by Bharucha and been X-rayed. When the X-ray is sent to Bharucha, I shall have to make another appointment with him and get the full report, which will be sent on to you.

*23rd June*

I didn't get very far with my letter-writing at the Vakils. There was so much noise going on. Also I was rather pre-occupied about trains. Every now and then I sent a man across to the station to find out when the trains would start running, for telephones were also out of order. At about 4 o'clock the station people said that all train services were resumed as usual, so I left immediately. Vatsala was to join me *en route* as she had made an appointment with Dr Cooper about my foot. The train was held up at a station called Elphinstone Road – there were three trains standing in front of ours – so that we finally reached the doctor at seven fifteen! The appointment was for five . . .

I think Psyche is finding it difficult to get away from Bombay for a long time. I do hate to be in any one's way, so I think we had better give up the Panchgani plan. At the moment this is what has been decided – we go to Poona on Wednesday morning and stay there. Then if we both feel like going to Panchgani we can always run up. I don't mind the rain if I'm dressed for it.

Your letter No. 15[3] has just come. I am writing to Dr Mahmud's

---

1. Mrs Coonverbai J. Vakil.
2. Maneckji Sorabji Captain (Mac): husband of Goshiben Captain (Psyche).
3. Letter not published.

daughters – I remember them well. The parcel of books arrived just as I was leaving for the station – I think I told you so in a previous letter. Re: the Indian publication of your *Autobiography*, the publishers are Padma Publications, not Hindustan Hamara.

A telegram has been posted to me from Allahabad – 'Panchgani meaningless come straight here. Bijju Chacha.' Isn't it just like him? I have also a charming letter from Chachi. [1]

I like your Hyderabadi letter paper. When I leave Bombay finally I shall have to do a round of visiting – Masi in Jaipur and Nani in Lahore. They are both very hurt that I haven't been to see them before.

I shall write to Agatha & Krishna. Is he still in the Strand, do you think?

Much love,
Indu

———————————————

115.                                   Ahmadnagar Fort Prison,
                                            26th June, 1943

Darling,
I have your letter of the 18th June from Bombay – No. 12. [2] I am glad you have got out of the heat of Allahabad. Probably you are in Panchgani now but I am sending this letter to Bombay. You will let me know your Panchgani address.

I was glad to see Vatsala Samant's report. It is satisfactory. I am not worried about your health, for worry is caused when something that ought to be done and can be done is not done. I am sure you are not guilty of such omission and are quite capable of looking after yourself. But naturally I do not wish to take any chances and your having to stay in Naini Prison in the hot weather was a very unusual occurrence for you which did cause anxiety. I repeated myself often enough in my letters to you, well knowing at the back of my mind that this was not necessary. Still a father is apt to be fussy about such matters and you must not mind. As I wrote to you, I am rather pleased at the way you have gone through this difficult period and this leads me to think that you have really laid the foundations of future good health. This is just the time when continuing care in essential matters secures these foundations. I am sure that within a year or so you will be healthy enough for a normal life in every way, without having to think of your body. A

1. Rameshwari Nehru: wife of Indira Gandhi's uncle, Brijlal Nehru. Active in politics, she was one of the founders of the All India Women's Conference.
2. Refers to letter No. 113.

healthy person does not think of the body; it is taken for granted. But a healthy person also develops habits which keep one fit. Most people, I find, have the most evil habits in small matters – food, rest, etc – and then they complain of ailments, as if they had not invited these ailments by their own misbehaviour.

I should like to see Dr Bharucha's report also.

Your reaction to Bombay after Naini is interesting but natural. I have seldom felt life's contrasts so much as when I went to London (with you) in November 1935. I had spent nearly four years in prison and the two or three months in Badenweiler had been quiet and anxious ones. The change to a great and wealthy city, with all its pomp and luxury, its strength and ceaseless activity, its social and intellectual life, had a remarkable effect upon me. I felt as if I was in a dream, or was I waking from a dream? Which was real and which was unreal? Dream-like almost, I went through my early engagements, and I remember that at the first short speech I made at a social gathering this contrast and sense of unreality coloured my words. Gradually, but soon enough, I adapted myself to the new environment and felt at home in it.

To a lesser extent that has been a frequent experience with me. Indeed long years in prison leave their permanent imprint on the mind and face, and nothing that can happen subsequently can rub it off. Ghost-like, that shadow-self of prison accompanies one through life's journey, often adding a deeper significance to the passing moment; sometimes, like a sentinel, barring the way to a particular feeling or sensation. It creates a self-made prison of the mind out of which escape is harder than from any other prison. Perhaps that is in keeping with the state of affairs in the world today.

You write that your mind works in a peculiar way and that you rarely find anyone who will sympathise or understand you. True enough for all of us who think, and yet, often enough, the fault lies with us rather than with others. Each one of us has, or ought to have, his ivory tower of thought, to which he retires from time to time. But no one can live in that ivory tower for any length of time without drifting away from the current of life and losing touch with those vital and human impulses which mean so much for us. Living so, we wither and shrink and become querulous and dissatisfied with others, and consequently with life itself. That is not good enough. Almost every person who thinks, imagines that he or she is a peculiar person, apart from the rest. And so, of course, every individual is. Then there is the feeling of lack of sympathy and understanding. True enough, again, for we are all, deep down, strangers to each other and even to ourselves. But the doors and windows of sympathy and understanding do not open out to us of themselves: they await our initiative. The more we give to others, the more do others give to us. Like most things in life, they come to us when we are not seeking them deliberately but thinking of something else.

I should like you to send me Tendulkar's snapshots – both the old ones taken in August and the new ones. I suppose they will get through.

About *Asia*, I am surprised to learn that both Puphi and you have been, or were, receiving copies. Betty wrote to me that it had long ceased to come. Of course I subscribe to it, or rather it is on the list I sent to Walsh [1] over a year ago asking him to subscribe on my behalf. If you have any copies of it for the last year I should like you to send them.

You mention that Madan Bhai is in Lucknow. Does that mean he is in prison there? Where is Upadhyaya? . . .

I suggested to you that you might write to Krishna; whether your letter will reach him or not I do not know. There is a book I have long wanted to get and have so far failed. You might ask him to send it. It is J. D. Bernal's [2] *The Social Function of Science* (Routledge, 12sh. 6d.). It is a fairly old book and was published some years ago. Also he might send one or two other books that he thinks might interest me and can reach me. The chances of his sending these books are strictly limited, but there is no harm in trying.

Here is a *rubai* (quatrain) by Hālī. [3] There is an English word in it – 'reformer'. Such words in Urdu always are difficult to make out as one does not expect them. This kind of verse dealing with social reforms and the influence of Western life on India was specially popularised by Akbar, the poet of Allahabad (*Akbar Allahabadi* he is called). [4] Akbar's son married a European woman and so Akbar was personally interested and he reacted strongly against this intrusion of the West, as he called it. These verses were topical enough a generation ago. Now they have dated. The following quotation is, however, not by Akbar but by another well-known Urdu poet, Hālī:

دھونے کی ہے اے ریفارمر جا باقی کپڑے یہ ہے جب تلک دھبا باقی
دھو شوق سے کپڑے کو پر اتنا نہ رگڑ دھبا رہے کپڑے یہ نہ کپڑا باقی
( حالی )

In Hindi: हाली-रुबाई

1. Richard J. Walsh: American publisher.
2. J. D. Bernal: British physicist.
3. Altaf Hussain Hālī of Panipat (1837–1914): a nationalist poet associated with Aligarh Muslim University.
4. Syed Akbar Husain (1846–1921): a satirical poet.

धोने की है ऐ रिफार्मर जा बाक़ी
कपड़े पे है जब तलक के धब्बा बाक़ी
धो शौक़ से कपड़े को, पर इतना न रगड़
धब्बा रहे कपड़े पे न कपड़ा बाक़ी ।।[1]

The language is simple enough. जा means जगह
Give my love to Psyche.

Love from your loving,<br>Papu

I have just received a letter from Puphi (Nan) in which she tells me that
Ranjit has had a bad heart-attack and has been transferred to Lucknow
for treatment.

---

116.　　　　　　　　　　　　　　　　　　　　　　Poona,
　　　　　　　　　　　　　　　　　　　　　　1st July, 1943

Darling Papu,
Psyche & I came here yesterday. Following your bad habit, I arrived at
Victoria Terminus after the guard had blown his whistle, but managed
to catch the train all the same. I have always liked the journey from
Bombay to Poona, but it is especially delightful in the monsoon. Silvery
waterfalls glimmering in the dark foliage, or against the inky rocks. After
the sticky heat of Bombay, Poona is very pleasantly cool. We are staying
with Nurie.[2] Her house isn't in Poona proper but nearer to Shivajina-
gar, two and a half miles away. It is very quiet. She has a small garden,
but it is not up to much yet, as the flowers and vegetables have only just
been planted. We shall probably leave for Panchgani on Tuesday next.
Our address there will be: Oomra Hall, Panchgani . . .

I am sending you today a basket of fruit. Puphi says she sent one
nearly a month ago – did you receive it? I am also sending two books:
*That Day Alone* by Van Passen and K. T. Shah's latest, *How India Pays
for the War.*

What is your weight now? I hope you have – or at least are making
an effort to – regain some of your lost pounds.

1. Hālī:　O ye reformer, clean the garment
　　　　　So long as the stain is there;
　　　　　Clean it as ye may;
　　　　　Pray, do not rub it so
　　　　　That it wears away!
2. Nargis Captain: granddaughter of Dadabhai Naoroji; a friend of the Nehrus.

Psyche and Nurie send their love. Nurie wants to know if you dream of Chand Bibi! [1]

Puphi – the big one – is staying at the Savoy Hotel. There was no room available at Pushkarbhai's. Rita was given a cocker spaniel by someone in Bombay and now I believe she has acquired another one in Mussoorie.

Lots of love,
Your loving,
Indu

117.                                    Admadnagar Fort Prison,
                                            3rd July, 1943

Darling,
I have your letter of the 23rd June. [2] I wonder if you are still in Bombay. Anyway this letter must go there for want of a better address . . .

I am sorry about Mac. Of course you should not come in the way of Psyche's normal programme. If you go to Poona, who will go with you? Psyche? And where will you stay? Where is Nargis nowadays?

Kashmir is so far away. Otherwise it is the obvious place for rest and a holiday – I cannot make out why people who have the choice, go to other places. You need not rule out Kashmir entirely, but for the present it does seem advisable to pitch your tent at some nearer and more accessible place. To be cut off more or less from events and people by going to Kashmir is itself an unattractive prospect.

You are right. You should do some visiting later. You have not seen Nani since your marriage, have you? A visit to her is long overdue.

I cannot give you any new address for Krishna. I do not think I have had a letter from him during the last three years nearly. You can try the old address in Strand.

No, I have not been spinning here. I did not have my *charkha* [3] for some months but even when it came I did not take to it. This was partly due to the pain in my arm. I had an idea that spinning aggravated it, or at least kept it going. Also, I was doing so much manual work in connection with gardening that no further manual labour seemed called for. Now that you have demanded yarn from me and my right arm is almost normal, I am thinking of going back to the *charkha*. Perhaps I may start

1. Chand Bibi: the pet cat of Jawaharlal Nehru in Ahmadnagar Fort. She was named after a famous queen of medieval India.
2. Refers to letter No. 114.
3. Spinning wheel.

our second year here with spinning. Only five weeks remain to it. I have some slivers (*punis*) but not much. You might ask Psyche to have a bundle of good slivers sent to me.

But surely you will not expect me to supply you with yarn enough for your requirements. That is beyond my capacity, especially as I do not propose to spin for more than, at the most, an hour a day. This does not carry one very far. Some of my colleagues here, better spinners than I am, have produced quite a lot. One of them has got about a dozen *dhotis* and saris, etc, made out of the yarn he has spun here during the last ten months.

Some of my old yarn – not much – was lying in my dressing room (left hand top or bottom drawer of the dressing table) and I asked Betty, when she was going to Allahabad, to get hold of it and give it to Psyche or the G.S.S.[1] I wonder if this was done.

In some of the old English papers I have seen an advertisement of a new book by Aldous Huxley. It is called *The Art of Seeing* (Chatto & Windus, 7sh.). Huxley's books are always interesting in some way or other but this particular book I am interested in because of the subject. Huxley lost his sight, or nearly so. He shows in this book how he recovered it by some psychological process, possibly some exercises. My sight is good enough but I am interested in bodily health. For the moment, however, it is Mahmud's eye trouble that has led me to this book. One of his eyes does not function at all and the other is seldom in good condition. So if it is possible to get this book, I shall be glad. I realise that this is no easy matter.

I should also like to have some time or other – no hurry – my book, *The Unity of India*. If it is possible to buy a new copy, I would prefer this. But the book was not available at the bookshops more than a year ago and there is little chance of fresh supplies having come in. With great difficulty a friend of mine managed to get a copy for me from a Calcutta bookshop, paying Rs. 30/- for it. Some profiteering! If a new copy is not available, get my copy from Allahabad, when you can easily manage this. I repeat, do not put yourself out for it.

Here is Urdu verse of a somewhat different type. It is called a *qata*, that is, four lines with a running thought, unlike the couplets which stand by themselves. It is by Wazir of Lucknow[2] (Wazir Lakhnavi) and is a gentle remonstrance and taunt at the Almighty for punishing him, although He is called the All-Merciful, etc. There are some words in it which you probably do not know, but you should know them, as they are in frequent use.

1. Gandhi Seva Sadan: a social service institution named after Gandhi.
2. Khwaja Mohammed Wazir (d. 1852): a poet of the city of Lucknow.

نه کر عوض مرے جرم و گناه بے حد کا  الهی  تجکو غفور الرحیم کہتے ہیں

کہیں کہیں نہ عدو دیکھ کر مجھے محتاج  یہ اسکے بندے ہیں جسکو کریم کہتے ہیں

(وزیر لکھنوی)

In Hindi: वज़ीर लखनवी—

न कर एवज़ मेरे जुर्मों गुनाह बेहद का
इलाही! तुज को ग्रफ़ूर उल रहीम क्हते हैं ।
कहीं कहें न उद्दू देख कर मुझे मोहताज
यह उसके बंदे हैं जिसको करीम क्हते हैं! [1]

एवज़ means बदला; ग्रफ़ूर=माफ करने वाला= who pardons; रहीम=रहम करने वाला=one who pities = the Merciful; उद्दू=दुश्मन= enemy; रुसवा=तकलीफ में= in pain; करीम=करम करने वाला=बख़्श ने वाला= the Giver, also one who forgives.

Some words, like *Ilahi*, are written in a curious way. These are the relics of Arabic in Urdu.

You must have made a fair collection of Urdu verses in your notebook by this time.

This is my letter No. 17. We are having plenty of rain.

Love,
Your loving,
Papu

---

118.                                                                  Poona,
                                                                3rd July, 1943

Darling Papu,

Your letter of the 26th June [2] reached me last evening. I have rather lost count of my letters to you. But if my letter of the 18th June was No. 12, I think this one must be No. 16. My last letter [3] was sent by hand to the Secretariat, along with some other things for you: mangoes, two books, one bottle of eye-lotion. The eye-lotion has been made up in Bombay from a prescription sent by Rajan Didda. Is this what you have been using? I was under the impression that you used 'Murine'. I tried to get some for you, but it was not available in Bombay.

1. Wazir Lackhnavi:    Pray, weigh me not for my countless sins, O Lord,
                       Thou art The Most Compassionate Pardoner!
                       Seeing me helpless, the enemies may not deride and say
                       'Look, here is he who serves The Most Benevolent One!'
2. Refers to letter No. 115.
3. Refers to letter No. 116.

Two snaps taken by Tendulkar I sent to you with letter No. 14.[1] Since then I have discovered another one which seems to be nicer. It is stamp size and I do not know what it will turn out like in an enlargement. I shall send it later. Tendulkar has also given a book for you: *Russian Fables* translated by Bernard Pares. Just in case anybody is learning Russian, it has both Russian and English texts! I shall send it on to you, after looking through it myself. Did you get Tendulkar's own book, *30 Months in Russia*? I have only just glanced at it, as I wanted to send my copy to Feroze, but I think it is rather a good book of its kind. The get-up and photographs are also good.

Verrier Elwin is writing a new book called – *Murder*!

I have sent airgraphs to Krishna, Agatha and Mami. Nurie says airgraphs take a whole month to reach England, so I shall not wait for Krishna's reply but will send him another one asking about the books, though I doubt if any books will be able to get through these days, or even if parcels of books are allowed. On second thoughts, I think I shall first enquire at the Bombay Booksellers if they have the books or if they can get them from England.

There is rather a muddle about Bharucha's report. Vatsala said she would go and get it and Psyche said she would, but Bharucha has such awkward hours, he is difficult to contact – so nobody has got the report! The simplest thing now will be to write to Bharucha to post it. So I hope you will eventually get it.

Upadhyaya is in Naini. Chandra Singh[2] was also there and had a sentence of seven years. On appeal this was reduced to twelve or eighteen months. He has now been transferred. Madan Bhai has been in detention since December. He had a terrible shock. His father, rather a grand old man, carrying his years remarkably well, was killed by dacoits when they came to plunder the house. Part of the house was destroyed and many goods stolen. Madan Bhai was arrested just as he had heard the awful news and was preparing to go to Hardoi. Chunneybhai is out but for some years he has been a permanent invalid. In any case neither of the brothers is capable of looking after and managing the estates as the old man did. I haven't been to Lucknow and so have no detailed news of the state of affairs in Hardoi.

Swarup – Raja's wife – also spent a couple of months in jail. Shona Chachi is still there. Now if I had only been with her I should be quite an Urdu scholar. I hear that she is very fond of and has a remarkable knowledge of Urdu and Persian poetry.

1. Letter not published.
2. Chandra Singh of the Garhwal regiment which refused to fire on a demonstrating crowd of nationalists in Peshawar during the Civil Disobedience movement of 1930.

Psyche greatly appreciated the *rubai* by Hālī. She had a letter from Bul a couple of days ago. Bul seems to be very depressed and unsettled. Unlike the rest of us, she says she cannot bear to read the classics in jail. She wants the latest news, the latest books and plenty of them. Psyche says it's quite a job to keep her supplied.

In an old article I found the other day a paragraph which I thought rather appropriate to the remarks you make about one's reaction to the outside world after months of seclusion in prison.

To go away, the French say shrewdly, is to die a little. But why has nobody ever made the parallel observation: 'To return is to know what it is to be a ghost?' For when you first come home you are always something of a ghost. They were sorry you went away, and they welcome you back with affection: but in the meanwhile they have adjusted their lives a little to your absence. They ask 'Where did you go? What was it like?' But you cannot tell them. For you cannot make them understand the essential point, which is that when you went away you took the centre of the universe with you, so that the whole thing went on revolving, just as usual, round your own head. How could they, indeed, be expected to understand this, when they know quite well that all the time the centre of everything stayed at home with them? It is a day or two, as a rule, before your universe and theirs merge and become concentric, and when that happens you know that you are really home!

I gave you my Panchgani address in my last letter.[1] Here it is again: Oomra Hall, Panchgani. You may remember it. Years ago[2] I stayed there with Mummie and Pilloo Vesugar.[3] We still have the snapshots taken there – they are the best ever taken of Mummie.

We lead a very quiet life here. I get up late, then potter about in the garden, write innumerable letters and sometimes listen in to the radio. In the evenings a short walk. In her garden, Nurie has planted all sorts of vegetables, but they do not seem to be doing very well, partly because of the lack of rain. Looking at the packets of seeds I thought of a poem we read in class in Badminton School. It was called 'The Seed Shop'.[4] I cannot recollect who wrote it or what the words were beyond the last three lines, which run:

1. Refers to letter No. 116.
2. In March 1932.
3. Pilloo Vesugar: son of the noted lawyer D. N. Bahadurji. Bahadurji family was on cordial terms with the Nehrus.
4. 'The Seed Shop' by Muriel Stuart.

Sealed in their shells, a million roses leap;
Here I can blow a garden with my breath,
And in my hand a forest lies asleep.

Nurie has a Zanzibar parrot, Pepite by name. She is a soft soft grey
with a brilliant red tail – such a lovely combination. Pepite fancies herself
as a singer and she & Psyche have duets every now and then.

Tons of love to you and *namaskars* to everyone else.

Your loving,
Indu

---

119.                                                Poona,
6th July, 1943

Darling Papu,

Your letter No. 17[1] came this morning. And this is my letter No. 17
in reply to it.

I am rather alarmed at the view you have taken on my remark about
your spinning. I don't exactly remember what I had said – but actually
we are not so much in need of yarn or cloth that you should risk a pain
in your already painful arm in order to provide it. Please do give up the
idea of starting to spin now. You were quite right – gardening is a more
healthful and also pleasurable occupation, and you should certainly not
give it up for spinning, especially when spinning hurts your arm and you
are not in the mood for it. It is a good thing that your arm is feeling
better but that is all the more reason that you should rest it until the
pain disappears completely. And even afterwards you must be very careful with it and not do anything which may cause the pain to return, or
in any way strain the arm. I have plenty of clothes and will not need any
for a long time. From what you said in one of your earlier letters I
gathered that you are also well stocked, so that there is no cause for
immediate worry. The future will look after itself. And from the state
of the few *Khadi Bhandars*[2] still open I deduce that soon there will be
no *khadi* – or very little – available. As far as I am concerned, it is high
time that I started producing my own yarn. So even if you did send
some I should be very truthful and not use it for myself. Besides it is
practically impossible to get any slivers. So please do give up the idea
of spinning now . . .

---

1. Refers to letter No. 117.
2. Shops for the sale of *khadi*.

You mention Huxley's book. I was going to get it for you in any case, but it has not yet come to India. It is sure to be interesting. For some years Huxley was following the treatment of a man whose methods seem rather similar to our Dr Agarwal's. This man was later accused of being a quack and a case was brought against him. Huxley and other well-known people were called as witnesses for the defence. I remember that Huxley spoke very warmly and enthusiastically and testified how this man's treatment had helped him – and many other practically blind men – to regain their eyesight. I think the man was acquitted – the case caused quite a stir in America.

I am sending you six packets of cigarettes, your cigarette-case (it has been mended) and the following books:

1. *My India, My America*
2. *Russian Fables of Krylov*
3. Two copies of *Life*
4. Two copies of *Manchester Guardian*
5. One copy of *Time*.

Shridharani's book I had sent for you a long time ago but apparently Rajabhai asked for it and said he would read it very quickly so Puphi sent it on to him. It has only just come back. Some of the Russian fables are rather good. Tendulkar gave me the book, but he was very keen on your having a look at it.

A letter from Panchgani says that it is very pleasant there and no rain. This sounds quite jolly for us but it is disastrous for the crops, & prices being what they are, things will be far from jolly for most people.

I hear that Rajabhai is better now and has regained 2 lbs. No further news of Pupha.

Keep cheerful, darling.

Much love,
Indu

---

120.                      Ahmadnagar Fort Prison,
                                        10th July, 1943

Darling Indu,
During the last week I have had two letters [1] from you, both from Poona. The last one was No. 16. I have received the two books you have sent me; also the parcel of *langra* mangoes. These mangoes were in good condition,

---

1. Refers to letters No. 116 and 118.

except for a few. It was delightful to have a good *langra* again. Some weeks ago I received the parcel of *Alphonsos* which Betty sent.

The eye-lotion has also come. I was somewhat surprised at it. I wanted Murine but having forgotten the name I asked Betty to find out from Rajan, who had originally introduced me to Murine in Dehra jail. I suppose this was not available and so Rajan sent some prescription. Now I have got the name from your letter but that will not help much.

I liked your pictures. In last year's snap you look about fifteen. You look a little older this year and the chin and jaws are firmer. Perhaps this means growth and development, both bodily and mental. But pictures depend so much on clothes and accidental circumstances. They capture a particular mood and fix it. In the course of the same day a person may look older and wiser or otherwise. Puphi (Nan) wrote to me that the 'service bob' suited you very well and you looked very boyish in it.

I should like to have your other snapshot which you mention. Also, if you can manage it, Mummie's pictures taken at Panchgani. When I came here I had a few odd snaps in my pocket book, Mummie's and yours. Now that you have added to them, I have stuck some of them up in some kind of frames and my room looks much gayer.

I am sending you to Panchgani some books which I no longer need. I want to get rid of such books so as not to keep on piling them here. After another two or three weeks I shall probably want to send some more. Where shall I send them? The old foreign periodicals are arriving in batches. Some of them are more than a year old but there is often something of interest in them and I am glad you sent them. I am returning them from time to time to Betty. Or do you want to have them?

The following books are being sent to you:

1. Macneile Dixon: *The Human Situation*
2. Mackenzie: *Myths of China & Japan* – (Psyche's)
3. Alva: *Men & Supermen of Hindustan*
4. Mark Twain: *Tom Sawyer*
5.   – Do –   : *Huckleberry Finn*
6. Tendulkar: *30 Months in Russia*
7. Mir Amman: *Bagh-o-Bahar*
   and 2 copies of the *Reader's Digest*, Nov. & Dec. 1942

One of these books, as marked, is Psyche's. Please give it to her. Have you read the Mark Twain books? They are interesting and make one understand to some extent the background in America in the early days. Both the books I am sending are Tara's copies.

The Urdu book is one of the earliest prose works in Urdu, written about

140 years ago. It was written especially at the suggestion of the officers of the East India Company to enable young factors from England to learn Urdu. It is simply written. The stories it contains are of course older.

I have received a letter from Amma from Lahore. Will you write to her and tell her that I have got it and that I shall write to her again later?

I was sorry to learn of the tragic circumstances of Madan's father's death. We have been particularly cut off from news of the U.P. The newspapers we get are from other parts and seldom give U.P. news. I do not yet know, except from what you have written, which of our friends or relatives are in prison there.

Where is Upadhyaya's family and Chandra Singh's wife? Are they in Allahabad still or have they gone to their respective homes in the mountains?

I got Mridu's long message which you conveyed to me and I was glad to have news of her. She is a very brave girl, one of the most courageous persons I know.

Poor Bebee has a way of [inviting] accidents. The number of them she has had, especially with cars. It is very foolish of her to continue to rush about in spite of her ill health. She is not going to solve the food problem this way. That is pretty desperate now and individual efforts cannot take one far. Still it must be difficult to see all this terrible suffering and sit idle.

Have vegetables been grown in any quantity in Anand Bhawan? Eighteen months ago or more I impressed Ladli Bhai with this and suggested that there should be widespread sowing of vegetable seeds. He was not keen and said we would not require all this. Of course not, but then there were our servants, our friends, our neighbours and indeed so many other people who would need them. I do not think he quite appreciated my argument; still he promised to make a beginning.

Our garden is taking shape now for the new season and, within a month, it should be in flowers. This is not a good season for flowers. But we have laid the foundation for a good display in the early winter.

One of our occupations just at present is to watch the new generation of birds come out of their nests. Our rooms are full of sparrows' nests; our verandah has many a *maina's* [1] nest and an occasional swallow nest. The other day we discovered a bulbul's nest right in the heart of a creeper, quite low down and accessible. It was a lovely piece of weaving, cunningly resting on and partly hung from the thin strands of the creeper. Two baby bulbuls peeped out of it and the rest seemed much too small for them. Between the bulbul parents and the *mainas* nearby there was continuous war, but fortunately no damage was done.

1. A kind of starling.

The first two days or so, when the nestlings come out of their nests, are a time of trial for them and their parents. The solitary neem tree [1] we have got in a corner of our yard contains a colony of kites, and they swoop down on the fledglings and sometimes succeed in carrying them away, but not if the parents are anywhere about. It is extraordinary how the small *maina* attacks a kite fiercely and pursues it, if the kite ventures to come near its young. I do not know how many of the fledglings have been carried off by the kites. Yesterday we actually saw one such tragedy – it was a *maina* babe. The bulbuls have, I think, escaped.

The bulbul in India seems to be a much more prosaic bird than its cousins in Europe or in Iran – the nightingales, *rossignols*, *Nachtigalls*, etc. In Iran it is called the *hazar-dastan*. It does not seem to indulge in much singing here. The bird which is continually attracting attention by its cries is the *koel*. [2] I suppose they have their nests round about somewhere. The parrots also must have a home nearby as they fly over us frequently. The wagtail used to visit us regularly but it has not been in evidence for two or three months.

Do not trouble yourself about my health or weight. I am in excellent condition – physically and mentally. My weight is now 133 lbs, which is just right. According to some rather silly theories of calculating weight with reference to height and age, I believe it should be about 140 or so. As a matter of fact I always gain about 5 lbs on release from jail, owing to better food, etc.

The quotation you have given from an old article [3] is singularly true and appropriate – much more so for those who go to prison than the writer probably imagined. We do become ghost-like for a while at least, and if the periods in prison have been long, some of this ghostly character clings throughout life. One cannot get out completely from that environment and it follows us wherever we may go.

What a lovely idea is contained in the three lines of 'The Seed Shop' poem! [4]

I have just been reading a review of a new Chinese book translated by Arthur Waley – or rather the book is an old one but the translation is new. It is a novel of which the central character is an old friend, Hiuen-tsang. It is called: *Monkey* by Wu Ch'eng-en, translated by Arthur Waley (Allen & Unwin, 12sh. 6d.). I do not suppose you can easily get it. But note it down and get it when you can.

Yes, tell Nurie that I often think of Chand Bibi. Inevitably so. She

1. Margosa tree.
2. Indian cuckoo.
3. See letter No. 118.
4. See letter No. 118.

has not appeared in my dreams when I am asleep but my waking dreams have often been full of her.

This letter is long enough already. So I shall give you only a single couplet of Ghalib:

رو میں ہے رخشِ عمر کہاں دیکھیے تھمے
(غالب)    نے ہاتھ باگ پر ہے نہ پا ہے رکاب میں

In Hindi:

रौ में है रख़्श उम्र कहां देखिये थमे
ने हाथ बाग पर है न पा है रिकाब में ।[1]

रख़्श=घोड़ा; पा=पैर

Your letter No. 17, dated 6/7[2] has just come – I had expected it from Panchgani but it is from Poona. Still I am sending this to Panchgani – this is my No. 18.

Love,<br>
Your loving,<br>
Papu

---

121.                                        Oomra Hall,
                                              Panchgani,
                                        14th July, 1943

Darling Papu,

Your letter No. 18[3] came yesterday. This is my 18th also.

Today it's just a week since our arrival in Panchgani, and the whole time it has rained almost non-stop. Today promises to be a little more cheerful. I go out for at least one walk a day whatever the weather. If it is clear Psyche joins me. Usually I go in the mornings before breakfast, while Psyche is still in bed. Unfortunately my raincoat – it is an old one belonging to Chand – is far from waterproof. I have written to Puphi to send another one. I have a cape in Allahabad but it has no hood and I do hate umbrellas, especially out on a walk. So Bari Puphi said that Chand's cape was a good one and I had better take that. I have borrowed a pair of ancient Wellingtons from Mrs Vakil.

1. Ghalib:    The steed of life
              Spirited does it go;
              Where does it stop, who can know?
              Neither our feet in the stirrups are
              Nor the reins do we hold!
2. Refers to letter No. 119.
3. Refers to letter No. 120.

I am vastly intrigued by a little bird. It appears to be the only bird in Panchgani apart from the babblers. It goes 'Ferdi', 'Ferdi' – 'tweet-tweet', rather like an insolent schoolboy. I haven't managed to get a glimpse of it yet.

About the snapshots. Mummie's is in Allahabad. I shall send it to you as soon as I get back. There doesn't seem to be much possibility of getting my one enlarged here. The old periodicals which were sent from Bombay recently were the ones I brought from Allahabad. I have seen them. So send them to Bombay. About the other batch of books I shall let you know later. We don't yet know how long we shall be here.

If you like, I could arrange for you to get the *Leader* or the *Pioneer*. They do have a bit of local news that may not find its way to other newspapers but otherwise they are not up to much.

Upadhyaya's wife and two daughters are in Allahabad. Also Chandra Singh's wife and child ... Upadhyaya's wife wanted to go up to her home in Almora – two of her daughters are already there. But Chandra Singh's wife kicked up an awful row and said she couldn't stay alone with all the soldiers and policemen just across the wall in Swaraj Bhawan. I offered to pay her fare to Almora so that she could also go, but she refuses to leave Allahabad. None of them are used to the heat and are consequently looking pale and sickly.

All sorts of seedlings were sown in our garden. And whilst we were in jail, I hear that some cauliflowers & cucumbers and other vegetables did come up. But I don't think anything has been sown this season. The *mali*[1] says that the porcupines come and eat up everything before it is time for them to be picked. I do not know how true this is. One or two porcupines were certainly killed by the *chowkidar*[2] after my release.

Puphi writes that none of the books you asked for are available. She has placed an order that if any of them turn up they should be kept aside for you.

I have a letter from Nora. She has now come down from Mussoorie. She is far from well. The Mussoorie doctors said that her present complaints are a clear indication that her erstwhile enemies, the tubercular germs, are resuming hostilities. Instead of resting a while, she has come down to the heat of Allahabad. Later she proposes to go to Simla to her mother. Nora had such a splendid opportunity for rest in jail but in spite of my repeated lectures on the subject, she persisted in leading what I thought was a very unhealthy existence – wrong food, wrong timings of sleep, and so on. No routine of any kind. If she couldn't do so in jail, it is extremely doubtful if she will be able to do anything about

1. Gardener.
2. Watchman.

it outside, with all the temptations of seeing friends and relatives and eating rich foods. The one big difference will be proper medical assistance and fresh vegetables and fruit.

There is only one post here, so I shall send this off to the Post Office now, so as not to miss the bus.

Lots of love to you – *namaskars* to the others.

Indu

122.                                    Ahmadnagar Fort Prison,
                                             17th July, 1943

Darling Indu,

Your letter No. 17 dated 6th July [1] reached me as I was finishing my last letter to you. During the last week I have had no further news of you but I expect to have a letter from you today. It usually comes on Saturdays.

I have received the cigarette case and the six boxes of cigarettes. Also the books you sent me (Shridharani's and Russian Fables, etc).

You are needlessly alarmed about my spinning. I never thought that I could supply you or myself with enough yarn to make any appreciable difference. I have long been thinking of going back to it chiefly because I rather like it and it is extraordinarily soothing – in relatively small doses. It is not going to take the place of gardening and I do not think it will affect my arm now. I shall probably spin a little daily and watch results. If these results are in any way unsatisfactory, I shall give it up. At the most I shall spin an hour a day, probably less.

I have had no trouble with my feet, as far as I can remember, for over twenty years in spite of *chappals* and the like. But I do think *chappals* are not good for the feet except for home wear. It is absurd to go for a long walk in them, and in a crowd they are a nuisance and sometimes give a great deal of trouble. I think my immunity from foot trouble has largely been due to my old habit of running which has kept the foot muscles strong and the arch of the foot firm in spite of *chappals*. For the last four or five years I have been wearing Peshawari *chappals* with a rubber heel added. This gives nearly an inch of heel. I find now that I feel uncomfortable in ordinary heelless *chappals*. My balance is upset a little and there is no proper grip. So I can quite understand your difficulties. You had better wear well-fitting shoes with inside supports when necessary.

Many weeks ago I asked Betty to write to Walsh, my publisher in America, and tell him to continue my subscriptions to various American

---

1. Refers to letter No. 119.

periodicals. She says she has done so, but she was doubtful of her letter reaching him as she had written to him repeatedly without eliciting an answer. I do not understand why letters should not reach America, especially more or less business letters. With so many Americans in India, there must be a big mail coming from the U.S. I suggest that you might also write to Walsh and give him the list of periodicals and tell him that I would be grateful if he could arrange to have them sent regularly, paying for them out of my royalty account with him. In case there is nothing left in this account (which is unlikely), I shall try to arrange for a remittance. Mention to him that Betty has already written at my instance but the list you are sending is a longer one than the one Betty sent. I had forgotten to add one or two papers then. Here is the list: *Life, Time, Nation, New Republic, Reader's Digest, Fortune* (for Feroze), *Asia, Amerasia, Pacific Affairs* (Quarterly), *Foreign Affairs* (Quarterly). Ten in all, to which he can add any others he considers appropriate.

You might also ask him to send a second copy of *Asia* addressed to you direct. It is a good magazine and two copies will be easily utilised. All my papers and periodicals should of course be sent to Anand Bhawan. I imagine this list will amount to about $60 or $70 (but you need not mention this to him).

In some American magazine I have seen a review of an American edition of my *Unity of India*, published by John Day. I have not seen this book yet. It appears that it came out in December or January last. Tell Walsh that I should like to see it, if it is possible for him to send a copy. Walsh's address is: Richard J. Walsh, The John Day Company Inc., Publishers, 40 East 49th Street, New York City, U.S.A.

The Times Book Club of London continues to send me some periodicals – *New Statesman*, etc – although I have not paid them anything for years. They have been very decent about it, possibly because I am one of their earliest members and subscribers. When you write to Krishna next you might ask him to settle my account with the T.B.C. out of any royalty monies he may hold on my behalf. Of course if he has no such money, he should not pay. Or perhaps it is easier for you to deal directly with the T.B.C. You can ask Bachhraj to send them £20 on account and write & tell them that you are doing so, asking them how my account stands. I suppose there is no difficulty in sending money to England. You might find out from the T.B.C. what papers they are sending me now – I am not sure. They should continue sending them till further instructions. The T.B.C. address is: The Times Book Club, 42 Wigmore Street, London W.1. My subscriber's number with them is I 2966.

Yesterday I had a letter from Puphi from Mussoorie. She gave me some news of Ranjit who is slowly progressing in the Balrampur Hospital.

As soon as you tell me of the address where they are to be sent to, I shall send you a few books. Among these will be Sylvain Levi's[1] *Le Théâtre Indien* which, after a lot of searching and hunting, Psyche unearthed for me from the library of the Bombay branch of the Royal Asiatic Society. Please give this book to her. But before you do so, you might glance through it yourself. The book is an old one, published in 1890, but it is nevertheless interesting. Probably you know very little about the old Indian theatre – very few people in India do. That is remarkable enough. And yet I think this subject is a fascinating one and tells us a great deal about our early beginnings and cultural background. Do not trouble to read the whole book. Big chunks of it are technical & dry. Glance through the introduction, the 'Histoire de la littérature Dramatique', 'Les Origines du Drama' (parts), 'L'Influence Grecque', and the two final chapters.

Do you remember the visit we paid in Paris to Madame Sylvain Levi in 1938? Her husband had died a few months earlier and she was inconsolable.[2]

I am returning *Life, Time*, etc, to Betty. Tell me if you want them and I shall send them to you direct. One number of *Life* I shall send you anyhow. This contains new kinds of charts and maps which can be cut out and stuck in some kind of rectangular blocks. You can try to do this. This is supposed to give a much clearer idea of the world as it is.

Here is something from Ghalib:

تو     اور  آرائش  خمِ کاکل

(غالب)          میں اور اندیشه ہاۓ دور دراز

In Hindi:

तू, और आराएशे ख़मे काकुल
मैं, और अंदेश हाए दूर श्रो दराज़![3]

ख़म   means curl; काकुल means the hair in front and sides; ख़मे काकुल= front and side curls.

1. Sylvain Levi (1863–1935): French orientalist.
2. Jawaharlal Nehru visited Paris both in 1935 and 1938. Since Sylvain Levi, the French orientalist, died in 1935, the reference to a visit to Madame Sylvain Levi in 1938 is probably a memory lapse. The visit may actually have taken place in 1935.
3. Ghalib: You and I, together,
              A picture we do make;
              You – engaged in plaiting and braiding
              the twists and twirls of your lock;
              And me – my eyes fixed on you – absorbed
              in the twirl of my thoughts!

This is from Amir:[1]

(امیر)
ہے آج جو سرگزشت اپنی
کل اُس کی کہانیاں بنیں گی

है ब्राज जो सर गुज़श्त ब्रपनी
कल इसकी कहानियां बनेंगी ! [2]

सर गुज़श्त = what is happening = जो वाक़्यात हम पर गुज़र रहे हैं.

This is my letter No. 19. No letter from you has come thus far. I shall wait a little longer and then send this off.

Love,
Your loving,
Papu

---

123.

Oomra Hall,
Panchgani
17th July, 1943

Darling Papu,

Here is letter No. 19.

Since my last letter to you, the Rain-God has been slightly less generous. We actually had an hour or two of rather watery sun, 'sending feelers towards the forgotten earth'.

Soon after I had posted your letter, Psyche and I nearly had a fit! With the post came a telegram from Feroze from Victoria Terminus saying that he was arriving in Panchgani the same evening! He is here now. Apparently somebody paid his fine, so with the remission on his year's sentence, he was released on the 10th. He is here now. I want to get over my visiting tour and then settle down to some work. Plans are still vague.

I wonder if while I was in jail, Puphi gave you any news of the *Herald*. There is an argument about it now. For some time Government have allowed an engineer to clean and oil the machinery every week, so that it may not get spoilt. All debts have been paid and there is enough at hand to pull on for a couple of years or so. Now Mohan Bhai[3] wants

1. Amir Khusru (1255–1325): a poet of medieval India.
2. Amir: What goes on with us today,
       Tomorrow tales of it
       They'll make!
3. Mohanlal Nehru: a cousin of Jawaharlal Nehru.

to sell off the Rotary and the Lino because a very good price can be had for them – almost double. Krishnaji[1] does not agree with this suggestion, his argument being that later on it will be practically impossible to buy any such machinery, for years to come.

There are some trees here – casuarines – that look like poor cousins of the pine, although I don't think they are related at all. When the wind blows through them it makes a sound like the waves of the sea.

I am missing you here more than these last months – for I know you would love it here. To walk on the rain-swept streets and breathe the clear fresh, completely dustless air. To look down on to the lovely soft browns and greens of the fields and the shiny silver of the rivers in the valleys, and the distant mountain ranges, blue as a painting by Roerich.[2] And nothing to cut off the view. The rain has been rather hard on the flowers – most of them have first been washed off, the few remaining are looking bedraggled and brown.

Cleaning out Mr Bahadurji's[3] room for Feroze, we found a book of common Indian birds, brought out by the Society of Natural History. Looking at the pictures, I was just wondering whether 'Ferdi', the bird, was a grey tit or nuthatch, for I had had a glimpse of its black head and greyish body – when he called out again and we rushed out for another glimpse. We saw a bright red patch under the tail. So everybody says it must be the red-vented bulbul. Also in the book I was able to identify the lovely brown and blue creature Nora and I saw in Naini – it is the white-breasted kingfisher.

Puphi writes that she is sending her own copy of *Unity of India*, no new ones being available. I do not know whether this has already been sent to you direct or whether it is first coming to me. She is very anxious that it should not go astray as it is her only copy.

I wrote to Hamidah Mahmud,[4] soon after you told me to do so. But she has not yet replied.

There are heaps and heaps of old *Punches* here. Browsing through them I found an old magazine which I had left behind years ago!

Do try and put on at least three or four pounds. I am sure you must be overdoing your exercises and running.

Very much love,<br>
Your loving,<br>
Indu

---

1. Krishan Prasad Dar: Manager, Allahabad Law Journal Press.
2. Nikolai Roerich: Russian artist.
3. D. N. Bahadurji: a friend of the Nehru family.
4. Hamidah Mahmud: daughter of Dr Syed Mahmud (see Political Circle).

124.                              Ahmadnagar Fort Prison,
                                           24th July, 1943

Darling Indu,

Since I wrote to you last week I have had two letters from you, your numbers 18 and 19.[1] You have now caught up to me. This is my letter No. 20.

I was not terribly surprised when I read in your letter that Feroze had arrived in Panchgani; indeed the surprise came earlier in another way. It so happened that I learnt of Feroze's release from a letter Narendra Deva received from his son in Fyzabad. He wrote that Feroze had been discharged on the 10th. Later I received your letter of the 14th and I confidently expected some mention of Feroze in it. Imagine my surprise to find no mention at all! I wondered if the news that had been conveyed to me was wrong and untrue. I came to the conclusion that possibly Feroze did not know that you were at Panchgani and hence the delay in informing you. I expected him to roll up suddenly at Panchgani – and so he did. It is just like him.

I hope he is well and his foot has recovered. I must now give effect to a resolution I made some months ago. Will you give Feroze, on my behalf, a Schick electric shaver – mind it is a Schick. The other ones are not, I think, so good. Draw the money for it from my account at Bachhraj's. You can find out from Betty where this shaver can be obtained in Bombay. I have now been using it daily for just over six months and I am a complete convert to it. It is undoubtedly an improvement on old-style methods. Only one cannot discard wholly the old razor as electric current is not always available in India.

Your letters leave me in doubt about your programme and how long you will stay at Panchgani. Anyway I am continuing to send my letters there till you send me a new address. I do not want my letters to go astray.

About the books I wish to return, I think I had best send them to Betty in Bombay. It is no good burdening you with them and perhaps take the chance of missing you. In any case you will pass through Bombay and you can then dispose of them. Tell Psyche I am sending Sylvain Levi's book to Betty. This, being a rare book and a borrowed one, has to be carefully looked after.

Betty has sent me my *Unity of India*. Also the eye-drops, Murine, as well as some other stuff for the eyes.

You need not trouble to send the *Leader* or the *Pioneer* here. I am not anxious to have them. I read newspapers of course but I rather grudge

1. Refers to letters Nos 121 and 123.

the time they take up. My own world at present is so far removed from the world of action that my interest in the latter is distant. Besides, the *Leader* came here for a week or two and it was so dull and uninteresting that we stopped it.

I am sorry to learn about Nora's health. She is quite extraordinarily careless and observes no rules or discipline.

I had not heard previously about the difference of opinion between Mohan Bhai and Krishnaji in regard to any disposal of our goods. Personally I am very definitely of the opinion that our goods should not be sold. Goods and things are far more important than money, especially in these days when so many things are almost unobtainable. So I agree with Krishnaji.

When you go visiting I suppose Feroze will go with you. He should do so, especially when you go to Nani. In Lahore you have plenty of friends and you will of course see them. Do not forget to call on our hostess, Ismet. [1] Also you should visit Bijju Chachi's mother, the Rani, and Ram Lall's wife, the Diwani.

I am giving you below three couplets of Ghalib. They are sad and written in utter disillusion, written after the tragic happenings of 1857 and 1858. Ghalib's world had come to an end, the shadowy Delhi court was no more, his friends were dead or in great distress. There was hardly any centre or place for the culture he represented. This feeling must have been widespread among the relics of the old world in India then. The shock had been terrible and had brought ruin to everything he valued.

رہیے ایسی جگہ چل کر جہاں کوئی نہ ہو
ہم سخن کوئی نہ ہو اور ہم زباں کوئی نہ ہو

بے در و دیوار سا اک گھر بنایا چاہیے
کوئی ہمسایہ نہ ہو اور پاسباں کوئی نہ ہو

پڑیے گر بیمار تو کوئی نہ ہو تیمار دار
اور اگر مر جائیے تو نوحہ خواں کوئی نہ ہو          (غالب)

In Hindi:

रहिये ऐसी जगह चल कर, जहां कोई न हो
हम सख़ुन कोई न हो और हम ज़बां कोई न हो
बे दर ओ दीवार सा इक घर बनाया चाहिये
कोई हम साया न हो, और पासबां कोई न हो

1. The wife of Mian Iftikharuddin, an eminent Punjab politician, who played host to Jawaharlal Nehru whenever he visited Lahore.

पढ़िये गर बीमार, तो कोई न हो तीमारदार
और अगर मर जाइये तो नोहाह्वां कोई न हो[1]

सख़ुन=बात; हम सख़ुन = a person with whom one converses; हम साया = one living in the same shelter; पासबां = guardian; तीमारदार = one who nurses an ill person; नोहाह्वां = mourner.

With love to you and Feroze,

Your loving,
Papu

————————————

125.                                                  Oomra Hall,
Panchgani,
26th July, 1943

Darling Papu,

Your letter of the 17th[2] came on the 21st just after I had posted a letter[3] to you.

I have sent an airgraph to Krishna about the books. That, I think, is easier than trying to send money to England. Of course if Krishna has got no money of yours, we shall have to send some from here. To Walsh I have written by airmail – I don't know if that helps, but still.

Today Psyche has gone to Bombay for four or five days. Our Panchgani programme is more or less definite. We leave on the 7th or 8th August. Feroze is coming up again tomorrow morning and will stay on until we all go down together.

I remember the *Life* with the new maps. I was solely tempted to cut them out! Did you also get a *Life* which had your photograph and your message to China?

Since parcels take a considerable time arriving, you had better send the books addressed to me c/o Chhoti Puphi. By the way, Chhoti Puphi has gone to Delhi for a change. She will be back in Bombay on the 31st.

Being alone has its advantages. After seeing Psyche off, I climbed up a nearby hillock, where Psyche & I have been a dozen times, and dis-

1. Ghalib: I long to live where I'm all alone;
   With none to speak to
   And none to share my thoughts!
   A dwelling without doors and walls it be
   With no neighbour and no guard;
   None to tend me if sick I lie
   And none to mourn if there I die!
2. Refers to letter No. 122.
3. Letter not published.

covered two lovely wild flowers. One plant of the butterfly orchid and dozens of tiny marsh gentians – at least that is what I think they are. The marsh gentians are such a pretty shade of blue, very pure and cold. Just shows how little we usually observe of the world around us . . .

While in Bombay I acquired a book called *Eat and Grow Beautiful*! The theory being that beauty is entirely dependent on good health; every cell and every organ in perfect condition. And perfect health is only possible if we eat the 'right' food, the right food being lots of vegetable and fruit, mostly raw. The author is probably a disciple of Bircher-Benner,[1] some of whose books you bought at the Vega restaurant for Tandonji.[2] The book doesn't have much new information – just what one has always known: calcium for good teeth and nails, iodine for hair, Vitamin A for eyes, and so on. But it is useful in that it gives lists of the foods that are rich in these necessary minerals and vitamins. Great stress is laid on drinking the juices of raw vegetables, such as spinach and carrots. Unfortunately the book is not very readable, being full of repetitions, numerous examples of various film stars and many pompous statements. I don't know what you can do in the food line, where you are. But for Dr Mahmud's benefit I am giving the list for eye-health: sea-foods, Scotch oats, cod-liver oil, watercress, beets, garlic, cabbage, spinach and egg-yolk. Rocquefort cheese & sea-foods of course you will not get but the other things are fairly simple. These things are supposed to contain a mineral called 'fluorine'. Apart from this mineral, Vitamin A is needed. The best foods for this are: liver, fresh butter, fresh cream, fresh milk, fresh cheese, mangoes. This book wouldn't do for Tandonji or Bircher-Benner, as they don't believe in milk or milk-products.

This is my letter No. 21. It will be posted tomorrow as today's mail has already left.

Since you are determined to spin, let me know when you want any *punis*. Feroze spun quite a lot in jail, but was not allowed to bring the yarn out!

Much love,
Indu

---

1. Bircher-Benner: Swiss dietician, inventor of the breakfast food muesli.
2. Purushottam Das Tandon: prominent Congress leader and colleague of Jawaharlal Nehru.

126.

Oomra Hall,
Panchgani,
6th August, 1943

Darling Papu,

Your letter No. 20 [1] came just after I had posted my No. 21 to you. [2]
It's simply ages since I wrote to you. This is my letter No. 22.

Panchgani continues to be wet and unpleasant. Now, in addition to
the rain, we have a terrific wind all the time, moaning and wailing
through the casuarina leaves.

I had intended leaving Panchgani on the 7th and [Psyche had agreed
to it before her] departure for Bombay. But instead of returning on the
1st, as settled, Psyche couldn't come until the 5th. She arrived looking
very tired and weary – so leaving on the 7th was out of the question.
Now the programme is as follows: we leave on the 11th – stay the night
in Poona – reach Bombay on the 12th. I shall stay about a week in
Bombay. Then a week or so in Jaipur – address in Jaipur,
c/o Pt. P. N. Kathju, 2 Club Road, Jaipur, Rajputana. After Jaipur back
to Allahabad. I have decided to postpone the visit to Lahore until the
winter. I shall let you know the exact dates from Bombay.

Yesterday came an airgraph from Agatha, dated July 13th. It is in
reply to my first one which I sent from Bombay on the 24th June.
Krishna is much better. Bhandari's daughters are now in Badminton
School. The school had to leave Bristol since the main building was
destroyed by fire. It is now housed in a large hotel at Lynton. They have
also spilled over into several nearby houses. Agatha went down there
one day to lecture on India. A month or so ago, Agatha and Krishna
were part of a 'Brains Trust' on India. There were five of them and
they had a strenuous time. The whole thing was arranged by some
League of Nations Union people. Agatha sends her love to you. So do
Mridu & Psyche & Nuri. Agatha writes:

> I was glad of the message from your father; there is much I would
> like to say to him but realise the restrictions on correspondence. I
> often think of him when looking after my tomatoes. I have some
> now in the front garden. Were he able to see them, he might smile
> patronisingly at them as he did before. But I would have him know
> that it is no small achievement to rear such plants in Albert Bridge
> Road.

1. Refers to letter No. 124.
2. Refers to letter No. 125.

Puphi – the big one – has also written to me. She has a letter from Frances Gunther. F.G. says she sent me a wedding present through the United States Government and Sumner Welles,[1] and that she knows it is now with the U.P. Government. She has asked Puphi to try and get it delivered to me before my golden anniversary!

Darling, this letter is most inadequate, I know, but these last days I have been feeling so very depressed. That is why I did not write earlier. And even now I cannot put my mind to anything. This isn't the time to be on holiday and yet one is so utterly helpless. There isn't anything one can do that will make any appreciable difference. Sometimes I do feel like Ghalib in those last couplets you sent – to go away into the wilds where there is nobody, nobody; to eat the wild leaves and to fashion clothes out of them and to live with the animals away from the ways of men.

In Bombay I am going to invest in a *charkha* and start spinning in real earnest. May be that will help in restoring mental equilibrium – Psyche says it does.

Our sheets and towels are wearing out and I don't know what to do about it – being without *khadi* is going to be very difficult.

Much love, Papu darling. I hope you are trying to put on a few pounds.

Indu

---

127.                                                    Ahmadnagar Fort Prison,
                                                          7th August, 1943

Indu darling,

You will be leaving Panchgani today or tomorrow, according to your programme. It is not clear where you go to, but I suppose Bombay is an inevitable halting place. Bombay just at present must be having a bad spell of weather – so Betty wrote to me. I suppose that was why she sought refuge in Delhi for a few days. North India, though warmer, is probably healthier now than Bombay.

I have communicated your list of foods containing ferrocene and Vitamin A to Mahmud and to others interested therein. There is a saying that in youth one thinks of love, in middle age of food, and later of medicine. I do not know what stage I am in but it is certainly not of medicine. Most of my colleagues here are, however, unfortunately full of medicine and even food takes a medical aspect. So this business of .vitamins and proteins and carbohydrates, etc, is of interest to them. I

1. Sumner Welles: American diplomat.

seem to prosper without giving much thought to these very necessary ingredients of one's diet.

Puphi's (Nan's) birthday comes off on August 18th (or August 23rd *Samvat* style). I should like you to send her some books on my behalf for that day. I cannot suggest what books, for I do not know what is available. You will be able to choose from such as can be had in Bombay. She is likely to stay in Mussoorie till the end of the month, so the books had better be sent there.

I hope you will not forget to get an electric shaver for Feroze – a Schick. This will be my gift to him.

I do not know when I shall start spinning or how long I shall keep it up. But you might send me some good *punis*. Bombay is the only place you are likely to get them easily.

In a day or two we shall complete one full year here. The day we arrived I noticed the new moon – a sight which always pleases me and cheers me up. Since then every new moon has been a signal of the completion of a month. Twelve of them have come, grown fat and round and then faded away. And now the 13th must have appeared two days ago, but I could not see it because of the clouds.

What a year it has been in the world, in India, and here in our tiny self-sufficient world of ours with which we are so tied up! Inevitably, I count up the balance sheet, the good and the ill, and I realise how terribly difficult it is for anyone to be truly objective. In all our thoughts we become the centres of the revolving universe, and judge most things in relation to ourselves. And yet we here at any rate inhabit a ghastly realm of limited physical surroundings and unlimited thoughts and ideas – both cut off from the world of reality. Yet again that world of reality itself seems a shadow show of marionettes performing madly and aimlessly, caught in the grip of forces entirely beyond their control or even understanding.

What have I done during this twelvemonth? I have read much and some at least of the books have been worthwhile and added to my knowledge and insight. But am I any the wiser for all this browsing and pursuing the printed word? I do not know. I have pottered about a good deal round garden beds, and dug with vigour, and played with the soft fresh earth, and watched the seedlings peep out from its surface and look with yearning towards the sun, and grow healthy and strong, and then flower and die. That at least has helped me tremendously to keep physically fit and mentally occupied and turned my mind from happenings that worry and distress.

Anyway I am a year older, as are all of us. But age, as it comes inexorably and relentlessly after a certain period of one's life, is no welcome visitor. The sense of the work to do, so little done, and ever less and less time to do it, oppresses . . .

I have just received a box of sweets from Betty – evidently Delhi sweets which she brought with her. Tell her that it has reached me. Also tell her that I received some time ago *The Unity of India* which she sent me. I had forgotten to acknowledge this in my letter to her.

This letter – my No. 22 – is being sent c/o Betty to Bombay.

Love,
Your loving,
Papu

---

128.                                                        Panchgani
                                                       August 1943

Darling Papu,

My letters seem always to miss yours by just a few hours. It is tantalising. A paragraph in your letter[1] was cut – I more or less guessed that it was about my wedding gift, since only two hours earlier had I written the same thing to you!

Have you seen Bharati's *The Well of the People*? Psyche brought back a copy. I liked it immensely. Bharati conveys so completely and vividly what is in her mind. It is beautifully written – occasionally a little heavy because of the wealth of imagery, one on top of the other. I feel it has captured something of the spirit of India. The book is beautifully got up too – the cover most appropriate and living . . .

*Poona*                                              *12th August*
I am posting this letter today without writing any more for I am very tired after the jogging in the bus. Shall write from Bombay. In a letter of Masi's I see that Nani is in Benares, where Mamu's children go to school. Masi says Nani has grown very weak and her eyes are bad.

Much love,
Indu

---

129.                                        Ahmadnagar Fort Prison,
                                             14th August, 1943

Darling,

I have your letter No. 22 of the 6th August[2] from Panchgani. According

1. Letter not published.
2. Refers to letter No. 126.

to the provisional programme you have given you should be in Bombay now. I am sending this letter there in the hope that it will catch you there. Even if it misses you in Bombay, it will be forwarded to the right address.

Your last letter is unlike you. Perhaps the stormy and inclement weather of Panchgani depressed you, and now that you are moving about again you will feel better. There is more than enough of course all over the world and in our own country to depress and irritate. Nevertheless I do not think we have any sufficient reason to feel that way, and anyway it does no good. It is during these difficult periods that individuals and nations really find themselves and build up a strong and enduring foundation for straight thought and effective action. We begin to appreciate and understand the real values in life and to get out of the superficialities of existence. Life is a queer business at all times. We are apt to slide along it without much thinking so long as everything is normal. Or if normalcy is disturbed, we take refuge in phrases and formulae which seem to explain life and bring out the essence of its problems. They are often helpful – these phrases and formulae – but they skim the surface of the problems and sometimes prevent us from probing down below. Perhaps it is hardly possible to probe too much and understand for, as somebody said, the only unchangeable law of life and the world is that everything changes. Still, there are some anchorholds. We may not understand much in this changing world, but we can endeavour to make ourselves effective instruments for thought and action whatever might happen. To those who are really old in years the future counts for little; the present grips them and exalts or oppresses them. But by that one unchangeable law of life, the present itself changes into something different, good or bad. And in that very present lie the seeds of that future of change. The real point is: have these seeds been truly sown and are they the seeds of noble and straight-growing trees? If the seeds are there, the harvest is sure.

Even if the wider scheme of things is beyond our control, our individual selves should be amenable to our wishes, and thus through them we can even influence that wider scheme. There is an amazing amount of shouting and lying and vulgarity in modern life and this reaches a peak in wartime. We are apt to be carried away by this, or, at any rate, to be powerfully affected. And yet I do not think all this shouting makes any essential difference to that scheme of things. Nature, in its widest sense, embracing humanity, carries on in accordance with its own rules and I cannot imagine that basically it is shoved out of those fundamental ways by the shouting or misbehaviour of human beings. I do think that man has made and can make an enormous difference but only by understanding the ways of nature and then using them for certain ends.

That is the way of science and that should be – but unhappily is not – the way of human beings. But through folly and killing and amazing stupidity somehow the experience of the race grows and leads to more desirable results.

For my part I can truly say that I have seldom any feeling of real and abiding depression. An abounding vitality fills me and the present seems such a transitory and passing phase that my eyes almost overlook it, searching for the morrow. If I feel that way, how much more should you, with all your vital youth and the promise of the future spread out before you.

Anyway, as I have said, even if the whole world goes wrong and awry, that is no reason why we as individuals should submit to fate. Do you remember what Beethoven said, Beethoven of all men in the wide world to be stricken with the misery of deafness? 'I shall seize fate by the throat. It shall never wholly overcome me.'

The individual has it in him or her always to rise above the caprices of fate. Whether it is just pride or some other basic quality which stands by him, I do not know. But he can, if he so wills, stand four-square to all the winds of heaven and hell. And by doing so, he influences and turns that very fate.

If you feel depressed at any time, think that the next day you are sure to get over this – it is just a passing mood. Depression usually comes from uncertainty and doubt – what to do, what not to do? That is a difficult question to answer, especially in an affirmative way. The negative, what not to do, is easier to answer. In spite of the difficulty, however, it is better to engage oneself in some activity of mind and body, however unimportant it might appear, for thus we maintain a certain poise of mind. Not to do anything and just to brood – 'the brooding sense of tragedy felt to be as much national as personal' – is not helpful at all and weakens our capacity for any effective work. It is just like being one of the unemployed who deteriorate so rapidly.

So cheer up, my dear, and let the old and the decrepit, with no vitality and no sense of the future, brood and brood.

So you are thinking of going to Jaipur. That presumably means that you will go right up to Delhi on your way back to Allahabad. It might have been worthwhile going up to Lahore from there as the journey is a relatively short one. But I do not know what the weather is like there at present and perhaps it is wiser to postpone the Lahore visit. Being cut off, I cannot really advise you. You will have all the relevant considerations before you and you can fix things up for yourself. Do not worry as to what you decide. Come to a decision and carry it out. Either way it does not matter much. Travelling and visiting have certain advantages, even in these days of overcrowded trains and extreme discomfort. They occupy the mind and prevent it from worrying.

I have Agatha's message about the tomatoes. I am sorry she thinks that I am not sufficiently appreciative of her tomatoes. Indeed I am. I think it is a feat to grow any vegetables or flowers in Albert Bridge Road. I am glad Krishna is keeping well.

When you go to Allahabad I should like you to send me two Hindi books. They are probably to be found in Anand Bhawan, though with difficulty. But it is better to send new copies as I want to give them to Mahmud. They are: *Sankshipt Shabdsagar*, a students' Hindi dictionary in one volume, published I think by the Indian Press and *Kavita Kaumudi*, Part I only (or Volume One), by Ram Naresh Tripathi. This was originally published by Hindi Mandir, Allahabad. I only want Volume One.

Certainly buy the *charkha*. It has its undoubted merits. But long before you can get into the rhythm of it, you will find it trying and irritating. All beginnings are so.

As for *khadi*, I suppose we can carry on, if necessary, for two or three years with our old stocks. Get Hari to produce all my towels, bedsheets, etc and use them up. Running short of a bathtowel here I managed to get a thick, rather towelish, bedsheet. This serves me excellently as a bathtowel.

Some little time ago I wrote to Amma and told her that you were likely to visit her some time later. I did not mention any particular time.

Here are two verses of Hālī. They are simple and well known – often recited in honour of a valued guest, to point out the inadequacy of the host's house in comparison with the radiance of the guest.

ان کے آتے ہی یہ کیا ہو گئی گھر کی صورت

نہ وہ دیوار کی صورت ہے نہ در کی صورت

ان کو حالی بھی بلاتے ہیں گھر اپنے مہمان

دیکھنا آپ کی اور آپ کے گھر کی صورت    (حالی)

In Hindi:

हाली: उनके भ्राते ही यह क्या हो गई घर की सूरत

न वो दीवार की सूरत है न दर की सूरत–

उनको हँसी भी बुलाते हैं घर अपने मेहमान
देखना आप की और आप के घर की सूरत! [1]

I wrote to you last week and asked you to send some books as birthday
gifts to Bari Puphi in Mussoorie. I hope you will not forget.

Love to you and Feroze,
Your loving,
Papu

---

130.                                                  20, Carmichael Road,
                                                              Bombay,
                                                  19th/21st August, 1943

Darling Papu,

I have two letters from you. The one dated the 14th [2] came two days
ago and the one dated the 7th [3] arrived today.

We sent a telegram to Puphi on her birthday. I shall see about the
books – there doesn't seem much to choose from. Electric shavers are
not available these days. The one you have was given by an American
friend. Meanwhile it is possible and also probable that Feroze will soon
be without electricity.

We went to the *Khadi Bhandar* yesterday and spent a lot of money
buying practically nothing – prices are terribly high. Amongst other
things we got two *charkhas* – Yeravada ones but made in Andhra. Also
a lot of *punis*, which are not very good but it was the best we could get.
I shall see if better ones can be made for you.

Psyche frightened me one day in Panchgani by insisting that the first
thing I should do on arrival in Bombay was to consult an oculist. So I
did, and was told that my eyes were good enough for an A.I. pilot's
licence! The next visit was to the dentist with not such happy results.
He advised the pulling out of my wisdom teeth – same as Prakash did
two years ago. So I've had one out already and made an appointment
for another for Friday. The other two will have to wait.

My programme is again changed. Mausaji [4] had to go on tour, so I

---

1. Hālī:   To my house she has just come;
           And look, how this door and wall,
           In fact, the very face of the house all is so changed!
           Hali too invites her to his place;
           Just look, look at him and his place!
2. Refers to letter No. 129.
3. Refers to letter No. 127.
4. Pyarelal Kathju, Indira Gandhi's uncle.

have postponed our visit to Jaipur. On next Tuesday or Wednesday I propose going to Allahabad. From there I shall go to Benares to see Nani & may be bringing her back to Allahabad with me for a few days.

From my writing you will see that I am still feeling 'unsettled'. That is one reason why I want to return to Allahabad first instead of going visiting.

Puphi was so impressed by your discourse on depression [1] that she has sent large chunks of it to Rajabhai, with whom the condition now seems to have become chronic. But most moods are so illogical, how can they be dispelled by reasoning? My moods come and go chasing each other, from elation to depression and back again. I know this happens. I know they don't last long and yet while I am depressed I see the world enshrouded in black and no light showing through. Then suddenly the veil lifts and I wonder what on earth I was worrying about! When you get to the bottom of it, all these depressing moods show a certain preoccupation with self. If we could see ourselves always as the microscopic and transient creatures that we are, should we get so agitated about our actions? On the other hand it is wonderful that being so insignificant we have been able to change the world and to harness the forces of nature for our use, as we have done. In so doing we have undoubtedly gained something, but we have also lost something. It is too early yet to say which is the more precious possession. We have gained knowledge at the cost of wisdom. We have gained a certain mastery over nature but we have lost our sense of proportion, our sense of union with the rest of nature, or as D. H. Lawrence calls it, our 'living organic connections with the cosmos'. In the details of day-to-day life – the reality of life as most people know it – we have forgotten the wonder of 'Life' in its wider meaning. And that, ultimately, is the cause of our unrest and our wretchedness.

*21st August*

Had my tooth out yesterday. It bled rather a lot – all night in fact. That is why I could not write yesterday.

We went to lunch with Psyche yesterday. I do like her house and the lawn.

For Puphi I have got a book on Confucius: *The Story of Confucius* by Carl Crow. [2] By the way, she writes that Frances Gunther's present has arrived and is with her. I am all curiosity but must contain myself until we both reach Allahabad. I am not sure about Puphi but Feroze and I will reach there on Friday night – the 26th.

1. See letter No. 129.
2. Carl Crow (1883–1945): American journalist.

In the hope that it will be allowed to you I am enclosing your yearly *rakhi*[1] from Tai and the accompanying card.

In a couple of days I shall send you the following books:

1. *Better Sight without Glasses*, by N. Benjamin
2. *The Improvement of Sight by Natural Methods*, by C. S. Price.
3. *Global War*, by Edgar Mowrer
4. *Monkey*, by Wu Ch'eng-en
5. *Destination Chungking*, by Han Suyin
6. *Ideal & Progress*, by Sri Aurobindo
7. *Escape with Me*, by Edith Sitwell

Of these *Monkey* belongs to Puphi & should be returned to her.

Lots of love,
Indu

---

131.                                     Ahmadnagar Fort Prison,
                                          21st August, 1943

Darling,

Your letter of August 12th[2] from Poona reached me five days ago and later I had a letter from Puphi from Bombay to say that you had arrived there. She also mentioned that you were having a tooth out. Was this the old wisdom tooth which had got all twisted up and which you showed to Prakash two years ago?

If Nani is in Benares and likely to stay there for a while you could go and meet her there. You might also induce her to spend some time with you in Allahabad. In view of her weak health and eye trouble I think it would be desirable for you to see her as early as you conveniently can. This would please her and cheer her up. Your meeting her in Benares or Allahabad will not take the place of your visit to Lahore. That visit will have to come off some time or other.

Yes, I had read Bharati's *The Well of the People*. Normally, I seldom enjoy this type of modern poetry – there are exceptions of course. But Bharati's poem is obviously full of sincerity and power. Some lines are fine, though some drag. The imagery seems to me rather heavy, and yet it is not inappropriate, for India is herself heavy with thoughts and images of the past. I think Bharati has done very well indeed. The

---

1. *Rakhi* is a coloured thread tied by a sister on the wrist of her brother as a mark of affection and trust on the festival of *Raksha Bandhan*.
2. Refers to letter No. 128.

writing of this must have done her a lot of good. To transfer from the mind to the printed page all the thoughts and images that fill it and burden it, and to do it effectively, is an art of creation which must bring a feeling of fulfilment in its train . . .

There is, as you know, Khusru Bagh in Allahabad. This takes its name from the son of Jehangir,[1] whose name was Khusrau and who rebelled against his father. He was imprisoned in Lahore, I think, by Jehangir and he died in prison. He is probably buried in the Allahabad garden – Khusrau was the half-brother of Khurram who became Shah Jehan.

In the early days, that is before and after the Mughals came to power in India, there was no Urdu language used as a literary vehicle. Gradually this Urdu developed as a camp and bazaar language, with its basic background of Hindi and with Persian and Arabic words thrown in. In those early days people connected with the court used to write poetry in Persian – the court language – or sometimes also in Hindi. This Hindi was what might be called pure Hindi. Thus Amir Khusrau. A later famous example was Rahim, a well-known Hindi poet of Akbar's day – Rahim or rather Abdul Rahim Khan-e-Khanan[2] was the son of old Bairam Khan who had been Akbar's guardian and whom Akbar pushed out as soon as he was old enough to do so. His son Abdul Rahim was a remarkable person. He was one of the biggest grandees of Akbar's court (Khan-e-Khanan was the highest title), he was a successful general, and a scholar in various languages – Persian, Arabic, Sanskrit & Hindi. He was very rich and recklessly generous. In fact he is best known today by these stories of amazing and sometimes ridiculous generosity. Having developed this reputation he was given to showing off far too much. After Akbar's death he got into trouble with Jehangir and was interned. Here is a *doha*[3] by Rahim.

बिगरी बात बनै नहीं, लाख करो किन कोय ।
रहिमन बिगरे दूध को, मथै न माखन होय ॥[4]

Rahim was a contemporary of Tulsi Das,[5] whom he must have known.

1. Jehangir (1569–1627): Mughal Emperor of India (1605–27); son of Akbar.
2. Abdul Rahim Khan Khana (1556–1626): a poet, scholar and noble in the court of the Emperor Akbar.
3. Couplet.
4. Rahim:   Honour once lost is never gained.
           Howsoever one may try;
           Milk turned sour, *O Rahiman*, butter does not make
           however much you may churn!
5. Tulsi Das (1532–1623): leading medieval poet, author of *Ramcharitmanas*, a very popular version of the Hindu epic *Ramayana* in Hindi.

The beginnings of literary Urdu took place in the early years of the eighteenth century when the great Mughal empire was fading away. Urdu, having become a spoken *melange*, was used by some bright person for some clever couplets – form and imagery Persian, language more Hindi than later. This caught on. It – the language – was called *Rekhta*. To begin with this was not considered serious poetry – that was in Persian. But this vogue grew – and curiously enough as it grew it became more Persianised in language and substance. There was no prose in Urdu then (*nasra* = prose) but only *nazm* – poetry. Prose came slowly in the early nineteenth century.

The early Urdu *nazm* is full of Hindi words and Hindi and even *dehati*[1] endings. These drop out later. Here is a simple couplet of an early Urdu poet – Mazhar – Mirza Jan-e-Janan:[2]

یہ حسرت رہ گئی کیا کیا مزے سے زندگی کرتے
اگر ہوتا چمن اپنا، گل اپنا، باغباں اپنا (مظہر جان جاناں)

यह हसरत रह गई क्या क्या मज़े से ज़िन्दगी करते
अगर होता चमन अपना, गुल अपना, बाग़बान अपना[3]

चमन = garden; बाग़बान = gardener.

Here is a clever couplet (of later days by a poet whose name I do not remember) with sarcasm in it:

یہ عجب میں رسم دیکھی کہ بروز عید قرباں
وہی ذبح بھی کرے مے وہی لے ثواب اُلٹا (مصطفیٰ)

In Hindi:

यह अजब मैं रस्म देखी के बरोज़-ए-ईद-ए-क़ुर्बां
वही ज़िबेह भी करे है, वही ले सवाब उल्टा![4]

The form of words is somewhat archaic. ईद-ए-क़ुर्बां is बक़ीद when animal sacrifices take place.

---

1. Rural.
2. Mazhar Jan-e-Janan (1699–1781): a medieval poet.
3. Mazhar Jan-e-Janan:　This desire of ours, alas, remained unfulfilled
　　　　　　　　　　　　What a life it would've been
　　　　　　　　　　　　If ours were the gardener,
　　　　　　　　　　　　　ours the garden, and ours the rose!
4. Funny are the ways of this world;
　　Look, he who kills on the Festive Day,
　　He gets the reward too!

Tell Betty I have received her letter of the 14th and the *rakhi*. Also that I got the Delhi sweets she sent. If you are not in Bombay when you get this, do not trouble to write about this to her. I have just received the Oxford book of quotations – a very sumptuous book indeed.

Thank Betty.

Love,
Your loving,
Papu

132.                                                        Ahmadnagar Fort Prison,
28th August, 1943

Darling Indu,

I have not had a letter from you for quite a number of days – twelve, I think. And even your last letter[1] was a brief note from Poona. Betty informed me of your arrival in Bombay and your intention to have a tooth out. I hope this did not lead to any trouble. According to your programme you should have left Bombay and gone to Jaipur. But I think it is safer to send this to Bombay, unless I hear from you to the contrary by today's post.

Betty sent me a *rakhi* for *Raksha Bandhan* and a sumptuous book – *The Oxford Dictionary of Quotations*. This book is a delightful companion. Betty inscribed it '*Bhaiya Dooj*'[2] although this day is still three months off. A mistake for *Raksha Bandhan*.

In my last letter sent to Amma (to Lahore) I asked her to send me some *supari*[3] (*bhuni supari*[4] with *elaichi*[5]) as she has sometimes sent me previously. Having written to her, I regretted it, for this meant giving her trouble. With her weak health and poor eyesight, preparing this might well become a burden to her. It would be better if she asked Bappi or someone else to prepare it.

When you go to Allahabad do not forget to send me one or more good snapshots of Mummie and the one of yourself you mentioned in a letter . . .

News of starvation and death in Bengal and Orissa is so harrowing that one feels sick at heart . . .[6] I want you to know that you can draw upon my account to any extent you like (subject only to the extent of

1. Refers to letter No. 128.
2. Festival sanctifying the relationship between sisters and brothers.
3. Arecanut.
4. Roasted arecanut.
5. Cardamom.
6. Deleted by censors.

the account) for any effective help that you can envisage. It is the fate of the children and the young boys and girls that upsets me . . .

This is my letter No. 25 to you.

*Later:* I have just received your letter from Bombay dated August 21st.[1] Also a letter from Betty dated 24/8 and a note from Amma from Benares. Amma complains she has not heard from you for a long time. Tell Betty I shall write to her on Tuesday next – Tai's *rakhi* has also come with the card. I propose to send my next letter to you to Allahabad.

Love,

Your loving,<br>Papu

---

133.

Anand Bhawan,<br>Allahabad,<br>29th August, 1943

Darling Papu,

This is just a hasty scrawl to send my love & a letter of Nani's which came to Puphi a long while ago but she mislaid it and it was found just as I was leaving Bombay.

The weather here is the same as in Bombay. This year it has rained more than usual.

Ladlibhai is complaining about Datadin. Datadin is very careless. Ladlibhai says it is entirely due to negligence that we have no vegetables in the garden. Ladlibhai gave the seeds to Datadin and even saw that they were planted. And yet nothing has come up although Ladlibhai's garden & the hospital garden are flourishing.

We are very busy meeting people. I am just in the mood to shriek at everybody for their complacency.

Bari Puphi is now in Lucknow, from where she will go direct to Bombay.

Much love,<br>Indu

---

134.

Ahmadnagar Fort Prison,<br>4th September, 1943

Darling Indu,

I had finished my last letter to you when your letter of the 21st August[2]

1. Refers to letter No. 130.
2. Refers to letter No. 130.

(your Number 24th) was given to me. I read it at first rather hurriedly as I wanted to find out where to address my letter. For no reason at all I became a little confused and I was on the point of sending my letter to Bombay. I recovered just in time, but the postscript I wrote bears traces of this confusion – you had written quite clearly about your programme; it was only my vagrant mind that made the mistake.

So now you must be in Allahabad, or perhaps in Benares with Amma. Give my love to her and tell her that I have written to her twice recently, on July 20th and August 11th. Yet she complains of not having received any reply from me to her letter. Both the letters were sent to Lahore, c/o Chand. The second one probably missed her in Lahore as she had gone to Benares. But the first should certainly have reached her before she left. These Hindi letters evidently take longer to reach their destinations.

The books you sent have reached me – all those mentioned in your letter, plus the *China Handbook*. It is a good and attractive selection. Mahmud is excited about the books on improving eyesight.

I have sent you to Allahabad the following books:

1. *Banking & Finance in China* by Tamagna
2. *Economic Development of the Netherland Indies*
3. *Ambassador Dodd's Diary*
4. J. B. S. Haldane: *Heredity & Politics*
5. Eddington: *Nature of the Physical World*
6. Gibbs: *America Speaks*
7. Ela Sen: *Wives of Famous Men*
8. Ben-Shalom: *Deep Furrows*
9. M. Thein Pe: *What Happened in Burma*
10. Alvah Bessie: *This is your Enemy*
11. Winwood Reade: *The Outcaste*
12. Adrienne Moore: *Interviewing Japan*
    and some old foreign periodicals . . .

I read with great interest your musings on philosophy. It is perhaps early for you to philosophise, and yet it is inevitable when the harsh facts of existence thrust themselves upon us. I have dipped into all manner of books on philosophy and science, from the Upanishads and Plato and Indian & Greek philosophy to many of the modern expositions and enquiries. It is a fascinating subject opening out innumerable avenues of thought, and yet it seems to lead nowhere. At any rate I do not think I am much wiser. Perhaps layer upon layer of their thoughts accumulate in the mind and give a certain depth. But my tendency is to turn away from metaphysical speculations. But no thoughtful person, however scientific he claims to be, can entirely turn away from some aspect of metaphysics, or let us call it the, for the present, unknown, if not unknowable. One simply must seek and enquire and delve deep – the Faustian attitude – whatever the consequences. (I am reading Faust again.) Recently I read Nietzsche. I remember reading him rather carelessly when I was in Cambridge. I dislike his fundamental thesis, but there is much that is attractive in what he says, or perhaps it is the manner of saying it that fixes the attention.

We come back after all to a certain pragmatic attitude. I think you are perfectly right in saying that our main trouble is a lack of organic connections with nature or life. We have gone off at a tangent from the circle of life, uprooted ourselves and thus lost the sense of fullness and coordination with nature. A peasant, at his very low level of living on the soil and for the soil, has that sense of organic connection. Hence, I suppose, his extraordinary tenacity and perseverance. But his level of existence is terribly low, and most of us had rather be uprooted than exist at that level. To live at a high level and yet to have that organic connection with life – that I suppose is the problem humanity is trying to solve now in its own crude, cruel and wasteful way.

Why does one do anything? Hardly because of reasoned thinking, though this may be behind the immediate urge to some extent. It is this urge, this impulse, overmastering and uncontrollable, that drives one on. Our moods depend even less on reason and the smallest things affect them, exalting them or depressing them. Often one forgets or hardly remembers the cause for this exaltation or depression, yet the mood prevails. I have felt sometimes extraordinarily exhilarated by the sight of a sunset sky, or the deep blue patch between the monsoon clouds, or even a flower which I had missed and have suddenly seen. For a moment I have felt at one with nature.

Why does one act? Impossible to answer unless one goes down deep into the depths of the unconscious self of man, a journey which is beyond our capacity. We may at best just glimpse into those depths and return mystified. Have you seen those lovely lines by Yeats on an Irish airman?

> Nor law, nor duty bade me fight,
> Not public men, nor cheering crowds,
> A lonely impulse of delight
> Drove to this tumult in the clouds.
> I balanced all, brought all to mind,
> The years to come seemed waste of breath,
> A waste of breath the years behind
> In balance with this life, this death.

I have been reading Virginia Woolf (*To the Lighthouse*). The more I read her the more I like her. There is a magic about her writing, something ethereal, limpid like running water, and deep like a clear mountain lake. What is her book about? So very little that you can tell anyone; and yet so much that it fills your mind, covers it with a gossamer web, out of which you peer at the past, at yourself, at others. Did you ever meet her? . . .

This is my letter No. 26.

Love,
Your loving,
Papu

135.

Anand Bhawan,
Allahabad,
4th September, 1943

Darling Papu,
The last letter I had from you was dated August 21,[1] which I got in Bombay a few days before leaving. This is my letter No. 26.

Feroze and I went to Benares the day before yesterday. Nani is there with three children: Ashok, Chitra and one of the twins, Om.[2] We spent the whole afternoon with her. She has been getting a temperature and her eyes are getting weaker. The two elder children go to school. Om is about fourteen months old. A couple of days ago he swallowed a pice and it has not come out yet! On top of that he has pneumonia. So with all these worries, Nani said it would not be possible for her to get away from Benares. Mamu[3] has gone to Murree on two months' leave. The other Mamu is getting quite fed up of being in England and is wanting to come back but they do not know if it will be possible.

Knowing that Bharati would be interested in having your reactions to her book, I copied out the relevant paragraph and sent it to her. I hope you don't mind.

A friend of Yunus's has written to say that with the greatest of difficulty he managed to get an interview with Yunus on the 13th of last month. Yunus seems to be quite well now . . .[4]

We met Malaviyaji[5] in Benares. It was pathetic to see him, so weak

1. Refers to letter No. 131.
2. Children of Chand Bahadur and Rup Koul.
3. Chand Bahadur Koul: uncle of Indira Gandhi. 'The other Mamu' refers to Kailas Nath Kaul.
4. Deleted by censors.
5. Madan Mohan Malaviya: veteran nationalist leader and founder of the Benares Hindu University.

he has grown. Mukund [1] was there. He said there was a great change this last month even. For the first few minutes Malaviyaji's voice was all right, then it dropped to a whisper and finally dwindled away. Towards the end of our talk we could hardly understand what he was saying. I felt it was cruel to sit there and make him talk but he would not let us go. Every time I made a move, he would say *'baitho baitho jaldi kyà hai.'* [2] He was distressed about Bengal and a great many other things as well. Malaviyaji asked after you and sent his love and blessings. He was perfectly sweet to us. After we had finally said goodbye and were getting into the car, he sent for Feroze and had another talk with him. Mukund stays with Malaviyaji almost night and day, looking after his needs and comforts. Kapildevji [3] is in Allahabad – back from Bhowali. He is better now.

Sri Prakasaji [4] was out of Benares. But I stayed with Chandrabhalji [5] and met Dr Bhagwandas. [6]

Nora is still here. Now she is thinking of going to Panchgani too.

Frances Gunther's present has reached me at last – three days ago. It is a silver flat cake spoon, with which you dole out slices of cake if the company is too polite for you to touch them with your fingers. It's rather a nice one.

The Indian Press people have sent word that the *Shabd Sāgar* has not yet been published. The *Kavita Kaumudi* I shall send soon. Meanwhile I am sending tomorrow:

a)  2 issues of the *M.G. Weekly*
b)  1 issue of the *Tribune*
c)  1 *Labour Woman*
d)  Some papers of the International Cooperative Alliance
e)  *The Death of the Moth* by Virginia Woolf
f)  *The Listener*

Yesterday I received a bill – or rather a reminder – from the Times

---

1.  Mukund Malaviya: son of Madan Mohan Malaviya; political activist and business-man of Bombay.
2.  Pray be seated, why are you in a hurry to go.
3.  Kapildev Malaviya: nephew of Madan Mohan Malaviya (see Political Circle).
4.  Sri Prakasa: eminent lawyer and politician from Uttar Pradesh; a close colleague of Jawaharlal Nehru; was later Governor of Assam, 1949–50, Madras, 1952–6, and Maharashtra, 1956–62.
5.  Chandra Bhal: younger brother of Sri Prakasa.
6.  Dr Bhagwandas Das: father of Sri Prakasa and Chandra Bhal; active in the freedom struggle; founder-member of Central Hindu College of Benares and of Kashi Vidyapith; member, Constituent Assembly.

Book Club. The bill is for £8 8sh. 3d. I am sending an airgraph to them referring to Krishna.

Lots of love,
Your loving,
Indu

---

136.                                             [Anand Bhawan,
Allahabad]
7th/9th September, 1943

Darling Papu,
Your letter of the 28th August[1] arrived the day before yesterday. This is my letter No. 27.

I am sorry I quite forgot to enclose the snapshots of Mummie in my last letter, although I had them out and ready to send. Here are two. I am not sending mine as the enlargement has turned out to be awful.

The *khadi* production money you mention is being seen to. The paragraph on Bengal – nearly two pages – have not arrived exactly as they were meant to be! . . .[2] Just before your letter came I had sent a cheque to Sapru's[3] *Leader* relief fund.[4] But money is not what is needed most. I have written to various people to see if anything more effective can be done. The students of the Vakil's School are doing a show for the relief fund on the 19th. They want me to go to Bombay to help. It's not long since I have been there so I am not keen on returning just yet. But if there is nothing much doing here I may go . . .[5]

Actually I went to see Tej Bahadurji because I had heard he wasn't well – he had flu but is now much better and holding his dates as usual – and also to consult him about doing something like Sind has done: that is to bring over batches of children to our province and look after them here. Tej Bahadurji and everybody else too says that this will not be possible here because we shall so soon be in the same position ourselves. I have been frantic trying to find out what a private individual

1. Refers to letter No. 132.
2. Deleted by censors.
3. Sir Tej Bahadur Sapru: eminent jurist and Liberal leader from Allahabad; a friend of the Nehrus.
4. Bengal was struck by a famine in 1943. *The Leader*, a nationalist newspaper of Allahabad, had instituted a relief fund to help those affected by the famine.
5. Deleted by censors.

like me can do. When this children's scheme fell through I thought of going to Bengal. I have written and talked to various people. But there again it is the same thing. Sir Tej says that the only good that one can do by going is to see for oneself just what conditions are like. I am now awaiting a letter from Abhayanandji.[1] The Math is doing real good work, I hear. Now there is a rumour that no tickets are being sold to get out of Calcutta – I do not know if this is true and if it will apply to people who come for brief stays from outside.

Meanwhile I am concentrating on the garden. Datadin has been very slack and lazy all these months, so naturally now there is a terrific lot to be done. I have engaged another man too, so that there are three of them now. I have put in cauliflower, carrot, radish & lettuce and am now having plots prepared for the winter vegetables and potatoes. We have such a lot of ground. Feroze suggests putting in wheat too. Ladlibhai said it would be a good idea if we could get competent people to cut it and do all the rest of the paraphernalia.

At the Sapru's they have dug up their *āngan*[2] for potatoes.

It is very hot and sticky here and the rains are not yet over. We have been having heavy showers these last two nights, which have done great harm to fields & crops.

Yesterday I had an airgraph from Mami in London. She is simply thrilled with her son. She writes:

Gautam[3] has grown into quite a big boy now and has a mass of bronze curly hair. People seem to be quite fascinated by him. It is such a shame that none of his relatives have seen him at this stage and boys change so quickly. He tries to speak both Hindustani and English. He knows Hindustani must be spoken to Mummy and English to people coming in . . . Two months ago Kailash was invited by the Cambridge University to deliver lectures to advanced students of Cambridge & London University. He stayed at the guest house of Emmanuel College and dined with the dons. They were all very pleased with him. Some time ago he was elected fellow of the Linnean Society and recently he has become the fellow of the Royal Asiatic Society also. His work keeps him very busy. Sometimes he works in the British Museum and has made some good contacts.

1. Swami Abhayanand: a disciple of Swami Sivananda of the Ramakrisha Math at Belur near Calcutta, to whom Kamala Nehru turned for spiritual guidance. Swami Abhayanand later became head of Belur Math.
2. Courtyard.
3. Gautam Kaul: son of Sheila and K. N. Kaul.

Nani is still having a temperature. Little Om has at last brought out the pice he swallowed but he still has a bad cough.

Lots & lots of love, darling one.

Your loving,

Indu

Enclosed: 2 snapshots.

---

137.                                      Ahmadnagar Fort Prison,
11th September, 1943

Darling Indu,

It seems quite a long time since I heard from you. Your last letter, dated 21st August,[1] reached me two weeks ago. A longer interval than usual was inevitable because of your return to Allahabad. Perhaps you went to Benares from there to see Amma.

I have had a letter from Amma from Banaras. She has received one of my letters to her. Surprisingly – and yet why be surprised? – she says that part of this letter was blacked out. You can imagine what I can write to Amma of all persons. How any of the purely domestic matters concerning various people's health outside should offend the sensitive judgement of the censor it is a little difficult to imagine.

Amma writes that Chand has taken two months' leave and has gone to Murree. Also that there is a chance of Kailas and Sheila returning from London. I suppose the new developments in the war situation will facilitate this return.

Yesterday's newspaper brought the interesting news that Feroze had been acquitted in appeal. Of course it is a minor matter that he had already served his full sentence of a year.

We have been having an abundance of rain during the last two weeks or so. Our little garden has revived and puts up a brave show. But far more important than the flowers in the garden are the crops outside and this rain has probably averted another tragedy.

When you were in Naini, or just after your release, I sent you a packet of flower seeds. We have collected masses of these seeds, rather indiscriminately, I am afraid. Would you like me to send you some more for Anand Bhawan or elsewhere?

I liked the book you sent me, Han Suyin's autobiography: *Destination Chungking*. It is very well written; her prose is clear and limpid and runs effortlessly. The descriptions of Chinese life during the war, and more particularly of the bombing of Chungking are vivid. I thought again and again of what I had seen in Chungking four years ago and more, of the

---

1. Refers to letter No. 130.

nightly air-raids and of the Japanese bombers shining brightly and look-ing beautiful as they were caught in the beam of the searchlight. Do you know the 'Epitaph' by C. S. Lewis? [1]

> She was delicately, beautifully made,
> So small, so unafraid,
> Till the bomb came
> (Bombs are the same
> Delicately, beautifully made).

Nightly they came, these shining, beautiful bombers, and the alarm shrieked out and we rushed into the shelters, peeping out sometimes to look at the planes far over us and the searchlights and the falling bombs. The next morning we inspected the craters and the debris covering what once were human beings.

This was four years ago and what a lot has happened since then. The bombers and the bombs, unusual sights, some things that only occurred in far away and backward countries like Abyssinia, China and Spain, are now the commonest of experiences for half the world at least.

And yet, sometimes, these four years seem to vanish away, as if they had not been, and I am back again in Chungking and Barcelona and Prague and Geneva, full of the excitement of the moment, full of anger at the folly and weakness of man.

It is an odd experience to go back to the past and live it again, almost forgetting the events that followed. Sometimes the old excitement returns in some measure, the joy and the pain, and then there is the sudden switch-back to the present and it takes a little time to adapt oneself to it. As if we had visited a theatre and seen a powerful play which gripped us, and in which, curiously enough, we were both actors and spectators. The play ends and we walk out into the cool night air, but our minds are still wrapped up in what we have seen and there is a veil before our eyes. Gradually it fades away and we are back to the present.

In prison, I imagine, this kind of mental throw-back occurs more fre-quently than outside. In the present here is still and stagnant and, lacking sensation, the mind searches for it in the pigeonholes of memory . . .

Love,
Your loving,
Papu

This is my letter No. 27.

---

1. Clive Staples Lewis (1898–1963): critic and novelist.

138.                                   Anand Bhawan,
Allahabad,
13th September, 1943

Darling Papu,

You are right – this is nice paper.[1] There is plenty of it here but all marked 'Anand Bhawan'. I am writing to Dehra for some for you, but I believe they take a long time. So I am also writing to Bombay; Puphi may be able to get more of the Travancore paper.

Your letter of the 4th[2] came last evening. It was your 26th. This is my 28th.

Puphi has returned from Bombay and is now in Lucknow. I have written to her quoting the paragraph dealing with Chand & Tara. She sent Sunder with some books and other things. Sunder tells me that Puphi has had the anti-cholera injection, prior to leaving for Calcutta.

In my last letter[3] I told you that I had written to Swami Abhayanandji of the Ramkrishna Math. His reply came this morning. He writes:

There is no dearth of workers in Bengal; some of the prominent Bengali and non-Bengali Relief Societies have already taken up the work of rendering help . . . Personally I would advise you to undertake the responsible task of collecting money, clothes, raw foodstuffs from other provinces and sending them to some of the Relief Committees. I feel it is wiser for people to work on the lines indicated above in other provinces for the help of the people of Bengal . . .

Along with my last letter I sent you yet another book of Virginia Woolf's, *The Death of the Moth*. I have not yet read it. I wish I had met her – even the books I only discovered after her death.[4]

Bharati sends the following message: 'It was good of Indu to send me what you have to say about my book. You can well imagine how happy it made me and how it cheered me. I had sent you the book together with an article on "Toller"[5] more than four months ago and I wondered why there was not a word from you until now when Indu wrote to me. Much love to you.'

A couple of days ago I received another airgraph from Agatha. A

1. Jawaharlal Nehru and Indira Gandhi always used hand-made paper for their personal stationery. Like hand-woven cloth or *khadi*, this reflected the cultural mood of the freedom struggle.

2. Refers to letter No. 134.

3. Refers to letter No. 136.

4. Virginia Woolf died in 1941.

5. Ernst Toller: German poet and playwright, a friend of Jawaharlal Nehru.

really sweet one! Perhaps you will be interested in this further news of her garden:

My garden is blossoming like the proverbial rose – a mixture of plants and vegetables. You would particularly love a mass of – what we call – tobacco plants. They only come out at night and when they do – they give out a glorious scent – not unlike the starry flowers that Indian women wear in their hair. Next door to us lives an interesting mineral-ogist, who understands all about soils – and the kind of nourishment different plants need. He is known in the district as an irritable person and he can be quite rude. But we have become great friends. He is experimenting in pumpkins that he trains up to his first floor and the gigantic fruits hang like golden lanterns. People come from all over to look at them, but the children in Battersea also go further and lean over to feel them. A strange commentary on the war situation is evidenced from their remarks – for they think it is a lemon plant, as, when small, they might be said to resemble this nearly forgotten fruit. Then one realises that children of that age have probably never known what a lemon is. I find that now the old doctor has put barbed wire round his precious experimental plant and a notice on the said wire, 'THIS IS A PUMPKIN PLEASE DO NOT TOUCH'. He is fearful lest these small people will be tempted to take my tomatoes that are now beginning to ripen and suggests that I, too, barricade them in some way. But I told him that I am going to experiment in the innate goodness of human nature!!! Up to the present this had worked, but one can never tell. Besides, several of these naughty children have become quite friendly and call out 'give us a flower, Miss' which I do – in the belief it may prevent them taking my precious tomatoes!

I foresee that I am going to have quite a struggle with our garden. But if eventually we can get anything out of it, it will be worth the trouble.

Sapru Saheb has had a relapse.

Re. bird watching – I have spotted two very regular visitors and hope to make friends with them soon: a lovely vivid oriole and a perky little robin. There are lots of blue jays too and in the afternoon just as I am settling down to a nap, I hear the call of the coppersmith – tuk tuk. But I haven't seen it yet.

Much love, Papushka[1] darling.

Your loving,<br>Indu

---

1. Indira is attaching a Russian diminutive ending to the familiar 'Papu'.

139.                                  Ahmadnagar Fort Prison,
                                          18th September, 1943

Darling Indu,

September is gradually creeping away and the days get shorter, the weather cooler. But our routine continues much the same; there is little of novelty in it. Only the mind occasionally rebels and wanders far afield, forgetting for a while the present with all its drabness and monotony. Latterly, as I wrote to you, I have taken afresh to spinning and I was pleased to find that my fingers had not lost their skill. I spin fairly well and fast but for only half an hour a day or so. And in half an hour not much can be produced; possibly in four or five days of half hours I spin enough yarn to make a pocket handkerchief!

I wrote to Amma a few days ago. As Kailas and Sheila are trying to come back – and they might well succeed – it struck me that perhaps they might be short of funds for the return journey from England. If so, and I asked Amma to enquire from Kailas, we might try to send them some money.

I have been looking through the two books on improving eye-sight that you sent us. They are very helpful and contain useful suggestions for simple exercises. I think these exercises would do you good, even though your eyes are in excellent condition. Some neck exercises are also worth doing as these relieve the stiffness & tension in the neck and thereby help circulation and prevent, to some extent, headaches. All this does not take more than five minutes. I remember how Dhan Gopal Mukerji[1] used to relieve headaches by gentle massage of the neck muscles.

I have had no news of Puphi (Nan) for some time and am not sure where she is. Probably she is back in Allahabad but there was no mention of her in your letter.

This is another reminder to you to send me snaps of Mummie and yourself.

Please get Hari and Khaliq to clean up all the books in the library and in my room. They get all musty during the rains.

Here are two simple Urdu couplets of Mir:

جی میں تھا اس سے ملیے تو کیا کیا نہ کہیے میر

ہر جب ملے تو وہ گئے ناچار دیکھ کر!    (میر)

یاد اس کی اتنی خوب نہیں میر باز آ

نادان پھر وہ دل سے بھلایا نہ جائے گا    (میر)

---

1. Dhan Gopal Mukherji: Indian littérateur settled in the United States.

मीर: जी में था उस से मिलिये तो क्या क्या न कहिये मीर
पर जब मिले तो रह गए नाचार देख कर !

याद उस की इतनी ख़ूब नहीं मीर, बाज़ आ
नादान ! फिर वह दिल से भुलाया न जाएगा [1]

Do you want me to continue sending you Urdu verses in my letters?
It is no trouble to me but I do not want to burden you with them unless
you are interested. They are not – far from it! – high-class poetry. But
they help us to understand a certain phase of India and of our people.
And they enrich our knowledge of the language.

Love to you and Feroze,

Your loving,

Papu

In your letter dated Sept. 4 [2] from Allahabad, you say it is your No. 26.
According to my calculation it is No. 25. The one before was dated
21st [3] August from Bombay. This letter is my No. 28.

---

140.                                    21st September, 1943

Darling Papu,
Your letter No. 27 [4] arrived yesterday.
    Puphi left for Calcutta last evening.
    The only Hindi dictionary in the house is an *Urdu–Hindi Kosh* by
Ramchandra Varma. I had it in jail with me. Is that the one you had in

1. Mir:   Much I thought if ever her I met
           I would say this and this and this;
           But look, when I met her
           I looked and looked at her
           And nothing I could say!
           Remembrance of hers, much, too much, O *Mir*,
           Will not be good for you;
           Contain yourself, so I say;
           You do not know, perhaps,
           So enduring will it be one day
           That you can ne'er defy!
2. Refers to letter No. 135.
3. Refers to letter No. 130.
4. Refers to letter No. 137.

Dehra Dun? And is that the one you want now? The other, *Shabd Sagar*, was probably in existence some years ago and is now out of print. Another edition will soon be ready, I am told by the Indian Press. *Kavita Kaumudi* likewise is not available anywhere.

It's a lovely day today. Raining and so cool – and the refreshing scent of wet soil. I do hope this is the last of the rains, so we can get down to the sowing. Ladlibhai suggests that we should have a really good *mali*, otherwise the vegetable garden will not be much of a success. As it is, Datadin and Gangu are eternally down with malaria. So I have asked Anna to acquire a good & experienced man from the Superintendent of the Alfred Park. He ought to know. If we can put down all those vegetables and potatoes successfully, then I want to try my hand at wheat and gram. There is such a ground, it's a pity to let it lie fallow. We might even have some *arhar*! [1]

These days Allahabad is having one show after another in aid of the Bengal relief fund. It is rather remarkable how even the poorer people are putting aside their own troubles – and they have enough – to give their mite to Bengal.

I am glad you liked *Destination Chungking*! I have not yet read any of those books. Living in Allahabad is really a nuisance sometimes. None of these new books ever seem to come to Kitabistan or any other local bookshop. And so few copies are received by the Bombay bookshops that they all get sold out within a couple of weeks and are never mentioned in catalogues and the like.

I am going to quote to you a poem about a Chinese friend of mine, Shelley Wang. [2] You may have seen it before and you may remember him too – you met him in London once or twice. It was soon after that that he returned to China and was killed. The poem is by John Hewitt and brings a very vivid picture of Wang. Here it is:

### In Memory of Shelley Wang

I cannot cheat my thought. I remember too well
his bland smooth face by that hearth, his cigarettes,
his explanation of the characters,
the firm fist with the bush held vertical,
his glinting glasses laminated thick,
his way of speaking of his early days;
his wise grandfather, poetry and tea,
Confucius, soya beans, and Mao Tse Tung . . .

1. A kind of pulse.
2. A Chinese writer who died in July 1939.

He was a restful man, a quiet scholar,
compact of wisdom, courage, tolerance
a gentle poet even of our hills
making a vivid stanza as he pass'd,
disliking our literal art's conceit,
and setting style and reason against despair.

For all his greatness life could offer him
only a little death in a vast campaign,
a manuscript unpublished, and a book
of badly printed verse on wartime paper.
Yet I do not think he would have understood
that sick word failure. There are other words . . .

With the coming of winter many birds will come from the Caucasus
and the Himalayas. Since I last wrote to you I have espied several new
species. The barbet, the coppersmith, the white-eye and the pied myna.
But you cannot really observe birds without a pair of good binoculars.
Some of them are so tiny. I am regretting that I did not invest in a pair
of binoculars before leaving England. Now of course they are non-
existent from the civilian point of view. Hari unearthed your old opera-
glasses, but they are quite useless for longer distances, and even for
shorter distances they don't help much.

I have just received a letter from a prisoner of war in Italy. It is dated
22nd June.

The hospital is doing very well these days. It is quite full and many
people have to be refused admission. So Vatsala is kept busy and she
does not grouse quite so much about the dullness of Allahabad social
life. The new Matron has not yet arrived. Isn't it strange that the Allahabad climate which suits Rohini Pooviah [1] so well should not agree with
any of her sisters!

I hope you are looking after yourself as far as possible and are trying
to put on some weight.

My *namaskars* to everybody and much love to you.

Your loving,
Indu

P.S. This is my letter No. 29.

---

1. Rohini Pooviah: Kathak dancer who was a family acquaintance.

141.                             Ahmadnagar Fort Prison,
                                    25th September, 1943

Darling Indu,

I have a sheaf of your letters in front of me. Three of them have come during the last week and they have cleared up a mystery and confusion that intrigued me previously. Your numbering of your letters seemed to me wrong, some of your references were not clear, and it was obvious that something was lacking. This could have been due to the blacked-out passages in your letters for they create a gap in understanding. But it was not that alone. Your letters reached me irregularly, in inverted order, sometimes a long while without any, and then in a bunch. Thus your letter of August 29th[1] came to me on Sept. 20th after I had received your letter of the 4th Sept.[2] Again your letter of the 13th[3] Sept. preceded the one dated 7th Sept.[4] I have now, I think, received all of them up to the one numbered 28. This proves the value of numbering.

The letters have come but with large patches blacked out. Evidently these deal with Bengal and Bengal is a sore point, little wonder. You will have to guess what has been deleted and hence has not reached me. Another reason for delay has been the inclusion by you in one of your letters of Nani's note in Hindi. Hindi takes much longer to get through, for a knowledge of Hindi does not seem to be among the accomplishments of the Bombay Secretariat.

I have received Mummie's snapshots – also Virginia Woolf's *Death of the Moth* and the foreign papers . . .[5]

I presume you did not go to Bombay for the show organised by Vakil's school – it is hardly worthwhile spending time and energy & money in travelling a long distance for one show – but of course sometimes this may be desirable.

In Bharati's message that you have sent me there is a reference to an article on Toller which she says she sent me with her book. Tell her I did not receive this article.

I was greatly interested and amused at the extracts from the airgraphs you have received from Agatha and Sheila. Gautam must be a comely kid! But then almost all children at that age are attractive and yet they grow up often into something very different. Kailas & Sheila are both good-looking and Gautam therefore should take after them. I am glad

1. Refers to letter No. 133.
2. Refers to letter No. 135.
3. Refers to letter No. 138.
4. Refers to letter No. 136.
5. Deleted by censors. See letter No. 145 para 2 for the extent of the deletions.

Kailas is doing well. It would have been a good thing if he had taken a doctorate of London University.

I hope your sending my Times Book Club bill to Krishna does not mean an additional burden on him. I have no idea how my royalty accounts stand there. For the last two or three years I have received nothing from London. Surely there must have been some income. Once I cabled to Krishna to give Kailas any sum that he might require – also to use the rest for any other suitable purpose.

Datadin is of course lazy & incompetent. You cannot rely upon him at all and the only way to make him work is to supervise him most of the time. He is too old a servant to be pushed out and so we must put up with him. But that is no reason why everything should be left to him. I am glad you have engaged another man to help. It is worthwhile & an investment to have more additional helps. It would be a good plan to put in wheat and potatoes. For wheat, get hold of a real *kisan*[1] to help – someone who knows. Preferably get someone we have known from our own district of Allahabad.

I received yesterday a long joint letter from Chand & Tara from New York dated 15th July. Large chunks of it were blacked out. It was a very interesting letter. They are so obviously excited and pleased – I shall send them a reply.

Here is a couplet by Ghalib:

قفس میں مجھ سے روداد چمن کہتے نہ ڈر ہمدم
گری تھی جس پہ کل بجلی وہ میرا آشیاں کیوں ہو ؟  (غالب)

In Hindi:

क़फ़स में मुझसे रूदाद-ए-चमन कहते न डर हम दम ।
गिरी थी जिस पे कल बिजली वह मेरा आशियां क्यों हो ? ? [2]

A bird in a cage is addressing an old companion outside. The two lines manage to compress in a few words a whole story of disaster which the bird is trying hard not to believe – क़फ़स = cage; रूदाद = वाकय = events; चमन = garden; हम दम = companion; आशियां = nest.

Love,
Your loving,
Papu

---

1. Farmer.
2. Ghalib:   Relate to me in the cage,
    Do not fear, my friend,
    In our garden what went on;
    The nest the lightning struck, ay,
    Why should it be mine alone?

142.                                  Anand Bhawan,
Allahabad,
30th September, 1943

Darling Papu,

I have just returned from a visit to Lucknow and Cawnpore, where we had gone in connection with the Legal Aid Committee. I found your letter No. 28 [1] awaiting my return.

According to my calculations my letter No. 25 was written on the 30th August. [2] The one dated 4th Sept. [3] was therefore No. 26. The former one seems to have performed the vanishing act or perhaps it may turn up later. This letter is No. 30. Rummaging in the Library drawer I have at last found the original & first two letters you wrote.

On my return from Cawnpore I found that in my absence it had been pouring with rain here. This has done much damage to crops and to our little vegetable plot. Benares is in floods and Vatsala tells me they fully expected the same state of things here.

Chhoti Puphi writes that she has already sent you some more of the Travancore paper. No reply yet from Dehra Dun.

Papu, could I have a godown for my furniture? Could you mention this to Puphi, please.

Hari says that there are some piles of old newspapers that you had put away a long time ago. I haven't yet seen whether they are files of the *Leader* or which newspaper. Do you want them kept or shall I dispose of them?

Puphi is expected back tonight. Pupha went to Bombay some days ago. Chhoti Puphi is, I believe, going down south for *Diwali*. Devki, a friend of Chand, is spending her *Dussehra* here.

There is a hospital meeting of trustees next week. Pan, [4] Psyche & Nair will surely come. The new matron has come. I do not think she will like it here. The hospital is packed full these days.

I want this letter to get off today, so I shall close now.

                           Much love,
                             Indu

---

1. Refers to letter No. 139.
2. Possibly refers to letter No. 133.
3. Refers to letter No. 135.
4. P. A. Narielwala: a friend of the Nehrus, a businessman associated with the House of Tatas, a leading name in Indian entrepreneurship.

143.                                          Ahmadnagar Fort Prison,
                                              2nd October, 1943

Indu darling,

I have your letter No. 29 of the 21st September.[1] Do not trouble yourself about the Hindi dictionary or the *Kavita Kaumudi*. I have managed to get a copy of the latter through Narendra Deva. It is an old library copy.

Now that Pupha is out – I hope he is well enough now after his long illness – you have got the best of expert guidance for the garden. If he has the time and the chance he will set things going in the proper way. But in any event a competent gardener is necessary and you have done well to ask for one.

I remember Shelley Wang very well, although I met him only twice, I think, at various parties in London. He had an attractive and rather distinctive face. When I went to China I enquired after him but could not get any straight news. There seemed to be some mystery about him. Then someone told me that he had wanted to meet me but was too far away to travel to Chungking. And then came news of his death. Everything seemed to be rather vague and indeterminate and hence the pictures in my mind are all mixed up. I remember definitely, however, that he had a certain premonition of death on the eve of his departure for China from London.

For some years past it used to be my custom to give some *khadi* clothing to the servants about this time of the year. Usually this amounts to Rs. 100/- worth. Also I gave *khadi* coupons for Upadhyaya's children. If you can carry on this practice I shall be glad. Probably it is difficult to get *khadi*. Anyway you will do what you can. The children of the servants as also Upadhyaya's little girls should have first preference.

We have been having very heavy showers of rain – an unusual phenomenon here. Partly due to this and partly to other reasons, it has been cooler here this year than it was at this time last year.

I asked you about flower seeds in one of my letters – I do not suppose you require them as you are concentrating on vegetables. Still, you might ask Pupha if he would like me to send some. We have masses of them, but inexpertly collected.

The swallows here have grown in number and have made their nests inside rooms and verandahs. I like them; they are so swift and quiet, so unlike the noisy and quarrelsome sparrows. It is rather fascinating to see a swallow's nest being built up, quietly, efficiently and without fuss. It seems to stick on to the bare wall or a corner without any visible

1. Refers to letter No. 140.

support. All feathers, soft and downy, collected probably from distant places and stuck together with some kind of cement.

Another frequent visitor is a kind of hummingbird, smaller than the average sparrow, and with a long pointed beak. It flits about from flower to flower extracting the honey. The Hindustani name for it is, I am told, *shakarkhora*. Then there is a great variety of butterflies.

There used to be a pair of binoculars in the house, rather ancient. I brought it in 1927 from Switzerland for Dadu. It may still be lying in some box or cupboard. Ask Puphi if she remembers it.

I have sent you back a packet of old foreign periodicals.

Here are two couplets of Ghalib:

جب ميكده چهٹا تو پهر اب كيا جگه كى قيد ؟
مسجد هو، مدرسه هو، كوئى خانقاه هو ! (غالب)

هر بو الهوس نے حسن پرستى شعار كى
اب آبروے شيوۀ اهل نظر گئى (غالب)

In Hindi:

ग़ालिब : जब मैकदा छुटा तो फिर ग्रब क्या जगह की क़ैद ?
मसजिद हो, मदरसा हो, कोई ख़ानक़ाह हो !
हर बुल हवस ने हुस्न परस्ती शेग्रार की ।
ग्रब ग्राबरू-ए-शेवा-ए ग्रहले नज़र गई ॥ [1]

The first couplet is easy – मैकदा means the wine shop or wine-saloon. ( मैं is wine) – ख़ानक़ाह [khankah] is the meeting place and the house of the Sufis (the mystics of Islam). There used to be large ख़ानक़ाहs where a well-known Sufi would live with his disciples and hold forth to the public.

The second couplet is more difficult. It is often quoted. It means, more or less: now that every parvenu and conceited fool has constituted himself as a connoisseur and judge of the beautiful, there is no honour or place left for those who have the eyes to see and appreciate.

1. Ghalib: When the tavern itself we're made to leave,
Why restrain to a specific place?
A seminary, a monastery or else a mosque,
Any place it may now be!
When professions of the greed-worshippers
admiring beauty soar,
The grace of the truly discerning ones
finds respect no more!

बुल हवस = हवस परस्त = greed-worshipper; हुस्न = beauty; शेमार करना = प्रपना तरीका बनाना; शेवा=तरीका; महले नज़र = Those with sight, i.e., those who have the capacity to appreciate beauty.

Mention of *khankah* reminds me of an interesting change in name of a famous *khankah* somewhere in Central Asia. This used to be a Buddhist monastery in the old days and, it is said, a thousand monks lived there. It was called *Nav Vihar*. Later, when Islam spread to Central Asia, this monastery became a *khankah* and, with a very slight change, it was called *Nau Bahar*. Very few people connected this new name with its Buddhist –Indian original.

Love,
Your loving,
Papu

This is my letter No. 30, which means about thirty weeks since I started writing to you afresh from this place.

*Later*
I have just received a letter from Puphi (Nan) dated 16th Sept., enclosing two press cuttings from New York about Chand & Tara. I have not so far received the copy of Tara's letter which she says she has sent separately. I shall return the press cuttings to her.

I have also received (from Betty) hand-made notepaper, *supari* & *elaichi* and some *murabba*. [1]

I am informed that a book of poems I wanted to send you for your last birthday has at last been obtained and sent on to you! I hope it has not been sent to Naini!

P

---

144.

Anand Bhawan,
Allahabad,
[October 1943]

Darling Papu,
I woke up at about one o'clock last night to find myself staring at Sirius and Orion. It was a lovely starlit night with the lady moon but two days old.

I was in such a hurry when I wrote my last letter, [2] I forgot to reply to most of your queries. I have already sent you two of the old Panchgani

1. Jam.
2. Refers to letter No. 142.

snapshots, one of Mummie and me and one of Mummie alone. I do hope they reached you.

Nani writes to say that she sent some *bhuni supari* and *murabba* to Chhoti Puphi, to be sent on to you.

Miss Darbyshire,[1] or 'The Darb' as the whole college used to call her, has sent me an airgraph. Rather nice of her, don't you think, especially when I know that she is always so busy with stocks of mail. She says that Somerville is thriving in spite of wartime difficulties, shortened courses, etc.

Hamidah Mahmud never replied to my letter, but I hear from Puphi that somebody did reply to her letter & that the other girl is now well.

Sheila Mami has sent a fairly recent snapshot of Gautam. He looks more like Mamu now than when he was tinier. He is over two now.

The books in your room have already been dusted. I have told Khaliq about the Library but that will take considerable time and when Puphi is here it is extremely difficult to get any servant for upstairs work. Hari, of course, is there but the job is too big for him single-handed. And I don't want the books strewn about when Psyche & Perin[2] come for the meeting next week.

I hope Psyche will stay on for a few days. I have a fair amount of work these days, with all the committees Feroze has formed – typing, meeting people, sending out notices and so on. But the rest of the time it is pretty lonely, being all alone upstairs. I go down for meals of course but it's rather formal – like a hotel or something. Feroze is out of town at present.

We have at last planted the potatoes, most of them, and the winter vegetables. These are the seeds Ladlibhai sent for: turnips, carrot, radish, cabbage, lettuce, cauliflower, papaya and tomato. We have been a complete failure as far as the lettuce is concerned and nothing has appeared so far. I want now to get some spinach & mint.

July before last we brought lots of bulbs from Kashmir, of spring flowers, such as iris, daffodil, tulip and lily-of-the-valley. In the months that followed these poor things lay in some forgotten corner of the house. On my return from Bombay I found them shrivelled and eaten up by insects. I gave the box to Bansi to throw away and to clear up the mess.

Apparently one bulb was still intact and without mentioning the fact to anyone, Bansi planted it in a flowerpot. Imagine my surprise and

1. Helen Darbyshire: Principal of Somerville College, Oxford, when Indira Gandhi was a student there.
2. Perin Captain: social worker and freedom fighter. Like Psyche, she was a granddaughter of Dadabhai Naoroji.

delight when yesterday morning I espied iris leaves shooting out beside a chili-plant! I hope it flowers too.

We have two guests here these days – Devki, a friend of Chand's, and Vimala Oberoi.

Darling Papu – I do miss you so much. I keep your room closed, for I hate going into it and finding it all empty and unlived-in. Sometimes when I see a new bird or something I feel like rushing in to call you to have a look and then of course I remember that you are somewhere in India, but definitely not in Anand Bhawan. Oh, it's perfectly awful. And the house without you is asleep and unresponsive and awaiting your return.

All my love, darling one,
Indu

P.S.

Do you want your subscription to the *Indian Journal of Social Work* renewed?

---

145.

Anand Bhawan,
Allahabad,
7th/8th October, 1943

Darling Papu,
Your letter No. 29, dated September 25th [1] reached me last evening. This is my letter No. 32.

Darling – I just don't know what to write. This last letter of yours has been very depressing and discouraging. Not because of anything you have written, let me hasten to add, but because of the state in which it arrived. Beginning from the last paragraph of page two right up to the second paragraph of page eight is blackout! I am mentioning this only so that you may have an idea of what you are allowed to write & what not to, so I hope the eagle-eyed censor will pass it!

*Vijaya Dashmi Day*
Makkhi [2] dropped in for a few moments yesterday with his wife Ganga and a crowd of other relatives. I hadn't seen Ganga for fifteen years. She was looking very lovely and was all 'a-glow'.

I do not know if Puphi has written to you – she is leaving Anand

---

1. Refers to letter No. 141.

2. Jai Kumar Atal (Makkhi Atal): a member of the Indian Civil Service; married Ganga Raina.

Bhawan and taking a house in Allahabad. Chhoti Puphi mentioned the fact when I was in Bombay but she said it was all very vague. On my return I asked Ladli Bhai and he knew nothing about it. But there was a great deal of whispering going on among the servants. I was reluctant to ask Puphi herself as I felt that if she had wanted to talk to me about it she would certainly have mentioned the subject herself. It was only three or four days ago that Puphi mentioned moving in my presence – and everything seemed to be so definite, I got quite a shock. I didn't know how to broach the subject so I wrote her a note, because it did, and does, seem ridiculous to me that I should occupy this big house on my own while the four of them are crowded into some 'bungalow'. Of course, having been kept completely in the dark so far, it was difficult for me to say anything. I told her that this move would hurt you and that if she was moving because of Feroze and me – surely we could come to some other arrangement. Feroze & I being only two and having so few belongings and encumbrances could easily go somewhere. In any case I shall be out of Allahabad most of the time when I start my visiting – Jaipur, Lahore, etc. And I want to go to Bombay too and if Feroze did come to Allahabad he would prefer to stay with his mother. But Puphi replied that her moving was not at all because of us and this was my home, and so on. I do wish she were not going. This is such a wrong time to set up house, and engage new servants and so forth. There are difficulties enough in life today without our making fresh ones – and such artificial and unnecessary ones too. However, she has made up her mind now. I do not know when she intends moving.

I told Hari about what you wrote concerning the wheat and the 'real' *kisan*. He was quite indignant, saying, 'Am I not a real *kisan*?' He says the wheat must be put in just two or four days before *Diwali*. Poor Hari is having a lot of trouble about his promised land with the Municipality. He sends his *salaams*.

The nights are slightly cooler now, especially towards mornings but it is still quite sticky and hot in the daytime.

I struggle along with a *charkha* too – though not too successfully! I hope spinning is not hurting your arms.

You asked about Tajo in one of your letters. She is well and seems to be getting on all right at the Isabella Thoburn. Puphi had asked her here for the *Dussehra* holidays but Tajo had already accepted an invitation from a college friend from Gorakhpur to spend the holiday with her.

Chunni, Hiralal's son,[1] came this morning with the *jaee*.[2] Hiralal,

1. Hiralal and Chunni: domestic servants of the Nehrus.
2. Oats.

poor chap, had diabetes and then got tuberculosis. He is rather bad. Kanhaiyalal also came some time ago and reminded me how Dadu had had Hiralal sent to the hills and had spent 1100/- over the treatment years ago! Both the brothers have become very thin.

Your letter No. 30, dated October 2nd[1] has just come. Long before your letter came mentioning the *khadi* for the servants, I have been trying to get some to give to the servants on your birthday. Rs. 100/- doesn't go very far nowadays, so we shall have to give less than usual.

Lots of love,<br>Indu

146.                                    Ahmadnagar Fort Prison,
                                              9th October, 1943

Darling Indu,

I have your letter No. 30 of the 30th Sept.[2] As you will notice, I am writing on Travancore paper which Betty has sent me. I think I have already written to you that I have received *supari* & *elaichi* and some *pethe ka murabba*.[3] I suppose Nani sent these for me.

Some two and a half years ago, when I was in Dehra, I received a letter from Mrs Robeson[4] from America. She wrote to me how their house in London had been smashed to bits during the London blitz and their library and records destroyed. She asked me if she could send me anything. I wrote to her and mentioned a number of books, not available here, which she might send – or rather I did not write to her myself but asked Betty to do so. Betty has now heard from her for the first time during these two or three years and it appears that not only did she write to her but sent her books and newspaper clippings (repeatedly). Neither the letters nor the books ever reached Betty. I am not sure about the newspaper cuttings as I remember getting a packet or two but was not sure who sent them. Betty will of course write to her and tell her so. But it would be a good thing if you kept in touch with Mrs Robeson also. Her address two years ago used to be: Mrs Paul R. Robeson, 555 Edgecombe Avenue, New York City.

Of course you can store up your furniture somewhere in Anand Bhawan. What a question to ask! I shall write to Puphi but my next letter to her is not due for another ten days or more. I wrote to her only three or four days ago. But surely it is not necessary for me to write to

1. Refers to letter No. 143.
2. Refers to letter No. 142.
3. Gourd-fruit jam.
4. Mrs Robeson: wife of Paul Robeson, the actor and singer.

her. Nor is it necessary for you to ask my or anyone else's permission. Naturally, when one lives together a certain cooperation is necessary and references have to be made. Mention the matter to Puphi and fix it up with her. Hari can then take charge of the job. There are at least three, and possibly four, godowns or places where old furniture, rugs, carpets, vessels and odds and ends are kept. Repeatedly they have been weeded out and numerous cartloads of useless stuff sold off or given away. Still a great deal of junk remains which can be disposed of with advantage – not monetary advantage but from other points of view. I dislike collecting old lumber. It is not used and simply decays.

There is much of course in these godowns which can be of use on special occasions, and some things have a sentimental value. Still, I think a cleaning up and weeding out are desirable, especially after the rains. I imagine the room at the back of Swaraj Bhawan, near the well, would be suitable for your extra belongings. It is a good clean room. There used to be some bookshelves in it. If these are properly arranged along the walls, the centre space can be cleared up.

I do not remember any old files of newspapers which I had asked Hari to preserve for me. I do not keep such files as they take up too much room, and anyway all manner of insects eat them up. I tried to keep some bound files of the old *Independent*[1] of 1920 and later. But the insects made a meal of them. So you might glance through these files and unless there is some obvious and compelling reason to keep them, dispose of them. Certainly I do not want to keep the *Leader* files. It is bad enough to have to read it for news on the day of issue. A duller newspaper I have not seen.

I hope Hari is airing from time to time my clothes, as well as the other things stored up in boxes and trunks. Also the books in the library & my room should be cleaned and aired.

I do not know what the condition of our servants' quarters is and whether they are all occupied or not. They should be looked after and kept in good condition for use should any emergencies arise, especially those near the old garage. This is a matter for Ladli Bhai to look into.

I have suggested to Puphi that the time has come when an ambulatory service might be undertaken by the hospital, tapping the nearby villages to begin with. That is an essential development in India and we should begin to think on these lines. I am afraid my suggestion was sent too late for the trustees' meeting. But it can be discussed, planned out and circulated. I hope Vatsala likes the idea. I do not like static conditions. That the hospital is doing good work and is crowded is not quite enough.

1. A nationalist newspaper started by Motilal Nehru from Allahabad in 1919.

It should be dynamic, progressive, experimental and model. Widespread medical service in India must have an ambulatory side.

Here are some verses by Ghalib of a different type from the ones I have been sending you. They deal with *bahar*, spring, but in India *bahar* in this sense is represented more by the rainy season.

پھر اس انداز سے بہار آئی     کہ ہوئے مہرومہ تماشائی

دیکھو اے ساکنان خطہ' خاک     اس کو کہتے ہیں عالم آرائی

سبزے کو جب کہیں جگہ نہ ملی     بن گیا روے آب پر کائی

ہے ہوا میں شراب کی تاثیر     بادہ نوشی ہے باد پیمائی

(غالب)

In Hindi:

ग्रालिब : फिर इस म्रन्दाज़ से बहार म्राई — के हुए मेह्र म्रो मह् तमाशाई ।

देखो ऐ साकिनाने-खित्त-ए-ख़ाक — इसको कहते हैं म्रालम म्राराई ।

सब्ज़: को जब कहीं जगह न मिली — बन गया रूए म्राब पर काई ।

है हवा में शराब की तासीर — बादा नोशी है बाद पैमाई । [1]

मेह्र or मेह्ल=sun; मह् = moon; sakinan = inhabitants; खित्त: = a place, मुक़ाम; खित्त-ए-ख़ाक = place of dust, i.e., this world; म्रालम = world; म्राराई = म्रारास्ता करना, सजाना; सब्ज़: = grass; रू-ए-म्राब = the surface of the water; तासीर = म्रसर; बादा or बाद: = शराब; बाद पैमाई = हवा का इस्तेमाल करना, हवा खाना (बाद = हवा).

This is my letter No. 31.

Love,
Your loving,
Papu

---

147.                           Ahmadnagar Fort Prison,
                                           16th October, 1943

Darling Indu,

Since I wrote to you last week I have had two letters from you, your

1. Ghalib:   With what a flourish
                The spring has come again!
                Even the sun and the moon are lookers-on!
                Look, ye dwellers of lowly dust,
                This is how to deck and adorn the world;
                Green, green, all is green,
                Even the scum on water has turned green;
                Wine's effect has the air,
                Breathing it in is drinking wine!

numbers 31 and 32.[1] I have also received a packet of miscellaneous foreign periodicals and two books: *Life and Letters Today* (Brazil) and *Recent Judgments*.

I am returning to you a number of old periodicals and three books: Han Suyin's *Destination Chungking*, Goethe's *Faust*, & Hogben's *Mathematics for the Million*. Some foreign magazines I have sent to Chhoti Puphi as they might interest Raja.

I am intrigued by the *Prescriber*. Who has started sending this technical medical journal to me?

I think you might as well continue the subscription to *The Indian Journal of Social Work*. It was at the editor's special request that I started getting it and I should like to encourage the venture.

I am glad you are giving *khadi* to the servants. I did not mention Rs. 100/- as a limit. That was merely what I used to set aside for this in previous years. Now prices are much higher and consequently more will have to be spent.

I suppose Psyche and Pan have been to Allahabad for the hospital trustees' meeting. Pan, being a captain of industry, will have just come for a day and returned; but I hope Psyche stayed on.

So one of my letters, No. 29 dated Sept. 25th,[2] had nearly six full pages blacked out! That certainly seems to be a record. I am afraid I cannot remember what I wrote, or rather I cannot specify what one particular letter three weeks ago contained. I do not write business letters to you which can be easily indexed and tabulated in the mind. I write as I feel at the moment. In a general way, of course, I remember what I have been writing about. But six pages surely could not have dealt with one subject. I try to avoid an invitation to the brush or blue pencil of the censor, for there is no point at all in my taking the trouble to write when the written word is going to be converted into a black smudge or a criss-cross pattern. But how to avoid this kind of thing I do not know.

Your last letter,[3] which came yesterday, has certainly upset my composure and led me furiously to think, or perhaps it is more correct to say that my mind has been wandering like a vagabond into all manner of dark lanes and passages. You were right in feeling that I would be hurt when I learnt of Puphi's intention of shifting to a new house. I had not heard of this before; no one had mentioned it previously. So when I read of it for the first time in your letter I was taken aback, amazed, and felt very tired, a feeling I do not usually experience. It is a small

1. Refers to letters Nos 144 and 145.
2. Refers to letter No. 141.
3. Refers to letter No. 145.

matter in our domestic sphere and in this world of big happenings we cannot afford to lose our perspective. And yet even such relatively small matters have a way of disturbing the mind. For many years past I have tried not to be influenced too much by personal factors for they often come in the way of larger undertakings. I had thought that I had achieved a measure of success, but repeatedly I have found how mistaken I was. Personal factors do count and make a difference; and without them life is apt to become dry and hard and somewhat dehumanised. I know a large number of people of all sorts and I manage to get on with them tolerably well. And yet really intimate personal bonds are of necessity few, very few. When these are strained, it hurts. Sometimes this becomes inevitable and circumstances beyond one's control drive one to it. But that, I think, is very rare and usually there is some defect in us, something lacking, that leads to such consequences. And the main defect is probably a want of perfect frankness. We nurse thoughts and misapprehensions when perhaps a frank approach would resolve them or, at any rate, lead us to an understanding of the other's viewpoint.

What do we aim at in life? Many things, personal and impersonal. In a sense every problem can be reduced, in the final analysis, to the problem of human relationships, the relation of one individual to another and to the group, and that of groups *inter se*. The group may be the family, a circle of friends, neighbours, city folk, nation and ultimately it becomes the international group, the world. Harmonious living in its smallest as well as its largest aspects is the ideal. In order to achieve it we evolve our political, economic, social formulae and isms, and even struggle with each other. But no formula or ism can take the place of the essence of harmonious living, which is a matter of judgment and balance, of tact and sensitiveness, of continuous adjustment and a consideration of others. If we succeed in this to some extent we gain poise and equilibrium even in a mad world.

Another way of putting the essential problem is how to strike a balance between the claims of the individual and of the larger social group – between individualism and some kind of communism. (I am not using the word in its usual and technical sense.) To suppress the individual is bad and stops growth, to allow individualism full play is to have anarchy.

Society in ancient China and ancient India tended to concentrate on a small group – the family. It did not encourage, at either end, the individual or the national group. It evolved, as nowhere else, the family system in a wide sense. It lost much thereby, but it managed to develop certain very desirable virtues also. There were far fewer self-centred individuals; there was a capacity for cooperation within the group, for adjustment, judgment, tact, poise, balance. One sees that still in China in spite of all that has happened. There is a real aristocracy and well-bredness about the Chinese which is impressive. I am afraid we in India do not show this, for we have undergone a long process of breaking up. Yet somewhere, I suppose, beneath the surface, that training of thousands of years must subsist.

In the West individualism was emphasised much more, with certain remarkable results in the shape of progress. It went too far and is now leading more and more to an inevitable socialism and communism. With all their manifest virtues, it is surprising how Westerners (individuals apart) lack poise and balance.

I suppose the East & the West, having explored life in different directions, are unconsciously or consciously going to pool their resources some time or other, and find a common path of harmonious living.

Meanwhile, I am naturally concerned with the sphere of work in which my lot is cast. It hurts me to see how in our individual conduct we falsify the larger ideal we claim to hold. How lacking in poise and balance we are; how self-centred and incapable of adjustment. For the narrow sphere of our lives has a large bearing on the wider plane of action.

I fear I can do nothing in family affairs or other matters while I am here, cut off from contact and activity. Each one of you will have to shift for yourself as best you can. For my part, where family affairs are concerned, my mind inevitably goes back to my father – Dadu – and I try to think what he would have preferred. Apart from my affection for him and my regard for his memory, I owe too much to him ever to forget his wishes.

I do not know if all this rigmarole will interest you. My mind is full of what I read in your letter yesterday and I wanted to share a part of it with you. I shall write to Puphi in the course of the next few days.

You say that you keep my room closed. Shall I tell you how I reacted to a somewhat similar situation when you were in Switzerland and England? Often I was quite alone in the house, for Puphi in those days was in Lucknow. I kept the door between your room and mine wide open. Every morning I visited your room and every night I went there to bid it goodnight. I wanted the room to look bright and airy and cheerful, almost as if you were living there and had just gone out and might come back at any moment. Sometimes I had flowers placed there.

I give below two verses by Hālī:

سرو و قمری میں یہ جھگڑا ہے وطن کس کا ہے
کل خزاں آکے بتادے گی چمن کس کا ہے

فیصلہ گردش دوراں نے یہ سو بار کیا
مرو کس کا ہے بدخشاں و ختن کس کا ہے

(حالی)

In Hindi:

सर्व व कुमरी में यह झगड़ा है वतन किसका है ।
कल ख़ज़ां आके बता देगी चमन किसका है ॥
फ़ैसला गर्दिश-ए-दौरां ने यह सौ वार किया ।
मेर्व किसका है, बदख़शां व ख़ोतन किसका है ॥[1]

सर्व is the name of a well-known tree in Persia; कुमरी is the name of a bird; ख़ज़ां = autumn; चमन = garden; गर्दिश-ए-दौरां = the rolling heaven = fate.

The three names in the last line are of places in Central Asia. They often occur in Urdu & Persian writing.

My love to you, my dear – keep cheerful and fit.

Your loving,<br>
Papu

---

148.                                   Anand Bhawan,
                                          Allahabad,
                                17th October, 1943

Darling Papu,

This is my letter No. 33. I am slightly late with it. Your letter No. 31, dated October 9th,[2] reached me on the day before yesterday. I haven't written earlier as I have not been feeling too well.

Psyche came and went, rather like a whirlwind. She and Nurie arrived at night on the 9th and left on the morning of the 11th. As there was so little time, we had to do all our talking late at night. I had already started getting a slight temperature, so with this extra strain I felt completely exhausted. I was just thinking of taking a day off and staying in bed when, quite unexpectedly, Masi turned up with her daughter, Sheila, and the baby Om who was with Nani. Masi had come to Benares for just a day to fetch Om, whom she is taking to live with her. She stayed here two days. Feroze and she left for Cawnpore on the 15th.

---

1. Hālī:   Who has the right on this garden?
           Both, the cypress tree and the ringed dove do contend;
           Whose is it?
           The autumn will soon pronounce on them!
           Time and again
           The ceaseless round of heavens has shown
           Who is to hold Marv
           And who to hold Badakhshan and Tartary!
2. Refers to letter No. 146.

Masi was going to spend four hours in Cawnpore and then go to Agra for a day, before proceeding to Jaipur. Masi really came with the intention of taking me to Jaipur too. But of course I cannot stir out of Allahabad just now.

Puphi is busy moving her furniture and such like, so there is a lot of noise and commotion. I believe she wants to settle Anna and Rita in the house in Mukerji Road before leaving for Calcutta.

I am afraid it is going to be very lonely for me to be all alone in this big house. Feroze is going to be out of town three weeks in the month in connection with the Legal Aid Committee. Fortunately I am more used to being alone than most people & I do not mind it so very much.

Puphi had an airgraph from Edward Thompson the other day. He was under the impression that his book of poems had not reached you. I am writing to him.

I have been wanting to get into touch with Essie Robeson, so I was glad to have her address.

I was glad you mentioned the ambulatory service for the hospital. That is something I have been very keen on even before the hospital started. In fact I discussed it with Bul and Mazumdar and various other people soon after my return from Europe. But, as the hospital had just been started, everybody said that we should wait and see how things went. Now with the shortage of petrol and general difficulties of any kind of transport the possibility of this kind of service seems even more remote.

Lots of love,
Indu

P.S.
I have a letter from Saralaben.[1] Mridu has been keeping bad health and the root of the trouble is now diagnosed to be chronic appendicitis and an operation may be necessary.

------

149.

Anand Bhawan,
Allahabad,
[21st October, 1943]

Darling Papu,
Your letter of the 16th October.[2] This is my letter No. 34.

I wonder if Puphi has written to you. She said she would. She left

------

1. See entry under the Sarabhai Family in Circle of Friends.
2. Refers to letter No. 147.

for Calcutta on the 17th and the next day, Rita and Anna moved into their new house, taking with them Rita's cocker spaniel, Punch, but leaving behind poor little Breezy, who was desolate. Fortunately she is quite happy now. In a way it is a good thing that she was not taken for Rita was so obviously partial to Punch that Breezy went about often with a hurt look in her eye. Breezy and I were both feeling rotten and very lonely, when luckily and quite unexpectedly Feroze turned up – back from Cawnpore. Since then we have both been very domesticated and busy. I have been clearing up godowns and taking stock of linen, etc. And it is by no means over yet. I want everything spick and span and ready to use. So that when you, or a dozen guests come there will be no last-minute rushing! Feroze has been spending all his time in the garden – flowers as well as vegetables.

I have just had a note from Pupha to say that he arrived last midnight, travelling from Rajkot via Bombay. He says he is not quite well yet and has a bad cold. He is leaving for Khali on the 24th. Pupha wants you to know that on the 15th inst. the typescript translation of Kalidasa's *Ritusamhara* together with the introduction was posted to you from Bombay on his instructions. Have you received it? . . . [1] *Prescriber* comes to Swaraj Bhawan. I sent it and a lot of other periodicals to you to find out which of them you would like. I don't quite know what to do with the newspapers that come for Swaraj Bhawan. Since my release I have been sending most of them to Naini to Upadhyayaji who passes them on to Sadiq Ali [2] and others. It is indeed a strange collection; for example, addressed to Sadiq Ali comes a thick well got-up magazine called *Mademoiselle* dealing exclusively with fashion for school and college girls!! Chand and Tara used to revel in it.

Your room is aired and cleaned every day. Hari had cluttered up your dressing room with some of my belongings. But I am having it cleared. A great problem is the accumulation of books. At the moment they have overflowed from the bookcases on to the floor.

I haven't seen Ladli Bhai yet about the servants' rooms near the garages. I did go to have a look at them and found that three of them were being used as godowns and that nobody had entered them for over a year. You can imagine the dust and cobwebs and armies of insects. I have had them cleaned. Jummi, the old and nearly blind widow of Medai, wants one of them for herself and her family. She is getting a small pension but rents are rising. So I have promised it to her. Kishori & Bitten are occupying two *kotharis*. [3]

1. Deleted by censors.
2. Sadiq Ali was General Secretary of the All India Congress Committee for several years.
3. Servants' quarters.

Chhoti Puphi wrote to say that she might come up for *Diwali* for about ten or twelve days. The original plan was to go south but in view of the bombing and the floods that trip may have to be given up.

The winter birds are coming in. I saw a redstart yesterday. Rather an amusing little fellow, the way he shivers his tail all the time. His call is exactly like the squeak of an unoiled bicycle wheel. There is even a slight pause between one squeak and the next, just enough for one revolution of the wheel! This morning a blue jay caught a baby mouse and sat and devoured it on our porch!

Lots of love,<br>Indu

P.S.
Rita's birthday is on the 24th but she is postponing the celebration of it to the 30th as Puphi will probably not be able to return much earlier.

Ballo is engaged to a girl called Swarup Razdan of Delhi.

Indu

---

150.             Ahmadnagar Fort Prison,
23rd October, 1943

Darling Indu,
Last week[1] I gave you my reactions about the proposal that Puphi should move into a new house. A few days later I wrote in more or less the same vein to Puphi. Inevitably one cannot write about intimate personal matters in letters from prison. Yet I felt I must let you and Puphi have some inkling of what I thought. Having done so, my job is over and I do not worry any longer over it. Nor should you. Yesterday I had a letter from Puphi, written a little before she went back to Bengal, and she mentioned this matter in it. And now, having disposed of this and put it by in some corner of my mind, I return, following Voltaire's advice, to my little cottage patch. But I want to know and feel that you will not burden yourself with what has happened or what I have written about it. Let us not occupy ourselves with the smaller difficulties of life when everything that is big is continually calling to us and demanding our utmost effort of mind and body.

Yesterday I also had a letter from Amma from Benares. Tell her that I received her *supari*, etc. Also that she might send me a further supply – a mixture of *supari*, *elaichi* and *laung*[2] with the *supari* slightly roasted.

---

1. Refers to letter No. 147.
2. Clove.

I have plenty left with me but by the time a second lot comes, I shall be in need of it. Maulana is the largest consumer of this mixture.

I wonder if you could find and send me my little foot-rug which I had in Dehra Dun and used for spinning and some exercises – *āsanas*? [1] I asked for it last year through Betty, when you were in Naini, but somehow it did not come. It is a product of Allahabad rural industry and was sent to me to Dehra by Puphi. It comes in handy, especially for the exercises. I used to have a coir-mattress in my room here but bugs – *khatmal* – took possession of it and multiplied exceedingly and so I discarded it. Against these bugs I wage unceasing war, with varying results. Without some kind of soft material to lie on it is difficult to do some of the *asans*. Hence the need for the foot-rug. But if by any chance you cannot find it, do not worry. I can raise a substitute for it.

So you are spinning. It is dreary work to begin with but as soon as one gets into the swing of it, there is a fascination about it. I am spinning more or less daily for about half an hour. This is not much and hence I am not producing much yarn, though I spin fairly fast. Since I began, seven weeks ago, I have spun about 11,000 yards of 25–30 count yarn. [2] I am told that about 30,000 yards are required for a sari. In another four months I might have enough for a sari for you!

What happened to the yarn I spun in Dehra? I gave it to Psyche and a small piece of it came for you last year at the time of your wedding. But I had given enough yarn, I think, for four saris or their equivalent. Having given it away I have of course no claim on it but I am interested to know its fate.

Some of my yarn from Dehra Dun (and subsequently) was left in the drawer of my dressing table. I remember asking once to send it on to Psyche. Did you do so? If not, you might hold on to it and add it to what I might send later.

We had very heavy rain for several days and then one morning I noticed a pair of wagtails, the first of the season. I prophesied a change in the weather and, sure enough, there was a marked change that very night. There was a nip in the air and our mild cold weather seemed to have started. Our friends here were impressed by my prophecy and began to regard me as a minor weather prophet.

Indeed the weather has changed here and is pleasanter; the change took place much later last year. The old familiar winter sky is beginning to appear. For some reason or other, I know this sky much better than the summer one, though normally we keep out much more in the sum-

---

1. Refers to Yogic exercises.
2. Refers to the thickness of the yarn spun.

mer. Perhaps the sky is clearer during winter; but the real reason probably is that I began to take interest in the night sky one winter long ago
and came to recognise many stars and constellations. And, because I
came to know them separately, a sense of friendly companionship arose
and every night I greeted them and made my bow to them. It is odd
how this kind of knowledge of stars, or birds, or flowers, brings them
nearer to us, as if there was some secret bond, a relationship which
others did not know but which we treasured. And stars, and the moon
of course, have a way of looking at you, and almost one can imagine a
sly wink or a friendly smile. Yet sometimes they seem so distant and
cold and unconcerned, as indeed they are.

During these October mornings, the first thing that I see when I wake
up (I sleep in a verandah) is Venus, the star of the morning. By its
position I judge whether it is time to get up or not.

When you were at Panchgani I suggested to you to glance through
Sylvain Levi's *Le Théâtre Indien* which I was returning to Psyche. I do
not suppose you had the time and the book went back to the library
from which it came. It was a fifty-year-old book and yet I found it
fascinating. I have now been reading a more recent book on the subject:
Keith's *The Sanskrit Drama*. It gives much more information and recent
discoveries but it is minus the poetic lilt of Sylvain Levi. Why are
scholars' books dull?

I am fascinated by the old theatre of Greece and India, the only two
countries which had it. China had something but it was not, as far as I
know, developed. The art of the theatre tells us more about a culture
and civilisation than most other things. It makes the past live and we
can see and understand it in terms of human beings. Greece & India in
this respect offer us very different pictures of the theatre. There is a
majesty about the Greek drama, a power which grips. On the other hand
the Indian drama is, curiously enough, a little more akin to our modern
conceptions (the analogy should not be taken far). The language is
majestic enough sometimes, and frequently it has an entrancing lyrical
beauty. But, above all, there is a human-ness about this Sanskrit–Prakrit
drama which is pleasing.

I am sorry that I do not know Greek chiefly because I cannot read
the Greek plays in the original, and I am sorry that I do not know enough
Sanskrit to be able to read Ashvaghosa and Bhasa, and Kalidasa and
Bhavabhuti. [1]

Do you know an interesting fact? The earliest known Sanskrit play

---

1. Ashvaghosa was a poet and philosopher at the court of Kanishka; Bhasa (AD 350)
wrote thirteen plays, and Bhavabhuti was a dramatist at the court of Yasovarman of
Kanauj.

(by Ashvaghosa) was discovered at Turfan on the edge of the Gobi desert! Some other early plays were discovered in Tibet. Turfan has long fascinated me as a place where several great cultures intermingled, far away, right on the edge of a great desert. I wrote something about it in *Glimpses*.

Old Ashvaghosa was a Buddhist propagandist. He was a resident of Ayodhya probably (round about the beginning of the Christian era). His mother's name was Suvaranakshi – rather sweet. It means 'the golden-eyed'.

Soon we shall have *Diwali*, the festival of light. Who will have the heart to celebrate it when darkness and sorrow grip so many the world over? And Bengal, the heartbreaking, whose long shadow falls all over the country.

Puphi wrote to me that Pupha had again been ill and had a mild attack of pleurisy. After his long stay in hospital, this relapse is very distressing. I am glad he is thinking of going to Khali.

Two more Urdu couplets but, tell me, do you want them? The first is by Akbar of Allahabad. It is a good definition, if the word may be used, of the conception of God or the supernatural.

تو دل میں تو آتا ہے سمجھ میں نہیں آتا

معلوم ہوا بس تری پہچان یہی ہے ! ( اکبرالہ آبادی )

In Hindi: अकबर इलाहाबादी :

तू दिल में तो आता है, समझ में नहीं आता
मालूम हुआ, बस, तेरी पहचान यही है ! [1]

تن کی عریانی سے بہتر نہیں دنیا میں لباس

یہ وہ جامہ ہے کہ جس کا نہیں سیدھا الٹا     ( آتش )

आतिश :

तन की उर्यानी से बेहतर नहीं दुनियां में लिबास
यह वह जामा है के जिसका नहीं सीधा उल्टा— [2]

उर्यानी = Nakedness.

Love,
Your loving,
Papu

---

1. Akbar Allahabadi:   To our hearts Thou dost come,
                      Beyond our reach Thou remainst;
                      Thus alone Thou dost manifest Thyself!
2. Atish:   No dress in the world is good
            As naked beauty is;
            A garment this,
            No wrong side which e'er shows!

151.                                    Ahmadnagar Fort Prison,
                                        30th October, 1943

Darling Indu,
Your last letter, No. 33 of Oct. 17th,[1] has worried me a little. I do
not at all like your getting a rise in temperature. Perhaps the changing
season is partly responsible, perhaps you have been tiring yourself
too much. You know how to look after yourself. Do so and take no
risks. It is desirable to keep in touch with your doctor. Not that
much doctoring is required but a doctor is helpful in finding out any
possible complications. Thus in this season malaria is often prevalent.
Jairaj Behari[2] used to visit our house. Does he still do so? He is
fairly reliable, though old-fashioned. You have Vatsala near you.
Kak[3] is also good . . .
    A few days ago I received the typescript of Pupha's translation of
Kalidasa's *Ritusamhara* – I liked it. Somehow this put me in mind of my
own MS which I wrote in Dehra and left unfinished. This was, in a
way, a continuation of my *Autobiography*. It is completely out of date now
and of little use. I have no desire to continue it and I grow less and less
interested in my own life during that period. There are some chapters
in it, however, which interest me from a different point of view. They
form a group containing a rapid review of Indian culture, etc. One of
them is called 'The Discovery of India'.[4] Because of these chapters I
should like to have this MS, or rather typescript, if that is possible. I
suggest that you might send it through the usual channel (the Bombay
Govt) and write a letter also to the person concerned (the Secretary to
the Home Department – [Political]). You might say that in case this
typescript is not to be sent on to me, it should be returned to you. I do
not want to lose it.
    You will find this in the steel cupboard in my dressing room – the
one nearer the bathroom. Probably the MS is there as well as a typed
copy. Send the typed copy, not the MS.
    More trouble for you – could you find out in the Library a copy of
the *All Parties Committee's Report* (commonly known as the *Nehru Report*)
which was issued in 1928? There are several copies about but it may
not be easy to spot them. Also I should like to have the four *Red Books*
(pamphlets) issued by the National Planning Committee in 1939–40.
They have red covers, unbound and are numbered 1 to 4 (the first one
is not numbered). These should be in my room or possibly in my

1. Refers to letter No. 148.
2. Dr Jairaj Behari: a well-known doctor of Allahabad.
3. Jainath Kak: a surgeon of Allahabad.
4. See pp. 46 n.2 and 526 n.1.

dressing room. If you can discover all these books please send them. I had them in Dehra with me.

I have noticed references in the newspapers to some new books published in India. These are probably easily available. I am in no hurry for them but some time or other I should like to have them. You might just note them down. These are:

1. *Modern Indian Culture – A Sociological Study* by D. P. Mukerji (India Publishers, Allahabad) Rs. 4/12
2. *Us: A People's Symposium* – Edited by Hiren Mukerji (Anti-Fascist Writers & Artists Association, Calcutta) 4/-
3. *Modern Islam in India – A Social Analysis* by Wilfrid Cantwell Smith (Minerva Book Shop, Lahore)

What a lot of trouble I am giving you! . . .

I have just received your letter 34,[1] undated. You do not mention your health, so I hope all's well. A big chunk in the letter is blacked out.

Love to you & Feroze,

Your loving,
Papu

152.                                   Anand Bhawan,
                                          Allahabad,
                                  5th November, 1943

Darling Papu,
Your letter No. 33, dated October 23rd,[2] reached me some time ago. I am really ashamed of myself for not writing earlier. I have not been too well – the usual temperature and so on – and as often happens at such times I felt very depressed and grousy. However I am all right now both physically and temperamentally.

Here we are in November. The nights are very pleasant but it is still very warm in the daytime. Some days we even miss the fans, which I have taken off and put by.

Your foot-rug has been found. I am sending it along with a pair of chopsticks. Puphi sent you a pair before leaving for Calcutta, but we heard from Poona that they arrived broken.

If you remember, my wedding blouse and handkerchief were made of your yarn. The material is quite ready. Some of it has gone into the

1. Refers to letter No. 149.
2. Refers to letter No. 150.

making of a sari which Psyche wants to present to Madame Chiang. Handkerchiefs have also been made out of it.

The yarn in your dressing table drawer is still there. I told Psyche about it last year but she asked not to send it immediately – so it's still there.

I was interested to learn how you look at Venus first thing in the morning. For many nights before *Diwali*, I would wake around five in the morning with a feeling that there was a light on my face, and open my eyes straight on to one of the biggest stars I have ever seen. It didn't twinkle so I guessed it was a planet, but I didn't know which. I used to lie looking at it and wondering if you could see it too. And then I would say good morning to it, hoping that the message would be passed on to you. The planet was so big and bright that on at least two nights the pillars and trees cast shadows that must have been due to its light – for there was no moon.

I did manage to glance through Sylvain Levi's book, though it was a cursory and unsatisfactory glance. There was so little time and Psyche was anxious to return it to the Library.

Pupha is expected back from Khali on the 9th. Vatsala and an American Mrs Gould went with him. Pratapji and Saraswati Bai[1] went direct from Bombay. Vatsala came back after a week, as she could not be away from the hospital longer.

Do you remember you asked me to order some hand-made paper from Dehra Dun. I wrote immediately. The reply came some time ago that the Forest Research Institute carried out investigations, on behalf of the U.P. Government, to improve upon and modernise hand-Made paper-making. The investigations were complete about a couple of years ago and the staff and equipment were transferred to Hand-Made Paper Centre, Cawnpore. The Institute very kindly forwarded my letter to the Director of Industries, Cawnpore, for disposal. From Cawnpore came the curt reply: 'The matter is under consideration and a further communication will follow.' This letter was dated the 16th October. There the matter rests.

Anna has just been. Puphi has a bad cold and Rita has a slight attack of flu.

After many months, I went to the cinema last evening to see a film that has been completely ignored by the public and practically unadvertised by the cinema – a Russian film, *In the Rear of the Enemy*. I liked it immensely. It was short and simple, good acting and photography and simply superb skiing. The film is about the ski-troops. Before the main film, there was a Russian short too, with different kinds of Russian

1. Pratap Pandit and Saraswati Bai Pandit: brother and sister-in-law of Ranjit Pandit.

music, some pretty bits of ballet & a lovely scene from *Rigoletto* for which I have always had a soft corner since it was my 'first opera'! I saw it in Rome with Mlle Hemmerlin.

My furniture has been stored for so long, Feroze said it would get spoilt if we did not use it for a short while. So we have rearranged the dining room. I have taken down all the old pictures and put up all the Roerich ones and a flag. The room is really looking lovely.

This is my letter No. 35.

Much love to you, Papu darling.

Your loving,<br>Indu

P.S.
Bachhraj have some income tax refund certificates for you. They want to know where they can send them so that refund can be claimed by you or your attorney.

---

153.                                      Ahmadnagar Fort Prison,
                                            6th November, 1943

Indu darling,

This letter will reach you probably a little before your birthday; my next will be too late for it. So this must carry an extra load of love and good wishes for you. You have turned the quarter of a century – how imposing it sounds! I remember when I was this age, I used to announce, when asked, that I was a quarter of a century old! That sounded impressive. Now that the half century for me has long passed, I am no longer eager to remember it. Unable to send you anything from here, I asked Betty (who was then thinking of going to South India) to get something for you from those lands of artistry and good craftsmanship, something that you would like, and to send it to you on my behalf. I hope she has done so, although her southern trip has fallen through. So, my love to you, *cara mia*, and may the difficulties and the distresses that surround us strengthen you in mind and body, and not abate the capacity to live wholesomely and beautifully and to take joy from the beauty and goodness of life, in spite of the ugliness and ills that lie around us . . .

I am very glad you have taken Anand Bhawan in hand and are rejuvenating it. It is young enough in years, but somehow it has carried with it the age and tradition of the older house. Like me, it developed a faded and *passé* look, and it was entirely beyond my capacity to change this. It was time it changed, and so I rejoice that you are putting into its thought-laden atmosphere some of your own brightness and vitality.

Shake it up and make it sit up and look round. It has become too introspective and stuck in the ruts. It should represent the life and activity of the younger generation, and not just the worn-out grooves of ageing people. Do not hesitate to spend some money over this transformation.

As for books, they go on accumulating and it is always a problem where to put them. The Library is full, my room is full, so is my dressing room. Some other rooms, like yours, have a good supply of them. From time to time I used to discard a number, or send them across to Swaraj Bhawan. The only thing that I can think of is to have bookshelves fitted in other rooms. For instance, in the big guest room on the first floor, low ones, like the kind I have in my room. Old books, which are not usually wanted, can be transferred to these new shelves. I want to keep a fairly select lot in my own room – old favourites and new books.

The shelves in my room were originally made by the Christian Workshop. Later I had them made by Lohia Pande of Muthiganj, who did the work rapidly and more cheaply. You can get into touch with him and ask him to send one of his men for measurements, etc.

Puphi writes to me that already you have made a great difference to Anand Bhawan. 'I wish you could see what Indu has done to the house. It has become alive and beautiful.' Well, I shall certainly see it one day – so go ahead.

What about fixing up one room as a kind of 'China room'? We have plenty of odds and ends from China lying about unused or wrongly used. Probably the big guest room upstairs would be suited for this – but these shelves full of books may not perhaps fit in.

It would be a good thing if you consulted Ladli Bhai occasionally about Anand Bhawan. He likes to be consulted. Not that he is at all up-to-date in the matter of house furnishing or arrangement.

Your last letter [1] had over half a page blacked-out – in the third page. What this was about I do not know.

Do not trouble to send me the *Prescriber* or anything so obviously uninteresting for me. But I like a variety of reading matter . . .

Your last letter which reached me was Number 34. [2] This letter of mine is No. 35.

Love,<br>
Your loving,<br>
Papu

---

1. Refers to letter No. 149.
2. Refers to letter No. 149.

154.                                          Anand Bhawan,
                                                 Allahabad,
                                          8th November, 1943

Darling Papu,
Your letter No. 34, dated October 30th, [1] arrived this morning just as
I was getting ready to go to the station to see off Feroze who has left
for Bombay. I raced about looking for the things you wanted. I have
sent with Feroze, a pair of chopsticks, your foot-rug, the *All Parties
Conference Report* of 1928, and some periodicals. I have also found your
typescript, but we thought it would be better to send it registered A.D.
[Acknowledgement Due]. I shall do so tomorrow morning. Feroze will
try and buy the Indian publications in Bombay and send them together
with the above-mentioned articles. In my haste I did not see the Planning
Committee pamphlets but doubtless they will soon be found . . .

Darling, I love doing things for you, it's little enough what we can do.
And it's no trouble at all. So please don't hesitate ever if you want
anything.

I don't mind typing and I am anxious to increase my speed. Besides
there is a great deal of sorting and arranging to do that it is really simpler
to do it ourselves.

Dr Jairaj Behari is still going strong. He seems to be doing business
in cars. Every time I see him he is in a new one . . . [2] My letter No.
34 [3] was written on the 21st October. This is my 36th.

There is a letter from the Mani Puthakasalai Publishers of Kumbakonam asking for permission to bring out a Tamil translation of the
*Glimpses* and the Tamil copyright. Hasn't the Tamil edition already
appeared?

The books – Aurobindo Babu's plays and *Soviet Communism* – have
arrived. Also the seeds. Datadin insists that it is now too late to sow.
But Anna does not agree, and she has taken some.
                                          Much love,
                                            Indu

P.S.
Your birthday is coming soon. Many many happy returns of the day. I
shall be thinking of you. All my love and good wishes.

---

   1. Refers to letter No. 151.
   2. Deleted by censors.
   3. Refers to letter No. 149.

155.                         Ahmadnagar Fort Prison,
                                   13th November, 1943

Darling Indu,

There has been a gap in your letters and I have not had any for just a fortnight today. Your last letter was No. 34.[1] (This is my No. 36.) I hope this simply means that you are busy renovating and putting new life into Anand Bhawan. That is a big enough job and a tiring one. But it is worthwhile and it must interest you. Now that the weather in Allahabad has become pleasanter and the sun is not too hot, I hope you will potter about in the open in the mornings and evenings. Good for the garden but even better for you. Gardening in the cool of the morning with the sun just pleasantly warm is health-giving. The sun and the soil between them are fine tonics and exhilarate. But do not overdo it, and certainly not if you feel at all tired.

I am sending back to you some old foreign periodicals – *Time, Reader's Digest, Common Sense, Listener*, etc. Also a copy of *Tomorrow* edited by Raja Rao & Ahmad Ali. Two copies of this little book managed to reach me, so I am sending one along to you.

Betty has sent me a number of new books. She has also sent a book to Mahmud, a good book which many of us will read but only Mahmud will be unable to do so, for the type is exceedingly small. It is Ilya Ehrenburg's[2] *Fall of Paris*. Kripalani has also got a new stock of books. So for the present we are well provided with literature, or at any rate interesting reading matter.

Why do you not invite some of your friends to pay you visits and stay in Anand Bhawan for a few days or weeks at a time? They could come one after the other, or together. This habit of people visiting each other – outside the family circle and except for so-called festive occasions – is not common in India. It should be encouraged. I am sure your friends will enjoy their visits and you will have agreeable company.

Do you know anything about Krishna's niece[3] who lives down away in Malabar somewhere? About two years ago or more she had to come to the U.P. for some examination. Her mother (Krishna's sister)[4] wrote to Puphi or to me about her. Then I wrote to the girl asking her to stay in Anand Bhawan when she came that way, and she was vastly excited at the prospect. I forget what happened. I think she came but I was not in Allahabad then and so I did not meet her.

You have plenty of friends in Bombay, Lahore, Delhi and elsewhere.

1. Refers to letter No. 149.
2. Ilya Ehrenburg (1891–1967): Russian novelist, poet and journalist.
3. Janaki Sethna.
4. V. A. Janaki Amma.

You have not met them for a long time. A little hospitality shown to them and a few days' pleasant companionship will be welcomed. It is true that travelling is a difficult job nowadays and not to be lightly undertaken; also that most people are occupied with their own work. Even the mood for outings is absent. Yet it may be worthwhile. Ismet for instance – Kupton's wife – whose guests we have been often enough.

Ever since I came here I have had no news of Uma Bhabhi.[1] Where is she? In prison?

I suppose you have not heard from Sarvar or Hamidah, Mahmud's daughters.

I am anxious about Raja – Betty writes that he has been having repeated and very painful attacks of asthma and has lost 22 pounds in weight. He was frightfully lanky and thin to begin with. What he must look now, I find it difficult to imagine.

By the way, among the books that might be sent to me at some future time is Laski's: *The State in Theory & Practice*. You ought to find it in my room – a copy given to me by Laski and inscribed by him.

Last week I sent you some lines from Ghalib. The following are a continuation of the same series:

یہ پری چہرہ لوگ کیسے ہیں ؟     غمزہ و عشوہ و ادا کیا ہے ؟
سبزہ و گل کہاں سے آئے ہیں ؟     ابر کیا چیز ہے ہوا کیا ہے ؟
"ہاں بھلا کر ترا بھلا ہوگا"     اور درویش کی صدا کیا ہے ؟
(غالب)

ग़ालिब:     यह परी चेहरा लोग कैसे हैं ?     ग़मज़ा औ इशवा औ अदा क्या है ?
सब्ज़ा औ गुल कहां से आए हैं ?     अब्र क्या चीज़ है, हवा क्या है ?
"हां भला कर तेरा भला होगा"     और दरवेश की सदा क्या है ?[2]

ग़मज़ा = wink;     इशवा = beauty's coquetry;     सब्ज़ा = grass;     अब्र = mist, fog;     दरवेश = a wandering faquir;     सदा = cry.

1. Uma Nehru: wife of Jawaharlal Nehru's cousin, Shamlal Nehru ('Bhabhi' means 'sister-in-law').
2. Ghalib:     What are these fairy-faces
             And their elegance, charm and grace?
             Whence this foliage green
             And the smiling rose have come?
             What are these carefree floating clouds?
             And what is this gentle breeze?
             'Ever do good
             And thou shalt be done good too!'
             What cry but this can a dervish raise?

The *darvesh's* cry, as given, was frequently heard in the streets. It has been well filled in.

I have had a letter from Amma from Benares. I shall write to her next week.

Love,

Your loving
Papu

---

156. 

Anand Bhawan,
Allahabad,
14th November, 1943

My darling one,

Thank you for your letter [1] which came on your birthday. Thank you for your good wishes and your love, which is to me the most beautiful and precious thing in the world. So do not bother about presents and the like. The loveliest present of all will be when you yourself are here again – just to see your smile and to listen to your voice and the going and coming of your footsteps.

Hari turned up exceptionally early this morning. He and Khaliq stood in the doorway of my room grinning broadly. For a moment I could not think what the matter was – then suddenly producing two bouquets and a goldy garland from behind their backs: *mubārak ho!* [2] The garland has been draped over and the flowers are around your picture which is on my writing-table. So you will know that we are all thinking of you today and every day.

Darling, I am not changing anything in the house until you are here to give your approval. Only the dining room has been changed – temporarily – I had to do that, for my furniture was getting quite mouldy from being so long in storage. In the other rooms I have merely moved around the furniture and given everything as thorough a cleaning as we could manage. The drawing room lights, for instance, how dingy and old they looked. Puphi said that that rather sickly shade of yellow was their natural colour but a little scrub with soap and water has made them clear and bright, as they were meant to be. That is the only rejuvenation the house is getting and it does need it badly.

I am, however, full of ideas of some changes I should like to make. But these must wait until you come and when the times are less troubled. Psyche suggested when she was here that our drawing room should be completely Indian – I do agree with her. It was then I thought of the

---

1. Refers to letter No. 153.
2. Congratulations.

'China' room – so we must be telepathic, you and I. But which room? Just now I am living in the upstairs guest room and using my own small room as a dressing room. Chhoti Puphi's room might do, except for the books, or Dol Amma's downstairs . . .

Pupha has got his old pleurisy again & is in Lucknow. Puphi is also there.

This is my letter No. 37. Your letter last received is No. 35.[1]

Much love,<br>Indu

P.S.

I hope you get some books from Bombay as a birthday gift from me – I have asked Psyche to see about them.

---

157.                                         Ahmadnagar Fort Prison,
                                             20th November, 1943

Darling Indu,

Your letters No. 35 and 36[2] have reached me. Also some books (*Life & Letters*, 2 numbers, *All Parties Committee's Report, Recent Judgments*); periodicals, foot-rug and the chopsticks, unbroken. Thank you.

You need not have rushed about to send these to me with Feroze just as he was going to Bombay. There is never any hurry for the books or other articles I mention to you. We do not live in a world of hurry here. Time moves slowly and at a dead level without ups and downs. I mention to you odd things as the whim seizes me, not requiring them urgently or, indeed, at all, but just for variety's sake. Especially old books, such as Milton, as I did in my last letter. I have enough and more to carry on for a long time but old habit persists. When I mention a book or anything else, I want you just to note it down and send it at leisure.

So I am mentioning another book. I have been reading a book by Charles Morgan.[3] That put me in mind of another book of his – *Sparkenbroke* – which was sent to me long ago by Louise Morin. I read part of it then but was too busy to finish it and then I forgot all about it. It struck me that I might as well read it through now, not only because the book is likely to be interesting but also because Louise sent it and I owe it to her to read it. So if you can find it – it is likely to be in my room – you can send it along.

---

1. Refers to letter No. 153.
2. Refers to letters Nos 152 and 154.
3. Charles Langbridge Morgan (1894–1958): English novelist and drama critic.

Have you had any kind of news of Louise and Jean-Jacques?

Odd, this reading of books. Once upon a time – this fairy story beginning is suitable – long long ago, when I had recently come back to India from Cambridge, I thought of the large number of books I wanted to read and of the little time I had for reading. Could I take myself away, I wondered, to some quiet retreat, preferably on the hills, for a year and just lose myself in books? It seemed one of those idle fancies which come and go, leaving a faint regret behind them, for it is so difficult to act up to them. No fancy or daydream then gave me a glimpse of the future; no shadow of what was to come fell on my mind's track. The years that followed saw that old fancy realised in a curious way, and it was not just a year but many years that I spent in retreats (shall we call them so?) and I had plenty of time to read. And even now the hunger is not satisfied and all these years seem just a beginning, a peep on the threshold of the world's books. Did I think then, in the pride and confidence of early youth, that a year would be enough? Even a lifetime now seems just a step on the long road winding ahead . . .

Betty has sent some books and some pictures by Amrita Shergil[1] which Kitabistan have issued on behalf of the Allahabad Roerich Centre. I like some of these pictures. Even more so they remind me of Amrita – did you ever meet her? I saw her only half a dozen times, usually at intervals of a year, but I grew to like her very much. She was unusual and was obviously very gifted. She wanted to do a sketch of me but this never came off. Just before my arrest in October 1940 I happened to be in Gorakhpur (it was for that speech in Gorakhpur that I was arrested and sentenced to four years). I was very busy but I managed to fit in a hurried visit to a sugar factory about eighteen miles from the town. Amrita was living with her people then and I went especially to see her. I was there for only a few minutes and then she motored back with me to Gorakhpur. A strange change had come over her since her return from France four years earlier. She was so full of confidence, so vital and self-possessed then; life was a straight and easy job except for those who were afraid. This self-assurance was no longer in evidence and life did not appear quite so simple or straight. She was quiet. Artistically, that is, in relation to her art, she was also changing. From painting typical French *salon* pictures she was drifting to India in many ways. I asked her to come for a few days to Allahabad and she promised to do so . . . I was arrested. The day after my release from Dehra Dun I heard on the radio that she had suddenly died. There was some mystery about it. Her poor mother went wild with grief; indeed she became quite demented and made extraordinary charges against some people.

1. Amrita Shergil (1913–1941): Indian painter.

I had quite a shock. She was not the kind of person one meets often. It was very sad that one so gifted should die in early youth.

My birthday! Yes, it is over and gone – nothing to shout about. It struck me that it was my fourth consecutive birthday in prison, apart from the other such days I have spent in prison. I have lost count of the number.

In your letter of Nov. 8,[1] towards the end, a small paragraph of four lines has been blacked out. What this was about I cannot guess . . .

Love,

Your loving,

Papu

This is my letter No. 37.

---

158.

Anand Bhawan,
Allahabad,
22nd November, 1943

Darling Papu,

I am typing this as something seems to be wrong with my pen.

This is my letter No. 38. Your thirty-sixth, dated November 13,[2] arrived on my birthday, as an additional and most welcome present.

I have just come in from the garden. A couple of months ago it was one mass of entangled weeds. And now – the hedges trimmed, lawn mowed, flowerbeds so neat with their tiny seedlings. All this due entirely to Feroze. If he had not taken the garden under his wing, I do not know what I should have done and I am sure I should not have got anywhere. Even Ladli Bhai had prophesied that with the existing servants, and the way everything had been neglected, we would not be able to do much this year. I know nothing whatsoever about gardens, so I was just about giving up in despair when Feroze took over. He has done a good job of it too – that's one thing about Feroze, whatever he undertakes he does thoroughly. I found that he has the necessary information too and that is what made all the difference in Datadin's work. And I must say Datadin has worked very creditably and hard. Feroze has bought some new tools and labour-saving devices for Datadin. From the portico to the gate on the right hand side (facing the gate) we have antirrhinum

---

1. Refers to letter No. 154.
2. Refers to letter No. 155.

and tuberose; on the other side, there are asters, verbena, calendula, petunia, phlox, candy tuft, nasturtium, pink, and larkspur. Dividing the lawn from the other beds is a long line of nasturtiums. Beyond that we have salvia, larkspur, aster, dahlias and hollyhocks. Bordering the road from the gate to about halfway up the drive there are more dahlias and from there right up to the kitchen we have sweet peas. The garden will be lovely when all the flowers are blooming. In pots and elsewhere there are carnations, pansies, gerbera, cineraria and mignonette. Now Feroze is putting in your coleus and morning glory. Our vegetable plot is being looked after even more carefully than the flowers and is just as attractive to look at. It is already providing us with our needs. We have got cauliflowers, beans, brinjal, tomato, spinach and radishes. These we are eating every day. Nothing from the bazaar could possibly be so tender and fresh and good to eat. Not yet edible are the French beans, peas, cabbages, turnips, lettuce, celery, parsley and mint. So far everything, including the potatoes and the wheat, is doing well. Our chief headache is the porcupine. They come in hordes to destroy our best cauliflowers and other things too. The squirrels nibble at the peas and the rabbits nibble at anything green!

I think I have sent you all the books you have asked for recently. I could find only [one] copy of Milton – your Harrow one. It has gone to be bound at the Law Journal Press, as the cover was in bits. As soon as it is ready it will be sent to you along with Laski's book.

I told you in a previous letter that I had received no reply from Hamidah but that she had written to Puphi.

This evening I am off to Jaipur at last. The journey is a long and tedious one and I am not looking forward to it. I shall have to waste a whole day at Agra. I propose spending a week with Masi. I am taking Khaliq with me. Feroze is staying on here.

I have never heard of any of Krishna's relatives. As a matter of fact I have always imagined him a family-less man, quite un-attached.

Uma Bhabhi now lives permanently with Anand Bhai in Lucknow. She did not go to jail. Puphi was telling me that Shammie Didda [1] came to Lucknow, some time ago. Kabbu Bhayya [2] is as sweet as ever and goes about dressed in Air Force uniform.

Darling, I won't write more today. I am so tired and there is a lot to be done before I leave.

1. Shyam Kumari Khan: a niece of Jawaharlal Nehru. Active in politics and social work (Didda = elder sister).
2. Kabir Khan: son of Shyam Kumari Khan.

I am sending a cheque. Please endorse it & return it.
Much love,<br>Indu

P.S.
What I have called a cheque is a Dividend Warrant – which you have to sign.

Feroze wrote to you some time ago. He would like to know if the letter has reached you. He sends his love.

---

159.                                        Ahmadnagar Fort Prison,
                                        27th November, 1943

Darling,
I have your letter No. 37 of Nov. 14.[1] I have also received my manuscript or rather typescript of Dehra Jail. Betty has sent me two books, one on your behalf and the other on Psyche's, as birthday gifts. Your gift – Havell's[2] *Ideals of Indian Art* – was particularly appropriate as I have long wanted to read it. It is not a new book for it came out, I think, round about 1920. But these years have been busy years for me and I missed it. I like Havell's approach. It is vivid and interesting, though not always wholly reliable.

Psyche's present is a fat 800-page book by the Beards of America – *The American Leviathan* – a very leviathan of a book! Yet on a subject which interests me and I shall certainly read it. Only recently I read the two fat volumes of Beard's *Rise of American Civilization* (Mrs Naidu's copy which Betty got for me through Padmaja).

Three countries interest me greatly at present, apart from my own. These are the U.S.A., the U.S.S.R. & China. Each of these attracts me for some different reason, for they are so different from each other. Yet essentially I think of them as countries with a big future, and countries which are bound to influence us here in a variety of ways. Somehow Europe does not attract me so much now. There is a lack of vitality, of freshness about it; far too much of the old ruts – very pleasant and comfortable ruts, some of them, but nevertheless ruts. Perhaps it is just because I have been so much influenced by Europe, till it has become

---

1. Refers to letter No. 156.
2. E. B. Havell (1861–1934): a former principal of the Government School of Art and Keeper of the Art Gallery, Calcutta; author of *Indian Sculpture and Painting, Benares the Sacred City* and many other books.

a part of me, that I am reacting in this way now. I want fresh fields, fresh avenues of thought, fresh reactions. I do not get these in Europe or from Europe now. But I do get them from America, Russia & China, though China is different of course. China is continually reminding me of India but in a curious way, a looking-glass way, where things are the same in many ways and yet different. China often helps me to understand India more, both appreciatively and critically. Somehow I cannot rid myself of the thought that we shall have a great deal to do with these three countries in the future – America, Russia & China. I wish I knew them more intimately and personally, but then my education is sadly incomplete. I make up for it by the reading of books, and so I welcome books which tell me of the past and present background of these three vast countries . . .

You mentioned in one of your letters [1] that Mani Puthakasalai, publishers of Kumbakonam, wanted to publish a Tamil translation of my *Glimpses*. I do not think any arrangements have been made so far for a Tamil edition but I cannot be certain. There is a kind of register – a big, long clothbound notebook – which contains information about my various publications. You might find this in the steel cupboard which contains my old MSS and papers. Somewhere about the middle of it you will find a note of mine, written in 1940, which collects all the relevant information. I added to this subsequently.

I would like, of course, a Tamil edition of *Glimpses* to come out but I do not want to agree to any copyright or permission till I am assured that the publishers are efficient, businesslike and have sufficient resources to carry through this task (the book is a big one). Also that the translation will be good & done by a competent person. I have had a lot of trouble with these translations, especially down Madras way, and I want to take no risks. If all these assurances are coming then I might agree. The usual terms are for translations: ten per cent royalty on price of books actually sold. This for the author. The translator should get five per cent royalty but that is a matter for arrangement by the publisher.

In these days of shortage of paper, it is doubtful if any small publisher can undertake this job. Kumbakonam is hardly likely to be the headquarters of a big firm.

As I was writing this I received a packet of books sent by you including the *History of Russia* & three National Planning Committee booklets. Also *Life & Letters* – Gordon Bottomley. [2]

1. Refers to letter No. 154.
2. Gordon Bottomley (1874–1948): English poet and dramatist who wrote plays on Shakespearean themes.

I have sent you three books and old periodicals. The books are:

1. Shridharani: *My India, My America*
2. Sitwell: *Escape with me!*
3. Julian Huxley: *Religion without Revelation*


The following are also being returned:


1. Liddell Hart: *The Strategy of Indirect Approach*
2. Roerich: *Fiery Stronghold*
3. Gibran: *The Mad Man*
4. Ezra Pound: *Poems*
5. Masefield: *Gautama*
6. Kendall: *Dum Dum*


The periodicals I return to you are pretty ancient. Still Pupha might be interested in them, so you might send on these foreign magazines, etc, to him.

I notice that Edward Thompson has come out with a new book: *The Making of the Indian Princes* (Oxford Univ. Press, 20sh.). Normally he would have sent this on to me. Anyway please note the name and get it when you can. It is a new book and is not likely to have reached India yet – not the booksellers anyway . . .

I have received a letter from Puphi in which she gives distressing news of Pupha's illness – the acute pleurisy he was suffering from. This is a bad job, more so as he is not careful enough. It is astonishing that over a month in the Balrampur Hospital was not enough for such a simple diagnosis.

Tell Puphi that I have also received a copy of Chand's letter dated 9th Sept. from Wellesley which she sent me.

Love,<br>
Your loving,<br>
Papu

160.                                   Ahmadnagar Fort Prison,
4th December, 1943

Darling Indu,
I have your letter No. 38 of Nov. 22nd.[1] This is my No. 39.

So you have gone to Jaipur. Have you ever been there before? It is an attractive city, famous for its town planning. I wonder if you will visit Amber, the old fortress some miles out of Jaipur. Few places have reminded me so vividly of medieval times, of knights in armour, and chivalry and the Rajput of old legend as Amber did when I visited it many years ago. As I stood on one of the battlements, looking down on the winding path below, almost I could imagine myself back in the Middle Ages and see a train of Rajput knights on horseback riding up to the main gate of the fort.

Your account of the progress that the garden has made is quite exciting. Obviously this is your and Feroze's doing. A beautiful garden looks far lovelier if personal labour has gone into its making. Does not that apply to most things?

By the way, do you know at all what is happening to the Swaraj Bhawan garden? Ask Feroze to have a look and find out. There used to be large quantities of vegetables there – who gets them?

I have received no letter from Feroze, so I imagine the letter he wrote was stopped. Why, I do not know, for I understand that in-laws, and especially a son-in-law, are on the approved list of those who can write and be written to. But all this is very vague. Till recently I wrote only to you, to Puphi, Betty and sometimes to Amma. Once or twice to Chand. For the first time I went beyond this circle and wrote to Ranjit Pupha some weeks ago. I was not sure that the letter would go through. But evidently it did, and so presumably a brother-in-law is approved. Why not a son-in-law?

I am sending back to you the dividend warrant for Rs. 40/-, duly signed. You can send it to the Punjab National Bank, Allahabad branch, and ask them to cash it and credit it to my account. Let them also keep the income tax certificate.

I suppose you know that letters addressed to me should now be sent to Bombay and not Poona. The Bombay Govt has moved to Bombay.

Betty has sent me, as a birthday present, an ivory *Nataraja*,[2] probably made in Travancore. It is a fine piece of work and, rather miraculously, it has reached me unbroken. I like it but it is not particularly suited to prison life. Delicate works of art do not fit in here.

---

1. Refers to letter No. 158.
2. *Nataraja*: Lord Siva in a dancing pose.

As is my uncontrollable habit, I am giving a list of books below. This has been made out of reviews and catalogues and most of them, I am sure, are unobtainable here. Still you might note them down, and if you come across any of them later on, get it.

| | | | |
|---|---|---|---|
| 1. | Viscount Wavell | : | *Allenby: A Study in Greatness* |
| 2. | – Do – | : | *Allenby in Egypt* |
| 3. | Stefan Zweig | : | *The World of Yesterday* |
| 4. | Ilya Ehrenburg | : | *Russia at War* |
| 5. | H. G. Wells | : | *You Can't be Too Careful* |
| 6. | Lionel Fielden | : | *Beggar my Neighbour* (Secker & Warburg, 3sh. 6d.) |
| 7. | Lin Yu tang | : | *The Wisdom of China and India* |
| 8. | L. H. Ajwani | : | *Immortal India* (Educational Publishing Co., Karachi) |
| 9. | Dr Quaritch Wales | : | *Towards Angkor* (Harrap, 1933) |
| 10. | Reginald Reynolds | : | *Cleanliness & Godliness* (Allen & Unwin, 12sh. 6d.) |
| 11. | Edith Sitwell | : | *A Poet's Note Book* (Macmillan, 10sh. 6d) |
| 12. | Kate Mitchell | : | *India* (Bodley Head) |
| 13. | J. H. Breasted | : | *The Dawn of Conscience* (New York) |
| 14. | Thomas Ryan | : | *Men in Chains* (Peter Davies, London, 8sh. 6d.) |

I am not sure of the full title of No. 1 – Wavell's book. The second book only came out in September in England & so can hardly have reached here – unless the Viceroy's books are rushed across.

Perhaps the easiest way will be for you to send the list to Kitabistan & see what they can get for you.

Did I write to you about *The Bible for Today* (or some such title)? This book used to be in my room. It was sent to me by the publishers. If found, it can be added to the next convenient lot.

Here is an Urdu couplet by Atish:

(آتش)      سن تو سہی جہاں میں ہے ترا فسانہ کیا

کہتی ہے تجھکو خلق خدا غائبانہ کیا

प्रातिश :      सुन तो सही जहां में है तेरा फसानः क्या —

कहती है तुज को ख़ल्क़-ए-ख़दा गाएबानः क्या ?[1]

फसानः = story; ख़ल्क़-ए-ख़ुदा = God's people, i.e., the public; गाएबानः = behind one's back.

Love to you and Feroze,

Your loving,<br>Papu

161.                           Anand Bhawan,
Allahabad,<br>8th December, 1943

Darling Papu,

I have not written to you for what seems to be years and years. I have wanted to write but could not do so for various reasons but you have been constantly in my thoughts.

Soon after writing my last letter[2] to you, I left for Jaipur. It is a tedious and roundabout journey, for I went via Delhi in order to be sure of a berth at night. I was lucky in getting good accommodation both coming and going. There is an innovation in the mail train service these days in the form of a new official: 'The Conductor–Guard' whose job it is to see to the comfort of first and second class passengers. The one on my train was the first smiling and pleasant railway official I have come across in India – efficient, too, without the usual fuss and noise.

This was my first visit to Jaipur. It was like going to India from a foreign land. In terms of history, Jaipur is quite young and yet it gives a greater impression of antiquity and a clinging to things past than many of our ancient cities, such as Prayag. I liked the wide swinging skirts of the women and the colourful turbans of the men. Englishmen and Anglo-Indians were conspicuous by their absence. Not so their influence, which was in evidence in a hundred little ways: society folk wearing

1. Atish:   Listen, if you please,
             The tales they tell;
             Do you know,
             There, everywhere, what they say of you?
2. Refers to letter No. 158.

suits. Picturesque streetnames, such as *Chaura Rasta* [The Broadway], side by side with Sir So-and-so road. Grotesque angels in the midst of an exquisite carving of Rajput dancers. Magnificent old trees being cut down, ancient gardens dug up to make 'modern parks'. The printing of Sanganer[1] and marble carving dying out for want of appreciation.

There is, however, no lack of lovely things. My visit was too short to fit in everything, but I saw some beautiful old Jain temples. And in the City Palace a remarkable collection of Rajput and Moghul painting. In this same collection was a Persian translation of the Mahabharata done, they say, in the reign of Akbar. I was interested also in the State armoury.

As you know, the city is in a valley surrounded by mountains which are covered by innumerable fortresses, and overrun with tigers and other wild animals, which often drift to the plain around about the city. To my great disappointment I did not see one even in the distance. (Do you remember, motoring in Ceylon one night we spotted two bright fiery eyes shining at us through the jungle – how excited we all were at the thought that they might belong to a tiger: it turned out to be a bullock!)

Jaipur is also the city of Mummie's ancestors. There is still the ancient house of Motilal Atal[2] in the *Chaura Rasta* – and numerous other relatives are scattered about the town. Babubhai is there too. I met Ganga and Ramji.

Masi's eldest son – Naresh – is a bright lad. He is not twelve yet. Drives beautifully. Can take a radio or a car engine apart and, what is more, fix it up again. He started learning swimming a few months ago and now does all kinds of fancy and trick dives. There is no suitable school in Jaipur and he has no outlet for his abounding energy. Masi is worried about him. She is thinking of sending him to a boarding school in Patna. It will be a pity if his interest in engineering is allowed to disappear for want of appreciation and help.

Kailas Mamu is trying hard for a passage home. He has written to Nani to say that he is trying to start by December. If he gets the passage, he ought to reach Bombay in January. Sheila Mami is expecting another child soon.

There is no news whatsoever from the Continent. Mlle Hemmerlin, Madeleine Rolland,[3] Louise Morin, Nanu, Lu – everybody is silent. It doesn't seem possible that they haven't tried to write.

Cawnpore has at last written to say that they can supply the hand-made paper. I have accordingly ordered some.

1. Sanganer is a village near Jaipur. In her letter Indira refers to a tradition of block-printing on textiles for which this village is famous.
2. Motilal Atal: great-grandfather of Kamala Nehru. He was Prime Minister of Jaipur.
3. The wife of Romain Rolland.

*Feroze and Indira on their way to India from Great Britain, April 1941.*

*Jawaharlal Nehru, Vijaya Lakshmi Pandit and Indira Nehru, Wardha, 1942.*

*Vedic ceremony on the occasion of the marriage of Feroze and Indira, foreground, L to R: Jawaharlal Nehru, Feroze, Indira and Sarojini Naidu, Anand Bhawan, 26th March, 1942.*

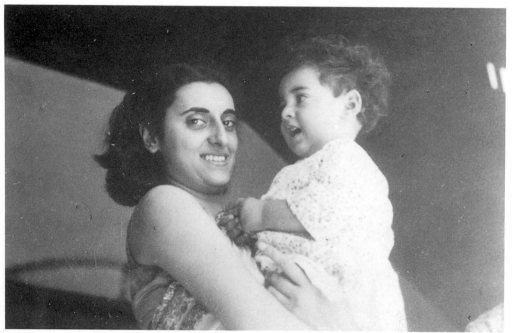

*With son Rajiv (born 20th August, 1944) in 1945.*

*With son Sanjay (born 14th December, 1946) in 1947.*

*Jawaharlal Nehru after his release from Ahmadnagar with Indira Gandhi, Feroze Gandhi and Rajiv Gandhi, Anand Bhawan, June 1945.*

*Indira Gandhi with Jawaharlal Nehru and a refugee girl, Jalandhar Camp, February 1948.*

*A view of Teen Murti House, New Delhi, from the north.*

*A group of children presenting flowers to Jawaharlal Nehru on his sixty-fourth birthday, 14th November, 1953. Indira Gandhi is by his side.*

*Prime Minister Jawaharlal Nehru, Indira Gandhi and Feroze Gandhi with Prime Minister Liaquat Ali Khan and Raana Begum, Karachi, 1950.*

*With Prime Minister Chou En-lai, Peking, China, October 1954.*

*With Prime Minister N.A. Bulganin, Kremlin, U.S.S.R., 1955.*

*(above) With Clement R. Attlee,
former Prime Minister of U.K.
New Delhi, 1953.*

*(left) Indira Gandhi and
Jawaharlal Nehru with Jammu
and Kashmir folk dancers.*

*With President Harry S. Truman, Washington, U.S.A., 1949.*

*With President John F. Kennedy and Jacqueline Kennedy, Washington, U.S.A., 1961.*

*With Nigerian leaders; from left: Indira Gandhi, Prime Minister Sir Abubakar Tafawa Balewa, the Governor-General, Dr Nnamdi Azi-Kiwe, Prime Minister Jawaharlal Nehru, Sir Ahamadu Belle, Lagos, September 1962.*

*Indira Gandhi and Pandit Jawaharlal Nehru with a group of visitors on the lawns of Teen Murti House.*

*Feroze and Indira Gandhi.*

*Jawaharlal Nehru and Indira Gandhi at an A.I.C.C. session, Madurai, 4th October, 1961.*

*Jawaharlal Nehru and Indira Gandhi at an A.I.C.C. session, Bhubaneswar, 1964.*

*(below) The body of Jawaharlal Nehru lying in state. Indira Gandhi is by his side.*

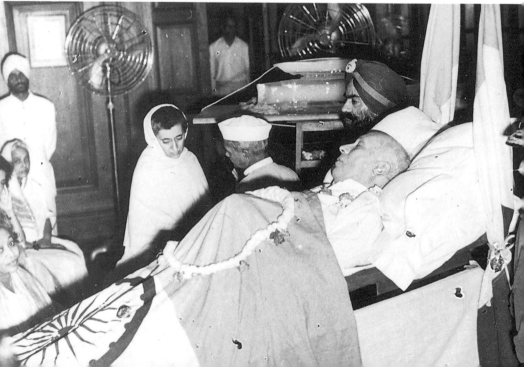

I am sorry I have not been able to find Laski's book in your room.

I have an airmail letter from Walsh dated October 6th. He says that Puphi's letter referring to magazine subscriptions has not reached him. He has my list now and is entering the ten subscriptions. About the American edition of *Unity of India*, Walsh writes:

> The small edition which we were able to import in sheets from England was exhausted long ago, and the English publisher has not yet been able to obtain enough paper to fill our order for more. It had not occurred to me to send a copy of our edition because it was simply sheets from the English edition, with our own title page inserted. And yet I think that perhaps your father would like to have a complete set of all his works in all countries. Therefore I think that I may be able sooner or later to buy back a copy from some bookstore and I will try to do so and send it to him. The only copy now in sight is our file copy which we feel we must retain, and indeed we have put it away in the safe as a matter of record.

I have your letters Numbers 37 and 38[1] ...
The servants send *salaams* and Feroze his love.
Much love from your loving,

Indu

162.                             Ahmadnagar Fort Prison,
11th December, 1943

Darling Indu,

I have not received any letter from you since I wrote last, but that was to be expected. There has been your visit to Jaipur and long railway journeys. I hope you found Bappi and family well. I have not seen her children for a long time and they must have grown, as children insist on doing. I shall hardly be able to recognise them when I see them next. They used to be charming kids. Pyare must be absorbed in his work. He has plenty of energy and this is just the kind of activity that should suit him and give scope to his ideas, though Jaipur is not too big a place.

Last week I wrote[2] to you that I had received no letter from Feroze. This passage in my letter has evoked a response from the mysterious individual who censors our letters in the Bombay Secretariat. A message has been conveyed to me that no letter from Feroze addressed to me

---

1. Refers to letters Nos 157 and 159.
2. Refers to letter No. 160.

was received or kept back. Further, that a son-in-law is entitled to write.

A week or two ago I asked you to try to get for me a new book by Edward Thompson, *The Making of the Indian Princes*. I have just been told that this book has been sent to me direct by Edward. To make sure that it reached me, he sent it through the Viceroy. It has not reached me yet. I shall let you know when I get it, so that you can inform Edward.

The copy of Milton's poems has reached me. I had an odd sensation when I saw the presentation card stuck in it dated: Harrow: Lent Term 1906. Over thirty-seven years ago, in the far-off past of my boyhood. Pictures of those days and other days that are gone rose up before me, and I thought of the great changes that have come over me. And then I thought of the future. What will India and the world be like in another thirty-seven years? I shall not be there to see them, but you and your generation will no doubt see and compare, and all that is happening today will then be but a story of long ago – *Hai aaj jo sargujast apni, kal iski kahaniya banengi.* [1] It is well that time passes and brings healing and forgetfulness in its train. How few are the moments of exquisite delight when we would like to say: O Time, stay thy flight, O happy hours, remain with us, do not pass us by –

> *O temps, suspends ton vol!*
> *et vous, heures propices,*
> *Suspendez votre cours!*
> *Laissez-nous savourer les rapides delices*
> *Des plus beaux de nos jours!* [2]

How few they are! And yet, if by some magic that passing hour stayed on, and, like a painted picture, represented an unchanging and unchangeable moment, would not the very magic of that moment go, and we would weary even of sheer delight? . . .

I received the books sent by Edward Thompson. There are three of them:

1. *New Recessional & Other Poems*
2. *The Life of Charles Lord Metcalfe*
3. *The Making of the Indian Princes*

1. The phrase in Hindi is a translation of the phrase in English which precedes it: 'all that is happening today will be but a story of long ago!'
2. Oh time, suspend your flight!
   And you, propitious hours, suspend your course!
   Let us taste the swift delights of
   the fairest of our days!
   (*Le Lac* by Alphonse De Lamartine)

The first of these was sent to me by Edward last year and it reached me here. The second (Metcalfe) has also been previously sent to me by him. I wonder if you remember it, for it came to me some years ago bearing not only Edward's signature but your name also (Indu). You had gone to visit the Thompsons in their house on Boar Hill at Oxford and he made you sign and then sent on the book to me. I am very glad, however, that he has sent another copy to me, for the earlier copy was lost, much to my distress. I had read it very carefully and valued it. But in one of its journeys between Anand Bhawan and some jail it disappeared somewhere in the jailer's office. So I am very glad to have this second copy. The poems are very welcome. As for the new book I have been eagerly looking forward to it, as you know.

I want you to write to Edward Thompson and tell him that I have received these three books. No gift that I could have had here could be more welcome, nor could I have wished for a better inscription than what he has written in the book on the Indian Princes. I often think of him and of the bond of friendship that ties us. Such bonds have helped me greatly to keep sane and sober, and not to allow 'black thinking', as they call it very appropriately in the language of prison, to find a home in my mind.

Let me know how Pupha is keeping. I am anxious about his health. And how is Nora? Does she still get a rise in temperature? Give her my love.

I think of Anand Bhawan in the delightful cold of December, with the warm sun flooding the house and the garden with its cheerful presence; and you and Feroze busy in the garden and inside the house, improving them and changing their aspect; making them full of joyful life – and the thought evokes many pictures in my mind, and I like them.

Love,

Your loving,
Papu

---

163.
Anand Bhawan,
Allahabad,
12th December, 1943

Darling Papu,
I was thrilled to see your handwriting on the envelope of your last letter – No. 39.[1] This has not happened since I was in Kashmir in July 1942. The dividend warrant has arrived safely, as also the two lots of books mentioned in a previous letter.

1. Refers to letter No. 160.

Imagine my surprise when I got a letter from Mridu from the Sara-bhai's Bombay residence. She was operated on the 7th – successfully – and is now progressing well. I have asked her to come to Allahabad when she is better and needing rest and a good climate.

Khaliq took your list of books to Kitabistan and brought back the answer that not one was available in India. It sounds rather exaggerated, so I am writing to Bombay myself. Taraporevalas [1] are already fed up with my orders. They never have in stock anything I want. When Feroze was in Bombay they asked him: where does she get the names from – we haven't even heard of these books! One of the books on your list I think you have read – H. G. Wells's *You Can't Be Too Careful*. At least you sent it to me in jail and it has your name in it.

I did visit a fortress some miles from Jaipur, way up on a hill. Was it Amber or Amba – I think the latter. It had a curiously lived-in atmos-phere, so that one was always expecting to hear the swish of a *ghagra* [2] or the clanking of swords and each new hall or dark pathway was surpris-ing in its emptiness. It was lived in quite recently – as late as the last Maharaja's reign. Masi told me that a relative of ours died there some years ago. Her baby was born unexpectedly and prematurely in the middle of the night and she was very ill, but the outside gate being locked and barred at nine p.m., no doctor could be summoned and the poor girl died before morning.

This is my fortieth letter to you.

Puphi returned to Lucknow last night. Pupha is much better – has gained about 8 lbs, I believe, and is looking well. There is also a slight improvement in Anand Sapru's [3] condition.

Much love,

From your loving,
Indu

---

164.                                        Anand Bhawan,
                                            Allahabad,
                                     14th December, 1943

Darling Papu,
I wrote my last letter [4] in such a rush – every time I started a paragraph visitors turned up – with the result that I forgot to mention several things.

1. Taraporevalas: a famous firm of booksellers.
2. A skirt from waist to ankle worn by Rajasthani women.
3. A. N. Sapru: youngest son of Tej Bahadur Sapru (see Circle of Friends).
4. Refers to letter No. 163.

With regard to the Tamil translation of the *Glimpses*, I am trying to gather more information about the firm of Mani Puthakasalai. Meanwhile somebody called Nagendra Nath Neogi,[1] connected with the Calcutta University College of Science, has completed an Assamese translation of *Letters From a Father*. He now wants to publish it. Do you know anyone who knows Assamese & is competent to judge the translation? Otherwise how does one get information about these obscure people? I am not applying the word obscure to the Assamese-knowing public but to the individuals and firms in various remote corners of India who wish to translate one of your books.

Allahabad is excited and pleased. The *Amrita Bazar Patrika* of Calcutta now appears simultaneously at Allahabad. They call it their *Northern Indian Edition*. The first edition appeared the day before yesterday – the 12th. I shall send you a copy. The poor *Leader* is putting up a frantic struggle for survival. Ever since the news of the *Amrita Bazar* was advertised, the *Leader* has certainly smartened up. They have a column for 'Legal Procedure', another called 'Allahabad Day-by-Day', which quite often collects all sorts of rumours current in the local bazaars, in an effort for local popularity. Even the news service has improved slightly. Various changes have been made in the staff. Brij Mohan Vyas[2] is their new manager!

Vatsala Samant is engaged to be married to an officer in the Air Force – Kumar Chaudhri.[3] He is a U.P. man, brought up in Allahabad. The engagement was officially announced in this morning's papers. Vatsala would like to continue in her work at the hospital, if the Committee allows it.

In a previous letter,[4] I told you about Anand Sapru. There is some improvement in his condition & Sapru Saheb was able to come down to Allahabad for a couple of days.

Lady Wazir Hasan[5] called a few days ago & especially asked that I should send you her love in my next letter.

Much love,

Indu

---

1. Nagendra Nath Neogi: a scholar who translated Nehru's work entitled *Letters From a Father to his Daughter* into Assamese.

2. Brij Mohan Vyas: Executive Officer, Allahabad Municipal Board, 1921–43; served on the staff of the *Leader*, 1943–8.

3. Kumar Chaudhri: an officer in Royal Air Force, 1940–5; Aerodrome Officer, Department of Civil Aviation, 1948–53.

4. Refers to letter No. 163.

5. Lady Wazir Hasan: active in the national movement. She was a member of the U.P. Legislative Assembly.

165.                                              Ahmadnagar Fort Prison,
                                                  18th December, 1943

Darling Indu,
I have your letter of the 8th December – No. 39, [1] which you wrote on
your return from Jaipur. This is my letter No. 41.

I was interested to learn of your impressions of Jaipur. Those impressions of old India would have been confirmed and emphasised if you had gone to Udaipur which is still, I believe, a relic of feudal times. Rajputana has an old-world atmosphere which clings to it and surprises a newcomer from outside. In spite of its misery, poverty and backwardness, there is a charm of history and tradition, of chivalry and blind courage, and one's mind inevitably travels back to those tales of long ago of brave men and beautiful women who cared for honour and self-respect more than for life or anything else. There also you find the remains of old artistry, and leisurely craftsmanship, alas dying now and almost dead. Havell, the English art critic, was an enthusiastic admirer of these craftsmen and master-builders and he tried his utmost to encourage them and revive these crafts. He cried himself hoarse in his attempts to have them employed for new buildings, for he hated the Anglo-Indian style of architecture which was rising in all our cities in all its ugliness.

How I regret that I did not explore these parts of India and many others when I had the chance and could do so unobserved and in peace. It fills me with rage that I should have spent so much of my time in places like Mussoorie and Nainital and Simla, when all this loveliness and charm were there to visit, to see and enjoy, and learn from. But that time went by, wasted, as so much of our life is wasted, in trivial things, and later it became impossible for me to have that experience in the right way. I went to some of those places but there was no peace for me then, no leisurely wandering. My mind was afire with other matters and I had become a personage who attracted attention and created a stir wherever he went. My visit became an event, upsetting many people and often raising new problems. No longer could I go wherever I chose for I had to consider the consequences of my going. No longer was I master of my self or my time; circumstances had enslaved me.

But though I could not go myself to many places, and even when I went, I rushed through, surrounded by crowds, my mind became more and more absorbed with this mystery of India in her manifold aspects. I tried to fathom this, to have glimpses behind the surface, to understand what this country of ours had been and was now. But the more I knew

1. Refers to letter No. 161.

of it, the less I claimed to understand it. Once, I remember, as we were journeying from Kuala Lumpur to Penang in the comfortable saloon carriages of the Malayan railways, I sat down to write about India. The mark of India on the other countries that I visited had impressed me and fired my imagination. I wrote a page or two and then there were interruptions and the mood passed. Somewhere still I have that page or two, and somewhere in my mind there is still that desire to put down on paper that groping of my being for an understanding of India . . .

Love to you and Feroze,

Your loving,
Papu

166.                            Ahmadnagar Fort Prison,
24th December, 1943

Darling Indu,

Your letter No. 41 dated 14 Dec.[1] has also reached me. This is my forty-second letter. I am writing to you a day earlier than usual – on a Friday instead of a Saturday – for tomorrow is Christmas Day and the day after is Sunday. The Post Office will be closed for these two days and so it has been suggested to me that I might send off my letter today.

I have received a parcel from Jaipur, sent by Bappi or by you when you were there, containing *supari*, dried fruits and various kinds of sweets. Some of these sweets, especially the *pethē kā murabbā* are obviously of the Agra variety. They are all good.

I sent you some days ago another packet of old periodicals.

You ask me about an Assamese translation of *Letters*. I am almost sure that I gave permission for this to somebody in Assam. If you can trace that register of mine in which all these facts are noted – a big book probably in the steel cupboard where my papers are kept – you will be able to find out the name and address. Giving permission, of course, does not mean that the translation has been published. Sometimes these translators and publishers take no further steps or delay publication inordinately. If you can get hold of the address, you might write and enquire. If the book has not come out so far and there is no chance of its publication, then I am absolved from my contract and can withdraw my previous permission and arrange with someone else.

I know plenty of people in Assam who could be referred to but I suppose most of them are in jail or detention and not approachable. As the person you refer to is connected with the Calcutta Univ. College of

---

1. Refers to letter No. 164.

Science, a reference might be made to Prof. Meghnad Saha[1] of that College. Saha is a Bengali and cannot judge Assamese. But he might be able to say something about Nagendra Nath Neogi. In any event I can only deal with publishers, not translators. A translator might well do his work and then be unable to get the book published. I do not believe in private publication by individuals. So Neogi might be asked, provided the book has not already been published in Assamese or is not likely to be published soon, what publisher is going to undertake the job. Also if he could get some competent opinion about the translation.

As these *Letters* have become popular and are included in prescribed courses, I have been anxious that as far as possible there should be no exploitation of students. So in all my recent agreements relating to them I have put in a proviso that if a public educational authority, a university or the like, wants to use the book, they can have the copyright from me free. I have given this copyright free for Urdu & Hindi translations to the Education Department of the U.P. Government. In the Bengali I have given it to Santiniketan. The U.P. Education Dept. were thus able to bring out the *Letters* very cheaply, almost at cost price. Even so they made some profit out of them and I suggested to others that this money might be used for scholarships for poor students. This was agreed to. What has happened since I do not know.

If you can get hold of the register referred to above, it would be worthwhile to write to my other publishers in India – there are quite a number of them in various languages – and ask them how matters stand.

The Jamia Millia of Delhi brought out, after long delay, an Urdu translation of about one-third of the *Glimpses*. This was a year or two ago. Have they proceeded with the work? . . .

This letter will probably reach you on the eve of the New Year. Time flows on inexorably and the days and the months and the years pass by, or is it we that pass? For it is we that bear the marks of this passing of time. A couple of days ago it struck me that we had been here just 500 days, each day like its forerunner, with no highlights, no new sensation, an ant-like existence, except for the activity of the mind. How we get used to anything and adapt ourselves to circumstances! But not the rebel mind which probes and wanders and dreams, forgetful of its environment. The real tragedy is when the mind itself gets dull and routine-ridden, incapable of new effort, lustreless.

So the New Year comes to the sound of the clashing of swords and the beating of war-drums and the bursting of bombs, and to the silence

1. Prof. Meghnad Saha: distinguished physicist; Professor of Physics, Allahabad University, 1923–38 and later at Calcutta University; Member, Lok Sabha, 1952–6.

of jails and prison camps. The human spirit, irrepressible, leaps over all this and thinks of the joy and beauty to come – some time.

May it be well with you, my darling one, during this year that is coming and the years that follow.

I have often written to you that you should arrange to give every possible help in Bengal relief work – financially to the extent of all my resources. I do not know what you have done, what moneys you have sent. Just now, when most people have got used to the Bengal tragedy and imagine that the worst is over, there will be even greater need of help. Get Rs. 1000/- from my account at Bachhraj's and use it for this purpose – more later when you want it. You need not mention my name.

Love,

Your loving,<br>Papu

---

167.                                           Anand Bhawan,
Allahabad,<br>27th December, 1943

Darling Papu,

I am ashamed of myself for not writing to you regularly. The whole trouble is that I have not yet got used to the irregularity of life in Anand Bhawan. There are days of quiet – writing letters, pottering in the garden, talking to leisurely visitors and reading. Then suddenly all sorts of things will happen all at once: take last week, for example, an important case in Gorakhpur that Feroze had to attend. Papers and data to be sorted out before he could leave. Feroze finally left, giving me instructions about various lists to be made. I had hardly begun on them when Sheikh Saheb turned up unexpectedly. He was here a couple of days until Christmas Eve. That day and the next I had promised to spend with Anna & Rita. Anna gave us a Danish Christmas Eve dinner & a Christmas tree. I got back rather late to find that Feroze had returned sooner than was expected.

Yesterday morning, Vatsala got married in a terrific hurry. The Pundit discovered that the only auspicious time for the wedding for a long time to come was the morning of the 26th. So Vatsala's father insisted that they should not wait for anybody but should have the ceremony on the 26th. She invited only a few close friends. Nobody could raise a present in time but we all turned up full of good wishes and regardless of other appointments.

I believe the hospital has given her permission to stay on. Her husband will probably come & live in her house, as he is all alone in Allahabad.

Anand Sapru is better. He was taking anti-rabies injections. He stood thirteen of them quite well, but at the fourteenth he got a stroke of paralysis from his neck downwards to his feet. Even the inner muscles, such as the stomach and bowels were affected. It was very difficult to feed him: it was done by means of tubes.

I have sent instructions for your pullovers, etc, with Sheikh Saheb.

Darling, I shall write a more coherent letter tomorrow. I want this one to be posted now.

Much love,

Indu

---

168.                                    Ahmadnagar Fort Prison,
                                         31st December, 1943

Darling Indu,

I had intended writing to you tomorrow, Saturday, on New Year's Day. But again I am told that tomorrow is a holiday for the Post Office and it is suggested that I write today instead. So I am writing to you my last letter of 1943, instead of my first letter of 1944. This is my No. 43 which means that I have been writing with some regularity for forty-two weeks. As a matter of fact the period is somewhat longer for I find that my letter No. 1 to you was written on the 5th March. [1]

So 1943 goes into history and becomes a memory, a spot in the long record of things remembered and forgotten. Two days ago I saw the new moon and it struck me that it was our eighteenth new moon here; there was a new moon to greet us here the day we came, just as there was a new moon for me when I was landed in Gorakhpur jail three years ago or more – the moon of *Id*, it was then – *Id ka chand*, [2] and *Diwali* had just gone by.

Sometimes I am fascinated by the idea of Time. We take it for granted as we do so many other things in life because we get used to them – the wonderful pageant of the stars, the sprouting of the seedlings bursting out from the womb of their mother earth in search of the sun, the flowering of the buds, and the soft rustling of the wind through the trees. Yet how amazing is this idea of Time! Is it Time that passes us, or rather is it we that pass and call our passing Time? As when we travel in a railway train and city and town and village appear in ordered sequence and pass us by, giving us the impression that they exist one

---

1. Refers to letter No. 93.
2. *Id ka chand* (Moon of Id): the festival of Id is indicated by the appearance of the moon after a succession of moonless nights.

after the other. Daily and hourly we change and each new aspect of ourselves is just a wee bit different from the last. So dead and past selves pile up behind us but the new self, itself a thing of the moment, ever changing, carries the impress of all these past selves upon it, past experiences and thoughts and trails, dreams and reveries, and the hard knocks of existence. Looking back, one sees this long and interminable succession of past selves, fading into each other like ghosts of things that were and are no more.

So 1943 passes and we stand on the threshold of another year, peeping into its dark and unknown recesses, and wondering what it may contain of good and ill. And we also grow reminiscent and think of the past that is over, standing on the razor-like edge of the present, with vast expanses of the past and future on either side.

Do you know that our ancestors of long, long ago had, unlike most people, a very powerful idea of Time? The ancient Greeks had no word for more than a myriad or ten thousand, the Romans stopped at the mille or thousand, and the Arabs also had no word beyond a thousand. But the old Indians had a definite notation, in a scale of ten, with names for numbers which went up to prodigious figures – over fifty zeros added to 1. They thought of time in terms of millions and billions of years and at the same time their smallest unit of time was $\frac{1}{17}$th of a second. But their most wonderful discovery, two thousand years ago, was that of zero. Every child knows this now but to evolve this zero idea for the first time must have been the work of a mighty genius. It has been called one of the great world discoveries of all time. On that is based all our modern arithmetic and algebra and so much else. *Shunya* (nothing) zero is called in Sanskrit and from that has come the Hindi *Sunna*.

Now zero is a very odd thing. If you divide anything by it, the result takes you to conceptions which are not easy to grasp – it is infinity. The old Sanskrit commentators, at a loss for a more homely comparison, compared this result to one of the attributes of God! . . .

In my last letter[1] I wrote to you again to arrange to give out of my account some financial help for Bengal relief. I suggested that you should get Rs. 1000/- (one thousand) from Bachhraj for the purpose. This to begin with. I have no idea how my account stands with them but I imagine you will be able to raise this much out of what is called the current account. I do not suppose relatively small sums like this make much difference, but they add up. Anyway I shall feel a little better if this is done. It is bad enough to learn of the suffering in Bengal, Orissa and elsewhere and not to be able to do anything worthwhile. Later, I should like to give some more money.

1. Refers to letter No. 166.

You can consult Puphi about the disposal of this money. Personally I would prefer it to go to the 'Save the Children Fund' started by the Women's Conference, for that is a definite object which goes beyond just feeding the starving. The idea of concentrating more on the children appeals to me.

There appear to be any number of relief funds and I suppose they are all doing more or less good work. The Ramakrishna Mission people do this work remarkably well, both efficiently and in a selfless, unostentatious way, and I admire them greatly. But theirs is, as it should be, general humanitarian work, chiefly, I suppose, giving food and medicine. They are rightly popular and, I imagine, they are getting enough money. So the 'Save the Children Fund' had better receive my contribution.

I hope this part of my letter is not objected to by the censor and blacked out. I see no reason for this, except possibly his desire that my name should not be given publicity. In this, if not in most other matters, I am in agreement with him. I do not want my name to be published in this connection. The donation should be anonymous.

Have you any news of Madan Bhai? I suppose he is still in jail . . .

So on to the New Year and all good luck to you.

My love,

> Your loving,
> Papu

---

169.

> Anand Bhawan,
> Allahabad,
> New Year's Day, 1944

Darling Papu,

Here is another year again. For most of us it has come in inauspicious circumstances. No hope of peace or goodwill. No sign of the proverbial silver lining.

Since my last letter [1] to you I have not been well – nothing special, just losing weight and looking & feeling awful. This morning I was feeling worse so decided to stay in bed until lunch time. However Vatsala turned up & was teasing me about starting the year well – then came a trunk call from Puphi from Lucknow so I had to get up and rush off to the hospital. Poor Pupha is very ill indeed & this last week he has become very weak and has great difficulty in breathing. He has been asking for Rita – so Puphi rang up to say that Rita & Anna should proceed to Lucknow as soon as possible, as Rita's presence would at

---

1. Refers to letter No. 167.

least set Puphi's mind at peace. Feroze and I are also going to Lucknow tomorrow night.

Raja Bakshi was here for three or four days. He left on New Year's Eve. Swarup is in Lahore.

I have an airgraph from Agatha. Appropriately enough it arrived on Christmas Day. Dr Bhandari is very ill & is in hospital. Overwork is the cause and his heart seems to have gone wrong. He has been in charge of Home Guard duties in addition to his heavy medical work and probably over-stepped his strength.

I airgraphed your message to Thompson, the day your letter came.

It rained a bit last night & this morning, but not enough for the crops. Having sown a little wheat ourselves we are able to sympathise more deeply with the needs of the *kisans*. If it does not rain very soon most crops will be completely spoilt.

Much love,

Indu

———————————————

170.
Lucknow,
3rd January, 1944

Darling Papu,

Feroze and I arrived in Lucknow this morning and since then we have been from one ill person to another. In spite of all I had been told, I was shocked to see Pupha so weak. I saw him only for a moment when oxygen was being administered to him. He is given oxygen every few hours. He was sitting bolt upright, propped up by innumerable pillows and cushions. Puphi tells me that is his normal position night and day for over a week now. There was plenty of fluid present in the lung – or wherever it is – but it seemed to have collected in various 'pockets' and could not be tapped. This caused him considerable pain. This afternoon Dr Bhatia tried tapping again and was successful – over a pint of fluid was taken out. It had to be done very slowly and took a long time. Since then Pupha is feeling relieved and we hope will pass a better night.

Pratapji & Saraswati Bai have arrived. I believe Chhoti Puphi and Rajabhai are also thinking of coming. I think they will leave Bombay on Wednesday.

Kishen Chacha has become quite weak. He has been having a series of heart attacks and is in bed. His home life and atmosphere are such as make any rest or peace of mind quite impossible. He is thinking of going to a hospital and I strongly agree with him. Apart from the comfort of expert nursing, there will at least be a doctor at hand in case of emergency. He told me that the night before last he had a bad attack and there was nobody to send for the doctor!

Vidya is now in Delhi working in All India Radio. She is getting a good salary and is, apparently, well and happy. She is having difficulty in finding lodging and is staying with the Shiva Raos. Padma [1] now stays at the Women's University hostel. She is in her final B.A. year.

Next we went right the other end of town – King George's – to see Anand Sapru. Apart from his physical state, his mind has gone completely to pieces. He just weeps and weeps endlessly. Knowing how visitors upset him, I did not wish to go inside the patient's room and went quite prepared only to have a few words with Mussorie Didda. However, she insisted on taking us in. Anandji started a long speech about how grateful he was for our visit and so on, accompanied by tears. Ramji Gurtu, [2] who was there, shooed us out but Anandji stopped weeping and said he wanted to talk, so we went in again and stayed for about twenty minutes, at the end of which Rajan Didda came and Anandji wept loudly. All this is a terrific emotional strain on him. Physically there is a slight improvement – he can now move his head from side to side, he can lift his hands a little and he can pass urine – a few drops – with the catheter. This last is still a very painful process, but it shows that the muscles of the bladder can move. Sir Tej goes to Allahabad every month for a day or two. Otherwise the whole family is here.

I have not brought clothes for more than a couple of days so I shall probably return to Allahabad in a day or two, and then come back to Lucknow.

Do excuse writing – we are spending the night at the Councillor's Residence and it is late and the light very bad indeed.

Much love,

Indu

---

1. Padma Seth née Nehru: niece of Jawaharlal Nehru and a second cousin of Indira Gandhi.

2. Ram Narain Gurtu: a barrister of Allahabad; later Judge of the Allahabad High Court; at present Adviser, Anand Bhawan, Jawaharlal Nehru Memorial Fund. A close friend of the Nehrus.

171.

Anand Bhawan,<br>
Allahabad,<br>
12th January, 1944

Darling Papu,

I wrote to you some time ago [1] of Ballo's engagement. There was some talk of the wedding taking place next year or at the end of this year. Imagine my surprise when on my return from Lucknow I find a letter from Bijju Chachi saying the wedding was on the 17th February and would take place in Allahabad, and could she have the use of the spare rooms of Anand Bhawan for about ten days, for the accommodation of guests, etc. Naturally I wrote at once that she could have the house for as long as she wanted. Ballo's cousin Hira Vatal is getting married on the same day to Bhaiya Sapru's daughter Satto. And around about that date, Ballo's future brother-in-law is marrying Kathju's youngest daughter. Quite an orgy of weddings! I sent an S.O.S. to Puphi asking what sort of present should be got on your behalf. The reply has just come – a household article worth about Rs. 150/-.

I have written to Bachhraj to send the 1000/- to Urmila Mehta, Secretary, Save the Children Fund.

Somebody who signs himself 'Jahalo' has written you a long letter – five typewritten sheets – from Los Angeles. Jahalo is obviously a pseudonym and there is no address or date on the letter, which is inspired by Shridharani's *My India, My America,* and deals almost entirely with Jahalo's childhood years. Towards the end he recommends one of his favourite books – Kahlil Gibran's *Prophet* – which he says he is sending to you. He wishes you a Happy Birthday, 'but since it can't be that, will wish instead that you can keep a resilient and creative mind, despite the limitations imposed on you'.

You ask about Brij Mohan Vyas. He took long leave some time ago and installed his son, just out of college, as officiating in his place. Soon after his return from leave, Vyas resigned, hoping that his son would be elected in his place. In the meantime Radha, Varma and others came out and the election has been postponed. Varma is trying for the job and there is terrific canvassing going on on all sides. Before Varma's release Shafi Ahmad Kidwai, Rafi's brother, who has been a good executive officer in Dehra Dun, was trying for the Allahabad post. I do not know if the two have come to any agreement – Varma and Shafi Ahmad, I mean.

Keshav's wife, Durga, has been running a temperature for months. We have now brought her to the hospital for a thorough overhaul.

---

1. Refers to letter No. 149.

Vatsala has gone to Bombay for a week's holiday with her husband. Choudhry is a U.P. man, a Kayastha. His family comes from a village near Bareilly.

Mohan Chacha[1] is well. I meet him occasionally. He was excited and busy these last days for Ratan[2] and Rajan and Rup Didda[3] all came to Allahabad for the Christmas holidays. The Law Journal Press has been bought over by Dalmia.[4] So far there have not been any changes in the staff and Kishan Bhai Dar remains the manager. There is a strong rumour that Dalmia is also wanting to buy the *Leader*. Other U.P. businessmen are also looking around, I hear, for newspapers.

Enquiries are being made about the Persian Grammar. There are two fat tomes in our Library: Phillott's *Higher Persian Grammar*. On closer examination, I do not think this could be of much use to you, as it deals with the 'differences between Afghan and Modern Persian'. The other book is the *English–Urdu Translator's Companion* (in Roman characters).

Munshi Aijaz Hussain is not connected with the *Khadi Bhandar* any more. In fact none of the old people are there.

I sent you a white woollen cardigan. Have you received it? I have sent instructions to the Srinagar *Khadi Bhandar* about the scarf and pullover. They have not replied to my letter but I hear from Sheikh Saheb that they have received it and have already commenced work.

I returned from Lucknow after a four days' stay on the 7th. The first night we stayed at the Councillor's Residence. The next day Feroze came away to Allahabad and I moved over to Anand Bhai[5] as that is more comfortable and also nearer to Pupha. Most of the day I was at Pupha's, although I only saw him for a few seconds on my arrival and departure. Puphi was looking very tired as they could not find a night nurse and she had to stay up herself. Now, I hear, that difficulty is solved. Pratapji and Saraswati Bai have also returned to Bombay.

Much love,

Indu

---

172.                                    Ahmadnagar Fort Prison,
                                         18th January, 1944

Darling Indu,

I did not write to you last week. Instead, I wrote to Puphi. On Friday,

1. Mohanlal Nehru: uncle of Indira Gandhi.
2. Ratan Kumar Nehru: a nephew of Jawaharlal Nehru. He was a member of the Indian Civil Service
3. Rup Vanchoo: daughter of Mohanlal Nehru; married to Hariharnath Vanchoo.
4. Dalmia: well-known industrialist.
5. Anand Kumar Nehru: a nephew of Jawaharlal Nehru.

January 14, I was informed that Pupha had died that morning in Lucknow. [1]

During the last week I have received more letters than usual – two from Puphi, three from you. All of them mention some slight progress in Pupha's condition, give hope of recovery. Some of them have come after the news of his death.

Your last letter, dated January 12, [2] came yesterday. You tell me in it of Ballo's approaching marriage and of two other weddings. It was odd to read of marriages when my mind was full of death. Yet, I realised that this was the way of life, and life and death, and sorrow and happiness are strangely mixed together. The world goes on along its appointed course, and even wars with all their vast horror and destruction do not deflect it overmuch. They are incidents covered over by the next season's harvest, as the harvest in Bengal will cover up famine and death, and a new generation will grow up and labour and suffer, and marry and beget children, and then fade away. But the memory remains, the memory that imprints itself on the mind of man and moulds his being, or which lingers in the consciousness of a people and a race and often determines their future actions.

I feel lonely as my friends and colleagues pass off into the unknown, and a feeling of weariness steals over me, a realisation that I too belong to a passing generation. The old and the ageing have a way of monopolising the stage, forgetting nature's way.

Puphi must be worn out after the long strain and the shock. She will require some peace and quiet and rest. Perhaps she could have more of these if she moved to Anand Bhawan. That is for her to decide.

Deaths in the family break the routine of existence and upset not only our minds but our ways of living. Gradually we adjust ourselves to the new scheme. There has been little of routine in all our lives, no settling down, and we have long been travellers in an unknown country, not knowing where our next temporary halt might be. So for us the process of adjustment is perhaps less difficult than for those who live more normal lives. Yet the effort has to be made to make the transition easier, to tone down the rough edges as much as possible.

You were right in placing the house at Bijju Chachi's disposal for Ballo's marriage. Everything that is there is for her to use as she wishes.

I have received the cardigan that you have sent me. But you need not and should not have sent your own. I do not require any warm things. My old pullover, full of holes as it is, and a warm waistcoat are more than enough for the mild climate we have here. Even when the new

1. Ranjit Pandit died on 14th January, 1944.
2. Refers to letter No. 171.

pashmina pullover is made it should not be sent to me here, lest the moths and the insects get at it. Soon *Vasanta Panchami* will be with us and then a fairly quick change of season. It is pleasant of course to wear your cardigan, because it is yours. I am using it. As the season changes I shall return it to you. I do not want to offer it as a feast for various worms & insects.

Do not bother about the Persian Grammar or indeed any other book. The one (Persian Grammar) in Anand Bhawan is no good for me. I have masses of books here, old and new, and they can keep me occupied for many months.

Some days ago I sent you a number of books. In this lot there were two books of Puphi's: Han Suyin's *Destination Chungking* and André Maurois's *Call No Man Happy*. Both of these I had previously received and read. Return these books to Puphi. Among the other books returned were: Havell's *Ideals of Indian Art* & Pearl Buck's *The Mother*.

I shall send you another batch of books in a day or two. This will also contain a book of Puphi's (Campion's *Towards the Mountains*).

I have received from you Morgan's *Sparkenbroke* and *Life & Letters* for July 1943.

Do not trouble yourself about Jahalo's letter. And do not send me Khalil Gibran's book if it reaches you. I have already read it.

I might be somewhat irregular in my letters to you for a week or two – I intend writing to Chand and Tara at the next opportunity.

In one of your letters you mention that you are losing weight and otherwise not feeling well. This distresses me. You should keep well –
　　Love,

Your loving,<br>Papu

---

173.                                                    Anand Bhawan,
                                                         Allahabad,
                                                   19th January, 1944

Darling Papu,
My heart aches for you. So far and with no work into which to immerse your sorrow. But what can one say – what consolation can one give? I have been in such a daze these last days. Life itself seems to be so pointless sometimes. From the minute we are born, with that first effort for breath, begins a lifetime of struggle. The years and years through infancy, childhood, manhood and old age are full of struggle, for something or the other, for health, for fame, for fortune. And then suddenly as if somebody had blown off a candle, pouff! it's all finished. The

individual with his likes and dislikes, his opinions and prejudices – in fact everything that makes him what he is, is no more, is just a 'body'. Dust thou art and to dust return. And when you have lost life itself, is it any consolation that you are remembered and mourned, that you have left a big or a small mark on the world and its affairs?

I am glad I went to Lucknow and had a last glimpse of Pupha. He was so weak but he smiled his characteristic smile and I couldn't imagine that he would not get well. And when the news actually came I kept on repeating to myself, 'It's all a ghastly mistake, Feroze must have misunderstood Puphi on the phone.' And even as I was repeating this, sitting in the car at Phaphamau, we sighted Puphi's car and in an hour or so it was all over – there wasn't even the body any more. Ladli Bhai & Feroze had got hold of Kanhayilal and others so that all arrangements for the funeral were complete before Puphi came.

Puphi and Rita are both bearing up wonderfully.

Bebee and Mrs Naidu are here, also Rajabhai and Chhoti Puphi. Saraswati Bai and Pratapbhaiji stayed at Mukerji Road and are returning to Bombay today. Raj Chachi[1] is also at Mukerji Road, with a Parsi girl she has engaged as nurse–companion. Janak Didda, Rajan Didda, Vidya, Shammie and Uma Bhabhi, Sharda and Subroto[2] all came for a couple of days and have now returned to their respective domiciles. Uma Chachi & Shammie will leave in a day or two. I do not know where they are staying.

My thoughts are with you constantly. All my love to you.

Indu

*21st January*

Bebee said she would send a message so I hung on to this letter but it isn't ready yet so I am now sending the letter off.

———————

174.                                          Anand Bhawan,
                                                    Allahabad,
                                          23rd January, 1944

My darling one,
Your letter to Puphi arrived yesterday. Beautiful it was – but so unbearably, heartbreakingly sad. I read it so quickly and yet the sentences have got burned into my brain, or so it seems, for all night through I tossed

1. Raj Dulari Nehru: wife of Indira's uncle Shri Shridhara Nehru.
2. Air Marshal Subroto Mukherjee: he was the first Indian to command an Air Force station at Kohat, 1943, later became Commander-in-Chief of the Indian Air Force. Sharda was his wife.

and turned and always they were in front of me. And your voice in
my ears. You have had, just as India herself has had, more than your
share of grief and sorrow. It is India's greatness as it is your own that
through it all you have remained stricken but undaunted. Perhaps it
is that the Providence that fashions us humans as we are, knows
what burdens we shall have to carry and accordingly endows some with
broader shoulders and stronger characters, bigger hearts and greater
endurance.

And meanwhile whatever we may feel, each absorbed in his own
personal sorrow – not only our family but the millions of other Indians
who are suffering untold miseries – the world goes on as it has been for
thousands of years. In the hospital next door babies are being born –
right here in our own compound the garden is brighter and more beautiful than ever before.

Much love to you,

Indu

175.                                        Ahmadnagar Fort Prison,
                                             25th January, 1944

Darling Indu,
I have had a letter from Betty from Anand Bhawan telling me of various
people who have come to Allahabad and giving me other news. Amma
has also sent me a telegram of condolence which has been forwarded
to me in the usual way by the Bombay Govt. Last week I wrote to Chand
and Tara to Wellesley.

All these happenings must have been a great strain on you, even more
so a mental strain than a physical one. You wrote to me that even before
all this you had not been feeling too well. I think you should take yourself
in hand and get over this indisposition. This is the best time of the year
in Allahabad and you should take full advantage of it to put by a reserve
of good health. You know well what to do. One thing, however, I should
like to emphasise again, as I have done previously. This is breathing
exercises. I am a great believer in them and I think they are more
important than other forms of physical exercise. In your case, particularly, they should do good. I am not referring to any fancy ways of
breathing but just regulated deep breathing daily, or, better still, twice
a day.

For some odd reason I did not feel too well either early in January
and developed a slight backache. It was nothing much but it put me off
exercise and spinning. Later the news about Ranjit depressed me greatly
and, as is usual in such cases, made me feel physically low. I have got

over these aches, etc, now and am gradually reverting to my exercises.

I had hoped to send a bundle of my yarn in December last. By that time it should have been enough for a sari. But I have been very irregular in my spinning and often there are gaps of a week or more. For nearly a month now I have not spun at all, so progress has been slow. It depends a great deal on the mood I am in and the quality of the slivers. As the slivers were none too good my spinning time & production were proportionately reduced. I shall go back to it now. Tomorrow is an auspicious day and so I shall start afresh then.

I wrote to you last week[1] not to send me any more books. Well, I have changed my mind. That shows how inconstant and changeable I have become! Mahmud wants one of my books and you should be able to find this in my room – it is Thompson & Garratt's *Rise and Fulfilment of British Rule in India*. It is a fairly heavy volume. As you are likely to send this, you might add another, if you can find it. This is a translation of the *Ten Principal Upanishads* by A.E.[2] and some Swami[3] whose name I forget. This book was sent to me when I was in Dehra by Bharati out of the Ambalal Library and I have failed to return it. It should be in my dressing room. As I have read some of the translations of the Upanishads, I want to compare A.E.'s version with them. The book is published by Faber.

Recently I have read in the newspapers an account of a memorandum on the industrial development of India issued by Tata House and signed by Jehangir Tata, Purshottamdas Thakurdas, Birla, Dalal, etc.[4] I should like to have this booklet or whatever it is, together with connected papers, if any. Will you ask Betty to write to people in Bombay and have it sent to me?

Bebee must be with you – give her my love – I hope she is keeping well.

This letter is rather a thin one – which, I suppose, indicates that my mind just at present is not as bright and overflowing as it should be. Perhaps too much reading with its attendant thinking is not conducive to a proper equilibrium. External activity is also necessary. As a matter of fact I have not even paid attention to our little garden lately and it is in a poor way, though this is just the time for it to flourish. Our efforts at vegetable-growing have not been conspicuously successful. I think

1. Refers to letter No. 172.

2. A slip for W. B. Yeats. A.E. was the poet George Russell, who was a friend of Yeats.

3. Purohit Swami (1882–1941): poet and novelist, wrote in Hindi, Marathi, Sanskrit and English; inspired by Lokamanya Tilak joined the freedom struggle, later turned to spiritualism.

4. Prominent Indian industrialists.

our soil is not good enough for them and then, in our eagerness for results, we have watered them too much. I realise now, as I had not done previously, that there is always a tendency to overwater our plants.

I have just seen a new book on gardening which seems to be helpful. This is E. W. Grindal's *Everyday Gardening in India*, published by D. B. Taraporevala Sons & Co of Bombay. You might get it for your own use.

Give my love to Betty, Raja and Feroze,
Love,

Your loving,<br>Papu

I have taken to a variation of a sea bath here! I remembered that when I was a little boy I used to see Dadu rub his body with rocksalt when bathing. So I got a chunk of rocksalt and began using it this way. I liked it. It produced a slight tingling sensation. I think it should be good for one. Try it. But be careful also. Sometimes it breaks and a sawlike edge comes out which cuts through the skin. This happened with me and in one vigorous movement I managed to get a number of scratches all over.

This is my letter No. 46.

P

176.                                    Ahmadnagar Fort Prison,
                                         1st February, 1944

Indu darling,

Two of your letters, dated Jan. 19 and 23,[1] came to me together soon after I had sent you my last letter.[2] They were full of the burden of sorrow and an emotional upheaval at the suddenness of death and all the questionings that this experience gives rise to. Out of this eternal questioning has arisen philosophy with all its problems, and throughout the ages innumerable people have wondered over this mystery of life and death. Philosophy has come to you early not only because of personal shock but also the larger tragedies that surround us. It depends on each one of us how we face these questions, how [we] react to them. Adequate answers we may not have but our imaginative self gives some kind of an unconscious response which affects our individual lives. We weaken under the stress and lose our sense of poise and equilibrium, or grow stronger and more capable of riding the storm and yet being not too much affected by it. Life is amazingly dynamic and, while it lasts, has an

---

1. Refers to letters No. 173 and 174.
2. Refers to letter No. 175.

extraordinary capacity to adapt itself and to express itself forcibly. We see this daily in the exuberance of nature and we are parts of that nature and have, or should have, the same exuberance and vitality. So we carry on along our appointed course and, though limited by circumstance, still endeavour to mould that circumstance itself according to the urge that is within us.

Reason and argument go some way to shape our minds and direct our activities. Yet in the final analysis we act because of that inner urge within us, which has been formed and conditioned by so many factors which have gone to our making – our own experiences chiefly, piling up one on top of the other from birth and childhood onwards, the influence of others, our heredity and our racial and cultural inheritance, our education, the sensations we have known and experienced.

So our reactions to events vary. Some, and among them have been wise men, think all this business of life a thing of sound and fury signifying nothing. Others have discovered or felt a meaning in it all. Yet others, uncertain whether there is any meaning or not, still are compelled by some force within them to adopt objectives and codes of behaviour and follow them with all their might. Perhaps that itself signifies some deep intuitive faith in a meaning. However that may be, most of us affirm life and it is right that we should do so positively, rather than just carry on negatively.

Twenty-five hundred years ago the Buddha addressing his followers said: '. . . while ye, O disciples, experienced this sorrow through long ages, more tears have flowed from you and have been shed by you, while ye strayed and wandered on this pilgrimage of life, and sorrowed and wept, because that was your portion which ye abhorred, and that which ye loved was not your portion, than all the waters which are in the four great oceans.'

A sad thought and though a true one, yet perhaps with an over-emphasis on the pain and suffering of life. Buddha was frequently emphasising this and many people therefore call Buddhism a religion of pessimism. Yet the face of Buddha in the statues that his faithful followers have made with loving care, and even more so in the image of him that I have in my mind, is so devoid of pain and sorrow, so full of peace and calm and compassion, that I cannot connect it with suffering. Or does it represent the conquest over sorrow? I do not think of him as a man of sorrows.

And then, going to the lands where Buddhism still flourishes, we do not find the people pessimistic at all. Where could there be more of the joy and affirmation of life than in the Chinese people? Is that a racial characteristic, I wonder, which has overcome and transmuted the pessimistic tendencies of the faith, or is it something else? I do not know.

But I do know that I am seldom depressed for long by events, however painful they might be for the moment, and a certain unreasoning faith in life rises up in me and keeps me going. I cannot argue about it but it fills me and therefore life is an affirmation to me and not a negation. Even if that subconscious faith were absent, I suppose, I would continue to function in much the same way, but that urge helps and gives me vitality. Experiencing this myself, I want others to share it with me.

What a letter I am writing! A vague and possibly unmeaning attempt at philosophy in its relation to life, or perhaps just a glimpse of that restless and wandering creature, my mind. I have written as I have done because I want you to have such glimpses and to realise, as I do, the extraordinary fascination of life's adventure. That pilgrimage would be no adventure if it lay in the ruts of normal experience and cautious conduct, safety first in everything, like the slow-moving river on an almost level plain. The body has its adventures and experiences, and many are worth having, but the real adventures are of the mind. Indeed, all feelings and experiences are ultimately of the mind, and the mind itself is part of the body.

There is the adventure of the individual, the adventure of the race, and finally the world adventure – and all tend to get mixed up together – and we can be parties to all these adventures. If the individual's adventure has an ending, the others continue and carry us to an endless future. Our country, tragic as she may appear to us at the present moment, has been carrying on her story and her quest since the dawn of history many thousands of years ago. That quest will surely continue and merge itself in the conditions of the modern world, into the world-quest for life and freedom and adventures of the mind and spirit.

I am sending you some periodicals and other books. One is Douglas Reed's[1] play: *Downfall*. And two are by Krishnamurti.[2] They contain some good pictures and some that are not good, as you will no doubt notice.

Love,

Your loving,<br>Papu

This is my letter No. 47.

---

1. Douglas Reed: British journalist and writer.
2. Y. G. Krishnamurti: the two books referred to are *Jawaharlal Nehru: The Man and his Ideas* and *Betrayal of Freedom*.

177.                                 Ahmadnagar Fort Prison,
                                         8th February, 1944

Darling Indu,

It is two weeks now since I had your last letter.[1] I await news of you and from you and want to be assured that you have got over the shock of recent events and are keeping well.

In one of your recent letters[2] you told me about Ballo's approaching wedding. When I first read of this I mistook the date to be 17th January and this seemed rather inopportune. Then I discovered that it was Feb. 17. I suppose this wedding and others will be taking place about the time you get this letter. You will give my love and good wishes to Ballo and his bride and suitable presents which are available. Also give my love to Bijju Chachi.

Last time I saw Ballo was, I think, in my flat in St James Street in the summer of 1938. He spent a couple of days with us there. He was big and manly looking then. I suppose he has grown bigger since. What has he been doing here since his return?

I understand that it is possible to get yarn woven here locally into cloth. Some of my companions, who are expert spinners and who produce much more than I can ever hope to, have had their stuff woven into various pieces of *khadi*. So it has struck me that I might well follow their example instead of sending you my yarn and then for you to send it on to Psyche and for her to find out weavers. I shall try to get a sari made when I have enough yarn for it. What is the usual length and width of *khadi* saris which you wear? Previously I believe saris used to be six yards long but since the advent of *khadi*, with its additional weight, etc, this has been reduced to five yards. Let me have the exact measurements. Also send me, if you can, any of my old yarn which you can find. I wrote to you once about it and asked you to send it to Psyche. But Psyche did not want it just then and so perhaps you have not sent it. If it is still with you in Anand Bhawan, then send it; otherwise not. It used to be kept in the left-hand drawer of my dressing table.

Betty sent me some time ago Tod's[3] *Annals of Rajasthan* – three volumes. I was a little surprised to get them but then she reminded me that I had myself asked for them. I remembered. I had thought of the book over a year ago in connection with your birthday. At that time it was not available. You were in Naini then. So the book was meant for you and it will be sent to you later. Meanwhile, I have been dipping into

1. Refers to letter No. 174.
2. Refers to letter No. 171.
3. Col. James Tod: a British civil servant in India and a scholar. Author of *Annals and Antiquities of Rajasthan* (1832).

it and reading large chunks of it. Many of the stories I know, having read them or heard them in my childhood. Perhaps even now you will find an old edition of Tod in the library. Going back to them after this long interval, I found a new fascination in them and for some days my mind has been filled with these tales of Rajput chivalry and courage which mocked at death. In most countries you will find similar stories of bygone days, and yet it will be hard to beat these tales of Mewar and Rajasthan. We, living in a more sophisticated age, grow cynical and reckless courage and audacity, which cared not at all for the consequences, seem a little foolish and belonging to the childhood of the race. Yet there is something about sheer heroism and bodily courage which holds one and thrills. Pride and honour and to keep the plighted word were the Rajput virtues, and though something else of importance must be added to them, they are still very much worthwhile and will remain so. The Rajput has not often been noted for wisdom or intelligence, much less for discretion, yet wisdom without spirit and intelligence without daring are poor, weak companions, symbols of age and not of youth both in the individual and the nation. *Si jeunesse savait, si vieillesse pouvait.*[1] And the Rajputs managed to preserve through a couple of thousand years or more magnificent bodily types before whom the average person of today in the East or the West seems puny and undistinguished. Tod is full of stories of Rajput women coming out in moments of peril and with sword and lance leading their troops into action. Also of course of that terrible thing – the *Johar*.[2]

So I have partly lived in the enchantment of the Middle Ages of India during the past few days, and after I have done with these books, I shall send them on to you so that you may also sense that enchantment and experience that thrill. As history Tod is not very accurate and he has the most fantastic ideas about words and their etymologies. But he has the great gift of a sympathetic imagination and so he builds up a picture which is truer in essence than a bold, dry history might be.

A few days ago I wrote to Betty (to Anand Bhawan) and asked her to arrange to send me a copy of the recent plan for the economic development of India issued by Tata House. I have received this now and so she need not trouble herself about it.

Today, or, to be perfectly accurate, early tomorrow morning, we complete eighteen months since our arrest. How well I remember that morning when I bade you goodbye and I was driven away as the dawn was breaking. You were standing by the car and the last glimpse of you

---

1. If youth knew, if old age could.
2. A collective act of suicide through self-immolation by women of Rajput (or warrior aristocracy) caste to escape capture and dishonour after defeat by enemies.

I had was when the car took a turn and passed on into the unknown.

Eighteen months! Yet twice before I have exceeded this period and spent over twenty months in prison, which was equivalent to a two-year sentence. Altogether, I suppose – I have lost exact count – I have spent about eight years in prison. I have developed a theory about this prison-going business, and though it is a general theory, there are so many ifs and buts and provisos attached to it that for the moment it applies to a relatively small number of persons. That number includes me. The theory is this: if a person keeps good bodily health, and if his mind can keep calm and in equilibrium, and if the minimum requirements of the body & mind are met, then the period in jail does not age one in the normal way. Bodily age comes from wear and tear of the body and a succession of sensations. Both these are reduced to a minimum in prison life. There is the mind, of course, and this affects the body, and it is more difficult to control. If it is not agitated and can keep more or less poised, its ageing process might be reduced also, though not so much as that of the body. The mind in prison lives a life of the imagination far more than that of sensations. It will depend on the quality of that imagination as to what effect it has on the ageing process. Generally speaking, and subject to the provisos, the period in jail will not age the body much. Almost, you might say that it does not count in the allotted span of a person's life – allotted in the sense of the amount of vital energy the person possesses which carries him through a number of years and then fades out with life. The face, however, being far more a mirror of the mind, shows age more. So there is a discordance first of all between the body as a whole and the mind, and then between the body and the face. Anyway, in spite of these discordances, life is apparently prolonged.

But only so if there is no illness of body or mind. There can be nothing worse than any such illness in prison. So you can ponder over this theory of mine and derive such satisfaction from it as you can! . . .

This is my letter No. 48.

Love,

> Your loving
> Papu

---

178.                                            Ahmadnagar Fort Prison,
                                                15th February, 1944

Indu darling,

What a long time it seems since I heard from you. Three weeks. Perhaps not so long after all. But I had got rather used to getting a letter from you every week, and this makes me expect it, and when it does not come there is a sense of emptiness as of something missing. Indeed during these three weeks I have hardly had any letter, except for a brief note from Betty which she sent from Bombay.

This absence of news has troubled me somewhat, for the last bit of information about your health was none too good. And so a cloud of anxiety has filled my mind. It should not be so for I can do nothing from here to help you in any way. Yet it is so.

Betty writes that you were not feeling well and that she had asked you to go to Bombay. Whether you are going there or not I do not know. If you feel unwell it is desirable to have yourself overhauled by the doctors and this cannot be done efficiently in Allahabad. Calcutta or Bombay are indicated and you can take your choice of them. In Calcutta you have Bidhan Roy, a doctor full of experience and good sense; in Bombay also there are good doctors whom you know.

It is quite cool still and in Allahabad it must be colder. But the change in the weather is creeping in and two months later it will be warm enough and the sun will begin to function for us in all its strength, and fans will be whirling over us. What will you do then? You should not stay in the plains during the summer months. Choose some place which appeals to you and go there. The hill stations of the Himalayas will probably not suit you for you will have to take a house or a cottage, or go to a hotel, and this will involve trouble. Nor is the atmosphere or the company there particularly soothing or desirable. There is Khali which is climatically, and in some other ways, very attractive to me. There will be no trouble fixing yourself there, whether you go by yourself or with Puphi. Then there are the Bombay hills where you spent some weeks last year. They seem to me a kind of halfway house between the hills and the plains – good enough and yet not very exhilarating. Kashmir also need not be ruled out although it is far and a little difficult to reach. For my part I would go to Kashmir whenever I have the chance to do so. It is worth the journey.

There is no particular reason why you should confine yourself to one particular place for the summer. Thus you could go to Khali for a while and then to Kashmir. In this matter you should follow your own inclination for, even more than the body, it is the mind that requires food in these mountain resorts. You are to some extent used to being alone, yet it is better not to be alone too much – Feroze, I hope, will be able to accompany you for a while at least. Perhaps he cannot remain with you all the time but he can visit you from time to time. If you can find another suitable companion, that would be desirable. To be alone, especially in the mountains, has its undoubted advantages for a while, if one can tune the mind to this kind of existence. But man, and woman, is after all a social animal and too much solitary living is not good. Cut off from normal contacts, we develop in a lopsided manner and though we may gain depth and inner experience thereby, we miss much that life has to offer. We must not turn our backs to life and pay too much stress on the negative aspects of our existence. The positive side is important. Some kind of a balance has to be struck between them, an equilibrium between the outer and the inner life, so that, when need arises, we can adjust ourselves to either or to a combination of the two. The shaping of our lives is not entirely in our power and circumstances entirely outside our control influence us greatly. Yet we can do much and control, if not the circumstances, at least our reactions to them.

I have had a long enough experience of isolation and, though used to it, can never get over its abnormality. I wonder, often, how lopsided I must have grown. I cannot judge, for no one can be subject and object at the same time. Sometimes I feel that this long-continued abnormal existence has made normality itself somewhat abnormal for me. And so always, wherever I might be, I am likely to be a round peg in a square hole.

But I have drifted to the not very important consideration of what I am or am becoming. What is more important is what you are or should become. I feel that you should not deny yourself company if you can help it. Unsuitable company is of course worse than none. But you have many friends and should be able to gather them occasionally around you. That will be good for you and good for them. We must not allow circumstances to corner us in our lives.

Mridu would probably be a good companion for you in the hills. She seems to have had a succession of operations and must require a restful existence for some time. Even apart from Mridu, there will be many others who will no doubt occur to you. I have a feeling that you live in your ivory castle a little bit more than is necessary or desirable. All of us must occasionally retire into that inner sanctum of our minds for peace and quiet reflection, and thereby gain strength and poise and that calmness of spirit which is unaffected by the storms of the outside world. Yet too much of that ivory castle disables us and lessens that very capacity to face unruffled the ways of the world.

Do not limit your activities and movements with the desire to economise. Economy is good in its way and waste is always bad. But I am no believer in economy becoming a controlling factor in our lives. We must take from life what we can whenever we have the chance to do so, and not hoard for future occasions which may or may not come. Money has to be spent, in a proper way of course, so do not hesitate to draw upon my account at Bachhraj's.

Betty has sent me her little book[1] and I have read it with great interest. It is well-written and there are many moving passages in it. She has obviously taken great pains over it and yet there is a certain spontaneity and simplicity about it which draws me. The canvas is a very limited one – just the family circle – and a film of sentiment covers it. Personally I avoid sentiment, perhaps because I am also just a wee bit sentimental, but it was right that Betty should write as she felt. I wonder how an outsider reading the book feels? I am too much an interested party to be a proper judge. Perhaps the book may strike one as too much of a eulogy of the Nehrus who have nearly all the virtues and hardly any failings. But the average reader in India will put up with much of this kind for he has taken kindly to the Nehrus, and when he feels that way towards anyone, he is not overcritical and will accept all praise.

Some time ago I thought of diverting my reading to French and to ask you to send me a packet of French books from our library. (There are no recent books but a fair number which I got in the late thirties – Romain Rolland, Paul Morand,[2] *Journal d'un homme de quarante ans*,[3] etc, etc.) Then I decided to postpone this diversion till I had finished a number of rather heavy books that I was reading – I now find that this process of reading goes on and on and there is no finishing it! I have been entangled in a heavy tome on Indian philosophy – also Plato – and the Bible! Do not imagine that I am taking to religion in the ordinary sense of the word. I was interested in the Bible because though I had read large chunks of it in the past I had never read it as a whole, and I like its language. Indian philosophy is, I fear, a little beyond me, at any rate its finer shades are beyond me as I am not metaphysical in my thinking – but nevertheless I found it rather fascinating reading. Adventures of the mind and the thought have always a certain fascination, and in our case in India there is an abundance of them. To some extent they help me to understand that very complex and mysterious entity called India.

Do not forget to send me the measurements for a sari – length & width.

Here is a couplet from Zauq:[4]

1. Krishna Hutheesing: *With No Regrets* (Oxford University Press, London, 1944).
2. Paul Morand: French diplomat and writer.
3. *Diary of a Forty-Year-Old Man.*
4. Muhammad Ibrahim Zauq (1789–1854): a well-known Urdu poet of Delhi.

گلہاے رنگ رنگ سے ہے زینتِ چمن

اے ذوق، اس جہاں میں ہے زیب اختلاف سے    (ذوق)

ज़ौक़:     गुल हाए रंग रंग से है ज़ीनत-ए-चमन ।

ऐ ज़ौक़, इस जहान में है ज़ेब इख़्तेलाफ़ से ॥[1]

ज़ीनत=ज़ेब=ख़ुशनुमाई, ख़ूबसूर्ती को उभारना; चमन garden; इख़्तेलाफ़=
difference, variety, opposition.

This is my letter No. 49.

Love,<br>
Your loving,<br>
Papu

---

179.                                    Anand Bhawan,

Allahabad,<br>
18th February, 1944

Darling Papu,

Is it days or weeks or months since I have last written to you? I don't know. I had lost all count of days and dates. I don't really know what came over me. Looking back on it, I can only analyse it as utter utter weariness, so tired that my mind and my body refused to work, so tired that I could not rest, could not sleep, could not eat. One didn't actually feel alive at all. Occasionally somebody would come and talk but I seemed to be so far away. I just couldn't grasp what they were saying. The only thinking I could do was: God, how tired I am! It was as if a terrible blackness or nothingness had stolen over me. I felt almost like Eugene O'Neill's Electra:[2]

> And day is night and night
> Is day again, and I have had no pleasure
> In sun or stars, for all things were to me
> As nothing.

---

1. Zauq:   Flowers of different hues
     do this garden deck and adorn;
   On the riot of colours alone, O Zauq,
     rests the garden's grace!

2. Eugene O'Neill (1888–1953): dramatist. The extract is from *Mourning Becomes Electra* (1931).

And all this due to nothing more serious than sheer physical exhaustion. Only once before have I had a more or less similar experience – our last days in Prague just before I had my first pleurisy.

I am only telling you all this because now it is all over. I have battled through the cloud and am again in the light and fresh air. Only a mild tiredness remains as a gentle reminder, so that since the last two days I am feeling sleepy all the day and I sleep well too! However, this, as I know from experience, is a good sign. So don't worry, please.

This exhaustion was due to several severe strains happening one on top of the other. I am going to have a baby and then all the recent unhappiness at a time when every nerve and emotion was taut to breaking-point. Vatsala & Chhoti Puphi insist that I should go to Purandare [1] in Bombay, for the event, which by the way is due in August or beginning Sept. Purandare says that I must be under his direct supervision from the six month onwards. So the programme is that I should go to Bombay as soon as it gets hot here and then go to some hill station nearby for a couple of months or so. By June I shall be back in Bombay or, if at all possible, in a hut at Juhu. Chhoti Puphi said she would make all arrangements but she has her hands full with Rajabhai's illness and his forthcoming return to Yeravada, so I have sent Feroze to Bombay to see what can be done. He left yesterday and will probably be back on the 24th.

Ballo's wedding has been postponed to May and will take place in Delhi. Bijju Chachi and crowds of other people are here for Savitri Sapru's marriage.

Much love,<br>Indu

180.                                        Ahmadnagar Fort Prison,
                                               22nd February, 1944

Darling Indu,
Another week has gone by without any letter from or news of you. It is just four weeks today from the day when your last letter [2] came. A long interval for one who waits, and I feel a little neglected. Yet I can well understand the many reasons which may have come in the way of your writing – activities, preoccupations, people coming and going, and, above all, the absence of the mood out of which a proper letter grows. That negative absence of mood has often afflicted me when I am outside, and

1. Dr N. A. Purandare: a well-known gynaecologist and obstetrician of Bombay.
2. Refers to letter No. 174.

I have found it difficult then to put pen to paper, except for what might be considered formal or routine work. It is as well not to write till the mind is more in tune and the urge to write reappears, for any attempt to force the pace is likely to result in form without content, a letter just missing that vividness of the touch and personality of the writer, those glimpses and that vitality which words and phrases have the power to convey.

What strange and mysterious things are words! The spoken word is powerful enough but even more so is the written word, for it has more of permanence. Image of thoughts and impulses, of the treasures of memory and stored fancies, the prelude and foundation of action, an idol with clear outlines or shapeless, and yet full of the breath of life! As with so many things to which we grow accustomed – the stars in the heavens, and flowers and green grass, and mountains, and the gentle rippling flow of water, murmuring as it goes – and growing accustomed to them, our senses are dulled to their astonishing beauty, so also with words. But when, in the morning of the world, words and language first burst upon the mind of man, how great must have been the joy of this discovery, with what reverence he must have looked upon this mighty thing, coming to him out of the unknown! Inevitably, he praised the gods he worshipped and called this new power of expression the language of the gods. Carefully he treasured it in his memory and handed it on from generation to generation, and out of that arose the books he called sacred, the scriptures of various lands and religions.

Sacred they were, as every word of power is sacred, as every attempt of man to understand the mystery of life and of his own nature, as the unfolding of his mind and intelligence, as his ceaseless challenge and struggle against the powers and principalities that would ignore him and suppress him. But words have become too common coin today, debased and often counterfeit, fit emblems of many of the human beings who use them.

If I knew that you were well, sound of body and calm of mind, I would not worry, even though your letters delay in coming, or, as was the case a year ago, cannot come at all. But that film of anxiety which covers my mind feeds on lack of news, and I wonder what may have happened to you. Perhaps it is just nothing at all that is significant, perhaps the fault lies partly at least with the censor.

In my last letter [1] I suggested to you that with the coming of the summer months you should think of a visit to the mountains. Apart from the question of your going away from the heat of the plains, I like the idea of your going to new scenes and pleasant places which would

---

1. Refers to letter No. 178.

refresh your mind and tone up your body, which depends so much on the mind. There was a selfish aspect to this also, for, through you, I can almost feel that I am travelling and breathing the invigorating air of the mountains, and meeting new people, and experiencing new sensations. That is something more than a vicarious enjoyment of the changing scene through someone else. I felt that way with Mummie and I feel that way with you.

Latterly I have been developing a mood for some kind of creative writing work. There is an urge to put away books and to write oneself, and there also is a hesitation in beginning. Between the two there is a tussle and, almost as a neutral, I stand by and watch. I do not know how things will shape themselves in my mind, and which feeling will have the mastery. I allow the mood to develop and, as it develops, ideas, words and phrases sometimes shape themselves in my mind, and then sink into the unconscious store of the mind. Perhaps one day the urge will be strong enough to impel me to give written shape to those thoughts . . .

A certain firm of publishers in Poona brought out some years ago a Marathi translation of my *Autobiography*. They have been engaged for some time in getting my *Glimpses of World History* translated into Marathi. They will probably write to you about it. You might, for safety's sake, look up my big memorandum book in which I have noted down particulars about my publications. (I wrote to you about this. It was kept in the iron cupboard which contains my papers.) Make sure that no previous permission has been given to anyone for a Marathi translation of the *Glimpses*. I am myself almost sure of this. You can then inform the publishers that they can go ahead with the work on the same conditions as applied to the Marathi edition of the *Autobiography*. If you cannot find the memorandum book, even so you can give permission. But tell them that the publication of the book should not be delayed and ask them in what form – number of volumes, etc – they are going to bring it out. They can use Horrabin's maps, but possibly, later, they may have to pay some small royalty for this to Horrabin. This won't be much and it will be a lump sum. The name and address of these publishers:

> Raghunath Ganesh Joshi
> Sulakha Rashtriya Granthmala
> 12 Tilak Road
> Poona – 2 . . .

This is my letter No. 50.
Love,

> Your loving,
> Papu

181.

Ahmadnagar Fort Prison,
29th February, 1944
Leap Year's Day

Indu darling,

At last your letter [1] has come and the coming of it has been a relief to
me, for there are few greater burdens than the blackness of silence and
absence of news, which may contain in its dark folds all manner of
strange things. The news that it contained was disturbing and soothing,
an odd mixture of the two, and yet, in the balance, I felt soothed and
comforted. How you must have suffered in mind and body during these
weeks when an utter weariness and listlessness seized hold of you and
life's rhythm seemed to be interrupted. To some extent that is understandable in the circumstances, for a while at least. And yet I wish you
were not quite so sensitive, so vibrant to external and internal stimuli,
for this sensitiveness strains the nerves and makes us feel taut and rigid.
It drains energy and makes us feel more exhausted than even action at
its highest.

Some people are not sensitive at all; thick-skinned and dull of mind
and imagination, they go through life at a low level, accepting what
comes to them without much comment or enquiry, and adapting themselves to changing circumstances. Who would change places with them,
even if that means an avoidance of the pain and sorrow which seem to
be so inseparably connected with life's journey? And yet I suppose there
is a middle way: to be in tune with life, to be sensitive and receptive to
what it offers in a thousand ways, to sense its sorrow and its ecstacy,
and not to be overwhelmed with either. Thus, perhaps, we may attain
a measure of equilibrium, and out of sorrow itself extract peace and
calmness of spirit, and so may achieve a certain victory over ourselves
and over circumstances, whose creatures we otherwise are.

I am glad that you battled against the cloud that enveloped you and
fought your way to light and air. There can be no submission to these
mists and vapours of the mind, which rise up in all of us from time to
time, whenever they find an opening, for submission to them is a denial
and a suppression of the real spirit within us, and without that we
become like empty shells.

Your pregnancy explains to some extent these changes and feelings
in you, for it is a vital time in [a] woman's life, and this mysterious
creation of a new life affects her mind and body in innumerable ways.
Because of this I do not worry myself much. If this had not been so, I
would have been troubled far more greatly. And yet pregnancy is not an

1. Refers to letter No. 179.

abnormal affair, though for each woman it is a novel and strange adventure. This act of creation, full of mystery as it is in human beings as in the simplest plant, is the fulfilment in some ways of a woman's being. She should be at her best during that period, for then perhaps she is more in tune with nature's ways than at any other time.

I am glad you are going to have a baby. There is no reason at all why you or anyone else should be frightened at the prospect. It is true that your lack of robust health is a hindrance and special care is therefore necessary. But I have a feeling, and I have had it long before I heard of this occurrence, that it might actually do you good, even physically, to have a baby. In other ways also it should prove beneficial to you. So accept this fact with pleasurable expectancy and without any trace of fear or apprehension.

But it is right that no risks be taken and every possible care provided for. What you have suggested in your letter seems to me the right course. Purandare is probably the best man in India for this kind of thing and you should put yourself under his charge and carry out his directions. Keep near him and when it is necessary go to some hill station near Bombay. Juhu will be pleasant in the early summer but not so when the rains commence. I hope Feroze has succeeded in making suitable arrangements for you in Bombay. Remember that you must not stint money in this matter. Draw upon my account at Bachhraj's unhesitatingly . . .

I have previously asked you to send me some books from the Anand Bhawan Library. There are two of these I am mentioning again here: Thompson & Garratt's *Rise and Fulfilment of British Rule in India*, and *The Ten Principal Upanishads*, translations by W. B. Yeats & Purohit Swami. Both of them you will find in my room or dressing room.

Also do not forget to send my old yarn which used to be in the drawer of my dressing table.

There is one other book I want but I cannot recollect its name – it is an odd name and is by one Mullick. It was published in England and is the size of an average novel. It used to be on the shelves in my room, near the door to your room.

I have often sent you names of books, mostly new and sometimes old, which I wanted you to purchase for me. But you could not get them at the usual booksellers. You might keep a list of those books with you in case they are now available. In particular I want you to note down the name of a good bookshop in Poona which often keeps books which cannot be obtained elsewhere. This is: The International Book Depot, Deccan Gymkhana, Poona Fort.

You might note the following names of books also which I want when available:

| | | |
|---|---|---|
| 1. Arthur Koestler | : | *Arrival & Departure* (Cape, 7sh. 6d.) |
| 2. – Do – | : | *The Gladiators* (Cape, 7sh. 6d.) |
| 3. H. J. Laski | : | *Reflections on the Revolution of Our Time* (Allen & Unwin, 15sh.) |
| 4. *Talking to India* | : | B.B.C. Broadcasts (Unwin, 7sh. 6d.) |

and Wavell's two books on Allenby.

I have sent you back some numbers of *Life*, etc. This packet also contains Wendell Willkie's *One World*. Perhaps you have seen and read it. It is very well worth reading. Not that there is anything very new in it. But in the context in which it is written and considering the author's background, it is really a remarkable book and I found it exhilarating. This concept of one world hanging together, all inter-linked, is still quite difficult enough for most people, in the East or the West, to grasp, even though they may hold advanced ideas. Even when it is partly grasped intellectually, there is no emotional appreciation of it. Yet I think that this is the basic idea of our present-day world and unless we imbibe it, our other ideas are apt to be airy and without reality. Thinking so, I liked Willkie's book.

I promised to send you Salim Ali's *Book on Indian Birds*. This has been delayed as some people are looking through it. Also because I am trying to make a list of Hindustani names of the birds – not all of course but a goodly number. For this I have to rely entirely on Asaf Ali, whose knowledge of bird-lore is considerable. The book will be sent to you soon and you should find it useful in identifying birds, especially in the hills.

Love to you and Feroze,

Your loving,
Papu

---

182.

c/o Mrs Hutheesing,
Carmichael Road,
Bombay,
24th March, 1944

Darling one,
Am writing with Puphi's pen – and I am afraid, not managing it too well . . .

Puphi must have written to you about Lin Yu-tang. I liked him immensely. He was rather like an Oxford don. That mild scholarly air, quiet and fondling his pipe.

He was just as excited to be in Allahabad, or rather Anand Bhawan, as we were to have him there. Amiya Chakravarty[1] had given him *With No Regrets* in Calcutta and Dr Lin came reading it in the train. When he arrived – Feroze, Rita & I had gone to receive him at the station – I introduced everybody but Dr Lin looked rather blank. Just as we were going up the bridge he suddenly stopped and asked, 'Are you Indira?' 'Yes,' I said. He grinned broadly & held out his hand. 'Now I know who you are,' he said, and we had to shake hands all over again! Something about Puphi's face reminded him of Madame Sun Yat-sen and he kept on muttering – 'Most extraordinary' every few minutes!

The day Dr Lin arrived we had an Indian meal at Anand Bhawan – not a great success as far as the food was concerned. We sat talking until three thirty when Dr Lin went to rest. For tea we all trooped to the Saprus. Ramji Gurtu & Dr Tarachand[2] were also invited. Then Feroze & I returned home and Dr Lin & Puphi went to Mukerji Rd. until dinner which was with the Chinese. Next day in the morning I showed Dr Lin the Library and your room. He also went up to the roof, where we had put the Chinese flag next to our own tricolour. Later I took him over to the hospital for a few moments. Puphi came for lunch. In the afternoon Dr Lin was taken to see Malaviyaji. And later was the tea-party I had given 'to meet' Dr Lin. At night Dr Lin had wanted to go for a moonlight picnic on the river. But it was so cloudy the moon did not appear and as Puphi had a bad cold we cancelled the trip. After dinner Feroze & I drove Dr Lin to the Curzon bridge. By that time the Lady Moon was peeping through the clouds and the river looked very lovely. Dr Lin enjoyed the drive and the moonlight. Early next morning he left for Benares. He wrote to say that he was most impressed with Radhakrishnan[3] although they met for a very short while. Dr Lin wanted to be remembered to you and he sent his very best greetings to you. When we gave him the Hospital Visitors' book, he thought it was the Anand Bhawan book and he wrote something like this: 'What a thrill it is for me to sleep in the room in which Motilal Nehru slept, to see the desk at which Jawaharlal Nehru works and to browse amongst his remarkable collection of books.' I didn't like to tell him that he had

1. Amiya C. Chakravarty: member of the academic faculty at Santiniketan, Secretary to Rabindranath Tagore, 1926–33.
2. Dr Tarachand: historian from Allahabad, also served as Indian Ambassador to Iran.
3. Dr S. Radhakrishnan: philosopher, later President of India, 1962–7.

made a mistake, so for the hospital I gave him a separate sheet of paper on which he wrote: 'To the eternal spirit of the pure Lotus', and he made a sketch of a lotus. Rather beautiful, I thought.

Dr Lin was quite engrossed in his three daughters and terribly thrilled that two of them – aged twenty and seventeen respectively – had written a novel each. He kept on saying 'Do you know anyone of seventeen who has written a novel?' I had to admit that I didn't.

*25th March*

*Naoroz* Mubarak. Puphi and I did not even know it was *Naoroz* today until Mausaji – 'Pyare' – rang me up. He is in Bombay to attend some conference. Did you know that the Maharashtrians also celebrate this day as their New Year. Only they call it something awful – it sounds like 'goody parva' – I'm not sure of the spelling. It is now the year 2001 of the Vikram Era.

By the way none of the books you mention have reached me. And Feroze has written that no parcels have come to Allahabad since my departure.

My address in Matheran will be: Rugby Hotel, Matheran.
Much love,<br>Indu

183.                                                Rugby Hotel,
Matheran,<br>28th March, 1944

Darling Papu,

We came up here yesterday. We got in a local train that stopped at every station. Neral was where we had to change to the Matheran (Hill) Light Railway. This train is the funniest thing – just like a toy. It goes at the rate of five miles an hour at its fastest. The route is rather nice, green woods brightened by the lovely orange blossoms of the flame of the forest and the deep red ones of the coral tree. There were also silk cotton trees and champas. And all along the route the tribes of children ran alongside the running train, offering grubby bunches of these flowers in exchange for a pice or two. The line is full of hairpin bends, but nobody was sick, probably because they could not see the bends & the speed of the train was so slow.

Matheran [1] is very very quiet. I think I am going to like it. The night was cool but in the day it is more or less like Bombay. It is very woody

---

1. A small hill station near Bombay.

and full of shady but rather small trees. Just outside our rooms, a white-whiskered bulbul has its nest. I spotted him almost as soon as I arrived. He has a cheerful song. A grouchy old Englishman told Rajabhai that there are all sorts of lovely birds here, including the paradise fly-catcher. I'm all excited to see him.

Rajabhai has brought his golden retriever, Spark, with him.

Do you remember the *murti*[1] that was lodged in the peepul tree in the Anand Bhawan compound but just opposite the Swaraj Bhawan portico? I had never seen it but Puphi & Bebee remembered having looked at it for years and years. This January, when Rajabhai & Chhoti Puphi came to Allahabad, Rajabhai had the *murti* dug out of the tree and brought it to Bombay. It now reposes on their verandah bookcase . . .

There is only one post from here and it is leaving in five minutes. So I must rush and post this.

Lots of love,

Indu

184.                                                                Rugby Hotel,
                                                                      Matheran,
                                                              3rd April, 1944

Darling Papu,

It's a lovely misty day today. Cool and fresh, everything looks so ethereal – unsubstantial and unreal. I have not seen any new birds and am quite disappointed. Rajabhai & Puphi are now thinking of leaving Matheran earlier, probably round about the 15th or 18th of this month. For a while I was rather worried as to what I would do when we went down. Now I hear from Mrs Vakil that she is going to Mahabaleshwar in May. I shall accompany her. For June & July I have had a big house in Juhu offered to me. The owners are going to Ootacamund until the end of July. By that time the monsoon will have started and Bombay will be cool.

I have brought your big memorandum book, in which you have noted down particulars of your publications, with me. In one of your recent letters[2] you ask me to write to the Sulabha Rashtriya Granthamala, Poona, with regard to the Marathi translation of *Glimpses*. These are the people who brought out the Marathi edition of your *Autobiography*, the translator of which – N. G. Goray[3] – is at present in jail.

I find from the memorandum book that you gave permission to R.

1. Idol.
2. Refers to letter No. 180.
3. N. G. Goray: socialist and author.

D. Shah for the Marathi translation of *Glimpses*. Publishers: Ratnakar Publications, Sangli. This was done on 3.6.41, and the book was to be issued within two months. No further information appears anywhere. I am writing to Ratnakar Publications before getting into touch with the Sulabha Rashtriya Publications.

Some time ago I wrote to you that N. N. Gogoi of the Calcutta University College of Science had asked permission to publish the Assamese translation of *Letters*. This permission has already been granted to someone else in May 1939. I am writing to them also.

Two other letters have come asking for permission. The first from K. Srinivas Kini, Headmaster, Board High School, Mulki, S. Kanara. He wants to reproduce the first chapter of *Letters* in a book of selections for High School pupils. It is not clear from your notes whether we can give him this permission without referring to the Law Journal Press or not. The second letter is from M. Krishna Pillai, Jagathy, Trivandrum. He calls himself a 'Vidwan[1] of Oriental Learning'. He has already translated the *Glimpses* into Malayalam and wants permission to publish it. He has, moreover, made several changes. The book has been divided into chapters without retaining its present form as letters. He has also omitted all 'personal and intimate touches'. The translation has been made from the 1934 edition and will comprise four or five volumes. This sounds rather doubtful to me. Bebee suggested that I should consult Rajaji[2] about all South Indian translations as we do not know any one else in the south. I am accordingly writing to him to see if he can help me to find out more about Mr Pillai and his abilities. According to the book, no Malayalam edition of *Glimpses* exists. The *Autobiography* & the *Letters* were published in Malayalam by Mathrabhumi, Calicut. On second thoughts, is it worthwhile investigating about Mr Pillai? He doesn't sound at all satisfactory. I am not doing anything until I hear from you about both these requests.

Some days ago I sent you two packets of incense sticks. Mridula has chosen them, as also the shells & the file. They are fragrant and keep away mosquitoes. I thought you might like them.

I hear from the Secretariat that the two books, *Mountain Way* & *Journal d'un homme de quarante ans*, were kept back for some reason but have now been forwarded to you.

Lots of love to you,

From your loving,
Indu

---

1. Vidwan: pandit or classical scholar.
2. C. Rajagopalachari: prominent leader of the national movement; was later Governor-General of India, 1948–50, and Chief Minister of Madras, 1952–4.

185.                                    Ahmadnagar Fort Prison,
                                             8th April, 1944

Darling Indu,
I have your letter of the 28th March [1] from Matheran, written soon
after you arrived there. I am glad your first impressions of the place
were favourable. I hope with further acquaintance you will continue to
like the place. Even though the days are warm, the cool nights and the
trees and birds must make a difference. Raja also I hope will improve
in those quiet sylvan surroundings.

A few days ago, on April 2nd, was *Ram Naumi*, the second anniversary
of your marriage. Did you remember it? I thought of you and Feroze
and of all the odd things that had happened since.

I think I wrote to you that I have received most of the things you sent
me in the big parcel – the yarn, cutlery, *pashmina* [2] shawl, etc. But the
various books you sent with this lot have not come yet. Books take their
time as they necessitate apparently a closer scrutiny.

I am glad to say that Fraser's book – *The Mountain Way* – has at last
managed to reach me. Also the first copy of Guehenna's *Journal d'un
homme de quarante ans*. I think I am going to like *The Mountain Way*. I
should like you to write an acknowledgment to Fraser and to tell him
how much I appreciate his gift. His address is: Rev. A. G. Fraser, Dial
House, Chipstead, Surrey, England. He is the Fraser who used to be the
principal of the Achimota College in the Gold Coast, West Africa. I
met him in 1935 or 1936 and ever since then he sends me from time
to time a book, usually of travel or arctic exploration or about the
mountains . . .

Will you tell Betty that instead of giving that very unfortunate picture
of the Brussels Conference in her book if she had given another, it
would have been more suitable. That other was a snapshot of a group
containing six or seven persons, including Ernst Toller, Willie
Munzenburg, [3] Betty & me. There were two or three others but I am
not sure who they were. I had this picture but lost it. Then I saw it
reproduced in one of Toller's later books which he sent me. That book
too seems to have disappeared from our library. It might have been *I
Was a German* though I think it was another one but equally small.
Toller's books ought to be traceable in Bombay and the picture will
interest Betty.

The mention of Willie Munzenburg's name reminds me of his tragic

1. Refers to letter No. 183.
2. A superior variety of woollen cloth made from the hair of a species of Himalayan
goat.
3. Willy Munzenburg: well-known German Communist leader.

end. He managed to escape from Germany by the very skin of his teeth within a few days of Hitler's advent to power in 1933. He was considered a particular *bête noire* by the Nazis and there was a regular hunt for him. He came to Paris and lived there among the German émigrés for a couple of years, probably organising anti-Hitler activities. It was a precarious life, for the French Government of those days did not like this kind of thing. When I was in Paris in January 1936 I was having tea in a café when, to my great surprise, Munzenburg suddenly walked up to me. He had that secretive haunted look so peculiar to those who live more or less in hiding and are engaged in secret work. I saw him again in the same café – he would not come to my hotel. Some months later I heard that he had actually been kidnapped by the Nazis and taken across the border to Germany and shot or otherwise killed.

How many of these dramas and tragedies have taken place, and take place from day to day, under the seemingly unruffled surface of life. Like the ocean which seems so calm and peaceful and innocent and then it opens its cavernous mouth and swallows up a ship, and again resumes its untroubled and innocent air . . .

Love,

Your loving,
Papu

I have just received your letter of April 3rd.[1] The incense sticks have also come. I shall write about *Glimpses*, etc, next week. Let me know definitely about your address for letters.

———————

186.                                            Rugby Hotel,
                                                  Matheran,
                                             9th April, 1944

Darling Papu,
Your letter of the 18th March[2] reached me the day before yesterday – I suppose it was the forwarding from Allahabad which caused the delay.

I have written to *The Hindu* and two letters to Tushar Kanti Ghose[3] – one to Calcutta and the other to Allahabad – so that wherever he is there need not be any delay in making the arrangements about sending you the papers.

1. Refers to letter No. 184.
2. Letter not published.
3. Editor, *Amrita Bazar Patrika* of Calcutta.

Most of the questions you ask have already been answered. As you know, Matheran was Rajabhai's own choice of a hill-station. He has an idea that the heat suits him better than the cold and this surely is the hottest 'hill-station'. Also both Puphi & Rajabhai were keen on being near to Bombay. Puphi, of course, dislikes any life that is dissimilar to the one she leads in Bombay. Rajabhai thinks that he likes the quieter and lovelier spots but after four or five days of quietness he too looks longingly at the advertisements of films running in Bombay! He has had several asthmatic attacks since coming up here . . .

I have no servants with me just now; nobody was necessary as we are staying in a hotel and with the rationing in Bombay any extra person is apt to be rather a burden. Towards the end of August, however, I shall send for someone, probably Hari. Just now Hari is rather busy. Last year in May he married off his son, daughter and a nephew. This year he is having another three marriages, two nephews and a niece. All these nephews & nieces are his brother's children. They all live with him, and as head of the family he feels the responsibility. By August he will be quite free to come. Khaliq, I am afraid, is a complete failure as an indoor servant. He is so clumsy and noisy and has no manners at all. Apparently it isn't possible to teach him either – he is too old to change his habits.

By this time you will have received the *pashmina* shawl. Keep it as long as it is needed and then you can send it to me to Bombay for safekeeping through the hottest months, or whenever the moths are most likely to attack it. Ahmadnagar is, I believe, much warmer than Poona in the summer. When I was with the Vakils I think I passed through once on my way to some other place. In those days Anandbhai was posted in Ahmadnagar and often when he had a holiday he would drive over to my school and take me out. He had a bright red open racing car which I used to love.

I have been reminiscing this evening. During my childhood I seemed to be so much older than other children are at the same age. Harsha is now nine and a half. He is a complete baby and somehow one does not expect him to be otherwise. And yet, I was under ten when I was in Europe. I knew three languages and could roam around the town of Geneva, or London. In boarding school in Bex we had to manage ourselves, and much else besides, completely unaided. Did I not also travel alone from Bex to Paris, where Dadu and all of you were staying just before leaving for London? I'm not sure of this. What an age ago it now seems! And what a strange thing is memory! Some things one remembers for no particular reason, quite unimportant and inconsequential events. Other seemingly more important and bigger events go completely out of one's mind. But to come back to Harsha and Ajit. Rajabhai does not approve of their going to boarding school. He says that Harsha is too sensitive for the knocks of such an institution and that neither of the boys will be happy. Puphi is willing to try out the Gwalior school for one term. And I think that would be a good idea – except that it would take more than just one term to get really into the atmosphere of any school. They must decide definitely before the end of the month so as to inform Mr Pierce in time for next term.

*10th April*

A parcel from you has arrived – it feels like the hanks of yarn. I have not opened it yet. The books have not yet come. Nor have I any news of the other parcels of books you have mentioned in one of your letters. I am writing again to Allahabad to verify this.

Chhoti Puphi was supposed to return to Matheran but she phoned to say that she couldn't come until tomorrow. The other Puphi is leaving for Allahabad on the 11th night.

These last two days Matheran has been very warm in the afternoons – uncomfortably so. Even at night, I did not need any covering until practically morning.

Much love to you,

Indu

---

187.
Rugby Hotel,
Matheran,
13th April, 1944

Darling Papu,

I have opened the parcel. It contained two lots of yarn – have you kept the other ones that I sent? The books you mentioned, the *pashmina* shawl and the woollen cardigan have also come.

We are definitely leaving Matheran on the 18th. It is just as well, for none of us relishes the idea of being next-door neighbour to Reginald Maxwell [1] – *The Times* says he is coming here for the season. Mrs Vakil went up to Panchgani for a couple of days to see what she could get in the way of accommodation in either Panchgani or Mahabaleshwar. I hear that she has managed to get a 'small place' in Mahabalashwar. So we shall probably leave Bombay on the 21st or 22nd. I do not yet know the Mahabaleshwar address so you had better send your letter to Sakina Mansion. It will be forwarded on.

1. Reginald Maitland Maxwell: he was Home Member of the Governor-General's Executive Council, 1938–44, and Adviser to the Secretary of State for India, 1944–7.

I have a long letter from Bebee. It would have been most unusual if she were quite all right. Just now she has had a bad attack of laryngitis, preceded by influenza. So she is in bed and, for the last nineteen days, has been absolutely dumb – what a predicament for any woman! She has recently met Cecil Beaton, the famous English photographer who has probably photographed more beautiful women than most of us have seen. Bebee writes that they had no time to discuss women, beautiful or otherwise, for Cecil Beaton was full of his visit to Assam and the wonderful birds and flowers he had seen there.

The Naidus also saw quite a lot of Beverley Nichols [1] when he was in Hyderabad. Nichols was attracted to their house, chiefly by Princess Numa Thai, the Siamese cat. He adores cats. Numa, like most cats, has always disliked strangers and visitors but from the minute she saw Nichols she was all over him. The two of them would romp on the floor, purring with sheer happiness!

As a child I used to dislike cats but as time goes on I like them more and more. I like them for their grace and also for their aloofness.

*14th April*

Your letter dated April 8th [2] came yesterday afternoon. As I have mentioned above, your parcel has arrived intact except for the old cushion cover! The hanks of yarn came tied with string and wrapped in brown paper. The shawl came in its original tissue paper.

I am glad you liked the shells. Unfortunately the prettiest ones could not be sent as they seemed to be much more fragile. It is true the shells were not strictly necessary, although anything that gives pleasure is, in a way, a necessity especially in jail. And so often the most beautiful things in the world have no special purpose or use.

Apart from getting better acquainted with the quaint and rather lovely red-whiskered bulbul, my bird-watching has been most unsuccessful. One day I had a glimpse of what might be either the blue rock-thrush or the Malabar whistling-thrush – the former is more likely. Then there are the calls of the green barbet. That is the whole extent of my adventures with the birds of Matheran!

I gave your message about the Brussels photograph to Chhoti Puphi. She says that the edition of *I Was a German* that she possesses has no photographs. The first edition of *With No Regrets* has sold out and I do not know when the second edition will be out – nothing has been done about it so far.

No replies have yet come to any of the letters I wrote to the various

1. Beverley Nichols: British writer.
2. Refers to letter No. 185.

publishers with regard to your books. I see from the 'Accounts' book that the Sulabha Rashtriya Granthamala (Marathi edition of the *Autobiography* and presumably also of *Glimpses*) has never so far replied to any letter asking for information. Something should be done about all these firms that do not reply to letters and sit tight on royalties. Shall I consult anybody about the matter?

Rev. Fraser has sent you along with the book a cartoon from the *New York Herald Tribune*. It got mixed up in my file of 'answered letters', hence the delay in sending it on to you. I was going to write thanking Rev. Fraser but did not have the address. I am doing so now. The cartoon is enclosed in this letter.

How is your weight these days? I hope you are keeping track of it and not letting it go down further.

Very much love,

Indu

---

188.                                   Ahmadnagar Fort Prison,
                                             15th April, 1944

Darling Indu,

The last week has brought quite an unusual number of letters from you. I mentioned one in a footnote to my last letter. This was dated 3rd April.[1] This was followed by a previous letter of yours dated 31st March,[2] and then came two more, dated 6th[3] and 9th April.[4] Quite a feast.

The packet of books you sent long ago, containing a number of French ones, has not yet come, though there is a rumour that it is on the way. It seems to me that French is not a language with which the Bombay Secretariat is conversant, and hence the delay in passing these books.

Your letters have produced a slight confusion in my mind about your programme – Matheran, Juhu, Mahabaleshwar seem all mixed up together. How long you stay at Matheran, where you go from there is all vague and uncertain. You write that Raja and Betty, tired of the seclusion and quiet of Matheran, were thinking of going back to Bombay. Presumably you stayed on. Not that it matters much whether I know your exact programme or not, except that I want to address my letters correctly. I do not want them to go astray.

1. Refers to letter No. 184.
2. Letter not published.
3. Letter not published.
4. Refers to letter No. 186.

Ahmadnagar is climatically not at all a bad place. Probably it is a cross between Poona and Matheran, though there is a lack of trees and foliage here, at any rate where we are kept. It is not as cold as I would like it to be in winter. The summer is not very hot and the rains are Poona-like, gentle showers as a rule. It is very dry and some people have trouble with their skin because of this dryness . . .

It was rather foolish of me to write at length offering my advice about Harsha's & Ajit's education. But I have an inveterate habit of giving advice. I wish I could cure myself of it. My own conceptions of men and things are not the usual ones and so my advice seldom fits in.

In your childhood I suppose you were a little more self-reliant than children of your age in India. The credit for that should at least partly go to your parents. I remember when you started going to the Ecole International in Geneva. You were about eight and a half years old then. I accompanied you to school, came back, went again to fetch you for lunch, again took you to school, came back, & finally went at four to bring you back. I seemed to spend the whole day in moving backwards & forwards between our pension and your school. After a few days I decided to let you go by yourself. It was a slightly tricky journey as it involved a change of trams. I spoke to the tram conductor, who had come to recognise you and who promised to look after you. I do not think Mummie was overpleased at this arrangement. However it worked. The tram journey was really more complicated than a railway journey. Later we moved to our flat in the Boulevard des Tranches. From there you used to walk to your school, which was about a quarter of a mile away.

I do not think you travelled all by yourself from Bex to Paris. As far as I can remember, I went to Bex from Berlin direct to fetch you, leaving Mummie & Chhoti Puphi in Berlin. They travelled by themselves subsequently to Paris. Dadu had gone previously. But I am rather vague about all this. Anyway you did travel by yourself by train in Switzerland . . .

This is my letter No. 57.

Love,

Your loving,
Papu

189.

c/o Mrs Hutheesing,
20 Carmichael Road,
Bombay,
18th April, 1944

Darling Papu,

We came down from Matheran a day earlier than we had meant to do – that is, yesterday. The train was crowded and late. We had to get off at Byculla, no coolies available. It was the most tiring journey I have had for some time. We left our hotel at two p.m. and reached Sakina Mansion at nine – seven long hours, which is perfectly ridiculous when you consider that Matheran is about sixteen miles from Bombay as the crow flies – forty miles by train.

Apart from the heat and the journey there was the worry about Bapu and the state of Bombay. We had got the very meagre news of Bapu's illness on the radio on Sunday night. Bombay's explosions[1] we heard and felt in Matheran. Only we did not know what it was. I was lying in bed reading just before tea when our building shook and all the windows rattled. I thought it was an earthquake and jotted down the time nine minutes past four p.m. by my watch. This was followed by distant rumbling which was repeated several times. Rajabhai had felt the shake too – so had the others actually, only they said it couldn't be anything as serious as an earthquake. The radio gave us news of the explosion. The next morning there was no mail, no newspaper. We were expecting a friend but the train did not turn up for quite some time. When it did come, there was one man from Bombay who spread the wildest rumours about the state of things. I don't think the censors will allow me to tell you more about things than has appeared in the papers – so I shall not attempt to do so. But the papers give very little inkling of the amount of work this tragedy has necessitated (does such a word exist or am I inventing it?). Great as is all the relief work of supplying shelter and clothes, food and medicine, how much greater and more difficult will be the problem of rehabilitating these thousands. Where will they live and what will they do – they have lost their jobs and many are from fairly well-off middle-class families. Very few will be able to retrieve any belongings from the ruins of their houses, shops or godowns.

Since early this morning I have been trying to get into touch with people and organisations who are doing relief work. Mridu was in Ahmedabad when all this occurred and has only just got back, so she is not in contact with people either. Finally I tracked down Hansaben

1. A fire broke out in a ship in the Bombay harbour on 14th April, 1944, and caused two explosions in which 500 people were killed and 2000 injured.

Mehta[1] who is in charge of the Women's Conference's relief work. I am meeting her this afternoon.

*20th April*

Writing a letter in Bombay is always a difficult job, but these days it has become almost an impossibility.

On the 18th I went to see the working of the A.I.W.C.'s [All India Women's Conference] relief office and then went around with Hansaben to one or two other places, ending up with Urmila Mehta[2] who is in charge of clothing. Naturally I offered my services for the few days I shall be in Bombay, though it is not possible for me to do any rushing about. I helped Urmilaben a little but apparently this was enough to gain me a large volunteer's badge! Anyway I was quite tired so we, Puphi & I, came home at about seven o'clock after a peep at the New Book Company where I got a couple of books for you.

On the 19th, next day, we had an appointment with Nagindas Master, the Mayor, who took us with him on another tour of relief centres. Mridu was with us. Rajabhai was not feeling very well so he didn't come. I brought Mridu home with me after this for a short while. At ten thirty I had to go again to help Urmilaben. We came home for lunch at one thirty. The whole afternoon I had to see various people.

At night I went to my first entertainment for months & months. It was a dance-drama 'Kovalan' got up by Mrinalini (now Mrs Vikram Sarabhai)[3] and Budi (Nandita Kripalani). Ira Vakil[4] also took part. Do you remember we met Mrinalini in Santiniketan on your last visit to Gurudev? It was, of course, long before her marriage. The whole Sarabhai clan came to Bombay for the first night. This evening they will leave for Kashmir. All of them are going except Vikram & Mrinalini. This South-Indian drama was originally being done for Malabar relief but since the Bombay tragedy, they decided to divide the proceeds between Bombay and Malabar.

I quite liked the show, perhaps more so because it is so long since I have been to any kind of show. And then I knew most of the performers and a large number of the audience. And it was good to meet old friends. Mrinalini is just a little too thin to be really graceful. Nandita was very

---

1. Hansaben Mehta: social and political worker; participated in the struggle for freedom; founder Vice-Chancellor, M.S. University of Baroda, 1949–58; member, Constituent Assembly, 1947–50.
2. Urmila Mehta: social worker.
3. Mrinalini Sarabhai: well-known dancer, married to Vikram Sarabhai, an eminent scientist and Chairman of the Atomic Energy Commission.
4. Ira Vakil: daughter of the Vakils.

good. Krishna Kripalani [1] is also in Bombay. Everybody asked after you and sent their love.

Did you get a book called *A Week with Gandhi*? It was sent along with some books that Puphi sent you from Bombay.

Did you send the *Book of Indian Birds* all by itself or were there other books with it?

The export of fruit from Bombay is not allowed now, so some of us made enquiries whether fruit could be sent to you from a local Ahmadnagar shop. I believe this permission has been granted, so the necessary arrangements will soon be made.

My departure to Mahabaleshwar has been slightly postponed – we are now leaving on the evening of the 23rd. We shall spend the night in Poona and take the morning bus on the 24th. The address in Mahabaleshwar is: c/o Treacher & Co., Chemists, Mahabaleshwar. Perhaps you had better add c/o Mrs J. J. Vakil after my name.

This morning as I got up I saw a *dhayal* or magpie robin. What an elegant little bird this is! I get quite excited when I add another bird to the list of the ones I have seen and been able to identify.

I hope you are getting the *Patrika* and the *Hindu* direct now.

Re. Marathi edition of *Glimpses*. R. D. Shah, the translator, who seems to be also the publisher, has written a long letter. He writes that the first part of the book was published on 1st August, 1941. He says he sent some copies to you, but that he received no reply to his letter or acknowledgement of the books. Soon afterwards Shah was arrested under D.I.R. [2] and his press was kept under police custody. Whilst he was in jail, his publishing house, containing all his publications, including 750 copies of the Marathi *Glimpses* was set on fire & reduced to ashes! Shah has just been released and has got his press back, although he is not allowed to use it. He writes that he is getting the book printed at Kolhapur. Of the copies originally printed only 250 were sent for sale – the rest were burnt up.

What does one do in such circumstances? I am trying first of all to check on Shah's story to find out if it is correct or not. To begin with, Shah must have been arrested in 1942 – so that still gives him one whole year. People here are saying that the Ratnaker Publications are most unreliable. Do you want me to try and get you out of these muddles? Naturally I shall not do anything without asking you first. But if I could get some kind of an authority from you it would help considerably.

1. Krishna Kripalani: scholar and writer from Santiniketan. Later became Secretary of the Sahitya Akademi (National Literary Academy).

2. During the course of the Second World War, the British Government adopted a series of rules conferring supra-judicial powers on the executive. These were known as the Defence of India Rules (D.I.R.).

Earlier in this letter I have mentioned something about sending you fruit. The name of a certain person, Motilal Firodia, has been sent to Government for approval. If they approve of him the procedure will be as follows. He will send you fruit from time to time. But if in between you want more fruit or other foodstuffs your 'Commander', or whoever is in charge, can order it for you locally, through Syt. Motilal Firodia, c/o Firodia Advocate, Ahmadnagar. Syt. Firodia will send me monthly bills. Mridula knows him and has had a talk with him on my behalf. He often comes to Bombay so I hope to see him myself soon. I am also writing to him.

I am sending the following books to you:

1. *The Story of Confucius*
2. *Mother Russia*
3. *The Loom of Language*
4. *A Book of Russian Verse*
5. *Poetry in War Time*
6. *King Oedipus* (Modern Version)
7. *Poems by Tagore*

I am leaving these books with Puphi who says she will have them sent to the Secretariat by hand. Other books may also be added.

Much love,

Indu

---

190.                                        Ahmadnagar Fort Prison,
                                              22nd April, 1944

Darling Indu,

I have your letter of April 13th.[1] Probably you are in Mahabaleshwar now but this letter is being sent to Sakina Mansion. Mahabaleshwar ought to be much cooler than Matheran. Here the temperature has gone up to 107°F and I realised that my comparison of Ahmadnagar with Poona was not quite correct.

All the books you sent, including the French ones, have now arrived, except one: *Warning to the West.* I suppose this is by Shridharani. Probably it has been kept back as not suitable for my morals . . .

Yesterday, as a particular favour, I suppose, I was given a brief note addressed to me by Bijju Chacha – but only after due enquiry about our relationship. The note contained the information that Ballo was

---

1. Refers to letter No. 187.

being married at Delhi on May 1st. He asked me, if it was possible, to send my blessings by telegram. This would not only be greatly appreciated but be of 'great spiritual value'. I do not know what spiritual value my good wishes might possess but certainly Ballo and his bride will have them in good measure. I do not propose to attempt to send a telegram as this cannot be done from here. At the most the 'telegram' is sent by post to the Bombay Secretariat and then, if it is passed and the stars and omens are favourable, and there is no obvious reason or rule why it should not be kept back, it might be forwarded by telegram. This is far too complicated and doubtful a process. But on receipt of this letter you might send a telegram to Ballo to Delhi, conveying my love and blessing to him and his bride.

Also write a letter to Bijju Chacha. Tell him I am happy to know of Ballo's marriage. Indeed I sent my good wishes, you will remember, some months ago when I thought that the wedding would come off in February. It is many years since I saw Ballo – five and a half to be accurate. That was when he came to our flat in St James's Street in London in 1938. He was big and well-built then. I am told that he has grown since then and is a fine specimen of a young man now. I heard of his return from England in an odd way. [1] On my way to Kulu two years ago I spent a couple of days in Delhi, staying with Ratan and Rajan. One morning, without previous notice, a motor bicycle rolled in and a very youthful and tall English officer tramped in and enquired for me. He was shown in and in a typical haw-haw manner he informed me that he had just flown over from England, that he was a product of Harrow, and that he had been commissioned by Lady Willingdon to convey her love to me! This tender and thoughtful message came as a surprise. Further, he told me that a young relative of mine had been his companion during the air journey. From his description I gathered that this was Ballo.

Tell Bijju Chacha also that I am continuing my *āsanas*, though sometimes I leave them off either because the mood does not fit in or, more usually, because some slight sprain or something similar gives a backache – nothing much but enough to stop the *āsanas* for some days.

Inform him also that Asaf Ali sends his love and good wishes to Ballo . . .

Love,

Your loving,<br>Papu

---

1. See also letter No. 80.

191.                                        Mahabaleshwar,
                                            7th May, 1944

Darling Papu,
This is a very brief note written in great haste. Yesterday's paper came
late last night & gave us news of Bapu's release.[1] Mr Vakil, Feroze &
I are leaving in a few moments for Poona.

  This is just to send my love & to tell you that I am well. Don't worry
if there is a delay or a gap in letters.

  Much love,

                        Indu

_____

192.                                        'Parnakuti',
                                            Poona,
                                            8th May, 1944

Darling Papu,
I dashed off a brief note[2] to you yesterday morning. Almost immediately
afterwards, we took the bus to Poona reaching here at three thirty p.m.
We had started off worried and anxious and not knowing whether we
should even be allowed to see him. I found a whole crowd here – Chhoti
Puphi & Rajabhai with the two boys, Psyche, Bebee & Mrs Naidu, and
a host of others including Mr & Mrs Munshi.[3] Apasaheb[4] and his
wife came with Martand[5] who now works in Aundh. Soon Puphi arrived from Allahabad. Quite like the old-time gatherings – so, of course,
we all missed you very much. Perhaps most of all Bapu. He asked so
many questions about you and sent his love.

  When I arrived he was sitting spinning and gave me a big grin and
the usual whack – only much much milder. He was looking very pale
and weak and tired. Contrary to doctors' orders he saw quite a lot of
visitors and consequently felt very tired. I hope the doctors are going to
be stricter in future. Since this morning they are making an effort, and
Bapu has at last promised to cooperate. Dr Gilder[6] said that all the

  1. Mahatma Gandhi had been imprisoned in the Aga Khan Palace in Poona and
was released on 6th May, 1944.
  2. Refers to letter No. 191.
  3. K. M. Munshi and his wife Lilavati Munshi: both were active in the struggle for
freedom; later became members of Parliament. K. M. Munshi held ministerial office in
the Government of Bombay and then in the Government of India.
  4. Apasaheb Pant: ruler of Aundh and later a diplomat.
  5. Martand Upadhyaya: connected with the Sasta Sahitya Mandal, New Delhi;
author of several books in Hindi for children.
  6. Dr M. D. D. Gilder: heart specialist who attended upon Mahatma Gandhi.

excitement had weakened him considerably. Fortunately today was the *maun*[1] day. Bapu was X-rayed and examined this afternoon and it has been decided that he should go to Juhu very soon.

Sushila[2] has cut her hair and wears *salwars*. She is looking so different I hardly recognised her – very pretty and ridiculously young, about sixteen!

Last evening we paid a visit to the Aga Khan's palace to pay our homage to the place where Ba[3] and Mahadevbhai[4] were burnt.[5] We took flowers and Sushila sang some *slokas*[6] and the usual prayer that Bapu was in the habit of doing every day.

What a hideous building is the Aga Khan's palace! I am told that the inside of the rooms occupied by Bapu and his party looked much nicer because all or most of the furniture had been removed. Bapu said: 'I should like to send him a message but it will not be allowed so what is the use!'

Chhoti Puphi left for Bombay early this morning. I am going early tomorrow morning. Puphi & Mrs Naidu will leave for Bombay on Wednesday. Bapu will probably stay in Bombay for some time so I hope to meet him again on my return from Mahabaleshwar.

Everybody, including Nandita & Krishna Kripalani, Raihana Tyabji,[7] Psyche and her sister Perin, send their love.

Much love to you,

　　　　　　　　　　　　　Indu

---

193.　　　　　　　　　　　　　Ahmadnagar Fort Prison,
　　　　　　　　　　　　　　　　13th May, 1944

Darling Indu,

I do not quite know where to write to you, for your last brief letter of

1. Silence.
2. Sushila Nayar: medical doctor and a close associate of Mahatma Gandhi; Union Minister of Health (1962–7).
3. Kasturba Gandhi: wife of Mahatma Gandhi who was active in social work. She was affectionately called Ba (mother) by the people.
4. Mahadev Desai: a close associate of Mahatma Gandhi who also served as his private secretary from 1917 till his death in 1942.
5. Refers to the cremation of Mahadev Desai and Kasturba Gandhi who were incarcerated, along with Mahatma Gandhi, in the Aga Khan Palace in Poona after the Quit India movement. Mahadev Desai died on 15th August, 1942 and Kasturba Gandhi died on 22nd February, 1944. Both were cremated in the grounds of the Aga Khan Palace.
6. Hymns of praise.
7. Raihana Tyabji: granddaughter of Badr-ud-din Tyabji (see Circle of Friends), and an associate of Mahatma Gandhi.

May 7th informed me that you were going to Poona to see Bapu. Yet, I suppose, you must have gone back to Mahabaleshwar and so my letter goes there. You have an advantage over me. You know always where to address your letters to me. I am not one of those flighty, unstable, restless individuals who move about frequently. I am a fixture – in Ahmadnagar Fort!

Bapu's release and his illness have naturally upset the still and rather stagnant waters of Indian life and there is a stir and an excitement and a going to and fro. Yet I wish our people would restrain their desire for *darshan*, [1] etc. We are a terribly inconsiderate people where illness is concerned – or, rather, 'inconsiderate' is not the right word. We overwhelm the person who is ill with too much consideration. I think one of Bapu's chief troubles has been this and he is seldom allowed privacy or rest. Crowds gather and gape and gaze at him, imagining that they are not interfering in any way. The worst offenders are those whom he encourages himself by his affection and personal interest. He has built up such a vast family and given a bit of himself to so many that each one of them considers it a right and duty to hover round him.

Normally I would not worry about his health, for he has considerable powers of recuperation. But it is his age that troubles me. He is nearly seventy-five, a good age for India, an age which I certainly do not expect to reach. For some years past I have noticed the obvious effects of advancing age on his physical frame. What the last twenty-one months have done to him I do not know, but I can make a guess. I hope, therefore, that he will be strong enough to take absolute rest till he is fully recovered and that others will help him to do so . . .

Love,

Your loving,
Papu

194.                                                    Mahabaleshwar,
                                                    19th May, 1944

Darling Papu,
Your letter of May 13 [2] arrived yesterday. I have written your message to Puphi. I have also written to all your publishers and am now awaiting their replies. I shall write to Walsh before the week is over.

I saw in the papers that Dr Bhandari's daughter Kamini has become

1. *Darshan* (seeing), the act of viewing a sacred person or object.
2. Refers to letter No. 193.

Sorensen's[1] secretary. Have you met either of the girls? There are two of them. They only come to stay with their father during their school holidays. The rest of the time they were with the mother who lived in Brighton or some such place.

Puphi is in Juhu in 'Gandhi Gram'[2] sharing a shack with Mrs Naidu and Bebee. This she found rather uncomfortable, so Bapu has made arrangements for her in Birla's House. As soon as Rita and Anna (who have been sent for) arrive, Puphi will move into her new quarters.

Here is Bebee's description of the place:

Nan & Mother and I have been sharing a shack a few yards away from Bapu's ... Nan has been doing some strenuous walking but I can only stroll about the sands. Unfortunately the evening crowds for *darshan* are growing every day and instead of dispersing after the prayers they are apt to linger about in the hope of having another glimpse of Bapu when he goes for his walk. Bapu is in some ways better than when you saw him. And yet his condition is far from satisfactory. The doctors are struggling to make him take some form of drugs but he is adamant and they are afraid they may not be able to control the anaemia. But it is surprising how much energy he seems to have in spite of everything.

Bebee's throat has been troublesome again. She writes that she may have to come to Bombay in two or three months to have her septic tonsils out.

Bebee says that after a week at Juhu her brain 'is at its worst' and the only suggestions she can make for the christening of Chand Bibi's offspring are:

1) Sher Shah (spelled Chere chat)
2) Popocatapetl (Popocat for short)

They are both rather idiotic, as she herself admits. She has promised to think out more names. But why not enlist Maulana's aid and have a nice Persian name?

Much love,

Indu

---

1. Lord Reginald William Sorensen: British Labour MP, Chairman, India League, and member of the parliamentary delegation to India, 1946.
2. Gandhi Gram: the residence of Sumatiben Morarjee in the suburb of Juhu in Bombay. Gandhiji often stayed with Sumatiben when in Bombay.

195.                                          Mahabaleshwar,
                                             26th May, 1944

Darling Papu,
Your letter of the 20th May[1] arrived the day before yesterday. I have
written to Walsh and am writing to Bachhraj.

The only reason I asked for the books to be sent to me was that that
is the only way to keep track of them. However now you had better hang
on to them and send them to Bombay when I go there.

I may stay on in Poona until the end of June. It will be better than
Bombay. I can stay with Nurie, if she is back from Panchgani by then,
or Sir Govind Madgavkar.[2] I should prefer Nurie's house as I have
stayed before and know her so much better.

Jivraj is here. I have met him several times. He is much better now
but still gets out of breath very quickly and looks rather pale. He cannot
walk long distances. His release is a great relief to me. He is the only
doctor in India who knows my case from the beginning and I have
perfect confidence in him. He knows Purandare well and will, therefore,
be able to deal with him more satisfactorily than all of us put together.

Jivraj says Juhu will be better than Bombay even in the monsoon, as
the air is always fresher and there are more opportunities for long walks.
Of course living in a shack is out of the question. One must stay in a
house and walk on *pucca* roads.[3]

I am writing to Ladli Bhai about Khaliq and the other servants' pay
lists. Khaliq's daughter is a bright girl. I see her from time to time. I
shall write to Khaliq direct about her.

Upadhyaya is still in. Why, nobody quite knows. I doubt if the persons
responsible know either.

I have not had news of Madan Bhai. Feroze could not get an interview.

The quietness of our stay in Mahabaleshwar has been interrupted as
friends are gradually discovering that I am here. This last week has
been, comparatively speaking, quite hectic. Apart from Jivraj and Hansaben there are quite a few people I know. Sir Govind Madgavkar was
here with his daughter Usha. He left yesterday. He was staying quite
close to our place and I saw a good deal of him. He gave me a long
lecture on the folly of not making a will at the age of twenty-one. He
was especially astounded that both Pupha and you, being lawyers, had
yet neglected making wills.

Another person who is taking a lot of trouble over us is Homi

1. Letter not published.
2. Sir Govind Dinanath Madgavkar: a retired judge of Bombay High Court.
3. Tarred roads.

Captain [1] – one of the brothers of Mac. He is here with his eldest son who is eighteen and a fine lad. Homi is taking me down to Panchgani on Saturday to have tea with Nurie.

I have collected from Chhoti Puphi all the books on children and babies that she possessed and have brought them here. I am rather awed by the responsibility of bringing a new person into the world and of having complete control over his life. Mistakes, which seem small enough to grown-ups, might have a lifelong influence. It is so difficult to know, since there is so little we remember of our own earliest years. I am more concerned that the new individual should be a happy one than almost anything else. There is so much unhappiness in the world and so few happy individuals. One unhappy person tends to make another unhappy, unconsciously, of course. I have here Ethel Mannin's, *Commonsense and the Child* and A. S. Neill's, *The Problem Child*. [2] Their argument is that the only way to 'bring up' a child is to leave it alone. Neill runs a school on these lines – a free school, he calls it, in Suffolk. He claims to have cured all sorts of 'difficult' children merely by allowing them to get rid of their repressions. The way Neill writes makes this method sound the only possible way to deal with children. And yet, the parent is not the only person with whom the child will come into contact. How can one reconcile a 'free' atmosphere at home with the usual orthodox school? Neill says that the child, if not forced to learn and have various subjects rammed down its throat, may start learning later but will learn faster and with more lasting benefit. He says the child must not have any kind of discipline thrust on it. Let it be dirty, if it so wills – let it stay up until it is tired enough to go to sleep, provided always that the child's wishes of the moment do not seriously affect your work or rest or sleep. Whatever method one means to follow must start from the beginning, from baby's earliest months.

One has heard and read so many jokes about the club bore but I had never actually met one. We do not go to clubs and the like but Mr Vakil has a friend, a man who has taken a degree at Harvard and has travelled in America and Europe. Can he talk, as the Americans would say! It is really quite wonderful to watch. This morning he came at about nine. He has been talking, believe it or not, all the time without pausing enough for anyone to say as much as yes or no. It is now one o'clock. This performance is repeated every time he comes. I have long since decided to give up all pretence of listening. I just go on with whatever I happen to be doing.

1. Homi Captain: brother-in-law of Psyche (Goshiben Captain).
2. A. S. Neill (1883–1973): founder of Summerhill School, he advocated liberal ideas in education. The novelist Ethel Mannin's book, *Commonsense and the Child*, was influenced by Neill's ideas.

Now about your publications:

1. Mr Chitnis, [1] who wants to bring out a book of your 'articles & utterances', writes as follows: The publishers are Nirmal Prakasan of Kolhapur. They have agreed to pay 10 per cent royalty on the sale price of the book. The amount will be sent to you as soon as the book is ready for sale. I have selected the following articles for the first volume. (1) Prison-land. (2) The Mind of a Judge. (3) India and the World. (4) The Last Letter to Indira. (5) The Question of Languages. (6) A Road-Side Interlude. (7) Students & Politics. (8) In a Train. (9) The Unity of India. (10) What of Us? (11) The Constituent Assembly. (12) A note to Members of the National Planning Committee. And portions from the forewords to *China Builds for Democracy* and *Frontier Speaks*.

Mr Chitnis says he contributes articles to the Marathi papers and has recently translated Minoo Masani's [2] 'Why this Starvation?' He says this translation 'was highly praised by each and every Marathi paper that reviewed it'. Also 'I shall not in the least mar the charm of Jawaharlalji's lucid style'!

2. The Mathribhum Printing and Publishing Co. of Calicut, who brought out the Malayalam edition of the *Autobiography*, have written to say that the first edition (1000 copies) is nearly sold out. They now wish to bring out a Malayalam edition of *Glimpses*.

3. Wide India Co. were given permission to bring out the Assamese edition of *Letters*. I wrote to them but have not received any reply. Now Narendra Nath Gogoi is asking for this same permission. He writes that to the 'best of his knowledge the Assamese translation has not yet been printed'. How can I find out if his translation is a good one? Gogoi's translation is already completed.

I have today sent you the *Reader's Digest* for March 1944.

Lots of love, Papu darling,

Your loving,<br>Indu

---

196.                                        Ahmadnagar Fort Prison,
                                            27th May, 1944

Darling Indu,

I have your letter of May 19th [3] – your 63rd.

The newspapers tell us that Mahabaleshwar has run short of food

1. S. L. Chitnis translated into Marathi Jawaharlal Nehru's *Glimpses of World History*.
2. Minoo R. Masani: socialist leader who adopted a liberal stance in post-1947 politics.
3. Refers to letter No. 194.

and army lorries had to be requisitioned to rush foodstuffs there. I hope you were not starved. That is not likely to happen, for Mahabaleshwar is not just any place in India but a spot where the elect go and their needs are always catered for.

It has been hot here and amazingly dry. I suppose the rains will begin soon and even before the regular monsoon starts, the winds change and are cooler. It is really surprising how dry this place can get. I thought that Allahabad and the north were dry enough with the hot *loo* blowing. But apparently there is something in the air here which beats Allahabad in this respect. This dryness affects the skin and produces an uncomfortable feeling. I did not know what this was due to. Others also complained and they said it was dryness. They took to oil massage but I dislike messing about with oils. So now I sleep with a pot of Vaseline next to me and if I feel 'dried up' in the course of the night I apply some of this stuff on my arms and legs. This gives relief. I suppose the rains will end this dryness of the air.

I do not think I ever met Dr Bhandari's girls, though he spoke to me about them and showed me their photographs. He was very fond of them.

I have received a number of books from Karaka[1] – his own productions mostly. One of them is a play, *Colour Bar*, by two Oxford men – presumably one of them being Karaka himself. It is not a very bright play.

I have been reading little lately and all the good books you have sent me repose in the bookshelf, which is over-full now. For the last six weeks I have spent a good deal of time in writing. I am beginning to tire of this and perhaps one of these days I shall put my pen and paper away and seek relief in reading. I am not very satisfied with what I have written. Yet, even though it may not be up to much, it is a useful discipline for the mind. It forces one to think precisely and to express oneself clearly. Indeed there is sometimes an element of surprise in seeing one's thought put on an attire of words and phrases and appear in black and white. Normally one thinks vaguely and the thought is all rounded up with no sharp ends; it fades off with wishes and odd fits of knowledge. In the old days education both in India and in Europe included a study of logic so that the student may know how to think and reason clearly. In Europe this was Aristotle's logic; India had and has her own system of *Nyaya*, which is still taught in the Sanskrit schools and colleges. Both these are out-of-date and far too formal in their approach. They tend to make the mind scholastic and rather rigid, and yet they served a useful purpose and did give a training to the mind. It

1. D. F. Karaka: a Bombay journalist.

is surprising how untrained most people's minds are now, even the minds of otherwise well-educated people. We cannot go back to Aristotle or *Nyaya* but the modern substitute is a scientific training, and especially practical work in science.

I remember, in my school days, there used to be a great argument in England, as elsewhere, of the relative value and importance of a classical and a scientific training. People used to grow quite excited and heated over it, each party or group emphasising the value of its own wares. I suppose science has now won all along the line and the classics are just tolerated. That is right in a way and it was inevitable. We simply can't do without science and the old rigid methods of classical education isolated a person from the world of today. And yet science by itself is pretty dry and the scientist is not always the most lovable of men. He lacks something, the poise and calm outlook on life which the classics often gave. Compare H. G. Wells[1] with Gilbert Murray.[2] Well, I suppose, we must combine the two somehow . . .

We have been here now for twenty-one months and three weeks. That reminds me that this is already my longest term. Previously no single term has exceeded twenty-one months – the sentence was usually two years but with remissions, etc, this worked out at about twenty-one months, or a little less. It is true that more than once two terms have often followed one another with only a brief gap in between – but there was a gap, and even a few days makes a difference. And then, previously, there used to be interviews and some kind of personal touch was kept up. Not so this time. So far as you are concerned, I did not see you for nearly two years in 1939–41. But that was not because I was in prison. You were in London, Leysin, etc, while I was in India, mostly out of prison, partly in Dehra Dun Jail.

How people must have changed, I often think, during these past twenty-one months or more. How you must have changed. When we meet, as I suppose we will some time or other, I shall be feeling about with the tentacles of my mind, trying to find what is new, what is old in you. So also with others. When we meet people frequently we do not notice the change for we are continually adapting ourselves to it. But after a long interval changes are more apparent. Children grow up amazingly and are hardly recognisable; boys and girls become men and women.

It is not merely the lapse of time that counts; it is what we have lived through that makes a difference. Recent years have been very abnormal

1. H. G. Wells (1866–1946): writer and novelist. His advocacy of the application of scientific method exercised a deep influence.

2. Gilbert Murray (1866–1957): classical scholar and distinguished interpreter of Greek ideas.

and each one of us has a particular stock of experience and a store of feelings and impressions, each one of which has made some little difference. And so strangers creep in where friends used to be.

I am very glad that Raja is definitely out.[1] Not that it made much difference whether he was in or out but this middle stage is upsetting, especially for a nervous person like Raja. He can now devote himself to improving his health, and that, from all accounts requires a great deal of attention. I understand that the children – Harsha and Ajit – are going to Gwalior after all.

Have you given my yarn to Psyche to get it woven?

Betty wrote to me that old Mrs Guzdar[2] of Allahabad died recently after a long illness. The news made me think how cut off we get from people we do not meet. I had not met her for a long time – did she come to your wedding? – and I had vaguely come to the conclusion that she had died. She was a good, kindly sort and I am sorry. Will you write a few lines to Nadir conveying my condolences?

G. D. Birla[3] has sent me a book written partly by him. It is in Hindi – *Rupaya ki Kahani*.[4]

Love,

Your loving,<br>Papu

This is my 63rd letter to you.

---

197.
Ahmadnagar Fort Prison,<br>3rd June, 1944

Darling Indu,

I have received your letter of May 26[5] – the 64th.

I am glad you have decided to go to Poona instead of Bombay from Mahabaleshwar. I suppose my next letter should be sent to Poona but I shall await your instructions in this matter. In Poona you will be comfortable enough either with Nurie or Sir Govind Madgaonkar (I am

---

1. Raja Hutheesing was also imprisoned in connection with the Quit India movement. He was released from jail towards the end of 1943 on account of ill-health, for a short period, and was required to go back to jail after he had recovered from his illness. But in May 1944 orders for his final release were issued.

2. Mrs Guzdar: wife of Nadir Guzdar, proprietor of the Raja Ram Motilal Guzdar & Co. in Allahabad and a close friend of the Nehru family.

3. G. D. Birla: industrialist.

4. *The Story of a Rupee*.

5. Refers to letter No. 195.

not sure if I have spelt his name correctly). Perhaps you will feel easier with Nurie because you know her well. Madgaonkar's house is a well-appointed one and he is a methodical person. Sarojini, who stayed with him, told me that the radio was functioning most of the time. Madgaonkar is a very decent person, though a bit censorious of others. I suppose that comes with age, especially when one lives a retired life and has nothing definite to do. Doesn't he talk a little like the 'Poonah' kind of Britisher? I do not remember having met his daughter Usha.

Jivraj's release is comforting and now you can have the satisfaction of knowing that he is at hand and can be consulted when necessary. He is a very competent and sound doctor.

I suppose it is right and inevitable that you should read books on babies and children. And yet there is always a possibility of overdoing this kind of thing – or rather of being so overburdened with advice that one's natural common sense hardly functions and one lives on edge, trying always to remember what to do next according to the directions. I remember Betty & Raja mugging up such books together and referring to them for advice at every time. This very attitude of doubt and hesitation with a tinge of excitement somehow affects the child sometimes in the wrong way, for children, like animals, are peculiarly susceptible to psychological states. The books you have been reading and which you mention are good in their own way and give a lot of sound advice. But it is as well to remember that many experts do not wholly agree with them and in fact there has been a tendency to turn away from this method of treating children. Probably it is a good method for the 'difficult' and 'problem' child, but many children are not, to begin with, problem children at all and in their case this treatment may not be wholly suitable. It may result in a normal child developing problem traits. There is a well-known school at Dartington Hall in Devon or Cornwall run on these lines and I heard rather curious stories about the children there. One father was quite worried about his son there, a lad of ten or so.

Problem and suchlike children have, I suppose, always existed but undoubtedly they are peculiarly common in our present age, especially in Europe and America. They are the products of this age of transition where everything is changing so rapidly that it is difficult to have any standards of values to judge by. Also the small families which are so usual today – one child or two – result in problem children. A larger family, several children, has disadvantages but from the child's point of view it is usually better and he has a more normal life with companions growing up with him. To some extent, but not wholly (except perhaps in a socialist country like Russia), school and a communal life can take the place of family life.

A child has to be treated as an individual and given every opportunity to grow as an individual. But it is at least equally important to treat him as a social being who can live at peace and cooperation with others. That makes one think of the kind of society he will have to live in – a difficult business today when society itself is changing. In any event the cooperative habits and traits have to be developed or else he will find it difficult to fit in anywhere. Usually single children, who have been looked after a great deal, have a hard time when they go out into the world and have to fend for themselves. Bertrand Russell says somewhere that parents are wholly unsuited to bring up their children; they are too intensely interested in them to take a dispassionate view or to treat them normally.

You say you want the child to be happy – of course. But then what is happiness? There is the solid content of a fairly prosperous peasant; there are higher grades of intellectual and emotional happiness. There is the happiness of the person who is drunk or who is under the influence of some drug. I suppose, if you analyse your mind, you will find that happiness is more often negative than positive – an absence of pain & suffering. And yet how is one to be happy if he knows and sees another in pain? A sensitive person will suffer continually on behalf of others. An insensitive person may escape that but at the cost of much that is fine in life. Long ago (probably 140 years ago) Leopardi, the Italian poet, [1] wrote to his sister on the occasion of her marriage: 'Thou shall have children, either cowards or unhappy; choose thou the latter.' That is perhaps an extreme view but there is some truth in it.

Ultimately we cannot be really happy till the whole world is happy and that is a large order. Mere avoidance of unhappiness, not easily possible, may itself result in isolation and boredom and a malaise which is worse than definite unhappiness. We are so organically connected with others & with the world that we cannot both live a full life and yet avoid the world's ills. Escapism does not pay in the long run, quite apart from its moral worth.

What then is one to do? That is a big question which has been asked almost since human beings began to think. It seems to me that the only thing to aim at is the power or capacity to extract happiness, or perhaps it is better to call it peace and calm, out of unhappiness itself. Not to escape from anything but to face it and yet be above it in a way; not to be overcome by it and to retain in spite of everything a sense of life and its larger purposes, a feeling of life fulfilment. How to do that is a difficult enough job and each person has to learn for himself and it

---

1. Giacoma Leopardi (1798–1837): author of many lyrics, some patriotic, and a prose work, *Little Moral Works*.

seems that only life, with all its waywardness and shock, can teach. The most we can do is to prepare the background for it.

Read your books by all means but do not attach too much importance to everything they contain. A story of Li-Po the great Chinese poet comes to my mind. A young man, desiring to become a poet, went to Li-Po and asked him how he was to train himself for the purpose; 'Master, how can I become a poet.' Li-Po said: 'Read all the rules and books and then forget them and observing nature put your feeling in words.' You mention Ethel Mannin's book.[1] She is a likeable person and I am sure what she says has sense in it. But it struck me suddenly – has she any children? I do not know but somehow I doubt it.

There is a passage in one of Gilbert Murray's books which might interest you. He says that we must be 'careful always to seek for truth and not for our own emotional satisfaction, careful not to neglect the real needs of men and women through basing our life on dreams; and remembering above all to walk gently in a world when the lights are dim and the very stars wander' . . .

Love,

Your loving,
Papu

This is my letter No. 64.

198.                                          Dunlavin Lodge,
                                                Shivaji Nagar,
                                              19th June, 1944

Darling Papu,
Your letter of June 10th[2] came yesterday. I have not heard from Jivraj yet, so shall stay on here until the end of the month. Even when I go to Bombay I do not know where I shall stay. Several suggestions have been made but until I see what each place is like during the monsoon I cannot decide. You had better continue to write to my Poona address until I let you know when I am leaving.

I have had no news of Anandbhai since I saw him last – in the first week of January – in Lucknow. He was feeling rather disgruntled in those days and had applied for long leave. I do not know if the leave was granted or whether he is still in Lucknow . . .

No news from Krishna Menon.

1. *Commonsense and the Child*, see letter No. 195.
2. Letter not published.

Nani is in Lahore with Mamu. She writes that she is much better now. Her address: c/o C. B. Koul, Imperial Bank of India, Lahore.

Bapu is here. He sent for us yesterday and we were with him for quite a while. He is looking so much better than when I saw him last, but still gets tired fairly quickly. He wants to have Oomra Hall for his stay in Panchgani. But Nurie doesn't think it will be very convenient for him. She, and others, have suggested various houses . . .

I was rather amused at your picture of me, rushing to consult a book every time the child was naughty! Rajabhai & Puphi do rather go to extremes sometimes. They discuss something and for a while it is 'the thing', then the enthusiasm wanes and it's completely forgotten. I do realise that the training of the child depends entirely on its individuality and personality, as well as its environment. But it is a help to know how other people tackle the various problems and difficulties that are bound to arise, and to know how other children have reacted to different kinds of treatment.

Ethel Mannin is a great admirer of Neill's, and sent her only daughter to his school. This daughter, Jean, must have been about eleven when Ethel wrote *Commonsense and the Child*.

You are right, my statement about happiness was rather vague. And when I started thinking about it, I got more and more confused. However, what I actually meant in my letter was not happiness in the widest sense of the word.[1] I only meant the carefree happy-go-lucky joy that is full of wonder at the mystery of the world – only a few children have it and for only a few short years. But in India it is very rare indeed. You see children dressed in unwieldy grown-up clothes with solemn faces, like little old men and women. It is hardly their parents' fault – the conditions of life are so difficult, there is a lack of all social amenities. But I do feel that for a few years at least the child should have the world as his kingdom. All too soon will come the realisation of the poverty and ugliness, of the many chains by which we are bound: social and economic and political, of the struggle that is life. But it is good to know that in the midst of all this there is much beauty.

Happiness is not content or satisfaction. I do not believe the insensitive can ever be truly happy. I feel that the ability to feel happiness is dependent on the ability to feel sorrow. And only those who have felt deep sorrow can feel deep happiness. Both sensations, at their most intense, are sharp and fleeting. One cannot stay at the climax long. Sheer happiness may turn into joy or delight, or at worst, content. Sorrow gets dulled into melancholy. Each is a passing emotion, but it leaves us the richer for having experienced it. Lin Yu-tang quotes a

1. See letters Nos 195 and 197.

seventeenth-century Chinese describing some happy moments – in each case it is an ordinary everyday occurrence – for instance: 'To cut with a sharp knife a bright green water-melon on a big scarlet plate of a summer afternoon. Ah, is this not happiness?'

Much love,<br>
Indu

199.

Dunlavin Lodge,<br>
Shivaji Nagar,<br>
Poona<br>
21st June, 1944

Darling Papu,

Your letter of the 17th[1] came yesterday . . .

Some time ago you asked to send *Mathematics for the Millions* to Dr Mahmud's son. I had previously written to Hamidah but had not received any reply. So before sending the book, I wrote to her brother that you wanted to give him this book and that I would send it to him after hearing from him as I was not sure whether letters were reaching them. No reply has come. So the book has not been sent. I did not want it to go astray. Now I shall send a registered-acknowledgement-due letter. But could you ask Dr Mahmud to tell his family to get into touch with me. If they find any difficulty with English, they can write in Urdu. I shall get the letter read by someone.

Krishna Kripalani and his wife are at Dinshaw Mehta's[2] clinic. Krishna has been ill for the past year and has been trying all sorts of treatments. He has been with Dinshaw for a couple of months but doesn't think that it is doing him much good. He is leaving today for Bombay. The day before yesterday, Nurie was going visiting, so I asked to be dropped at the clinic. I had no intention of disturbing Bapu but to just ask about him and to meet Krishna and other friends. But at five o'clock, Nandita had been asked to sing for Bapu, while he was spinning – so I went in too and sat for about ten minutes whilst she sang. It was Bapu's silence day so he just gave me one of his characteristic grins . . .

Puphi must have sent you Eve Curie's[3] book. I was trying to get hold of it, without success. Puphi had a copy of her own. I hear it is not a very good book. Shridharani's *Warning to the West* has been returned to me.

1. Letter not published.
2. Dinshaw Mehta: a nature cure specialist.
3. Eve Curie: daughter and biographer of Marie Curie, the distinguished scientist. She had visited India in the course of her travels.

That is the big disadvantage of not living in Bombay – one always misses the new books. These days so few copies come through that they are almost invariably picked up before being put out for sale. And the booksellers don't even bother to keep them aside, or post them, even if you have repeatedly asked them to do so.

Here is a quotation about books, from Anatole France. [1]

What is a book? A series of little printed signs – essentially only that. It is for the reader to supply himself the forms and colours and sentiments to which these signs correspond. It will depend on him whether the book be dull or brilliant, hot with passion or cold as ice. Or if you prefer to put it otherwise, each word in a book is a magic finger that sets a fibre of our brain vibrating like a harp string and so evokes a note from the sounding-board of our soul. No matter how skilful, how inspired the artist's hand, the sound it makes depends on the quality of the strings within themselves.

The parcel of periodicals has come. Do the *Time*, etc, come to you direct from America, or are they sent by someone in India? I am asking because none of these American periodicals has come to the Anand Bhawan address, except a copy of the *Reader's Digest*.

It is not at all necessary for either Mami or Masi to come for my confinement. They dislike leaving their children and their home even for a short while. To come to Bombay will mean a long and uncomfortable train journey and needless expense. Then where will they stay in Bombay? As I shall be in hospital they cannot be with me for any length of time. I have tried to explain all this to Masi. Evidently she has not conveyed the message to Nani. I am writing to Nani.

Puphi has arrived in Poona. She is staying only until the 24th. She writes that she will be with Bapu every evening, so I shall meet her there. It is rather difficult for us to go to Koregaon Park, where Madgavkar lives, because of the lack of petrol.

Much love,
Indu

---

1. Anatole France (1844–1924): French novelist, noted as a free-thinker, socialist and satirist.

200.                                          Dunlavin Lodge,
                                              Shivaji Nagar,
                                              Poona
                                              22nd June, 1944

Darling Papu,
It isn't only the 'artistic temperament' that lets things drift! I wrote to
you that when Jivraj left for Bombay, he had promised to write to me
and to let me know as soon as possible about his talk with Purandare,
and when Purandare would be able to examine me. Well, I waited and
waited. Yesterday by the merest chance Nurie and I went to the clinic
because Nurie wanted to read out to Bapu a letter she had received
from Horace Alexander. We found Jivraj there on the point of leaving
– this was in the evening and early this morning he was due to leave for
Panchgani. Then I was told that Puphi and Jivraj had gone to see
Purandare together, Purandare told them that he was leaving for Nasik
and would not be back until the end of July – when I had seen him, he
had especially told me that he wished to examine me at the end of June
– but that as the seventh-month examination was important, I should
get it done by his son, who is also a doctor. With regard to the confinement, he said that he could not promise a room – he did not 'book'
rooms in his hospital – but if everything was full up I could stay in what
he calls his 'drawing room'. This is an upstairs room with no bathroom
attached. When Puphi asked whether he would himself conduct the
confinement he said, 'Well, if I am not there, there is always my son'!
You see how vague everything is. I am afraid I got rather upset. I don't
like the idea of having everything so indefinite and uncertain up till the
last moment and having taken so much trouble to stay here, around
Bombay, for all these months just for Purandare's sake, I don't want to
get shunted on to his son. Then there is the expense. The whole thing
– that is the ten days in hospital – is going to cost Rs. 1000/- or more
and it's a bit thick if after spending so much I can't even have ordinary
comfort. When I told Jivraj that I did not want to be examined by
Purandare's son, he said then I would have to wait until the end of July.
Also before getting an appointment I must write to Jivraj, who is going
to be in Panchgani, to fix up the appointment with Purandare and let
me know – that, apparently, is the only way to get a fool-proof appointment. So if for some reason I should need help or advice, I just cannot
get hold of Purandare! Rather a strange state of affairs, isn't it? As I am
keeping so well – in fact everybody says I am looking better than ever
before – I thought I might as well save myself all this expense and go
home and get good old Maggie for the case. But Puphi says no.
    However, I am going to Bombay with Puphi on the 24th morning. I

shall stay only for a couple of days or so. I shall meet Purandare's son and see the hospital & the 'drawing room'. Also other hospitals. (I have also some other odd jobs.) And in those couple of days I must decide definitely.

Rajabhai is at Dinshaw's. He is going to be with Bapu for some time, with a fortnight's break from the 2nd to the 20th July. He and Chhoti Puphi will be taking the children up to Gwalior on the 8th or so. On their way back they will go to Delhi. Rajabhai has brought some books to be sent to you. Do you want them or shall I keep them?

1. *Mathematical Recreations* (sent by Pan)
2. *More Pocket Cartoons* by Osbert Lancaster
3. *New China* by Nym Wales

There are also some periodicals which I am sending to you.

Aryanayakam [1] has thought of a most wonderful – from his description – nurse & midwife who has spent some time with Gurudev & Pratimadi [2] and whom you have also met. He says she will be delighted to come to be with me during my confinement and after. Let us see if she materialises.

Much love,<br>Indu

P.S.
Puphi rang up to say that she thought I should now leave Purandare for Shirodkar [3] – I shall see how the land lies when I get to Bombay.

———————————

201.                       Ahmadnagar Fort Prison,
1st July, 1944

Darling Indu,
I have your letters dated 21st and 22nd June [4] – Nos. 69 & 70. It is extraordinary how casual people are. Jivraj is a methodical and careful person who can be relied upon to do a job he has undertaken. And yet even he seems to have suffered from a lapse. As for Purandare I hardly expected any kind of smartness from him. He is good at his work but his looks and ways of dealing with his patients give little comfort. I hope

1. E. W. Aryanayakam, of Sri Lanka, was Secretary to Rabindranath Tagore for some time and later an associate of Mahatma Gandhi.
2. Pratima Devi: daughter-in-law of Rabindranath Tagore.
3. Dr V. N. Shirodkar: a well-known obstetrician and gynaecologist of Bombay.
4. Refers to letters Nos 199 and 200.

that you have fixed up everything during your visit to Bombay. I do not know Shirodkar – never heard of him. That of course is not against him, for my knowledge and experience of the world of doctors and surgeons is strictly limited. Obviously in a city like Bombay there must be many competent gynaecologists. Purandare is good and experienced but he is not the only one. The main thing to do is to fix up definitely with someone and have the assurance that you can refer to him whenever necessary.

It certainly will not be right for you to return to Allahabad for the confinement. Not that I think badly of the facilities available in Allahabad. But obviously Bombay offers many additional facilities and it is safer to be near these. You have already spent some months round about there and it is worthwhile continuing for another two months or so. There is really nothing to worry about. Your present health is excellent and this is the basic factor. For the rest, one should take every precaution during these months and not worry. It is Purandare's casualness that must be irritating. If something definite is fixed up then you simply carry on normally and almost forget about doctors. During the seventh month some extra care is usually called for. Do not worry about the extra expense. Often that saves trouble and expense later.

I was amused to learn that Raja had entrusted himself to Bapu's care and treatment. I am not particularly enamoured of his methods of treatment and yet there is much in them, especially for an asthmatic case like Raja's. I am firmly convinced that one's health depends on one's way of living, food, exercise, mental occupations, etc, far more than on medicine, though medicine is certainly useful occasionally. Bombay flat life is far removed from any natural life – it is cut off from nature, fresh air and exercise & there is a tendency to lounge about. But then, as you say, Raja is so used to this existence in a Bombay flat that he feels bored elsewhere. The change ought to do him good if he can stand it.

I should like to have news of Rafi Ahmed and Raghunandan Saran. Both have been ill for a long time. Could you ask Feroze to find out?

Mahmud's son, Said, has been unwell for some time and some lung trouble is suspected. He has recently gone to Bhowali, though whether he will stay there or not for any length of time I do not know. I can understand Hamidah not answering your letter for she must feel shy about writing in English. As a matter of fact she can write rather broken and incorrect English. Said has been eager to get Hogben's book – *Mathematics for the Millions* – and ever since he has heard that I am having it sent to him, he has repeatedly enquired about it. I am therefore surprised at his not answering your letter. Perhaps there was some delay in the letter reaching him. I think you might send the book to him to the Chapra address, that is if it is convenient for you. If the book is lying about somewhere in Allahabad and you cannot easily reach it, then do not trouble yourself over it. Better give a full address: Said-ur-Rahman, Dr Syed Mahmud's house, Haque Manzil, Chapra, B.N.W. Ry. – Bihar.

It will be a good thing if you can get that very wonderful nurse and midwife whom Aryanayakam recommends. He is a fairly good judge.

I have glanced through Eve Curie's book – read about fifty pages at the beginning and the chapter about her visit to Anand Bhawan. I rather liked it and am going to carry on with it. It is of course just good reporting but that reporting is done well. She writes smoothly and has the knack of observing little things which help to make a picture vivid. Being a reporter's account the book is likely to date. Perhaps I like the book because I rather liked her and then she has so many nice things to say about me! The personal touch counts.

I am surprised at your asking me how I get my foreign periodicals. I was under the impression that they were all sent to Anand Bhawan and then forwarded, via the Bombay Secretariat, to me. I cannot tell how they come as they reach me without their covers. Once a *Reader's Digest* arrived with a cover and I was a little surprised to notice that it was addressed to me, c/o Home Department, Government of Bombay. I wondered how the *Reader's Digest* people got hold of this address. Probably, I thought, Walsh had given it. Walsh has fixed up with all these American periodicals on my behalf. That is convenient for me as he can pay the subscriptions out of my royalties, if he has any. It is possible that he has given the Bombay Govt's address to all of them. I am getting quite a number, though many numbers are missing, and I do not get them in proper order. I have been getting *Life, Time, Foreign Affairs, Pacific Affairs, Asia* (odd numbers), *Reader's Digest, Nation, New Republic, Amerasia*. There are also other odd papers which come to me without my having subscribed to them – such as *The Jewish Frontier*. I have never read so many American periodicals more or less regularly before, because I could not afford the time.

Does Feroze get *Fortune* and do you get another copy of *Asia*?

The three books you mention – one sent by Pan for me – might be forwarded to me.

I have been reading in the English papers references to the books of L. H. Myers who died recently. Two of his books are especially commended. These are novels dealing with Akbar's time in India. That is an interesting period and I should like to read these books. Probably you will not be able to get them – they were published originally round about 1940 & 1941. However I am giving these names for you to note them:

L. H. Myers:          *The Root and the Flowers*
  – Do –:          *The Pool of Vishnu*

Bombay has no doubt larger and better bookshops than other places but Poona has a place – The International Book Depot, or some such name – which often keeps books not available elsewhere.

I think you are right in not encouraging Rupa[1] or Bappi to come for your confinement. That would mean trouble for them and no advantage to you.

We have had some rain again after a long gap.

Love,

Your loving,
Papu

This is my letter No. 68.

———————————————

202.                              Ahmadnagar Fort Prison,
                                        8th July, 1944

Darling Indu,

I have had no letter from you since I wrote last,[2] but that was almost expected as you had gone to Bombay. I hope everything was fixed up satisfactorily there.

Tomorrow is a kind of special day for us here. We complete one hundred weeks – 700 days – and incidentally twenty-three months. It so happens that is Sunday also, the day we arrived here. These round figures somehow fix special and red-letter days, although they have no particular importance, for every day is more or less alike.

We have a little rain occasionally, not much, but enough to keep us cool. There has been a lack of rain this season. I hope this does not apply to other parts of the country, for bad crops would mean a terrible addition to starvation and misery.

There are some books which I want to return but they are not likely to interest you – for instance Mullick's book on philosophy. Instead of sending them to you it would be better if they were sent direct to Anand Bhawan. Who shall I address them to? Feroze or Ladli Bhai?

Puphi has sent me photographs of Chand and Tara and Betty has sent pictures of Harsha and Ajit. They are all good.

1. Rup Koul: wife of Indira Gandhi's uncle Chand Bahadur Koul.
2. Refers to letter No. 201.

This letter is a brief one for a change, and for this relief you will no doubt feel grateful. It is my No. 69.

Love,

From your loving,
Papu

---

203.

[c/o Mrs Hutheesing,]
20 Carmichael Road,
Bombay,
9th July, 1944

Darling Papu,

Again I have been slack in writing to you and two letters[1] have come from you. However both the Puphis have written to you so I hope you have not been anxious . . .

I am going to Poona for a week tomorrow morning. The doctor wants to see me every fifteen days – three times more – so I have to be back on the 19th.

Rajabhai, Puphi and the boys left for Gwalior yesterday afternoon. Parents are not allowed to stay for more than three days, so on the 12th they will go to Delhi. They are expected back on the 18th. The boys will get twenty days' holidays in October, which they will spend in Bombay and another ten days for Christmas for which they might come to Allahabad as it is so much closer than Bombay.

Anandbhai is still in Lucknow and still very disgruntled. He had a son in May. They have called him Arun and he is the image of Anandbhai. Thank you about Anna. I am writing to her. She is in Bangalore . . .

I think I wrote to you in my last letter[2] how well Rajabhai was looking when I saw him at the clinic. Soon after that he started running a temperature and by the time he came to Bombay he was his old thin self again complaining of all sorts of aches and pains. I believe he has written to Bapu that he will not come to Panchgani as the climate will not suit him.

I shall be in Poona – Dunlavin Lodge, Shivaji Nagar, P.O. Poona-5 – until the 19th July.

This is my 71st letter. Your last letter was No. 68.

Much love,

Indu

---

1. Refers to letters Nos 201 and 202.
2. Refers to letter No. 200.

204.

Dunlavin Lodge,
Shivaji Nagar,
Poona,
15th July, 1944

Darling Papu,

Your very brief letter of the 8th July,[1] No. 69 came a few days ago. It is certainly not a relief to have a short letter – you know how I love your letters and look forward to them, especially now when that is the only means of contact.

Poona is perfectly delightful. I am glad I came for even this short period. The monsoon has come a little late but now there is plenty of rain. I do not know what it is like up North. How about Ahmadnagar?

On Thursday the 13th – a taxi drove up and out came Bul. It was so unexpected – we were just thinking of collecting various articles that she had asked for. Bul is always so smartly dressed. Nobody could have guessed that she was coming from two years of jail instead of getting off the fashionable Deccan Queen![2] In jail she used to dress in smart and well-cut shorts or slacks most of the time. She was looking very well and chirpy and brown. She wanted to rush off to Panchgani immediately but it was too late for the bus so she left early next morning. She sent you her love and what she calls her usual message – 'keep cool'.

You must have read in the papers about Amarnath Jha's[3] visit to Bombay. He came from Delhi and brought with him some tins of China tea, which were sent or brought from China for you and were with Rajan Didda. I am sending one tin. I am also sending some books:

1. *New China*
2. *More Pocket Cartoons*
3. *And One Did Not Come Back*
4. *Interglossa*
5. *Mathematical Recreations*
6. *Beatrice the Ballerina*

Chhoti Puphi wrote from Gwalior that the boys seemed to be happy and had already made friends. Puphi and Rajabhai will be returning from Delhi on the 17th. I shall go to Bombay on the 19th.

Here is a poem of Walter de la Mare that I rather liked:

---

1. Refers to letter No. 202.
2. Deccan Queen: well-known express train which ran between Bombay and Poona.
3. Amarnath Jha: eminent educationist, who was Vice-Chancellor of Allahabad University.

## Alone

I sit alone,
And clear thoughts move in me,
Pictures, now near, now far,
Of transient fantasy
Happy I am, at peace
In my own company.

Yet life is a dread thing too.
Dark with horror and fear.
Beauty's fingers grow cold,
Sad cries I hear.
Death with a stony gaze
Is ever near.

Lost in myself I hide
From the cold unknown:
Lost, like a world cast forth
Into space star-sown:
And the songs of the morning are stilled,
And delight in them flown.

So even the tender and dear
Like phantoms through memory stray –
Creations of sweet desire,
That faith can alone bid stay,
Cast off the cloak of the real
And vanish away.

Only love can redeem
This truth, that delight,
Bring morning to blossom again
Out of plague-ridden night,
Restore to the lost the found,
To the blinded, sight.

Mridu and the Sarabhais are back from Kashmir. Sheikh Saheb sent his *salaams* to you and the Maulana especially, and greetings to the others. Mridu stayed a day at the Sarans[1] in Delhi. Raghunandan Bhai has been ill for a long time – dysentery and all sorts of internal disorders.

1. Raghunandan Saran and his wife Raksha Saran: see Circle of Friends.

He is a little better now but still far from well. Mridu herself is looking pretty ghastly. She had an appendicitis operation at the beginning of the year. Now adhesions are forming.

Aryanayakam's daughter was very ill with bronchitis so he had to rush down to Sevagram. I had a letter from Barbara Hartland, the nurse Aryanayakam had suggested. But now that Shirodkar is providing his own nurse for ten days and after that there will be Anna, it seemed unfair to send for Miss Hartland as well. She is doing good and useful work – she is in charge of a children's home run by the Friends' Ambulance Unit in Contai, Midnapore. I should feel ashamed if she had to leave her work and come all this way just because of me.

How is your garden doing? . . .

This is my letter No. 72.

Much love,

                         Indu

---

205.                              Ahmadnagar Fort Prison,
                                      15th July, 1944

Darling Indu,

Yesterday I received your letter No. 71 of the 9th July from Bombay. [1]
I hope this letter of mine will reach you in Poona before you leave for Bombay again on the 19th.

Yes, I had news of you from the Puphis. I am glad you have fixed up with Shirodkar. As a matter of fact I had come to the conclusion some time ago that Purandare was not satisfactory – not because of the lack of competence, for he knows his job, but because of his sloppiness and casualness. I dislike this kind of thing greatly. Perhaps also he is too old to be smart. I did not write this to you as I did not want to interfere with arrangements already made. Now that you have made new arrangements with Shirodkar I feel much more at ease. It is not clear from your letter whether you propose to return to Poona after each visit to Shirodkar.

I wrote to Puphi (the elder one) day before yesterday and, would you believe it? I dated my letter 20th July instead of the 13th. And this after consulting the calendar! I remembered that it was Thursday and just skipped a week. This shows how one loses the sense of time in prison. A mistake of a day is frequent enough and normal, but a whole week is very unusual. It can only mean either absorption in work or an approach to dotage.

---

1. Refers to letter No. 203.

Another instance. I apply oil rarely to my head – usually about once a fortnight. The other day, in an attempt to do so, I put on a fair quantity of undiluted Dettol to the head! It was only after a little while that I discovered something was wrong. Again, later I reversed the process and put some oil in a tumbler of water for the purpose of gargling! Pretty bad, isn't it? Though not quite as bad as it looks, for I keep the two in very small unlabelled phials and a mistake is possible. Still, I was put out by this succession of lapses. I remembered reading in an American magazine recently about a chaplain who began to forget little things he had to do. He could not remember the number of the prescribed hymn in chapel; he forgot some engagements. Thinking that he might be suffering from overstrain, he consulted his doctor. There was apparently nothing wrong. However the investigation proceeded, various X-ray photographs were taken, and a faint shadow or some other indication was noticed in the region of the brain. It was decided to operate and the beginnings of a small tumour were removed. He recovered rapidly and got back his memory; there were no further lapses.

All this does not mean that I am suffering from a softening of the brain or any other ailment. I think my mind and brain are in very good condition, and as for my body it is as fit as it has ever been. I continue my exercises & especially the *āsanas* and breathing ones. I am convinced that, short of accidents and deep mental shock, physical health can be maintained by anyone who cares to do so and has some sense and knowledge of the body.

Some days ago I received three bottles of Mahabaleshwar honey either from you or from Betty. It looks good and is rather swanky as each bottle bears the name of a different flower – rose, *akara*, *pangla*. What is the *akara* and the *pangla*? I do not know them. But I had a shock when I noticed the price marked on one of the bottles. This is Rs. 7/4 and the bottle is a small one, not containing more than 1¼ lb. It is scandalous paying so much for honey, especially in these days. Please do not send any more at this or like price. Tell Betty also. Anyway this honey will last us a long time as we use it with all due care and reverence.

I am sorry Raja had a relapse. This combination of asthma and other ailments is very troublesome. A course of treatment that may do good to one of them, may at the same time be injurious to the other. The only thing to do is build up bodily resistance. Even that is made difficult by repeated attacks of asthma.

Love,

Your loving,<br>Papu

This is my letter No. 70.

206.                                              Dunlavin Lodge,
                                                  Shivajinagar,
                                                  Poona,
                                                  19th July, 1944

Darling Papu,

Your letter of July 15th [1] – No. 70 – has just arrived. This afternoon I am leaving for Bombay and will now stay on there. There is no point in journeying back and forth all the time – the trains are crowded and uncomfortable. Though I should have liked to stay on in Poona – it is so pleasant. In Bombay the very air is stale and heavy and one feels so cramped and shut-in in the compact flats. I long to sit under the open sky and see some little bit of greenery. Perhaps it may be more agreeable in Juhu, although during the rains Juhu can be very dismal and dreary.

Darling, I was amused at your worrying about growing old so soon. Isn't it funny how when one is very young, anybody just a few years older seems to be very old? There is rather a delightful story I remember coming across in a moth-eaten book some years ago. Two little chaps are discussing the age of a third, and the one reflectively remarks: 'Well, I don't 'zactly know how old Charlie is; but he must be very old, for he blows his own nose.' The author makes some such comment as – happy and far distant days, when such an accomplishment seemed to be characteristic of a remotely future age! Then there was the little boy whose mother had a maid, who seemed to him to be extremely old. He longed to know her age but was too polite to ask a direct question. Eventually he discovered in the Book of Knowledge the fact, or is it only a saying, that the aloe flowers only once in a hundred years. This was his opportunity, so he sweetly asked the maid, 'Mary, have you often seen the aloe flower?'

As we ourselves gain in years, old age seems to recede further and further back. Now that in four years I shall be thirty, fifty seems to me to be quite young. My own ideas of old age have been modified greatly since I have been observing our old man – Bapu. What a wonderfully clear brain he has! How straight he picks his way through the fine points and arguments, the sense and the nonsense that are talked to him. With what patience he listens to everybody and yet lets nobody confuse him – all these clever lawyers and politicians and other bigwigs.

I am afraid I am to blame for the honey, but there seems to have been some confusion. I wanted to send you one big bottle of rose honey – I was informed that the price of the small bottle was Rs. 3/12/-. However the honey was not available in the Mahabaleshwar shop so I just

1. Refers to letter No. 205.

remarked that it was a pity since I wanted it for you. Apparently the Madhukosh people have taken matters in their own hands.

I had a very woe-begone postcard from Chhoti Puphi – by the way, I have now started calling her Chitti (which is Tamil for aunt) to avoid the constant confusion between the two Puphis. She is missing the children very much and the children are missing them. Harsha has written to her: 'I shall die if you don't come immediately.' Ajit says, 'I can't eat anything because you are not here.' I do hope she & Rajabhai don't do anything hasty and take the boys away from school before they have had a chance of getting used to their companions and their surroundings. Their first holidays will be in October for *Dussehra*, Chitti will bring them to Bombay.

You will remember I wrote to you some months ago [1] about the *murti* that Rajabhai had had dug out of the peepul tree in Anand Bhawan and had brought to his flat in Bombay. Apparently everybody who saw it told him that he should not have done so, that it would bring ill-luck and that such *murtis* should never be disturbed, and so on. Both Rajabhai and Chitti were quite upset. The *murti* has now been removed from its place and is reposing in my suitcase waiting for someone to take it back to Allahabad when it will again reign supreme over the peepul tree. I am not sorry, for I did not much like the idea of its coming to Bombay in the first place, specially when Bebee told me how long it had been in our garden.

With very much love and a big fat hug,
Indu

This is my 73rd letter, I think.

---

207.                                            Ahmadnagar Fort Prison,
                                                   22nd July, 1944

Darling Indu,
I have your letter No. 72 dated 15th July from Poona. [2] I suppose you have paid your second visit to Shirodkar in Bombay and returned to Poona – hence this letter goes to Poona. I intend sending you a few books on Monday next. Among these there will be two or three of Betty's which you can return to her. They bear her name.

The six new books that you have sent have not yet reached me – I suppose they will come in the ordinary course. Meanwhile, a bundle of

1. Refers to letter No. 183.
2. Refers to letter No. 204.

Communist literature has been sent to me by Puran Chand Joshi. [1] There are two or three books and a large number of pamphlets – some published in Moscow, some in Bombay. They deal mostly with the war in Russia. Will you convey my thanks to Joshi if you can get into touch with him. Altogether I have received twenty-one books and pamphlets from him.

Mention of books reminds me that August 18th is Bari Puphi's birthday. I should like you to choose a number of good books as a birthday gift to her on my behalf. Of course if you can choose a more suitable present for her, do so by all means. My mind runs to books only.

I like de la Mare's poem which you have sent me. [2] Amazingly musical he is and imaginative, living on the borderland of fact and fantasy, with a secret nostalgic longing for some elusive feeling or emotion. I like him not only because of his good writing but also because he evokes sympathetic responses in me. I feel in tune with him and his mood – and that, I suppose, is as good a test as any of successful writing. His lines linger in the memory and often take one out of the present into a world of imaginative existence.

I know Barbara Hartland quite well – that is to say I have seen her many times during the past seven or eight years. She used to work in the Friends' Hospital in Itarsi and whenever I passed through Itarsi, and that was pretty often, she was almost always at the station to meet me. I did not send her any previous intimation of my passing through, but she managed to find out about it. When going to Wardha we had to change at Itarsi and spend some hours there. Someone from the station usually went and informed the Friends' Hospital people and Barbara and sometimes others also trooped up at the station. On several occasions I went and had a bath and a meal at their house. She is a very earnest, enthusiastic kind of person, as Quakers often are, and a hard worker. I think you have decided rightly in not asking her to leave her present work. To run a children's home in Bengal is just the kind of work she will do well and it would be a pity to draw her away.

I suppose you saw the eclipse of the sun last Thursday. It was a bad day, cloudy and with an occasional drizzle of rain. But we managed to have many glimpses of the crescent sun looking like a two-day-old moon. At least ninety per cent or possibly even ninety-five per cent of the sun's disc was covered at the height of the eclipse. Because of the clouds there was no sudden darkening as usually occurs during such eclipses, leading to much consternation among the birds. I remember almost a

1. Puran Chand Joshi: Marxist leader and General Secretary of the Communist Party of India, 1935–48.
2. See letter No. 204.

total eclipse which I saw when I was a small boy – probably eleven or twelve years old. The total eclipse took place some distance away from Allahabad, at Buxar in Bihar, and many scientists and astronomers went there from all parts of the world. Such a total eclipse lasts only a second or two but that fraction of time is rather unique, for the whole disc of the sun is covered and some kind of rays and emanations emerge from the edges. Einstein's theory of the curvature of light rays, mathematically arrived at, was confirmed by observation and photographs of a total eclipse of the sun. This took place in Java, I think. Sometimes, it so happens that all the big astronomers foregather at the appointed place, ready with their instruments and special cameras, all tensely waiting for that mystic second, and then a cloud floats by and covers the sun and the moon and makes observation impossible, rather like those tensely expected moments in life when we hope for so much, and then the moment comes and passes and life has eluded us again. The gods laugh, making fun of the petty hopes and ambitions of poor mortals.

I presume now with the development of aircraft and helicopters it should be possible to overcome this disability of clouds screening the sun at the right moment.

One rather odd and unexpected thing we saw during the eclipse. This was a huge, faintly rainbow-like halo round the sun, making a perfect circle. I suppose this effect was due to the rain-laden clouds.

The Chinese tea you have sent will be welcome. It is a pleasant change and a diversion for us with its golden colour and soothing aroma and faint but delightful taste. Over a year ago Bari Puphi sent me a large packet which had come from China. We used it sparingly, once a week on a specially appointed day, after dinner, and made it last nearly a year. It brought us memories of other places and other days.

I am glad Bul is out and is looking well and as smart as ever. Give her my love. Why has Mridu not profited by her stay in Kashmir? I think she worries too much.

Our garden has been neglected for many months; chiefly my fault as my mind turned to other things. We have now put in a number of seedlings suitable for the rainy season. Probably by the end of August they will flower.

Love,

Your loving,
Papu

I am returning the dividend warrant for Rs. 40/- after endorsement. You can send this on to Bachhraj. This is my letter No. 71.

208.                                          [c/o Mrs Hutheesing,]
                                              20 Carmichael Road,
                                              Bombay,
                                              27th July, 1944

Darling Papu,
I came to Bombay on the 19th – the next day was the eclipse. Did you
see it? Puphi and Rajabhai looked at it through a bit of smoked glass.
Puphi said it was the most beautiful she had ever seen. People in my
condition are not supposed to look at an eclipse – or indeed to do
anything in the way of sewing or cutting and so many other things during
the eclipse. Puphi practically shut me in my room and in order to avoid
the numerous taboos I lay down and read *The Song of Bernadette*[1] until
one o'clock. *The Song of Bernadette* is the story of the Lourdes grotto
where all the miracle cures are supposed to take place. The book is
actually written by a Jew, who got stuck in France, starving and miserable, at the time of the German occupation. He vowed that if and when
he reached America safely, he would tell the world the story of Lourdes.
    The Chinese tea sent to you in my last parcel has come with the
compliments of Mr & Mrs Shen Shih-hua, Commissioner of the Republic of China.
    Rafi had come out on parole due to his father's illness. He is now
back in jail. His father's blood pressure had shot up to 255 but it came
down to 185 the day before Rafi Saheb left Barabanki. Rafi Saheb
himself is not too well but there was not enough time for him to get
thoroughly examined or to have any treatment prescribed. For the last
twenty months he has been running a slow temperature. He had lost 45
lbs in weight but says that he has regained 20 lbs in the last few months.
He has grown very weak. Feroze writes that Rafi Saheb has some kind
of nasal trouble, but Rafi himself does not mention it. Examination both
in jail and outside did not disclose anything seriously wrong but the
doctors have not been able to diagnose the cause of the continuous
fever. Rafi sends you his *salaams*.
    Shammie Didda has had a baby daughter whom she wants to call
Nandita.
    I wrote in my last letter[2] how miserable Harsha and Ajit were at
school. They seem to be settling down now. Ajit is completely happy and
absorbed, Harsha will take more time. They write long and characteristic
letters. Harsha's are more frequent and full of unhappiness. Ajit writes

1. *The Song of Bernadette* was written by Franz Werfel.
2. Refers to letter No. 206.

about what they are doing and wants news of his friends here. The two brothers are so different.

It is amazing how the minute the price of any particular thing is controlled, that article disappears from the shops. All this time I have managed to get along. My wants are so few. If one thing was not available, one bought a substitute or did without. But now I have been going about with my list of necessities – the most ordinary things, hydrogen peroxide, milk of magnesia and so on, and everywhere the reply is the same: Madame, you will only be able to get that in the black market! Can you guess what the black market means – nipples for a baby's feeding bottle which in ordinary times would cost from 2 to 4 rupees, are sold for Rs. 35/- each in the black market! It's exasperating to say the least.

Much love,

Indu

P.S.
Your letter No. 71 – with the dividend warrant – has just arrived. [1]

---

209.                           Ahmadnagar Fort Prison,
                                      29th July, 1944

Darling Indu,
My last letter [2] was sent to the Poona address. After I had despatched it I got yours of the 19th July [3] – No. 73 – in which you say that you intended staying on in Bombay.

I have received the following books from you:

1. M. Kraitchik: *Mathematical Recreations*
2. Hogben: *Interglossa*
3. Nym Wales: *New China*
4. Osbert Lancaster: *More Pocket Cartoons*
5. *Beatrice the Ballerina*
6. *New Kashmir*
7. *Correspondence with Mr Gandhi* (Govt. Publication)

And I have sent you to Bombay:

1. Carl Crow: *The Story of Confucius*

1. Refers to letter No. 207.
2. Refers to letter No. 207.
3. Refers to letter No. 206.

 2. Croce: *History as the Story of Liberty*
 3. Mullick: *The Real & the Negative*
 4. – Do –: *The Individual & the Group*
 5. Thompson: *The Making of the Indian Princes*
 6. Burchett: *Wingate's Phantom Army*
 7. Koestler: *Arrival & Departure*
 8. Brock: *The Mountains Wait*
 9. Ilya Ehrenburg: *Russia at War*
10. Karaka: *Chungking Diary*
11. – Do –: *We Never Die*
12. *Colour Bar*
13. Beverley Nichols: *The Living & the Dead*
14. Mead & Chattopadhyaya: *The Upanishads*
15. Gibran: *The Prophet*
16. Agarwala: *Hindu–Muslim Riots*
17. Tendulkar: *Rūs mein Tees Mahine* (In Hindi)
18. *Merchant Seamen and the War*: I.L.O.

And *I.L.O. Review – Visva-Bharati* & other periodicals. A separate bundle of periodicals has also been sent. The following further books, etc, are now being sent:

19. Louis Fischer: *A Week with Gandhi*
20. Eve Curie: *Journey Among Warriors*
21. *Beatrice the Ballerina*
22. Lancaster: *More Pocket Cartoons*
23. Kate Mitchell: *India*
24. *Mudra-Rakshasa*
And *Hindustan Quarterly* & *Visva-Bharati*.

I liked the two books of cartoons. Several of these books are Betty's – please return them to her.

Eve Curie's book was not so good as I expected it to be. It is diffused and too much of day-to-day reporting. But it makes interesting reading, especially the part dealing with Russia. *Wingate's Phantom Army* has a brief reference towards the end to Moti Kathju. He died just when they were on the point of reaching India on their way back.

I decided, not without an effort, to read Karaka's books.[1] How astonishingly silly he is. His ideas about most things are peculiar but his knowledge of Indian conditions is fantastic. He means well I suppose and so I am prepared to take an indulgent view, but why write when

---

1. See letter No. 196, para 5.

there is such woeful emptiness in the mind and ignorance of the subject? Probably he would be in his element if he wrote about Bombay racing or nightclubs.

If you want to give an average person a headache commend to him Benedetto Croce's book. It is full of learning and thought and makes the reader think also. But what a jumble of semi-metaphysical speculations and ideas about history – after condemning metaphysics and the like. I am glad I read it but it was no easy journey.

You are right about our changing views of age. These really derive from an important psychological truth. We are always apt to make ourselves the measure of things – almost all things. As individuals we judge others by our own standards – physical, mental, moral. If we are tall, others appear short and stumpy. If we succeed in life we are likely to consider those who do not as fools or inefficients. Nationally, we are equally apt to consider our country as the standard of measurement and other countries appear odd and foolish. Our religion, our philosophy, our ways of life – everything seems natural and in the proper order of things because we have been used to them from our childhood. In the old days, when communications were very limited, this exclusiveness was much more marked and there was a strong tendency to consider all foreigners as barbarians because their ways were different. The Chinese, the old Indians, the Greeks, Romans, Arabs, Iranians always referred to foreigners as barbarians, as people living outside the pale of real civilisation. Now that process has been reversed and the Europeans and Americans, because of their obvious material progress, are convinced that they are the elect and others are backward races, decadent or rather primitive. Within the European group, each country considers itself the chosen one and the others not so favoured. Travel and contacts with other countries and peoples help a little to get over this narrowness, but not much, for each individual and group has an amazing capacity to live in its own shell, and the barriers of the mind are much harder to get over than physical differences. And so we are all apt to spot the mote in the other's eye and ignore the beam in our own . . .

You asked me about our garden. I must tell you about an entirely private affair of my own – a kind of window decoration. This is not a window-box, but a creeper growing out of a bottle. I do not know the name of the creeper. It has green leaves with yellowish white patches. No flowers so far. It grows at the rate of about a foot a month. I have had it now for over six months and it goes right across my window and back again, trained along thin pieces of string. It is a delightful decoration for a window. At first the leaves were small and the growth rather slow. Then I started adding a fertiliser tablet to the water in the bottle and immediately the leaves doubled in size and developed a richer colour. Three- or four-inch-long aerial roots are now coming out. I change the water of the bottle once a week.

Here are the names of two books which you might note down for purchase when they are available:

*Indigo* by Christine Weston (Collins, London, 10sh. 6d.). This is a novel about India.
*The Mirror of the Past* by K. Zilliacus (Gollancz, 7sh. 6d)

Love,
Your loving,<br>Papu

This is my letter No. 72.

———————————◂▸——————————

210.                                          [c/o Mrs Hutheesing,]
                                                20 Carmichael Road,
                                                            Bombay,
                                                2nd August, 1944

Darling Papu,
Your letter of the 29th July [1] and the first lot of books have arrived. I have noted down the books you have asked for.

Anna has agreed to come, but she will not be able to join me until the first week of October. Since leaving Puphi, she has been looking after Mrs Cousins in Bangalore. Mrs Cousins is getting on in years and her sight is not what it was. Besides, she has had various accidents which forced her to stay completely in bed. So Anna has been having an exhausting time and she feels that she needs a holiday before starting anything new.

In the meantime I am having great difficulty in finding a suitable *ayah*. [2]

Puphi says *Indigo* is not worth buying, so I am sending you Chinnibhai's (Sundaram) [3] copy to read. I am also sending Stefan Zweig's *The World of Yesterday* and some periodicals.

Let me know when you finish the tin of Chinese tea. There are three more tins waiting to be sent.

You asked me some time ago to find out if the U.P. Govt were giving

1. Refers to letter No. 209.
2. A female attendant or maid-servant.
3. C. R. Sundaram: son of C. P. Ramaswamy Aiyar. The latter was a famous lawyer and politician who served in various Princely States.

scholarships to poor students out of the profits of the sale of *Letters*. Their reply has now come. They write that Rs. 2939/7 was deposited in the Treasury in September 1942, to be utilised for this purpose 'in due course'.

The Law Journal Co. has been referred as to the remittance of further amount accumulated under this head and as soon as this is settled a scheme will be framed for its utilization in awarding scholarships to poor and deserving students. A further communication will be addressed to you when the scheme materializes giving you full information on the point as desired.

You also asked about the publishing of the Hebrew translation. This appeared some time last year or the year before but was promptly banned in Palestine. A copy managed to reach Chhoti Puphi and is now with me.

Have you read *Mission to Moscow*?[1] And if not, shall I send it?

Masi insists on coming to Bombay. Both she and Nani will feel hurt if I say no. Besides Masi has lots of friends here so she will make her own staying arrangements. Puphi is not coming now as she will have to stay with Rita after her operation in Calcutta.

I conveyed your message of thanks to P. C. Joshi. In reply he writes that he has sent you another batch of twenty-three books and pamphlets and would like an acknowledgement through me.

With much love,

Indu

---

211.                                                  Ahmadnagar Fort Prison,
                                                            5th August, 1944

Darling Indu,

I have your letter No. 74 of July 27th.[2]

With the coming of August there has been a subtle change in the weather. It is cooler and fans are no longer needed. We have little rain now and the sky is often brilliantly clear. I suppose Bombay is close and unpleasant and next month there is likely to be worse. It is a pity you have to be there during these months. But then there is no help for it.

The Chinese tea reached me some time ago. I hope you or someone thanked the Shen Shih-huas for it. We have not tried it yet. It is being

1. *Mission to Moscow* by Joseph E. Davies.
2. Refers to letter No. 208.

preserved for a special occasion – the occasion will soon be with us – August 9th, the second anniversary of our coming here.

That very expensive honey you sent is not particularly good. The previous consignment, which you yourself extracted from the comb, was far better.

So you did not see the eclipse of the sun. You did not miss much, and yet one likes to see these unusual occurrences and they become landmarks in the dull routine of our lives. I do not believe in most taboos, certainly not in those associated with eclipses, and my own tendency is to break them. But if one feels that way it is best to avoid doing anything which is associated in our minds with ill-luck. Betty, or Chitti as you call her, seems to attach considerable importance to taboos. I should have thought that there was so much misfortune and ill-luck in the world that anything that we might or might not do would make little difference. The world certainly will not be affected, but it is true that we ourselves might be affected by our own beliefs and apprehensions.

I am sorry you are having difficulty in obtaining the most ordinary necessities. It is scandalous that you should have to pay Rs. 35/- for the nipples for a baby's feeding bottle. The black market, I suppose, is a symbol of much that is black and dark and gloomy.

It seems rather absurd to try to control prices in such a way so as to drive those articles from the open market and force a person either to do without them or to pay outrageous prices for them. I see in the newspapers huge long lists of articles with their controlled prices marked opposite their names. I suppose that means that those articles have disappeared and lie somewhere hidden for secret sale. What is the black market? The same persons, I presume, who sell goods in public.

I hope you will remember to send a birthday gift on my behalf to Bari Puphi for August 18th.

After your confinement, if all goes well, as I am sure it will, how long will you have to stay in Bombay? I suppose about three or four weeks. Bombay has horrid weather in October and the sooner you get out of the place the better. Allahabad will be delightful then.

I was glad to have news of Rafi. I am very fond of him and admire him in many ways.

I am at present reading, for the second time, Tolstoy's *War and Peace*. I read it first I think about twenty years ago. It is a mighty book both in size and content. War and Peace: war, one can understand though one may regret it, peace one hopes for and dreams about. But this world and all of us seem to drift into a strange condition which is neither war nor peace – a kind of unreal existence in an unreal world. It reminds me of the story of Trishanku[1] in old Indian mythology. Trishanku, having become very powerful, wanted to storm the citadel of the gods. The gods, as is their way, got frightened and were unable to check him. So they went to higher powers and sought their help. The result was that they succeeded in stopping Trishanku but could not wholly defeat him or send him back. So old Trishanku hung between heaven and earth, and there I suppose he is still suspended.

Love,

Your loving,
Papu

---

212.                                          [c/o Mrs Hutheesing,]
20 Carmichael Road,
Bombay,
7th August, 1944

Darling Papu,

The air is full of rumours of your release. Of your transfer to Dehra Dun with Pantji. About the end of the war and a dozen other things. And we poor sheep are in the unenviable position of just having to wait and see and hope for the best.

Feroze writes that your room is aired and swept and dusted every day, just as it used to be when I was in Allahabad. At the beginning of the monsoon, it, along with the rest of the house, got a thorough cleaning.

Vatsala is on leave and is in Bombay. She expects her baby towards the end of September and will return to Allahabad at the end of October.

We have a Mrs Prasad staying at Anand Bhawan. Feroze has put her in Bibi Amma's room. She is the wife of Rajendra Prasad, brother of Jai Prakash. Poor Rajendra Prasad who had a good job was arrested for no special reason when Jai Prakash was being searched for. Mrs Prasad was expecting a baby. What with that and grave financial difficulties, she went completely off her head, to such an extent that no doctor would have hesitated in certifying her insane. She was brought, along with her small baby, to our hospital. Vatsala did not know what to do. There was nothing wrong with the woman physically and maternity hospital is

---

1. A mythological story which refers to the desire of King Satyavrata to ascend bodily to heaven. While the dynastic priest, Vashishta, could not help him, another sage, Vishwamitra, performed the necessary sacrifices to enable him to do so. However, the gods in heaven were loath to accept a human ruler in their midst, so that the king, now renamed Trishanku, remained suspended between heaven and earth with his head pointing downward, visible as a star in the heavens.

hardly the place for a mental case. Mrs Prasad's blank stare, so typical of the mentally deranged, terrified the other patients. We put her at Rai Amarnath's [1] place with a woman to look after her. She was there for months but the arrangement was not at all satisfactory and she was very unhappy.

We kept on getting messages from her husband that she should be taken away from there and some arrangement should be made for her in Bombay. I am trying my best at this end but so far with little success. Meanwhile Mrs Prasad seems to be quite normal again – Feroze writes that she spends her time with Mrs Upadhyaya. The trouble is that she has no family to go to and has no money at all. There are so many many people needing help, one doesn't know what to do.

Bul has gone to Sevagram with Bapu. Rajabhai returned home to Bombay. He seems to be better.

Rita's operation is due on the 11th or 12th, so it will probably not be possible for Puphi to come to Bombay, as she has planned to do.

We are rather worried about Kailash Mamu – no news has come from him for over two months. These flying bombs are a real menace. [2]

What news of the kitten and the chick? [3]

Along with the books mentioned in my last letter, [4] I am sending Ajwani's [5] *Introducing India*. The bookseller insists that it is the same book as *Immortal India* which you asked for some time ago.

Much love,

Indu

This is letter No. 76.

⸻

213.                                      Ahmadnagar Fort Prison,
                                            12th August, 1944

Darling Indu,

I have your letter No. 75 of August 2nd. [6]

Since writing to you last week we have celebrated the second anniversary of our arrival here. Two years! A big part of one's life concentrated

---

1. Rai Amarnath Agarwal: businessman of Allahabad; member, U.P. Legislative Council, 1936–52, and Council of States, 1952–60.
2. Kailash Mamu was still in London. The flying bombs were the 'doodlebugs'.
3. Pets 'adopted' by Jawaharlal Nehru in Ahmadnagar Jail.
4. Refers to letter No. 210.
5. L. H. Ajwani: noted author.
6. Refers to letter No. 210.

in one place – the same people, the same surroundings, the same routine.

Gradually one fits into it and all that has happened previously becomes a distant memory, rather unreal, a vague stretch with a number of prominent landmarks. There is a sensation of seeing things in a dream, but which is the dream, the present or the past, one does not quite know. For the present also has a certain dreamlike quality, an absence of sharp outlines, something that one cannot fully grasp. This present will also fade away some day and then the other dream will become the reality of the moment. So we live two lives, like those who have developed split personalities and jump from one life to another. When the next jump comes for me I shall take some time to wake up to the new life.

We had the Chinese tea you sent us as part of our celebration. It was different from the previous lot which Puphi had sent last year and not so good. That had been chrysanthemum tea and we had got used to its gentle flavour and soothing effect. I suppose this present lot is the usual kind of Chinese tea – you need not send any more of it, for the present tin will last some time.

This is your last month and I suppose you will find it a little trying and your mind will be in a state of expectation. It is curious how the most normal and ordinary processes of life are so full of mystery. So many things happen daily which we take for granted and which are yet very odd when we start thinking about them. Each individual is a mysterious person living in a private universe of his own, different from the world other people live in. Is it ever possible for one person ever truly to understand another? But few people ever worry themselves about such everyday matters and everyone thinks that his world is the only possible world and all others are deviations due to cussedness, knavery or just simple ignorance. And yet when we come face to face with the beginning of a life or the ending of one, suddenly we find ourselves peering into the dark unknown. How little we really know. Death, too, for all its effect, passes and becomes a memory. But new life is an amazing, fascinating thing, full of the wonder of existence, of change and growth, and so always the process of giving birth to anything vital has been the most tremendous fact of existence in this world, for because of that the world continues in spite of the hateful instincts of man. The pain that sometimes accompanies it becomes trivial in comparison with the supreme satisfaction of creation.

I read in some newspaper that Feroze was going to Bombay and intends staying there for a month or more. I am glad he is there.

If Bappi is coming to Bombay well and good. In a practical sense she can be of no help. But I knew that Nani would not be happy unless she came herself or sent someone. So it is as well that Bappi is coming.

I have already written to you the names of the books received by me which you had sent. In referring back to one of your previous letters, I find that one book you sent has not reached me – this is Ahmad Abbas's *And One Did Not Come Back*. Probably it was held up by the censor. I am merely mentioning this to you so that you can get back the book from the Bombay Secretariat . . .

I hope your search for an *ayah* will succeed. It will be a nuisance if you cannot find a suitable one.

This is my letter No. 74.

Love to you and Feroze,

Your loving,<br>Papu

I am sending you a bundle of periodicals: *Foreign Affairs, Pacific Affairs* – 2 *Asia, Life*, etc.

I have just received your letter of August 7th. [1] Do not worry about rumours.

P

---

214.                                    [c/o Mrs Hutheesing,]
                                         20 Carmichael Road,
                                                  Bombay,
                                         12th August, 1944

Darling Papu,

I have your letter of August 5th, [2] No. 73, I presume.

Bombay is quite pleasant these days. There is a fair amount of breeze and occasional showers of rain. It is in September and, even more so in October that the town will become unbearable. I shall probably have to stay on for about forty days after the baby's arrival, so the sooner it arrives the better.

You are needlessly upset over the honey. As I wrote to you from Poona, it is most probably a present from the Madhu-Kosh. I have received no communication or bill from the Madhu-Kosh people. When Bapu was in Juhu, I wanted to send him some Mahabaleshwar honey, but when I made enquiries about buying some, the owner of the Madhu-Kosh said that he would like to present the honey to Bapu himself. So the whole thing was taken out of my hands and the man

1. Refers to letter No. 212.
2. Refers to letter No. 211.

travelled from Mahabaleshwar to Juhu laden with six or seven bottles of rose honey. The same thing happened in Poona. Soon after Bapu's release I wanted to get for him a copy of *A Week with Gandhi*, so I sent a man to the International Book Co., to buy the book. But when the manager heard for whom it was, he said he would like to present the book himself, which he came and did. But I am sorry the honey is not good.

Mehr Taj's fiancé is Yahya Khan – Yunus's brother. He is forty. He is the person who spent a week with Feroze and me up in Mohanmarg, in Kashmir – quite a nice person, quiet but not young for his age!

Nani has at last heard from Kailas Mamu. He seems very worried and anxious and is trying to send Mami and the children out of London.

Mridula and Tendulkar are bringing out a 'birthday volume' for Gandhiji. Actually many persons are concerned in the venture – the book is to appear simultaneously in several languages but Mridu and Tendulkar are the guiding lights especially of the English edition. I believe Chalapathi Rau[1] is also helping them in editing the book. The book is to contain articles on Bapu and some photographs and paintings. They wanted to include something written by you and the others at Ahmadnagar. I don't know what they have done about the others, but for you they have compiled a short article consisting of extracts from the *Autobiography*. They asked for and received by cable from Krishna, Lane's permission to use an extract of 5000 words, subject to Puphi's approval. Mridula did not wish to bother Puphi during Rita's operation, so she brought the extract to me. It is, as such a thing is bound to be, a little disjointed in places. I suggested that they should put . . . at the end of each separate quotation to make it clear that they were separate. In two places they have presumed to correct your English and punctuation. I was most annoyed and have told them that no such changes could be allowed. Apart from this it seems to be all right. Have you any objection to its being included in the book?

I do not know what the book is going to be like. The editors have scrapped, as not being good enough, articles by such people as Sophia Wadia,[2] Sri Prakasa, etc. They returned the articles to these people with copious suggestions re corrections and omissions. Naturally the contributors refused to change what they had written.

Much love,
Indu

---

1. M. Chalapathi Rau: a well-known journalist and author, who served on the *National Herald* as Assistant Editor and later Editor.
2. Sophia Wadia: eminent theosophist; editor, *The Aryan Path*.

215.                                        [c/o Mrs Hutheesing,]
                                               20 Carmichael Road,
                                                          Bombay,
                                               16th August, 1944

Darling Papu,
Your letter No. 74 of the 12th August[1] came yesterday. This is my
letter No. 78.

I have today sent you some periodicals. The books, *Indigo*, etc, have
not been sent as you do not want them just now.

I have also sent off Puphi's birthday parcel – Stefan Zweig's *The
World of Yesterday* was your present. Actually I had got the book for you,
but Chhoti Puphi and I spent quite some time in the bookshops searching for a suitable book to send to Puphi on your behalf. There was
absolutely nothing which Puphi would have liked.

Rita's operation was successfully performed on the 12th. Feroze will
be coming here on or about the 17th. Actually he was due on the 17th.
But I have wired to him to bring along Mrs Prasad, so that may delay
his departure. We are trying to make arrangements for Mrs Prasad in
Wardha.

Harsha & Ajit have thirteen days' holidays for *Dussehra*, beginning on
the 23rd September. They are very keen on coming home for the holidays, instead of going camping as all the other boys are going to do.
Either Puphi or Rajabhai will probably go to Gwalior to fetch them.
They seem to be happier in school now so I hope there will be no
trouble about their going back. Sami, Shammie Didda's stepson, is also
in the school.

After all, Masi may not be able to come. Mausaji has resigned from
his post in Jaipur. I do not know what he is going to do or where he will
stay. Masi wrote that he wants to have two months' holiday before taking
on any job. Several posts have been offered him but he has not decided
anything yet.

Chhoti Puphi's second edition is going to be out in a couple of days
or so. I believe you asked her for the reviews of her book – I am enclosing
four.

Agnes[2] has left Puphi of her own desire. She is keen on taking up
nursing. But when the day for leaving came, she was full of tears and
self-reproaches. Harsha and Ajit wrote her very sweet letters: 'you will
make a great name in this world of ours', and so on. I must say the boys

---

1. Refers to letter No. 213.
2. Agnes: a nurse who looked after the children of Krishna Hutheesing.

can write very charmingly when they can summon enough patience to sit down and concentrate.

Chhoti Puphi has been so sweet to me – these days it is no fun having people staying with you for weeks and weeks, especially when they are in my condition and requiring all sorts of special consideration. Often and often she must be upsetting her own programme because of me; and then preparing things for me – that has needed considerable time and expense and bother. I don't think anybody has ever spent so much time and thought over looking after me in every way and not only physically. I am deeply grateful to her but just do not know what I can do to thank her. I should be glad if, when you next write to her, you say a few words on the subject.

Much love,
Indu

---

216.             Ahmadnagar Fort Prison,
19th August, 1944

Darling Indu,

I have received your two letters: No. 76 and 77 dated 7th and 12th August. [1] You mention rumours about us. These rumours have seldom any basis, and even when there is some justification for them it is slender and people are apt to exaggerate and distort so as to make them fit in with their wishes. The best thing to do is to ignore them completely. Last year you wrote to me some lines by A. Athenison, 'Actual evidence I have none', etc. They contain a good picture of the origin and growth of rumour.

Your account of Mrs Prasad has led me to think of the wider question of giving relief to the many who must be in desperate need of it. I am very glad Feroze has been devoting himself to this work. It is difficult to tackle such a big problem but the fact that it is big is all the more reason why we should tackle it. I should like to help. Indeed you should have drawn from my account for relief work without any special authority from me. I suggest that you give Feroze Rs. 100/- a month from my account and, whenever you think it necessary, a further lump sum . . .

I have no objection to extracts from my *Autobiography* appearing in the 'birthday volume' which Mridu, Tendulkar and others are preparing for Bapu. It would be desirable to have dots between two separate quotations. As for correcting my English and my punctuation, I am not prepared to say that I am above correction. But Mridu and Tendulkar are hardly the persons to undertake this. Chalapathi Rau – I suppose

---

1. Refers to letters Nos 212 and 214.

he is the *Herald* man – is a good choice for editing. I like him both as a person and for his capacity. He is quiet and efficient at his job. If there is an obvious error in my writing, there is no reason why it should not be corrected, provided it is obvious enough and you agree. As a matter of fact if I had the chance to revise my *Autobiography* I would make many alterations in it. I never had the chance to revise it with any care. After my first writing of it, it was typed by Upadhyaya without any revision by me. I took this typescript with me to Badenweiler and rather hurriedly looked through it there. I could not apply my mind to it then and I was in a hurry to be done with it. The book was then published. I never tried to read through the printed book and of course the proofs never came to me. Krishna made himself responsible for its publication, proof correcting, etc. So, oddly enough, the book was not revised by me at any stage. There was no occasion for it and I find this business of revising what I have already written very boring. It is a trying job even to read through it all again, though parts of it are sometimes referred to or re-read.

Then came the American edition. This was an abridged version and everything in connection with it was done in New York without reference to me. It was not possible for such references to take place owing to wartime delays, and so I left it to Walsh and asked him to consult Krishna. Walsh complained that Krishna did not even answer his letters.

This American edition reached me in Dehra Dun Jail and for the first time I read my *Auto* in print right through. I was taken aback by some of the abridgements, which made no sense. There were also minor changes to suit the American public, especially in the spelling of words. I accepted these minor changes but pointed out to Walsh a number of errors. These corrections were, I believe, carried out in a subsequent American edition. But the English editions presumably remained unchanged.

It is difficult to make any changes in a printed book for this upsets the arrangement of the plates. The slightest change, for instance the addition of a comma, means changing the plate. A whole page may thus be changed but then care has to be taken not to affect the next page in any way. If a word or sentence is taken out in any page something in its place, occupying the same amount of space, must be given. All this is exceedingly tiresome and I have therefore refrained from interfering with the present arrangement of the book, although there are many changes which seemed to me to be desirable.

As for punctuation, it perplexes me frequently. I am sure I make mistakes in it, as well as in grammar generally. Not having paid much attention to grammar, except to a slight extent Latin & French grammar, I am rather at sea with questions relating to it. I have to go by sound and sight. That helps probably in style and I have a sense of words and the hang of a sentence. But minor errors are apt to creep in. Do you know the story of some eminent English writer – I think he was Oscar Wilde? He was asked how he had spent the day. He replied that he spent the whole morning in putting in a comma, and the afternoon in taking it out again!

*Glimpses* was first published in India (by Kitabistan) without any revision by me at any stage. I did not even see the typescript made by Upadhyaya and this, as I discovered subsequently, was full of errors. The result was that the printed book was a horror and I could hardly look into it without extreme irritation. The English edition was hurriedly revised by me, chiefly on board ship when I was going to Europe in 1938.

If Mridu, Tendulkar & co. are going to sit in judgment on people like Sri Prakasa, etc, they will have their work cut out for them.

I am glad Bombay is pleasant now.

This is my letter No. 75.

Love,

Your loving,<br>Papu

---

217. [c/o Mrs Hutheesing,]
20 Carmichael Road,
Bombay,
19th August, 1944

Darling Papu,

I wrote to you some time ago [1] of the Hebrew edition of the *Autobiography* and the news concerning it given to Chitti by somebody who came to India for a short visit on his way to South Africa. Today I have received a reply to my letter of enquiry. A charming letter. Mr Benton [2] writes that apart from your telegram of March 10th, 1942 he has received no communication from you. On the other hand he has sent several letters and a telegram 'of sympathy and appreciation on account of his arrest' which have not reached us. He writes that the book was to appear towards the end of 1942 but the whole edition was seized by the police before it reached the public. However, a few months ago the ban was lifted. The book is now on sale and is 'extremely popular' with the Hebrew-reading public.

1. Refers to letter No. 210.
2. William Benton: U.S. Senator, 1949–53; met Jawaharlal Nehru in March 1937 at Allahabad.

It has suddenly become quite hot and sticky. But Chitti and Rajabhai have both got bad colds and I am sitting smothered in eucalyptus as a precaution.

Puphi writes that Rita's appendix was five inches long but everyone says that is not possible because an appendix cannot grow long but only broad and there is not so much room – perhaps she means that the surgeon had to make a cut of five inches. Whatever it is, Rita is progressing satisfactorily and, from her letter to me, seems to be quite cheerful. Banerjee intends to keep her in the nursing home three full weeks.

*3rd September, 1944* [1]

Darling Papu – The above is rather ancient news now but I am sending it on. I wrote it on the evening on the 19th and it would have reached you days ago if I had not been interrupted by a visit from Ballo and his wife. Later, when I woke up at three a.m., I had an urge to finish the letter but did not do so because I was afraid of waking Feroze if I put on the light. By five a.m. it was too late to write!

I have been wanting to write since the 21st, but it is so uncomfortable in bed. Besides the routine of the day tires me out completely. The evening is the only time when I could sit up & write but there are always visitors.

I am still running a temperature of 99° – it isn't much but when it continues day after day it tires one out. My cough and cold also persist. The worst of it is that I keep on giving them to baby. Poor little chap, he is too small to be able to spit out the phlegm, so he has an uncomfortable time – the only way he can bring it out is by vomiting. True to the superstition that day babies always sleep in the day, he spends most of the night yelling.

Puphi tells me that she has sent you the list of names that she and Rajabhai got out of various books. I like most of them. Satyavrata and Suvrata are too common. And I do not much care for Abhimanyu and Indrajit. I have always had a special liking for the name Rahul. I feel that a child is sometimes rather embarrassed by a long-winded or very uncommon name, like Nichiketa. Otherwise it sounds rather nice, doesn't it? I like Rajeeva and Rajat and Karna, Gokarna and Raivata and Chakradhara. I had better stop now or else I shall be adding the whole list by bits. You had better choose out of Puphi's list.

It was Rajabhai's idea too that we should give two names, one a Persian – if a good one could be found. None of us know of any. I wonder if Maulana Saheb will be able to help us out of the difficulty.

1. Rajiv Gandhi was born on 20th August, 1944. This event explains the sudden termination of the letter dated 19th August and its resumption on 3rd September.

A name not included in the list but rather nice is *Sanjaya*. Also *Nakul*.

I had a letter from Madanbhai. He sends his love to you. He writes that he is a little better and has gained 3 lbs. Rafi is also in Lucknow. Madanbhai says that Rafi's heart is in such a condition that it can take him a long time to get anywhere near normal health.

The weather here is so treacherous, it changes from hour to hour. I am hoping to go to Allahabad by the end of September. You know what Jivraj is. He gets agitated about nothing. He was making a lot of fuss about my temperature, and wanting me to be X-rayed and so on. In the meantime he has gone to Madras for fifteen days for some medical conference, so by his own instructions everything is held up. I personally feel that I shall improve in Allahabad. For the baby too it is better to go before Allahabad starts getting cold, otherwise it will be rather a sudden change from the heat and stickiness of October in Bombay to the cold crisp air of Allahabad. Feroze will probably return by the 15th Sept.

With very much love,
Indu

---

218.                                             Ahmadnagar Fort Prison,
                                                 21st August, 1944

Darling,
So you have made me a grandfather!

I received the message yesterday in the afternoon. It had apparently come by telephone. I felt very happy that this tension was over and that you had successfully launched into motherhood. Pantji managed somehow to produce some very good and fresh *peras*[1] at teatime to celebrate the occasion. I hope it is well with you and the little one. All our friends here send both of you their love and blessings.

All my love,
Your loving,
Papu

---

219.                                             Ahmadnagar Fort Prison,
                                                 26th August, 1944

Darling,
Your letter No. 78 of the 16th August[2] reached me three days ago. It

1. A variety of sweetmeat prepared from milk.
2. Refers to letter No. 215.

seems rather ancient history, for since it was written you have become a mother and I have attained the dignified status of a grandfather. I am trying to find out how it feels to be a grandfather. Thus far I have experienced no particular change in my constitution but I suppose I shall grow into this new status, though I fear I lack the dignity for it.

I have had excited letters from Betty and Puphi and a few lines from Rita. Also a telegram from Amma and Rup. I suppose women are more excitable than men, but I have long had a theory that India as a nation – that is, the Indian people as a whole – is rather feminine. That is why I suppose India is so lovable in spite of her many failings. I do not easily get excited but I experienced a deep feeling of contentment when I heard of the arrival of the newcomer. I was happy that it was all safely over and that you were well. There was also a vague and comforting sensation of the future gradually pushing out the past, as it always does. This is usually a mixed feeling, for one is usually attached to the past and does not like to break with it. Of course there is never an actual break; it is an unending and continuous flow, link after link in a chain which has no visible beginning and apparently no end. Yet the future always represents hope, though why it should do so has seemed to me one of the oddest traits of human nature, but it does so nevertheless, while the past is a curious mixture. There is always something of the promise of spring about the future. It seems young and growing and full of new life and the next winter seems far off.

The renewal of life from spring to spring, from generation to generation, has an amazing fascination. Therein lies the essence of immortality not only of the species but of that vital precious thing that is life, and, in human mind, of memories and ideas that grow from age to age and link the past with the ever-changing present. So a nation and a people taste of immortality and even a family lives on and on.

I am happy to learn that you had an easy delivery. That shows how essentially healthy you are. You will of course take care of yourself during the next month or so, and then you can live your normal healthy life, not remembering the ailments of the body which have sometimes worried you in the past.

Feroze I suppose reached Bombay just a day or two before your confinement. I am glad he was there in time for it.

You have added to the population of India. That is supposed to be – I doubt the figures but I shall accept them for the moment – four hundred million. Roughly speaking, we might say that the newcomer is the 400,000,001st. That is a formidable number and it will take a lot of living up to.

Betty says in her letter that she had offered prayers to Hanuman [1] and Ganesh. [2] I am glad there is somebody in the family who prays to the gods, for some of us, like me, are utterly lacking in this respect. But why choose these rather inhuman representations of the powers beyond us when there are so many beautiful and lovely creations of the imagination? Anyway old Ganesh has a very human twinkle in his elephantine eye and there is something irrepressibly humorous about him, and a merry look and laughter are gifts from the gods . . .

I am returning the four reviews of Betty's book which you sent me. Please return them to her.

Love,

Your loving,<br>Papu

This letter is No. 77.

---

220.               Ahmadnagar Fort Prison,
4th September, 1944

Darling,

Betty has been keeping me informed of developments. Her last letter came three days ago. I am sorry you and the infant both managed to catch a slight cold. I hope it has passed. Such things happen in spite of every care. The only real remedy is to have enough powers of resistance. Unfortunately these powers are limited in the early days. Now that the infant has attained the respectable age of a fortnight he will no doubt act in accordance with the responsibilities of that age. I hope Betty will write to me frequently – as frequently as the rules governing Ahmadnagar Fort permit – and keep me informed. My mind is with you all the time and I think of you and the infant, and the babe growing from day to day. I am glad you have kept nurses. Hold on to them and do not be in a hurry to part with them. Little things count at this stage and it would be folly to save money at the cost of worry. That will interfere with your own return to normal health as well as the baby's. For the babe depends ever so much on the mother. Also without proper nurses, Betty will inevitably have more to do and that will not be right. She is of course a perfect brick and it is a great comfort to me that she is with you. About expenses generally you should not worry. They are not your look-out.

Darling, I understand that you people have been referring to the infant as Rahul. Indeed Puphi wrote to me that this name was suggested

---

1. Hanuman: Hindu deity venerated for his devotion to the epic hero, Lord Rama.
2. Ganesh: worshipped as the god of wisdom, good luck and the remover of obstacles.

some months ago and all of you had decided that it was going to be a boy. Well, Rahul is not a bad name – that was my first impression. But some further information I have gathered from Narendra Deva has made me change my mind. Rahul of course was Buddha's son and this tradition and connection are in its favour. But do you know what it means? It means a fetter, something that binds – a *bandhan*. The story is that when Buddha, or Siddhartha as he then was, was told of the birth of his son, he exclaimed that this was a fresh *bandhan* or fetter attaching him to the life he was leading and from which he wanted to get away. That word of his – Rahula – caught on and became the name of his son. It has since been seldom used as a name, except rarely by Buddhist monks and the like, so the name is hardly suitable.

Betty says that you have prepared a list of possible names. She was going to send this list to me but apparently could not find it at the time. When it comes I shall let you have my reaction after consulting friends here. Meanwhile, I mentioned the matter to Narendra Deva and the next day he came out with certain historical names from Sanskrit litera-ture. They were unusual and worth considering. But I shall wait for your list and then write more about it . . .

Feroze, I presume, is with you. He should remain with you and not hurry away. I hope that by the end of this month you can go to Allahabad so that the infant and you can enjoy the delightful cold weather there.

Love to you both,

Your loving,
Papu

---

221.                                                    Ahmadnagar Fort Prison,
                                                         9th September, 1944

Darling,

I have spent quite a bad week, though why I should behave in this way I do not quite know. I thought I could control my feelings and emotions better, but I realise how one's mental discipline and hard-acquired wisdom are swept aside for a while at least by the surge of feeling. On the 1st of September I got Betty's last letter in which she told me of your cold and fever and the little one's cold. I was a little worried, but not much. I hoped to have further and better news within two or three days. As the days went by and no further news came a growing apprehen-sion seized me and I grew restless in mind. I was thinking of you and the babe most of the time and wondering how both of you were. You would soon get over your cold I hoped, but the little one, a few days old, how would he fare? I remembered the time when you got a bad attack of influenza when you were a few months old – about six. A very vivid picture of you then, lying in a cot in Dol Amma's garden room, in what is now Swaraj Bhawan, came to me. Under instructions from Ranjit Singh (the gallant Major), who was treating you, all the doors were closed and the room was full of some kind of vapour – eucalyptus or some such thing. A long-necked, rather primitive apparatus produced this vapour and its nose was so arranged so as to be near your tiny face. I presume they have better ways of treatment now. Anyway I remembered that scene and all the trouble you were having with your breathing and coughing. I felt so helpless. Fortunately you got over your troubles soon.

For eight days I have had no letter at all from anyone to give me news of you. This was a big gap and I worried and could not make out why this was so. I think this is yet another sign of age. Or is it the usual thing for grandfathers to do? I thought of how I must take the little one in hand and help him to build up a strong and healthy body. A delusion I suffer from: that I know a great deal about the rules of health and that anybody who follows them must of necessity remain healthy. Really it is only another aspect of my general tendency to interfere with other people. You and Feroze will have to hold me in check.

As I was beginning this letter, at last a letter was handed to me in the usual On His Majesty's Service envelope. I peeped in and saw it was from you. It was dated August 19th.[1] Welcome as it was, I felt disappointed. Oh this was your old unfinished letter and contains no later news. But as I read it I found that there was a later addition dated Sept. 3rd. I felt better. But I am not entirely reassured. I do not like this continuing temperature and cold. I have no doubt that both you and the baby will improve rapidly in the Allahabad climate. But not just at present, as September is not a good month there. October is just right, not cold but pleasant and slowly cooling off with November. But it would be desirable for you and the babe to get rid of the cold completely before you travel. A long journey might aggravate an existing distemper. Also I think it would be as well, before you go, to have yourself X-rayed, etc. In this matter, as in others affecting your health and the babe's, you should follow Jivraj's advice. He is cautious and sound and knows your history.

About the names, Betty has not sent me the list. I shall await that list before consulting Narendra Deva again. I shall also ask Maulana. It has struck me also some time ago that an additional Persian name would be desirable.

I was interested to learn about the Hebrew edition of my *Autobiography*.

1. Refers to letter No. 217.

When you feel better, I should like you to write to Mr Benton, or whatever his name is. Tell him that I was happy to have news of the book. I received none of his letters or his cable. I wrote to him also in March 1942, in addition to my cable, but evidently he did not receive my letter.

Some little time back I wrote[1] to you to arrange for a payment of Rs. 100 monthly to Feroze for his relief work. In addition will you please arrange for a lump payment of Rs. 1000/- to him from my account. I am sure he will put this to good use in giving relief to people standing in need of it. Apart from this Rs. 100/- a month should continue.

I am glad to have news of Madan Bhai and Rafi. I think I told you that the book you sent me dealing with the Chinese Medical Mission – *And One Did Not Come Back* – did not reach me.

I am sending you today a bundle of old magazines and periodicals.
Love,

Your loving,
Papu

This is my letter No. 79 . . .

---

222.                                [c/o Mrs Hutheesing,]

20 Carmichael Road,
15th September, 1944

Darling Papu,

Your utterly sweet letter of the 9th[2] came yesterday. I was distressed to read of those anxious news-less days you had – all that worry could so easily have been prevented had you received Puphi's letters in time. Unfortunately we know only too well the kind of people in whose hands these matters rest.

However, now the wee one and I are both well again. We are still having trouble with the wee one's feeds – he doesn't get enough and is not putting on as much weight as the doctor would like. Otherwise he is very good. The nurse has left today. She was rather good with baby. We were lucky to have her. I do not know if Puphi told you that years ago this nurse came to Dakshineshwar with Jivraj, to act as assistant to Dadu's nurse.

Dr Coelho, who is treating baby, is also very good. It is reassuring to find a doctor who is not in a hurry, and who is interested enough in

---

1. Refers to letter No. 216.
2. Refers to letter No. 221.

each case to remember every detail. Dr Coelho has had a bad attack of
infantile paralysis, so that for him walking about and going from place
to place is not the effortless job that it is for most of us. He has a
peculiar metal contraption on his right leg and has a man to help him
get up and sit down. In spite of this, he is on the go from 8.30 in the
morning until late at night. (By the way, Mrs Coelho had a baby in
Shirodkar's hospital about twenty days before my wee one arrived and
she was in the same room that later I occupied.) Dr Coelho has been
to see baby about four times. We ring him up every morning and evening
and give him a full report of how baby is and he gives his instructions
– if he is doubtful about anything, he comes himself the next morning.

Some months ago when I was at Matheran, Masi wrote saying that
she had heard from some Parsis that it was written in their ancient book
that a Hindu girl of high family would marry a Parsi and their son would
do great things – religious reform and so on. Masi asked me to enquire
into the matter but it quite slipped my mind. Last evening my mother-
in-law came in a state of great excitement. She had also heard something
of the sort, a slightly different version. According to her, the son was
the reincarnation of the Shah Behram [1] of Persia!

Baby's *patra* [2] has arrived. I am enclosing it. It is written in Gujarati
but I suppose you will be able to get it read. I am also enclosing an
English translation of the *jyotishi's* [3] remarks. I am sending all
this registered – please do the same when you return it. The good
thing about it is supposed to be that there are five planets in one
house.

I am allowed to go out for drives, but Rajabhai's car is not working
so the drive has not materialised yet. Bapu sent word that he would
come and see me. But he gets so exhausted and has no time, so when
he heard that I was allowed to go for drives, he remarked, 'Why cannot
she come for a drive to Birla House?' If I had suggested anything of the
sort, Jivraj would have given me a long lecture but as it was the Mahatma
who asked, Jivraj said, 'Certainly she can!' So baby and I went for a
short while. Fortunately baby was asleep all the time. Bapu was lying
down but he held baby for a while and afterwards gave both of us his
birthday *prasad* [4] of almonds & raisins. Bapu said to me, '*Teri shakl to
bilkul badal gayi hai.*' [5] Whereupon Rajaji held forth on the effects of

1. Shah Behram: a famous emperor of Iran.
2. *Janam patra*: horoscope.
3. Astrologer.
4. Food offered to a deity and distributed among the devout.
5. Your appearance has changed completely.

motherhood on a woman and added, 'No woman is complete unless she has borne a child, she remains an unfinished experiment.' Fancy saying this to Bapu of all people and then in a roomful of women who are not likely to get married!

We are wondering what you thought of the names we sent. Vatsala has called her daughter 'Sasmitha', which means 'with a smile'. I like the meaning but not the sound.

As I have written above, I am enclosing, along with baby's *patra*, a rough English translation of the *jyotishi's* reading of the *patra*. This translation is Rajabhai's. No doubt Narendraji and maybe some others who are with you will be able to read the *patra*.

In my next letter I hope to be able to send a snap of the baby. In five days he will be a month old.

We hear from Puphi that Rita has malaria. So they are both still in Calcutta.

Much love to you, darling,

From your loving,
Indu

---

223.                                              [c/o Mrs Hutheesing,]
20, Carmichael Road,
Bombay,
3rd October, 1944

Darling Papu,
Bombay is getting stickier and hotter than ever. Puphi wrote some time ago that there was a lot of flu in Allahabad and the weather was pleasant. Feroze said don't come yet: it's hot in the day and cold at night. Now he wires that the weather is very good and we should come soon! Fortunately, I had stuck to my previous arrangements regardless of all their conflicting advice. I had booked for the 8th and that still stands. Six of us are going. Feroze's mother, Mrs Vakil, Ira, Anna and I and the *ayah* – not to mention the wee one.

Puphi will not be in Allahabad when we reach there – she has just wired that she will be away from the 5th to the 11th. We do not know where she is going, probably Delhi. By the way, has her list of names reached you?

The wee one is still yelling a lot – his tummy seems to be eternally upset. In between he rather alarmed us by putting on a pound in a week. I think he is settling down gradually.

I don't know how or why London gets excited about your health every now and then. I didn't mention your cold to anyone until after the report in the papers, when everybody asked if I had had any news from you.

The boys are returning to Gwalior on the 7th. Malati's mother is taking them back. Now that the day is drawing near, they are feeling unhappy at leaving home.

The periodicals you sent have arrived. I am sending you the following books:

1. *On Living in a Revolution*
2. *Reflections on the Revolution of Our Times*
3. *Battle Hymn of China*
4. *Reshaping Man's Heritage*
5. *Lady Precious Stream*
6. *Indigo*
7. *Mission to Moscow*

I am also sending a cigarette case. Chinnibhai (Sundaram) has given it to you. It is made in Travancore. Two other books that I had got for you have gone to Allahabad in Feroze's luggage by mistake. I shall send them when I get there.

I note what you have written about money gifts to the servants. Also about the cigarette-holder. The Persian primer I seem to remember having seen in Anand Bhawan just before leaving.

I have given the payment order to Puphi.

The *janam patra* has also arrived.

Much love,<br>Indu

224. Ahmadnagar Fort Prison,<br>21st October, 1944

Darling Indu,

I have had no news of you since your return to Allahabad. The first few days must have been rather full, for you had been away from home for many months . . .

Ever since Mahmud has left us and gone out we have read with some surprise the statements made by him or about him in the papers. But the biggest of all surprises came when we read an account of our life here which, *inter alia*, said that the older people played chess or cards 'and in the evening some girl inmates take to badminton'. Girls! Considering that we have not seen anything resembling a girl or a woman ever since we left Bombay twenty-six and a half months ago. And yet there it was soberly stated in *The Leader* as well as in the *Patrika* in some agency message. Both the Allahabad papers agreed in this and I wondered what our friends and others reading this would think of it. Evidently the sub-editors had found nothing odd about it and so it was possible that others might also imagine that benevolent and benign Govt had taken some steps to cheer us up by arranging to send some girls to play badminton in the evenings. But no. They did not come from out-side, they were the 'girl inmates'. Who were these girl inmates? Where exactly do I come in, for I play neither chess nor cards?

A reference to some other newspapers brought some light. Apparently the word 'agile' had been converted into 'girl' in the process of trans-mission. The editors of *The Leader* and *Patrika* were not clever enough to spot this or even to doubt the accuracy of the message.

We were informed two or three days ago that we would be permitted to have fortnightly interviews in the future under the usual jail rules. You must have seen this piece of news in the newspapers. After two years and two months and more we have forgotten all about interviews and only vague memories persist of what people outside our little group are like. For various reasons which I need not go into – some are obvious enough – we have decided not to take advantage of this generous offer and so we propose to take no interviews and to carry on as we are. Need I say how much I would like to see you and others again? But it is better to hold ourselves in patience and wait for the day, distant or otherwise, when we can meet in more normal circumstances. I have written to Betty and informed her of our decision. Will you tell Puphi also? She is thinking of going to America and both she and I would have liked to see each other before she goes. But there are so many things that we want to do and yet cannot and sometimes deliberately refrain from doing. That is all part of this game of life and we must accept it with good humour even when it hurts. [1]

We were supposed to have interviews with those to whom we are allowed to write. That means, so far as I am concerned, you and Puphi and Betty and Amma. Amma had also better be informed, though I suppose there was hardly any chance of her travelling two thousand miles in her present state of ill-health in order to have a brief interview with me.

So that is that!

1. On 17th October, 1944 Government announced that the interned Congress leaders could interview close relatives in prison but the leaders refused to accept the offer. Abul Kalam Azad, as President of the Congress, wrote that 'the general attitude of the Government towards us during the past twenty-six and a half months, and the rigorous isolation to which we have been subjected, even in spite of personal tragedies, are not calculated to incline us to take advantage of the personal facility'.

I see from the papers that Kailas and Sheila are returning at last with their two babies. I suppose they will travel via the Mediterranean. They ought to reach India early in November.

I have sent you back the following books & pamphlets:

1. Shakespeare's Works, Vol. IX
2. Gustav Stolper: *This Age of Fable*
3. *Mahabharata* (abridged)
4. *Dayananda and the Indian Problem*
5. Stalin's Report No. 17
6. *Peace Front and People's War*
7. Stalin: *War of Liberation*
8. Earl Browden: *Victory and After*
9. Orel
10. Kharkov
11. Sebastopol
12. *France Fights for Freedom*
13. *A New Germany in Birth*
14. *Spotlight on Yugoslavia*
15. *I.L.O. Man-power Mobilisation for Peace*

Also some periodicals.
Love,

Your loving,<br>Papu

This is my letter No. 85.

---

225. Anand Bhawan,<br>Allahabad,<br>14th November, 1944

Darling Papu,
This is to send you my very best wishes and my special love. We shall be thinking of you and missing you even more than usual. I have not even sent you a present this year – I just could not lay hands on anything worth giving which would also be suitable for Ahmadnagar Fort. But the search is not at an end, so I hope you will not mind getting it later.

The students had a *prabhat pheri*[1] this morning. It was well done. How long it is since we last had one! It is good to be awakened by good and enthusiastic voices. There is a meeting in Swaraj Bhawan in the evening. The municipal elections are on today, so there is a lot of noise and confusion and no *tongas* or *ekkas*[2] are available.

The Vakils left on the 5th. Two days before their departure Nani and Masi arrived unexpectedly and have been here ever since. They are leaving tonight. They will go to Lucknow for a couple of days to get together Kailas Mamu's things. Since their arrival I have been having rather late nights and no sleep in the day – with the result that I am quite fagged out. Masi and the little boy, Om, had had colds but they all insisted on sleeping under a fan at night. Not unexpectedly I caught the cold too and have been feeling rather wretched. The worst part of it is the wearing of a handkerchief mask while attending to baby. It's so stuffy and uncomfortable but I dare not risk his catching cold again after all the trouble we had last time. Rajiv is getting on very well. He sleeps most of the time and for the rest is content to be awake smiling to himself and making all kinds of peculiar sounds if any one is there to speak to. We had him vaccinated on the 27th Oct. It is all over now and he is settling down to his routine nicely. I want to keep him out in the open for as long as possible and fortunately he loves it. In the morning it is rather cold for him to leave the room before sunrise but if he is delayed for a little after seven thirty he starts yelling and only stops when he is out. He stays in his pram in the garden until nine fifteen, which is bathtime. Then after the ten o'clock feed his cot is put out on the verandah and he stays there until four o'clock, when he again goes downstairs in the garden until six. On the hospital weighing machine – which does not seem to be too accurate – baby's weight is 11 lb 13 oz . . .

Upadhyaya has gone to Almora for ten or fifteen days.

There seem to be several fountainpens in the house but none of them in working order. There is no cigarette-holder like yours but there is one of another kind. I shall send it to you.

Thank you very much for the cheque. I am accumulating all my birthday presents in advance this year!

Mrs Naidu has only to take a pen in hand to turn out prose that is sheer poetry. I wish she could write or at least get some of her letters published. Some of them are so much more beautiful than her poems. This telegram from her has just arrived: 'Our hearts turn in love today towards one whose prison is the nation's sanctuary.'

Bul and Mahmud sent a joint telegram addressed to Rajiv *ratna*:

1. *Prabhat pheri*: a tradition of taking out processions on festive occasions. The tradition was utilised for political purposes during the freedom struggle.
2. Refers to varieties of two-wheeled carriages drawn by horses.

'Many happy returns for your first celebration of grandfather's birthday.'
   With very much love from us three,
Indu

---

226.                                  Ahmadnagar Fort Prison,
18th November, 1944

Darling Indu,

It is a little over three weeks since I had a letter from you. I suppose Rajiv keeps you pretty well occupied and the multifarious new duties following motherhood fill the day and tire you. That is inevitable at this stage and so I do not expect you to be very regular in your letter-writing. I should, however, like to have news of Rajiv. Puphi mentioned in a letter she sent from Lucknow that he had been vaccinated and his arm had swollen up. He must have been unwell and very restless and requiring constant attention. I hope he has got over this completely and is now well and prospering. In another two days he will be three months old. More and more he will resemble a human being. Can he sit up now without support? I should like to have a good picture of him to find out how he is growing and what he looks like now.

I have received two books, apparently under your instructions: *Gandhiji* – the anniversary volume – and Laski's *Reflections on the Revolution of Our Time*. Have you purchased Laski's book or has it been borrowed from someone? I ask this as I have found some passages in it marked in pencil.

Last week I wrote [1] to you that I had received some books from Edward Thompson and also a message about his illness. There was some brief information about his sons also. The younger one was serving in the army in Italy, the elder one was, it was stated, on some secret mission and no letter had come from him for some time. Yesterday I read in the papers of the death in June last of this elder son. He was working then with the partisans in Bulgaria – a dangerous job. There was thus a sufficient reason for his not writing to his father, for he had been dead for many months. The news has distressed me greatly, though such things must happen in war. He was a very bright boy – his school & college record had been thus far brilliant – and his father was tremendously proud of him. And yet, even in 1938, Thompson was obsessed with the thought of the coming war and used to say that all their bright young men were destined to die in them – just cannon fodder they were.

---

1. Letter not published.

This death must be a great blow to him. The younger son was at school in 1938. He wrote me a letter once from school.

Is it possible to write a cable to France now? If so I should like to have news of Louise Morin and Jean-Jacques – also of Nanu. How people disappear from our lives behind the black curtain of war!

Puphi is, I understand, busy with her passages and her priorities. I was astounded to learn from her letter that an air passage from India to New York in an American plane costs $900. If that is the kind of price one has to pay for air travel in the future, then I am afraid there is little chance of my indulging in it, much as I prefer it to other methods of transport.

This is my letter No. 89.

Love,

From your loving,<br>Papu

---

227.

Anand Bhawan,<br>Allahabad,<br>24th November, 1944

Darling Papu,

I sent you a brief and rather inadequate letter on your birthday. There was so much I wanted to say. All day I was poignantly aware of the emptiness of the house. Many people celebrated the day and some sent messages to me. But nobody seemed to understand how almost unbearably it hurt to remember that this day you spent your birthday in jail for the fifth time in succession. It seems a poor reward for all that you brought into the world fifty-five years ago – a new vision of hope and beauty for all the downtrodden people of the earth. However, it is not in our tradition to grieve and I know how much you would disapprove if we did. So, let us, instead, offer thanks to whatever gods there be for you and all you mean in this tragically unhappy world. I was proud of the moving tributes that were paid to you – Edward Thompson's was rather beautiful, wasn't it? I hope all these greetings brought cheer to your day and lifted it out above the monotony of life in the fort . . .

I miss you so much when I am with baby. You would love to watch him learn and develop day by day.

Much love,

Indu

---

228.

> Anand Bhawan,
> Allahabad,
> 14th December, 1944

Darling Papu,

You must have seen in the papers that Puphi arrived in America on the 8th. There is naturally no news of Rita yet.

Kailas Mamu has got his old job in the Lucknow University . . . He is staying with a friend in Lucknow, as he has not been able to get his house. Mami and the children are in Lahore with Nani. I hear the children are unwell; after all their travelling amid strange people and custom and food, I am not surprised. Pyare Mausa [1] is going to America too. He is being sent by some business firm. He has now got his passport, visa, etc, I believe, and is awaiting his passage.

I am enclosing a dividend warrant – it is an old one – to be signed. Also some snaps of Rajiv. They are taken at different times – I have written the dates on the back of the picture. Two are enlargements and two are in the original size. They are so small and quite a strain on the eyes. Because of the paper shortage it is not easy to place large orders for enlarging or even printing. At the moment we have no more films. I have written to Rajabhai to get one in Bombay and send it to us. As soon as it arrives I shall send a snap of mine – or I might get photographed at Zaidis. I am not really looking any different, only a little fuller . . .

My *ayah* – her name is Roffin Roberts – is indeed very good with Rajiv. She is Goanese Catholic, fond of babies and competent and hardworking . . .

Yunus has got engaged to a young Christian girl from Lahore, Lajwanti Rallia Ram. You may not remember her but you have met her at a party in Lahore. I don't know her very well but I liked her immensely when I met her for a brief while. She is very good-looking and bright. The engagement ceremony took place in October in Yunus's absence and in great secrecy . . . Yunus's family are in the know and just a very few friends. Lajwanti has now written to me that Yunus wants you to be told. Yunus has had made a pair of Peshawari sandals for you and would like to send them to you . . .

Swami Abhayanand sent two bottles – not very large – of honey, one for Puphi and one for me. Mrs Vakil was here when mine came and we used it up almost immediately. (You and I are the only ones in the family who like honey and eggs.) Puphi has left her bottle to be sent to you. It

---

1. P. N. Kathju, uncle of Indira Gandhi. 'Mausa' means maternal uncle.

is not difficult to send it if you would like to have it – there is often somebody going to Bombay.

Your yarn is with the G.S.S. [Gandhi Seva Sadan]. Every now and then I remind Psyche about it but she says it is not possible to get it woven well these days and it would be a pity to spoil it. I have written to her to try and get it done in Andhra if possible, as that is the best place for fine yarn.

With much love from all of us,

Indu

<hr />

229.                                           Anand Bhawan,
                                                   Allahabad,
                                      20th December, 1944

Darling Papu,

Greetings to you for the New Year. There was a time when New Year's Day was a day of hope and of making plans and resolves. But now the future looks gloomy and even blacker than the grim present.

Mrs Naidu passed through Allahabad on her way to Calcutta yesterday. She had made a special request that Rajiv should go to the station to meet her with some food! The *Amrita Bazar* reporter thought Rajiv was eight months old, or so he says in this morning's paper. What short memories people have.

Actually Rajiv is exactly four months old today. We were invited to tea at the Parkers (Chand's old Woodstock principal who is now at the Ewing Christian College). They have a daughter of nine months. Being so much older, she was sitting up and munching a crust of bread but she did not have the bright and alert look that Rajiv has.

Dr Katju, [1] who is the chairman of our local hospital committee, has appointed me the joint secretary. I do not yet know who is going to be the other secretary.

Chandrashanker Shukla, [2] who used to be in charge of the *Harijan* office in Poona, wants to translate & publish one of your articles, 'slightly condensed', written in reply to Soumyendranath Tagore [3] and published in *India and the World,* in a Gujarati volume containing selections of appreciation of Bapu. Full acknowledgements will be made.

The National Publishing Co. of Madras wish to reproduce your birth-

1. Dr Kailas Nath Katju: lawyer and nationalist leader who later held ministerial office in the Government of India.

2. Chandrashanker Shukla: writer and journalist; Mahatma Gandhi's Secretary, 1933–4; editor of the Gujarati edition of *Harijan,* 1933–40.

3. Soumyendranath Tagore: Marxist leader and intellectual.

day letter to me from *India and the World* in their *Selections from English Literature*, edited by Prof. M. S. Doraiswamy B.A. (Oxon), Professor of English, Osmania University. The book is intended for the use of High Schools in India.

I am glad you liked the fruit. I should like to send some more if I can find anyone to take it.

Jivraj Mehta is coming on the 30th or so. I shall send the fruit with him if it is not too ripe by then.

I have now procured a copy of *Anna Karenina*. But Chhoti Puphi writes that she has sent you one in French, so I presume you do not want the English one.

Much love,
Indu

---

230.                                          Ahmadnagar Fort Prison,
                                              23rd December, 1944


Darling Indu,
Yesterday I read in the papers that when Sarojini was passing through Allahabad you went with Rajiv to the station to meet her. Rajiv was described as eight months old. This was of course just double his age, but I wondered if he was big enough looking to delude people. I suppose he is growing fast. For another three months or a little more, Allahabad will be just right for him, but then the warmer weather will not be so suitable. I am not a great believer in children being protected too much from our normal climate. They should get used to it or else they become misfits and physically somewhat unstable. But still I think that it will be better for him to spend his first hot weather in a better & cooler climate. I wonder if you have thought of it? The average hill-station is always a nuisance and expensive, but since the war began, it has become even more unattractive and difficult of access. I think it would be good for both Rajiv and you if you took him to Khali. [1] Except for the fact that it is somewhat out of the way and not easy to reach, everything is in its favour. The climate is delightful and the pine-clad hills are full of health. Personally, from a psychological point of view also, I fancy the mountain air and atmosphere for a growing child. It broadens his vision and gives him new perspectives. Khali will also require very little in the way of

1. A place in the Almora hills in uttar Pradesh where Ranjit Pandit owned a house.

special arrangement for you. Only the journey will be a little trying. From the point of view of Khali also it will be good for one to live there for a while. It is far too much neglected.

If you go to Khali, it would be desirable to ask Sheila and her children to join you there. These kids may also find their first hot weather a little trying and the change from London in wartime to the open air of the Indian mountains will be very good for them.

It seems a bit odd for me to think and write about the summer when we are still in the early stages of our winter season. All manner of fresh developments may take place in this little world of ours during these coming months and it is not always wise to make plans too far ahead. Yet it is better to accept things as they are and plan for them, rather than to wait for something to happen. Plans can always be changed to fit in with changing circumstances. Very little planning indeed is necessary. All you have to do is to inform the Khali people well in advance so that they can keep the house clean and ready. This will anyway keep them up to the mark. I do not know who is running Khali now. Puphi wrote to me that she had asked Krishnaji[1] of Lucknow to look after it in some way or other. Probably this had more to do with the garden produce and the cottage industries that are or were carried on there. You can write to Krishnaji and tell him of your intention to visit Khali in the summer. Upadhyaya should also write to Chandra Singh at Khali – I hope I have got the name right. If you go to Khali you should take Upadhyaya with you. He will be useful there and knows the people in Almora. Also it will do him good.

Sheila has had a hard time during the past five and a half years. I should like her to have some rest and a holiday. She and her children should of course be wholly our guests at Khali and no burden of expense should fall on her. Do not mind the expense of your or her going there. You should draw on my account for it. I suppose about mid-April will be the right time to go there. It is still spring there then and very delightful. On your way to Khali you could break journey at Bareilly for a little rest. Anyway, you have to change at Bareilly. Our friends, the Dwarka Prasad[2] family, will be happy to have you in Bareilly. Where Dwarka Prasad is now I do not know – in prison or out. But he has a huge family . . .

How is Madan Bhai getting on? Have you any fresh news of him?

Betty writes to me that she intends going to Allahabad at the end of January and to spend a month there. I am glad.

1. Krishna Narayan: a businessman of Lucknow.
2. Dwarka Prasad: a *zamindar* or landlord of Bareilly, active in the freedom struggle.

You should get this letter on the eve of the New Year. So again all my love and good wishes to you and Rajiv.

Your loving,<br>
Papu

This is my letter No. 94.

---

231.

Ahmadnagar Fort Prison,<br>
30th December, 1944

Darling Indu,

This is my last letter to you written in 1944. What a year it has been all over the world and in India, and what a contrast between the wars and tumults outside and our quiet unchanging life here. Every new year brings the promise of youth and yet it ages soon and the bloom fades off. So we shall enter 1945, inevitably affected by some psychological process of change and with our minds stretching out into the future. How one clings to the future in spite of repeated experience that this future is often enough just a continuation of the stale past.

After a long interval I have returned to you some books. These are:

1. R. Mehta's *Pre-Buddhist India*
2. Munshi's *The Glory that was Gurjardesh, Parts I and III*
3. Dr Sarma's *The Renaissance of Hinduism*
4. *Reshaping Man's Heritage*
5. *Prayers, Praises & Psalms*
6. Masani's *Socialism Reconsidered*

There are many other books that I have to return. I must get rid of my accumulations. I shall send them to you in small batches next month by post.

Some newspapers have come out with a story of the many books I have been reading recently. You must have seen the long list given. As a matter of fact out of that long and varied list I have only received three books, the others you could not obtain for me. The list represents many of the books I have asked for during the last year or more, not the books I received. I wonder how the newspapermen got hold of these titles. Probably Betty keeps a list and someone saw this and made a foolish and incorrect use of it. But it is a trivial matter and does not make any difference.

As you keep a list of books wanted, you might add to it Aldous Huxley's new novel: *Time Must Have a Stop*. Huxley is one of the authors one does not like to miss. I suppose it will be some time before this book appears in India . . .

I have had no letter from you for two weeks. I hope all is well with you and Rajiv.

Love to you and Feroze and the little one.

Your loving,<br>Papu

This is my letter No. 95.

---

232.
Anand Bhawan,<br>Allahabad,<br>New Year's Day, 1945

Darling Papu,

Well, here's another year. Somehow it doesn't seem appropriate to say 'Happy New Year'. Each year seems to be worse than the last, and what chance is there that 1945 will mean anything but more misery, more killing and more corruption. Even the weather is cheerless and grey. We have been having delightful sunny cool days but at about one o'clock last night the clouds started gathering and it rained. Now it is damp and cold and so dark that I have to have the light on in my room.

Rajiv likes the cold. Anyway he has solved the problem of clothing him warmly enough when it is especially cold, by snuggling under a thick blanket and sleeping all day. He is getting on well and has started having a teaspoonful of rice water every day.

Jivraj Mehta was to come here after the conference in Cawnpore but he got flu and a toothache and so decided to go straight back to Bombay. Vatsala was very upset as she had put aside a lot of matter concerning the hospital to be dealt by him.

I like your suggestion regarding Khali. You know that I dislike the conventional hill-stations and that I was enraptured by the very short glimpse I had of Khali and its surroundings. But I must first find out if it is all right to take Rajiv to such an out-of-the-way place for his first summer, especially as he will be teething about that time. Vatsala advised against Kashmir. And Kashmir will be very expensive until Rajiv is a little bigger and can rough it. I wonder what conveniences there are now to get to Khali. The rationing of petrol must have made a considerable difference. However, I shall write to Krishnaji and Mami.

The only alternative to Khali is Ootacamund, from Rajiv's point of view. The only disadvantage is the distance, and the necessity of breaking journey in Bombay.

Mami is still in Lahore but is now staying with her parents – or rather

her mother, for the father died while she was in England. Mamu came
again for a day to fetch the luggage that they had left behind.

Much love,<br>Indu

---

233.                                       Ahmadnagar Fort Prison,
                                           5th January, 1945

Darling Indu,

Today, probably for the first time since we came here, the temperature
registered a sudden fall and reached 38°F or possibly lower. Having got
rather used to long spells of warm and equable weather this change has a
sting in it, or may be my bones are getting older. My hands are quite cold.
I am almost regretting having sent back some *kurtas* [1] and pyjamas,
though I have enough to carry on with and the cold will not last many days.

I received two letters from you on the 31st Dec. – dated 14/12 and 20/
12. [2] Why there should have been this delay in my getting the earlier letter
I do not understand, especially as it bears a pencil endorsement – probably
made in the Bombay Secretariat – that it was received there on 28/12. It
seems to have taken two weeks to go from Allahabad to Bombay.

Rajiv's pictures are good. He looks quite human. He is attractive and
has got a good-humoured look. In some of them he resembles you, in one
there is a marked resemblance to Feroze. Don't forget to send me a good
picture of yourself. The idea of your getting fat amuses me . . .

I have received a letter (No. D.O.G./9549 of Allahabad, Dec. 9,
1944) from W. G. P. Wall, Director of Public Instruction, U.P., together
with a copy of a scheme he has drawn up for the 'Kamala Nehru
Scholarship Endowment Trust Fund'. I do not know if this came
through you or direct. Anyway I do not propose to write to him directly
as this might involve special requests to Govt Will you, therefore, please
write to him and give him my message? Tell him that I have received
his letter and scheme and I am grateful to him for all the trouble he has
taken in this matter. As for the scheme, he is in the best position to
judge and to fit it in with Govt. rules and regulations. So he can go
ahead and do what he thinks best. There is, however, one basic suggestion which I am making for his consideration, but it should be understood that this is just a suggestion. He can decide as he thinks best
under the circumstances. The suggestion is this: It seems to me that it
might be better to use the income as it comes in rather than to accumu-

---

1. A loose shirt without collar and cuffs.
2. Refers to letters No. 228 and 229.

late it and only use the interest. This will yield a much larger sum for use immediately. From his letter it appears that a sum of Rs. 3904/14 has so far been collected in the course of the last four or five years. That means an annual income of between Rs. 780/- and Rs. 975/-, say Rs. 800/-. Whether this is likely to be a regular income or not I do not know. Even if we put it at Rs. 600/- per annum, this means Rs. 50/- per month. If it is possible to use this sum immediately it could be divided up into scholarships of Rs. 10/- each. Rs. 5/- a month seems rather a small sum to give. If most of the income is being used up as it comes in, then of course there is no chance for a permanent fund to grow up, but immediate results are obtained. As I have said above, he can decide as he thinks best.

Chandrashanker Shukla can publish my old article in reply to Soumyendranath Tagore.

The National Publishing Co. of Madras can also reproduce the birthday letter. This is really the first one in *Glimpses* and normally the publishers have to be consulted. But in present conditions this might be dispensed with. It will be desirable however for some token payment to be made. I suggest that they pay Rs. 25/- to the Kamala Nehru Memorial Hospital.

I think you had better send me *Anna Karenina* in English. Betty has not sent this book in French to me. Anyway there are others who would like to read it in English. There is another book that I would like you to send: W. Macneile Dixon's *The Human Situation*. This was with me here a year and a half ago – I sent it to you to Panchgani in July 1943. I find now that Maulana would like to see it. If you can trace it easily, have it sent. Otherwise do not bother.

Could you ask Feroze or someone else to find out from the Professor of Physics, Allahabad University, some names of, more or less, recent books on modern developments in physics, especially the Theory of Relativity and the Quantum Theory. If he can supply the books, all the better. They will be returned to him. There is another way also of finding out about these books. You can ask Betty – she will probably be in Allahabad soon – to write to Homi Bhabha[1] at the Bangalore Institute of Science to get the information.

I am glad you have become joint secretary of the local hospital committee . . .

Love,

Your loving,
Papu

---

1. Homi Bhabha: eminent scientist; later became Chairman of the Indian Atomic Energy Commission.

234. Anand Bhawan,
Allahabad,
7th January, 1945

Darling Papu,
Your letter of Dec. 30.[1]

I am sending you today the following things: forty guavas, a tin of guava cheese, a bottle of guava jelly. Also two books.

These books: *In Russia Now* by Walter Citrine, and *Russia Triumphant* by George Sava, belong to Mr Jinarajadasa.[2] He is a leading Theosophist come to deliver lectures in Allahabad. Yesterday Vatsala Samant and I went to the Seva Samiti office in connection with the hospital. Mr Jinarajadasa walked in – he is staying in the building – and we talked about you. He said he had brought many new books from England and would like to lend you some. So here they are.

He is very impressed with the South American peoples. He said he would like to meet you and introduce you to the South American civilisation. Mr Jinarajadasa is over seventy years of age, I think, and a fine figure of a man. He has a beautiful voice.

Your list of wanted books must have leaked out through Mridula. I was complaining to her one day of the difficulty of obtaining the books, as I was mostly out of Bombay and the books get sold almost as soon as they arrive, and she asked for a copy of the list. This she deposited with some booksellers.

The rain has stopped but it is very cold. I do not know if the cold has increased or if my resistance is lower, but I never remember wearing so many warm clothes as I am found to do nowadays.

Much love,
Indu

---

235. Ahmadnagar Fort Prison,
12th/13th January, 1945

Darling Indu,
I have your letter[3] written on New Year's Day – No. 91.

I am glad you like the idea of going to Khali. Of course your plans and movements will largely be governed now and for some years to come by that young tyrant Rajiv. It was thought of him chiefly that led

1. Refers to letter No. 231.
2. C. Jinarajadasa: President of the Theosophical Society, 1946–52; author of over forty books.
3. Refers to letter No. 232.

me to suggest Khali. I should like him to become acquainted as early as possible with the Himalayas, have sight of the snow-covered peaks, look down into the deep valleys, and breathe the fragrant and health-giving air of the pine-clad hillsides. The more I think of it, the more I like the idea. Your fear that Khali is perhaps too out of the way and isolated is not really justified. We have got into the habit of thinking of places at some distance from a railway station as out of the way. Khali is for all practical purposes a suburb of Almora and can be reached from there within an hour or less. The motor road now almost touches the Khali estate. You can reach Khali from Allahabad within thirty-six hours, though it is preferable to proceed in a more leisurely fashion. As for medical facilities, Almora is as well provided as any average Indian city – apart from the big cities like Calcutta, Bombay, etc. There is a hospital there, a civil surgeon, an assistant civil surgeon and a number of private practitioners. The doctor I would recommend is Dr Khazan Chand[1] who is fairly competent and who would no doubt go out of his way to be of service to you. He has a car and can easily run up to Khali whenever wanted or at regular intervals. He is not a children's specialist of course but as a general practitioner he is as good as any in Allahabad.

In these days of rationing you will probably be better off in Khali than in most other places. There will be an abundance of fruit, vegetables, eggs, good milk, and most other necessaries can be obtained in Almora.

The journey to Khali seems troublesome and a little alarming but it is not really so. Indeed it is probably easier and more comfortable now than a long railway journey to the south. Both from the health point of view and that of accessibility, Ooty is not a patch on Khali. In a sense you would be more cut off there than in Khali, certainly removed from Allahabad. It will also be much more expensive.

The normal method of going to Almora is to go by motor bus or private car. Motor buses run regularly but obviously they are not indicated for Rajiv or you – I do not think there will be the least difficulty in getting a private car. Indeed Pantji[2] says that a letter from him from here can fix this up, though this is not necessary.

I would, however, suggest to you not to go by the motor road but to take to the bridle path instead. This suggestion, no doubt, surprises you for all of us are so used to travelling and even thinking in terms of the automobile. I am all for the automobile as a rule but its virtues are not so overwhelming in the mountains. The last time I went to Almora I decided that on the next occasion I would travel in a more leisurely way

1. Dr Khazan Chand: medical practitioner. He was Chairman of Almora Municipal Board.
2. Govind Ballabh Pant.

by the bridle path, either on foot or on horseback. Old memories came back to me and I remembered faintly how I had enjoyed that journey long ago, before the automobile had descended on these mountain roads. I was only eight or nine then, and at that age one can enjoy almost everything new. The whole family trekked – and it was a large family – and there used to be a long procession of ponies, *dandies*,[1] luggage porters, etc. That was Dadu's way of doing things. From Almora we had gone to the Pindari glacier – again that tremendous procession with additions, for we had to carry some tents also and food for the journey. When the family returned to Allahabad at the end of the summer they left me behind in charge of the headmaster of the local high school – a man named Thomas. I lived with his family for many months.

My next visit to Almora took place a long long time afterwards: it was in 1934 when I was taken to the Almora Jail! During the intervening years I had often been to Naini Tal and even beyond but I never managed to reach Almora. Once I almost got there. I was on my way to it when I got a telegram at Ranikhet that Mummie was very ill and I hurried back. This was I think in 1929 when Mummie and you were at Mussoorie.

But I had occasion to travel by the bridle path from Kathgodam to Ramgarh (on the way to Almora) in 1921 to see Dadu who was resting there.

The distance from Kathgodam to Almora by motor road is over eighty miles. By bridle path it is thirty-eight miles with three resting places on the way – Bhim Tal, Ramgarh and Piura – where there are good dak bungalows[2] or rest-houses. Each stage is about ten miles or less and it is pleasant going, shady as a rule, with ups and downs. Starting after a good breakfast, one can easily reach the next stage by lunchtime and spend the rest of the day there. Or, one can carry lunch and have it *en route* whenever one feels like it. The dak bungalows have cooks.

Some people, unused to this kind of travelling, may be a little frightened at the prospect. As a matter of fact it is very easy going and comfortable – probably far more so than the tedious and crowded railway journeys nowadays. One need not of course travel in the sumptuous and complicated way which Dadu favoured. Besides there are many facilities now which were unobtainable in the old days. For instance, all the heavy luggage can be sent on by lorry from Kathgodam to Almora, only bedding, some clothes and warm things and a few other necessaries need be taken with one. Each stage of the journey is an easy walk but naturally for you and Rajiv and the *ayah*, *dandies* would be necessary. If

---

1. Litters carried on men's shoulders.
2. Rest houses for travellers along main roads.

I had to go that way I would walk, keeping a pony for emergencies.

It is usually possible to arrange for *dandies* and ponies at almost a moment's notice at Kathgodam. But it is safer to fix them up a day or two ahead. It is quite easy to do so by writing or by sending someone (say Upadhyaya) a day before. A line to Pantji's family in Naini Tal (Chandra Dat) would facilitate matters.

This kind of journeying appeals to me but it is quite possible that it may not appeal to others who have less of the savage in them than I have. It depends really on a mental approach – even, you might say, a philosophy of life. Most of our journeys nowadays are looked upon as troublesome but inevitable affairs leading to the desired goal. So we put up with all manner of inconveniences on the way and arrive exhausted at journey's end. The goal and the journey's end are there of course but why not make the journey itself a part of the goal, giving health and pleasure, even apart from the more distant goal? The holiday, if one can call it that, should begin the moment we set off and not when we arrive at the other end. Life becomes fuller this way, the process of living consciously and actively is a continuous one and not a thing of fits and starts. There is also a sense of freedom about it, a lessening of dependence on others, apart from the communion with nature that it gives. All this trouble about petrol rationing vanishes. For Rajiv, who will be about eight months old by that time and able to sit up and take an intelligent interest in his surroundings, it should be a stimulating experience. He will have to go in a *dandy*, which is unfortunate. A year or two later he could have done a little walking or riding. I remember carrying about Betty in the front of my saddle in Naini Tal when she was about ten months old.

Thus the journey from Kathgodam to Khali becomes a delightful excursion with the minimum of worry. From Almora it would be desirable to go by car to Khali. It is only six or seven miles.

In Almora of course there are hosts of people who will be eager to help you in every way. Upadhyaya knows a lot of them. Probably the most useful person is Rudra Dat Bhat, a merchant. Then there is Badri Dat Pande.[1] And of course Gertrude and Boshi Sen.[2] The best time to go up is the middle of April. It will not be cold then and travelling by bridle path will be pleasant. Later it may become rather warm.

Of course if you prefer going by car, a private one can easily be fixed up. An advantage of Khali over Ooty will be that Feroze will be able to pay you frequent visits.

1. Badri Dat Pande: active in the national movement.
2. Boshi Sen and his wife Gertrude Emerson-Sen. They were friends of Jawaharlal Nehru and lived in Almora.

It is possible that Madan Bhai may be out and available by the time you go up. You should invite him to join you there. His health must be pretty well shattered up and rest at Khali will be good for him.

Have you heard about the Brewsters again? Thinking of Almora, they came to my mind. I have had no news of them for many years.

From the American papers I find that the Ramkrishna Centre of New York has issued a new translation of the *Gita* by Swami Nikhilananda. [1] This is very highly spoken of. I wonder if it is possible to obtain this from our friends at Belur Math. They ought to have it. You might write and enquire.

I am sending you back some books:

1. Gandhi: *Nonviolence in Peace & War*
2. Smith: *Modern Islam in India*
3. Gunther: *D-Day*
4. Thompson: *Burmese Silver*
5. Sampurnanand: *The Individual & the State*
6. De Silva: *The Four Essential Doctrines of Buddhism*
7. Ajwani: *Introducing India*

Yesterday we received a parcel of guavas which I suppose you had sent. They are excellent and maintain worthily the reputation of Allahabad. Also I received with them a bottle of guava jelly and a tin of guava cheese.

I have received a letter (dated 2/1/45) from the manager of the Allahabad Law Journal Press, informing me that the period of the sole agency for the sale of *Letters from a Father to his Daughter*, which was given to the Oxford University Press, expired on 31.12.1944, and the Oxford University Press want the agency renewed till 31.3.1949. Will you please tell the A.L.J. people that before I can send a proper reply or make any suggestions for the future I must have full particulars and information? I have no idea of what the terms of agency were or are. These were fixed up by Kitabistan without any previous reference to me and I was only informed of them later and then only, so far as I remember, partially. It is odd that a reference has now been made to me only after the expiry of the period of agency. This should have been done well in advance of it to enable me to consider the matter. Situated as I am, delay in consultation is inevitable. I do not, however, wish that existing arrangements should be upset suddenly because of this delay.

---

1. Swami Nikhilananda: Head of the Ramakrishna-Vivekananda Centre in New York and co-translator of many Sanskrit classics.

The Oxford University Press should be informed that I am waiting for some relevant information before coming to a decision; as soon as I receive this I shall communicate with the A.L.J. Press about future arrangements. Meanwhile, to avoid any confusion or gap period, I am agreeable to the Oxford University Press continuing the old agency on the old terms for another year, that is to the end of December 1945.

The A.L.J. Press to be requested to supply me with the following particulars:

1.  Copy of agreement with Oxford University Press.
2.  Statement about royalties received by them on my behalf during the past three years. What part of them have been paid over to me or to someone on my behalf? – and to whom? Any balances standing to my credit to be sent to Bachhraj & Co. Ltd., Bombay.
3.  Are the A.L.J. Press functioning both as printers & publishers of the book? Have Kitabistan any further interest in it?
4.  Is the book being issued in one uniform edition or in different formats – for students & the general public? What is the sale price of the book for both these categories of people?
5.  Is the book sold solely through the Oxford University Press? Do the A.L.J. Press not sell it directly to any booksellers?
6.  What institutions, so far as is known, have adopted it as a textbook? I understand that the Calcutta University adopted it for the matriculation exam. Has any other university or education department also done so – I am referring of course only to the English edition?
7.  Is there any continuing general sale of the book, apart from the sale as a prescribed textbook, and is this general sale specially catered for?
8.  Any other relevant information might be added.

Further, the A.L.J. Press might be asked if they have now any dealings with any of the translations of the book, apart from the Hindi & Urdu ones which they print for the U.P. Education Department. Do they issue any Hindi or Urdu edition for general public sale (apart from students)?

This is my letter No. 97 – I am getting on to the century!

Love,

Your loving,
Papu

*Later*

I have just got your letter of Jan. 7th [1] in which you mention the guavas, etc, Jinarajadasa & the cold. The guavas I have received, not the two books so far. I have not met Jinarajadasa but I have known of him ever since the days when I joined the Theosophical Society at the age of twelve or thirteen. He should really have been the President of the Theosophical Society after Mrs Besant [2] if Arundale [3] had not cut him out.

As for the cold we all seem to have felt that way. The news Pantji has received from Naini Tal is quite exciting – houses snowed up, etc.

I have also got today a letter from Puphi from New York sent soon after her arrival there. She complains of the cold also and at the same time of the overheated rooms. But her biggest grouse is the expensiveness of everything. She has not fallen in love with New York and dislikes its skyscrapers.

P.

236.                                        Ahmadnagar Fort Prison,
                                               20th January, 1945

Indu darling,

Accounts in the newspapers of the snow and cold in the north have exhilarated and excited me. Mussoorie and Simla and Naini Tal all snow-bound; people having to dig their way out of their houses; the roof of Hakman's Hotel collapsing from the weight of the snow; even Dehra Dun becoming all white with snow. Khali must have become one mass of snow and the house must have been half buried in it. I remember how I enjoyed a light snowfall in Almora in 1934–5 and hoped for more. In Dehra Dun I could only look wistfully at the snow on the neighbouring hills and hope that a favourable wind might bring some snow to my little yard also. Well, I suppose, this brief spell is past and is already a memory. Here, after a few days of cold weather, there was a rather sudden and marked change and now it is definitely warmish. I was surprised to discover that *Vasanta Panchami* had arrived – usually it

1. Refers to letter No. 234.
2. Annie Besant (1847–1933): theosophist and reformer, President of the Theosophical Society from 1907 till her death; participated in the nationalist struggle in India and presided over the Indian National Congress in 1918.
3. G. S. Arundale: President of the Theosophical Society, 1934–45.

comes off early in February. I remembered Vidya's marriage and connected it with this day, a favourite one for weddings. I hope the wedding
went off well and Vidya is happy about it.

We are ten now for Dr Prafulla Ghosh [1] has left us, exactly a hundred
days after Mahmud went. A century of days has become a useful unit
for us to note the passing of time. Months are over too soon and a year
passes slowly. That reminds me that in another six days – on the 26th
January – we shall complete 900 days here.

Dr Ghosh has, I read from the papers, said something about our
respective physical conditions and has pointed out that I am getting
older. True, none of us grows younger with the passing of time and all
our efforts to delude ourselves or others are childish and vain. But I
think Prafulla Babu has rather exaggerated, so far as I am concerned.
A person's activities or the lack of them depend so much on the passing
mood, which indeed is affected by the physical condition, but depends
also on many other factors. Generally speaking, I keep very well and I
propose to continue doing so. It is difficult to take an objective view of
oneself, though I try to do so. Compared to my companions here I am
a shining example of good health. Prafulla Babu has mentioned Pantji
also. That is more to the point and I have long been concerned about
him. These two years and a half have pulled him down in a variety of
ways and he is continually suffering from a number of ailments. Being
made that way, he tries to make light of them and would like others to
ignore them or at any rate not to worry about them. But that is not good
enough and I worry about him.

I have sent you the following books:

1.  *China Handbook 1943*
2.  *Global War*
3.  *Recent Judgements in India*
4.  *Pantopia*
5.  Tendulkar: *30 Months in Russia*
6.  *Grain-Standard Labour Money*
7.  Radhakrishnan: *Education, Politics & War*
8.  Shah: *Principles of Planning*
9.  *Ethics of Buddhism*
10. *Beautiful Valleys of Kashmir*

I have just received the two books which Jinarajadasa gave you:
Citrine's *In Russia Now* and George Sava's *Russia Triumphant*. Am I to

---

1. Dr Prafulla Chandra Ghosh: participated in the struggle for freedom and jailed,
1930, 1932, 1940, 1942–4; later was Chief Minister of West Bengal.

return these to you when I have finished with them? Or is there a way of my returning them direct to him?

More than a year ago Betty wrote to me that Mrs Robeson had sent her a letter in which she had mentioned sending me books from time to time. I told Betty that I had received none. Now Chand mentions this again in a letter to me. This is odd for I do not remember ever having received a book from Essie Robeson. When I was in Dehra in 1941 I received packets of newspaper cuttings from her. Indeed I wrote and asked her then for a number of books. I suppose the books she sent were lost in transit or were suppressed by the Censors. You have not, by any chance, received any book sent by her?

Betty must be with you – I wonder how she liked the cold. A long stay in Bombay is not a suitable preparation for facing real cold weather. How she and Raja used to shiver in Dehra Dun! Give my love to her, and to Rajiv and Feroze.

Love,

Your loving,<br>Papu

This is my letter No. 98.

237.
Anand Bhawan,<br>Allahabad,<br>23rd/26th January, 1945

Darling Papu,

I found your letter of the 12/13 Jan.[1] on my return from Lucknow. The books you sent have also arrived.

In my last letter to you, I believe I wrote about several enclosures. None of these were sent. I am now enclosing the dividend warrant in this letter. The press cutting and pamphlets are being sent separately. Some periodicals and three books, from Mr Jinarajadasa, have also been sent. Also the *Human Situation, When the Moon Died.* I should like to send *Best Stories of Modern Bengal* if you have not already read it.

The two last named books have been sent to me by Nilima.[2] Perhaps you have heard of the publishing house she has started. The Signet Press, it is called. These two books are samples of their work. They are well got-up, are they not? Nilima wanted to write to you to 'request you to allow them the privilege of publishing the Indian edition' of whatever

1. Refers to letter No. 235.
2. Nilima: writer and publisher.

book you may be writing. The aim of the Signet Press is to raise the standard of book-publishing in India to compete favourably with foreign publications, using Indian paper, Indian printing and Indian artists as illustrators. The above-mentioned books are the only English ones they have so far published. But they have brought out about a dozen Bengali books . . .

*Independence Day*

We have had the usual flag ceremony at home. Rajiv helped me to hoist the flag! He also made weird accompaniments to the flag song. This year we have had a flag-hoisting in the Civil Lines [1] as well – over the *Patrika* building.

Your letter of the 20th [2] has come.

You asked me some time ago for some tubes of Bengue's Balsam. There are none in your bathroom, nor anywhere else in India. Chitti says that Thermogene is very good. We are trying to get some for you.

Yes, the news of snowfalls all over was exciting, but here it was a wet cold which is not so agreeable. The last days have been warm but yesterday we had a spot of rain and people are prophesying another cold spell.

No books have arrived from America either from Essie Robeson or anyone else.

Do you want to renew your subscription to all the American magazines that you are getting? You have been getting reminders from all.

Mr Wall writes that he is considering your proposition. If you like you can return Mr Jinarajadasa's books direct to C. Jinarajadasa, The Theosophical Society, Adyar, Madras.

Chitti is here and writing to you so she will probably give all the news regarding Vidya's wedding. It went off quite well and Vidya seems to be happy, which is the chief thing. They had a civil marriage in the evening followed by some puja . . . Vidya will keep her maiden name for her work. I was glad I went, chiefly because Vidya was happy to have me and I was very useful to her. I dressed her for the wedding and the next day. Chhoti Puphi, Shammie Didda and I did all the packing of presents and other effects, made lists of clothes, presents, etc, and a whole heap of other jobs as well. Of course on top of all this were the usual chores of cutting the vegetables, serving and so on. Bijju Chachi came, also Mohanbhai and Bhabhi, Rajan Kale and Manoharbhai. [3] I saw Radha after many years. How she has changed! All her beauty is gone. She was looking thin and plain. She has taken up nursing.

1. A suburb of Allahabad outside the medieval walled city complex.
2. Refers to letter No. 236.
3. Manoharlal Nehru: nephew of Jawaharlal Nehru.

I had a talk with Sheila Mami about her going to the hills. She is going to Secunderabad to stay with her brother and does not want to go anywhere else.

I am still pondering over Khali. Chhoti Puphi is going to Kashmir. You have made the bridle path journey sound very attractive but with Rajiv's feeds and teething it cannot be very pleasant. I have not been able to continue feeding him myself and he now gets Ostermilk. This complicates things considerably . . .

Rajiv does not sit up yet but he makes valiant efforts to raise himself while he is lying down.

With lots of love,<br>
Indu

238.                                             Anand Bhawan,<br>
Allahabad,<br>
9th February, 1945

Darling Papu,

There has again been a long gap in my letters to you. It seems I can do just so much and no more. Just when I had got Rajiv settled to a routine which allowed me time to attend to my letters and visitors and other odd jobs, Puphi came along. Of course that does not affect Rajiv's routine except that he gets an extra amount of cuddling, and loves it too! But I wanted to give Puphi as good a time as Allahabad can provide, knowing that she finds it dull enough usually. So we went out quite a lot and had people in to meals, and so on. I think she liked it. Now we are having a hospital week and she has been helping us.

Collecting money is a terrible job. It takes so much time and energy. We started off rather well with Sir Tej's cheque of Rs. 500/-. The day before – on the 7th – Sir Tej was returning from a party when he passed the hospital. He admired the building. Fortunately Ladli Chacha was with him and was able to persuade him to go in and have a look. Sir Tej was very impressed. I decided to go to him for funds while the impression was still green. Sir Tej is very keen that a statue or bust of Mummie be put in the hall. He advises that a separate appeal be issued for this purpose – he will himself subscribe.

Puphi changes her plans every day but she has finally decided to leave Allahabad on the 13th for Delhi.

Much love,<br>
Indu

239.                        Ahmadnagar Fort Prison,
17th February, 1945

Darling Indu,

I have your letter of Feb. 9th.[1] Now that I know that both you and Rajiv are keeping well, it does not matter much if your letters do not come regularly. So do not trouble about this. Write only when you feel in the mood for it. It is seldom worthwhile to write when there is no particular urge to do so. I write fairly regularly as there are only a limited number of activities here and inevitably one develops a routine.

I have read in the papers the answer which Mudie,[2] the Home Member, gave in the Central Assembly about the health of the internees in Ahmadnagar Fort. He said that I had had an attack of lumbago but had recovered from it. We are used to odd and novel statements made on behalf of the Government and try not to be surprised. But it was something of a surprise for me to associate lumbago with myself. I looked up the word in the dictionary for I was not clear about its precise significance – I found that it was a 'rheumatic affection in loins'. Certainly I have not had, recently or at any other time, any such 'affection', and so I conclude that I have never had lumbago. There appears to be something wrong about the sources or channels of the information that reaches Govt. Normally this error is the outcome of a desire to tone down something or make it appear, as far as language can help, to be something other than it is. But there was no particular reason for saying that I had lumbago when I had suffered from no such malady. I imagine that the lapse was due to carelessness or inefficiency somewhere, or mixing me up with another person here who did have lumbago. It is true that I had a slight pain in my left shoulder and round about it for some days. It was not much but it interfered with my sleep and exercises. What annoyed me was that I should have had it at all, for any bodily weakness or disability irritates me. I got over it by massage and fomentation and especially sunbaths. I have been completely free from it and have been indulging in my exercises as usual. The plague inoculation came in the way but that too is over, with all its after-effects.

I have received the two books and a pamphlet which Jinarajadasa sent you. They are:

1. Sean O'Faolain: *The Great O'Neill*
2. H. Fortes Anderson: *Borderline Russia*

1. Refers to letter No. 238.
2. Sir (Robert) Francis Mudie: Chief Secretary, U.P. Government, 1939–43; Home Member, Viceroy's Executive Council, 1944–5; Governor of Sind, 1946–7; Governor of West Punjab, 1947–9.

3. Jinarajadasa: *Economics & Theosophy*

*The Human Situation*, which you mentioned, was not in this lot.

I might mention that I have also received two new books from Rupa & Co., who sometimes send me books. These are: Wavell's *Allenby in Egypt* and A. L. Rowse: *The English Spirit*. Wavell's book was in a list of books required that I sent you last year. You can strike it off from it.

I have returned the following books to you:

1. Julian Huxley: *On Living in a Revolution*
2. Shaukat Ansari: *Pakistan*
3. Borodin: *Soviet & Tsarist Siberia*
4. Nym Wales: *New China*
5. Tikhov Semushkin: *Children of the Soviet Arctic*
6. *History of the Communist Party of the Soviet Union*
7. Alexei Tolstoy: *My Country*
8. Dean of Canterbury: *The Socialist Sixth of the World*
9.      – Do –      : *Soviet Strength*
10. *Correspondence with Mr Gandhi* (Govt Publication)

Semushkin's *Children of the Soviet Arctic* I found rather fascinating reading. It is simply written, but the account of change creeping in, or rather sweeping in, to those remote areas is very interesting. Apart from this, the Arctic and wide stretches of snow and ice have always attracted me.

I have read in the newspapers that Rafi has been transferred to Naini Prison. Why he should have been transferred to a place where special medical attention is not easily available is difficult to understand, more especially at this time of the year with the summer looming ahead. I wonder if you could arrange to send him fresh fruit regularly. What the jail rules are about this I do not know but you can easily find out if you do not know them already. You can put Upadhyaya in charge of it and either he or Khaliq can carry the parcel, say once a week.

Probably Rafi will appreciate books even more than fruit. Books are apt to get waylaid or lost when sent to prison. I have lost many that way, including a parcel of them sent to Rafi to Bareilly in 1942. But that was not his fault, as the books apparently never reached him. There is less danger of loss or disappearance if they are sent and recovered by messengers. Anyway the risk has to be taken, for I should like Rafi to have good reading matter. You can pick out such books as you think suitable – a packet of three or four at a time can be sent and recovered when the next packet goes.

Also foreign periodicals, even though they are pretty old. I asked you in my last letter to send some of these to Sucheta Kripalani. Some might be sent to her, but I would like a more regular supply to go to Rafi – *Life* & *Time* & other magazines are likely to interest him . . .

As I was writing this letter I received a packet of books from you:

1. *The Human Situation*
2. Swami Nikhilananda's *Bhagavad Gita*
3. Vivekananda's *Lectures from Colombo to Almora*
4.    – Do –     *Letters*
5.    – Do –     *Karma Yoga*
6. Nilima's *When the Moon Died*

and some pamphlets, including a reprint of some old speech of mine – also Thermogene – thank you.

Betty seems to have decided to go to Kashmir. She suggests that you might accompany her. If you could manage it, it would be excellent. You know that for me there is no place like Kashmir. But you have to take Rajiv into consideration. There is no obvious reason why he should not benefit by a visit to Kashmir, in spite of the long journey. Anyway you will be the best person to decide. Khali just by yourself & Rajiv is not an attractive proposition.

Love,

Your loving,
Papu

This is my letter No. 102.

---

240.                                          Anand Bhawan,
                                                    Allahabad,
                                        17th February, 1945

Darling Papu,

Poor little Rajiv has been shoved in the background by the hospital week – I have hardly seen him this last week. Fortunately he does not seem to miss me at all!

Actually our week should have been over on the 15th but we have extended it as it was physically impossible to finish the collections in that short time. This was my first experience of collecting funds or indeed of doing any such work all on my own – so, in spite of many mistakes, I do not think we have done badly. The brunt of the whole collection fell on Vatsala and me, the other members of the committee helping us not at all. Then, Dr Katju had so worded his appeal that it was directed to the citizens of Allahabad alone. This is the first time that no money from outside has come in. In 1943, when the week was last celebrated, Rs. 4000 only [was] collected in Allahabad, Rs. 6000/- came from outside. This year we have already got Rs. 7500/- from Allahabad and by the end of the week the figure will rise to Rs. 10,000/- we hope.

In the process of collecting I have lost 4lbs in weight and am thoroughly fagged out. I shall be glad when the week is over, although that will not be the end of the collection. The Allahabad Culture Centre is giving us a show and we have to sell the tickets. The Allahabad Friends of the Soviet Union is giving us the proceeds of a Russian film. But since that Society has died a natural death – or at least is lying dormant – I can see all the arrangements for it coming to my door.

I hope the reaction to the plague injection has settled down. I hear it is a painful one. I have never had it, although I was in Poona when plague was raging there and there was an unending procession of carts loaded with corpses passing by our gate. I was spared the inoculation because at that time I had one of my usual attacks of tonsillitis.

The prospect of Khali has receded way into the background. Chhoti Puphi is very keen on going to Kashmir – last year she could not go because of me. At my suggestion she wrote to Dewan Ram Lall[1] and he has offered us his house. It seemed a pity to let that lovely house go [to] waste so we have decided that I should also go there. So my plan is to go to Lahore as soon as Allahabad gets hot and to wait there for Puphi and her family, so that we can all travel up to Srinagar together.

The key of the godown containing Dadu's law books is with me. As soon as I have a little time I want to clear up the place – list the books and so on. The *Rajtarangini*[2] have been removed to Puphi's Mukerji Road house.

Kapildeva Malaviya's[3] daughters are attractive girls – the middle one is at the University and the youngest at the Crosthwaithe.[4]

Lots of love,
Indu

---

1. Dewan Ram Lall: brother of Diwan Chaman Lall (see Political Circle).

2. A poem composed in Sanskrit by Kalhana, which narrates the history of Kashmir from the earliest times to the twelfth century, translated by Ranjit Pandit into English during his imprisonment. The translation was published in 1945.

3. Kapildev Malaviya: nephew of Madan Mohan Malaviya; a leading criminal lawyer of Allahabad; active in the national movement.

4. Crosthwaite: refers to a well-known girls' school in Allahabad, Crosthwaite Girls' High School.

241.                                    Ahmadnagar Fort Prison,
                                          24th February, 1945

Darling Indu,
I have just received your letter of the 17th Feb.[1] – No. 96. I read something about the hospital week in the papers. This collection business is
always very troublesome; in India more so than elsewhere for here people
expect personal visits. I have an extreme dislike for doing such work.
However, it has to be done, I suppose, and it helps us to gain an insight into other people's minds and habits – not always a pleasant sight
to see. We cannot expect much financial help from other parts of India,
for after all the hospital can only cater for local needs. So it is as well
that the people of Allahabad should feel that it is their responsibility.

I am glad you have decided to go to Kashmir with Chhoti Puphi –
Kashmir must always remain first choice for a holiday. Your going there
means that a bit of myself also goes and I feel a sense of exhilaration at
the prospect. Ramlal's house is good. But do you propose to spend most
of your time in Srinagar? Probably Betty would prefer that and anyway
Srinagar is pleasant enough and many small excursions can be arranged
from there. I don't think a houseboat is particularly healthy for a small
child, though many children live there. A tent is much better. Perhaps
later on you might move to a higher valley for a while. That depends
on how Rajiv fares with his teething. Normally I should not worry about
any very special arrangements for him.

Is Anna going to stay on with you and will she accompany you to
Kashmir? Anyway you had better take Tulsi and Hari.

There are rumours again about our possible transfer to a U.P. prison.
I have always attached little importance to these but perhaps there may
be some slight basis for them this time as, in any event, Pantji is in need
of an operation. An operation of course does not necessitate a transfer
to the U.P. It means Pantji's transfer to a good hospital where a good
surgeon is available. Some people in the Central Assembly and elsewhere seem to be anxious to get us transferred, though why they should
feel that way I do not know. For my part a prison is a prison anywhere
and minor changes make little difference. It is the prison that counts,
not the place where the prison is situated, except to some extent in
regard to the climate. The prospect of a summer in the U.P. plains is
not exactly alluring – that is in a prison. Still it really does not make
much difference, and if one day we are told that we are being sent
elsewhere, like some commodities who have no choice in the matter, we
shall gather up our belongings and march out, in due secrecy, from one

1. Refers to letter No. 240.

enclosure to another. There will be a break in our routine here, a bustling and an unusual activity, and then quiet will again reign here, and elsewhere we shall settle down to another routine.

The only possible advantage of a transfer to one's province is to facilitate interviews. That advantage does not apply to us and I do not propose to take interviews elsewhere. So it makes not the slightest difference whether you are a hundred miles or a thousand miles away from me, for in either event the barriers remain.

As for interviews the reasons which actuated us not to take them remain, but, apart from them, there is a personal reason which counts with me. Jail interviews are seldom satisfactory and often disturbing. There is no normality about them and a sense of tension persists. The conditions under which they are usually held are irritating. Emotionally they are rather upsetting; feelings long restrained and dammed up have a glimpse of a narrow outlet and yet are unable to adapt themselves to it, and the half-hour or so passes rapidly without any adjustment and leaving a hollowness and hunger behind. All this is normal in prison even when interviews have been a regular event. We have, of course, often had these interviews.

But it is a very different matter to be isolated for two and a half years and then to have this brief restricted and uncomfortable interview under the grim shadow of jail walls and under the supervision of jail officials. When I meet you again, wherever that may be, I might remain silent for some time, just looking at you and trying to find out what you are now, how you have changed, what private universe you inhabit; or I might break out in unmeaning talk as a reaction from the long silence, a torrent of words trying to cover my own shyness and uneasiness, reaching out and seeking for something which eludes me. Gradually, as we see more of each other, we shall adjust ourselves as we understand each other afresh. But this cannot and will not happen in a jail interview, and though even sight, after the long absence of it, fills a vacuum somewhere, a heartache remains and is accentuated, and the gnawing feeling of emptiness continues. And so I feel that it is better for me to avoid these jail interviews. When I see you, I want to see much of you, quietly, normally and with a feeling of freedom and leisure. Till that is possible, I had rather not meet you.

It is odd to think that for over two and a half years I have not seen women or children. Even the men we have seen have been strictly limited in number and quality – and so our conception of Homo Sapiens must undergo some change. It will not be particularly easy to adapt oneself to the wider world after this experience and always there will be a sense of unreality about it or of a double life.

Yet of course we shall adapt ourselves, though we may carry that work on our foreheads and in our eyes. I think I am peculiarly adaptable for I have gradually reduced the mental luggage I have to carry. That is why, I think, I can go off to a distant country at a moment's notice without much inconvenience. Betty, in her last letter, said something of the many arrangements necessary for the proposed visit to Kashmir. I suppose all that is necessary. And yet I would be prepared to go to the Arctic regions or to any other faraway spot without much mental or other preparation.

I have sent you the following:

1. Katrak: *Oriental Treasures*
2. Pandya: *The Holy Gita*
3. Nilima: *When the Moon Died*
4.          : *Hungry Bengal*
   and periodicals.

The pamphlet of the Hindustan Hamara people which you sent me – containing a speech of mine – has reached me. For a moment I could not place it. Yet I realised soon enough that it was a speech of mine, though when and where delivered I do not know. Obviously it was an extempore speech and the text has been taken from a newspaper report, and like all such reports it is faulty. I have no objection to the Hindustan Hamara people issuing it, but they should have sent previous intimation. What is more important is that they should have stated the occasion, place and date of the speech and the fact that it was taken from a newspaper report. A careful revision by a competent person would have removed some of its obvious errors and redundancies.

Among the books which you are noting down for me, please put down Toynbee's *A Study of History* – I have an idea it is in my room but I am by no means sure. If you cannot find it there, you will have to purchase it. There is no hurry. I have plenty of reading matter with me. Toynbee's book is big, more than one volume, I think.

Only three days ago I wrote to Betty not to send me any honey as there was always danger of breakage. Yesterday four big bottles full of honey were delivered to me, sent by her. Now that it has come, we shall of course consume it with pleasure.

Once you wrote to me that you proposed to fix up a Chinese room, and one especially Indian room in Anand Bhawan. Did you give shape to your ideas?

Love,

Your loving,
Papu

This is my letter No. 103.

242.                                             Anand Bhawan,
Allahabad,
25th February, 1945

Darling Papu,
Your letter of the 17th.[1]
Darling, of course I have the urge to write and much more than once a week too. In fact I always seem to be writing to you in my mind, so that when I actually do sit down with pen and paper I am not always sure what I have written on paper and what in my mind. It all sounds a bit confused, I know, but then I am confused just now. Perhaps that is why I felt I must write to you even though it is very late for me. I hold a mental consultation with you about all sorts of things and before all decisions. It seems to comfort me. But just now it is small comfort.

Rajiv is ill again. I don't know how it started or when. He is getting pus in his ear and the little fellow is in agony. He is getting a temperature and feels like a hot water bottle to the touch. He won't touch his milk or anything else in the way of food. All last night he did not sleep but he rested for a few hours in the day. He has such a small cry – so pathetic, so sweet. One doesn't know what to do. He has got a very bad throat and has to have it painted. The stuff that is put in his ear – mostly rectified spirit – burns like anything. Poor little fellow all peaked and thin and pale. Doctor Kak is looking after him. We had Rajiv's blood counts taken today.

I shall write again tomorrow or the day after.
Very much love,

                      Indu

---

243.                                             Anand Bhawan,
Allahabad,
1st March, 1945

Darling Papu,
Suddenly and without warning, summer is here. It is hot and glary and even when there is a cool breeze, it is a summer coolness. *Holi* is supposed to bring in the summer but I did not remember it to be so sudden a change.

Rajiv is much better now. He still gets his throat painted and his ear cleaned, which doesn't hurt him at all but he yells his loudest all the same, probably because he has got those operations associated in his

1. Refers to letter No. 239.

mind with pain. He did have terrible pain in the beginning, poor mite. My temperature is also down – I have not gone downstairs for days! I find that going up and downstairs is the most tiring thing.

I have a letter from Bari Puphi. Also news of her through Prof. Meghnad Saha and Dr Lokanathan.[1]

I have sent Rafi some periodicals and some other articles that he had asked for. The jail people here are very disagreeable and make a lot of trouble about accepting every little thing.

Chitti – Chhoti Puphi – has a habit of exaggerating. I was annoyed at the selling off of some of my things and also because I was so terribly tired those days. In fact it was only because of this fatigue – you know how I feel when I am tired: 'let anyone do as they like but for heaven's sake leave me alone' – that I let everything happen as it did. However all these things are not important enough to get upset over.

The Communist Party has sent you another batch of books. Twenty-one in number. All of them have been passed by Government. Of the first lot several were withheld. They wanted to send you *People's War* but the Government says that they will not send it to you unless you ask for it. So they – the Communists – request you to ask for it! Mohan Kumaramangalam writes that yet a third batch of four books has been despatched.

After the numerous letters I have been writing to Raksha for the past year, I have at last a reply. She writes that Nandan is much better on the whole. But he cannot walk more than fifty yards without the aid of a stick and he cannot stand for even five minutes. The main trouble is his sensitive tummy. When that is upset he gets a lot of other ailments too.

Bijju Chachi is very anxious to have an interview with you or at least to write a letter. I have told her that neither is possible but that she should communicate with the Bombay Government.

I hear that it is fairly definite – your coming to the U.P. Will that make a difference to your taking interviews?

Very much love,

Indu

---

1. Dr P. S. Lokanathan: noted economist who was later Executive Secretary of the U.N. Economic Commission for Asia and Far East (1947–56).

244.                    Ahmadnagar Fort Prison,
                                  3rd March, 1945

Darling Indu,
I have been sending you lately rather longish letters and I think you
need some relief from them. Anyway a short one for a change ought to
be welcome. Or, perhaps, the real reason is that my mind today is rather
a blank so far as letter-writing is concerned. It is not quite a blank of
course, for there is much that fills its odd corners and leads me to muse
and travel leisurely along its corridors. Sometimes these wanderings
lead to what appear to be blind alleys, and sometimes there are distant
and alluring vistas. So we build up, each one of us, private and individual
worlds of our own, touching and overlapping other people's worlds, and
yet remaining always our very own, different from the others. And these
worlds become a refuge and a shelter, and sometimes also a prison
through whose invisible, and yet nonetheless effective, iron bars we peep
out at others and the wide world outside us. Those strong bars of the
spirit rather isolate us and we feel incapable of crossing over to the other
side, but occasionally they seem to melt away and we become one with
others and sense a feeling of communism with nature and the world.

*Holi* has come and gone, the spring festival, which has already the
promise, or is it, in India, the threat, of the coming summer. It is, I
think, the most delightful of our festivals, or should be such if we had
not got so tied up in our minds and activities, not knowing exactly what
to do and what not to do, pulled in different directions and constrained
by circumstance, doubtful of each other and ourselves and what we
stand for. *Holi* is the essence of spontaneity, of exuberant joy and merry-
making, of a breaking of bonds that separate and a meeting together of
all on an equal and democratic footing. How far it is from what it should
be and probably used to be – for we lack spontaneity and the spirit of
merry-making, and joy is a scarce-known visitor.

*Holi* was Dol Amma's birthday. Most of these festivals of ours are
associated in my mind with some event, some happening in my life.
*Vasanta Panchami* was my wedding day; *Raksha-bandhan* and the *Dussehra* bring numerous memories; so also *Diwali*.

I have been receiving letters occasionally from Puphi from America.
They are interesting and fill in somewhat the brief accounts of her
activities that appear in the papers. I write to her sometimes but the
long delay in receiving letters – the average period for an airmail letter
is about five weeks – rather puts me off writing. I am asking her to bring
me a gift: a new Parker pen of the latest type – No. '51', I think it is
called.

When do you propose to go to Lahore on your way to Kashmir? I

suppose you will remain in Allahabad for the whole of this month.
Love,

Your loving,<br>Papu

This is my letter No. 104.

---

245.

Anand Bhawan,<br>Allahabad,<br>4th March, 1945

Darling Papu,

I don't quite know where to send this letter – Dame rumour has it that you have already arrived in Bareilly. However I think I had better stick to the Bombay Govt until there is more definite news about your transfer.

Rajiv is all right now but still a bit pale.

Our collections are still going on in some form or the other. There is a society here called the Allahabad Culture Centre. It is founded by a Mrs Dutt, a great pal of Mrs Naidu. The Culture Centre is giving us a variety show which includes Shaw's *August Does His Bit*. So we are selling tickets now. The collection has gone up to Rs. 12,000/-.

Ladlibhai came yesterday after a long long time. He had a look at the servants' quarters and will see to the repairs. Lado Chachi has gone to Bombay with Manno Didda who was here on a visit.

The other day Dhawan[1] came into the Library for a moment and saw that book *Mathematical Recreation* on the table. He opened it and saw your name. Oh, he said, Panditji must be making a deep [study] of Marxism, otherwise why should he study mathematics! Nothing I could say by way of explanation was able to alter his conviction. How these people's minds work. Dhawan's little son calls Stalin, Uncle Stalin.

Yunus's fiancée, Laj, has at last been able to interview him. She was very thrilled and excited. Yunus has grown a beard but is otherwise looking very well, although he is no fatter.

Much love,

Indu

---

1. S. S. Dhawan: lawyer and judge of the Allahabad High Court; later Indian High Commissioner in the United Kingdom, and Governor of West Bengal.

246.                                Ahmadnagar Fort Prison,
                                           10th March, 1945

Darling Indu,

Two letters from you have reached me dated 25/2[1] and 1/3[2] – Nos. 97 and 98. The first one with news of Rajiv's ear trouble rather worried me. I imagine that some infection had affected his throat and this had spread to the ear. It is very difficult to prevent these infections, for innumerable microbes infest the air. It depends ultimately on the individual's power of resistance. A baby can hardly be expected to have much of this. I gathered from people here that children often have some kind of ear trouble and, though painful, it is not considered serious. Serious or not, it is very distressing to see a child suffer. I can never forget your face and your plaintive cry when you had your tonsils removed at Juhu when you were five years old.

Your second letter mentions that your temperature is also down. This is the first indication I have had that it was up. I hope this was due to some passing and minor trouble. It is clear anyway that both you and Rajiv have to go away for the hot weather. Kashmir will put you two right.

There seems to be quite a lot of talk about our transfer to other jails though no official intimation has come yet. The papers contain all manner of contradictory reports and Naini, Bareilly and Dehra Dun are mentioned so far as I am concerned. Having some considerable experience of U.P. jails, I am not likely to be sent to a jail which has not been previously haunted by my presence and thoughts. So wherever I may be sent I shall soon fit into an accustomed groove. And yet there is always some trouble and jail people have a way of making themselves disagreeable over little things. You mention the trouble you have had at Naini about some things sent there for Rafi – Naini and the larger prisons are usually more disagreeable in such matters. Still, I would continue sending books, etc, to Rafi. Let the jail people refuse them if they want to do so.

My transfer will make no difference to interviews, that is to say, I shall continue *not* to take them. I think I have already written to you about this. So the transfer, if and when it comes, should make no difference to your programme. All that you will have to do will be to address your letters to me differently. Even about that I do not know what the proper address then will be: direct to the jail or through the Provincial Govt. You can find out after you learn of our transfer . . .

1. Refers to letter No. 242.
2. Refers to letter No. 243.

I have not received so far a fresh batch of books from the C.P. people. It may come later and add to my luggage. A few out of the books they send are good, most are mediocre, and some are no good and are just propaganda sheets or pamphlets. As for their weekly, *The People's War*, I am certainly not going to make any request to Govt. Normally I do not do so and more particularly I have no intention of singling this out as an exception.

I have sent you a parcel containing the following books & pamphlets:

1. Davies: *Mission to Moscow*
2. Anderson: *Borderline Russia*      Belonging to
3. Jinarajadasa: *Economics & Theosophy*      Jinarajadasa
   (pamphlet)
4. *Bushido*
5. Aronson: *Rabindranath Through Western Eyes*
6. Vakil: *To Europa*
7. H. Kabir: *Mahatma & Other Poems*
8. Gertrude Murray: *Verdict on Beverley Nichols*
9. & 10. Agarwal: *Gandhian Plan of Economic Development of India* – 2 Parts
11. *Kadambari*
12. *Finland Unmasked*
13. Krishnamurti: *Vishva-Bharati*

I have still with me one of Jinarajadasa's books, *The Great O'Neill*. I have finished with it but some others are looking through it. I shall return it later and then you can send it back to Jinarajadasa.

I have received an account of Frank's (Edward Thompson's son's) death in Bulgaria. As you must have met Frank, and the story is a moving one and must interest you, I am giving it to you here. The original account is from an eye-witness of the incident.

Frank had a very exceptional gift for languages. He knew the European classics (Greek & Latin) well and a large number of modern European languages. He was eighteen or so when the war started. He joined up and served later in Libya, the Sicilian landing, etc. Apparently he added to his stock of languages during these war years and learnt or improved his knowledge of Persian, Arabic, Russian, Polish, Czech, modern Greek, Serbo-Croatian and Bulgarian. A very remarkable achievement for a boy who died at the age of twenty-three. He was also, I understand, a poet of some distinction. He was attached to an important intelligence unit of GHQ, Cairo and held a very responsible post in it. But he felt ashamed of the easy life of headquarters in Cairo and was deeply stirred by the courage & sufferings of the Yugoslav patriots. So he volunteered for the dangerous work of assisting Bulgarian partisans and in January 1944 was parachuted into Yugoslavia. His work there was very good and much appreciated. In March his colleague was surprised and killed but Frank just escaped and wandered about for ten days in the forests and hills. He joined another unit and then, although he had a safer alternative, deliberately courted danger by marching off with a band of Bulgarian patriots. He felt that not to go with them would be unfair and would lead them to think that he was afraid of sharing their risks. There were running battles and he just escaped being killed – a dictionary stopped a bullet. He refused to leave his wounded wireless operator. They were nearly starving when they were rushed and captured on May 31. They were not allowed to sleep and were repeatedly interrogated. He claimed that as a liaison officer, captured in uniform with all his papers in order, he & his colleague were protected by the laws of war. He refused to give away his wireless code or military secrets.

On June 10 he was sent to Litikovo, a village some thirty miles from Sofia where thirteen of them were tried – five officers (Frank, one American, a Serb and two Bulgarians) and eight others. Fifty-seven partisans had already been shot out of hand. Frank sat in the village public hall where the trial was taking place, smoking his pipe. The hall was packed, and it is said that the intention of the authorities was to rouse the crowd to a fury, to lynch them, so that it could be claimed afterwards that their deaths were the result of a spontaneous outburst of public indignation. But the people were on their side. When summoned, Frank, to everyone's amazement, spoke in fluent and correct Bulgarian. He was asked why he, an Englishman, fought against them & entered their country. He replied: 'To me this war is something far deeper than a struggle of nation against nation. The biggest thing today is the fight of fascism against anti-fascism.' 'Do you not know that we shoot men who hold those opinions?' 'I am ready to die for freedom and I am proud to die with Bulgarian patriots.' The crowd burst into weeping and an old woman flung herself forward: 'I am only an old woman, it does not matter what you do to me. But you are all wrong. We are not on your side, we are with these brave men.' She was struck down to the ground. The judges hastened the trial and finished it in twenty minutes. Major Thompson took command, led his comrades to the place where they had to stand and raised his hand in the clenched-fist salute of the Fatherland Front. It was struck down, but he called to the people: 'I give you the Salute of Liberty.' At the castle all of them, as they died, died lifting this salute, with the spectators weeping.

Frank, it is said, has already become a Bulgarian national hero. The story of the Thirteen Partisans of Litikovo has become part of Bulgarian legend and history and above all the courage of the young English officers' leader (Frank) is admired there. Later, in November, the Bulgarian Govt gave the partisans of Litikovo a great ceremonious funeral; there were 50,000 spectators as the coffins were carried shoulder-high. Bulgaria is raising a memorial over their common grave.

That is the story as it has reached me. It is sad that young men of such promise should be snuffed out almost in boyhood. But heroism for the sake of an ideal is always inspiring and a splendid death surely is better than a long life, without purpose and meaning.

Your visit to Kashmir will mean considerable additional expenses. Draw on my account at Bachhraj's for them.

Love,

Your loving,<br>Papu

This is my letter No. 105.

---

247.

Anand Bhawan,<br>Allahabad,<br>14th March, 1945

Darling Papu,

... I am in a strange mood these days. Whilst I had my cold I was naturally banned from baby's room. Anna came to sleep upstairs and I went to my own room. I had my first full night's sleep after many months. Then the next day I thoroughly enjoyed myself in spite of the sneezes and shivering. I collected some books of poetry, classics and moderns, and my favourite records; got into my most comfortable dressing gown; had nothing for lunch except toast and two half-boiled eggs. And I had a lovely time.

Do you remember some time last year we had a brief discussion in our letters about people imagining that they were 'different'. But really I think that with me it is more than just imagination. It is actually so. I'll tell you why I think so. In the whole of this country I hardly know anybody (who is anywhere near my age) who likes the kind of things that I like. Puphi and others are always chiding me for not going out to parties and such. Every now and then I do go. The kind of parties there are in Allahabad are deadly. I get so bored. It seems to be such a waste of time, the people discussing such futile things.

Much love to you,

Indu

---

248.                                     Ahmadnagar Fort Prison,
                                              17th March, 1945

Darling Indu,

I have your letter No. 99 of March 4th.[1] I can well understand your difficulty in deciding where to address your letters to me. There are so many rumours about our transfer and every day some new story crops up in the newspapers. Yet here we are still in Ahmadnagar Fort. The local correspondent of the Associated Press is responsible for some of these stories and there are the newspapermen in New Delhi and elsewhere who pick up scraps of news and conversations and then give vent to their imaginations. It is an interesting game, though it must confuse many people. The latest story is that aeroplanes are kept ready for our transfer and we shall be carried through the air in a day or two. This appeared in yesterday's papers. Also that we are all ready and packed. The fact of the matter is that we know nothing definite and no information has been supplied to us. All we know is from the newspapers. I have given no thought to my packing. Why should I till I know definitely? It is rather absurd for me to pack up and upset my day's routine and then wait from day to day for something to happen. Packing really consists of putting my numerous books in boxes. So, in spite of some inevitable mental disturbance, we carry on as before – and I think you had better do so also till you have clear information about a change in our place of habitation.

I wrote to you that I was asking Puphi to bring for me, on her return from America, a Parker '51' pen. Somehow I managed to forget writing about this to her. So if and when you are writing to her you might mention this. Also I want her to get for me a Schick Colonel dry electric shaver. I am not sure if she can get either of these in wartime. The style of nib I use is more or less medium fine – that is rather a poor description and individual tastes vary greatly. But that is all I can say about it.

According to the lunar way of reckoning the new *Samvat* year – 2002 – started with the new moon two days ago. Our *Nauroz* usually comes a fortnight or so later. But I am not sure this time, as this year an extra month is added for purposes of adjustment to fit in with the solar year. If you know the date for *Nauroz* let me know.

I am glad you have news of Yunus looking well. But I do not approve of his newly-acquired beard. I suppose he will be coming out very soon and then the beard will go.

For many months past I have not been receiving any English periodicals – *New Statesman, Time & Tide, Tribune*, etc. I wonder if this means

1. Refers to letter No. 245.

that my subscription has expired. The American periodicals come in more or less regularly, sometimes with a slip attached that the subscription has expired. I wrote to Chand two or three months ago asking her to get Walsh to renew these subscriptions.

Love to you and Rajiv and Feroze.

Your loving,
Papu

This is my letter No. 106.

———————————— ■ ————————————

249.                                                                Anand Bhawan,
                                                                        Allahabad,
                                                                 20th March, 1945

Darling Papu,

All these rumours in the papers are most unsettling. Now you are being transferred to Naini, to Bareilly, to Dehra Dun. Now you are not being transferred. Now you're coming by air. I have some books for you and some papers but I am keeping them since there is no point in adding to your luggage at the last moment.

Rajiv is seven months old today. Weighing him is a tricky job. The hospital is not very accurate & baby keeps jumping or kicking or making some movement which makes the needle fluctuate from one end to the other. However we guess that Rajiv's weight is about 18 lbs 14 oz, which means that there has been a gain of only 2 oz in the last week. Rajiv makes a great effort to talk, trying to imitate the various sounds made by grown-ups. If someone is within sight of him, but not taking any notice, he will keep on saying *ay* until the person looks round and talks. About the only sound that Rajiv can manage accurately is *ka ka*, when he sees or hears the crows. But he now recognises several words – *mam* for drinking water; *jhanda* – he looks up at the flag when you say *jhanda* – and so on. He is intrigued with *chutki bajāna*[1] and tries hard to do it himself. He is really fun to be with and to watch. He doesn't mind the heat in the daytime for he loves being without a lot of clothes on, but at night he is restless and wakes up many times to have a drink of water. Every night he gets badly bitten by mosquitoes.

*23rd March*

I am sorry this letter has got delayed. In the meantime your letter of the 17th[2] has also come.

1. Snapping with fingers.
2. Refers to letter No. 248.

You ask about *Naoroz*. I think I mentioned to you that it was on the 15th March – the first day of the moon – or so Vatsala told me.
Much love,

Indu

---

250.                                                  Anand Bhawan,
Allahabad,<br>26th March, 1945

Darling Papu,
Rajiv has cut his first tooth today – a lower central one. I can't see it yet but it is quite clear to the feel and sharp as a razor. Moreover he has slept comfortably after many days of restlessness, so that what we thought was his naughtiness was really this tooth troubling him. Rajiv is progressing so normally and 'according to the books' – it's a great satisfaction.

Dr Krishnan [1] has sent the following books for you. Would you like to have them all? If not, you can let me know the numbers of the ones you want.

1. *Doctor Darwin* – H. Pearson
2. *Famous American Men of Science* – Crowther (2 vols)
3. *The A.B.C. of Psychology* – Ogden
4. *Invention and Their Uses* – Stafford Hatfield
5. *Mathematician's Delight* – Sawyer
6. *What Happened in History* – Gordon Childe
7. *Experiment and Theory in Physics* – Max Born
8. *Living Thoughts of Darwin* – Julian Huxley
9. *Living Thoughts of Shopenhauer* – Thomas Mann
10. *Growth and Form* – Thompson
11. *The Universe in Space and Time* – Van den Bergh
12. *The Renaissance of Physics* – Darrow
13. *Frontiers of Science* – C. T. Chase
14. *Unsolved Problems of Science* – Haslett
15. *Men of Mathematics* – Bell
16. *Science in Progress*

I have a letter from Mr W. M. Benton, Vice-President of the University of Chicago. He is also the Chairman of the Board of the *Encyclopaedia Britannica*. He says he visited you in 1937 and is one of

---

1. Dr K. S. Krishnan: eminent physicist who taught in Allahabad University; later became Director, National Physical Laboratory, 1947–61.

TWO ALONE, TWO TOGETHER

your 'thousands of American admirers'. In consultation with Frances Gunther he has subscribed to the magazines *Fortune* and *Foreign Affairs* in my name, to be sent on to you. One copy of the *Foreign Affairs* has already come. Also two books and some pamphlets issued by the Committee for Economic Development. This is a new war-born group, now active in America, of which Mr Benton is the Vice-Chairman of the Board of Trustees. This is the most important business group in the United States interested in economic and political problems after the war. Mr Benton feels that you will be particularly interested in their forthcoming publications dealing with international trade. Mr Benton writes: 'If there is anything that I as an individual can do to assist your father, or to lessen the ardours of his confinement, I would regard such an opportunity as a privilege. I would like to hope that you can think of some ways to call upon me.'

With the same post came a letter from Frances Gunther introducing Mr Benton and adding, 'he (Mr Benton) is a swell guy and devoted to the Nehrus and India'. Frances says she is enclosing a clipping on Lincoln for you. But it hasn't come. She probably forgot to enclose it for there is a note from the Censor saying that the clipping was found to be missing when the letter was opened by the Censor. Apparently this is quite a usual occurrence, for the Censor's note is a printed one and bears the number 5468!

I see you have returned Gertrude Murray's *Verdict on Beverley Nichols.* Have you also read Nichols's book, *Verdict on India?*

Authoritative circles feel that things are on the move and fast. So fast that I may have to postpone leaving Allahabad! However I shall stick to my programme until the last moment. Whatever happens, Rajiv must go to the hills in Kashmir, since that is what has been decided upon. But since I have a good *ayah* as well as Anna, I can easily leave the three of them in Kashmir and come away myself. In spite of all these plans I don't dare hope for much. And yet such thoughts – even if they prove to be mere wishful-thinking – give relief. It will be fun to have you out. It's been so long. By the way, why has poor Kripalani been sent to Karachi? Do you think there is a chance of your being sent to Kashmir, the abode of your ancestors!

Love,
Indu

251.

Ahmadnagar Fort Prison,
27th March, 1945

Darling Indu,

After five or six weeks or more of deep and intensive thought, careful staff work and complicated arrangements, it does at last appear that we are going to be sent away from Ahmadnagar Fort to other and various prisons. If the dispersal of ten persons from one place involves so much time, labour and expenditure of mental and physical energy, I have wondered how much trouble is involved in the movement of armies and arrangements for their food and quartering – logistics as all this is called. If you add to this the opposition of enemy forces which has to be met and overcome, the problem, tackled in this leisurely way at least, becomes prodigiously difficult. No wonder that wars drag on and on.

All this preamble means that we have for the first time received definite information about our impending transfer. Or rather, the information is not very definite for our destination is still supposed to be a major state secret. But that we are going away soon somewhere, somehow, may be taken now for granted. Because of this fact I am writing to you today, Tuesday, which is unusual for me, for I have almost always written to you on Saturdays ever since I came to Ahmadnagar Fort.

I cannot tell you much about my movements or destination, but you will no doubt find out about them soon enough, probably before you get this letter. Yet I felt like writing to you today and sending you what is likely to be my last letter from Ahmadnagar Fort. It is my 108th letter to you from here, thus representing over two years of weekly correspondence.

Though we go from here to yet another prison, and life will be much the same for us, though in different environments, still it means a big break for us. For 961 days today, two years seven months and eighteen days, we have existed here like some plant or vegetables rooted to the ground. And now we are going to be uprooted, transferred and transplanted in some other barren and stony soil. But there and elsewhere later in life, the memory of these years spent in Ahmadnagar Fort will endure and colour our vision. The days have passed and the months and the years, but each day, each moment, has left its impress, and layer upon layer of these impressions and experiences will be embedded in the recesses of our minds.

It will be a change to go out and see the trees and broad fields and human beings moving about as we travel across India. Everything changes and yet everything continues to be much the same as it was. The change is really within us, each one of us, and the world and nature continue ever young, though generations of living beings are born, grow up and fade away. Yes, it will be a change to go out because we shall see everything with different eyes. And when others see us what changes will they find in us? We cannot say or even know.

Some time, when I have the chance, I should like to see high mountains, snow-covered, with rivers of ice flowing down their sides, and wide spaces and deep ravines. So I would try to adjust my mind and vision to distance and depth again, and breathe the invigorating air that comes from those snow tops. Too long I have lived and moved in a narrow quadrangle and looked at its cheerless and hard walls. Only the sky offered distance and depth and mystery.

Enough of this. You will of course make the necessary adjustments consequent on my transfer. Letters and periodicals to be sent to a new address (I am sending you today a packet of periodicals: *Life, Time, Asia, Commonsense,* etc). I have been receiving here, addressed to me, two daily papers: *The Hindu* of Madras and the Allahabad *Patrika.* Please ask Upadhyaya to inform them both of my new address.

I have still with me one of Jinarajadasa's books: *The Great O'Neill* by Sean O'Faolain. I am having this returned to him direct to the Theosophical Society, Adyar, Madras. I hope you have returned his other two which I sent you. Inform him that I have sent the *O'Neill* direct to him.

Some time back I asked you to try to get for me a Persian dictionary through Kitabistan. I wonder if this is available. Anyway please ask Upadhyaya to get for me from Ram Narain Lal, bookseller of Katra, Allahabad, his *Students' Practical Hindustani–English Dictionary.* The 10th edition came out in 1940. There should be no difficulty in getting this. Tell Upadhyaya to send it on to me to my new jail address, wherever that might be.

Yesterday I received a huge parcel of *khadi* stuff sent by Mridula – she chose rather an odd time to add to our luggage. There were six full *thans,* [1] three bedsheets, six towels. Obviously they were not meant just for me and I have succeeded in distributing the lot except for two *thans* which are still with me. They were good *khadi* and are bound to come in useful, though I do not require them at present. In these days of cloth scarcity in most parts of India, it seems rather selfish for me to hang on to them. Will you thank Mridu?

I follow the temperature of Allahabad in the weather reports in the papers. It grows warmer with unusual rapidity. You had better fix up your departure for the north and escape before the full heat descends upon you and the little one.

Love,

Your loving,
Papu

---

1. Length of cloth.

252.

Anand Bhawan,
Allahabad,
31st March, 1945

Darling Papu,

It was wonderful to see you even for that brief while.[1] I was so over-whelmed I couldn't do anything but look at you. It was a shock to see you so thin. Don't you think you should drink milk or Ovaltine or something? You should certainly do something about it. It's not good for you to be so thin. As a matter of fact all of you looked rather shrunken – almost as if you had not even had enough fresh air. And of course in a way you did not have any fresh air. I was sorry I had not taken Rajiv to the jail. It was really stupid of us. But everything was so uncertain. We did not even know until when you came out whether all of you were being transferred or not, whether we should be allowed to go anywhere near you or not. But still I realise now that we should have taken the risk. The other difficulty was that our own car was not functioning and we had to crowd into someone else's four-seater. So now again there is nothing to do but to fall back upon old Dame Hope. May our optimism be justified! Sometimes everything points one way and then suddenly branches off in another direction. Like your car did last evening!

I hope you had a comfortable journey and that Pantji will find Chandra Dutt and everything else he needs at Bareilly.

Darling – it was lovely to see you.

Lots & lots of love,

Indu

P.S.

Your last letter[2] from Ahmadnagar has just come. I am not in a hurry to go to Kashmir. So far the heat is not interfering in any way with Rajiv's health or mine. We have not even started using fans yet. The afternoons would be disagreeable if one had to go out but a room with the *chiks*[3] down is cool enough.

---

1. On 28th March, 1945 Jawaharlal Nehru was transferred from Ahmadnagar Fort Prison to Bareilly Central Prison. He travelled through Allahabad and spent a day (30th March) in Naini Central Prison. Indira had a brief glimpse of her father at the gate of the prison and her letter reflects her emotions on this occasion.

2. Refers to letter No. 251.

3. Thin screens which can be rolled up. They are made of slit bamboo and are often covered with cloth on one side.

I wonder if you will be able to dash up to Kashmir for a breather[1] before rushing around meeting people and discussing the old old things that assume new shapes from time to time.

Did you notice the moonlit Jumna last evening?

Our peepul tree has been invaded by crowds of interesting mynas. The Bark Myna, the Brahmini Myna, and the Pied Myna which is the most elegant of the lot. What a noise these little things can make! There are also the rose-coloured starlings, also known as the 'Rosy Pastor'. This is the first time I have seen them. I wonder if they are migrating to Central Asia, for that is where they are said to live most of the year, coming to India only for the winter. [They] also breed in Eastern Europe and Western Asia.

With much love,

Indu

---

253.                                       Bareilly Central Prison,
                                              3rd April, 1945

Darling Indu,

We are settling down – gradually. The process is slow, requiring not only physical arrangements but mental adjustments. After two years and nearly eight months of Ahmadnagar Fort, changes followed rapidly. The mere coming out of the Fort was an event for us, though it was dark and we could not see much. It was the night of the full moon. We had reached Ahmadnagar on August 9th, 1942, just when the new moon was beginning its brief life of light and growth, and it was appropriate in a way that our stay there should end with the full moon, though many a moon had waxed and waned in between – was the number of these thirty-three or thirty-four?

It was exciting to have movement by car and train, to see crowds and hear them shout, to watch the morning steal over the fields, recently harvested, to remember the stations as they came one after another. And then Naini, on the threshold of Allahabad, and the old prison I knew so well. The meeting with old friends there with all the excitement that this involved.

And when I came out of the Naini Prison gate, to see you and Feroze standing by – and you looking just as you looked three years ago, a dainty and lovely slip of a girl, apparently unchanged by the passage of

---

1. It was believed that Jawaharlal Nehru was about to be released in the spring of 1945. Indira wonders in this letter whether Jawaharlal will have the time to spend a brief vacation in Kashmir before he is caught up in politics.

years or by motherhood. More friends at Phaphamow, and another journey by train. Again distant horizons and the familiar Oudh landscape. And so to a little station near Bareilly where we were taken off the train and motored (part of the road was villainous) to Bareilly C.P. There we bade goodbye to Pantji.[1] And so here we are.

We are settling down slowly. Conditions here are different, for this is a proper, or rather regular, jail with all that this means. And there are swarms of flies and mosquitoes and, above all, dust. Even as I write the paper I write on gets covered with a layer of dust. But we get used to these minor inconveniences soon enough. It will take a little longer to adjust oneself emotionally, for the three days of our journey from Ahmadnagar to Bareilly were very full of experiences to which we had become so unused.

It was good to see you even for a brief while. I feel refreshed and vitalised by this outing and the sight of friends' faces and the sound of their voices.

From Naini I sent you one or two odd articles. Arriving here I discovered many more unnecessary things with me and so, rather hurriedly, I sent a suitcase, my box *charkha*, and a small packing case to Upadhyaya. These contain some odd books, clothes, warm coverings, etc. Also an ivory Nataraja which Betty had sent me and which I hope will reach you intact. There are also two boxes full of small stones picked up in our yard at Ahmadnagar Fort. Some of these are rather attractive, though they are valueless, and I was wondering if you could not have a few set properly in the form of a brooch. That would be a souvenir of my stay in Ahmadnagar!

I have still far too many things with me and I have little or no use for them here. Indeed they are a bit of a nuisance for there is no proper place to keep them. In Ahmadnagar there were cupboards & chests of drawers, etc, and there was little dust. Here things have to be kept in boxes and even of these I have not enough. So I am thinking of sending you, in the course of a few days, a packing case containing old clothes, books & various oddments. I suppose this can be easily sent as a railway parcel. The clothes I might return are of little use to me here or elsewhere, they are worn out and can be given away.

I am told that, as at Ahmadnagar, I can write two letters a week and receive four. So there need be no change in regard to this. I shall write to you once a week. Letters to me have to be addressed to Bareilly Central Prison.

I do not like the idea of your delaying your departure for Kashmir

---

1. Refers to the release of G. B. Pant from prison.

and waiting for developments. This living in a state of uncertainty is unpleasant. Personally I do not think that anything is going to happen soon enough to upset your programme. I suggest that now you should provisionally fix up your programme so as to meet Betty in Lahore when she gets there. That will be about the 26th, if I remember rightly.

Love to you and to babe,

Your loving,
Papu

---

254.                                          Bareilly Central Prison,
                                              7th April, 1945

Darling Indu,

I have received your letter of March 31st[1] – No. 101. You just completed the century while I was in Ahmadnagar Fort. This is my letter No. 110 to you.

Did I look thin and shrunken when you saw me? You and others who see me after a long interval are better judges than I can be. Changes creep in slowly and are hardly noticeable from day to day, and we get used to them. In the aggregate they must amount to a good deal. To be thin is not always a disadvantage. It may even be a change for the better, as I think it is, within limits, in my case. But to present a shrunk-up appearance is not advantageous, as age is not by itself a welcome factor. Yet both have to be accepted. I do think, however, that I am pretty fit and healthy. But neither I nor anyone else can write off two and three-quarter years at a time of life when physically at least one must be on the decline. As for milk, etc, which you suggest, I have been taking some regularly for many months. Not too much, for I am not used to it.

I had not allowed myself to hope that I would see you on my passage through Allahabad, though somewhere at the back of my mind there was that expectation. It is better not to expect too much from life and take it as it comes. About Rajiv I had definitely not expected to see him, so it was no disappointment. In view of the uncertainty of our meeting and the late hour, when he must have been asleep, it was not worthwhile carting him about from place to place and upsetting him. Of course I would have loved to see him. And yet I am not sure that I would have

---

1. Refers to letter No. 252.

been glad to have my first glimpse of him when he was upset and possibly grumpy. Anyway all that is over now and I hope that I shall see him some time or other in a more suitable environment and in the bright light of day. That will be much better than a prison gate at night.

About Kashmir, you will fix up your programme as you think best. After all, you are in a better position to judge than I am. What I do not like is for anyone to hang on to rumour and uncertainty, and it seems to me there is far too much of this rumour business and wishful thinking.

Yes, I would like to go to Kashmir, more especially if you are there – to go there as soon as I can, even if I can only stay there for a few days. The combination of you and Kashmir will be just the right tonic for me. I do not think it will make much difference to anything or anybody if I am away for ten days or a fortnight. Yet life is so much like an octopus and its tentacles grip and hold me to activities which may have little essential importance. I sometimes wonder how much of what we do has much basic importance!

I see from the papers that Padma is getting married in about three weeks' time. I should like you to send her some kind of a gift on my behalf. If you have difficulty in fixing this up, send a cheque for Rs. 250/-. This should be sent to her direct and not to her parents. Also you will convey to her and her parents my love and good wishes.

Some time back I asked you to get Rs. 500/- transferred from my account with Bachhraj to my account at the Punjab National Bank, Allahabad branch. I wonder if you had this done? If not, please take the necessary steps now. While at Ahmadnagar Fort I used to issue cheques on Bachhraj to the Bombay Govt for cash. That was convenient there, but it will no longer be convenient here. The Punjab National Bank is more suitable here. So I want some money there to draw upon whenever needed.

I have been receiving various newspapers here – all those that I wanted, except the *Leader*. I had not mentioned the *Leader* to you pre-viously as I expected to be able to get it here. Curiously enough a copy of it came here by post addressed to me but then it stopped. You might therefore ask the *Leader* people to send their paper to me. It will keep me informed of local happenings . . .

Will you send me a copy of the pamphlet containing the marriage service which we had prepared at the time of your wedding? There used to be a bundle of these in my dressing room. I want to give it to Narendra Deva.

And that reminds me. My last day in Ahmadnagar Fort was March 28th. I remembered that it was the anniversary of your wedding – the third. Was I right about the date? Three years.

Love to you and Rajiv & Feroze,
                    Your loving,
                        Papu

I was sorry to learn that Radhey [1] was suffering from typhoid. I like him very much and am rather anxious about him. I hope he is getting better.

---

255.                                    Bareilly Central Prison,
                                          13th April, 1945
                                            Baisakhi Day

Darling Indu,
Two of your letters, which you had sent to Bombay, have been forwarded to me here. They are dated March 20th/23rd [2] and 26th. [3]

I am glad to know that Rajiv's first tooth is out and that he is keeping well. His efforts to talk are most interesting and they must fascinate you. Does he not sit up yet? Surely it is time he did so. It is an extraordinary thing, as old as humanity and yet ever new, how a child develops his consciousness of the outer world. There is all the sense of unending adventure, of continuous enquiry, of a peering into new phenomena, and everything is new, as it must have been for those remote ancestors of ours who came into being at the dawn of human existence. Rapidly, so very rapidly, the child passes through millennia of human history, and subconsciously, or partly even consciously, lives through the history of the race. If we grown-ups could only retain in some measure that spirit of adventure and enquiry and delight at ever-renewed discovery that is a child's heritage, and add to it the knowledge and wisdom that the ages have accumulated for us, how excellent it would be! But unhappily we grow too soon out of that wonder of childhood and yet do not reach mature manhood with all its compensations. Somehow we manage to miss both, and though we grow in years we remain babes and sucklings in mind but without the vitality and the spirit of growth of the child.

Please thank Dr Krishnan for the books he has sent you. They were originally required for the Maulana but to send them to him now is out of the question. [4] Nor would I like you to send them all here – they are too many and I do not want to burden myself unnecessarily. I am not a fast

---

1. Radhey Shyam Pathak: a Congress leader of Allahabad.
2. Refers to letter No. 249.
3. Refers to letter No. 250.
4. Maulana Azad at this time was still in Ahmadnagar Fort Prison and was expected to be transferred to Calcutta at any time.

reader. If I think a book is worthwhile, I like to take my time over it. The following books out of the list, however, are likely to interest me:

1. Ogden: *The A.B.C. of Psychology*
2. Van den Bergh: *The Universe in Space and Time*
3. Darrow: *The Renaissance of Physics*
4. C. T. Chase: *The Frontiers of Science*
5. *Science in Progress*
6. Thompson: *Growth and Form*

If you like, you can send me these, or two or three of them.

I remember W. M. Benton very well. He paid a visit to me in Anand Bhawan some years ago. He first introduced me to *Time*, which he arranged to send me for a year or two. He was at the time the head of a big advertising firm in America and was probably also connected with *Time*. It is odd how these business people suddenly develop into heads of universities in America. Probably he looks after the business side of the University – and this is a very big job there.

It is good of him to send me *Fortune* & *Foreign Affairs* – the latter I have been getting already through Walsh, but that does not matter. As for *Fortune*, do you or Feroze not get it? It was included in the list I sent Walsh. Please write to Benton to thank him and tell him I have pleasant recollections of him. It produces a warm feeling in me to know how friends remember me. As for his enquiry – what he can do for me 'to assist me in lessening the ardours of confinement' – that thought itself and the goodwill that prompted it goes a long way to help. For, after all, this is largely a matter of psychology, a question of the mind and its reactions, of waves of thought, important always and everywhere but more so in confinement. If he will occasionally send me a new book which he thinks might interest me – I have fairly extensive interests – this will be welcome to me not merely for the book's sake but more so for his sake, and will make me think of him and of America. Write to Frances also and send her my love.

No, I have not read Beverley Nichols's book – nor am I particularly anxious to do so.

I have sent you a railway parcel containing clothes and books. This has been booked to Prayag. Probably you will have received the railway receipt for it. If not, enquire at Prayag station. The clothes sent are some old and tattered ones, some new or more or less new. Give away the old ones. You will find in the lot three coloured shirts which Betty sent me – these are quite new and unusual. I did not require them and I prefer white ones, in prison especially. A full list of clothes, books, etc, has been placed inside the box at the top. A number of old foreign periodicals have also been returned in this box. You can deal with them by sending them on to others, as previously.

Now that I have sent you in this parcel and through Upadhyaya quite a number of articles which I had accumulated, I feel lighter. How things accumulate even in prison! Even now I have far too many clothes and books about me. But I like to be prepared for all contingencies and for the moment I have enough to carry me on through the summer and the rainy season. Of course when winter comes – and it is cold here – I shall require some warm things. But that is still far off and much may happen in between . . .

Has Upadhyaya returned or is he still with Pantji?

Love,

Your loving,<br>Papu

---

256.                                   Bareilly Central Prison,
                                           19th April, 1945

Darling Indu,

I have your letter of April 8th. [1] This was your No. 104 – I am continuing the old numbering. This letter of mine is No. 112.

I am glad you have decided to go soon to Lahore and Kashmir. There was no point in your delaying your departure. Perhaps by the time this letter reaches Allahabad you will have already left. I might have sent this to Lahore to catch you there but on second thoughts I have decided to address it to Anand Bhawan. That appears to be the safest address and it will I hope be forwarded to you wherever you might be. Please let me know your future address for letters, or addresses on given dates, so that I can send my letters to the proper place. I hope you have arranged to have the foreign periodicals sent on to me here regularly. Also where am I to return them and to whose address? That applies to books also. Shall I send these from time to time to Feroze, Anand Bhawan, or Upadhyaya?

I wrote to you from Ahmadnagar Fort and asked you to arrange to send me Ram Narain Lal's Hindustani–English dictionary. I should like to have this and Upadhyaya ought to be able to get it easily. There are two other books, or one book in two volumes (I am not sure) which is somewhere in the Library. This is Romain Rolland's book on Rama-

1. Letter not published.

krishna and Vivekananda. If it is not found in the Library, ask Upadhyaya to get it for me. The Indian edition has been published by the Ramakrishna Centre near Almora – the Advaita Ashram in Mayavati.

Talking about books, I am rather keen on reading Aldous Huxley's and Somerset Maugham's new novels: Huxley's *Time Must Have a Stop* and Maugham's *The Razor's Edge*. I wrote about them to you previously. Perhaps they are not easily available yet. It is just possible that you might be able to get them in a Lahore bookshop. I am looking forward to a parcel of books which Puphi sent me from New York two or three months ago. But if letters take six weeks by air, parcels must take many months. I do not know where she has addressed it to me – perhaps care of the Bombay Govt.

The packing case I sent you was despatched over a week ago by passenger train and should have reached you. Yes, steel trunks are useful in prison. I managed to get one in Ahmadnagar and I am trying to get another here. Books and papers have some protection inside them. You need not trouble to send a trunk to me.

I have had a small note from Kishen Bhai informing me of Padma's marriage. I am not writing to him myself as this would come in the way of my other letters. But you will have, I hope, sent the wedding present or cheque on my behalf to Padma with my love and good wishes.

That reminds me that something has to be done about Yunus's marriage, which you say is coming off towards the end of this month. I really can't suggest what you should give him as a wedding gift. The choice nowadays is limited. You cannot send him a cheque as in Padma's case. That would not be appreciated. Try to get something in Lahore or later in Srinagar, although that will be after the event. You can spend anything up to Rs. 200/- or Rs. 250/- for it. And also of course you will convey to him and his bride my love.

I have not written to Amma (Nani) for over three months, and meanwhile, I have received two letters from her. You will apologise to her on my behalf and tell her I am well. After all, that is about all I can write to her. I find it hard to fit in extra letters as my usual correspondents – you, Puphi and Betty and occasionally Chand or Tara – exhaust the number of letters allowed me. I have been writing fairly regularly, once a fortnight, to Puphi in America. As she is far away I felt she ought to have some news of us. But so far she has not received any of my letters. They take a mighty long time to get through the various hurdles on the way.

Soon you will be in Kashmir – what a delightful prospect for you and Rajiv. He ought to flourish there and imbibe not only health and strength but some of the fascinating and mysterious beauty of the place. I shall be with you often in mind and enjoy this charm and beauty through you, vicariously and yet intimately enough . . .

Give my love to Nani, Chand, Rup and children in Lahore, and to other friends there.

It is still not too warm here and the nights are definitely cool.
Love,

Your loving,
Papu

---

257.

Anand Bhawan,
Allahabad,
24th April, 1945

Darling Papu,
I have your letters. [1]

We have been looking for the books you want. I have now made out a clear list for Upadhyaya. I am sending some books – the ones from Dr Krishnan. Upadhyaya will send the Hindustani dictionary & Romain Rolland's book in a few days. I have got Rolland's books in French. One volume on Ramkrishna and two on Vivekananda. But Upadhyaya is looking for the English versions. There is a Persian–Urdu dictionary available but no Persian–English. Do you want the Urdu one?

Your packing case of old things has come.

I have a brief note from Bari Puphi – her second. It has not much news except that Rita is in a coed school in Vermont.

We are leaving Allahabad on the 25th, tomorrow evening. We reach Delhi next day at eleven o'clock. I had hoped to leave the same evening but we are finding great difficulty in getting reservations. We may have to go by the day train, but this will be very tedious for Rajiv and it will not be easy to fix his feeds, especially if the train is crowded, as all trains seem to be these days. I shall be in Lahore for a couple of days. From Pindi one goes by what is called a super-bus! No – or at least very few – cars are available. But the super-bus is supposed to be very comfortable & does the journey in a day. My address in Kashmir: c/o The Postmaster, Srinagar (Kashmir & Jammu State).

What strange weather we have been having. It is very pleasant, except in the afternoons. It is delightful to sit on the lawn in the evenings. The season for flowers is over but there are some perennials that continue

---

1. Refers to letters Nos 255 and 256.

to bloom very prettily – the cannas and verbena, for instance. The whole garden is bathed in the red glow of the gulmohars.

You can send the periodicals to Feroze.

Much love,

Indu

P.S.

I am sending a dividend warrant – please sign and return it.

Upadhyaya says that the *Popular Hindi–English Dictionary* which came out in 1940 is out of stock now. It may be available at Benares. He is finding out. We have got a *Students' Hindi–English Dictionary* here. It is a 1920 edition. Would you like to have it if the other is not available?

Much love,

Indu

---

258.　　　　　　　　　　　　　　　Bareilly Central Prison,
　　　　　　　　　　　　　　　　　　27th April, 1945

Darling Indu,

I have been wondering where you are likely to be now and where I should send my letters. Your last letter [1] came two weeks ago and you mentioned in it that you intended going to Lahore on or about the 21st April. So I suppose you are there now. Betty wrote that she is going to be in Lahore on the 30th and 1st for Yunus's wedding. Presumably you will also stay on for this although you have not said so in your letters. So I am sending this letter to Lahore, c/o Chand, where I suppose you are staying. Chand and family, from the address, live in a flat. Your party will probably rather crowd them up. Not you, for you take little room, but the babe and his companions spread out a lot.

As you travel north to Lahore and Kashmir, I manage to accompany you in my mind and visit these places and see old friends again. I wonder how they look like now and to what extent they have changed. Your journey becomes almost (it is an odd comparison!) like a silent film with one picture succeeding another. Have you any plans about the length of your stay in Kashmir? I suppose not and there is no need to plan far ahead at this stage. Betty apparently intends to return early in July when the boys' holidays end. July, though the rains have begun then, is not a healthy or comfortable month in Allahabad. So you might as well stay on in Kashmir, though Srinagar then is not too pleasant. Is Feroze going to visit Kashmir during your stay there?

1. Letter not published.

You will give my love to Amma and Rup and Chand and tell them all about me – how well I am keeping, etc. Chand's and Rup's children must have grown up. Where are they now?

I have had another letter from Puphi from America. She is evidently feeling more and more at home there and fitting into a life of continuous travelling about. Her stay is being prolonged for she has entered into a year's lecturing contract with a firm arranging these lecture tours. That has somewhat taken me aback for it means that she will not be back for another year, or at any rate till early in 1946. In spite of all my past practice in public speaking, the prospect of such a contract and having to speak day after day for months rather terrifies me. I would soon get bored with the audiences, with myself and what I went on saying and repeating, for repetition there was bound to be. Fortunately I have to put up with no such thing and do not propose to let myself in for it at any future time. I feel I have had enough of public speaking, though no doubt when I have the chance I shall shout again.

From the point of view of Chand, Tara and Rita it is good that Puphi is staying on longer. Chand will graduate soon and may get temporary jobs there in newspapers, etc. Occasionally I get letters from her. They please me for they show how well she is shaping in mind and spirit. There is something rather fine about Chand. She is straight and frank, sensitive and yet not very self-conscious, determined and enquiring, naturally troubled by many things and events but always trying to find out and get on her feet. Her visit to and training in America have undoubtedly done her good and she ought to make something worthwhile of her life. It is inevitable that she and others in her position, with mixed and conflicting backgrounds, should have to face difficulties in the future. To some extent all of us have to in these days of change and transition. And yet perhaps the conflicting elements are greater between the Indian and American background. The two countries are in many ways as the poles apart. America and Soviet Russia, for all their many differences, are much nearer to one another in spirit. I am convinced that we in India have to develop to a great extent that spirit, not losing our own backgrounds of course. And so it is well that young people should go to America for training, though how they react to it is another matter. There is always that risk when one ventures out of harbour into the open seas. The risk has to be taken and must be taken for we have been anchored for too long and our minds have become clogged and fixed in grooves of thought. It is a continuous source of astonishment to me how mentally and spiritually our people have starved and isolated themselves – and none are so narrow and isolated as some of those who have changed superficially and imagine themselves to be very modern and in tune with the changing world.

The change will come in India – it is obviously coming. It will be rapid enough and yet gradual, so far as large numbers of people are concerned. It is a struggle in the spirit and soul of India. Individuals who change more rapidly than their environment have a tendency to get stranded and cut off, and they must suffer for that. Yet they are very necessary.

I have been reading Swami Vivekananda's *Lectures and Letters*. Many of these letters are from America where he lived for over a year and toured about a lot. That was over fifty years ago and yet his letters have a good deal of topical interest. He was a remarkable and fascinating man with enormous energy and a fire and passion which drove him on and eventually consumed him when he was barely forty. He was born about the same time as Dadu and Gurudev, and yet he seems now as belonging to a distant past age. It was odd to discover that he had never spoken at a public meeting anywhere, either in Bengali or English, before he appeared at the Congress of Religions in Chicago in 1893. He was totally unknown then and more or less starving and shivering in his inadequate attire – the yellow *sanyasin's*[1] robe. He spoke extempore and created a sensation. That sensation was a continuing one wherever he went, and he came to be known in the U.S. as the 'Cyclonic Hindu'. Later he travelled over Europe and went as far as Constantinople & Cairo. Halide Edib, the well-known Turkish woman writer, once said that Vivekananda visited her school in Constantinople when she was a little girl. She had forgotten what he had said, but she remembered still how impressed she had been by his presence.

We have been having unusual rains here. That has cooled the air. This reminds me – are you now liable to colds? I have long had that failing, and though it does not amount to much, it is certainly a nuisance. For the last four months – and that is a long period for me – I have been entirely free from them. There may be many reasons for this, but I have told myself that one of these is a new habit I have developed: to gargle every morning with warm water with a good pinch of common salt dissolved in it, also to sniff this up through each nostril. Rock salt – *lahori namak* – is good for this purpose. It is clear and pure and can be ground into powder. It is also stronger than sea salt.

I find that, almost unthinkingly and unawares, I am often giving you grandmotherly advice – I suppose this habit comes from advancing years. After all, I am a grandfather.

Love,

> Your loving,
> Papu

---

1. An ascetic.

259.                                          Bareilly Central Prison,
                                                  1st May, 1945

Darling Indu,
I have received your letter of April 24th[1] – No. 105 – sent from
Allahabad on the eve of your departure for Kashmir. Four days ago I
wrote[2] to you to Lahore. I wonder if this letter of mine managed to
catch you there. You must be on your way to Srinagar, if you have not
already reached there. I read in the papers of your misadventure at
Delhi station.[3] This kind of thing is very irritating and I imagine the
journey must have been a trying one both for you and Rajiv. Well, I
hope you will soon recover from it in Kashmir. From weather reports I
find that Srinagar is still pretty cold . . .

So the European war is over or almost over. The end was long
expected and yet it came with some dramatic suddenness. War is not
over yet and will continue for yet a while in other parts of the world,
and even in Europe real peace is still a long way off. Nevertheless a long
and terribly bloody and horrible chapter closes. In the years to come we
shall gradually think of it as past history, something over and done with,
and the passions of the day will fade off to some extent. It is well that
the war, or rather this part of it, is over. We have had a superabundance
of horror and cruelty and inhumanity and stark suffering which pass
comprehension. Our minds and feelings get numbed and incapable of
normal responses. For the present, this feeling of horror and numbness
remains. Except for China, many parts of Europe have experienced this
extremity of war and destruction more than any part of the world, more
even than China in several respects. What a shambles eastern and central
Europe have become, a vast pit of destruction and ruin and ashes. From
Stalingrad and the Caucasus in the east this trail of fire and death
stretches right across Germany to Holland and Belgium. Of the great
cities of continental Europe how many have been reduced to dust and
rubble. Paris and Rome and Prague are still there, externally not greatly
altered, and yet I wonder how far the spirit and soul of these cities is
the same as before. It cannot be the same again, but it may recover
some of the old atmosphere. But Warsaw and Kiev and Stalingrad and
Budapest and Dresden and Leningrad and Berlin have ceased to be as
they were, and they will have to rise again and anew from their ashes.

Five years and eight months! My mind goes back to the day in Chung-

1. Refers to letter No. 257.
2. Refers to letter No. 258.
3. Refers to an incident (reported in *The Hindustan Times*, 27th April, 1945) wherein
Indira Gandhi was prevented from travelling in a train by the presence of two British
Army officers in a compartment reserved for ladies.

king when I first learnt of the German invasion of Poland and the outbreak of the war in Europe. For all its horror, what an extraordinarily dramatic period this has been with its sudden ups and downs, and uprooting of humanity, and strange turns of fortune! But to go back still further – the last twelve years since Hitler came to power – what astonishing changes and developments, what brilliant successes and down and out failures these have witnessed. To go back still further – the end of the last war and the tortured years that followed. So two dramas of history have been played before our eyes and the story goes on. The war has not actually ended in Europe, it appears, but it must end soon. It cannot go on. And then the war in the East. This may continue for some time to come, but that too will end. And then? Other kinds of conflicts, a piling up of problems and difficulties, realism and idealism, a search for a real peace that is so elusive and difficult to attain.

It is well that you are in Kashmir and can have some peace of mind and body in that enchanting country. Give my love to Bijju Chacha and others and remember me to Sheikh Saheb.

Love to you and the little one,
Your loving,<br>Papu

This is my letter No. 114.

———————————

260. 21 Bikman Road,
Lahore,
[3rd May, 1945]

Darling Papu,
Travelling has to be seen to be believed these days. We have had quite a hectic time. We left Allahabad on the 25th in a compartment which had no switch – just two wires sticking out. If you wanted the light on or off you had to fiddle about with the wires to get the desired result. The bathroom lights have been removed long ago. The bathroom door had no handle. We spent the day in Delhi with Raksha & Nandanbhai. Puphi & Rajabhai, who had arrived the night before and were staying with Bijju and Fory, came to see me. The same night we left for Lahore. This time we had in our compartment a Muslim lady with a son of about twelve who was very ill with malaria; an Anglo-Indian lady with a dog who was about to have pups!

I hadn't realised that I knew so many people in Lahore. It has been a rush to see them all, especially as Nani would like me to spend all my time with her. I called on Rai Saheb – Ladobhai is also there. Shama, who is now Mrs Chopra, lives here too. Then there was Yunus's wedding on the 30th. Beltie Shah Gilani[1] is the bride's maternal uncle. Yunus had a civil marriage & the bride wore a thick *salwar kurta* the yarn for which had been spun by Badshah Khan. Dr Khan Saheb came and Wali.[2] Also Mehr Taj, who has grown quite fat, and her husband.

Ifti[3] is the same as ever and Rajabhai teases him a lot. Ifti & Ismet send you their love. Dr Mahmud is also here.

Rajabhai & Puphi are leaving tonight for Rawalpindi, Dr Mahmud for Delhi. Anna, Rajiv & I will leave tomorrow night. Rajabhai, etc, are staying a few days with the Watals[4] first. I am sending up Tulsi & Dewan Ram Lall's man on the same day as Puphi, so that the house will be cleaned & the food ready when we arrive.

With much love,

Indu

---

261.                                      18 Gupkar Road,
                                                 Srinagar,
                                                 Kashmir,
                                          9th May, 1945

Darling Papu,

Your letter of May 1st[5] and April 27th[6] both reached me yesterday, one in the morning and the other, the one you sent to Lahore, by hand through the Imperial Bank in the evening. It was the day the Germans surrendered and the bund here was all bedecked with flags and *divas*.[7] What excitement there must be in London and the big cities of the U.S. And yet peace is a long way off. Will there ever be a real peace – or will it be just a period of preparation for the next war?

Here in Kashmir there is little evidence of the war – except perhaps in the rationing of wheat & rice & sugar and the shortage of petrol. Otherwise everything is so much the same as I remember it from 1942 and further back in 1934. The same lovely material & other handicrafts in the shops and the same sort of crowd to buy them. More visitors are expected this year than there have been for some time. Lots of people

---

1. Beltie Shah Gilani: a Roman Catholic who sought to promote nationalist feeling among Indian Christians; suffered imprisonment during the freedom movement.
2. Abdul Wali Khan: son of Khan Abdul Ghaffar Khan.
3. Mian Iftikharuddin. Ismet is his wife.
4. Avtar Krishna Watal: a friend of the Nehrus.
5. Refers to letter No. 259.
6. Refers to letter No. 258.
7. Small earthen oil lamps.

we know are here or are intending to come. The whole Sarabhai clan, with the exception of Mridu, is here, complete with secretaries and the usual paraphernalia. Hannah Sen[1] & family. Yunus & his wife. And many others. Kitty Shiva Rao[2] comes every year now that her brother-in-law is Prime Minister.

The Government does not come to Srinagar until the 10th. So Bijju Chacha is not yet here. Sheikh Saheb has gone to some conference – I met him in Lahore . . .

It is cold here – colder than I had thought it would be. An extra blanket would be very welcome. But now each day will be warmer, so I hope. Gulmarg, I hear, is still covered with snow. Here in Srinagar it is cloudy & windy and each day the surrounding ranges seem to have a fresher & whiter layer of snow. Around about our house the air is full of some awful cotton-looking sort of thing. I think it falls off the poplars. From a distance it is just like snow falling. But it is horrid stuff and gets into one's nose.

This house has a beautiful situation. It is one of the last houses on the Gupkar. The building of houses was prohibited since they came too near the palaces! We are just under Shankaracharya, on the side away from the lake. In fact I can see the temple from my bed. I have also a most gorgeous view of the whole snow range. Rajiv, Anna, *ayah* & I are living in an attic. Rajiv & I sleep in an alcove which has glass windows all around – hence the view. We also get lots of sun, when there is any. But it has its disadvantages too: the bathroom roof is slanting & somebody or other is always banging their head against the rafters. Rajabhai, Puphi & the children occupy two quite luxurious suites downstairs. But they have no view and no sun. However, when the sun is out it is very pleasant to sit out in the garden.

I have no definite plan as to how long I shall stay. July & August, though not as hot as May, are nevertheless rather unpleasant months in Allahabad, full of illness and insect bites.

Mamu has two big children – Ashok who has just started college & Chitra who will do her matric soon. Then there are the twins, Hari & Om, aged about four or so. They are all in Lahore.

I think I wrote to you that Puphi had written to say that she had sent some things for baby through a Santosh Mahindra. Well, I contacted Santosh in Lahore and have got a suit which fits Rajiv very well. I have

---

1. Mrs Hannah Sen: Director, Lady Irwin College, New Delhi, 1932–47; Honorary Adviser, Ministry of Relief and Rehabilitation, 1947–9; President, All India Women's Conference, 1951–3.

2. Social worker and wife of the distinguished journalist and nationalist, B. Shiva Rao.

had him photographed in it. The photograph ought to be here in a day
or so.

We have met Nikkubhai[1] and are going to dinner with him the day
after tomorrow.

I have received the dividend warrant and the periodicals.

Much love,

Indu

P.S.
You mention colds. Right now all of us except Anna have terrible ones.
I always get one when I am tired, then there is all the dust and the cold.
And I cannot treat myself here as I would at home.

---

262.                                        Bareilly Central Prison,
                                                11th May, 1945

Darling Indu,
I have your letter from Lahore, undated but probably written on May
3.[2] It is your No. 106. I hope you have now settled down in Srinagar
after all the long and troublesome journeys. Yes, travelling in India must
be pretty bad in these days. These early experiences of Rajiv will not
dispose him favourably to it, and at the back of his baby mind he will
store up resentment against this moving about and being shaken up and
out of his normal comfortable routine. Modern civilisation aims at and
has achieved comfort to an amazing degree. But when it breaks down,
it becomes an ugly ramshackle affair, worse than the hard and simple
ways that preceded it, just as you see the astonishing difference between
the up-to-date houses of today and the slums of today. The mud hut
surrounded by the fields, bad and uncomfortable as it is, is better than
the city slum. So in travelling also, if we have the wherewithal and
opportunity, in luxury airlines or air-conditioned coaches or, on the
other hand, in tightly jammed third-class carriages where it is difficult
to breathe or even move your little toe or finger. The stagecoach and
the bullock cart are almost wholly extinct now for purposes of travelling
– not quite in parts of India. They were bad enough in retrospect. Yet
they were more comfortable than the present-day third class in our
Indian railways. Nobody wants to go back to the stagecoach or the
bullock cart and anyway that is not possible. But it is pretty rotten to
have to put up with something which is even worse and which, in

1. Kanwarlal Kathju (see Kinship Circle).
2. Refers to letter No. 260.

addition, somehow lacks the human touch. It is nauseating to see third class carriages packed with human flesh and blood, all individuality sinking almost in one pulsating and panting mass. Travelling conditions are after all a reflection of life in general in India and what applies to travelling applies in an equal degree to the way the masses live, or rather exist.

It was this distaste of travelling in these conditions that had led me some months ago to write to you on the delights of trekking in the mountains. Our city dwellers, unused to this kind of thing, are frightened at the prospect of being far from a railway line or a motor road. Yet the disadvantages of trekking are far less, and the advantages in the mountains are obvious. Of course that does not apply to the plains and it is impossible to walk or ride or drive from Allahabad to Kashmir, unless one has the facilities which the Grand Moghul's imperial train provided in the old days.

So you are in Kashmir now. What does it look like at this season? What flowers are blooming, what fruits hang from the over-burdened branches? I suppose the peach blossoms are over now, so also the rhododendrons. The lotus must be still in bud or even in an earlier stage. It blossoms on the Dal Lake in July, if I remember rightly. Cherries will soon be out and apricots and apples and peaches. I am getting rather mixed up about their respective seasons – they vary somewhat in different parts of the country.

Where is Ram Lall's house where you are staying? Is it in Gupkar or thereabouts – I suppose I have spelt this name wrongly? Somewhere between the city proper and the Chashme Shahi? I heard some time ago that the Chashme Shahi had been practically enclosed by the Maharaja's private gardens and was hardly open to the public. That indeed would be a misfortune. Even in 1940 these private gardens had spread out to the Chashme Shahi building and had cut off a road leading from the lake to the other side. How extraordinary is this desire to wall up and isolate large tracts of nature for one's private pleasure and deprive others from sharing in the abundance provided, which grows no lesser by the sharing. And the Nishat and Shalimar Baghs – what do they look like now? Is the Dal Lake much the same as ever or have the fancy boulevards made much difference? What birds chirp and sing in the trees?

I think of all these scenes treasured in memory's chambers, but even more I visualise the higher valleys leading up to the snows and glaciers, with their ice-cold brooks gurgling and rushing down to the vale below where they join the Vitasta.

I suppose, in spite of difficulties in travelling, Kashmir still attracts crowds of visitors, chiefly from the Punjab. Many of our friends may be there now or might come up later. How is Siddhartha doing – Nikku's son? He must be a grown-up boy now.

I like going to Lahore, chiefly because there are so many old and young friends there. The city also is developing in a way the air of a great city, though this is still rather superficial. The mixture of old historical tradition and modernity is rather appealing in its contrasts, though they clash frequently enough. Probably what I like is a certain vitality about the place. It is like a growing child, very immature in many ways and yet with an air of sophistication. But of course grown-up people, that is grown-up in years, who are still very ungrown-up and immature in mental outlook, are not always attractive. They may become very tiresome. Gaiety is always to be welcomed. In Lahore however there is an atmosphere of a fake and superficial gaiety which is not so welcome. Yet, for all that, I like Lahore. Do you know that some of my earliest years, that is before I was ten, were spent in Lahore? Dol Amma was in a sense a Punjabi. She was born there and till her marriage lived there. Often she used to go on long visits to her mother, brother and others, and of course I accompanied her.

What has happened to the lovely pony which was presented to you by a friend – I forget his name – in Lahore in 1942 summer?

I am glad you consulted Dr Bharucha about baby. I do not know much about such matters – deficiency of calcium, etc. Why should there be this deficiency? Can it be made good pretty soon with right feeding, etc? It denotes a certain weakness of the bodily structure and we do not want Rajiv to be weak in any way. He will be nine months old soon and I suppose he is taking some other food now besides milk, though milk is the best stuff for providing calcium. Have you had his *khir chatai*.[1] And did you ever have a formal name-giving ceremony? How does his weight compare with a normal nine-month old? The main thing is that he should keep generally healthy & cheerful and he will himself supply any deficiencies.

Love,

Your loving,
Papu

This is my letter No. 115. Should I go on sending letters c/o the Postmaster or to your proper address?

P.

---

1. Formal feeding ceremony of a child.

263.                               Bareilly Central Prison,
17th May, 1945

Darling Indu,

Yesterday I got your letter of the 9th May[1] from Srinagar – your No. 107. You do not tell me what the motor journey was like. Are the so-called super-buses comfortable? And how did Rajiv fare during the journey?

Kashmir continues of course much the same as it used to be. Nobody, and not even gross mismanagement on man's part, can take away the beauty of the place. Yet how much more agreeable and desirable it could be made if the mass of human beings there were put on the road to betterment. Every year bigger crowds of visitors go there from other parts of India and this I think is to be welcomed. Many of them are decent people, going in search of rest and health and beauty. Still I do not take kindly to the class that flourishes so well in these days – the high dignitaries extravagantly paid without much reference to their brain capacity, the war contractors and profiteers, and the hordes of others of high and low degree who seem to sprout up in wartime like weeds in a badly kept garden and eat up the soil to the vast detriment of the more legitimate plants and flowers. It is this variety of people who are most in evidence, I suppose, at all the holiday resorts, and especially in Kashmir. That is why I prefer the quieter higher valleys where there is less flaunting of ill-gotten monies. Not that I do not like pleasant and intelligent society – I am no recluse – but the contrasts of India are so marked and painful.

There is no need for you to fix up your programme in Kashmir definitely or to decide on the length of your stay there. Enjoy your holiday and do not bind yourself down to anything. There is no particular point in your returning to the plains when the rains have started. That is not a healthy season. Now that you have gone so far, you might as well stay on there as long as possible. Your last visit in 1942 was, I am afraid, cut short chiefly because of me. This should not happen this time. Srinagar may not be an ideal place to stay in from July onwards. You can then pitch your tent elsewhere. There is no lack of places to choose from.

I am looking forward to Rajiv's new photographs. Even more so I am thinking of the time when he will begin to toddle . . .

It is pretty warm here now, yet not so hot, I imagine, as at Allahabad. The nights are pleasant. It is not the heat I mind so much as the dust

---

1. Refers to letter No. 261.

when the *loo*[1] blows. Within a month the rains ought to commence –
the *chhotai barsat*[2] to begin with. So there is not long to wait. It is
surprising how rapidly the days and weeks go by. Only occasionally they
stick.

What is Nikku doing now? Is he working in Watal's factory? . . .

Puphi seems to have been having a rather hectic time in San Francisco. Her stay there must be ending as she was going to Chand's
graduation at Wellesley.

This is my letter No. 116.

Love,

Your loving,<br>
Papu

---

264.

18 Gupkar Road,<br>
Srinagar,<br>
Kashmir,<br>
19th May, 1945

Darling Papu,

Your letter of the 11th[3] arrived yesterday. Like all your letters, it
cheered me up and gave me fresh energy – regular tonic.

Yunus had come here to spend the day. He and Laj have been staying
in Baramulla all these days – they came up to Srinagar on the 17th
evening for a couple of days or so. They want to be very quiet and are
now proposing to live a month near – or rather twenty miles from –
Patan. Afterwards they want to go to Sonamarg. They are pressing me
to join them but I have not made up my mind yet. The chief reason
Yunus wants me to come is so that I may persuade Laj to wear *khadi*!
Yunus is still weak, gets tired very quickly. Did I write to you about his
wedding? On his wedding night he had a bilious attack and was quite
ill for the next few days. It's not an encouraging prospect for the new
bride.

What short memories we have! It is unpardonable of me not to have
written to you in greater detail of Kashmir & Lahore and everything,
remembering as I do how I felt about such things when I was in jail.

Coming up from the plains – the dry hot dusty roads, the scorching
sun – you can imagine what a relief it was to the eyes to see miles and
miles of fresh green. We came by super-bus. It has six comfortable seats

---

1. See p. 168 n., letter No. 97.
2. See p. 205 n.3, letter No. 108.
3. Refers to letter No. 262.

– almost, but not quite as comfortable as a car. And at the back a separate compartment for servants. I had sent Tulsi & the Ram Lall's servant on ahead the day before. Anna, *ayah*, Rajiv & I all sat in the front part. We had a comfortable though rather dusty journey. Rajiv behaved very well & slept all the way. We reached here about eight thirty p.m. and had to settle the house because Puphi & her family, although they had come up a day before, were staying at the Watals for a few days.

This house has a most beautiful situation. It is on the side of the 'Takht' or Shankaracharya mountain. It is near the palaces. You can say that it is between the city and the Chashme Shahi & other Moghul gardens. (There is a state guest-house near the Chashme Shahi. It is said to be very lovely and is reserved for special favourites.) Our house here has lots of room for a garden and there are indeed a few flowers but that is all. There is no proper planning. It is a pity, for with practically no effort and very little cost, they could have had masses of roses or other blooms. When we came up the wild iris were just ending and now there are no wild flowers in the valley itself. On the slopes of the 'Takht' there are some yellow flowers which are quite attractive. I have not been to the Shalimar or Nishat yet. It is so cold and damp. Nor have I seen any especially nice private gardens. One exception is the rose garden at 'Lambarts' the Chemists. It has the loveliest blooms, red and pink and white and yellow, some extra large ones and other ordinary creepers with all the colours of the sunset. In the Dal there are as yet no signs of the lotus or the lotus lilies. We were too late to see the fruit blossoms. Only the chestnut trees are in flower. The first cherries and strawberries are coming to the *bazar* – also plums.

You will be interested to hear of a recent flying accident here. Some Americans – a married couple, a friend and the pilot – were coming to Srinagar for a holiday in an American plane from Delhi. Mr & Mrs Tweedy were the couple. Mr Tweedy is in the American Air Force – his job is to take supplies & things to China. His wife is expecting a baby – it's her fourth month. Mr Tweedy was used to flying over danger- ous and high mountains. He always wore especial warm kit fitted up with brandy flask and other essentials in case of a crash. But this trip, being on holiday, nobody even thought of such things. Well, they were over Kashmir when they lost their bearings. They were caught in clouds and could get neither above nor below them. They had no idea where they were but suddenly the snowy ranges were towering around them and they prepared to bale out as there was no hope of saving the plane. Mrs Tweedy had the presence of mind to change her summery cotton dress and get into woollen slacks but of all the things she could have put into her pockets, she chose her lipstick! She was the first to jump out. She landed on the snows and again showed how alert she was by pulling in and bundling her parachute under her as she touched the ground, otherwise the wind could have dragged her away. Her first job was to look for the others. Within half-an-hour she had found her husband. The other passenger found them late in the evening and the pilot not until the next day. Two days they were in the snow, 1400 ft high with no food, no warm clothes at all. Then they heard a distant sound and saw some smoke. What prodigious luck to land in the one place where they could get quick help – for they soon discovered they were near Kishtwar, the sapphire mines which are strongly guarded by police. They were given something hot to drink and some *charpies*,[1] which they put on the flat roofs of the police huts and for one whole day and night they slept, so exhausted they were! Then they trekked down the mountain to the place where cars were awaiting them. They are all perfectly well – not even a cold. It's remarkable.

You ask about the birds here. Half the joy of being here is that there are no crows and no babblers. There are mynas but they are not as noisy as in the plains. The birds that are constantly in the garden are the white-whiskered bulbuls, shrikes, golden orioles and different kinds of tits. All such lovely creatures. I'm longing to see the paradise fly-catchers – they say there are lots here. It is truly a heavenly bird.

Somewhere on the journey Rajiv got something in his eye. Both his eyes became very red with matter coming out. Puphi said it was due to his cold, so we did not pay much attention. But he started yelling so I had the doctor in. Now they are quite all right. His cold is better too but we both have coughs.

I have not had a name-giving ceremony or *khir chatai*. I did not feel like having anything with no elders around. Rajiv has not had proper *khir*[2] yet. But he has been having *suji*[3] since he was six months old. Now he is having other things as well – Quaker oats, almost all vegetables, potatoes, egg-yolk, rusks. Soon he will begin having milk-puddings. According to the books, he should be put on a three-meal basis, now that he is nine months old – breakfast, lunch & supper. But I don't think it will be possible to stick to that routine in India for with the kind of life we lead how can we expect the child to go to bed at six thirty p.m. I don't think the calcium deficiency could be very serious. He has had no trouble with his teeth and now has five of them. He is beginning to crawl now but still does not sit up on his own. Otherwise he seems to be healthy. He is not fat but has a good weight – 20 lbs.

1. Cots.
2. A sweet dish made of rice, milk and sugar.
3. Semolina.

He is good-natured and friendly to all – even strangers. He rarely cries, only if he is wet or uncomfortable in any way. He seems to be very interested in his surroundings. He doesn't care for toys but loves playing with torches, hand-fans, buttons and, above all, paper!

I shall soon be sending you some new snaps of Rajiv.

Puphi sent Rajiv a suit from America with Santosh Mahindra. He looks very sweet in it and it just fits beautifully.

Lots of love,

Indu

P.S.
Greetings from Sheikh Saheb, Yunus and all other friends.

---

265.                                          18 Gupkar Road,
                                                   Srinagar,
                                                    Kashmir,
                                              23rd May, 1945

Darling Papu,
Srinagar is really lovely. Rajiv woke up at five this morning. After a whole night's rain, the sky was clear and cloudless and studded with stars, and the mountain ranges glistening silver with the freshly-fallen snow. It was a cold night and the snow seems to have fallen much lower down. Later on, at about seven, came the dawn, starting with the merest touch of pink on the highest peaks, then gradually spreading the rosy glow until the whole range was bathed in sunlight and stood out against the sky, looking whiter and whiter. It was a glorious sight. The river is lovely too, with the water rushing around the tortuous bends and the chinar and other magnificent trees leaning over its banks. The current is very strong these days, probably due to the rain and some melting snow.

Yesterday we climbed to the Shankaracharya temple. Going slowly and leisurely, it took us forty or forty-five minutes, which is supposed to be average going. Later in the day, when Yunus came to visit us, I was amazed to hear that Laj had once run up to the temple in seven minutes. I am afraid I cannot quite believe it – she says she is a very fast runner as well as walker – but seven minutes to climb a thousand feet! The view from the top was beautiful. We went up the usual long-winded way but for coming back we chose a narrow and slippery path, which looked as if it were coming straight down to the house. Instead, it took us to the other side of the mountain into a most delightful and fragrant grove of pines. The ground was strewn with pine cones and needles, and growing nearby were tall marguerites and masses of iris and prickly wild rose bushes.

Puphi and family left for Gulmarg this morning. They are staying in a hut leased by Munus Didda but now rented from her by Rajabhai's brother Narottambhai for Rs. 800/- for two months. Munus Didda has had this hut for the last four or five years but has never yet stayed in it! This year she was determined to come but apparently Amrit could not resist renting the hut! Narottambhai arrived in Srinagar some time ago with his wife and two children and three other children – nephews and nieces. First they had rooms in one hotel then they changed to another hotel. None of the children had any warm clothing! Their daughter Rita, aged fifteen, has asthma. Because of her they could not make up their minds whether to go to Gulmarg or not – whether they should even stay on in Srinagar or return to Ahmedabad. Eventually Narottambhai has gone to Gulmarg with Raja to see what it is like and if it is fit for the rest of the family.

Bijju Chacha is insisting on my moving to his house. I have decided to move over in the first week of June, if he agrees to this proposal. Just now there is no one there except Bijju Chacha & Fory.

We had tea with Lady Maharaj Singh the other day. She is staying in a dream of a houseboat. It is a small one – two bedrooms – but perfectly made and beautifully furnished. It is complete with good modern books, electric kettle and other appliances, silver, and so on.

When the sun has been out all day it gets quite warm. I must make some arrangements about going higher up. I love the scenery of Pahalgam and the smell of the pines. It is one of the healthiest places in Kashmir. The water is good too. But in July & August it becomes the stronghold of the Punjabis. That is its only disadvantage.

I should like to do at least one small trek. In one of the guide books there is such a lovely description of the road to the Tragbal Pass near the Nanga Parbat, that I cannot resist the temptation to go and see for myself. If Rajiv is well, I can easily leave him for a few days with Anna & the *ayah*. But with whom can I go?

I am sorry this paper is so thin & the writing goes through to the other side. Anna got it. I must get another one.

Lots of love,

Indu

266.                                  Bareilly Central Prison,
                                            31st May, 1945

Indu darling,

I have received two letters from you dated 19th and 23rd May[1] – Nos. 108 and 109. The latter of these came this morning.

I love your descriptions of Srinagar and the neighbourhood, of the dawn touching the snowy peaks and gradually creeping down and spreading over the lowlands. Some time ago I read an airman's account of the dawn. He was flying high up and was enveloped in the early morning sunlight, but the earth was still a dark shadow and gradually it emerged from the gloom. So it must feel also if one is on a high mountaintop.

I remember the Gupkar area fairly well. In 1940 I spent some days there and much earlier, over a year before you were born, the whole family lived in a large house almost at the foot of Shankaracharya. Gupkar was not built over then as now and there were few houses. Nor had the Maharaja's palace spread out in all directions, enclosing the land round about Chashme Shahi. We went frequently to Chashme Shahi and up Shankaracharya. Janki Chacha – do you remember him? – he was one of Dadu's closest friends – was staying with us and he was a great walker. Every morning, before most of us were up, he had his little constitutional which usually meant going up Shankaracharya by one route and coming down on the other side.

The guest-house near Chashme Shahi I remember very well. What a lovely situation! The view from its balcony over the Dal Lake and towards the mountains is hard to beat – In those days in 1916 Swamiji (Swami Sant Deo) used to live there. He was in high favour with the old Maharaja Pratap Singh[2] (the uncle of the present one[3]), and a crowd of Punjabis, especially women, was always to be found round about him. Dol Amma and Bibi Amma thought no end of him and we used to go to him frequently and consume the lovely fruits of his garden which he gave us in abundance. I lost sight of the Swami for many years and then, in 1940, on my way back via the Jammu route, I met him somewhere halfway in the mountains. I used to like him. He was (and I hope still is) a jolly, cheerful person with plenty of commonsense. I wonder if he is still flourishing. Nikku should know, for his family was greatly attached to the old Swami.

1. Refers to letters Nos 264 and 265.
2. Maharaja Pratap Singh: the third Maharaja of Jammu and Kashmir who ruled from 1887 to 1925.
3. Maharaja Hari Singh of Kashmir (1895–1961): succeeded as Maharaja, 1925; withdrew in favour of his son Karan Singh in 1949.

Whenever Tej Bahadurji goes up to Srinagar he stays as the Maharaja's guest in the Chashme Shahi guest-house. I visited him then in the summer of 1940. It brought back old memories to me and I gazed for long at the magnificent view spread out before me. And now even 1940 is an old memory.

If Bijju Chacha wants you to shift over to his house, it would be well to agree to his proposal when it is convenient for you to do so. Perhaps so long as Betty and Raja and their children are staying on in Srinagar you had better continue where you are. Bijju Chacha's house will be quite comfortable for you. You are likely to have much more company there, for he likes to have his friends round about him.

There are ever so many places in Kashmir which invited one to trek. Pahalgam, itself a lovely spot, is a fairly good spot. There is a lake, rather high up, but just one day's good trekking, which is worth a visit. A place I liked is on the way to Kolahoi, also one day's easy trek from Pahalgam. I forget the name of the place but there were beautiful meadows skirted by pinewoods. There is a fairly decent rest-house there with two good rooms. You could easily go there and even take Rajiv with you. It is always desirable to have a pony with you when trekking. Pahalgam has that disadvantage you mention – too many visitors go there during the summer months, many of them invalids, and a small place easily gets crowded.

Last Saturday – the 27th – was rather a special day, but very few people in India took notice of it, although we have a vast number of festivals and holidays and a passion for anniversaries. It was the *Vaisakhi Purnima*, the full moon of the month of Vaisakha, the last day of that month, leading on to the *Jyeshtha*, or more simply *jeth*. Tradition says that Buddha was born on this day, attained enlightenment on the anniversary of that day, and finally died also on the *Vaisakhi Purnima*. The Buddhist era begins from the date of his death, thus this day is the Buddhist New Year's Day and is celebrated as such in the Buddhist countries. I remember the celebrations in Ceylon when we were there in May 1931. Last Saturday began the 2489th year of this era. Historically speaking, Buddha was the greatest person born in India and it is right that we should remember this day.

We are right in the middle of the hot weather here and it is pretty hot. Sometimes, though not frequently, the nights are bad. But then there is one peculiarity of Bareilly, due to its nearness to the hills – suddenly a cool wind comes at night and makes a difference. We have been having very hot and sticky nights. But last night turned cool rather suddenly and some warm covering was required in the early morning. We sleep in the open – it is as hot as ever today.

What an extraordinary story of misadventure and good luck you have written [1] about – the exploits of the Tweedy family. Kishtwar is one of the most out-of-the-way provinces of Kashmir, very seldom visited by tourists or others. In my mind it is connected with an old legend that the women of Kishtwar are very beautiful!

I don't think you need worry at all about Rajiv's health. He is doing well, his weight is good and he keeps cheerful – that in itself is a sign of health. It does not matter if there is slight delay in his sitting up or walking. That will all come in good time. I think you should have a simple ceremony soon now both for the name-giving and the *khir chatai*. It should not be delayed much longer. Kashmir is a suitable place for it and there is Bijju Chacha to help you fix it up. He is sure to be interested. So ask him about it.

Love,
Your loving,<br>Papu

This is my letter No. 118.

267.                                                 18 Gupkar Road,
Srinagar,<br>Kashmir,<br>2nd June, 1945

Darling Papu,
Here are two photographs of Rajiv's taken in Lahore. In the dressed up one he is wearing a suit sent by Puphi from America. He now sits up and also crawls. He still has only five teeth but they seem to be ample for eating even the hardest toast! He says 'mamma', but he means his food not me. He also makes many sounds such as '*akka*' and '*appa*'.

I am sending separately a *Gita* which Bharati has sent for you & a copy of *Foreign Affairs*.

Srinagar is lovely but it has become impossible to enjoy it when one sees the temperature of the plains. I think of you continually. If it weren't for Rajiv, I don't think I could have stayed on here. I hope to be able to send you some cherries in a few days.

Shall write again tomorrow or the day after. Anna wants to take this to the post as it is Saturday.

Much love,
Indu

1. Refers to letter No. 264.

268.                                                      18 Gupkar Road,
                                                              Srinagar,
                                                               Kashmir,
                                                          3rd June, 1945

Darling Papu,

I am feeling desperately depressed. It must have been growing hotter
and hotter on the plains for a long time. And yet I only became conscious
of the fact a few days ago and suddenly I cannot bear it here. The more
beautiful it is the more I hate it and the more I long to be down in the
plains and the heat. And how irritated I become with all these people
here, dressing up in gaudy clothes, buying expensive things for themselves, yet grudging a few extra annas to the *tonga-walla* [1] or the *shikara*
man, [2] constantly complaining of petty discomforts such as the shortage
of sugar etc. I do wish I were in jail too.

Puphi's book, *Prison Days*, has arrived. I am sending you your copy.
I have only just glanced at it but I feel that she has missed out much –
the enjoyment we took in little things, the sad cases of many convicts,
the anguish of not having news of you, and so many many incidents,
interesting or exciting or humiliating. I think she has made our jail life
sound dull – it wasn't that for me. And in all the ranges of feeling and
emotion that I went through in those nine or ten months, there was no
room for boredom. But the book has brought back a host of memories,
though most times I have seen and interpreted the same incidents rather
differently. But I suppose that for each person the same things have
different meanings.

About my arrest, Puphi says that we were arrested before we could
hold a meeting. That was not so. We had a meeting of about 3000
people for three whole hours from five p.m. to eight p.m. The police
started trying to arrest me from about five thirty onwards! I am rather
proud of that evening. To collect and keep so many people together in
the days when the general public was of two minds – some full of
bravado, wanting to throw stones and pull wires, the others cowed and
afraid, not daring even to go to the cinema for fear of getting involved
in something – everybody was amazed and said it was quite an achievement. We had two brief speeches and the rest of the time we sang or
shouted slogans. And all the time the police trying to beat the people
away. The people were absolutely non-violent and under our control.
The 'scuffle', as Puphi calls it, started when we squatted on the road
and refused to be arrested – and the crowd said that it would *not* let us

1. Driver of a *tonga* or a horse-carriage.
2. Boatman.

be arrested! What days those were! Whether all that happened was right or wrong, the enthusiasm and the spirit of ordinary people were wonderful – as Voltaire said of the French Revolution: it was good to be alive 'but to be young was very heaven'.

Darling, when you are out, do come up here for a breather – Kashmir will be perfect with you. And it will do you a world of good. The fresh air and the comfort of the cool snow to the eyes. Remember three years ago – you were somewhere in the heat, Wardha or Bombay and I wired to you from Gulmarg – I wish I could send you this coolness and beauty. Raihana Tyabji says that if she concentrates on a thing hard enough she can see it as clear as if it were actually before her eyes. Last year when I went to see Bapu in Poona immediately after his release, Sushila Nayar took Raihana & me and some others to the Aga Khan's bungalow (I refuse to call such a ramshackle old place a palace!). Suddenly Raihana said, 'That's where Ba sat and read the Ramayana.' 'This is where Bapu lay,' and so on. 'Why, yes,' said Sushila, 'you must have come here during the fast.' But this was Raihana's first visit to the house. She told us that during the fast, she was praying almost continually and in her concentration on Bapu, she could actually see him and his surroundings! Isn't it strange and remarkable? Raihana is rather a strange person herself. She looks at people's hands – not palmistry, not the past and the future and so on – but just to see what kind of people they are, what they are capable of doing and that sort of thing. I was sitting one day with my arm hanging over the back of the chair. Raihana was coming up from behind – she did not recognise my back but she came up and asked me, 'Child, do you draw?' When I turned around she knew who I was and embraced me. 'Why should I draw?' [I asked.] 'Because you have a remarkable talent for line drawing – don't waste your time on painting!' And here I am with not a single drawing lesson to my credit. But now that my train of thought has led me to Raihana and my drawing, I think I will invest in a pencil and a drawing pad.

I have seen Sheikh Saheb only once or twice. He seems to be very busy, making money, amongst other things. He takes contracts to supply things. I hear he is increasingly being influenced by the Communists. Many of the Punjab Communists come up here every year and have a more or less free holiday, and unload their ideas on politics in general and India in particular. Speaking of Communists, have you received another batch of books from them?

I have written to Louise Morin. Also to Lu [1] for news of Nanu. Re. Edward Thompson, I think Agatha or someone wrote to say that he was

1. Louise Geissler.

miraculously cured. I am not sure exactly what she was talking about, but I shall find out by looking up the letter.

We took Rajiv out to the gardens in a friend's car. We went on a Thursday and spent the whole day there. The fountains play only on Sundays and so hardly anybody goes there on weekdays. We had everything to ourselves. It was beautifully quiet and peaceful. We brought back a large *gharha*[1] full of water from the Chashme Shahi.

I hear that Bijju Chachi is here with Ballo's wife. If they have room in their house, I shall move over on the 7th or 8th.

The Sarans are in Naseem Bagh. It is miles from here but very beautiful. Raksha has asked me over for a week or ten days. I might go.

I wanted to go to Pahalgam for July & August, if I stay so long. Yunus & Laj are also going, so we thought we might share a hut. But a hut costs Rs. 1500/-. It's much too much. Yunus is looking around for tents. Avtarbhai Watal has offered me his hut, but I do not know if I can keep it for so long. Money is very useful sometimes!

Either I have been walking too much or because I tried a spot of fasting to set my inside right, or it may even be that I do miss you so much and it upsets me to be in all this loveliness when you are in a veritable hell, whatever the cause I have suddenly lost weight and am much thinner. All my *salwars* have to be pinned up!

All my love,

Indu

P.S.
Puphi's back from Gulmarg. She seems to be in a very cross mood!

---

269.                                           18 Gupkar Road,
                                                     Srinagar,
                                                     Kashmir,
                                              5th June, 1945

Darling Papu,
Your letter of the 31st May[2] has just come. I was considerably relieved to hear that you have a cool breeze occasionally. What a difference it must make! Here in Srinagar it is warming up too. Today Rajiv has discarded his woollen vest for the first time in Kashmir.

Now that he has got rid of his cold and cough, Rajiv is happy and flourishing again. I am sending yet another snapshot of his. Feroze took

1. Pitcher without a handle.
2. Refers to letter No. 266.

it in Anand Bhawan – just outside the Library – a few days before we left for Delhi. Behind us is the gulmohur, or the Flamboyant, in bloom. He is thinner now.

Feroze writes that they had a terrific gale in Allahabad. It has damaged some of our nicest trees. The electric wires snapped and most of the whitewashing on the outside verandah has fallen off!

The Banerjees are a most peculiar family. Nora has been divorced for some years now but she continued living in the same house and referring to P.K.B. as 'my husband'. Now he has married a girl from Delhi. Nora, I hear, has started wearing what she thinks is the Hindu widow's garb but she is still going to live there all together.

Last evening we had a party here: about twenty-eight people, just all those who had invited us out to meals. It went off quite well. The only people who could not come were the Watals. Shama Watal has gone to Lahore as one of her relatives has died.

Chhoti Puphi is going to Pahalgam tomorrow. *En route* they will visit Achibal & Martund. They will spend a few days in Pahalgam and then go up to Kolahoi with Sheikh Saheb. They expect to return here by the 15th and then to proceed to the Gurez valley. I want to join them on the second trek. The description of the road to the Tragbal pass is too tempting. So I am hoping that Kolahoi, which is their first trek, will not tire or disappoint them.

After Puphi leaves for Pahalgam, I shall move to Bijju Chacha's. Their house is always so crowded ... When Puphi returns from the Kolahoi she will also stay there ...

The day we went to dinner with Nikku Bhai there was much talk about some Swamiji. Nikku Bhai had met him recently but I felt rather out of it as I had no idea who it was. I will ask him when we meet next.

The Watals have a most beautiful house – full of lovely things. I wonder if their Pahalgam hut is also well got-up.

I shall be sorry to leave this house. We have been so quiet and peaceful. And the view is so wonderful. One would think that Srinagar was a city of trees – no ugly houses at all. Bijju Bhai's house has no view. It is wedged in between Nedou's & Regina Hotel.

Actually from the point of view of my American baby book, Rajiv has sat up at the right time. They say eight to nine months he should sit up. But most Indian children sit at six or seven months. As a matter of fact, the book disapproves of babies sitting or walking early, arguing that the longer the baby lies the stronger his back. Early sitting & walking often mean a curved spine & bandy legs, which is a common enough sight in India.

All my love,

Indu

270.                                    Bareilly Central Prison,
                                               7th June, 1945


Darling Indu,

Was it last week that I wrote to you about my recently acquired freedom from colds? Well, I was a little premature, for, soon after, a tiny wee bit of a cold, hardly noticeable, crept in somewhere within my system, and like the camel nosing itself into the tent, began to spread. An odd moment to choose, for we are at the apex of the hot weather. So for some days now I have had a cold, nothing much, but there it is, and a cold is a cold and a bit of a nuisance.

The heat here has revived old memories. For some years I had had no such experience. Ahmadnagar was, after all, a plateau of nearly 2000 ft. altitude and the hottest day there was mild compared to the northern variety. Besides, conditions there were different. There is a certain ferocity about the *loo* in northern India which is comparable to nature's wilder outbursts. It does not last very long, for it heralds the monsoon. Here too I suppose the rain will come soon. It is possible, however, that we may be transferred to a cooler jail from here.

Feroze has sent me a parcel of mangoes – *dasehris* grown in Anand Bhawan. There were just 100 of them, all in a raw state. They are being preserved in the right way so that they may ripen. Tell Feroze that I have got this parcel. Along with it came another from Bombay – *Alphonsoes* sent on Betty's instructions, four dozens of them. On the whole they were in good condition. What a gorgeous thing is the mango – surely the king of fruits.

I enclose a letter which came to me here from Maria Lorenzini, a lady living in San Francisco. Her book of poems – *Seeding Democracy* – also reached me here. I want you to send her a proper appreciative reply. The poems were interesting, though rather beyond me occasionally. Most of them were reactions to musical pieces, and as I was ignorant of the music which inspired them, it was not easy for me to react in the same way. But of course you are not going to say all this to her. You will write a proper, nice, agreeable letter to her which should give her a moment's pleasure. It was good of her to send her book to me.

The lady has sent me a cutting containing her picture (I enclose this also). It is a powerful face and I feel like wilting before its pleasant but stern gaze – perhaps this feeling is more due to the Bareilly weather.

One of the advantages of being in jail evidently is that other people have to answer your letters.

Love,

Your loving,<br>Papu

This is my 119th letter.

---

271.                                            Srinagar,<br>
Kashmir,<br>
11th June, 1945

Darling Papu,

I moved here on the 8th evening, as previously decided. Shortly after my arrival came two other guests: Mr Kumarappa[1] and Manoharbhai. Mr Kumarappa is giving a series of lectures, Bijju Chachi presiding, on 'World Security'. I missed the first two because on the 8th night at about ten thirty p.m. Sheikh Saheb and Mr Beg[2] . . . came to see Bijju Chacha. S.S. mentioned that they were both going to Pahalgam the next day to make arrangements for Rajabhai's trip to the Kolahoi and would I like to go too? I decided to go to make arrangements for my own stay in Pahalgam later on. We left on the 9th at about twelve thirty. Stopped at Anantnag for lunch (my second!) at Mr Beg's house. Reached Pahalgam at about five p.m. We met Padma and her in-laws, the Munshis & other acquaintances, who were all staying at the Plaza Hotel. We were told that Rajabhai and family had gone to Chandanwari. However they were soon back. The Motilal Setalvads[3] are in Pahalgam and also Chhaganlal Gandhi[4] of Sevagram. And Yunus and Laj of course. Pahalgam was lovely as ever. I love the smell of the pines. I stopped the night with Rajabhai at the Watals' hut. We had a huge camp-fire after dinner. I felt so fresh and frisky that instead of walking like a sober citizen, I ran all over the place with the result that today I am feeling stiff all over! We spent just the day there, leaving Pahalgam for the return journey yesterday at five. We were in Mr Beg's car. We dropped him at his house in Anantnag & went to the dak bungalow at Khanebal,

1. J. C. Kumarappa: economist; an associate of Mahatma Gandhi.
2. Mirza Mohamad Afzal Beg: active in the political movement launched by Sheikh Abdullah in Jammu and Kashmir.
3. Motilal Chimanlal Setalvad: eminent jurist; Advocate-General, Bombay, 1937–42; Chairman, Law Commission of India, 1955–8; Attorney-General of India, 1950–62. His wife was Vimlagauri Setalvad.
4. Chhaganlal Gandhi: Mahatma Gandhi's nephew and associate.

a couple of miles away. Until quite recently this dak bungalow was reserved for His Highness, so it is much nicer than most, with a beautiful garden and good furniture. We had tea there, then caught the mail bus to Srinagar. I thought of you a lot and missed Rajiv, otherwise I enjoyed myself. There is only one hut which can be rented and is 'far from the madding crowd'. I have asked Yunus to write the details about rent and so on. If it is not available, I have decided to pitch two tents either on or near Yunus's site. It is a beautiful site and it will save us a lot of bother if we all mess together, otherwise, I shall have to collect crockery, cooking utensils & all sorts of things which Yunus has in plenty. It will also come cheaper for both of us.

I miss the Gupkar Road house – we had so much more space. And the meals here are very irregular. Last night I was so tired after my trip but dinner was not over until ten forty-five p.m.

Rajiv didn't miss me at all the two days I was away! He tries hard to talk now. He says *ph* when he sees flowers and *bat* for *batti* and other such sounds. [1]

Rajabhai will return here on the 16th. Kishen Chacha & Chachi are also coming.

Much love,

Indu

272.                                                    Almora Jail,
                                                  12th June, 1945

Darling Indu,

I am writing to you from a new address – though not so new. I have come back to the old place almost exactly ten years after I left it so suddenly to fly to Europe. It has changed somewhat but many of the old landmarks are still there, well-remembered nooks and corners and tops of trees peeping over the walls. We cannot see the mountains at all as the jail is situated over a ridge and the walls prevent a distant view. In winter and during the rains, I remember, this sometimes produced a strange and rather pleasant sensation of being in the clouds or near them, cut off from the rest of the world.

As I was looking round this old-new environment, faint memories began to stir within me, memories not so much of the material objects surrounding me but of the vague intangible past with all its associations, and gradually more vivid pictures took their place. This train of thought

---

1. Flowers are referred to in Hindi as *phool* and *batti* means a light. Rajiv, as an infant, referred to such objects through monosyllabic diminutives.

was started by a gentle soothing sound, of which I was hardly consciously aware for some little time but which seemed to envelop me and whisper in my ears. There was a dream quality about this sound, something that distinguished it from the more obvious noises of the waking day. Or perhaps it was rather like that middle state which lies between waking and sleeping, when vague ideas float through the mind and pass away leaving no trail behind. It had a slightly hypnotic effect on me, and then I realised that I was listening to the rustle of the breeze through the deodars. There are no deodars within the jail enclosure, but just outside there are a few of them in a clump, and I can just see the tops of two or three of them quivering as a slight wind passes through them. What a lovely sound it is, arising as it were out of nothing and passing off into nothingness, and thus rising again with its slow rhythmic motion, emblem of nature's basic harmony. Sometimes it reminded me of the advancing and retreating tides on a distant beach.

After a little gap I got a sheaf of letters, among them three [1] from you. Two of the letters were actually given to me as we were leaving Bareilly and I read them in the car. Rajiv's snaps also came. The old boy looks bright and healthy and energetic. I think you are right in saying that it is not desirable for infants to sit up or walk too soon. This premature growth looks attractive and pleases the fond parents but I have an idea that one has to pay for it in some way or other in later life. I think a slower and more solid growth, both physical and mental, yields better results. I do not want particularly to hold myself up as an example but I have an idea that my own growth was by no means too fast. In some ways it was perhaps even retarded. Anyway I am still growing!

I wrote to you in my last letter [2] that I had developed a cold. It was not much of a cold but taken with the heat – what a combination! – I felt poorly. There was some loss in weight also in Bareilly. The Superintendent there was anxious to feed me up and produced all manner of things which, during the course of a fairly long life, I had so far managed to avoid – Ovaltine and Horlicks, etc. Well, I swallowed them – Horlicks for the first time in my life! There was nothing much the matter with me. What intrigued me was that I could not quite find out what was the matter with me. I was examined and found to be sound in the obvious places. Probably it was just an odd combination of various circumstances – my getting a cold whilst it was so hot and some other minor factors, not important in themselves but helping each other to produce a derangement of the bodily functions. What a delicate thing is the body!

1. Refers to letters Nos 267, 268 and 269.
2. Refers to letter No. 270.

It is a matter for continuous surprise to me how this intricate structure functions so satisfactorily in spite of persistent misuse and unfavourable environments. Has it ever struck you as odd how the body maintains a more or less even temperature even when it is far hotter or colder all round it? If there was not some delicate apparatus to maintain this even temperature imagine the result – with the atmosphere temperature at 112°F or more we would all develop terribly high fever and pass out, or when the temperature is below zero, we would freeze to death.

I am sorry you have lost weight. What is your present weight and what has been your maximum? The gradual reduction in my weight at Ahmadnagar and Bareilly has brought my weight back to what it was when I was in my middle twenties – a slim lad who had once coxed a boat. This going back to the past has its advantages in many ways and I am not sure that I would not like to go back. But there is one very serious drawback: there would be no Indu then – she would just be a hope and an aspiration.

It is unusually warm here in Almora but still there is a world of difference between Bareilly and Almora. Measured in Fahrenheit degrees I suppose the difference is about 25°. It is pleasanter here and my old body is approving of the change. It is important of course that the body should approve independently of the mind. The body, though intimately connected with the mind (and indeed the mind is part of the body), has a way of going its own way despite the advice and the reasoning of the mind. The mind is of course much more highly developed and perhaps because of that its natural functions have been covered up or directed by thoughts and urges. But the body is comparatively more primitive and still reacts more naturally. As somebody said, a mind can and often does lie, a body can hardly do so.

So I expect to be quite fit again within a few days. The mere feel of the mountains has a tonic effect on me. And though you are still far from me, it is pleasant to think that we are both in the Himalayas and, as the crow flies, not so far after all.

I have received Puphi's little book: *Prison Days*. It is rather thin. In fact it is hardly a book. What there is of it is well written and is easy reading. This business of keeping a diary in jail is a tricky affair. What must one or can one write? The trivial happenings which fill the days? Yes, sometimes, for even the apparently trivial has sometimes a deep significance for us. What do we write for? For ourselves or others? It is very difficult for the average human being to be absolutely frank about himself or others. So even in our personal diaries we tend to be circumspect, thinking of the future when other eyes may read them. And this leads to triviality and artificiality.

Isherwood's [1] translation of the *Gita* (which Bharati sent) has also reached me. This was welcome as I had been reading reviews of the book in American papers and stories of Isherwood becoming a Hindu mystic. From what I have seen of it, I like the translation.

If Edward Thompson has recovered this is certainly something on the verge of the miraculous. I do not think anyone, and certainly not Edward himself, expected recovery . . .

Tell Yunus that I have received his letter. He wants me to send him word, through you, if I want anything from Peshawar – what am I likely to want here, except good news of him and his bride?

Perhaps you have moved to Bijju Chacha's house already. Anyway this letter is going to the old address.

We have been here in Almora just two days. We came all the way from Bareilly by car – we started at six a.m. – (and that meant my getting up at four which is really three) and reached here at about two p.m. It was not a very strenuous journey but I felt tired at the end of it, partly because of the heat and partly because I had not been feeling well. Here, for the present, I am resting mostly.

The Anand Bhawan *dasehri* mangoes have been slowly ripening and are quite good. We have brought them along with us here. Here we found fairly good apricots and the tiny variety of pear which is rather delicious. What do you call this kind of baby pear?

This is my letter No. 120 to you. The three letters which I have received from you are dated 2/6, 3/6 and 5/6 – Nos. 110 to 112.

Love,

Your loving,
Papu

---

*[ Jawaharlal Nehru and other prominent Congress leaders were released from prison in June 1945. This release was due to the fact that the British Government had, at this juncture, decided to initiate a constitutional dialogue with the leaders of India.]*

1. Christopher Isherwood: novelist and playwright.

# PART III

# Towards Freedom
## (1945–1946)

273.                                                    Running Train,
                                                       30th June, 1945

Indu darling,
I was sorry to leave you in bed and my thoughts are with you. Take care
of yourself and you will be well in three or four days. Don't be in too
much of a hurry to move about. This will only delay recovery.

I hope to go with you to Kashmir but I do not know how things will
shape. Anyway I shall join you there. I shall keep you informed of my
programme. Perhaps I might have to stay in Simla for two weeks. If so
you need not wait for me, provided you are well enough to travel. There
is also this possibility of your joining me in Simla to recuperate for a
few days before you undertake a longer journey.

The last eleven days with you have been lovely though I am afraid I
have spent most of my time away from you. I wish I had not to go away
so soon. But I hope to be with you soon.

Love,
                          Papu

---

274.                                                       Armsdell,
                                                            Simla,
                                                       1st July, 1945

Darling Indu,
Feroze's telegram about you reached me this afternoon. I am glad you
are improving but I am afraid your recovery will take a few days. This
must put you out but such untoward happenings have to be accepted
and put up with. I am anxious that you should not start on a long journey
before the doctor agrees to it.

I am afraid I shall have to stay here for a fortnight or so. I see no
escape from it. Maulana wanted me to stay with him so here I am. That
was as well, as Amrit Kaur is almost crowded out of her little house.
This house (Armsdell) is Government property and used to be occupied
by a member of the Viceroy's staff. It is well appointed and I suppose
we are in a sense the Viceroy's guests. Red-liveried *chaprasis*[1] are in
evidence, and both the soap and the notepaper are embossed 'Viceregal
Lodge'! I find it quite impossible to use this Viceregal notepaper, though
I have succumbed to the soap. Rather odd this atmosphere for me. I do
not feel too happy about it. The Viceregal chef, or at any rate the person
who functions here, is not too good.

1. Orderlies.

Maulana, Pantji & I are here with our respective secretaries, but some other people also feed here. I have a double room with two bathrooms and a dressing room. So if you happened to come here for a couple of days, you could be easily accommodated.

The journey from Allahabad to Simla was a sore trial. I had hardly any rest during the day or the night and the vast crowds at some of the stations exhausted me. My voice is very hoarse. I can't make out why I attract these crowds. Very gratifying, no doubt, but also very trying and often irritating. Here in Simla I have had to go out to the balcony and verandah frequently to give *darshan*. I doubt if I shall ever be able to go out for a walk because of crowds following, except at dead of night . . .

I am dead tired and so I am going to sleep now. The bed is soft and comfortable.

Love,

Papu

---

275.                                             [Anand Bhawan],
                                                      Allahabad,
                                                   2nd July, 1945

Darling Papu,

Just a line to send my love. I hope you are looking after yourself and resting whenever you can. Don't worry about me, I am quite all right now. All day yesterday my temp. was 99. And this morning it is 98. I am feeling a bit weak and rather groggy about the knees but that is all.

I have just sent you a telegram.[1] I have provisionally fixed my programme as follows. I leave Allahabad on the fourth night with Puphi. Spend the day in Delhi. Leave on the 6th for Pindi. This is of course unless I hear from you. I don't feel that you will be able to get away as easily or quickly as you thought you might. And I am increasingly worried about Rajiv. Now Anna writes that the *ayah* is not well and has a bad cold, etc. Srinagar is terribly hot too and that is upsetting the little one. Naturally I shall change or modify my programme if I hear that you are able to come away on a definite date and that soon.

Anyhow Puphi and Rajabhai will be with you in Simla and will probably accompany you to Kashmir. I can't say that I am terribly thrilled at this idea. I had so looked forward to having you all to myself for a few days. It's been so long since I've ever seen you properly! But now that must wait for Kashmir would have been the only opportunity – a tiny island in a sea of activity. Afterwards there is so much to do. I do not

---

1. Telegram not published.

even know how much you will be in Allahabad, or where your head-quarters will be. Really, it's a shame. No, that's unfair of me, isn't it? And selfish too. Why shouldn't other people come too? But honestly if I felt that it meant as much to other people as it does to me then I wouldn't mind sharing you even those few days in Kashmir.

Well, anyhow – don't get too tired and eat properly.

Lots and lots of love,

Indu

---

276.                                   [Armsdell],
Simla,<br>5th July, 1945

Darling Indu,

You must be in Delhi today if your old programme holds. I am glad you decided to rest there for a day or two, *en route* to Kashmir.

Your letter of the 2nd[1] reached me yesterday. No, I don't worry about you. I think you can look after yourself and also that your health is generally sound enough. Of course some care has to be taken.

I suppose you will move away from Srinagar immediately to a cooler place. Somebody the other day offered his Gulmarg hut to me and I was thinking of informing you of it. But I have completely forgotten now who he was.

I have received a telegram from Yunus from Gulmarg saying that he wants to see me and proposing to come here if my stay here is prolonged. I have wired to him in reply that my stay here is of uncertain duration and it would be better for us to meet later in Kashmir. It is not worthwhile for him to come all the way here. I am kept pretty busy here from morning till late at night – committee meetings, delegations from innumerable groups, meeting people from all over India after three years or more, etc. As I wrote to you, it is likely that I shall have to stay here till the 16th or so. As soon as I am free here, I shall go straight to Kashmir – so I intend. At first I shall go inevitably to Srinagar and then to whatever place you and Rajiv may be in.

Bijju Bhabhi has written to me inviting me to stay with her and suggesting that I shall have a quiet time there ... Anyway I do not intend to remain in Srinagar more than a day or two to begin with. I should like to get away to a quieter place as soon as possible. Later, on the eve of my return, I might spend another two or three days in Srinagar. I should like to have no public or semi-public engagements to begin

---

1. Refers to letter No. 275.

with. These should be reserved for the end of my visit and should only be fixed up after consultation with me. Please tell Sheikh Saheb of this and also that I am looking forward to meeting him. After I meet him and have a talk, we shall fix up things.

The Gurez Valley trip attracts me greatly. If you can fix it up it would be a good thing. But I am not going anywhere without you. I have no idea how long I shall be staying in Kashmir. Or put it at a fortnight. If I can pull it out to three weeks I shall be happy, but the difficulties in my way are obvious.

I do not know Betty's & Raja's programme and how long they will stay in Kashmir. It would be good if they come. I shall see to it in any event that I have as much of you as possible . . .

In spite of the rush and hustle here I am feeling a little better. The improvement would be more marked if I did not keep very late nights. That is really my fault. Finding no time to meet old friends in the day time, I ask them at night and then talk on.

I hope Hari is going with you with my extra clothes.

Love,

Papu

---

277.                                        3 Clive Road,
New Delhi,
5th July, 1945

Darling Papu,
Your letter.[1] Thank you so much. I wonder if you will get to Kashmir this year. It seems well nigh impossible. If the new Executive is formed, then the working of it will leave little time for mountaineering. There will be the meeting of the A.I.C.C. and a thousand other things.

I am leaving Delhi by the Frontier Mail tomorrow night. I shall reach Srinagar on the 8th. I plan to go to Pahalgam on the 10th or 11th. I shall stay there until the end of this month or middle of August, according to what you advise and what fits in with your programme. And then I shall come straight back to Allahabad. Srinagar and the Punjab will be boiling hot so there will be no point in stopping anywhere *en route*.

I am taking Hari with me – shall I send him to you to Simla? He can get a direct connection from Rawalpindi.

---

1. Possibly refers to letter No. 274.

Lots of love to you and the best of luck in all things,
Indu

I have brought a *Rajtarangini* from Alld. Puphi will bring it to Simla.

---

278.                                                        Armsdell,
                                                              Simla,
                                                        7th July, 1945

Darling Indu,
I suppose you are somewhere on the way to Kashmir – probably round
about Pindi. I hope you have not been silly enough to send Hari here.
Not only do I not require him here but he is likely to be rather a burden.
Keep him with you till I come. And come I will, in spite of the obstacles
and impediments in the way. My repeated statements about going to
Kashmir, often reported in the press, have convinced not only me but
others also that I shall ultimately go there. Every one asks me when I
am going. Even Lady Wavell[1] put me this question when I went to have
tea with her. But what is alarming is that people intend to follow me to
Kashmir – all manner of odd people whom I hardly know. I am just
coming back from dinner with Dr Khan Sahib at the Cecil. There I met
a young ruler of a small State who informed me that he had prepared
a fifteen-year plan to socialise his State and eliminate himself, more or
less! He wanted to consult me about it and as I was busy here he would
come to Kashmir where he imagined that I would have plenty of time
to devote to the affairs of his State.

I have received your letter[2] from New Delhi. Unless the unforeseen
occurs I should be free to leave Simla within ten days – say the 17th.
Add a day or two more if you like to provide for contingencies. I intend
going straight to Kashmir from here, without stopping anywhere *en route*.
I might reach Srinagar on the 22nd or 23rd according to this. I cannot
be sure of the date but I just do not see how it can go beyond the 25th
at the latest. This has nothing to do with the outcome of the conference
here. In either or any event I shall try to get away for two or three weeks.
More time I cannot find, for I shall have to come back for the A.I.C.C.
If I stay on for the A.I.C.C. then I shall get caught in a round of activities
and all ideas of going to Kashmir will have to be given up. So I shall
have to go direct from Simla. No date has so far been fixed for the
A.I.C.C.

1. Lady Wavell: wife of Lord Wavell the Viceroy of India 1943–7.
2. Refers to letter No. 277.

In Kashmir I am in your hands. I want to be with you all the time or nearly all the time. If it suits you, you can arrange an excursion into the Gurez Valley. I have heard so much about it that the desire to go there is strong. I understand it is a week's trip. I have a growing fear that wherever we may go, many people will want to accompany us. How to deal with them is a problem. Sheikh Saheb, I suppose, will insist on making the arrangements and it is difficult to refuse him. He will do everything on a sumptuous scale and we shall move about in state with crowds of companions and camp-followers. In so far as this can be reduced, an attempt might be made to do so. But I fear it cannot be wholly avoided and we shall have to reconcile ourselves to it . . .

I am feeling sleepy now. It is one twenty a.m. on the 8th and I have still to read the day's papers. I cannot find time for this in the course of the day.

Love,

Papu

---

279.

c/o Post Master,
Pahalgam,
12th July, 1945

Darling Papu,

After much confusion and difficulty and the braving of Bijju Chacha's 'strong disapproval', we have at last reached Pahalgam. The place is swarming with Punjabis but I hope they will not interfere with us in any way. I had hired a site next to Yunus's but on arrival we found that someone else had pitched his tent there. However, they are moving in a couple of days. In the meantime we have had to instil ourselves on Yunus's site. A friend in Srinagar has lent me his tent, which has turned out to be a very grand affair with doors and windows.

Rajiv has gone very thin and his whole face has changed. That sturdiness he had is gone. I am worried and don't know how to set about to build him up again. It would almost have been better if I had taken him down in the heat instead of leaving him in Srinagar on Anna's responsibility. She is most unreliable and more concerned with her own personal comfort than anything else. However I hope this lovely pine-laden air will soon do us all good.

Sheikh Saheb is so busy these days that it is impossible to get at him but I saw him for a few moments and told him what you would like to do if you could come to Kashmir. He insists on the river procession because, he says, it will be the least tiring for you. He is also arranging the trek. The Tragbal-Sonamarg trek will take over ten days. There are so many alternatives something is sure to be fixed up.

Lots of love,

Indu

---

280.                                    Lahore,
Night of 25th/26th August, 1945
12.45 a.m.

Darling Indu,

I have just returned from an odd and exciting experience and I am a little tired. Yet because of the excitement I have gone through I am wide awake and am therefore writing to you.

The Frontier visit was pleasant in spite of certain rather depressing factors. It was good to meet old friends. As one grows older oneself one appreciates all the more the friends of one's youth. The depressing factor was really nothing new. It was the realisation once again how immature human beings are and how they fall out on the most trivial of matters. Temperament is usually more powerful than logic. Yet my visit I think did good all round, whether temporary or fairly permanent I do not know.

From Nathiagalli we went to Abbottabad, Havelian and Haripur. And then to Taxila. Badshah Khan & Dr Khan and several others accompanied us. Near Taxila, at Wah, there is an old Moghul garden with a spring and a small pool of wonderfully clear water. I had intended having a dip there but as no one else was prepared for this, I had to refrain also. We fed there, our host being Sikandar Hyat's[1] brother who owns the place. Chaman Lall, Helen[2] and some others joined us there. There we visited Taxila and I spent over two hours there and yet did not see some of the excavations.

And so to Pindi, where a vast meeting of about 100,000 was waiting for us. The night journey to Lahore was a troubled one but not so bad as it might have been. On arrival at Lahore the first news I heard was of Iftikhar's resignation[3] and the statement he had issued. This was not unexpected and yet the time and the manner of doing it hurt me and rather upset me. As happens with me, my face developed a tired look and a sense of weariness stole over me. However the day's programme kept me busy. I paid a short visit to Chand's flat and found that Nani

1. Sikandar Hyat Khan: a leader of the Unionist Party and Chief Minister of Punjab, 1937–42.
2. Wife of Diwan Chaman Lall.
3. Mian Iftikharuddin: left Congress in 1945 and joined the Muslim League.

had been, and was still, rather ill. She is suffering from anaemia, which in her case is a bad sign. I am going there again tomorrow.

Tonight there was a public meeting – and what a meeting! Among my vast experience of large crowds, I do not think I have ever seen anything like it. I imagine there were 200,000 people there, and there might well have been 250,000. The loudspeakers of course broke down and even the platform partly collapsed. Fear invaded the people round about the platform [and] on it and this is an infectious affair. I stood on a table on the collapsing platform and surveyed the seething mass of humanity. Many people urged me to go but I refused to budge and said that I would not leave the crowd and would make a speech even if I had to stay all night. Men & women & children fainted and I was told that two children had died (this is probably not true). But I was in a savage mood and said I did not care what happened; I would stick on. Piteous appeals were made to me to go but I was harsh in my replies and was especially hard on poor Ifty. Something of my morning's irritation, I think, induced me to behave in this manner. Yet I was perfectly cool and laughing at the fear and discomfiture of others. How hard and cruel I was! I was myself surprised at this savage aspect which revealed itself unawares. Ultimately I jumped into the crowd and was pushed and tossed about by it. I carried a large part of the crowd away and delivered several short speeches at various places in the midst of the crowd. I saw that the women – there were many of them – went away. Then I returned to the platform – again went down and returned. These excursions led to a thinning of the crowd and at last only about 50,000 remained. Then I addressed these people from the platform (without a loudspeaker) I spoke for a good while and have grown rather hoarse.

Having a sense of the crowd and being popular with it, I had no great difficulty in dealing with it, though it was a terribly tiring business. Anyway, my staying on and speaking at the end at some length (and briefly at various places) pleased the crowd and lessened its irritation. How easily such a crowd can become a savage & aggressive mob! But, being expert at the job, I managed to add to my popularity with it.

And so we finished after midnight and we returned with thousands of frenzied people escorting us.

The experience and excitement of all this worked away my irritation and I feel better.

And now I must go to bed.

Your loving,<br>Papu

A lady in Nathiagalli gave me a rather pretty gold bangle on *Raksha Bandhan* day.

281.                                                        Hut46½,
                                                          Gulmarg,
                                                 29th August, 1945

Darling Papu,
Your letter from Lahore [1] has just come.

Yes, we were all rather surprised at Ifti's resignation coming just then – although his position has been becoming more and more untenable. We heard some talk the other day of a Muslim remarking at the Gulmarg club that he had had a 'very nice letter' from Jinnah [2] in which there was reference to Ifti's joining the League. Of course I do not know if this story is true. Such things are bound to be said, especially after Qayyum's [3] resignation.

I met Ismet for a brief while but no reference was made to politics. The boys were very pleased with the sticks and, I believe, are writing to thank you.

We are keeping fairly busy. We had lunch today at Dr Jawaharlal's. [4] His cottage is next door to ours. It is a nice family, I like them. Doctor Saheb's daughter-in-law had a nasty fall from her horse a couple of days ago. She was galloping downhill! . . .

The day after my arrival in Gulmarg, we went to lunch with Pestonjee [5] & his son. They have a hut called 'The Pinnacle', which is the highest in Gulmarg. It has nice grounds and is the only place here where one can have any privacy. It is on the hill which is on the left-hand side of the 'Gap'. Niloufer [6] always stays there.

Yesterday morning, Kitty, [7] Anna & I set forth at seven thirty a.m. for Allopathar. I had a very bad horse and a worse saddle but by now I am so used to all kinds of horses and saddles that I didn't mind much. We had a glorious day. The view of Gulmarg and the main valley was magnificent, otherwise Allopathar lake itself is not up to much and the last lap of the way is not even beautiful. Anna bathed in the lake. We had lunch there and started on our way back at twelve thirty; that was

1. Refers to letter No. 280.
2. Mohamed Ali Jinnah: President of the Muslim League, 1916, 1920 and from 1934 till his death. Founder of Pakistan.
3. Abdul Qayyum Khan: Congress member of Central Legislative Assembly, 1937–42; joined Muslim League in 1945 and was Chief Minister of the North-West Frontier Province, 1947–53; was later in Z. A. Bhutto's ministry, 1971–7.
4. Dr Jawaharlal Rohatgi: a doctor and Congressman of Kanpur; suffered imprisonment during the freedom struggle; was a minister in the U.P. Government after 1947.
5. Kuverji Peston: a Congressman of Lucknow.
6. Princess Niloufer: a Turkish lady of aristocratic descent and wife of Prince Moazzam Jah, second son of the Nizam of Hyderabad.
7. Kitty Shiva Rao.

just when other people started arriving. We were thankful to be leaving. On the way down we met over fifty people coming up, among them Sapru's granddaughter, Savitri, and her husband. We stopped at Khillenmarg to have strawberries and cream and arrived back home at three forty p.m. Once the saddle of my horse (it was not attached to the tail of the horse) suddenly jumped and landed on the horse's neck not far from his head. For a second I did not guess what had happened and I wondered what had happened to the horse's neck! Instinctively I had pulled the reins so tight that I did not fall.

Poor Kitty was rather afraid of her horse and clung to the saddle and shouted out whenever the horse showed signs of moving less slowly. We had a good day but I thought of you incessantly and missed you dreadfully. We found lots of edelweiss. Rather a poor lot, though.

Sheikh Saheb is still in bed. The eye is better and the sight of it is safe – another quarter of an inch and that would have been gone. But it is very painful. Sheikh Saheb has to stay in a completely dark room for about a week. I usually telephone to Beg's house every other day.

Your letter[1] was very interesting. The description of the Lahore meeting was so well written and vivid that I could see the whole scene almost as if I had been there myself. I can well imagine how tiring it must have been for you. As for Ifti and the others – it doesn't take much to frighten them and most of them are more used to drawing rooms than the electric atmosphere of a public meeting.

This was your first visit to Taxila. You must tell me some time what you thought of it.

I am sending you a wire to Delhi about my programme. I propose leaving Gulmarg on the 10th and Srinagar on the 15th Sept. Is that all right? Or do you suggest anything else? I suppose you will be in Bombay then.

Rajiv has received a birthday cable from Lekha, Tara, Rita.

Have you any further news of Puphi?

Lots of love,

                                        Indu

P.S.
I hear Feroze's foot is giving trouble again.

---

1. Refers to letter No. 280.

282.

Hut46½,
Gulmarg,
30th August, 1945

Darling One,

Today is one of those glorious days that one has sometimes in the early autumn in England and other European countries: deep azure sky and not a cloud in sight, and just cool enough for one not to mind the sun. How vividly I remember that just such a day was September 3rd, 1939, the day when England declared war on Germany. I was in Penn, Buckinghamshire, that day.

Anna and I went out for an hour's riding this morning. It was my first real ride and I had for my mount a Pindi racehorse called 'Succa'. This was probably my own fault for I kept telling the *chowkidar*[1] that I must have a fast and big horse. Anyway, when we were setting forth, the syce and *chowkidar* frightened me by repeated reminders of how fast 'Succa' ran and how it was impossible to stop him, and so on. Moreover 'Succa' had two pairs of reins and I was rather confused as to how to deal with them. I had to keep the reins loose all the time, the slightest tightening and 'Succa' would gallop and the only way I could stop him was by turning him round. We went along the outer Circular Road, trotting gently most of the time. But the last bit homewards I galloped. It was great fun but next time I should like a slightly slower horse!

The view of the mountain ranges is magnificent. We can see the whole of the Nanga Parbat in all its grandeur. Also Haramukh and the Kolahoi peak. These are the only peaks I recognise.

I don't know if and when my wire will reach you. The line was faulty and subject to delay.

Yesterday's phone call to Beg's house revealed that Sheikh Saheb will have to remain in the darkened room for another three or four days. The doctor has pronounced him out of danger but he still is not allowed to move even in bed. He gets severe pain in the eye by fits and starts.

Yunus is standing here and wants me to send you the following message. He is anxiously awaiting a reply from you to his letter, the one you received in Srinagar. Also about the things he talked over with you. Yunus says that he is not at all disturbed by Qayyum's resignation. He says it has a great propaganda value for the League but it will not affect the movement in the Frontier. Qayyum was not at all in touch with the people of the Frontier and no one liked him. Yunus is writing to Qayyum to tell him that he never wishes to see his face in the future. Yunus has

---

1. Watchman.

also written to Qazi Ataullah [1] and others to look into the electoral rolls for the Central Legislature and see that they are properly amended and to find a more suitable candidate because Qayyum may have his eyes on the seat. He has got a few votes, though Yunus does not think that he has any chance in this or in the Provincial Assembly. It seems that Jinnah had offered Qayyum the leadership of the League Party in the Central Assembly several times, and Yunus thinks that they may give him something even now. All this has practically been dictated to me by Yunus.

I gave Yunus your message about Mahesh Babu. But we have not heard from him at all, and we do not know his address. He had told me that he would write to me first.

Lots of love to you from us both,

Indu

---

*[Jawaharlal Nehru was now fully caught up in political events. He toured several provinces during this period to campaign for elections to the Central and Provincial Assemblies, which were to be held between November 1945 and March 1946.]*

283.
[Anand Bhawan],
Allahabad,
17th November, 1945

Darling Papu,

You come and you go, almost like a flash of lightning. It is wonderful to have a glimpse of you, but even before one has got used to the fact of your being there, it is time for you to leave. I can't tell you how empty everything feels when you are not there, [and] if it weren't for Rajiv, I could hardly bear it.

I am annoyed with Chhoti Puphi. As soon as I knew that I was not going to Bombay, I wrote to her to get me a birthday present for you – any small token of a deep love. Allahabad doesn't boast of a single good shop – books or otherwise – I had already searched. Well, she didn't write or let me know whether she was getting anything. It was only when you arrived on the 16th that Hari brought a note saying that she was sorry she couldn't get anything. So your birthday present will have to wait. I am so sorry.

In the meantime something terrible has happened – at least I am hoping and praying most frantically that it doesn't turn out to be what

1. Qazi Ataullah: a minister in the North-West Frontier Province Government, 1947.

we think – I have got mumps! I don't mind for myself but poor little Rajiv has been with me all evening & it is terribly infectious. I am writing this with a mask on. I am going to the downstairs room & will be locked in with Ram Kumari – no other servant to come near. If it does turn out to be mumps, it will mean a two to three weeks' isolation, plus much pain. Of all the things to happen! I am so disgusted & terribly worried about Rajiv. I am so annoyed that I let him be with me but I didn't dream of mumps. There is still a slight chance that it may be something else – *inshahallah*! [1]

Much love,

Indu

---

284.  [Anand Bhawan],
[Allahabad],
New Year's Day, 1946

Darling Papu,
Just to say once again – a Happy New Year to you. That sounds rather trite and it is far from likely that 1946 will bring a sudden change of heart or policy either here in India, or in Asia or even in war-ravaged Europe. The picture of the world is dismal beyond hope – and yet, being human, hope we must. And since we must fight, let the fight be a clean and good fight. And because we are in the right we must come out on top . . .

With love from us all,

Indu

---

285.  [Anand Bhawan],
Allahabad,
25th February, 1946

Darling Papu,
Here are three letters. I have also had one from Eva [Geissler]. It has come very quickly – it is dated Feb. 18, '46. She is naturally very worried about Nanu. She writes that the only news she has came through a personal messenger, who informed her that N. was taken to Braunschweig in the British Zone in July or August of last year. [2]

1. God willing.
2. A. C. N. Nambiar (Nanu) was an emigré freedom fighter located in Berlin during the course of the Second World War. As an Indian national he was taken by the British authorities to the British zone in post-war Germany.

The Brailsfords [1] are staying on until the 27th morning. I like them both – we talked until quite late last night, mainly about Europe. This morning I discovered that we have much in common – our taste in music and art, for instance. Mrs Brailsford hails from Westphalia.

Lots of love, darling,

Indu

P.S.
Puphi had definitely cancelled the Sultanpur programme and could not be persuaded to take it on again. She is, however, taking up the rest of your tour – Orai, Chargaon, Jhansi, etc. Pant [2] and Venu Chitale [3] are going with her, Chitale is moving to Puphi's house to stay and may go to Lucknow when Puphi becomes a minister! [4] This tour ends on the 1st. But Puphi will be in Allahabad once or twice in between. Am going to Mirzapur on the 27th for a day.

*Au-revoir, cheri,*

Indu

Excuse pink envelope.

286.                             Statistical Laboratory,
87 Barrackpore Trunk Road,
P.O. Alambazar,
Bengal,
10th March, 1946

Darling,
I have lost my Parker 51 to which I was getting rather attached. This disappeared from my pocket in the crowd after a large meeting at Howrah. Before I go to Malaya I should like to have another pen. Will you please send with Hari to Delhi the new Parker 51 sent by Kesh Naoroji for me. You will find this in the top left-hand drawer of my writing desk in a case.

The last two days in Calcutta, etc, have rather taken it out of me. I have just returned by air from Dacca & Chittagong. It is seven p.m. and

1. H. N. Brailsford, British political activist and author sympathetic to the Indian cause, and his wife Evamaria Brailsford.
2. Pitamber Pant: leading statistician and economist, who was close to the Nehru family.
3. Venu Chitale: political activist of Allahabad.
4. Mrs Vijaya Lakshmi Pandit was likely to be appointed minister in the government of the United Provinces.

I am so tired and sleepy that I am going to bed for an hour or so.

I leave by train tomorrow for Bombay. Delhi I reach on the 16th afternoon.

Love,

Papu

---

287.

Statistical Laboratory,
87 Barrackpore Trunk Road,
P.O. Alambazar,
Bengal,
11th March, 1946,
12.45 a.m.

Darling Indu,

I wrote to you a short note [1] on return from an air journey today and then went to bed. I slept for two hours, had a bath & then dinner at a rather late hour. After dinner I had a longish talk with my host & hostess who told me many stories of Gurudev.

It has just struck me that I am not likely to see you till after my return from Malaya. That is not very long after all, but any trip abroad somehow involves a break. I do not like long absences now, perhaps because I am growing older.

Two days in Calcutta & Bengal have been very tiring. I have one consolation: that this is the last of the election business. I have had more than enough of this. My host has been greatly shocked at the way people exploit me for election or other purposes. It has quite upset him. I have suggested to him to form an S.P.C.J.N. – Society for the Prevention of Cruelty to Jawaharlal Nehru. Will you be one of the office-bearers?

Malaya is likely to be strenuous but not so bad as this electioneering business. And then Delhi with all its burdens.

You might talk to Puphi about the possibility of your going to Khali for a month or so.

Hari should reach Delhi on the 16th morning.

Love,

Papu

---

1. Refers to letter No. 286.

288.                        In moving train,
12th March, 1946

Indu darling,

As I was leaving Calcutta Nilima presented me with two copies of my new book,[1] fresh from the binders. They had been hurriedly done up for me and had not been pressed, etc. So at last the book is out, or will be out within ten days or so. I do not fancy the design on the back of the binding.

Will you please ask Padmaja where she will be during the next week or two and where her mother will be. I want to have the address to which the book should be sent. At first I had given Nilima the Hyderabad addresses. Please inform Nilima direct.

This is a long journey – two nights and a day and a half.

I have given one of the two original copies of *Discovery* to Horace Alexander who is travelling with me. I shall try to preserve the other – which I call the first copy – for you. But there are many dangerous corners to tackle and these are full of highwaymen.

    Love,

Papu

Bidhan Roy has given me his pen and I am using it now.

---

289.                          [Anand Bhawan],
Allahabad,<br>15th March, 1946

Darling Papu,

Your letter of the 12th[2] has just come.

I am so thrilled about the book and can hardly wait to see it. How disappointing that everything about it is not up to scratch – darling, you are much too lenient about these things. You always let people do as they like. The inside of a book is the only thing that matters but it does make a difference to have an attractive get-up. Good Papu and so on. Did Nilima not show you the cover design and ask your advice about it? She should have.

I have appealed to old 'Hanuman' to guard the first copy from all highwaymen and other perils of the journey.

---

1. Jawaharlal Nehru: *The Discovery of India*, Signet Press, Calcutta, 1946. This book was written by Jawaharlal in Ahmadnagar Fort Prison during the five months, April to September, 1944.

2. Refers to letter No. 288.

Poor little Rajiv has still got 100° temperature and is looking pale and peeked. He woke up at four a.m. and said '*Inquilab*'[1]! . . .

Bebee says that it is best for the books to go to Hyderabad as she is not sure of her own or her mother's programme.

Madame Morin writes that the money has arrived. Is this what I had sent, or have you sent something through the Reserve Bank? I have not yet heard from my bank.

Look after yourself, darling.

Very much love,

Indu

---

290.
Butterworth,
Near Penang,
18th March, 1946

Darling Indu,

We have nearly arrived at the end of our journey[2] but there has been a slight hitch here and so I have sat down to write to you. We left Delhi at eleven thirty a.m. yesterday – direct non-stop flight to Dum Dum where we arrived at four p.m. We had to wait three hours there & change planes, so we went on to Bidhan Roy's, met him & had a heavy tea with him. Back again and on to a Dakota with just narrow benches. Another four-hour run to Hunbay (or some such name), an airfield thirty-five miles from Rangoon. Another stop of nearly two hours & change over to another plane. Reach Butterworth at six a.m. All this is Indian standard time. Local time here is two hours ahead & it was really eight when we reached here. We ought to have gone on from here an hour ago but after we got back to the aircraft some technical hitch was discovered – magneto trouble – and we were bundled out. We are waiting now for this to be repaired. It may only take half an hour or much more. Meanwhile plenty of people are also waiting in Singapore.

The journey has been a fast one & we flew at the rate of 200 miles per hour. It was uncomfortable, especially during the night when we sat huddled up and dozed. Arrangements for washing, etc, here are primitive and it was with some difficulty that I could shave. There was some hint of an explosion here some weeks ago which did much damage & this has upset arrangements.

In Delhi day before yesterday I felt very much below par – perhaps

1. Revolution.
2. Jawaharlal Nehru travelled to Burma, Malaya and Indonesia to meet the nationalist leaders of these countries. He also called on Lord Mountbatten, at this time the Supreme Allied Commander stationed at Singapore.

because I had not slept much the night before or whatever the reason was. But yesterday, after a good night's rest, I felt better. Now I am feeling fine in spite of the troubled & disturbed night we have had. It is warm here.

You asked me if I had met Lakshmi – yes of course I did. She is a delightful babe. She really has not grown up at all, which is an attractive trait in so far as it goes – I liked her – or a babe may get into trouble.

Singapore,
19th March, 1946

We arrived here three or four hours late yesterday & kept everybody waiting. Big crowds – a curious mixture of official & crowd welcome. This is going to be a heavy week, perhaps exciting occasionally. Singapore looks well in spite of everything.

Love,

Papu

---

291.                                    18 Hardinge Avenue,[1]
New Delhi,
2nd April, 1946

Indu darling,
I have just arrived here and on arrival have remembered something. In Malaya I was given two National flags which the I.N.A.[2] have used in action. One of these had been taken to Kohima and planted there on Indian soil. These were specially given to me and I brought them carefully wrapped in a piece of paper in my suitcase. I wanted to bring them here to Delhi but forgot about them.

On enquiry from Hari I understand that he gave all these flags and banners to you. Will you please try to find these two flags out and keep them separately. If and when you come here you should bring them with you.

Love,

Papu

---

1. Jawaharlal Nehru's cousin, R. K. Nehru, lived here.
2. The Indian National Army: a volunteer army of Indians located in South-East Asia, led by Subhas Chandra Bose, the distinguished nationalist leader who sought to liberate India through armed intervention. During the closing years of the Second World War, the I.N.A. fought the British on the Indo-Burmese frontier, and, as Jawaharlal Nehru observes in this letter, liberated the township of Kohima in the North-East of India.

292.                                      Royal Hotel,
Nainital,
17th May, 1946

Darling Papu,
We arrived here a little while before lunch. The lake is lovely with yachts and small rowing boats. I had not remembered Nainital as pretty as this. The hotel is nice too. We have very comfortable rooms. Puphi has had to take a suite specially for me – I can have it until the 24th when it is booked for somebody else. But I don't think I shall stay so long.

It started raining soon after tea last evening and has been pouring the whole night and this morning. It's the kind of rain one usually gets in July. Consequently it is cold, and damp too. I wonder if it is also raining in the plains – it will rot the crops and finish off the few mangoes that remain.

Just as I was writing this I remembered the Cabinet Mission's [1] statement which was to reach Puphi after I went to bed last night, so I rushed to read it. It isn't independence and it isn't ideal but it is something workable. But I feel that the scheme will give rise to a whole new set of complications.

Rajiv is being very naughty. He hates being indoors and can't go out because of the rain . . . [incomplete]

---

293.                                      Royal Hotel,
Nainital,
25th May, 1946

Darling Papu,
It was good to hear your voice. It is a great disappointment that you cannot come up even for a few days but I do realise how important the

1. In March 1946 Prime Minister Attlee sent a special mission of three Cabinet Ministers to India to discuss constitutional issues with the nationalist leaders. The members of this mission were: Lord Pethick-Lawrence, Secretary of State for India; Sir Stafford Cripps, President of the Board of Trade; and A. V. Alexander, First Lord of the Admiralty. The proposals of the Cabinet Mission sought to create a Confederation within India, with provision for regional groupings of Muslim and Hindu majority provinces.

Faridkot and Kashmir [1] affairs are. I wish it had been possible for you to have just a few breaths of mountain air before undertaking these strenuous and irritating trips . . . [incomplete]

---

294.                                    18 Hardinge Avenue,
                                               New Delhi,
                                          13th June, 1946

Darling Indu,

I am just leaving 18 Hardinge Avenue and shifting to *20 Akbar Road* where the Maulana is staying. Rajan went to Simla three days ago & Ratan is also going soon. The house will be closed up soon.

Lady Cripps [2] is here and she has made repeated enquiries about you. She is very sorry that she could not meet you.

This business of the Cabinet Delegation drags on & on interminably. It is a most exhausting affair. Yesterday I had a talk with the Viceroy lasting one and three-quarter hours!

I have no news of you or Rajiv. Write to me sometimes.

I am still trying to find time to go to Kashmir.

Love,

                          Papu

---

295.                                    20 Akbar Road,
                                               New Delhi,
                                          16th June, 1946

Darling Indu,

. . . My programme is still entirely uncertain. The Provisional or Interim Govt is still far off, indeed it is for the present fading away. There is a lot of talk of a break in negotiations. There is no actual break, though there is an impasse. I do not myself think that there will be an actual break, for no one really wants this to happen. Probably this evening

---

1. Faridkot and Kashmir: Jawaharlal Nehru defied a ban on his entry into the Princely State of Faridkot. The then Government of Kashmir had arrested Sheikh Abdullah and was proposing to put him for trial in June 1946. On hearing of this, Jawaharlal Nehru decided to go to Kashmir in order to assist in the defence of the Sheikh. Letters Nos 296, 297, 298 and 299 deal with Jawaharlal's decision to defy an order of the Kashmir Government, banning his entry into the State. On entering Kashmir, he was arrested and subsequently released. At the same time, the Kashmir Government adjourned the trial of Sheikh Abdullah.

2. Dame Isobel Cripps: wife of Sir Stafford Cripps.

there will be another development. What this will be, good or bad, I do not yet know – so anyhow we are stuck up here.

At the same time I am anxious to go to Kashmir,[1] though it is very difficult to leave Delhi even for a day. I have decided, subject to unforeseen developments, to leave for Kashmir on the 19th morning by air to Pindi and thence by car to Srinagar. We expect to reach Srinagar on the 19th evening by seven p.m. It is quite possible that I might return by the same route on the 22nd morning. What happens in Srinagar is again an uncertain factor.

My programme, you will notice, is made from day to day. You must not depend upon it. Fix up your programme according to your own convenience. If any change has to be made in it later because of other developments, well, it will be easy enough to make it . . .

The railway strike also should not come in the way. Whether it takes place or not is still doubtful, and if it takes place no one knows how long it will last.[2] To avoid the strike altogether, you have to go down so as to reach Allahabad by the 26th. That is too early. There is another viewpoint. If the strike comes off, perhaps Khali is a better place to be in than Allahabad. I think you should not allow this possibility of the strike to interfere with your programme. Stay in Khali till you are clear that you must go down. That means, stay on and see what happens.

Delhi weather has been bad, as bad as Bombay can be, stuffy and humid. Allahabad is also likely to be equally bad. The monsoon has its advantages but sometimes it makes one really uncomfortable.

I enclose a note from Louise. Could you send her a snap of Rajiv? I hope you got the pictures Feroze took in Khali. He sent them here with Upadhyaya and later I posted them to you. They were good.

I have received a fat cheque for my royalties on the first impression of *Discovery*. I feel others should share it with me. So I suggest that you give a bonus of a month's salary to all our servants – I shall send you a cheque for this if you will let me know how much it is. Do you want any money for yourself?

Love,

Papu

I have arranged for the *Hindustan Times* to be sent to you for three months – the minimum period.

———————

1. This was in response to the arrest of Sheikh Abdullah by the Kashmir Government.
2. The rail strike did not, in fact, take place.

296.                                                        Domel,
                                                    [Jhelum Valley,
                                                          Kashmir],
                                                  19th June, 1946

Darling Indu,
After weeks of exhausting talks and debates and a gradual oozing out
of spirit and vitality, I have had a little tonic today. What has recently
happened in Delhi had been peculiarly depressing. I had hoped that
this very brief Kashmir visit would provide a diversion. My hopes have
been amply justified. This is only the first day and I do not know yet
what tomorrow will bring. So we must offer thanks to the Kashmir Govt
for the astonishing folly with which it conducts its affairs. It tried to stop
me at Kohala. It did not succeed. I spent five hours there getting more
& more bored. Then we sallied out and faced the Kashmir police and
pushed forward. I felt in my element as I always do when there is a
question of forcing a barricade. Asaf Ali & Chaman Lall & Yunus (who
had joined me at Pindi) became infected with the excitement and led
the first line! It is a long story which has not ended yet. Ultimately the
police retired and we drove on to Domel, where we reached at eleven
p.m. I am very tired. What has been happening in Srinagar today I do
not know.
    What an odd mixture is my life. There is talk of a Provisional Govt
and at the same time I function as a law-breaker!
    Love,

                                    Papu

_____

297.                                                        Domel,
                                                     Jhelum Valley,
                                                           Kashmir,
                                                   20th June, 1946
                                                           9 p.m.

Darling Indu,
I am told that the radio has announced that I am injured. Also there are
odd rumours in Pindi that there was firing at us last night. All this is
not true. I am quite well and unhurt. It is true that it was touch-&-go
last night and a bayonet might easily have hurt. But all of us escaped.
    I have spent the day resting here and sleeping. I like the place but it
is too warm in the daytime. After Delhi of course it is a vast change for
the better. And then there is the sound of running water with the Jhelum
flowing past below us.

There is some talk of our being taken to some other place. We are détenus for the present under the Defence of Kashmir Rules. I would prefer being taken higher up. It will be cooler and nearer Srinagar. For I am bent on going to Srinagar.

I have no idea how long I shall have to stay in Kashmir. I suppose this business will last some days at least. I do not mind remaining here in the least but I am afraid other people must be minding greatly.

There is just one thing that rather worries me. Krishna Menon is due to reach Delhi on June 22nd. I wanted to be there then. However, things will adjust themselves somehow.

Love,

Papu

---

298.

Dak Bungalow,<br>Uri,<br>Kashmir,<br>21st June, 1946

Darling Indu,

The third day of this adventure. First day Kohala – second Domel – third Uri. How often we have passed these places and looked upon them as mere stages for lunch or tea, a brief halt or a passing glimpse, and then further on. Now each place is being associated with a particular experience and a special memory. Not only is the environment of each place imprinted on my mind – the rumbling Jhelum below Domel; the crystal-clear water of the Kishanganga meeting the muddy reddish Jhelum; the shape of the hills and especially the trees standing on the ridges, clearly defined in the sunlight; the huts and houses on the hillsides, the main road running in between – but also the marching to and fro of the Kashmir army and police, the lorries and buses rushing by, small groups collecting in the distance trying to peep in but not daring to come nearer. Today Uri, tomorrow where? There is a rumour that we shall be shifted again tonight.

There was some doubt yesterday as to our exact position. This has been cleared up now. We have been served with orders of detention under the Defence of Kashmir Rules. We are détenus – all of us, that is apart from me, Yunus, Mathai,[1] Hari, Tajammul Husain of the I.N.A. who joined at Pindi, and a young Pindi Saheb, Dalip Singh. Asaf Ali and Chaman Lall were not so served as they went on to Srinagar

---

1. M. O. Mathai: member of Jawaharlal's personal staff, 1946–59.

for Sheikh Abdullah's case. We expect them back this evening to tell us news of what is happening.

For we have no news or newspapers. Scraps of rumour reach us occasionally, third hand reports of what the radio has announced.

I imagine I have managed to upset many an applecart. Well, what am I to do about it? If the Kashmir Govt wants to behave with crass stupidity and discourtesy, things will happen. I offered them an opportunity to adopt a correct course gracefully and without loss of dignity. They were too conceited to accept my suggestion which was merely to allow me to go to Srinagar for a day or two. I expressed my desire to meet the Maharaja. But no, they took a different course and now they will have to face the consequences.

And so the Kashmir forces are on the move and the whole political situation in India is affected. Frankly, I am not at all sorry. Let people realise the forces that are astir in India and not imagine that everything can be settled by using a few soft words. As a matter of fact the Kashmir Govt has been lacking even in the soft words.

Sitting here on the verandah of the dak bungalow my mind goes back to childhood days when we used to come to Kashmir by *tonga*. It took us nearly three days, I think, from Pindi to Srinagar. Once Dol Amma was rather ill and she could not travel by *tonga*. So a phaeton or rather a landau was engaged and the interior was converted into a bed where she lay and I often sat beside her. I was about six or seven then. We proceeded slowly to avoid jerks and took full five days for the journey.

Do you know the story of Nur Jehan [1] and the Kishanganga which meets the Jhelum at Domel? Nur Jehan reached Domel on her way to Srinagar with Jehangir, hot and tired and dusty with smarting eyes. She bathed her eyes in the water of the Kishanganga and felt relieved and refreshed. So she named the Kishanganga *nainsukh*. [2]

Domel was very warm – Uri is less but I expected it to be cooler. At night we required a thin shawl only.

As I was going to Srinagar for a day or two only I brought very few books with me; unlike my usual habit. One of them was Pattabhi's [3] new book – *Feathers & Stones* – nothing very exciting or interesting. I glanced through it during my air journey. The only other book was a little one, *Poems from India*, by members of the forces. A good collection. Then I borrowed a collection of English plays from the District Magis-

1. Nur Jehan: wife of the Mughal Emperor Jehangir. She was an accomplished lady of great beauty.
2. Joy of the eyes.
3. Dr Pattabhi Sitaramayya: Congress leader, active in the freedom struggle; Governor of Madhya Pradesh, 1952–7; author of *History of the Indian National Congress* (2 volumes).

trate. I have asked Chaman Lall to get me some books from Srinagar –
they may reach me tonight.

The District Magistrate with whom we have had to deal is the Governor of Kashmir, Maharaj Kishan Dar. You will remember his
daughter-in-law visiting Bijju Chacha's house last year. She is my cousin
Birjan Kaul's daughter.

Some Urdu papers from Lahore have come. They contain fantastic
headlines about Chaman Lall & our being injured by bayonets. As I
have told you, none of us has been injured in any way, though of course
it was easy enough to be injured when bayonets are being flourished
close to one.

Keep well and cheerful. Love to you and Rajiv,

Papu

We reached Uri at three fifteen a.m. this morning or night? We left
Domel after eleven p.m. and it was slow going in the night.

---

299.

Almora,
22nd June, 1946

My dear – How can I tell you how much my thoughts have been
with you. I listened to every news bulletin but they are so hopelessly inadequate.[1] I can well imagine how you must be feeling at
returning to Delhi like this. Now with events marching as they are, you
are bound to come into conflict with more and more States, because
they are sure to make one last effort to hold on to the old ways which
they feel are slipping away forever. Kak,[2] however, is more keen
on his own power and authority. I doubt if he cares a hang for the
Maharaja except in as far as his own power is dependent on the
Maharaja.

Tomorrow the Working Committee decision will be out finally. There
doesn't seem to be much to say for either alternative. It's disgusting how
most Congressmen are out to grab whatever crumb is offered. They're
in office and they want to stay in office. I am not saying that the Government offer is not good, or is good. It is just that most people do not
even want to think of the disadvantages.

1. Refers to Jawaharlal's visit to Kashmir. See letters No. 295, 296, 297 and 298.
2. Ramchandra Kak: Prime Minister of Kashmir, 1945–6.

The postman is waiting so I am closing now but shall write tomorrow. I enclose a letter[1] I wrote days ago – it seems petty & trivial now but I am sending it all the same.

Much love,

Indu

---

300.                                                'Khali Estate',
                                                    P.O. Binsar,
                                          District Almora, U.P.,
                                                24th June, 1946

Darling Papu,

Your letter of the 13th[2] has just this minute arrived. Eleven days seems rather a long time for a letter from Delhi. I wonder if the censorship is still continuing?

I sent a letter yesterday[3] to you to 18 Hardinge Avenue. Will you have it fetched, please? . . .

I am keeping well too. But I dare not go for long walks yet.[4]

We have had a lot of rain these last three days. Yesterday a whole crowd came up – Sampurnanandji[5] with a party of ten. They went up to Binsar Estate and returned here for tea.

I finished reading the *Discovery* days ago. It is a fascinating book. Some passages are so beautiful, one has to read them out aloud like poetry.

At the moment I am reading Van Loon's *Story of the Pacific*. He suggests that the Polynesians originally came from India. But he thinks this exodus must have taken place before the introduction of 'Brahmanism' throughout the Indian peninsula, as the Polynesians' religion shows no 'Brahmanical' influences. But the Polynesians are quite different racially from any of the groups inhabiting the other Pacific islands. Also they had a knowledge of a great many crafts which were being practised in India of that time – thousands of years before the Greeks had ever learned how to make a crude stone-wall or to forge a steel sword. Unfortunately, as they got more and more separated from the homeland (both in space and time) their hand began to lose its cunning and their technical skill gradually dwindled. They were such expert marine engineers that they explored the whole of the Pacific in their small

1. Letter not published.
2. Refers to letter No. 294.
3. Refers to letter No. 299.
4. Indira Gandhi was expecting her second child in December 1946.
5. Sampurnanand: Congress leader from Uttar Pradesh, its Chief Minister, 1955–60; Governor of Rajasthan, 1962–7.

canoe-like boats. They were the original discoverers of the Pacific.

Lots of love to you,

Indu

P.S.

I do wish I could be with you when you go to Kashmir again. It's so much less worrying to be on the spot than to be hanging on to the radio for news.

———————

301.                                                  Anand Bhawan,
                                                        Allahabad,
                                                 13th August, 1946

Darling Papu,

Your letter of the 8th[1] from Wardha & your telegram have arrived.

I was distressed to hear of the tiresome journey you had. When one is already so over-burdened, all these incidents take much out of one ... We have had a hectic two days while Rafi[2] was here yesterday & the day before. There were always about fifteen cars on the premises and Rajiv couldn't make up his mind which one to sit in!

But now all is quiet. Even Feroze went to Lucknow with Rafi. He is expected back tomorrow morning. So is Shah Nawaz.[3]

Darling, every day brings you more responsibility and more work. I wish you would also think of your responsibility towards yourself. Try to drink orange juice every day, especially when you are tired.

Much love from Rajiv &

Indu

———————

302.                                              [Anand Bhawan],
                                                        Allahabad,
                                                 15th August, 1946

Darling Papu,

Your telegram.[4] Mathai & I were discussing only yesterday morning that you would surely have to go.

1. Letter not published.
2. Rafi Ahmed Kidwai.
3. Shah Nawaz Khan: served in the Indian National Army of Subhas Chandra Bose; taken prisoner and tried in the famous Red Fort Trial, 1945; sentenced to transportation for life but sentence commuted; later entered Lok Sabha and held important ministerial posts.
4. Telegram not traceable.

I hope you got my letter in Bombay.

Radhakrishnan wrote to ask when the librarian could come to fetch the law books. So I am expecting him any day now . . .

Shah Nawaz is here. He arrived yesterday & was just as surprised as the rest of us to read in the papers that his tours had been cancelled because of Ramzan.[1] Nobody seems to know who gave the news to the press. Shah Nawaz is naturally worried, having made this long & troublesome journey for nothing. He wants to proceed with the tours if it can be arranged. There is trouble about the house Mridula took for him. The owner's son has been transferred to Allahabad & wants the house for himself. Nadir Guzdar[2] is trying to put him off but I don't think it's possible – or fair to him.

Feroze did not return yesterday as expected. This morning a telegram has come from Krishna Menon from Calicut. He says, 'Srinivasan agrees. Wire him date arrival Madras. Also have informed Swaminathan.'

Mathai will tell you that there are innumerable difficulties in getting your manuscripts bound. I have asked him to bring them back here until you decide what is to be done.

A circular came from the Government specifying the accommodation available for members of the Constituent Assembly.[3] They expected a reply before the 20th. What have you decided? Will it not be inconvenient to you & to Raja if you stay there the major part of a year?

Feroze has just arrived – he will book one of the rooms suggested by Govt.

Look after yourself, darling – especially about food and sleep.

Much love to you from us all,

Indu

P.S.
Rajiv has tried to telephone you twice. And once when the phone rang, he picked it up and would not give it to me, saying, *Nana Baba ko bulata hai.*[4]

---

1. Ramzan: the holy month during which Muslims observe a fast.

2. Nadir Guzdar: proprietor of the firm Raja Ram Motilal Guzdar & Co. in Allahabad and a close friend of the Nehru family.

3. The Constituent Assembly of India came into existence in July 1946. It was an indirectly elected body; since it was created by the Provincial Legislatures, on the basis of one member of the Assembly representing a population of one million. It first met on 9th December, 1946.

4. Grandfather is calling Baby.

303.                                      18 Hardinge Avenue,
New Delhi,
19th August, 1946

Darling Indu,

I have been wanting to write to you but partly from sheer fatigue and partly because of the uncertainty of our programme, I did not write. Even now I am entirely uncertain. It is quite possible that I might go to Allahabad within two or three days.

I was very tired out when I arrived here two days ago. Fortunately I have had more leisure here than I expected and I have slept a lot. I fall asleep at odd times of the day.

Please do not send here the various periodicals that come to Anand Bhawan. I shall keep you informed by telegram of my probable programme.

The binding of my MSS had better wait till my return. You can keep them till then.

Ask Krishnanand (who I am told stays in Upadhyaya's house) about the States People's Conference Office address. Or send the papers here and I shall hand them over.

Love,

                 Papu

---

304.                                      [Anand Bhawan],
[Allahabad],
21st August, 1946

Darling Papu,

Your letter[1] has just come. Your telegram of the 20th[2] came this morning.

Shah Nawaz left for Bombay the day before yesterday – 19th. I shall inform him. He is staying with Dhiru Desai.[3]

Feroze is leaving for Madras via Itarsi today.

Upadhyaya arrived this morning. He passed through Alld. on his way to Lucknow on the night of the 19th.

I was glad to hear that you have been getting some sleep, even though it was at odd moments. If you could sleep like Bapu you would conserve

    1. Refers to letter No. 303.
    2. Telegram not traceable.
    3. Dhirubhai Desai: son of the eminent advocate and Congress leader Bhulabhai Desai (1877–1948). Bhulabhai Desai led the team of lawyers who defended the accused in the Indian National Army trials. Dhirubhai was later Ambassador to Switzerland.

a lot more energy. Don't bother to write unless there is something special – knowing what a rush you are always in, I do not expect letters.
  My thoughts are with you always.
  Much love,

Indu

I enclose five letters.

---

*[On 2nd September, 1946 the Viceroy, Lord Wavell, reconstituted his Executive Council to include Jawaharlal Nehru and other leaders. Jawaharlal Nehru became Vice-President of the Executive Council and was allocated the portfolios of External Affairs and Commonwealth Relations. Congress circles regarded the reconstituted Executive Council as a 'Provisional Nationalist Government'.]*

305.                                          Circuit House,
Patna,<br>3rd November, 1946,<br>10 p.m.

Darling Indu,
After a few minutes of mental conflict I have decided to stay on here. Having come to this decision my mind feels clear and light. I had to stay. The immediate need was here in Bihar and all else became secondary. [1] We have heard ghastly stories here and what we have seen is pitiful enough. Stories of Noakhali, [2] etc, bad as they were, became more and more exaggerated as they spread from mouth to mouth and inflamed the Hindu peasantry. For the last week or more the idea of revenge for Noakhali spread – a queer idea of revenging themselves on innocent people for others' faults. They have been terribly cruel – the lust for murder is a horrible thing and to it is added arson and looting. A repetition of Noakhali minus the forced conversions and abductions. No one knows exactly how many people have been done to death . . . Patna is full of refugees – miserable weeping men, women and children. Mass misery has a curious numbing effect.
  I have sent on Mathai to Delhi just when I wanted someone here with me. We are trying to arrange to get the plane back here tomorrow and to stay here. If this is fixed up, and I hope it will be, please send

---

  1. Jawaharlal Nehru travelled to Bihar in the winter of 1946 in order to control communal rioting there. This letter and the next (306) refer to the communal situation.
  2. A district in Bengal which was the locus of communal rioting in October 1946.

Upadhyaya and Hari on it with some additional clothes for me. I am certainly staying here for two more days, probably more.

Love,

Papu

I have no bedding at all here and the shawl I had bought seems to have been left in Calcutta.

Upadhyaya will be perhaps more useful here than Mathai as he knows the language. My shaving brush has also been left in Calcutta. Please send another.

---

306.      Circuit House,
Patna,
5th November, 1946

Darling Indu,

Horror has piled on horror during these past two days and I feel quite numbed. But the urgency and necessity of the moment has kept me up and will keep me up so long as I am here. After that there may be a reaction.

I do not yet know how long I shall have to stay here. Tomorrow I am here certainly and also the day after – Nov. 6 & 7. I am not going away till I see some light in this midnight of Bihar. At the earliest therefore I come back on Friday or perhaps on Saturday.

Upadhyaya & Hari came here yesterday and they were welcome although they have very little to do. But that little makes a difference to me in the stress and strain of existence here.

Do not worry about me. This is just another layer of feeling and experience on the numerous other experiences which have gone to make me what I am. It will change me somewhat, I suppose, as others have done.

This letter is being taken by Nishtar [1] who goes off to Delhi tomorrow morning. I am keeping a small expeditor plane for my use here and I shall probably return in it to Delhi when the time comes.

Love to you and Rajiv,

Papu

---

1. Sardar Abdur Rab Nishtar: leader of the Muslim League in North-West Frontier Province; Finance Minister, N.W.F.P., 1943–5; Minister in the Government of Pakistan, 1947–9 and 1951–3.

307.                                                    Congress Nagar,
                                                              Meerut,
                                                 22nd November, 1946

Darling Indu,
Thank you for sending me the papers and the blanket. I have not seen
the blanket but I suppose it has arrived. Ajaya came this morning and
is of course vastly excited.

Arrangements for our stay here are satisfactory – food is clean and
good, the tent is relatively comfortable, the girl volunteers who stand on
guard smart and efficient. Of course I refer to what is called the Leaders'
Camp – I do not know what other places are like. Sarojini & Padmaja
are staying at the Circuit House.

Work is proceeding here thus far according to plan. We ought to
finish on Sunday night. On Monday morning we shall have a meeting
of the A.I.C.C. and I hope to return by Monday noon or lunchtime.

You would have liked being here of course but you were wise in not
coming. The journey and the stay here would have tired you. I met
Hiralal Atal[1] last night. It appears that he is not too popular with
G.H.Q. because of his supposed relationship to me! He has been passed
over several times and the plums have gone to others.

I am quite fit & well except for a slight backache due to a too sudden
attempt to do the *sarvangàsan*[2] in Delhi the other day. This will pass
soon.

Love to Rajiv and your own little self – even though you are full
twenty-nine!

                                        Papu

———————————

308.                                                          Karachi,
                                                 30th November, 1946

Darling Indu,
. . . We reached the airport at six fifteen p.m. A crowd there, a long
procession of cars with crowds *en route*. The distance is eleven miles.
As we approached Karachi it grew dark and the crowds increased,
preventing our progress. We were in an open car. I controlled myself
for quite a long time but then I broke loose – back or no back – and
dived into the crowd. There was as usual a great deal of pushing and

———

1. Brigadier Hiralal Atal: Liaison Officer of the Government of India in Kashmir,
1947; later was Ambassador to Ethiopia.
2. Refers to a yogic exercise.

panting. Anyhow I emerged & got into somebody else's car and drove to the hotel. Surprisingly enough, all this rough business had no effect on my back. Indeed I am feeling better tonight than I have done for some days. I dined with Lalji Mehrotra [1] and have just come back. We leave tomorrow morning at six fifteen a.m.

Look after yourself. You can send me messages through Harish Dayal. [2]

Love,

Papu

---

309.
Shepheard's Hotel,
Cairo,
1st December, 1946

Darling Indu,

Why I am writing to you at this hour – it is midnight – I do not know, for I should hurry and get as much sleep as I can. In less than three hours I have to get up. We leave the hotel at three forty-five a.m.

It took us just twelve hours from Karachi to Cairo with an hour's halt at Basra. Owing to the difference in timing we arrived here at four p.m., Cairo time. I have had a very full evening meeting people – Indians, Egyptians and others. I went to sign my name at the Palace and then called at various places. Nahas Pasha [3] rather upset my hurried programme. He had to dress up in order to see me and kept me waiting, and then came and embraced and kissed me and had a long and, for me, trying talk in French. Then he insisted on accompanying me back to my hotel and having another talk ... I left a card (it was fortunate that I possessed a few) at Sidqi Pasha's, the Prime Minister. [4] Ganeshilal had of course had to take me to his house where a crowd of Indians had gathered. In between, large number of Indian soldiers came to visit us ...

Hari did not come here but he has the satisfaction of knowing that his bedding has visited Cairo. Thus we see the advantage of having a number of secretaries to look after arrangements. The bedding is travelling back to India.

Love,

Papu

---

1. Lalji Mehrotra: businessman and political activist.
2. Harishwar Dayal: Political Officer in Sikkim, 1948–52, and later Ambassador to Nepal.
3. Mustafa Nahas Pasha: Egyptian statesman and leader of Wafd Party.
4. Ismail Sidqi Pasha: Prime Minister of Egypt, 1930–3 and 1946.

*[Indira Gandhi's second son, Sanjay Gandhi, was born on 14th December, 1946. Since father and daughter were living under the same roof at this juncture, her notes and letters to Jawaharlal Nehru do not contain any reference to the event.]*

PART IV

# In the Prime Minister's House
## (1947–1962)

*[On 15th August, 1947 India became a free country. Jawaharlal Nehru was sworn in as Prime Minister on the morning of the 15th. The ceremony was conducted by Lord Mountbatten, the last British Viceroy, who became the first Governor-General of India after the attainment of freedom. Indira Gandhi watched her father being sworn in as Prime Minister of India.]*

310.                           Mussoorie,
21st August, 1947

Darling Papu,
Even though he cannot yet negotiate a phone, Rajiva was thrilled by your call yesterday. He got so excited *Yeh hamare Nanu hain?*[1] I think he enjoyed his birthday. He looked very grown up in an *achkan*[2] and *tang*[3] pyjamas. On the 19th morning I spent an hour at the phone, only to discover that everybody I know had gone down to the plains. But Dr Prakash, the dentist, came to the rescue with his twins aged six and two other tiny relatives.

Feroze rang up to say that he had got a house,[4] the only flaw of which is that it has some mutiny graves in the compound. It's rather gruesome, isn't it? Still I suppose one has to take what one gets – ghosts and all!

Mussoorie is lovely these days. It rains & rains like the deluge and then suddenly the sun is out and the roads are quite dry and we have a magnificent view of the snows, fresh and sparkling white. The slopes are full of wild flowers.

Bebee sent a cake for Rajiv – just a little larger than yours.
                   Much love,
                   Indu

---

311.                             Lucknow,
5th December, 1947

Darling Papu,
It's such a nuisance not having a phone. I have no news of you, except

1. Is it my grandfather?
2. A long coat reaching below the knees with a buttoned-up collar. The coat has a little flare.
3. Narrow.
4. After her marriage Indira lived with Feroze in Allahabad for a couple of years. In 1946 Feroze joined the Governing Board of the newspaper, *National Herald*, based in Lucknow. Indira accompanied him to Lucknow after her brief holiday in Mussoorie. She is referring to a house that Feroze had rented in Lucknow.

for what appears in the papers. I hope, quite in vain I suppose, that you are less tired and that the tension has lightened somewhat.

Lucknow goes along its own rather dreary way, getting gradually more and more narrow-minded. What a peculiar deadness there is in our provincial towns. And what makes the atmosphere sickening is the corruption and the slackness, the smugness of some and the malice of others. Life here has nothing to offer the not-so-intelligent (and they form the bulk of any class) middle-class young men. It is not surprising that the superficial trappings of fascism attract them in their tens of thousands. The R.S.S.[1] are gaining strength rapidly. They have been holding very impressive rallies in Allahabad, Cawnpore, Lucknow – except for very minor details following the German model almost exactly. I was given a vivid description of the Alld. show by one of the Malaviya boys. The rally was held in Alfred Park. There were thousands of uniformed volunteers. As each spectator arrived he was given a card for his cycle (as they do for cars in Govt House) or other vehicle. Seating was on the ground but clear white sheets had been spread and each person was allowed just so much room to sit in. People were seated in rows – very orderly. They had to take off their shoes & *chappals* & here again were given cards so that the shoes should not get mixed up or lost. At the appointed time the announcement was made that proceedings were now starting and that nobody would be allowed to move from his seat or to talk or interrupt in any way. Five minutes were then given so that all who did not wish to stay until the end of the meeting should leave. After that the Guruji[2] & others spoke in pin-drop silence.

It is really surprising that this sort of rally is allowed when Section 144[3] is still operating in the province. Some of the ministers ignore the whole thing and others say that they have orders from Delhi not to interfere. But the growth of this organisation is so amazingly like the Brown Shirts of Germany, that if we are not very quick on our toes it will grow beyond our control and beyond the control also of the industrialists who are now financing it (just as happened to Thyssen & others in Germany). The recent history of Germany is too close for us to be able to forget it for an instant. Are we inviting the same fate to our country? The Congress organisation has already been engulfed – most Congressmen approve of these tendencies. So do Government servants of all ranks and positions.

My optimism and my faith in the ultimate sanity of the human race

1. Rashtriya Swayamsewak Sangh: a revivalist Hindu organisation.
2. Madhav Sadashivrao Golwalkar, popularly known as 'Guruji'. He was head of the R.S.S. from 1940 to 1973.
3. Section 144: an Indian Penal provision prohibiting the assembly of more than five persons in a public place with a view to maintaining peace and order.

is high and I feel sure that we shall be able to pull through all these dangers. But doubts do creep in. Is it wishful thinking? So did the German social-democrats & others persist in believing that somehow, at some stage, the Brown Shirts would be suppressed or that the movement would die a natural death. And that was the undoing of the German people. Let us not fall into the same trap.

My cough has gone almost completely and I am feeling rested but it is not enough. I must put on some weight. I am staying very quiet – just visiting a few people, dealing with letters accumulated in the last weeks. I am also dabbling with Rural Uplift![1]

Darling, I am ashamed to find that this letter has grown so long. But I am so agitated about the whole thing.

The children are well. Rajiv talks of you often, mostly in connection with standing on the head.

Much love,<br>Indu

312.                              17 York Road,[2]<br>
New Delhi,<br>
6th December, 1947

Darling Indu,

Thank you for your very interesting letter.[3] Yes, all this is happening and future prospects are not bright. Recent experiences have so dulled our senses that we do not react to events as we might have done earlier. I do not know that I believe in the ultimate sanity of the human race, and yet, somewhere at the back of my mind, there is a lurking faith. I have an idea that this depends greatly on one's physical & mental health. As I am fortunately by and large a healthy person, or so I imagine, my view tends to be more optimistic than facts warrant.

I went to Jammu today – Puphi went with me. I met the Yuvaraj[4] for the first time and liked him. He is a very bright boy . . .

I am glad you are much better. I think you should stay on in Lucknow

1. Indira was involved in a Gandhian programme for rural development.

2. When Jawaharlal Nehru was Vice-President of the Viceroy's Executive Council (1946) he resided in a bungalow at 17 York Road, now known as Motilal Nehru Road. Later, on 2nd August, 1948, he moved into Teen Murti house, which became the official residence of the Prime Minister. Indira accompanied him to the new residence.

3. Refers to letter No. 311.

4. Dr Karan Singh: son of Maharaja Hari Singh of Kashmir; Regent of Jammu and Kashmir, 1949–52 and Sadr-i-Riyasat, 1952–65; held important ministerial portfolios in successive governments in the 1970s; was Indian Ambassador to the United States (1989).

for some weeks longer – with gaps. You are of course coming to Allahabad for the 13th & 14th. I propose reaching [there] on the 13th morning
by air about ten thirty. Puphi, Tara & Rita will accompany me. We shall
all have lunch that day with Dr Sapru. I shall be dining out also at the
University. On the 15th morning I go to Calcutta for a day.

I have decided to go to Jaipur on the 19th morning returning on the
20th afternoon to Delhi. Puphi, Tara & Rita may also go with me there.
I should like you to come too if you feel up to it. If so you could come
to Delhi with me from Allahabad on the 16th – that is I would pick you
up at Bamrauli on my way back from Calcutta.

After Jaipur you could return to Lucknow for two or three weeks or
more and rest there.

Love,<br>Papu

I shall take Mathai & Hari with me to Allahabad.

---

313.                                              [Anand Bhawan],
                                                      [Allahabad],
                                              13th February, 1948

Darling Papu,
Pantji came to the house about five thirty p.m. He was sorry to have
missed you but he must be pleased with your telegram to him. Everything
did go off very well. It was very moving and solemn and dignified. [1]

Sumitra [2] – one of Bapu's granddaughters – stayed the night and has
just left for Benares by car.

By the way, did you notice that as the procession passed the cathedral,
choir and priests stood outside singing Bapu's favourite hymns?

Much love,<br>Indu

Here are some telegrams.

---

1. Mahatma Gandhi was assassinated on 30th January, 1948. Indira Gandhi and
Jawaharlal Nehru attended the ceremony marking the immersion of Mahatma Gandhi's
ashes at the Sangam, the confluence of the rivers Ganga (also known as the Ganges),
Jumna and the mythical Saraswati, near Allahabad on 12th February, 1948. In this letter,
Indira shares with her father her impressions of the solemn and moving ceremony.

2. Sumitra Kulkarni: daughter of Mahatma Gandhi's third son, Ramdas Gandhi;
married Gajanan Kulkarni, an economist; resigned from the Indian Administrative
Service in 1972 to join the Rajya Sabha.

314.                                                    [Srinagar],
                                                  14th May, 1948

Darling Papu,
I do hope you will be able to come again soon. It is so peaceful and
quiet and perfectly beautiful. Couldn't you come for the weekend every
week or, at least, every fortnight? You could bring your files and the
stenographer and get a lot of work done besides breathing in this lovely
fresh and clean air. Nobody would disturb you at the Chashmeshahi
house but if you would like to be quieter still and nearer the mountains,
we could go up to Pahalgam or Sonamarg. Do, do think about it, please.
I am sure you can manage it if you make up your mind to do so.
    The day you left we moved into the Guest House No. 1. It hasn't got
lovely grounds like the other but it has the advantage of being within
walking distance of most places we visit, so we have been able to dispense
with the car and save petrol for the Govt.!
    We have been meeting and talking to a lot of people – all kinds. The
result is most depressing. For over a year, because of lack of visitors,
transport difficulties or whatever, trade has been almost completely at a
standstill. The hotel-owners, houseboat & *shikarawallahs*, shopkeepers
and artisans, labourers and *hanjis*:[1] all are starving or on the verge of
it. Salt has come down in price – 2/8 per seer. But that is still too
expensive for the poor. Besides, the distribution is bad and there is even
some black-marketing in it. All these things breed discontent, and
finally, hostility.
    Although Sheikh Saheb and Bakhshi[2] are personally tremendously
popular, the other members of the Govt are not. And just now the
morale of the people is at a low ebb . . .
    There are two main reasons for this political attitude. Most of the
officials, in the police, etc, are still the old ones and they are all Leaguers.
I believe they go about expressing their views quite openly in the club
and elsewhere. The other reason is that the only paper that has been
coming regularly to Kashmir is the *Civil & Military Gazette* of Lahore.
I presume that other Pakistani Urdu papers must also have been coming
in and spreading their vile propaganda. Only since the Dalmia–Jain
service has started, do they bring Dalmia's paper, the *News Chronicle*.
    This is the talk of the town. They say that only Sheikh Saheb is
confident of winning the plebiscite . . .
    Personally, I feel that all this political talk will count for nothing if

1. Boatman.
2. Ghulam Muhammad Bakhshi: leading member of National Conference in Kashmir; Deputy Prime Minister, 1947–53 and Prime Minister of Kashmir, 1953–63.

the economic situation can be dealt with. Because after all the people are concerned with only [one] thing – they want to sell their goods and to have food and salt.

The Kashmir Government is finding it impossible to collect any revenue – this loss will have to be made up by the Indian Govt.

Communications with India must improve. It should not take very long to make an all-weather track at the Srinagar Aerodrome.

But most important of all – and, I feel, the only thing that can save Kashmir for India and the Kashmiris – will be an influx of visitors this summer, preferably from Bombay & Ahmedabad, since those are ones [who] buy the most. I am sure if there had been enough publicity, people would have flocked to Srinagar. Both the Kashmir & Indian Govts should go all out to assure people that Srinagar is SAFE. Just now it is cheaper, cleaner, healthier and more beautiful than any other hill station. Mussoorie, Simla & Naini Tal are overflowing and charging exorbitant prices besides spreading illness because of the congestion. But whatever is done must be done NOW to have any effect. Even if Govt could ask Govt Servants to send their families up, it would make a difference. Papu, please do consider these things seriously. I am sure if you appealed to people to spend the summer here, they would come in thousands. If nothing else counts they should regard it as a patriotic duty. And what a pleasant one it will be too!

Feroze has an idea that some of the research offices or other such departments that don't have to be in Delhi could be temporarily transferred here. Although these people won't buy they will occupy hotels & houseboats and consume food. Every little will count in our favour.

Sheikh Saheb's Govt have restricted the sending of money outside Kashmir to Rs. 2500/- per week, so people have placed standing orders at the various banks that their whole account should be transferred to Allahabad or Agra or some such place at the rate of Rs. 2500/- a week! Of course this money will come back in a jiffy when people have some feeling of security.

Darling, I am sorry to take so much of your time with this long letter but you know that I only write when I must – when I feel so strongly about something that it cannot be kept quiet. You will remember that last long letter [1] I wrote from Lucknow. How right I was & what tragic consequences followed. [2] Feroze went off to Uri (and

1. See letter No. 311.
2. The reference is to the assassination of Mahatma Gandhi by Nathuram Godse, who was associated with the R.S.S. In her letter No. 311 Indira had spoken at some length about the activities of the R.S.S. (see p. 548).

beyond?) yesterday afternoon with Kachru.[1] They are due back this evening.

Last night we – Rita & I – dined at General Thimayya's[2] headquarters. Feroze couldn't go because of the Uri trip. We had a pleasant evening. Sheikh Saheb comes every day for tea and we are being well looked after.

The weather has held – the sun is out every day and it is warm and lovely.

I hear the Convent is opening soon – if it does I plan to send Rajiv there. It is just across the river from Mamu's house. Mamu's house is rather dark and damp but now that the sun is out I don't think that will matter & all the surrounding water will soon dry up.

I miss you here – do try and come up as I suggested. It will be good propaganda too. And the weather is ideal for swimming or riding.

Much love,<br>Indu

---

315.

17 York Road,<br>New Delhi,<br>19th May, 1948

Darling Indu,

Thank you for your letter[3] which I found most interesting and instructive. It is rather silly of you to apologise for that letter because you know that I like very much having any kind of a letter from you, more so a letter which gives so much useful information.

The points you have mentioned had been vaguely before us, but they have now been emphasised by you. We should do what we can in this matter. I imagine that the situation may well be clearer and more helpful from the point of view of visitors and transport within a fortnight or so . . .

I had four very quiet and restful days in Mashobra. I did no work at all, although I took many papers. I was not in the mood to work. We visited Narkanda one day and on our way went to a village fair which was very interesting with the coloured garments and head-dresses of

---

1. Dwarka Nath Kachru: General Secretary of the Indian States People's Conference; joined Jawaharlal's Secretariat in 1947 to deal with the Princely States; died in an aircrash, 1950.

2. General K. S. Thimayya: Commander, Indian troops in Kashmir, 1947–50; Chief of Army Staff, 1957–61.

3. Refers to letter No. 314.

the village women. I had so much of this sun during my visit that the skin on my face is peeling off . . .

My programme is as follows:

24th & 25th – Mussoorie.
28th – Gwalior.
31st May to 3rd June – Ootacamund.

Rita is likely to accompany me to all these three places and Krishna Menon will go to Mussoorie with me. For the rest I am likely to remain in Delhi. Perhaps I might think of coming over just for a day to Srinagar about the middle of June. But it is rather difficult because of the Mountbattens' coming departure.

Feroze is leaving tomorrow morning for Lucknow.

Do write to me as often and as long as you like. The oftener and the longer the better.

I get a large number of letters marked Personal. In order to distinguish these from the really personal ones I propose to have the latter marked on the envelope 'For Himself'. So please remember this.

I have not received yet the bill for the shawl or for the other purchases I made in Srinagar. Please have these sent to me.

Love,
Papu

---

316.                                    c/o The Imperial Bank,
                                              Srinagar,
                                         20th May, 1948

Darling Papu,
Your letter [1] has just come and as there is a possibility of Kachru's going to Delhi tomorrow I am dashing off a few lines . . .

If you come in the middle of June I could return with you to Delhi for the Mountbatten parties and departure.

I suppose Krishna is coming with Lady Mountbatten.

I haven't got the silver bracelet but I know which one you mean & shall get it for Pam. [2]

I was so glad to hear that you had a real good rest at Simla and were able to prolong your stay by a day. When you come here, it will be tiring

1. Refers to letter No. 315.
2. Pamela Mountbatten: daughter of Lord Mountbatten; married David Hicks in 1960.

to come only for a day. Why not make it a weekend: come on Friday evening and leave early Monday? . . .

The day before I came over here to stay, the Sheikh came to see me. He was very depressed about everything – his relations with H.H. [His Highness the Maharaja of Kashmir] and the States Ministry. He has a feeling that the States Ministry supports the Maharaja as against S.S. [Sheikh Saheb] and that it is due to his being a Muslim. That is a very dangerous feeling for him to have at this stage – or any other for that matter. The Maharaja is being very stupid about the little as well as the big things. Sheikh says that when he asked for the Chashmeshahi Guest House for you the Maharaja did not give his consent until the evening of the 8th! These are small things but irritating. On the other hand you yourself saw how the National Conference loses no opportunity of pinpricking Their Highnesses in front of them or behind their backs. [1] It is so ridiculously childish. But now I suppose it has become a matter of prestige. According to the Sheikh, the only solution is that H.H. should abdicate in favour of his son and that a council of regency should be set up – consisting of the Maharani, a representative of the Indian Union (they should naturally like to have someone whom you trust rather than one appointed by the States Ministry) and one other.

Talking of the States Ministry, you will remember I told you once that Mahajan's [2] name had been suggested by Sardar. It seems that that is what he himself has been telling people here. Also that whatever he (Mahajan) did in those days of crisis was at the advice of Sardar. The Maharaja, also trying to push the blame for his own stupidity and mis-deeds on someone else, says that when he ordered your arrest, and the manhandling, etc, Sir Olaf Caroe [3] was practically sitting beside him the whole time, telling him what to do next.

It is a pity the contract for running the air services to Srinagar has been given to Dalmia. His is the worst service and the worst reputation too. The planes that are coming here are not passenger ones at all, and consequently have no conveniences. There are no racks for small lug-gage, papers, etc. Nothing on the floor and no curtains, so that the people who sit on the sunny side have the full blast of sun on their faces

1. The National Conference was a secular party organised by Sheikh Abdullah for securing the democratisation of Kashmir and its integration with India. Because of its stand, there was considerable tension between the National Conference and the Maha-raja of Kashmir.

2. Justice Mehrchand Mahajan: Prime Minister of Jammu and Kashmir State, 1947–8; later Chief Justice of the Supreme Court of India.

3. Sir Olaf Caroe (1892–1981): Chief Secretary, Government of N.W.F.P., 1933–4; Foreign Secretary to Government of India, 1939–45; Governor, N.W.F.P., 1946–7.

for three hours at the hottest time of the day and the hottest days of the year. On top of that they are not properly cleaned, everybody has been complaining of the stink. This is hardly an encouragement for people who want to go for a pleasure jaunt. Sheikh says that other airlines had also volunteered and one had offered to do the trip much cheaper. But Dalmia got the contract because of influence with D.G. civil aviation. I do not know if this is true.

The cherries are coming in now & will probably rot away unless they can be transported to Delhi every day. The fruit is very delicate and doesn't keep and the season for it lasts only about two or three weeks.

Are you eating properly and looking after yourself generally?

Very much love,

Indu

---

317.

c/o Imperial Bank,
Srinagar,
23rd May, 1948

Darling Papu,

Thank you for your letter[1] & the enclosure . . .

To come back to the topic of the day – Kashmir. There is one thing more that strikes me. I have not discussed it with Sheikh Saheb & do not know if he has already done anything about it. There seems to me to be a woeful lack of political propaganda on behalf of the Kashmir Govt. The 'Azad Kashmir' radio is blaring out the most brazen lies night and day and there is nothing to counteract them. The Jammu radio gives only news and a normal peacetime programme. This is not good enough. Sheikh should have a powerful transmitter here and a well-planned scheme for having loudspeakers at the 1st Bridge and other parts of the city. Every day there is a fresh crop of rumours, probably spread by the 'fifth column', which seems to me to be powerful and active. It is a whispering campaign. Only radio can reach into the lanes and byways of Srinagar and give authentic news and contradict the ridiculous stories spread by the 'Azad Kashmir' radio. Do you know that the day you left Srinagar, the 'Azad Kashmir' radio announced that on your arrival in Srinagar you were met by one lakh of people waving black flags & shouting 'Go Back!'!!?

Must stop now.

Much love,

Indu

---

1. Letter not published.

318.                                          c/o Imperial Bank,
                                                      Srinagar,
                                                9th June, 1948

Darling Papu,
There has been no news of you for some time.
    I am booking my seat to Delhi on the 14th morning.
    I have been wanting to write to you but did not like to do so by post.
Srinagar, with all the rumours and whispering, is becoming increasingly
depressing. One would be so much happier if one could take the world
as it is, with all its limitations. One always expects too much from people.
And alas, the standard of the normal – the normal that is and not the
normal that should be – human being is woefully low: in honesty and
intelligence and, even, common sense.
    I am looking forward to seeing you.
                                              Much love,
                                                  Indu

I hear Sheikh Saheb is planning to come to Delhi on the 15th.
    The Convent, which is a lovely building & specially built for a school,
is being forcibly taken over from the nuns, so that is the end of the only
good school in Srinagar and one less attraction for people to spend the
summer here – for most people like to go somewhere where their children can attend school. The Convent is being taken over for the new
Jammu–Kashmir University. With so many important projects on hand
why this particular one should be rushed is difficult to understand. Why
cannot the Kashmiris attend any university in India? Of all peoples they
have perhaps the narrowest outlook. It is essential for them to get out
& meet people & exchange ideas.
                                                  Indu

---

319.                                          c/o Imperial Bank,
                                                      Srinagar,
                                                9th July, 1948

Darling Papu,
Your telegram [1] came this morning just as I was going off to the refugee
camps. Since then Krishnaji [2] has been to see the house. I don't know
when we can move.

    1. Telegram not published.
    2. Krishna Mehta: a friend of the Nehru family; engaged in the rehabilitation of
refugee women and children in Jammu and Kashmir; member, Lok Sabha, 1957–62.

The refugees here are housed in hotels and other houses, there are no camps as such. [1] As far as living space goes, they are comfortable enough. I did not find them exceptionally dirty, but Krishnaji says that they were much dirtier the day she went. Somebody told her that Kashyap Bandu had a big cleaning drive after her visit. Since then the doctor has also been doing the rounds of the houses regularly. Everywhere we went the chief complaint was about the rations. They get one pan of *ata* [2] per person per day. This is, apparently, not enough. Besides the quality is terrible, full of *bhusi* [3] or some such thing. The rice is also very bad: broken grains mixed with a lot of dirt and *kankar*. [4] Some families have clothes but others are in rags. Krishnaji did not take me to the Rambagh Camp which is supposed to be the worst. Besides these there are refugees living in the city and being looked after [by] the local Pandits.

I suggested to Krishnaji that a list be made of the most needy; also of able-bodied men for whom employment could be found – some of them are already earning. Accordingly we collected some women and at the meeting some girls offered themselves for doing this work. Krishnaji has also got the loan of a hall in an Arya Samaj School, where she proposes to have classes for spinning wool.

Some of the women seem to be good workers and enthusiastic, so I am sure the work will progress satisfactorily. Krishnaji is really most energetic. She has spent the whole of today going from house to house practically rounding up these women. It is a good thing that she is doing this quite independently of the various groups here.

The Maharani has asked me to lunch but I am not sure of the day.

I am hoping to take the children for a swim tomorrow.

Much love,
Indu

---

1. The invasion of Kashmir by Pakistan had obliged numerous citizens of the State to take refuge in Srinagar. Indira, along with her friend Krishna Mehta, was engaged in social work in these camps.
2. Flour.
3. Husk.
4. Gravel.

320.                                                  Claridges,
Brook Street,
London,[1]
6th October, 1948

Indu darling,

This really should be dated 7th as it is two a.m.

We had a good and comfortable journey – a lovely bed – stops at Basra, Cairo & Geneva. Just before reaching Geneva we passed Mont Blanc. It was dusk and there was a sea of clouds above which rose, clear and silvery bright, Mont Blanc.

At Geneva some of the local functionaries, and Dhiru & Madhuri[2] of course, insisted on taking me for a drive round the city and I recognised many well-remembered landmarks, and to a meal at the Hotel Richemond.

After the reception at Heathrow Aerodrome, Krishna took me to the Mountbattens' flat where I met them. The flat, though big for London, has tiny rooms and it is a change from Govt House. I came to my hotel about one a.m. and have just had a bath. My rooms here are very posh. This is supposed to be the royal suite.

Both Edwina & Pammy asked tenderly about Hari and Trilok Nath[3] and expressed their great regret that they had not come! Especially Pammy – you might convey their sentiments to the persons concerned.

Tomorrow evening I am going off to Broadlands.[4] Puphi joins me the next day.

Love to you and the children,
Papu

---

321.                                                  Claridges,
Brook Street,
London,
18th October, 1948

Darling Indu,

I have not written to you since the day of my arrival when I sent you a brief note.[5] Somehow I am kept fully occupied all day and till late at

1. Jawaharlal Nehru attended the Commonwealth Conference in London in October 1948.

2. Dhirubhai Desai and his wife Madhuri Desai. See also p. 539, footnote 3.

3. Trilok Nath: a member of the domestic staff of the Nehrus.

4. Broadlands: Lord Mountbatten's house in Romsey, Hampshire.

5. Refers to letter No. 320.

night but little solid work is done. I have had many odd and new experiences here and I could write much if I had the time.

Last night at midnight I returned from Paris after a two-days' stay. Paris is such a beautiful and gracious city that it is always delightful to be there. But it was painful also to see the gradual disintegration of a great and famous nation. The people seemed to have lost their soul and with it hope and faith. The foreigners there – including us – lived in luxury and sumptuous food and wines were abundantly provided and wasted when vast numbers of people were in great trouble. The U.N. crowd distressed me.

Lekha & Tara came with me to London. This is Tara's first visit to London & England. They will leave some days before me and stay in Cairo. From there they will accompany me to Bombay.

My programme is:

Oct. 26th: go to Paris
Oct. 27th to Nov. 1st: in Paris
Nov. 2nd: Paris to Cairo
Nov. 3rd, 4th: in Cairo
Nov. 5th, 6th: Cairo to Bombay
Probably I shall reach Delhi on Nov. 7th.

Lekha & Tara will stay in Bombay for a few days before going to Delhi.

Tonight for the first time I went to a theatre with L & T. It was an all Negro cast. The play was *Anna Locastor*. Wonderfully acted but the play itself was rather thin. Tomorrow we are going to a show with Edwina.

Love to the children and to you,<br>Papu

322.                                            Hotel George V,
                                          31 Avenue George V,
                                                       Paris,
                                          28th October, 1948

Darling Indu,
You have not written to me since I left India. I have not been too good a correspondent but I have at least sent you two letters.[1] Also you get some news of me from the papers.

I have been here in Paris for two days. I like Paris but the present

---

1. Refers to letters Nos 320 and 321.

atmosphere is not conducive to enjoyment. Last night we went to the Opera – a gala performance in honour of the U.N. delegates. There was a ballet – fairly good. I am not much of a judge but on the whole I liked it. For the rest, I hope to visit the Louvre and go occasionally to the Bois de Boulogne. This living in expensive hotels is rather unnerving. And the food that is wasted here and in every restaurant gives one repeated shocks. The French have not lost their love of food even though France may be disintegrating.

I rather enjoyed my stay in England, especially my two weekends in Broadlands. I suppose that was natural, for I had to react in that way to the welcome and friendly approach I found everywhere. Perhaps also my vanity was tickled for there was praise enough. I am told I made a hit, from Buckingham Palace downwards. Even Winston Churchill went rather out of his way to be friendly to me. All this was partly me but much more so the growing importance of India which is dawning upon the outside world. The *Economist* comes out with an article on 'India – the new Great Power'. So I basked in all this praise and adulation. But at the same time I felt rather uncomfortable and somewhat out of place and counterfeit.

The Mountbatten family derived a lot of amusement from a letter Dickie received from a gentleman in Calcutta suggesting that in the interest of Indo-British friendship Pamela should marry me!

This evening I had two long interviews – nearly two hours with Dulles,[1] the prospective Secretary of State in the U.S.A., and nearly three hours with Vyshinsky.[2] An interesting but at the same time an exhausting business.

Love,
Papu

---

323.

Bangalore,
26th December, 1948

Darling Indu,
I have been missing you every day during my stay in Hyderabad and here. It has been a wonderful experience even for me with all I have seen in the past of public enthusiasm and big gatherings. I doubt if this kind of thing can be repeated. My visits appear to produce a human convulsion or earthquake and vast numbers of people gather from afar and develop a frenzy of enthusiasm. It is deeply moving and rather

1. J. F. Dulles: American statesman; Secretary of State, 1953–9.
2. Andrei Vyshinsky: Foreign Minister of the Soviet Union, 1949–53.

terrifying. Everywhere I go this happens, more especially in the south where I come so rarely.

I shall be returning to Delhi on the 29th, reaching there about lunch-time. You must know that I have promised to address a public meeting in Allahabad on the 1st January at four thirty p.m. This means that I shall have to start early from Delhi. I want to go to Anand Bhawan first, spend a little time there, and then go to the meeting. I shall try to reach Bamrauli by three p.m. I shall let you know of course the exact time of arrival.

I expect to return from Allahabad to Delhi on the 4th January – the exact time to be determined later.

I should like to visit Tej Bahadurji on the 1st Jan. preferably before the public meeting, if I can manage it. Perhaps I could go there just for a few minutes on my way from Bamrauli.

Love,<br>Papu

324.                                                              Basti,
                                                   10th February, 1949

Darling Indu,

Today is the end of the fifth day of this particular tour – another four days and I shall be back home. As the tour progresses I count the days and even the hours when I shall be back. It is hard and tiring work and the roads here are terribly bad. My throat and voice are giving out.

I hope to be back on the 15th morning. I do not know yet whether I shall go by train or car from Benares. I shall let you know by phone or telegram. Ranbir Singh may accompany me to Allahabad.

I hope you are keeping well.

Love,<br>Papu

325.                                            [Government House],
                                                        [Bombay],
                                                   28th April, 1949

Darling Papu,

As you see we have stayed on at Govt House. It seemed the simplest and most convenient. Juhu is too hot to be bearable. But I have been going out a good deal – there are so many people to see.

There has not been much opportunity for swimming. The boys go to the beach most days at six thirty in the morning and if I am up I join them. Later on the beach can become quite unpleasant. Rajiv & Sanjay are having a good time. They have bought some expensive toys, which I have locked up – to produce again on Rajiv's birthday!

I have been to the oculist who confirms that my eyes are as good as ever, and the dentist who prophesies that if I am not careful about my gums all my teeth will fall out!

Our host & hostess send their love to you. H.E. usually visits us at eight thirty when we are having breakfast in our cottage . . .

I approve of the house in Govt House – early meals and so on. One gets so much more time to oneself. But the Bombay Govt is really stretching things a bit too far. There is now a law that all entertainment must stop at midnight and Morarji[1] is quoted as saying that he will put all Bombay to bed by nine thirty p.m.! I suppose gradually there will be so much regimentation that nobody will be allowed to have any private life at all. It is a pity that so much time and effort should be devoted to such unimportant things when there is so much constructive work to be done in every line.

Our thoughts have been very much with you – it must have been a difficult time and most people are pleased with the way you managed the conference and feel that the decision taken was a personal triumph for you.[2]

I hope the weekend at Broadlands was refreshing and that you will return looking less tired than when you left . . .

Much love,<br>Indu

326.                                      3rd May, 1949

Indu darling,

I am on my way from London to Zurich. We started at nine fifteen a.m. and are expected to reach Zurich at eleven forty-five. I go on immedi-

1. Morarji Desai: eminent politician; was Chief Minister of Bombay, 1952–6, Union Minister of Commerce, 1956–8, and Finance, 1958–63; Prime Minister of India, 1977–9.

2. The Commonwealth Prime Ministers' Conference of 1949 had to take a crucial decision regarding the terms on which India would become a member of the Commonwealth. At Nehru's initiative, it was decided that India's membership of the Commonwealth was to rest on the understanding that she accepted 'the King as the symbol of the free association of its independent member nations and as such the Head of the Commonwealth'. For details about this Conference and Nehru's contribution to it, see S. Gopal's *Jawaharlal Nehru: A Biography*, volume II, 1947–56 (Delhi, 1979), pp. 52–3.

ately by car to Berne. On the 5th night we start from Geneva by Air India, reaching Bombay on the 6th night.

Bajpai[1] is going on ahead and will take this letter. He will also take some Petit Suisse for you and today's London newspapers. In the *News Chronicle* you will see a picture of the Churchills and me. Suddenly, on my return from Broadlands yesterday, I received a message from Winston. He was very keen on my having lunch with him. I could not manage it as I was having Ernest Bevin[2] to lunch. I was busy the whole evening and had a reception at eight thirty. But Winston insisted and so we fixed an early dinner. He and his wife went out of their [way] completely to be friendly to me. The old man is a very likeable person and his wife is charming. He told me frankly that after much painful thought he had changed his opinion about India and he had been deeply moved by the recent decisions and more especially by my magnanimity. He drank the toast of India and said he would stand by India. I am sure he meant it in his own way.

The feeling in England among all classes and groups, except perhaps the Communists, is overwhelmingly friendly towards India. It is full of gratitude, as of escape from some impending disaster. They feel that after a succession of misfortunes and mishaps in the world, something has happened which in some deep but indescribable way indicates the turn of the tide. Winston said to me that he felt as if a friend whom he had given up for dead had suddenly come back to life. If Winston feels that way you can imagine how others feel.

That is the British side. In the letter[3] which you have sent through Puphi you describe the mixed Indian reaction. That was partly to be expected. Yet I do feel that we have not only done well but done it in the right and gracious way – the Gandhian way. I am sure that we have done right for India and the world. We have not given up an iota of our freedom, of anything that matters, and we have gained much. The objection can only be on sentimental grounds and that too on false sentiment and hangovers from the past.

I return a little more light-hearted than I went, a little surer of myself, a little fresher in mind and body. I have not had much rest. Perhaps two days in Switzerland will further tone me up – my two visits to Broadlands were very delightful. It is a lovely place which fits in with my mood and I wish you could also visit it.

I spent seven hours in Dublin and had a warm-hearted welcome there. The Irish are a lovable people and Dublin is a charming city.

1. G. S. Bajpai: Secretary-General in Ministry of External Affairs, 1947–52; Governor of Bombay, 1952–4.
2. Ernest Bevin: at this time Foreign Secretary (1945–51).
3. Letter not traceable.

Bajpai is taking some of my extra luggage. He will leave it in Bombay and I shall pick it up when I come. I suppose you and the children will accompany me to Delhi on the special Tata plane. I should like to start on the 7th morning at about eight a.m.

Puphi was telling me that she had suggested your going to Mashobra. I think this is an excellent idea. The house at Mashobra lies empty and can be had at any time. It is a delightful house with gardens, an ideal place for a quiet holiday.

Give my love to the Maharaj Singhs.

Love,<br>Papu

---

327.

6 La Place,<br>Shahnajaf Road,<br>Lucknow,<br>U.P.,<br>10th December, 1949

Darling Papu,

At last our plans for the immediate future are taking shape. We shall arrive in Delhi on the 3rd January. That will give me five days before leaving for Colombo with you. Feroze wanted me to leave the boys here but you have not seen them for some time and the *ayah* is really not capable of looking after them on her own. So they will come along to Delhi. Feroze has not yet decided about himself. Anyhow he will come before the 26th January.

I hope Farrukhabad was not too dusty and tiring. I hear Tandonji wants to change its name and that of every town which ends in 'bad' into 'nagar'.[1] If this sort of thing goes on much longer I shall be provoked into calling myself 'Zohra Begum' or some such thing!

Lots of love from us all,<br>Indu

P.S.

Now that Christmas is coming, you will be receiving cards from the various embassies. Do you think we shall send some too? – New Year cards? Or perhaps we could get something specially printed & send

---

1. 'Bad' is a Persian suffix for a town or city, while 'nagar' is a Sanskrit suffix for the same. The change of names was in keeping with the President of the Provincial Congress, Purushottam Das Tandon's, emphasis on the Sanskritisation of India.

them out for the 26th Jan.?[1] There isn't much time left. Let me know if there is anything I can do.

Love,<br>
Indu

---

328.                                                          Lucknow,
                                               16th December, 1949

Darling Papu,

I don't quite know how to begin this letter. The politics of this province stink so much that it is becoming difficult to ignore or be indifferent – at least I cannot live in such an atmosphere. Every day Lucknow discloses some new scandal.

And now the rottenness has come right into my house. Perhaps you know that there is a meeting of the shareholders of the *National Herald* on the 18th. The chief business on the agenda is the election of two directors. I don't know if you have realised that Pantji likes to have only 'yes' men in the province & the whole ministry is very annoyed with the present set-up at the *Herald*. They don't like the way the news is presented & they don't like the editorials. I am not showing any favouritism when I say that the *Herald* is the only newspaper worth reading in India with the one exception of the Madras *Hindu*. It is also very fair in its reports, as far as it is able to be. With regard to the Kisan March[2] for instance. I was an eyewitness & I can swear that the account of the March given by ministers like Kher[3] are pure lies & wishful thinking.

1. Since 1930, the Indian National Congress observed 26th January as Independence Day. The first celebration of Independence Day followed the adoption of a resolution by the Congress, at its annual session in Lahore in December 1929, stating that the objective of the freedom struggle in India was the achievement of *Purna Swaraj* (or complete independence) instead of Dominion Status. After independence, India was formally proclaimed a Republic on 26th January, 1950, and this day is since annually observed as Republic Day.

2. Several thousand *Kisans* (peasants) from all parts of Uttar Pradesh held a demonstration on 25th November, 1949 in front of the Council House in Lucknow (the capital of U.P.) after having marched through the main streets of the city in a big procession. Their main demand was the abolition of Zamindari (or landlordship) without compensation. The procession was led by a number of socialists, namely, Acharya Narendra Deva, Dr Rammanohar Lohia, Damodar Swarup Seth and Raghukul Tilak, and it also included some Communists. During the course of the procession, there was a clash between the socialists and the Communists and a number of the latter were injured.

3. B. G. Kher: Congress leader of Bombay; Chief Minister of Bombay 1937–9 and 1946–52; High Commissioner in London, 1952–4.

The *Herald* report is what any unbiased person would have written. But the Govt was up in arms about it.

All this was the preamble. The point now is that Pantji or Chandra Bhan Gupta [1] (I do not believe that Chandra Bhan Gupta would act on his own without sanction from Pantji) have moved the whole Govt machinery to collect proxies in favour of two people: Radhakrishan Agarwal, a petty businessman of Hardoi and Kishorilal Agarwal, a local shopkeeper. Both have rather unsavoury reputations but Kishorilal Agarwal is a known black-marketeer. Pantji has himself written to Dahyabhai Patel [2] to collect the Bombay proxies. Gupta has mobilised the entire rationing dept. to collect the proxies district-wise. The local Congress Committee has also been working hard in its mohallas. [3]

Tandonji has made over the proxy for the 1200 shares of the Provincial Congress Committee to one of the above mentioned gentlemen. By the way, the way these shares were made over to the P.C.C. is quite illegal and had you not been the Prime Minister, the *Herald* could have started proceedings about this matter.

You tolerate a lot of things but are you willing to have the *Herald*, which everybody associates with your name, run by black-marketeers? That is what it will amount to.

I don't know what you can do about this because now, with Pantji's & Gupta's letters and putting pressure on people, they have already secured the proxies for 6000 shares – a clear majority. But I feel sure something could be done. Why not have a talk with Rafi Saheb?

I am writing this against Feroze's wishes. It makes one's heart bleed to hear everyone say that it is no use bringing anything to your notice since you don't do anything about righting things. This matter is not a small thing – it is indicative of the way the mind of the Govt works & even you must admit that it is very ugly. But the worst is that your name is involved.

Can you not move Tandonji to cancel the proxies of the 1200 P.C.C. shares?

I don't know what you can do but I do know that if you don't call Pantji to order for interfering in this way (with the full strength of Govt machinery & personnel including District Magistrates) in the business of a newspaper, then please stop in future talking about democracy &

1. C. B. Gupta: Congress leader from U.P.; held various important ministerial portfolios in the U.P. Government, was also its Chief Minister from 1960 to 1963.

2. Dahyabhai V. Patel: son of Sardar Vallabhbhai Patel (see Political Circle); leader of the Swatantra Party in Rajya Sabha.

3. *National Herald* was managed by a company, and according to Indira, G. B. Pant was attempting to mobilise the votes of those shareholders in Bombay who could not attend the meeting at Lucknow.

the freedom of the press in India. With all our other ills let us not also have hypocrisy.

Indu

Papu,

This is rather a long letter and I know you are always rushed but PLEASE take a few minutes off, as you would have if I had come myself, and read it properly.

Indu

What happens to the *Herald* will make a big difference in my life.

---

329.                                       [Prime Minister's House],
                                                      New Delhi,
                                          16th December, 1949

Darling Indu,

Your letter of the 16th[1] reached me this afternoon. I can quite understand your distress, nevertheless it does not help to be a victim of it. I have heard something about what is happening regarding the *National Herald* meeting on the 18th. Probably there is a good deal of truth in the stories that have reached us. Probably also there is much exaggeration. In any event the whole business appears to be pretty bad. I do not myself think that anything terrible is going to happen. Indeed, at the worst, nothing terrible can happen. Something has already been done to check this business. If we are to lose our balance because of such things, then life would be a very short business. I have to face much more difficult and distressing situations almost every day.

You are irritated at me because, as you say, everyone says that I ignore such matters and do not help. Perhaps everyone is right. One can only function according to one's own capacity. But most people are rather shortsighted and apt to lose their heads and that does not help. It is just like many persons always shouting out for war against Pakistan or asking us to bring more pressure on Pakistan to do this or that.

As I have said above, I do not think anything terrible is going to happen. We must not lose our perspective, more especially when we have to fight something that we consider evil. You must remember that I am sufficiently interested in the *Herald* not to be a silent spectator of

1. Refers to letter No. 328.

any injury to it. I like the *Herald* and agree with you that it is in some ways the best and the most readable paper in India.

I have made some arrangements for the printing of New Year cards.

Love,
Papu

---

330.                                           Lucknow,
17th December, 1949

Darling Papu,
Your letter[1] has just come.

If you thought that my distress was entirely due to this *Herald* business you would be right in saying that I was losing my balance. But unfortunately it isn't. At the worst the *Herald* will be another 'Ji-Huzoor'[2] paper, although I hope that all decent people connected with it will resign by then and force it to close down. But that is by the way. What is the root of my trouble is the general trend in the country, in all the provinces, although I myself can speak for only this one.

I know you have a lot of big and intricate problems and that it is impossible for you to deal with such small matters. But it is these very small matters which are causing the rot in the country. These are the small drops which have combined to make the giant wave of unpopularity that is inundating the Congress and the Provincial Govts. Can you deny this unpopularity? That what support the present regime has is due to your personal prestige and the fact that the people have no alternative to choose from? What do you think this is due to?

You say I exaggerate. I should be grateful if you would specify just which particular item you consider an exaggeration. Would you like to have a list of the officials who exerted pressure for the collection of proxies? Would you like to meet the officials? How can the truth be proved to you?

And should it be proved that the Govt did in fact use its officials, would you call that corruption or not? Or do you think it is a minor thing for a Govt to act despotically as a matter of course and habit? If they have done so now, what is there to prove that they are not doing it all the time in other matters too?

Indu

---

1. Refers to letter No. 329.
2. Obsequious.

331.                                            Lucknow,
                                        23rd December, 1949

Darling Papu,
You will be off on a tour in a few days so I must hasten to send you my
love and good wishes for the coming New Year.

Darling, I go off the track occasionally – small things by their mere
proximity assume gigantic proportions and one is depressed and frus-
trated. Amongst the myriad articles and tributes that appeared on your
birthday did you see an open letter to you by Saiyidain?[1] In case you
didn't I should like to quote from it because it is so true:

> ... those who criticise you most strongly for all that has not been
> achieved in India ... pay you, entirely unconsciously, a very great
> compliment. They seem to believe that you could have achieved a
> socio-political miracle within two years and that not only is Govern-
> ment an important agency that can revolutionise at will the pattern
> of national life and thought but that you personally can mould the
> Government and its administration into any shape that you like!

And yet you have performed scores of little miracles, achieving so
much that seemed impossible, smoothing out the strings of many a
situation that seemed hopelessly entangled.

And through everything have shone, bright and beautiful as the stars
on a dark night, your courage and your faith. You have truly reached
the heights. What greater glory can I wish for you?

So I shall wish instead that in this New Year, the Indian people may
have real faith in your vision and your tremendous efforts, that they may
take your words to heart and act upon them and that they may partake
of your courage and integrity. And so may 1950 bring us closer to the
fulfilment of your dreams.

                    With all my love to you,
                              Indu

——————————————————

332.                                         Doon Court,
                                             Dehru Dun,
                                           5th July, 1950

Darling Indu,
As I left Delhi this morning at six the rain clouds gathered and it started

1. K. G. Saiyidain: educationist; Secretary, Ministry of Education, Government of
India.

drizzling. Later on the way it rained fairly heavily. It has been very pleasant here – first with the rain in the morning, then the rain stopped and the garden looked lovely. Later the sun came out and Mussoorie was topped by the deep blue sky. I am returning to Delhi tomorrow morning at six fifteen.

I hope you are having a good time at Chakrata. If not then the fault must be yours and not Chakrata's. I am told it is very delightful round about Chakrata – and then there is Deoband which you were so keen on visiting. I suppose you know that the people living in Chakrata tahsil – the Jaunsar people – are rather unique. They have both polygamy & polyandry.

The ex P.M. of Nepal – Juddha Shamsher Jang Rana [1] (the man who gave us the big brass Ganesha) – came to see me today. He said his wife the Maharani was rather ill. She was anxious to see you and give you some mementoes. I wonder if it is possible for you to go to his house for ten minutes or so on your way down. He lives in Young Road, Dehra Dun. It would be worthwhile for you to go there. I suppose anyhow you will break journey at Dehra Dun. The District Magistrate could direct you there. Or, on your way down, stop at the police station at Rajpur and ask for his house.

There is no particular necessity for you to go to the Maharani and you need not put yourself out for it. If it can be arranged easily then you can go.

Love,
Papu

333.

Forest Rest House,
Chakrata,
U.P.,
7th July, 1950

Darling Papu,
Your letter [2] came last evening while I was being fêted by the 'élite' of Chakrata! Afterwards we motored to Chilmari, a rather lovely spot on the road to Mussoorie. Mussoorie is thirty-six miles by the bridle path. In the opposite direction is Simla. In fact you pass the outskirts of Chakrata if you walk or ride from Mussoorie & Simla. The Srinageshs [3]

1. Maharaja Juddha Shamsher Jang Bahadur Rana: Prime Minister of Nepal, 1932–45.
2. Refers to letter No. 332.
3. Mrs and General S. M. Srinagesh. General Srinagesh was Chief of Army Staff, 1955–7, and later Governor of Assam, 1959–62, of Andhra Pradesh, 1962–4, and of Mysore, 1964–5.

went with us. He is a great walker and does about eight miles or more every day. Last evening we walked about a mile on the Mussoorie road. The boys had great fun picking wild flowers – there are not many except daisies – and trying to catch butterflies. Suddenly the top of the highest mountain seen from here appeared above the clouds – the name is Bander Punch, I'm told. Mrs Srinagesh asked Sanjay, '*Woh pahār ki chotī dekhī?*' [1] to which he replied, '*Hamko to khāli pīth dikhtī hai*!' [2] He was right in a way, for it looks much more like a back than a peak. Another remark of his which caused much amusement – he was rushing down a rather sharp incline and the paths here are wet and slippery and full of sharp slatey rocks jutting out, so I yelled out: '*Aste jao!*' [3] Sanjay replied: '*Ham to bilkul aste chalte hain, yahan ki zamīn hi tez hai!*' [4]

After this excursion we walked through the quaint Sadar Bazaar. It is on two sides & the top of a hill with stone steps going up both ways, reminding one of the Valletta in Malta. There is one other bazaar consisting of three shops, called the *lal kurti*! [5]

We usually have a couple of clear hours every day but the rest of the time it pours as if the very heavens had burst. General Srinagesh has sent his car down in advance so as not to risk its being stuck here because of landslides. I wondered if I should do the same.

We are having a good time in spite of not having seen very much of the surroundings. My greatest good fortune is that I manage to enjoy myself or at worst not to be bored wherever I may be & however difficult the circumstances – jail, for instance. In the mountains I am in my element. I love them and the leaf-covered winding paths and the cold rain on my face.

We propose to leave at seven a.m. on the 10th. We had not planned to stop in Dehra except for petrol, but a few minutes at Juddha's won't make much difference.

Much love,
Indu

*Rajiv aur Sanjay Nanu ko pyar bhejten hain.* [6]

---

1. Do you see that mountain peak?
2. I can only see its back!
3. Go slow!
4. I try to walk slowly, but the steep slope makes me run!
5. Red shirt!
6. Rajiv and Sanjay send their love to grandfather.

334.                                         Nasik,
17th September, 1950

Darling Indu,
Nasik has been a surprise – from the weather point of view. When I
arrived here it was cool and even slightly chilly. At night I used a blanket
inside my room. I could have used a warm *sherwani* if I had it here. But
it is not really needed. Probably this is unusual weather.
    Your note [1] has just come.
    I enclose a page from a Bombay paper which might interest you.
                     Love,
                     Papu

---

335.                            The Retreat,
[Mashobra],
30th October, 1950

Darling Papu,
I hope you had a really restful time in Srinagar.
    Mashobra is quite changed since I was last here. The haze of the
monsoon and the damp have gone. The view of the snows is magnificent
– a huge quarter circle from North to East. It is colder in the sense that
the temperature is lower but it is a dry cold which I don't mind and it
feels lovely on one's face.
    Dr Chandravati Parmar, whom you have met at Kurukshetra – called
on me & today I went to lunch with her at Sanjauli. I like her enormously.
Such energy and zeal and enthusiasm. She is now the Assistant Director
of Health in charge of maternity & child welfare in the East Punjab
States. Tomorrow very early in the morning I am going with her to
distribute dried milk to some remote village in the interior beyond Narkanda. We shall probably spend the night at Narkanda.
    Lots of love from us all,
                     Indu

P.S.
My hand is nearly frozen, that is why my handwriting is worse than
usual!

---

1. Note not traceable.

336.　　　　　　　　　　　　　　　　　　[Prime Minister's House],
New Delhi,
1st November, 1950

Indu darling,

Thank you for your letter.[1] I am glad you are enjoying your stay at Mashobra and the dry cold is doing you and the children good.

My two days in Srinagar were pleasant and enjoyable, though they were fairly occupied with engagements. Still, I had some little leisure and I went to the Forest Reserve and then right into the forest for some miles. I had hoped to see a bear or at least a stag. But no animal of any kind was visible. I was surprised to find wild rose bushes with big red berries, almost like cherries. I have brought a number of these. I did not know that a rose tree produced such a berry . . .

I have not been previously attracted much by the papier-mâché work of Kashmir. But on this occasion I was rather struck by it. They have made considerable progress and there are some very attractive designs . . .

Rajiv has evidently improved his Hindi, as appears from his note to me. I am enclosing something for him. I am looking forward to seeing the children pink and healthy when they return from Mashobra.

I have been staying in my new room. I rather like the change. The new room appears a little cosy, although it is big enough, or perhaps I was tired of the old room, having been there now for over two years. I suggest that when you come back, you might arrange the furniture quite differently in the old room, so as to give an appearance of newness.

Love,
Papu

---

337.　　　　　　　　　　　　　　　　　　Srinagar,
28th May, 1951

Darling Papu,

It is so peaceful here, not at all cold but fresh. Except for a brief while in the evenings, one does not need woollens. This evening we walked up to the Chashme Shahi garden and sat on the grass. Rajiv & Sanjay had taken some of their toys, tiny models of a jeep, a bulldozer and a steamroller. In a few moments we were surrounded by some very beautiful & lively children who were quite fascinated by the toys. They exam-

---

1. Refers to letter No. 335.

ined them minutely and asked a lot of questions, and stayed with us the whole time we were there.

The Yuvraj came yesterday. Today I thought I would call on him & the Yuvrani but they were out fishing.

We are moving into a houseboat on the 1st for just one day to allow Tulsi to take the luggage, tents, etc, to Pahalgam. We will follow on the 2nd.

The children are well and send their love. Rajiv says he will write soon.

I hope it is not too hot in Delhi and that your day is slightly less strenuous. I hope later on after the trip to Kathmandu you will be able to take a couple of days off and come here.

Love,<br>
Indu

---

338.                                              Pahalgam,<br>
20th July, 1951

Darling Papu,

I felt so guilty coming away when you are staying in that awful weather. Pahalgam is lovely. I believe they had torrential rains while I was away but since yesterday the weather has behaved, which is a good thing for I have got a dreadful chest, cold & cough.

The people here are very worried – Liaquat Ali's [1] statements & the talk of troops has created a panic amongst the visitors & they are rushing to book their seats for the return journey. [2] I think the Govt should issue some kind of statement that there is no danger. Janki Nath [3] & others are pressing me to stay on a bit as my staying might reassure the others. I have bought a lot of odd things I don't need – only because the hawkers are so pathetically eager to sell & there is hardly anyone to buy.

Love,<br>
Indu

---

1. Liaquat Ali Khan: Prime Minister of Pakistan, 1947–51.
2. Refers to the development of a tense situation on the Indo-Pakistan border as a result of some speeches of Liaquat Ali Khan.
3. Janki Nath Shurga: husband of Jawaharlal Nehru's cousin, Brij Mohan Rani.

339.                                            [Prime Minister's House],
                                                       New Delhi,
                                                    23rd July, 1951

Indu darling,
Your letter.[1] You need not feel guilty at all. The thought that you and
the children are at Pahalgam makes me feel better than I would otherwise do. I really do not mind the heat. I hardly think of it. There are
too many other things to think and worry about.

I think you should certainly stay on in Pahalgam. What is the point
of returning early? It does not matter if the children lose a few days'
school.

I don't think there is going to be any war. If there is a war then
Pahalgam might well be a quieter place, and perhaps safer also, than
Delhi!

Maulana has brought rather a good painting and a piece of *zar-baft*
(gold tapestry) for us from Iran.

Yesterday – or was it day before – Mathai took me to the swimming
pool in Govt House in the evening.

I enclose a copy of the best of exercises I showed you. Some of them
are good. Try them.

                              Love,
                              Papu

___

340.                                                   Pahalgam,
                                                    27th July, 1951

Darling Papu,
Your letter[2] came last night. What a time you have been having! I can
well understand that the weather is the least of your troubles.

Here it is cold and since my arrival we have been having cloudy
weather with rain off and on. Everybody says that as it is still so hot in
Delhi, the children will probably lose all that they have built up these
two months in Kashmir within a few days in Delhi. I don't know what
to do. We can't stay on indefinitely. Rajiv has missed three weeks of
school because of chicken pox just before the holidays. On the other
hand their health is more important than school and this muggy heat is
not healthy like the dry heat.

1. Refers to letter No. 338.
2. Refers to letter No. 339.

Apart from this small personal problem, the failure of the monsoon will have terrible results as far as crops are concerned.

I heard from Tara that Gautam's youngest sister is getting engaged to V. P. Menon's[1] son.

Darling, you don't have to reassure me about the war! I am not afraid of such things and in any case there are plenty of people looking after me. What I was concerned about [was] the effect on the tourists in Kashmir – large numbers left in a panic. Pahalgam is quite empty & I believe Srinagar also.

The boys continue their riding. Now Sanjay also rides on his own without the syce holding on to his horse. They also bathe in the river every sunny day.

We have a youth camp quite close to us. There are sixty-three boys. The camp commandant is an Australian, Mr Edwards, who belongs to the Bisco Missionary School in Srinagar. He is a queer character but loves the boys and I am sure they love him. We are joining their camp fire tonight. Sheikh Saheb's two sons are in the camp.

Rajiv, Sanjay, Anna & I are going to Aru[2] for the day – tomorrow – if it doesn't rain.

Love,<br>Indu

341.                                [Prime Minister's House],<br>                                            New Delhi,<br>                                   28th January, 1952

Darling Indu,

This is just to send you my love – come back soon. You have had enough of these elections.[3] After my return from touring on the 21st night, my mind turned away from elections and I hardly have the patience now to read the long lists of election returns.

I am anxious to have you back here before you fall ill and take to bed. Puphi is bedridden. I have been, in a way, having a quiet time. Not very quiet, and there was plenty of work. But there was more rest than usual

---

1. V. P. Menon: eminent civil servant; Reforms Commissioner, 1942–7; Secretary to the Government of India, Ministry of States, 1947–51; member, Finance Commission, 1951–2.

2. A picnic spot about ten kilometres from Pahalgam.

3. The first General Election held in India on the basis of the new Constitution which had come into force on 26th January, 1950 took place between October 1951 and March 1952.

and Boshi Sen rubbed and thumped me twice a day. That has done me good and I feel rested. Boshi will be going away tonight.

There is a Shakespearian play here (Eric Elliott's company) on Feb. 1st night. Try to come by then if you can manage it without inconvenience. You will like it.

The next month is going to be a heavy one for me. Heavy not only because of work but more so because of decisions to be made.

Edwina writes to say that she might come here in the second or third week of February on her way to Japan, etc.

Give my love to Feroze and keep a lot of it for yourself.

Love,
Papu

---

342.                                                  M.S. *Batory*, [1]
                                                     21st April, 1953

Darling Papu,

Because of favourable weather, we are making good time and have saved a day – we are reaching all our ports, including Southampton, a day ahead of schedule.

Last evening we spent a few hours at Aden. How enormously it has changed and grown since I saw it last. It is full of huge modern buildings. Our consul there is one Thadani[2] – he is related to Jairamdas Doulatram. [3] He told me that the Indian community there is very backward, especially the women. When Kamaladevi[4] was passing through some time ago the community gathered together to arrange a meeting for her. Although she was very tired and reluctant to speak, she spoke on the emancipation of women – this offended them deeply and when she was leaving not a soul went to see her off!

Thadani said there is a lot of discrimination and it is growing. Indians are not allowed in the cinema, or swimming pool or club, where Europeans go. At first Thadani was given a diplomatic pass but as he was the only Asian, they didn't like the idea much and have now withdrawn all diplomatic passes and diplomats – they are only at the consul's level

---

1. Indira Gandhi was on her way to London to attend the coronation ceremony of Queen Elizabeth. Her father (see letter No. 347) joined her in the month of May.

2. A. B. Thadani: Commissioner of India in Aden, 1952–3; First Secretary, High Commissioner of India, Karachi, 1955.

3. Jairamdas Doulatram: General Secretary of the Indian National Congress, 1931–4. Later a minister in the Indian Cabinet.

4. Kamaladevi Chattopadhyaya: socialist and pioneering leader of the women's movement in India.

of course – have been asked to apply again. Thadani says that he has been in Aden for a full three years – when K.P.S. [1] passed through he mentioned of his own accord that he would write to Ext. Off. about a transfer. I believe Papi [2] is in charge of this side.

We have a most luxurious suite – in fact it is known as the 'bridal' suite. It was going empty so the captain very kindly offered it to us without any extra charge. We have two spacious cabins on the promenade deck with a special entrance from the deck and two bathrooms.

There are a lot of Pakistanis on board – the ship touches at Karachi. What is happening in Pakistan? We get the scantiest of news.

Love from us all,<br>Indu

Amongst the passengers is a K. B. Lal. He was Dist. Magistrate of Bidar when you went there.

343.            Camp: Ludhiana,
                 25th April, 1953

Darling Indu,

I am writing to you from an odd place – Ludhiana. It is easier to write or dictate from such places than from Delhi where I get immersed in my normal work. I have come to Ludhiana for a day and a half to see some military exercises that are going on here. I am here, therefore, in my capacity as Minister of Defence.

I do not quite know where you are at present. I imagine you should be round about Port Said. I hope the voyage has been pleasant. In any event, the unpleasant part in the Red Sea and the Suez Canal must be over. I gather that you are travelling in great luxury in some kind of a royal suite. This letter is timed to reach you when you arrive in London.

Padmaja came to Delhi soon after you left. A day or two later Papi's birthday was celebrated and we were made to dress up for the occasion. Of course, it is easy to dress up when I can provide gowns in various shapes and colours to any number of persons. Padmaja has decided to accompany me during my Maharashtra tour. I shall be glad to have her of course, but I am a little nervous about her capacity to stand the strain of this kind of touring. I am going to travel more than 200 miles a day, apart of course from meetings and speech-making. Padmaja says that

1. K. P. S. Menon: member of the Indian Civil Service, later became Foreign Secretary of India.
2. Leilamani Naidu (Papi): daughter of Sarojini Naidu; served in the Indian Foreign Service, 1948–58.

she will rest while I am attending meetings. I am rather looking forward to some parts at least of this tour as I have not been to that part of the West coast before. This includes Ratnagiri, Kolhapur and Ahmadnagar. In Ahmadnagar I shall, of course, visit the old fort and have a look at the place where I lived with others for nearly three years.

We have changed the venue of our conference [1] in Switzerland from Lucerne to a place near Lucerne (about fifteen kilometres away) which is much quieter and, I am told, very beautiful. In fact, it is specially meant for quiet conferences. I forget the name. I think it is called something like Bergenstock. You can find out the actual name from Mr Kher. I think this place will be better than Lucerne which will be crowded with the ordinary tourists. It will be easy for us to go to Lucerne when we want to.

The chief piece of news is that Rita has got engaged to Avtar Krishna Dar of our Foreign Service. Rita broke the news rather suddenly. I suppose she was hurried into some kind of a decision by the fact that Dar is being transferred in about a month's time to Cairo. Puphi is giving us all a party to relatives and others soon to announce the engagement formally to them. Dar appears to me to be a good boy, quiet, rather retiring and shy. He is hard-working.

Last night, I saw a puppet dance show. This took place at Rashtrapati Bhawan and a large number of people were invited to it. I liked the show and I think that we should encourage this kind of medium both for our children and adults.

The military exercises here are on a large scale. The idea is that two hypothetical countries have had a quarrel and one of them invades the other rather suddenly. In these exercises they name these countries Nark and Swarg and a third country nearby is Sansar. Nark is an unfortunate name to give to any country. I tried to get it changed, but it was too late for it. So now the armies of Nark and Swarg are supposed to be locked in armed conflict. There is, of course, a great deal of make-believe about it all. But it is rather fun. We have press communiqués being issued by the respective Governments in justification of their action and we have, in a small way, all the paraphernalia of war without any actual firing. There is also a good deal of makebelieve in another sense. A motor truck may represent half a dozen tanks, the reason being that, as far as possible, we want to save our tanks. Large numbers of umpires move about and declare that a certain tank is out of action or

---

1. Jawaharlal Nehru attended the coronation of Queen Elizabeth II and the Commonwealth Prime Ministers' Conference in London in May–June 1953. He also spent six days (17th–22nd June) in Switzerland where he held a meeting of Indian Ambassadors in Europe.

that somebody is a casualty. Aircraft hover above and are supposed to bomb. The umpire declares that a place has been bombed.

In spite of all this makebelieve, there is a good deal of reality about the organisation and it is very good practice and experience for the officers and men. Headquarters officers with all their paraphernalia as well as Division or Brigade Headquarters suddenly move backwards and forwards and establish themselves in a new place. They are camouflaged, telephone lines have to be laid quickly and a constant supply of news has to come from various fronts. An amusing incident took place. One tough N.C.O. refused to retire when, by all the rules of the game, he was surrounded and ought to have retired with his men. He said that he would not retire and that if he was disabled, his men would fight on! The General had to tell him that he would declare him a casualty and have him carried away if he did not retire.

The general level of our younger officers seems to be quite good. Some of the foreign military attachés present here have been impressed by them.

You will see Betty and Harsha. Please give my love to Harsha and tell him that, by the time I come, I hope he will be fit and strong.

I have received a special invitation to visit the Indian section of the Victoria and Albert Museum. I should like to go there if I have the time. Try to go there yourself and take the children. Take the children also specially to the South Kensington Museum. I am sure they will enjoy it.

If Isobel Cripps is within reach, you should try to see her; also Mrs Laski.

My love to you and Rajiv and Sanjay,
Papu

——————————————————————

344.                                            Camp: Ahmadnagar,
                                                   1st May, 1953

Indu darling,
I am writing this letter to you from Ahmadnagar. I have just completed four days of my Maharashtra tour. Two more days remain and then I go to Bombay, and thence to Delhi, on the 4th May.

As usual, the tour has been a heavy one and my average journey for the day works out at over 200 miles by road, with a number of meetings roped in. In addition, I have to stop my car every few miles because a crowd gathers there. The meetings have been on a big scale. Yesterday I had a very big meeting at Sholapur, estimated at nearly two hundred thousand and three other meetings each going up to a hundred thousand. I suppose, at a moderate estimate, during these six days, I shall have covered about a thousand miles by road and directly addressed about a million people, apart from those I pass on the roadside. I never cease to be astonished at this response of the people and their excitement at seeing me. Naturally, I am deeply moved. The Maharashtrians are not supposed to be demonstrative, but they have been quite excited about my visit, not only the urban people, but perhaps even more so the rural people.

My main purpose to come here was to see the scarcity areas and the works undertaken there. On the whole, the Bombay Government has dealt with the situation with promptitude and more or less effectively. There are a large number of works. The people working there did not seem to me to be emaciated at all. Only in some free kitchens where the old go to are there signs of emaciation.

My first day landed me at Sawantwadi, a small State which is now merged in Ratnagiri district. Sawantwadi was the original home town of Ranjit Pandit's father. The ex-ruler of the place, an attractive young man, was our host. His mother is the sister of the Maharaja of Baroda who was recently pushed out in favour of his son. His wife is the daughter of the same ex-Maharaja, which is rather an odd combination for India. Sawantwadi was a pleasant little place in the hills, not far from the sea, but rather stuffy.

The next day we went on to Ratnagiri and later to Kolhapur. This was my first visit to this area. Ratnagiri, by the seaside, is the real home of the *Alphonso* mango. Unfortunately I have been unable to do full justice to the *Alphonso*, because I have not yet completely recovered from the little upset I had even while you were here. However, the situation is well under control.

Apart from some tour on the hills on the first day, we have been mostly moving about in the plains and it has been pretty hot, the temperature usually being 110 in the shade. There was very little shade in some of the arid plains we passed through. Occasionally, however, there was the Gul Mohur all aflame. That reminds me that Delhi at present is full of bright flowering trees. Mathai took me specially to see them in Connaught Circus, which was a blaze of colours because of the Gul Mohur trees. Elsewhere the cassia or laburnum are in bloom, and then there is the jacquaranda (I do not know the spelling correctly). Our garden is not showing off any of these trees particularly well, but elsewhere they are in full glory. Padmaja has thus far kept up to the mark, although the pace of this tour is hard on her. Our hosts have been interesting folk. The first night the Raja of Sawantwadi; the second, the District Magistrate of Kolhapur, a young Muslim with an intelligent wife; and the third night at Sholapur the District Magistrate who is a

Parsee. Here in Ahmadnagar, the District Magistrate, who is also a Muslim, though he has rather a Hindu name . . .

   Love to you and the children,

Papu

---

345. Dhulia,<br>West Khandesh,<br>2nd May, 1953

Darling Indu,

Yesterday at Ahmednagar I dictated a letter [1] to you. I forgot to mention in it the very thing that had impressed me most and rather moved me. This was my visit to the fort where I had spent over two and a half years of my life. Inevitably all kinds of memories assailed me and I stayed on rather longer than was intended and upset my subsequent programme.

To my amazement I found a board up in the wrong room indicating that I had stayed there. This was not a slight mistake. They had put me as well as the others in a different wing altogether. Why? I was told that they had done this on the best authority! Indeed they were reluctant to accept my evidence! I realised how very easily history and even the most obvious facts are likely to be distorted. If I had not gone there, the wrong room in the wrong wing would have been permanently fixed as my place of residence.

There was a pomegranate tree also which was described as having been planted by me. I did not plant it.

Today I completed my fifth day of tour and I am feeling somewhat worn out. It has been hard going and the heat and the dust and the frequent stops at almost every village have exhausted me – another day and then I go back to Delhi . . .

Love to all of you from,<br>Papu

---

346. 48 The Grove,<br>Isleworth,<br>Mdx.,<br>5th May, 1953

Darling Papu,

What a shock it was to get up this morning and see the word 'Bomb'

---

1. Refers to letter No. 344.

practically jumping out of the headlines to meet the eyes! Afterwards, I was weak with relief. Fortunately Mathai had had the good sense to send a cable yesterday.

Dr Bhandari, Dharam Vira[1] & somebody called Zaman came to Southampton and brought us here by car. Surrey is one of the loveliest spots in England. And England in spring is really unbelievably beautiful. After a very wretched and long winter, the day we arrived was really the first day of fine weather. I hope it stays like this. It's just perfect – warm but fresh and bracing too – the trees dressed in such shiny new leaves; the countryside bright with yellow gowan and the different pinks of blossoms: peach, cherry, plum. The rhododendrons are out too and the gaudy-coloured tulips and daffodils and the gentle anemones, irises, lilies of the valley.

In London itself there is feverish activity: poor old Eros is being put into what looks like a gilded cage. All the statues and columns are being polished up and cleaned. Hideous stands all along the 'route'.

The children had a most wonderful voyage, enjoying every minute of it. And here they are so full of excitement at everything they see, I almost feel as if I too were seeing London for the first time. Yesterday we went to town & bought them a new suit each. Rajiv has got himself a pair of leather gloves which he refuses to take off. This afternoon I am taking them to see *Peter Pan*, a Walt Disney film.

Dr Bhandari has a nice house – we have a lot of space and a garden but oh so so suburban. I think one should live in the heart of a city or the heart of the country. This in-betweenness is too depressing.

We went to see Harsha in hospital. He is very depressed, poor chap. I heard (not from the Hutheesings who probably don't know) that if the leg had been left as it was fixed in Bombay, he might have had to have it amputated later on. As it is, it will surely heal but one doesn't know if it will be shorter than the other leg. I hope not.

I rang up Krishna – will see him tomorrow. This place is so very far out, it takes an hour to go anywhere. I don't know how to manage the museums. Perhaps, when I move to Kher it will be easier. I go there on the 11th.

Love from us all,

Indu

---

1. Dharam Vira was Principal Private Secretary to Jawaharlal Nehru in 1950–1. At this juncture he was Commercial Adviser to the Indian High Commissioner in London; was later Cabinet Secretary and Secretary to Union Council of Ministers, and Governor of West Bengal.

347.

[Prime Minister's House],
New Delhi,
8th May, 1953

Indu darling,

Mathai will send you the revised version of my programme in London. [1]
This is getting filled in. I am anxious to keep a good deal of time free
because I shall have to see many people there, individually and separately. There are a number of Prime Ministers. I shall have to give a
good deal of time to the Pakistan Prime Minister. [2] Also to the Ceylon
Prime Minister [3] and, of course, Sir Winston and St Laurent, [4] apart
from others.

As you perhaps know, I shall proceed on arrival in London direct to
Mr Kher's house. From there I shall go to India House for a couple of
hours or so, returning for an early dinner with Mr Kher. After dinner
I intend going to Broadlands. Probably Edwina will come and call for
me at Kher's house.

I hope you will be coming to Kher's house for dinner that evening,
if not earlier. I should, of course, like you to come to Broadlands. I am
sure Edwina will love it. But it is for you entirely to decide what you
would prefer to do during that weekend. I shall return from Broadlands
on Sunday night.

I understand that we shall be staying at Claridges. I shall therefore
go to Claridges on Sunday night and you can also come there then.

The Mountbattens will probably reach London a few days before I
do. I think you should pay them a visit. Edwina wants to fix up some
theatres to go to. I know nothing about the places at present.

During the next few days in London, you will be accompanying me
to many functions. To some, like Prime Ministers' Conference, you
will not of course go. You can fix up your own programme for those
occasions.

I suppose you will accompany me to Spithead to the Naval Review. I
intend going on board our cruiser *Delhi* at that time. Probably before I
go to the *Delhi*, I shall visit for a while Lord Mountbatten's flag ship.

Krishna Menon must have met you. I need not tell you that he
requires a friendly and affectionate approach. He feels rather out of it
and frets a great deal. I have fixed no time to see him. Probably I shall

1. Refers to Jawaharlal Nehru's programme during his proposed visit to London to
attend the coronation of Queen Elizabeth.
2. Mohammad Ali: Prime Minister of Pakistan, 1953–5.
3. Dudley (Shelton) Senanayake: Prime Minister of Sri Lanka.
4. Louis Stephen St Laurent: Prime Minister of Canada, 1948–57.

see him on arrival for a little while and then I can fix up other times when I am in Claridges.

I have been terribly busy since my return from the Maharashtra tour. Among other things, our honourable two Houses of Parliament nearly came to blows with each other over a relatively trivial matter. However, I have succeeded in pouring oil over these troubled waters! I am likely to be hard-worked right to the last moment of my departure from Delhi. I had hoped to go to Allahabad for a couple of days, but that seems difficult now. I also wanted to go to Kashmir for a weekend . . . That too seems difficult for a variety of reasons.

I received your letter [1] from somewhere *en route*, probably Port Said, and I was glad to know that the children had been enjoying themselves. I do not know where you are now and where you will be when this letter reaches London. Perhaps you might have gone to Switzerland. I shall not see them till I reach Switzerland myself. Give my love to them and tell Rajiv that I got his card and liked it.

I have noted what you have said about the Consulate at Port Said and I shall enquire about it . . .

Padmaja is here and will stay on, I suppose, as long as I am here.

The big Jaipur lamp has been shifted to its place just above the stairs. This is very effective and, in the evenings, the light and shade effect on the stairs and the surrounding walls is very attractive indeed. It looks like a piece of tracery. I am very fond of this lamp and it cheers me up whenever I see it.

Love,<br>
Papu

---

348.                    9 Kensington Palace Gardens,

London,<br>
11th May, 1953

Darling Papu,
Your letter from Ahmadnagar [2] – or rather, about Ahmadnagar.

I have just come from the House of Commons where Churchill spoke on foreign affairs. He seems to have undergone as much of a change of heart as the Russians. I sat in the diplomatic gallery and quite near by there was a bejewelled gentleman (Nepalese, perhaps) who snored throughout the speech. And whatever else Churchill may be, he isn't ever dull.

---

1. Possibly refers to letter No. 342.
2. Refers to letter No. 344.

We moved from Bhandari's today after a most exhausting morning. While Rajiv & I were inside the house, packing, Sanjay was playing in the garden. It seems he suddenly conceived the idea of going for a walk on his own, arrived at the Great West Road – one of the worst from the heavy traffic point of view – and then couldn't remember which turning to take for the way home. He wasn't a bit upset, just walked up to someone & said, 'I've lost my way.' The man phoned the police, who sent a car to pick him up and there he sat at Brentford Police Station, happily sucking a toffee! In the meantime all of us at home were searching frantically for him. Finally I rang the police and within ten minutes I spoke to him on the phone and 'got his story'! He didn't know the address but he did tell them that he was staying with Dr Bhandari. But being an Indian name and with his special pronunciation they couldn't make out what it was. His own name also they couldn't understand & he wrote it out for them in large block letters! Throughout he behaved so calmly and nonchalantly that the police thought he must be used to getting lost! He is really very sweet.

I must say I am feeling very proud of the children – they have been so good, helping me in every way they could. There were so many children on the ship and here one sees them in the park and everywhere but everyone remarks how well behaved these two are and at the same time obviously happy and enjoying themselves. They are happier here in this house because the Kher's grandchildren are here, aged twelve, eight, & two and a half, and the house is touching on Kensington Gardens. I have taken care to make Sanjay learn this address.

I have seen Krishna Menon several times; he comes to all my functions and I have had lunch & dinner with him. He seems to be remarkably fit and cheerful. At the dinner he was complaining of some pain but he ate well and was full of jokes and stories – in fact it was quite difficult to break up the party at midnight! I see from the papers that he is standing for the Council of States.

I should prefer *not* to go to Broadlands the first weekend – if you are definitely going there again. But we can decide later.

Much love,<br>Indu

---

349.                                    [9 Kensington Palace Gardens],
                                                        London,
                                                  17th May, 1953

Darling Papu,

...I am going off to Switzerland tomorrow morning. Our Cottage

Industries exhibition is opening on the 27th, but there is a press preview on the 26th, so I shall return on the 26th morning or evening of the 25th. I didn't want to stay here but Kher Sahib is insisting and it is rather awkward. I should like to take rooms somewhere near the exhibition.

This house is so lovely – beautifully furnished – but rather dead. I'm terribly disappointed in Kher Sahib. He is so easily taken in, so hedged in with prejudices. Full of talk of India's culture and Sanskrit and yet terribly flattered when some ex-Governor of Bombay asks him to a meal. He isn't really interested in politics or foreign affairs. He seems quite unaware of the currents & cross-currents. He doesn't seem to have contacts with anybody except those old fogies of ex-justices & ex-Governors. He can at best act messenger boy for you – he can't possibly have any initiative or even understanding of your policies. Some of the younger men in India House think that the Foreign Office make fun of him by telling him things that practically everyone knows but asking him to keep it confidential. Whereupon he is tremendously flattered & hesitates even to mention the matter in a cable to you! Somebody – not Haksar [1] – told me that Haksar has to write out the simplest things for him. It is a really distressing situation. Even Agatha, who is so mild, is agitated. Kher is quite good socially, but politically he is quite insignificant. These are *such* critical times. Can there be any poverty worse than this poverty of men? At a time when we can influence people and practically change the world there doesn't seem to be anyone for these important posts . . .

For the club function four thirty to six is quite enough, I think, and you should put your foot down. Anyhow I have done it for you & told Kher Sahib that you will be leaving at six at the latest and we are putting forward the India League function to seven (you can arrive later of course) so that you will be quite free by eight thirty for dinner & Broadlands. Otherwise you would have to eat at seven thirty, immediately after a heavy tea at the club & would be late for Broadlands. I hope this won't create a fresh situation with Krishna.

Talking of Broadlands, I have changed my mind. I will come with you the first weekend. The second I go to Bristol.

Is Edwina doing anything about plays? It will be very difficult to get good seats. You don't seem to have a single evening free. Kher Sahib hasn't been to a play, concert or any kind of good entertainment since he is High Commissioner!

---

1. P. N. Haksar: member of the Indian Foreign Service, was at that time Counsellor, Indian High Commission in London. Later became Principal Private Secretary to Indira Gandhi when she was Prime Minister. Also author and distinguished intellectual.

To go back to Krishna, I know he is quite moody & extremely irksome but he does have a brain and a keen awareness of the world situation. Agatha is quite dazzled at the way he handled the U.N. She says that everyone was full of admiration and that it was a truly wonderful bit of work. She says she knows that Krishna had a great deal to do with the tone of Attlee's speech and even indirectly of Churchill's. Selwyn Lloyd [1] told her that Krishna sometimes drives him crazy but he has to turn to him for consultation and advice because with his vast knowledge & interest combined with his experience, he is quite useful.

What a problem it is. Krishna's staying in London can never be a success while Kher is here (he is just as childish about this as Krishna himself) and Kher will feel burdened, & unhappy. But if Krishna leaves London, we will lose touch with the centre of things and will sink to our former position of running behind & trying to catch on. And lastly if you remove Kher, who *can* you have? Nobody can think of a single name. It's the same in China. It's all very depressing.

Krishna himself hasn't spoken at all except about students' affairs & his not being able to see you when you are here. This I have fixed with Dharam Vira, that a car should be sent to take Krishna to the airport and to see that he comes in the V.I.P. enclosure.

Krishna gave Sanjay a Brownie box camera. You should have seen the way his eyes shone. He, Sanjay, told me that I must not interfere – he went alone to buy the films and would not accept any advice about focusing or anything else. The snapshots, especially one of me, have come out quite well and he is mighty proud of himself!

I haven't been able to see Bee. Just no time. The India House boys are most alarmed at her taking over the tourist publicity. They say she is more interested in getting invitations than anything else.

You must have heard that Harsha's stitches were removed the day before yesterday. The whole family was in a state – I went to give moral support. The leg has healed beautifully. Tomorrow Harsha will take his first step with crutches. He can leave hospital on the 21st.

Much love,
Indu

---

1. Selwyn Lloyd: British Foreign Secretary, 1955–60; later held the post of Chancellor of the Exchequer, Lord Privy Seal and Speaker of the House of Commons.

350.                            Prime Minister's House,
New Delhi,
19th May, 1953

Darling Indu,

Thank you for your letters.[1] Your account of the beauty of the English countryside now makes a strange contrast with Delhi in May. I am rather looking forward to getting away from this treadmill and breathing some fresh air for a while. Meanwhile, I am trying my hardest to get through as much work as possible. I have a slight feeling of apprehension as to what [will] happen here during my absence. There is so much petty trouble and always a chance of its growing.

Anyway I shall be with you in just ten days from today and I am greatly looking forward to seeing you.

On the 29th when I arrive I shall be going to India House in the afternoon. I would like to visit Harsha also that day.

I have decided to spend the next weekend in Srinagar – Saturday & Sunday. Padmaja will probably go there also – she has never been to Kashmir.

When I was in Maharashtra I got a message from the Vice-Chancellor of Cambridge informing me that the Senate had decided to confer an honorary LL.D. on me. But my presence on June 4th morning was essential. This clashed with the P.M.s' Conference and so regretfully I had to tell the V.C. that I could not come. There the matter ended. Two days ago I learnt that Winston Churchill had heard of this and in order to suit my convenience, he has postponed that session of the P.M.s' Conference. So I shall be going to Cambridge on June 4th morning – will you come with me? It will be a rush by car there and back, but the countryside will be pleasing.

All my love,
Papu

———————————————

351.                            Embassy of India,
Moscow,
25th June [1953]

Darling Papu,

K.P.S. tells me the bag closes tomorrow so I must dash off these few lines to send my love.

I am so excited to be here and deeply moved too. My first impression at

———

1. Refers to letters Nos 346 and 348.

the airports of Minsk and Moscow and during the drive in town was almost of being in some part of India. The weather is like March in Delhi. But of course Moscow is quite unique. Nowhere else are there such wide, wide streets and such enormous squares. The traffic, vehicles & pedestrians, look quite scanty now but the streets are being planned for future years.

I went to 'Volks', the people who look after foreigners, this morning. K.P.S. had drawn up a rough programme but I told Prof. Dinesov that if he had any suggestions we could change or add to the plan. The Prof., a most genial man with no hair (it's shaved off), remarked, 'Now isn't that just like a woman – to make a plan and to want to change it?' I replied, 'No, it's like the Soviet Union. You make plans but you want to achieve more than the plan.' The old man was very pleased and immediately drank a toast to Indian women!

I have already been to a ballet – the *Bronze Horseman*. Spent two hours in the Metro, and two hours driving around the town, getting off at strategic points such as the Red Square, Gorky Park, new University, etc. This evening K.P.S. had a diplomatic reception. Volks are sorry the children did not accompany me – they had prepared a special programme for them!

Volks have asked me to speak on the radio. I didn't give any definite answer as I wasn't sure what I should say. I said something about making statements without knowing a country, whereupon they replied that they didn't want me to talk about the U.S.S.R. but about India.

Do take a couple of days off if you possibly can.

Lots of love,<br>Indu

I shall be in Moscow until the 2nd.

---

352.                            [Prime Minister's House],
New Delhi,<br>1st July, 1953

Darling Indu,

So I am back to the dust and heat of Delhi – very much to the dust and heat! Except for a brief shower before I came, there has been no rain here and a pall of dust surrounds us. The air services are affected and I was held up for a day in Bombay.

It is depressing to come back to the same old problems – not the major ones but the others which irritate. Dr Syama Prasad Mookerjee's [1] sud-

---

1. S. P. Mookerjee: Hindu Mahasabha leader of Bengal; Union Minister for Industry and Supply, 1947–50; founder of Jan Sangh; died in detention in Kashmir, 1953.

den death in Srinagar has excited people greatly, especially in Bengal, and all kinds of allegations are being made.

It was delightful to have you and the children with me for a few days. But it has its drawbacks – I miss you later.

Feroze is here, not looking too happy but otherwise well. Padmaja has come back from Kashmir. Meanwhile Kashmir is a cauldron of unreason and intrigue.

We have had a diversion – the Everest Party – and numerous functions in their honour. Tenzing [1] is a very decent man – I like him. His wife and daughters have also come. He is going off to England from here. He has hardly any clothes and so I had a bright idea and gave him a boxful of mine, which fit him tolerably well.

Last night we saw a film taken by our Air Force of Everest. It is excellent and our I.A.F. boys are justifiably proud of their feat. They flew round and round Everest for over an hour.

I enclose a picture from the *Illustrated Weekly* – I like it.

Love,<br>Papu

---

353.

Embassy of India,<br>Moscow,<br>17th July, 1953

Darling Papu,

I am always rather shaky after a big plane trip and we have just come from Sochi – five and a half hours. But I am told the bag must leave immediately.

Your telegram [2] about my making statements. I had no intention of doing so here or in India. Everywhere we have been there have been dinners and toasts, confined to peace, greetings to the Indian people, closer cultural relations, health, etc. I don't think this pattern will change in this country anyhow.

Everybody – the Russians – have been so sweet to me. The trip has been wonderful. In Tashkant (Uzbekistan) I rushed about madly and saw every different kind of institution. We went to Samarkand, for the glory that was. Then Tiflis (Georgia) which is quite quite different – all the young men looked like Stalin and all the women like his mother! Everywhere we saw people of different departments and asked hundreds of questions – some quite impertinent!

1. Sherpa Tenzing: mountaineer; the first to scale Mt. Everest, along with Edmund Hillary in May 1953.
2. Telegram not traceable.

The last three days in Sochi were just for holiday and it was a very thorough one. I don't think I have had such a holiday for years. We stayed in a small house reserved for Government officials right by the sea. The Black Sea was very calm and like a lake or the Mediterranean. She must have sensed my disappointment because the very next day there arose a storm and then she was changing her dress every five minutes and nobody could decide which was the most beautiful. It was fascinating to watch. We swam and lay on the pebbly beach – uncomfortable but quite lovely because of the different coloured stones. And believe it or not got sunburnt – really burnt. Red & swollen and painful! But in spite of it I am feeling and looking very well.

I have a few days in Moscow. Aruna Asaf Ali is here in hospital. She has to be operated upon for a tumour but is so anaemic that she has to have some treatment first. I don't know if visitors are allowed. I have asked to go & see her. I also want to meet 'La Pasionaria' – Dolores Ibarruri. [1] She may be out of Moscow.

I am being treated like everybody's only daughter – I shall be horribly spoilt by the time I leave. Nobody has ever been so nice to me.

K.P.S. & Mrs Menon and Prakash Kaul (Second Secretary to the Embassy) were on the trip. I was rather embarrassed because the Russians always gave me the place of honour. K.P.S. gets very easily tired, can't climb stairs or walk much, so most of the time we had to leave them at home. Prakash was very useful. He speaks Russian well and seems to have taken some trouble to find out as much as possible (which isn't much) about the country. Anyhow he got on very well with our companions. We had three. One official from Protocol dept. of the Foreign Office. One from Protocol dept. of Volks (the Society for Cultural Relations, whose guest I was) and an interpreter.

Well, lots of love,
Indu

---

354.                                            Hotel Astoria,
Leningrad,
25th July, 1953

Darling Papu,
We came here yesterday – I am accompanied by Madame Kislova,

---

1. La Pasionaria (Dolores Ibarruri): leader of the Communist Party in Spain.

Vice-Chairperson of the All Union Society for Cultural Relations with foreign countries, a protocol officer of the same society, a protocol officer of the Foreign Office, an interpreter & Sathe, First Secretary to the Embassy of India. The evening we left, the Society gave what they called an informal dinner and I was loaded with presents. We came to Leningrad by train – the Red Arrow – I think it is one of the old pre-Revolution ones, like the *wagon-lit* Pullman cars, but rather slow.

Leningrad is a truly beautiful city – the present Govt has done its utmost to preserve the architectural harmony of the city. Many many buildings still wear the scars of the last war but from all accounts the reconstructional work has been quite monumental. It is still the city of Peter the Great – we saw the little house in which he lived as well as the palaces built later. The Hermitage Museum has a wonderful collection of European paintings – also collection of arts from China, Ancient Egypt and a small one consisting mainly of armour from India.

I have a suite of rooms – bedrooms, bathroom, sitting room, dining room and study. Wallowing in luxury! The hotel has a lot of foreigners – they may have come for the International Free Auction.

With lots of love,<br>
Indu

355.                              Prime Minister's House,
                                           New Delhi,
                                    2nd August, 1953

Darling Indu – I have two very interesting letters[1] from you from Russia. I have not written myself as I was not sure where to catch you. This is a brief note sent to the school in Suisse – I hope you will get it and with it all my love.

Tomorrow Parliament begins at eight a.m. Meanwhile Holland,[2] the New Zealand P.M., is here with wife and daughter. But my real headache is Kashmir where Sheikh Saheb has turned many somersaults and is bitter against India and me. The situation there is explosive and anything may happen.

Krishna Menon is coming here tomorrow for brief consultations. He will stay here for five or six days & then go back to London and New York for the U.N. which meets on Aug 17 You will miss him.

We are all looking forward greatly to your & the children's return.

1. Possibly refers to letters Nos 351 and 353.
2. Sir Sidney George Holland: New Zealand politician and Prime Minister (1949–57).

The house will wake up again. Padmaja has been here looking after me and has taken a lot of trouble over it.

All my love to you & Rajiv and Sanjay,

Papu

356.                                           Copenhagen,
7th August, 1953

Darling Papu,

I have just arrived here and am already feeling sorry that I did not spend these extra days in Norway. I liked Norway so much – it's one place that I would really like to come back to and to live in. The people are frank and free and friendly – one could discuss every subject under the sun. It was so wonderful to meet and talk to 'real' socialists. They are the government, so they are fully aware of their problems and responsibilities. And they have vision and broad interests, idealism combined with practical sense. There is just now a tremendous interest in India – 'Travancore',[1] to be more exact. And everywhere the question: how can we help more? Nurses, students, doctors want to go out and work in India! Quite a few people are learning Malayalam! Some are regularly getting the weekly edition of *The Hindu*. I met the Foreign Minister who gave a lunch for me, and the Health Minister, the Director of the Dept. for Cultural Relations, & the Minister for Social Affairs, plus many other lesser but equally interesting people.

I stayed [with] a Quaker family – Mrs Lund had been to the U.N. as one of the Quaker group and had met Puphi & Krishna. The son is an active member of the executive committee of the International Union of Socialist Youth. Mr Lund, Senior, is in Quilon, in charge of the Norwegian project in Travancore.

Lots of love to you,

Indu

I hear from London that the boys are well & happy and increasingly boisterous.[2]

1. Travancore: a Princely State in the south-west of India. After its integration into the Indian Union, it became a part of the State of Kerala.

2. Rajiv and Sanjay were in Great Britain while Indira Gandhi went to various capital cities in Europe.

357.                                    [Prime Minister's House],
                                                New Delhi,
                                           9th August, 1953

Darling Indu,

It has been difficult to keep pace with your movements and hence not easy to write to you. I sent you a letter[1] to the Swiss School. I had intended giving a note for you to Krishna Menon who left late last night. But at the last moment I forgot. I was very tired and went to bed.

You will see Krishna and he will tell you something of how we are. In a week or so you will yourself be here after your long wandering. The house and its present occupants await you with eagerness.

Life is not dull here at least. In Kashmir, after a continuing crisis, things have boiled over. The Cabinet there split up and Sheikh Saheb carried on a bitter campaign against India and to some extent against me. Last night the *Sadar-i-Riyasat*[2] dismissed his ministry and called upon Bakshi to form a new Govt. We have no further detailed news yet.

Send a message to say when you are arriving here. I want to be in Delhi on that day.

                         My love to you & the children,
                                        Papu

                         ———————————————————————

358.                                               Zurich,
                                           10th August [1953]

Darling, darling Papu,

I got the Kashmir news in a Swiss paper this morning.[3] It is a heart-breaking thing to happen – I do realise that everyone concerned must have thought and thought before taking this grave step. And it must be justified and right. And yet – it wasn't a shock, for I was dreading such a thing since your letter[4] and some other Kashmir news I got – but somehow one is never quite prepared. I am filled with a terrible and deeply penetrating sadness. I suppose one has to do some things for the greater good but it is like cutting a part of oneself . . .

I wanted to take the next plane to India but since you were so anxious for us to go through these examinations I shall carry on to London &

1. Refers to letter No. 355.
2. *Sadar-i-Riyasat*: the Governor of Kashmir was known as *Sadar-i-Riyasat* or Head of State.
3. Sheikh Abdullah, the leader of Kashmir, was removed from office and arrested on 9th August, 1953.
4. Refers to letter No. 355.

try to get away as soon as I possibly can. How I wish I were in India — I am feeling absolutely wretched and in no mood to talk to people.

My love to you,

Indu

---

359.               [Cable]              Zurich
[11th August, 1953]

Jawaharlal Nehru
New Delhi.
Wish could be with you these difficult days going London today coming soonest possible much love

Indu

---

360.            Post Graduate Medical School Hospital,
13th August, 1953

Darling Papu,
Your telegram came last night and your letter of the 9th, [1] this evening.

I arrived in London on the 11th late in the evening and the very next day was whisked off to this hospital for the 'check-up'! It isn't a usual hospital as you can see by the name but it is full of specialists and would-be specialists. The latter are young and cheerful and awfully nice. That helps a lot, for can there be anything more dull than lying in bed trying to think of all your childhood ailments and, at intervals, having all kinds of disagreeable tests made? Nobody can tell how long all this will take. If my tests are over before the children are ready to go, I have even thought of leaving them behind & letting them catch a later plane.

I see from the papers that Mohd. Ali is with you. In spite of the relief of having things settled one way or another, you will doubtless be besieged by a whole set of new problems.

I had lunch with Krishna. He was very uncommunicative – unusually so.

The boys are staying with the Khers. I have engaged an elderly governess for them, Miss Stewart.

1. Refers to letter No. 357.

On my return to Delhi, I do want to reorganise my life and get out of all the silly committees. I am so sick of people doing social work as a step up [the] political & social-set ladder, and equally sick of the vague goodness of the so-called Gandhians.

Lots of love,<br>Indu

---

361.                                              [Anand Bhawan],
                                                       Allahabad,
                                              23rd December, 1953

Darling Papu,

My tour here has been planned almost on election lines. I go off after having lunch at ten a.m. and return covered and lined with dust around seven forty-five p.m. So far – in two days – I have covered Chail Tehsil, Soraon Tehsil & Phulpur, several meetings in each, and many wayside halts complete with gates, garlanding and flower throwing. In the Soraon area, I visited the flood-affected area which is still in a bad way. People have not been able in many cases to rebuild their houses. Wells have been so damaged that they are unable to water their fields, which have a dried-up appearance. The demand is still for food and cloth.

The response to my appeal for volunteers for our camp has been quite good. We have already got eighty women. I don't know how many of them will turn out to be capable of taking any training or doing any work later on in their villages.

In every constituency, I am accompanied by the M.L.A.[1] Phulpur, Shivji Kathju's[2] domain, is the most prosperous but it didn't seem to be at all organised. The Congress candidate lost in the town area election.

There is great resentment against the pilgrim tax.[3] Everywhere the *kisans* spoke about it, the womenfolk were specially vociferous. They said that even in British times this sort of thing had not been done and in spite of our trying to explain the reason for it, we failed to convince them. The worst of it is that the tax has been made the basis for all

---

1. Local elections were being held for the Gram Seva Dal (Village Service Organisation). Indira Gandhi went to the region for electioneering purposes and in every constituency she was accompanied by the local member of the U.P. Legislative Assembly.

2. Shiv Nath Kathju: elected to U.P. Legislative Assembly from Phulpur constituency in 1952.

3. Pilgrim tax: Prior to 1947, the state used to collect pilgrim tax to compensate itself the cost of managing temples and religious fairs. The reference here is to such a tax which was levied on the occasion of *Kumbh Melá*.

kinds of wild rumours – such as that the *kisans* will have to pay a rupee per *dupki*[1] and that money will have to be spent at every turn. The poor *kisans* are genuinely distressed and feel that even this, which was one of the few things available for them, is now becoming inaccessible and more for the *shahri log*.[2]

Talking of spending money, I have heard talk – just the usual rumour mongering – that Mrs Munshi[3] intends to organise a collection during the *Melá*[4] for her scheme of homes for destitute women. In view of the tax to be levied and the growing concern of the *kisans* about the expense of being a *yatri*,[5] I wonder if such collections will be proper or wise.

I am going to the *Melá* grounds this morning to attend a meeting of the *Melá* Planning Committee and to have a look round. I believe the arrangements have been going very well. There is admiration for the way the army has handled the job, though amongst the city contractors there is considerable heartburning, as they feel they have been done out of their legitimate earnings. Lalluji, who is the solitary contractor for beds, tents, etc, is charging exorbitant rates & people are therefore trying to get things from outside.

There is also some heartburning among some social welfare agencies because of the money that Mridula was able to get from the Social Welfare Board for our camp. But none of them would have been able to get women out of the villages. We hope and plan that the best out of our women volunteers will form the nucleus for a permanent camp run on the lines of the Kasturba Scheme . . .

Shammie is not here.

Love,
Indu

---

362.                       Mashobra,
1st June, 1954

Darling Papu,

The house is so quiet and empty since you left. There is one sentry on

1. Dip.
2. Townsmen.
3. For Mrs Munshi see letter No. 192, footnote 3.
4. *Kumbh Melá*: the most important Hindu religious fair. It is held every three years, rotating between Hardwar on the Ganges; Ujjain on the Sipra; Nasik on the Godavari; and Allahabad, at the confluence of the Ganges, the Yamuna and the mythical river Saraswati. Bathing in these rivers during the *Kumbh Melá* by the devout Hindu is seen as an act of great religious merit. The 1954 *Kumbh Melá* was held at Allahabad.
5. Traveller.

duty and one man who trails us on walks, who saves us from charging panthers!

I saw a panther on my way back from the Winter Sports dinner on the 30th: a long body leaping out of the beam of headlights and then two huge glistening eyes staring from the brushwood.

The dinner was not too exciting except for two very beautiful skiing films from Norway. The Norwegian Minister had brought them, especially for the meeting. You must see them – they take only ten minutes each. Mr Lyke has offered to lend them when I come down to Delhi.

We are going to lunch with the Sarabhais tomorrow, tea with my Mamu and the C.P.N.'s [1] reception to the President. On the 5th I am lunching with the President.

I am rather bothered about my tour in the interior. I now find that it takes seven whole days horseback, carrying *all* provisions, to reach Sangle & the same to return. Fifteen days – it's no fun doing it alone. I had originally planned to take the children but Auntie Vakil feels that I should not take them for such a long period, especially as we have asked Miss Clark from the Welham School to come up to coach Rajiv. The other problem is that I have got only two pairs of *salwars*!

It has grown a little warmer since you left.

What do you think of having our big dining room air-conditioned?

The day you left we went to see Wild Flower Hall. It is really an enchanting place. I quite fell in love with it and don't feel like staying in 'Retreat' [2] any more. What a pity that it cannot be run as a hotel any more!

Lots of love,
Indu

---

363.                                                    [Prime Minister's House],
New Delhi,
2nd June, 1954

Indu darling,

I returned from Bhopal today. My day and a half at Bhopal was interesting. The place was slightly less warm than Delhi and the evenings were cooler.

The police put up a tattoo and made it a good show. One item in the programme was a display of dresses of different States by girls. This

1. C. P. N. Singh: educationist; Vice-Chancellor of Patna University, later was Ambassador to Japan, and Governor of Punjab.
2. A cottage in Mashobra, about eighteen kilometres from Simla, the summer capital of India during the British Raj. The cottage was maintained for viceregal vacations.

was well done. It struck me that we should have some pageant of dress in our Republic Day parade. I think there was some such suggestion in your meeting. Whether the parade will be quite suitable for this or not, I am not quite sure. But we might add that as one item in the Stadium show.

I have received your letter of June 1.[1] Also Rajiv's and Sanjay's letters.

It seems to me that your tour in the interior, if it is going to last for fifteen days, is not good enough for you to undertake. This will involve great strain. I certainly agree that the children should not go with you in this long tour.

My programme remains uncertain, and I do not know how and when I can finalise it because the situation at Geneva[2] and in Pondicherry[3] and in some other places is very tricky, and I do not want to be out of touch with it. Perhaps my being at Mashobra would not matter so much because I would be on the telephone. But going beyond the reach of the telephone might make things difficult. Anyway, I propose to remain here in Delhi till the 20th June or a little after. If I can manage to find four or five days about that time and before the end of June, I might go to Mashobra. I would have liked to go by jeep to Rampur or the end of the jeep road. I take it that a visit there and back takes three days at least, possibly four. You might find out from Dr Parmar.[4]

In Bhopal, I met a remarkable person. I have heard of him first and saw some papers about him which excited my curiosity. He is a man named Ramakrishna and comes from a Tamil family long resident in Mysore. Although he knows some Tamil as a home tongue, he really knows Kannada much better. He comes from a large family of eight brothers and sisters. His father was some petty employee. He took his degree in Agriculture and later took service in Bhopal as an Entomologist. He is now connected with the Planning Department of Bhopal and is now getting Rs. 300/- a month. This salary too has been recently increased in spite of some opposition from the Public Service Commission because he had been given two increments. He is twenty-nine years of age now.

Ramakrishna, some three years ago, took part in a world contest

1. Refers to letter No. 362.

2. In the month of May 1954 an international conference was held in Geneva to resolve the problem of Indo-China. Through his special emissary, V. K. Krishna Menon, Jawaharlal Nehru played an important 'behind the scene' role in this conference.

3. Refers to the negotiations with the French Government for the merger of the French colony of Pondicherry in the subcontinent with the Indian Union.

4. Dr Y. S. Parmar: Congress leader from Himachal Pradesh; its Chief Minister, 1952–6, 1963–77.

sponsored by UNESCO. He stood first in this and got a prize of Rs. 11,000/- or more as well as an offer of a post in UNESCO in Paris subject to his being married. Apparently they have a rule for this post that a person should be married. He was not married and would not agree to get married. In fact, he actually returned the prize money to UNESCO. The essay of his, however, which had got this prize, brought him a doctorate from the Sorbonne in Paris. Later, he got another doctorate because he won in another world contest. He has never been out of India although he has been asked to go.

T. S. Eliot met him about two years ago and was tremendously impressed by him. I am sending you some odd papers, copies of correspondence about him. Also a copy of his essay for which he got a doctorate. This is about children's training, etc. If you read these papers, you will get some idea of what he is and what he is thought to be by very eminent men.

I met him for a short while yesterday. He is modest and a fairly attractive person. Naturally, I had no opportunity to know much more about him. It is obvious, however, that he is an unusual type and that he should not be allowed to spend the rest of his life in some minor Government post. He is getting married now within a few days in Bhopal. The girl he is marrying is also from Bangalore but is a Hindi M.A., and is a teacher at present in Bhopal.

In view of Ramakrishna's very special interest in children, I immediately thought of him in connection with our Bal Bhawan. I have asked him to send me a note on his idea of Bal Bhawan, and later to come here to have a talk with you and me when you are here. [1]

Delhi had some little rain yesterday and is slightly cooler.

Love,
Papu

---

364.                                          [Prime Minister's House],
                                                       New Delhi,
                                                  6th June, 1954

Indu darling,
I have received today a letter from Mridula with which she has sent me a copy of a letter dated June 5th, which she has addressed to you. This

---

1. Around this time, Indira Gandhi and Jawaharlal Nehru were discussing the possibility of instituting Bal Bhawans, or institutions for stimulating social activity among the young; such an institution was formally established in 1956.

relates to what she calls Working Children's Welfare Board, Delhi State. I have sent her a reply, a copy of which I enclose.

I am afraid Mridula is setting about this in the wrong way. All this idea of big committees is wholly beside the point. Some small scheme should be drawn up for one centre without fuss or even publicity to begin with. We can easily find a little money for it, say Rs. 10,000/-, to start with. With the experience gathered there, we can then expand. Government will help in a small way. If, later, the scheme becomes a big one, you may even get more money. But that must wait. I entirely dislike the kind of board or committee that Mridula has suggested and of which she wants you to be Chairman.

As you know, the Delhi State Government is at present in a bad way because of the internal quarrels. To ask them to undertake anything of this kind would lead to nothing. Everybody is always agreeable to starting a board and becoming office-bearers in it. It seems to me extraordinary how this is done without carefully working out what has to be done. Mridula, of course, has a way of thinking and acting in a grandiose way. She is herself a very energetic and good worker. But this is not good enough for a scheme which has to function well and permanently.

If this board is started, as Mridula suggests, the result will be that a big part of the burden of it will fall on you and others will be more or less pro forma members.

As I told you, the idea is good and we should work it out, beginning in a small way.

I have been keeping well. The *hakim*[1] came to see me two days ago and has prescribed various pills and tonics for me. I have to take Benafsha every night and Majum in the morning. All this is mainly to please you.

Love,
Papu

---

365. The Retreat,<br>Mashobra,<br>Simla Hills,<br>9th June, 1954

Darling Papu,
Your note[2] on the working children's scheme has just come. One point I want to rectify – Mridula has been the initiator and the motivating

---

1. Physician of the indigenous Unani system of medicine.
2. Refers to letter No. 364.

power throughout. Of course I am tremendously interested in this problem.

I agree that Govt cooperation is essential for tackling this problem effectively. But since Govt cannot take it up just yet, why cannot some of us start in a very small way, taking only a few of the children in hand. I do not think they are all vagrants or delinquents – some of them are just poor and forced by their parents to earn. We might pick out a few of the less hardened ones and see how we succeed with them. I am sure I can collect some more money to add to your 10,000/-. But while the whole venture is in this experimental stage, I would prefer not to have either Saiyidain or Humayun Kabir[1] or indeed any Ministry involved. If the experiment is a success, we can see what the Govt can do to expand it or help in the financing, etc. Before you come up here again, I shall draw up a note, which we can discuss with Dr Ramakrishna[2] too.

Bhimsen Sachar[3] had thought that it was better for me to combine Congress work with that of the Social Welfare Board. That means stopping longer at each place, so that the week's tour (drawn up by Mathai) would be extended to two or even three weeks. As I have meetings in Delhi from the 2nd to 7th July, I would have to be away the whole of the month. I don't think this would be very good for the children – especially as Rajiv is going off to school soon after. So I am wondering if I could not do the week's tour for the Social Welfare Board from 9th to 16th July and then return to Mashobra. After Rajiv goes to Dehra Dun I could tour the main places for other work. It is a bit complicated but what else can be done?

*10th June*

We walked down to Mashobra bazaar this morning. The short cut down is very steep, we took it for going down but came up the long way.

Kacker & Parmar are coming down in a little while with some local Congress people. In the evening we are thinking of going to Naldera, the golf course.

Much love,
Indu

---

1. Humayun Kabir: Educational Adviser, Government of India, 1948–56, and Education Minister, 1957–63. For Saiyidain see letter No. 331 footnote.

2. See letter No. 363.

3. Bhimsen Sachar: Congress Leader of Punjab; Chief Minister, Punjab, 1949 and 1952–6; was later Governor of Orissa and Andhra Pradesh, and also High Commissioner in Sri Lanka.

366.                              Prime Minister's House,
New Delhi,
15th January, 1955

Darling Papu,

I am off to Simla tonight with the boys & Jessie. It has been very raw & damp here since you left, so Simla must also be really cold. I hope we all survive it!

I am feeling much better & I am sure the snow will do me good. I shall be back in Delhi before you.

Andhra must have been tiring – *Blitz* has some biographical sketches of the Congress candidates, comparing them with the Communist candidates.

Give my greetings to Sri Prakasaji.

Much love,
Indu

---

367.                                     Camp: Madras,
16th January, 1955

Indu darling,

I have just come back from Pondicherry and received your letter of the 15th.[1] I am glad you were going to Simla with the children. Look after yourself there and don't exert yourself.

Pondicherry had a festive air.[2] The town was decorated with numerous arches and buntings and large crowds from outside had come there. In the various functions French, of course, was dominant. It was interesting to see how people there took pride in their French as many of us have done with our English. At a college function French poetry was recited with great gusto.

I visited the Aurobindo Ashram and met the 'Mother'.[3] The lady has grown quite old and looks fragile. She produced no great impression of spirituality on me. I saw the boys and girls there, and indeed the

---

1. Refers to letter No. 366.

2. Jawaharlal Nehru visited Pondicherry in connection with the celebrations marking the merger of Pondicherry with the Indian Union.

3. Mirra Alfassa (1878–1973), popularly known as the 'Mother', was the principal associate of Sri Aurobindo (1872–1950) in the activities of the Ashram and the spiritual movement initiated by the latter in Pondicherry. As is well-known Sri Aurobindo was a very distinguished nationalist, revolutionary and thinker. After 1910 he withdrew from formal politics to lead a life of contemplation and reflection and established the Ashram mentioned above.

grown-ups too, indulge in athletics. They were quite good at it. What was interesting was that the girls of all ages were clad in the most diminutive of attire.

You will remember showing me Bijji Kaul's [1] letter about the Chinese delegation's visit to Madras. I have not discussed this matter with anyone here, but I have gathered the impression that the delegation was quite happy here. I am inclined to think that Bijji Kaul dramatises little events. There was some faint reference here to people from Delhi trying to boss everybody here.

Love,<br>Papu

---

368.                                              Camp: Raj Bhawan,
                                                           Madras,
                                                 18th January, 1955

Indu darling,

I hope the Simla weather is suiting you and that a week's stay there will make you quite fit. If you are lucky, you might have some snow there and the children can play about.

We have today finished our Steering Committee work. Tomorrow morning we begin at Avadi, fifteen miles away from Madras, and start our public sessions, first with the Subjects Committee and then with the Open Congress . . .

Tonight we had a performance here at Raj Bhawan of Bharata Natya [2] by Balasarasvati. [3] I do not know if you have seen her dance. She is supposed to be the best. Indeed, she is the person chiefly responsible for the revival of Bharata Natya in Madras and other parts of the country. Previously it had almost died and there was a movement by worthy reformers. They had started an anti-Nautch society. [4] Balasarasvati started dancing at an early age in the late twenties . . .

I learnt today something which I did not know. Apparently all the commentaries on Bharata Natya were written by Kashmiris, in Sanskrit of course. Some King of Kashmir married a girl named Kamala who knew Bharata Natya and his Minister wrote a big treatise on the subject.

1. General B. M. Kaul: Chief of the General Staff, 1961; Coordinator of Goa operation, 1961; Corps Commander in North-East Frontier Agency, 1962.
2. Bharata Natya (also spelt Bharata Natyam): a classical dance form of India.
3. T. Balasarasvati: one of the foremost exponents of Bharata Natya.
4. In the nineteenth century dancing in India was associated with decadence. Hence, various social reformers had initiated a movement against public dancing. These movements were led by anti-Nautch (anti-dance) societies.

All the earlier commentaries have been lost and only one remains. This one is also by a Kashmiri. It was found in the Malabar and was written about the tenth century.

I enclose the programme for the dance recital this evening. This might interest you.

Love,<br>Papu

369.                      Himachal Winter Sports Club,
Simla,<br>20th January, 1955

Darling Papu,

It is just like you to take the time to send me a few lines[1] when you must be in the midst of a million things. Thank you.

You always accuse me of the possessive instinct when I talk about acquiring a small place in the hills but I feel that life would be much pleasanter if there was a tiny small house where one could go for a weekend or longer without upsetting governmental machinery and a lot of fuss and bother. As Justice Khosla[2] says, 'The Himalayas are essential to my emotional existence.' I read his book almost at a single sitting.

The children are having the time of their lives. Yesterday I suggested they might try skating. Rajiv sulked and almost had to be carried there but once at the rink they both enjoyed themselves immensely and have made arrangements to go every evening! I enclose a snap taken yesterday at the rink.

The weather is delightful – sunny and fresh. I just can't understand how anybody can '*not*' like it. Yesterday the Bhandaris had said they would come at five p.m. At about four fifteen there was a snowfall. The children wanted to go out so we three went for a walk. It was very pleasant and not at all cold – we just had on our Delhi clothes plus an overcoat & gloves. We hurried home so as not to be late for the Bhandaris, only to get a telephone call saying that they could not come because of the snow! Mind, for they were anyhow coming in a closed car!

Lots of love to you from us all,<br>Indu

---

1. Possibly refers to letter No. 367.
2. Justice: Gopal Das Khosla: Chief Justice of Punjab High Court.

370.                                                      India House,
                                                            Aldwych,
                                                    London, W.C. 2.
                                                    1st February, 1955

Indu darling,
I suppose that the children have gone to Dehru Dun and you have accompanied them there. Sanjay might feel a little unhappy to begin with, but I am sure he will not only adapt himself to the school, but will enjoy it later. I am anxious that you should look after yourself well and take plenty of rest.

I have got some mechanical toys for the children. The arrangements of the Conference here are not quite so tight as they used to be. Partly this is because of the old man Winston Churchill who requires plenty of rest, and partly because they are having separate conferences dealing with defence matters, NATO, SEATO, Middle East, etc., and I am not concerned with them. I have, therefore, a little more time at my disposal than I expected. Yesterday, I went out shopping and bought some shirts, a hat and toys from a special little shop as well as Harrods. I have more or less finished my shopping except perhaps books and except also some things for you. Please let me know immediately what kind of things you would like me to bring for you. Send me a small telegram L.T. addressed to 9, Kensington Palace Gardens, W.8. Do not hesitate to do so. I feel in a somewhat expansive mood when I travel abroad.

This house is much more attractive now than it used to be. It is rather ornate or sumptuous of course. One small sitting room especially on the ground floor is very tastefully fitted up and is definitely restful. Eden [1] came to see me [the] day before yesterday and immediately remarked on the restful character of the room.

Our business here will proceed more or less according to schedule. Probably, we shall finish the Conference on the 8th February. The next two or three days are full up with other engagements here and also a visit to Cambridge. Most probably I shall go to Broadlands for the weekend and then to Paris. I am asking Harsha and Ajit and Naresh [2] to come here for a day.

The situation in the Far East is a difficult and dangerous one because two great countries with high ideas of their own prestige and 'face' and with a good deal of passion are at loggerheads. In the balance, I do not

---

1. Anthony Eden was at this time Secretary of State for Foreign Affairs. He succeeded Churchill as Prime Minister in 1955.
2. Naresh Kathju: son of P. N. and Swarup Kathju (see Kinship Circle).

think that war is likely, but one never knows. Eden and R. A. Butler [1] have a fair understanding of the situation, but Winston Churchill is difficult. His face has deteriorated and become more flabby. Sometimes, he has quite a child-like impression, a kind of second childhood. Yet, occasionally his mind works well, but he cannot get rid of his past background. As for the other P.M.s, as usual, Menzies [2] talks a lot with little sense. St Laurent is restrained and cautious and is respected more than anyone else. [Sir Sidney] Holland, Pakistan and Ceylon have little to contribute. South Africa and Rhodesia even less so.

The weather here since I came has been pleasant and not at all cold. In fact, it might almost be Delhi at this time of the year.

St Laurent has come here with one of his daughters, not the one who accompanied him to Delhi. She resembles her sister very much.

Eden and his wife Clarissa will be coming to Delhi early in March for two or three days. Clarissa is rather frail and not too well. I had lunch with them today.

I am going to the theatre tonight with the Mountbattens.

Love,<br>[Papu]

---

371.                        Prime Minister's House,
New Delhi,
8th February, 1955

Darling Papu,

It was lovely getting your letter [3] just a few moments ago. My thoughts have been constantly with you, knowing the intricacies of the situation and the key role you would have to play in trying to smooth out the knots. It is really amazing how people refuse to learn from experience. Every time you have to extricate them from the results of their folly. And for this dependence they dislike you heartily.

Papi Naidu turned up last evening with the latest American report on you. It's from the *Fortnightly Review of Radio and Broadcasting*. They say you are afraid of me and since my husband is a Communist, that 'affects his actions towards the reds'!

The house is in a turmoil. Repairs and renovations all over the place.

---

1. Richard Austen Butler: Conservative member of British Parliament; Chancellor of the Exchequer, 1951–5; Leader of the House, 1955–61; Home Secretary, 1957–62; Chairman of Conservative Party, 1959–61.

2. Robert Menzies (1894–1978): Prime Minister of Australia, 1939–41 and 1949–66.

3. Refers to letter No. 370.

In order to come to my room, Bebee has to go down her stairs, walk the length of the house, and then climb my staircase! However everything will be spick and span for your return.

There is an exhibition of Chinese crafts. There are some beautiful things but on the whole it is not very exciting.

We have had some bad accidents. One night one plane [crashed] at Nagpur, in which Rajiv's best friend at Welham lost his life. The little boy was his parents' only child. And others: railway accidents and a mine disaster.

The weather is perfect and the garden very lovely with the peach trees in bloom.

The boys are in school. Sanjay was rather unhappy to see me leave. He has since written rather an untidy postcard, ending with, 'Mummy dear, I love you very much'!

Don't bother to bring me anything. I have far too many possessions already.

I hope you have been keeping well and will [not] get tired out in Cairo.

Lots of love to you . . .<br>Indu

---

372.

Geneva,<br>14th February, 1955

Darling Indu,

We are for the moment held up here and so I am writing this brief letter to you. We are travelling by one of the Super-Constellations, which are in the habit of developing small engine trouble. We have already been delayed two hours and we shall certainly be here for another hour at least.

It was snowing in London when we left and the countryside was white. So also in France. But the sun came out in Paris and it was cold and pleasant. Mendès-France[1] had arranged a sumptuous lunch. We had a good talk. I liked him. He has a fine face. I gave him a copy of Madanjeet Singh's book on Ajanta; also as a parting gift, my sandalwood baton! At the London Airport and in Paris we were televised. At Geneva we had an official welcome from the cantorial and municipal authorities and television of course – I was asked to make a 'declaration'. Having

---

1. Pierre Mendès-France: Prime Minister of France, June 1954 to February 1955, he negotiated the end of the seven-year-war with Indo-China with great skill, but was forced to resign when defeated over his policy in North Africa.

finished our official business and interviews, we prepared to depart. We were informed of engine trouble. And so here we are.

I have been round Geneva: to the Palais des Nations, to our Consulate General, to the Air India Office and to our showrooms. And now we are waiting in Bertoli's [1] office.

There are plenty of Indian children here, all looking chubby and healthy and jabbering away in French – I met Ella Maillart [2] here also. She is going to India soon.

Darling, I am greatly looking forward to be back home and to see you again.

Love,<br>Papu

Edwina has given a lovely book of flower paintings for you.

---

373.                           Prime Minister's House,
New Delhi,<br>15th July, 1955

Indu darling,

I hope you will reach India fairly fresh and not too tired. [3] I am trying to get back to normal life. This is not easy as people insist on lionising me.

Ring me up after your arrival – say between three thirty & four thirty p.m. I shall be in my office in External Affairs – Number 31360, New Delhi.

I found the children well – Rajiv had a slight difficulty in bending fully his right arm but this was gradually passing. The X-ray examination in Dalhousie had revealed no fracture. There had been a big swelling of his arm, round about the elbow, and this had almost entirely subsided.

Feroze had an X-ray taken here by a more competent man and better apparatus. This revealed that there had been a small fracture which had healed but some other small bone-formation had developed (I can't explain all this but it was nothing much). So the surgeon decided to immobilise the right arm by putting plaster round it. He said that in about ten or twelve days the small growth of bone will be absorbed and all will be well. This surgeon is very good – exceptionally so. He has

1. Bertoli: Air India Official based in Geneva.
2. A Swiss lady who was friendly with the Nehrus. She was a traveller and author of repute.
3. Indira had accompanied her father on his visit to the Soviet Union in June and remained in Europe for a few weeks after his return.

recently come back to India from England – his name is Doraiswamy.

So if you see Rajiv with plaster round his arm do not worry.

Rajiv & Sanjay just came in. They are going to the swimming pool. Sanjay to try to swim and Rajiv to look on.

Love,
Papu

---

374.                                          Bombay,
                                   17th October, 1955

Darling Papu,

I am utterly exhausted – it is very hot and sticky and the programme is very badly planned. We spent most of the time racing from place to place. I feel that the whole thing has been a waste of time. I am much too tired to know what I am saying!

C.P.N. [Singh] has wired from Chandigarh that it is not possible to postpone the Taradevi programme. So I had better go. Perhaps a day in a cold place will do me good.

Lots of love,
Indu

---

375.                                          Jog Falls,
                                   19th October, 1955

Darling Papu,

Here I am after all. And truly it's a sight worth seeing. The scenery all along the road was very lovely too, although the road itself is deplorable.

Just as I was being told that there was no likelihood of seeing any wild animal at that time of the forenoon and in this season when water is plentiful throughout the forest, a tiger, magnificent creature, sauntered across the road just in front of our car.

When I wrote[1] to you from Bombay, I was so tired out that I could not imagine what would happen the rest of the day and the rest of the tour. But almost as soon as I had written to you, I seem to have rallied some latent energy and turned up at the civic reception in the evening (after a series of other engagements) looking, and what is more strange, feeling as fresh as if I had just had a long rest.

---

1. Refers to letter No. 374.

I am again tired today because of having unexpected meetings at stations throughout the night, between Bagalwat and Hubli. But I am sure that this will pass before I see you!

Lots of love,<br>
Indu

---

376.　　　　　　　　　　　　　　　　　　　　　　　　[January]
　　　　　　　　　　　　　　　　　　　　　　　　　　　[1956]

Papu

Mr Kanungo[1] rang me up this morning. He is very anxious that some high up Congress person should go to Orissa. It seems that Dhebarbhai[2] had half promised to go on the 31st. Kanungo vaguely hinted that it might be a good thing if you or Pantji could go, but I have told him that this is quite impossible because of your Bangalore trip – and Pantji because of his health. It would be a good idea if Dhebarbhai could be persuaded.

It is almost definite now that I shall not be able to go to Orissa. Do you think it is worthwhile my going to the U.P. for three days while you are away in Bangalore?

I am lunching with Mrs Middleton to meet Mrs Macdonald.

Love,<br>
Indu

---

377.　　　　　　　　　　　　　　　　　　　　　24th January, 1956
　　　　　　　　　　　　　　　　　　　　　　　　　　2.35 p.m.

Darling Indu,

Of course neither Pantji nor I can go to Orissa now. Apart from this difficulty of finding the time, I do not think it is desirable. Dhebarbhai will be going there on the 31st.

I think, on the whole, it will be desirable for you to go to Orissa. Of course this visit cannot be for a tour as previously thought of. This

1. Nityanand Kanungo: Congress leader from Orissa; Union Minister; Governor of Gujarat, 1965–7, and Bihar, 1967–70.

2. U. N. Dhebar: prominent Congress leader; Chief Minister of Saurashtra, 1948–54 and President of the Congress, 1957–9.

would be just to give moral support to Noba Babu[1] and others. Noba Babu is a very fine man but unfortunately he does not get much cooperation from his colleagues in his Cabinet or the P.C.C.[2] or even his wife. I should like him to feel that we are with him. So it would be a good thing for you to go to Cuttack (and perhaps to Puri also) – no public meetings, etc, but private talks, etc. You can go in addition to Dhebarbhai, who agrees with what I have written above.

                                                    Papu

---

378.                                    Prime Minister's House,
                                                New Delhi,
                                            23rd April, 1956

Darling Papu,
I feel I should put some of my thoughts before you.

You know that I have never cared much for Deshmukh[3] as a person, although recently his vision with regard to our economics seems to have broadened and his views regarding the Five-Year Plans seem more balanced.

But on the issue of Maharashtra my sympathies are entirely with him. There is no getting away from the fact that the vast majority of Maharashtrians and most non-Maharashtrians, except Gujeratis, are for a certain proposal.[4] How is it possible to ignore their demand?

The M.P.C.C.[5] made many initial mistakes. They may be foolish but they are not bad. We seem to be trying to cut off our nose to spite our face.

It is most unfortunate that Morarjibhai has a closed mind on the subject. Most people have certain ideas about which they cannot be balanced. There is a growing feeling in Congress circles – this extends to many members of the Working Committee also – that you are tending more and more to accept almost without question, the opinions of certain people with regard to certain parts of the country. Morarjibhai for Bombay, Gujerat, Maharashtra, etc, Bidhan Babu for Bengal, Bihar.

1. Nabakrushna Choudhry: Orissa Congress leader and politician; Chief Minister of Orissa, 1950–56; later joined the Sarvodaya movement of Vinoba Bhave.
2. Provincial Congress Committee.
3. C. D. Deshmukh: Governor, Reserve Bank of India, 1943–9; Finance Minister, 1950–6.
4. Indira Gandhi wrote this letter in the context of the territorial redefinition of the States of the Indian Union on the basis of language. The phrase 'a certain proposal' probably refers to a draft scheme for creating a composite state for the Marathi speaking people, to be called Maharashtra. C. D. Deshmukh hailed from this region.
5. Maharashtra Provincial Congress Committee.

Kamaraj[1] for Tamilnad. These are very fine men and our top leaders, but no one is big enough or detached enough to be the only word on matters of their area. This complete trust in a very few creates dissatisfaction in many and cuts at your contacts with all those who hold different views.

Sorry to inflict this on you but I just had to get it off my chest! . . .
Indu

---

379.                                           [Prime Minister's House],
                                                          New Delhi,
                                                 3rd November, 1956

Papu,
I was quite amazed to see the circular that has been sent around to the artists on the works of art to be executed on the various public buildings. It is really shocking that the Chief Engineer and other dignitaries of the C.P.W.D. [Central Public Works Department] should sit in judgement on our foremost artists or to pretend to know anything about modern art.

I do not think it is enough to speak to Sardar Swaran Singh.[2] You should come to some decision so that this sort of thing may never be repeated.

I had something to do with the decision that a certain percentage of money should be spent on decoration of public buildings. But I do feel very strongly that it is far better to have no decoration at all than to have the sort of thing that is likely to be approved by the present committees.

The only way out seems to be to have other non-official people on the committee. I should normally like to be out of these things, as I have far too much on my hands already, but I am deeply distressed about the present state of affairs and, if it is the only way out, I should like to be on the committee. There should naturally be other names, perhaps, such as Mr Narielwala and others.

I showed Lala Lajpat Rai's portrait[3] to Dhebarbhai and Khandubhai.[4] They also liked it immensely. I have written to Shri

1. K. Kamaraj: a Congress leader and Chief Minister of Madras, 1954–63; President of Indian National Congress, 1963–7.

2. Sardar Swaran Singh: a very distinguished politician who held important ministerial portfolios in successive Congress Governments after 1947. At present regarded as a senior statesman in the country.

3. This portrait of Lala Lajpat Rai (1865–1928), a prominent nationalist leader, was painted by the noted artist Satish Gujral. It is located in the Central Hall of the Indian Parliament along with those of other distinguished political figures.

4. Khandubhai K. Desai: active in the struggle for freedom; Union Minister for Labour, 1954–7; was later Governor of Andhra Pradesh.

Ananthasayanam Ayyangar[1] suggesting that the matter may be considered again. It would be a good thing if you could also mention this to him when Parliament meets.

You can yourself judge of the taste of the present Parliamentary Committee by the paintings of the artist whom they wish to do Dadu's portrait. I hope you will be consulted before the chairman of the Parliamentary Committee is appointed in place of Dr Chakravarty.

Indu

380.
[Anand Bhawan],<br>Allahabad,<br>17th February, 1957

Darling Papu,
This is just a very hurried line being written at the crack of dawn as I leave for Fatehpur. Shall not be back until midnight.

Every day's programme is like that. I am enclosing a copy of the schedule as far as it is complete.

Punjab was strenuous but most exhilarating too. I had a 100,000 people in Rohtak just for me – imagine that! The other meetings were good though not as big and Choudhury Ranbir Singh[2] looked after me as if he were my grandmother!

It has suddenly become cold again – there was a cold wave – and there is a chill wind.

Much love,<br>Indu

P.S.
It is too late now to bother about making the programme lighter – one can only pray with Tagore to gain the physical strength to go through with it! Tagore said, 'Let me not pray to be sheltered from danger but to be fearless in facing them.'

381.
Khaga,<br>4th March, 1957

Indu darling,
Please put an end to your touring now. You can stay on in Allahabad

---

1. M. Ananthasayanam Ayyangar: distinguished parliamentarian; Speaker, Lok Sabha, 1956–62; Governor of Bihar, 1962–7.
2. Choudhari Ranbir Singh: a Congress leader from Haryana.

but at least have long rest in the night and in the afternoon. It is folly to overdo this business. I am told that you are pressed to go to Jabalpur. You should not go. I have just been there.

Lal Bahadur[1] tells me that Hakim Usmani[2] saw you – I think it would be a good thing if you took his tonics. Hakim Usmani, I am told, said to you that the P.S.P. [Praja Socialist Party] people are threatening Muslims in the city. You can assure Usmani that no one should worry about these threats. We shall deal with the matter adequately if anyone misbehaves.

All my love,<br>
Papu

---

382.                                   Anand Bhawan,<br>
Allahabad,<br>
7th March, 1957

Darling Papu,

It was so nice hearing your voice on the phone.

Immersed as I am in all this election excitement – and you know what a low level Allahabad has reached in this respect – I find it very difficult to imagine any social functions such as you must be having just now for the Danish Prime Minister.[3]

I am afraid you are going to be very angry but I am taking the risk and the responsibility is entirely mine. Seth Govind Das[4] is very much perturbed about Jabalpur and, apart from his numerous telegrams and telephones, has now sent his nephew. I believe your speech in Jabalpur is being misinterpreted and Sethji feels that my going is the only thing that might help a little. Lal Bahadurji had offered to go instead but Sethji was not very happy about this. Also, I feel that it is not right for Lal Bahadurji to be out of Allahabad just at this stage. So, I have decided to go to Jabalpur tomorrow afternoon. Lal Bahadurji is giving me a twin-engined Beechcraft for the journey.

The day after that is your last polling in Manjhanpur. This is the place where you had a Kisan Sabha[5] a few months ago. After the polling I fly to Sultanpur for a meeting in the town.

---

1. Lal Bahadur Shastri: eminent Congress leader from U.P.; held various positions in the Union Cabinet between 1952 and 1963; Prime Minister, June 1964–January 1966.

2. Hammad Usmani: Principal of Unani Medical College, Allahabad.

3. Hans Christian Hansen: Prime Minister of Denmark, 1955–60.

4. Seth Govind Das: Congress leader and parliamentarian.

5. Peasants' Association.

This is indeed a tiring programme. But I am sure I can stand it and will be able to rest after the 12th. As you know, staying in Allahabad is really just as tiring because there are a series of meetings and constant noise & movement.

Please do not worry about my health. I was a bit low two days ago but am quite all right now. There is no point in people feeling that I have let them down at the last moment.

I went to Mirzapur the day before yesterday and had a very good meeting there. They had had a hailstorm and it was quite cool. Allahabad had warmed up considerably but has cooled down again since yesterday.

There is much talk of C. B. Gupta being given a seat from Nainital or some such place. I personally feel that he should not contest for some time – at least a year. If he had lost by a thousand or less, it would not have mattered much but 11,000 is quite a figure, especially in a town like Lucknow which is far from ignorant or illiterate. His being given a safe seat soon will create a very bad impression on the public. The trouble is that Pantji will not say no.

Much love,<br>Indu

383.                                              [Prime Minister's House],
                                                           New Delhi,
                                                    11th April, 1957

Papu,
The day before yesterday I went to see Papi at the Willingdon Hospital and was shocked to see that the beautiful mobile dental clinic which was given by the German Government has not been used at all and is lying in the servants' quarters of the hospital. Until a short while ago it was lying on the front lawn but because there were so many remarks and criticisms it was removed where it cannot be seen.

I do feel this is a great pity. There is so much need for such mobile vans in India. The K.N.M. Hospital has a health van and it is doing so much good work that we wish we had several, and in a short time it has done thousands of miles.

I do wish this dental van could be given to somebody who could put it to proper use.

Indu

384.                                Prime Minister's House,
New Delhi,
14th June, 1957

Darling Papu,
Yadunath Singh [1] has just been to see me regarding your letter to the President about the appointment of Mrs Mathai [2] to the post of Deputy Comptroller of Govt Hospitality. Yadunath says that the President has asked him not to take action since he wishes to discuss the matter with you on your return.

It seems that the President has a proposal that R.B. [Rashtrapati Bhawan] should be taken out of the G.H.O. [Government Hospitality Organisation] and that he should be given increased allowances and be allowed to look after the guests who will be put up at R.B. I suppose this means that he will not be accountable to anyone for the expenditure on the guests.

Yadunath expressed the hope that it would not be desirable to have 'a regrettable controversy between two high V.I.P.s'. He certainly is bumptious to say the least.

I am writing this to you not to bother you on your trip [3] or to make you take any action or write to the President but only so that you may have time to think the whole thing over & that it should not burst upon you like a bombshell on your return to Delhi.

Some very ugly things are happening right around you. It is of course the familiar green-eyed monster jealousy. What can one do?

Lots of love to you, darling,
Indu

---

385.                                        Raj Niwas,
Simla,
18th June, 1957

Darling Papu,
It seems now that our motives for building the small house are in doubt.

---

1. Major-General Yadunath Singh: Military Secretary to the President, 1955–6.
2. Mrs Mathai: Deputy Comptroller of Household who looked after Teen Murti House.
3. Jawaharlal Nehru went on a four-week tour of foreign countries in mid-June 1957. He visited Syria, Denmark, Finland, Norway, Sweden, Netherlands, Cairo, Sudan and London (where he attended the Commonwealth Prime Ministers' Conference, 26th June–5th July, 1957).

It is said by some that it is a ruse so that we will have 'two houses'. [1]

I have sent a message to Sachdev [2] not to go ahead until you sanction the estimates. Anyhow it will take time to prepare the ground to perfect the plan.

It is warm here. The house is lovely but full of guests, dogs & flying squirrels! They have some lovely bird houses which we should copy for our garden.

Lots of love,
Indu

---

386.                                [Oslo],
21st June, 1957

Darling Indu,

Ever since I reached Damascus I have been kept on the move, except for the periods of flight. On the 14th June I got up in Delhi at five a.m. That night I retired to bed at four a.m. (Delhi time). That is I had a twenty-three hour day, with some rest in the plane on the way to Damascus. In other places it was not quite so bad but the evening or night found me rather tired – a brief night's sleep refreshed me.

I have thoroughly enjoyed my visits to Copenhagen, Helsinki and here at Oslo. The weather has been near perfect. At Copenhagen it was so warm that a fan would have been welcome. The P.M. of Denmark, Hansen, insisted on taking me to the Tivoli. I was expected to praise it and I did so. But I was quite overwhelmed by the garish lighting. Henceforth I shall not criticise Brindaban near Mysore. [3]

Everywhere people ask me about you and remember your visit. You have evidently many friends in these countries. At Helsinki, a friend of yours who was with you in Switzerland (I forget her name) asked me to convey her love to you.

I have had very warm welcomes from the people. Crowds gather wherever I go, sometimes waiting in the streets till midnight. All this has been a heartening experience.

I hope you and the children are keeping well – I am fit and impressing everybody with my fitness.

---

1. There was a proposal to create a small residence as a retreat for the Prime Minister but the proposal was shelved.

2. M. R. Sachdev was secretary in the Ministry of Works and Housing.

3. Brindaban Gardens near Mysore were illuminated at night.

In the new house that is being built for us, I think the study room should have built-in bookshelves, as many as possible.

Love,
Papu

---

387.

Raj Niwas,
Simla,
21st June, 1957

Darling Papu,

We have been reading of your trip with great interest. From tomorrow we will be cut off as we shall be constantly on the move and may not see any newspapers.

The trip is through Bilaspur, Suket, Mandi, Kulu, & Kangra. We shall go to Mandi for an evening and a night & to the hydro-electric works at Jogindernagar. Those are the only parts of the programme which are unconnected with social welfare. Since we were passing so close by I thought the children would enjoy those visits.

We reach Jammu on the 29th and go on to Srinagar where work will keep me until the 6th. After that we might take a week off and go to some quiet place. I hope to be back in Delhi by the 14th July or a couple of days later.

Much love,
Indu

---

388.

9 Kensington Palace Gardens,
London, W.8 [1]
27th June, 1957

Indu darling,

On arrival here two days ago I received two letters from you, one dated 14th June and the other 18th June . . . [2]

I was much impressed by my visits to the Scandinavian countries and I believe that my visit did a lot of good also. Certainly I had rather extraordinary welcomes there from all classes of people. Sweden, which is supposed to be rather a formal and rigid country, did not behave to me in that way at all. The newspapers there were full of my visit with innumerable pictures. Very little was said in the London papers about my visit to Scandinavia. Almost it was ignored.

---

1. Jawaharlal Nehru went to London in connection with the Commonwealth Prime Ministers' Conference.
2. Refers to letters Nos 384 and 385.

I have now been here for two days. Tomorrow evening I go to Chequers for the night. The next day I shall proceed to Broadlands for another day and night. Then return to London. It is very warm here, almost like early October weather in Delhi.

Last night I had to go to Windsor for a banquet there. I had never been to Windsor Castle before. I must say that I was impressed by the collection of treasure there. The rooms are very gorgeous indeed. The room we dined in contained pictures of the people who attended the Council of Vienna in 1815 to settle the fate of Napoleon. There is a story that when De Gaulle visited that room and saw all these pictures, he said: 'What a lot of people it took to face Napoleon.' When Bulganin and Khrushchev[1] went into that room, they spotted immediately a big painting of Czar Alexander I and referred to him: 'Oh, there is our national hero.'

But the most attractive part of Windsor was the library which contained fascinating old books and prints.

Suhrawardy[2] was there. He was rather glum during dinner partly because Mrs Diefenbaker, wife of the new Canadian Premier, who was sitting next to him ignored him completely and was overwhelmed by Prince Philip on [her] other side. After the dinner, and no doubt during it, Suhrawardy consumed quantities of alcoholic drinks. A little before we left late at night, Suhrawardy became quite boisterous in his behaviour. Indeed, the Duke of Gloucester gently told him that he was losing control of himself.

Nevertheless, Suhrawardy is a clever man and he is being made much of here. He is out to pour out, privately at least, the most vitriolic and false propaganda about India.

Krishna Menon received a letter from Chhoti Puphi today. As usual with her letters, this is quite an extraordinary document threatening all and sundry with dire consequences. It deals with the Rossellini[3] episode. Why she has brought poor Krishna in the picture, I do not know because he has had hardly anything to do with it. I am writing a letter to her, a copy of which I enclose . . .

Love,
Papu

---

1. N. A. Bulganin was Prime Minister of the Soviet Union from 1955 to 1958. In 1956 he headed a delegation to the U.K., accompanied by Nikita Khrushchev, at this time First Secretary of the Central Committee. Krushchev succeeded Bulganin as Prime Minister in 1958.

2. H. S. Suhrawardy: leader of Muslim League in Bengal; Prime Minister of Pakistan, 1956–7.

3. Roberto Rossellini, the Italian film director, visited India earlier in 1957.

389.                              29th June, 1957

Darling Papu,
Your letter from Oslo [1] has reached me here today. It was very welcome.

As you know I have been constantly on the move – each night in a different dak bungalow . . . But the boys have enjoyed being with me & have had fun on the whole. Our two holidays – a day in Manali and a day in Barot – were perfectly delightful. Even Rajiv, one of the most ardent lovers of Kashmir, had to concede that Manali is one of the loveliest places on earth. It is still unspoilt & peaceful. However the boys enjoyed Barot most because of the added excitement of the funicular and staying in a log cabin. Barot is a tiny village tucked away behind the ranges at Jogindernagar, right at the foot of the snow mountains, which looked very clean & fresh with a layer of newly fallen snow & there was crispness in the air even where we were.

Today was our worst day. It is very hot here & tomorrow will be equally bad until we reach Srinagar.

Love from us all,<br>Indu

---

390.                            Prime Minister's House,
New Delhi,<br>1st May, 1958

Darling Papu,
I should not presume to advise you but I have been thinking over our little talk of an hour ago.

Having once suggested giving up the Prime Ministership and started a train of thought and discussion, is it wise to go back to the *status quo*? Will it not have an adverse effect? So much is rotten in our politics that everybody sees things through his own avaricious myopic eyes and is quite unable to understand nobility or greatness. There will therefore be a feeling that you had no intention of giving up the P.M.ship and were only bluffing.

Let them try to manage by themselves, otherwise they will only drag you down with their own rottenness. If you are outside, it may at least reassure the general public that you are not responsible for all the wrongdoing.

I have so much to say but there is no time.

All my love to you,<br>Indu

---

1. Refers to letter No. 386.

391.                            In flight Beirut–Geneva,
                                       15th July, 1958

Darling Papu,

Rajeshwar Dayal[1], Jansen[2], etc, turned up at the airport. Dayal said he had only gone to bed at two, so it was really nice of him to come to receive me at six twenty. They did not know very much more about Iraq than we had already heard.

If our young writers were not so concerned with competing for the title of 'Angry young man' what material they could get for stories and plays out of the tragi-comedy, or is it comi-tragedy of Lebanon.[3] Dayal says that there is a great deal of shooting but most of it is in the air. Naturally if someone happens to come in the way, he's had it, as they say. Chamoun[4] & party, who control the newspapers, are very angry with the U.N. observers. Also they are deliberately trying to minimise the Baghdad happenings. Dayal feels that if the General gets elected on the 24th there will be peace, since both the parties support him. But it is difficult to prophesy what impact Iraq will have on Lebanon. It is the strangest civil war. The army is completely neutral, in the sense that they are not fighting and at least forty per cent of the people don't care one way or another & will support whoever is top dog.

*Later*

Switzerland is so clean it strikes one forcibly every time.

                           Love,
                           Indu

---

*[In February 1959, Indira Gandhi was elected President of the Indian National Congress.]*

1. Rajeshwar Dayal: Permanent Representative at the United Nations, 1952–4; Ambassador in Yugoslavia, 1954–8; concurrently Indian Ambassador to Greece, Jan–June, 1958; member, U.N. Observer Group in Lebanon, June–Dec, 1958; High Commissioner in Pakistan, 1958–62; Foreign Secretary, 1967–8.

2. G. H. Jansen: Press Attaché, New York, 1952–5, Djakarta, 1955. Later became a journalist specialising in West Asian affairs.

3. Unrest in Lebanon during the summer of 1958 amounted to virtual civil war. On 14th July, U.S. troops landed at Beirut at the urgent request of the Lebanese Government to restore public order.

4. Camille Chamoun: political leader who served as President of Lebanon from 1952 to 1958.

392.                         Prime Minister's House,
                                     New Delhi,
                                23rd April, 1959

Darling Indu,

I am leaving Delhi for Dehra Dun and Mussoorie and you will be coming here. I have been missing you and worrying a little about you. I hope you are keeping more or less fit. I see from your programme that we are not likely to meet till early in May. We appear to move like stars in their courses without coming in contact.

Pantji has had the attack which I always feared he might get. It is called a mild one but even so it means many weeks in the nursing home and rest afterwards.

The Tibet situation is getting more serious so far as we are concerned. It is going to be heavy weather all round.

I shall be seeing Rajiv and Sanjay.

                             Love,
                             Papu

---

393.            In running train between Tiruppur & Erode,
                                    5th June, 1959
                                    7.50 p.m.

Darling Papu,

You must be speaking at Mettupalaiyam just now. We missed the train there by just a few minutes & caught it at Coimbatore at 6.20. I have now had an hour's sleep & am feeling a little more alive. This is a very shaky & sooty compartment.

At Erode our compartment will be detached from the main train. I shall give this note to someone who is going to Delhi. Dhebarbhai, Sadiq Ali[1] & some others are at the other end of the train. They are going to Madras & some of them will proceed to Delhi.

The more I think of it, the more I like the idea of the boys coming south. We shall, of course, have to travel third, otherwise it would be too expensive but I am told that one can get small third class compartments.

Going to the Doon School & living at the P.M.'s House, they are not at all in touch with the life of an average Indian, especially in the villages. It would be a good experience for them to spend some time at Gandhinagar, see the village life of the area & then see Ooty, Kotagiri, Kodaikanal etc. What do you think?

1. For Sadiq Ali see p. 290 n.2, letter No. 149.

Travelling third will be a tremendous experience too. I should like them to know something of my work & life.

Love,<br>Indu

We reach Erode at 8.30.

---

394.                                                    In flight,
                                              20th June, 1959

Papu,
I do not know what line your discussions with the Kerala Govt will take. I just want to mention some points.

1. There is no point in calling the agitation communal. It is communal only in so far as everything is communal in Kerala, including the Communists. The Communists very cleverly played the Nairs against the Catholics & now are trying to play the Ezhuvas against both.

2. If we are going to ask the local Congress to withdraw from the present movement, we must outline some other programme for them. They cannot just stand aloof.

3. If the Education Bill is to be discussed, the question of textbooks is important. Naturally I have not checked them myself but the newspapers reported that they tell a lot about Stalin and Mao Tse-tung, nothing about modern India except our foreign policy. This matter was taken up with the Union Ministry of Education – Dr Shrimali[1] is reported to have replied that Education was a State subject. This is not good enough. We should not permit any anti-national bias in education.

Love,<br>Indu

P.S.
Since I have talked with Dhebarbhai this is rather out of date but am still sending it.

Much love,<br>Indu

---

1. Dr Kalu Lal Shrimali: Minister for Education, 1958–63.

395.                                New Delhi,
                                      30th October, 1959

Darling Papu,
It is now three forty-five a.m. It must be twenty years since I have felt compelled to get up at an odd hour of night to write letters! This will show how agitated I am. I just had to write to Pantji and I am sending you a copy of the letter to enlist your support in withstanding the 'affectionate pressure' which is being put upon me. [1]

Many reasons, all equally valid and cogent, can be given for my wishing to discontinue. But deep down there is always 'the real reason' which one does not tell about because no one would understand.

Each person probably feels that he is different from the rest of humanity, but in my case there may be some justification for this thought. We are moulded by our experiences and our reactions to those experiences.

Few people could have had the fortune of such truly wonderful parents, and also rather remarkable grandparents – Dadu was known and admired, but not many discerned the deep compassion & understanding of my Nani. Since earliest childhood I have been surrounded by exceptional people and have participated in exceptional events. This has given me a somewhat unusual attitude. I am not terribly concerned with public acclamation or the reverse, nor do I feel any honour in holding a high position. Some people are attaching importance to my presiding over a Congress session & delivering the address. To me it has no special meaning or attraction.

The circumstances in which I passed my girlhood – both the domestic and public spheres – were not easy. The world is a cruel place for the best of us and specially so for the sensitive. We are apt to guard ourselves with whatever armour we can lay our minds on . . .

. . . So it was at a comparatively late age that I began discovering the world and people and, above all, myself.

This brought a realisation of the richness of life but also of my debt to the world. I felt a burden on me and these last eight years or so, I have worked harder and longer as the years went by, always feeling that I could never do enough. Last year there suddenly came a moment of lightness, as if the last of the debt had been paid off. By the time I became President, I just was not in the mood for this sort of work and I have felt like a bird in a very small cage, my wings hitting against the bars whichever way I move.

---

1. Congressmen were putting pressure on Indira to retain the Presidentship of the Indian National Congress for a second term. However she refused to hold the office for more than one term.

The time has come for me to live my own life. What will it be? I don't know at all. For the moment, I just want to be free as a piece of flotsam waiting for the waves to wash me up on some shore, from where I shall arise and find my own direction.

The experience of being President of the Congress has been exhilarating at times, depressing at times, but certainly worthwhile. But I have already begun thinking of it in the past tense – my mind is racing ahead and I can only be warped & unhappy if I have to continue.

Sorry to inflict so many pages of illegible handwriting on you first thing in the morning.

All my love,
Indu

---

396.

Prime Minister's House,
New Delhi,
9th November, 1959

Darling – I am enclosing a cheque for Rs. 500/- ten days before your birthday so that you might buy something you like.

All my love,
Papu

---

397.

9 Kensington Palace Gardens,
London W.8,
1st May, 1960

Indu darling,

I arrived here about a couple of hours ago. The journey was fairly comfortable and uneventful. The aircraft was very crowded, but that did not make any difference to me. I slept a little before Cairo where we reached at four o'clock Cairo time or six thirty Indian time. After that, I could not sleep as it was daylight. At the Cairo Aerodrome Ratan, Rajan, Avtar and Rita,[1] apart from the Egyptian officials, came to see me. Then we stopped at Rome for nearly an hour . . .

Chhoti Puphi is still staying at 9 Kensington Palace Gardens.

Love,
Papu

---

1. See Kinship Circle.

398.                           [Prime Minister's House],
New Delhi,
3rd May, 1960

Darling Papu,
It is around midnight. We returned to Delhi around ten fifteen. Just because I was telling everyone in Bombay how cool & pleasant Delhi was, the weather has changed with a vengeance & even at this hour it is terribly hot. In the daytime it is like a furnace.

All your side of the house is in a shambles – scaffolding is up & all kinds of repairs are being undertaken. Hence the lift is unusable.

The situation in Turkey seems to be worsening. [1] Apart from everything, it does not seem right to be the guests of a Government against whom the people are agitating & with cause. The Turkish Govt may be too preoccupied to think of anything but how to deal with the riots – should you or Mr Pillai [2] not send a message suggesting that in view of their difficulties the visit might be postponed. Those few extra days could be spent in some cool place nearby. I am not worried about the physical but the political aspect of your visit.

Love,
Indu

399.                           Prime Minister's House,
New Delhi,
4th May, 1960

Darling Papu,
Your letter of the 1st [3] came this morning. I was glad to read of your visit to Harrow and your joining in the singing.

I saw Dr Radhakrishnan this morning. He feels very strongly that you should take a complete holiday for longer than two or three days. The state of the Congress & Parliament is deteriorating. Firm guidance and attention to detail is imperative but you are not feeling fresh & alert enough to give it & your programme is so crowded with appointments & tours – good in themselves but secondary in importance to the other

1. A commission appointed by the Turkish Government on 18th April to enquire into the alleged subversive activities of the Turkish Opposition party banned all political activity and thereby sparked off violent anti-Government demonstrations in Ankara, Izmir and Istanbul.

2. N. R. Pillai: Secretary-General in Ministry of External Affairs, 1952–60.

3. Refers to letter No. 397. Indira read about the visit to Harrow in *The Hindustan Times* of 4th May, 1960.

things. So many good ideas and programmes are being channelled in the wrong direction, there is so much drift in our political life, only because no one has the time or inclination to keep an eye on them.

About Turkey also, the Vice-President agrees that your visit will be greatly misunderstood in other countries. It is not possible for the Turkish Govt to ask you not to come. They will naturally want to use your visit to bolster their prestige at this critical moment. But for us it should be quite easy to tell them that you do not wish to trouble them or add to their difficulties.

If the visit is given up I hope you will use those days to good purpose – that is a quiet & cool place without official engagements. Could the Cairo dates be changed so as to enable you to have the holiday to Europe, before going to Egypt?

If Seshan[1] is not busy with your work, could he come to the airport on the 14th when I am passing through?

Love,
Indu

---

400.                                                New Delhi,
                                                   [June, 1960]

Darling Papu,
I feel so bad going off to Srinagar & leaving you all alone in this terrible heat. But the children are badly in need of a change.

I do hope you can come for more than a couple of days. You need to get away every now & then and we shall all be missing you.

Lots of love,
Indu

---

401.                                        Prime Minister's House,
                                                   New Delhi,
                                                11th June, 1960

Indu darling,
Thank you for your note[2] from the station. There is nothing at all for you to feel bad about me. I think you have done the right thing to take the children to Kashmir for a short spell there.

1. N. K. Seshan: Personal secretary to Jawaharlal Nehru and subsequently to Indira Gandhi.
2. Refers to letter No. 400.

Today, at your instance, Krishna Mehta came to lunch with me. She grew lyrical in praise of Kishtwar and round about. Of course she has done this previously and for many long years I have wanted to go to Kishtwar because of the accounts I have read of the beauty of the scenery there which, some say, surpasses the valley of Kashmir.

The novel element introduced by Krishna in her talk was to make me realise that this is fairly easily accessible. I had an idea that it took several days' march. Now it appears that a good road has been built from Batote and the distance is about fifty miles. Buses run on this road. I was told there was even an airfield in Kishtwar, but how big it is I do not know. Krishna tells me that even the road from Batote goes through magnificent mountain scenery. It is worthwhile to go along that road for ten or twelve miles even though we may not go further. You are going by car from Jammu to Srinagar and you must have passed Batote. Presumably you will come back the same way, at least up to Jammu. Why not go to Kishtwar for a day or two? If that is not feasible, why not at least go along that road for some distance?

As I told you, I am vaguely thinking of going for a day or two to Kashmir. The real object is to go to Leh in Ladakh. Perhaps I might be able to fix this up about the first week of July. I would then go, let us say, for two days to Srinagar and one or two days to Ladakh. On my return journey, I should like to pay a visit to Kishtwar for a day or so. That would probably mean coming back by car up to Jammu. All this is very vague. But if I do so, I should like to fit in with your return date so that we might come back together.

Love,<br>Papu

402.

Prime Minister's House,<br>New Delhi,<br>13th June, 1960

Indu darling,

I had a talk with Subroto Mukherjee[1] today about my going to Ladakh. He said that this could easily be arranged, but he would like it to be as early as possible in order to avoid the early rains. He would have liked me to go some time during the last week of June. That is not feasible because I have a good deal of work to do here. On the 1st of July, there is the celebration of Ghana's new Republic, and I should like to be here then. So the earliest I can leave Delhi is the 2nd July.

1. For Subroto Mukherjee see p. 333 n.2, letter No. 173.

This means that the earliest I can go to Ladakh is the 3rd July. At first I had intended going to Leh, spending a night there, going on the next day for a flight over our eastern border and possibly getting down at Chusul, and returning to Srinagar. There is one snag about this programme. If I reach Leh and the second day is not a good day for flying, I might get hung up there till the weather clears.

Therefore, it seems better to go to Leh from Srinagar and come back the same day. The next feasible day I go for the flight to the border and also come back the same day. On both these days I shall have to start early, about six a.m., as that is the best time for flying. I should return by twelve noon or perhaps a little earlier.

Provisionally, therefore, I am arranging to reach Srinagar on the 2nd July forenoon. If the weather is good, I shall go on the 3rd to Leh early morning and come back before midday. Probably on the third day, if the weather is good, I shall fly to the border and come back.

My present intention is, subject to developments, to stay in Srinagar for four days, including the visits to Ladakh. This means from the 2nd to the 5th. On the 6th, I should like to start on my return journey. As I have written to you, I should like, if possible, to pay a brief visit to Kishtwar as well as the other place nearby (I think it is called Bhadarwah) from where Krishna Mehta comes. Although there is said to be an air strip at Kishtwar, I think it will be better to go by car as this will enable me to see the new tunnel also and go over the mountain road from Batote to Kishtwar. Probably I shall have to spend the night round about there. The next day I could go to Jammu by car and take the plane from there to Delhi. This is a rough idea of what I have in mind at present. I do not know how this will fit in with your programme.

I am writing briefly to Bakhshi Saheb about my visit. I do not know where I should stay at Srinagar. I would, of course, like to be near you, but perhaps that may not be feasible because you are in a houseboat. In any event, I should like to spend much of my time with you and the children. I do hope that Bakhshi Saheb will not have functions for me.

Delhi continues to be as hot as ever. I am pretty well used to it. On the whole, I am having a fairly easy time as after a succession of Cabinet meetings, we are having an interval. Pantji is probably going tomorrow to Naini Tal for some days.

The Akali demonstrations,[1] morcha,[2] etc, were a big show yesterday. Our police behaved rather well and with great restraint. The Akalis were very violent. But, in spite of all this violence and stone-throwing from

1. Refers to an agitation by the Akali Party for a Punjabi speaking state in North India.
2. A militant campaign.

houses, and especially from the Sisganj Gurudwara, which is a several-storeyed building, there was no firing and not much in the way of lathi charges. Tear gas was used several times. In spite of the violence and aggressiveness of the Akali crowd, the police held them, prevented the procession, and ultimately cleared Chandni Chowk.[1]

I hope you are having a good time.

Love,<br>
Papu

---

403.

H.B. Argonaut,<br>
Nagin Lake,<br>
Srinagar,<br>
15th June, 1960

Darling Papu,

Your letter[2] came last evening. The day we arrived was very warm but since then it has been cool, even cold. It rained a lot yesterday & the mountains are covered with fresh snow. Somehow one is much closer to Nature in a houseboat than in a house & it is very peaceful.

Sanjay & I went swimming only once – it was cold, cloudy & windy but the swim was very refreshing. We have one of Tito's canoes & Bakhshi has sent us a rubber rescue boat. We had planned to go to Sonamarg for a couple of days but if the weather does not improve there is not much point in going. We hear much of a place called Desu which is just above Kukernag & might go there instead.

Nikkubhai doesn't think much of Kishtwar. He says it is not a patch on the valley; however he is not necessarily a good judge. I am so happy you are coming.

Love from us all,<br>
Indu

---

404.

H.B. Argonaut,<br>
Nagin Lake,<br>
Srinagar,<br>
16th June, 1960

Darling Papu,

I wrote to you this morning but your second letter[3] came a short while

1. Chandni Chowk: the central plaza in the walled city of Delhi.
2. Refers to letter No. 401.
3. Refers to letter No. 402.

ago. It is certainly good news that you are coming. About your staying we could all move to wherever you stay but it would be a pity if you had to stay in the State guest house. They are both so centrally situated & hot & full of flies and give no opportunity for sitting in the garden. I have just had a bright idea – though I doubt if Bakhshi Saheb will take kindly to it. Our houseboat is in a lovely, very quiet spot. Just five minutes' boat ride from us are two houses belonging to Pandit Upendranath Kaul.[1] Puphi stayed in the bigger house when she was last in Srinagar. He is himself in the smaller house now but is moving in three or four days. (We called there this morning.) There is a garden, a lovely big chinar & a magnificent view of the snowy ranges, as well as Shankaracharya & Hari Parbat. I wonder if it would be possible for you to stay there? I am sure Kaul would gladly offer the house. We are about three and a half miles away from the guest house where you normally stay – the road is a good one.

The Director of Tourism & everybody with whom I have discussed Kishtwar says that there is *no* motorable road right up to Kishtwar. I did not mention your name but said that I might go. They discouraged me strongly & say that it would be a tiring trip with nothing worthwhile at the other end. Would you care to go to Desu instead – it is around forty-five miles from here? The drive to Jammu would be most dusty, hot & unpleasant.

Love,<br>Indu

P.S.
Bakhshi Saheb went off to Pahalgam for three days, last evening. He was looking unwell – his eyes watering, face swollen. So he may not reply to you immediately. Rashid, Bakhshi's brother, is here.

*17th*
He says it would be best to fly to K[ishtwar]. Otherwise [I should go by] jeep.

---

405.

H.B. Argonaut,<br>Nagon Lake,<br>Srinagar,<br>18th June, 1960

Darling Papu,
Today is the first clear day since our arrival & it is a truly magnificent

1. Member of a prominent Kashmiri family which was on cordial terms with the Nehrus.

sight. In Kashmir there is always an element of sadness, or is it melancholy. Perhaps it is due to the willows & their droopy look, reminding one of Davies's poem on the kingfisher

> So runs it in thy blood to choose
> For haunts the lovely pools, & keep
> In company with trees that weep.

The boys are busy. Sanjay swims, rows & takes photographs. He is very independent & loves this life close to nature, observing dragonflies & kingfishers. Yesterday a kingfisher came right into our sitting room – a swift perched on Rajiv's shoulder. Rajiv seems to have become a much more town's person. He has not been able to swim because of a bad cough ... I hear Lekha has come to Bombay to hunt for servants!

Let me know about the house. I have not spoken to anyone yet. Bakhshi Saheb returns on the 20th – in time to receive Krishna Menon.

Love,
Indu

P.S.
Will it be possible for the four of us to return to Delhi with you?

From the point of view of fresh air & relaxation I wish it were possible for you to stay around here. Someone is sure to be coming from Delhi to see about security. Could he come & see me, so that I can show him the house?

Here is our favourite kingfisher bringing our love.

Indu

---

406.

H.B. *Argonaut*,
Nagin Lake,
Srinagar,
19th June, 1960

Darling Papu,
Bakhshi Saheb is returning this evening. Ghulam Mohd – (I can't remember what his present designation is but he is an older man whom we have known for some years & who seems to have been appointed our guardian by Bakhshi Saheb. He comes every other day with fruit or nuts or sweets or trout.) – came last evening & I mentioned your visit & the question of where to stay. He will speak to Bakhshi Saheb, to whom he is very close, but he is sure that Bakhshi Saheb will offer you

the choice either of Kaul's cottage (since we have made the suggestion) or Dachigam, the forest bungalow which is about sixteen miles from Srinagar. Dachigam will be cooler & has more opportunities for walks. You know it well. Just now the lakeside is cool & very pleasant but if the temperature rises appreciably it can be warm too. The cottage has its own bathing *ghat* surrounded by yellow lotus lilies & the boys will be proud to row you around. Besides, although you will be very quiet & peaceful, you will still be much nearer town & the airport.

I don't know what you will decide about Kishtwar. It is not possible to fly as only a small plane can land & I do not think you should use a small plane to go over the Banihal. The road trip is too long, dusty & hot – about 202 miles Srinagar to K. & 157 from K. to Jammu.

Please send a cheque for Rs. 500/- to Mrs Naresh Kathju – a belated wedding present. She leaves for England on the 3rd July. The office has P. N. Kathju's address.

Love,
Indu

———

407.　　　　　　　　　　　　　　　　Prime Minister's House,
　　　　　　　　　　　　　　　　　　　New Delhi,
　　　　　　　　　　　　　　　　　　20th June, 1960

Darling Indu,
I shall probably reach Srinagar airfield early on July 2nd at about eight thirty a.m. It is better to fly early in the morning. I shall start by Viscount at seven a.m. from Palam.

The next day I shall go to Chushul, etc, starting at six a.m. for Srinagar airfield.

Bakhshi suggests that I should stay at Dachigam. That will be very far from the airfield and therefore rather inconvenient.

He also suggests that all of you should shift to Dachigam. That I think is not at all necessary. You should stay on in your houseboat.

Love,
Papu

408.

Prime Minister's House,
New Delhi,
20th June, 1960

Indu darling,

This morning I wrote a hurried letter[1] to you. The President went off to the Soviet Union at six a.m. from Palam. We all went to see him off, although that meant getting up very early. On my return from Palam I wrote to you.

On coming to the office later in the morning I received two letters from you, one dated 16th and the other dated 18th June.[2]

As for staying in Srinagar, I should very much like to stay somewhere in Nagin Bagh, in a house or in a tent. The more I think of it the more I do not approve of the idea of staying at Dachigam. That is much too far and is closed in. If you like, you can speak to Bakhshi Saheb about the house. Even a tent would be good. I am also writing to him on the subject.

As for going to Kishtwar, it is possible for me to fly there in a small plane. Subroto Mukherjee has agreed to fly me there, although I told him that I would prefer to go by road. Anyhow, he will keep a small aircraft ready. Now that I have said that I would go there, I should like to keep my promise. I should have liked to go to Bhadarwah also. This is in a slightly different direction. This is the place from where Krishna Mehta comes. I doubt, however, if this would be possible. In any event, if I go to Kishtwar, I shall have to spend a night there and from there I shall have to fly to Jammu in a small aircraft. From Jammu I can come back by the Viscount. In flying from Srinagar to Kishtwar or Kishtwar to Jammu I am told that I should do this in the early morning before ten o'clock.

All of you can, of course, come back with me to Delhi from Srinagar. There will be no difficulty about that.

Love,
Papu

---

409.

H.B. *Argonaut*,
Nagin Lake,
Srinagar,
21st June, 1960

Darling Papu,

As Rajiv has written, we are planning to go to Daksun on the 23rd.

1. Refers to letter No. 407.
2. Refers to letters No. 404 and 405.

Bakhshi Saheb will join us on the 24th & we shall return together on the 25th. If it is really very attractive we may even stay on an extra day.

The new Chashme Shahi guest house seems to have been built to spite the Yuvraj. It has a wonderful situation but the design is the old stereotype one.

We are all so tired of eating fish that fishing has had to be banned for the family.

It continues to be chilly & windy.

Rajiv has a tutor for Chemistry every morning. I do a bit of English with the boys & am trying to learn Spanish myself.

Love,<br>Indu

---

410.                                             H.B. *Argonaut*,
                                                 Nagin Lake,
                                                 Srinagar,
                                                 22nd June, 1960

Darling Papu,

This evening I received a letter from you dated the 20th.[1] You mention writing earlier the same day but the other letter[2] has not reached me. I hear that Bakhshi Saheb has decided that you should stay at the Chashme Shahi rest house. The Yuvraj has offered it. His mother is temporarily moving to the Kabutar Khana, now known as the Lakshmi Villa. Feroze wants to leave at the end of the month and he has a meeting of the P.A.C.[3] on the 1st. I cannot figure out how we can accompany you back to Delhi. The big plane on which you are coming will probably return to Delhi on the same day & will return to Jammu in time to pick you up again. On the small plane there will not be room for us all. Perhaps we could motor to Jammu but we shall have to leave a couple of days early. However don't be bothered about all this – it will sort itself out. But do please ask some P.A. to let me know the exact programme.

We leave tomorrow for Daksun.

1. Refers to letter No. 408.
2. Refers to letter No. 407.
3. Public Accounts Committee: a Committee of the Indian Parliament created for the examination of the annual finance accounts of the Government of India and various bodies which draw their monies from the Government.

The Chilean Ambassador has written to say that his Govt have invited me to Chile. Has anything been decided about Africa?

Love,
Indu

I am not too keen on taking the children or going myself to Kishtwar as it will be hot, dusty & full of insects.

---

411.                    Prime Minister's House,
New Delhi,
23rd June, 1960

Indu darling,
I returned this afternoon from Gujarat. I had a good tour there even though the heavy rains came in the way and I could not go to some places because of them. My return journey this afternoon on the Ilyushin was again a rather unpleasant experience. However, I have recovered.

I have had a letter from Bakhshi Saheb in which he tells me that he is making arrangements for me to stay at Chashme Shahi rest house. Karan Singh has also written inviting me to go there. I suppose I had better stick to this now. I however hope that I shall be able to spend some time with you and the children at Nagin Bagh.

I shall write to you more about my possible programme later.

I was happy to receive the little notes from Rajiv and Sanjay.

Love,
Papu

---

412.                    Prime Minister's House,
New Delhi,
24th June, 1960

Darling Indu,
I have your letter of the 22nd June.[1] I wrote to you last night.[2] I have now had a talk with Subroto Mukherjee. It seems to me that the proposed visit to Kishtwar is rather a complicated and dusty affair. This will involve my going to Jammu and spending the night there. Subroto has now ruled that he will not permit me to go by air anywhere in the afternoon. Possibly, therefore, I shall give up the Kishtwar visit and

---

1. Refers to letter No. 410.
2. Refers to letter No. 411.

return to Delhi direct from Srinagar. We can fix this up after our arrival there.

Bakhshi Saheb wants me to reach Srinagar airport at twelve. I do not like this at all as this will break up my first day there. I have, therefore, arranged now to reach Srinagar airport at 9.00 a.m. on the 2nd July.

There will be no difficulty in regard to you and the children returning with me. For the present my programme is to go on the 3rd to Chushul, coming back by midday to Srinagar and to go to Leh on the 4th. Thimayya and Subroto Mukherjee will accompany me. From Chushul I would like to go by helicopter to the forward areas. The helicopter can carry only four persons.

Love,<br>Papu

---

413.

H.B. Argonaut,<br>Nagin Lake,<br>Srinagar,<br>27th June, 1960

Darling Papu,

We returned yesterday afternoon from Daksun. It is a pleasant place, pine and fir forest & trout streams. It was a nice change. There is a grains preserve [or store] & later on when the maize is ripening, the big grizzly bears come down to raid the fields. There are also stags & other wild animals. The boys fished one whole afternoon & evening & the next morning Rajiv & I went for a longish walk. Feroze got so anxious that the *chowkidar* was sent to search for us!

We are planning to go to Sonamarg just for the day tomorrow. Rajiv is keen to see it.

Last evening we went to the middle of the lake for a swim & were caught in a storm. We had to seek the aid of the motorboat to tow us home & arrived drenched & looking like drowned rats. Sanjay enjoyed it immensely & thought it was the best part of our stay.

There is no news from Delhi.

Love,<br>Indu

---

414.

H.B. Argonaut,<br>Nagin Lake,<br>Srinagar,<br>27th June, 1960

Darling Papu,

On our return from a very pleasant swim, during which Sanjay learned

to water-ski, we found three letters from you dated 20th, 23rd & 24th. [1]
We are all looking forward to having you with us here. For the time
being we are keeping on the houseboat. After your arrival we shall
decide whether to give it up or not. It is also possible to have it moved
to the Dal Lake, nearer to the Chashme Shahi. But it would be nice if
you could spend an evening with us on the Nagin – the late mornings
& afternoons tend to be hot. But the evenings are delightful. I hope you
are staying until the 7th.

    Feroze leaves on the 1st.

Lots of love,
Indu

---

*[Indira Gandhi lost her husband, Feroze, on 8th September, 1960. He died
of a heart attack aged only forty-eight. What this tragic loss meant to Indira
is poignantly expressed in a letter to an American friend: 'At times of stress
and difficulty, Feroze was always by my side...' Indira also confessed to
someone later: 'The most important death in my life was my husband's...']*

415.                                 The Carlyle,

35 East 76th Street,
New York 21, N.Y.,
29th September, 1960

Indu darling,
I have been here four full days now, but it seems to me that we came
to New York about a month ago. [2] The measure of time is sometimes
a very deceptive one, more especially when we get out of our usual
rounds. This does not mean that I have been frightfully busy here,
though I have been mostly occupied, without doing very much. The
result is some tiredness at the end of the day. Most of the kind of work
I do is visiting and being visited; going out to meals or parties and, more
often, inviting people to meals, including breakfast. There are here at
present a multitude of Heads of States and Governments with innumerable aides and Ministers and hangers-on. Apart from this crowd, New
York appears to be full of three categories of persons: policemen who
crowd the streets and are bustling about all the time and shouting,
plain-clothed security men in equal numbers, and photographers. Anyhow, wherever we go, we come across these three kinds of men. I asked
a photographer how many of his kind were in New York. He replied,
'Fifteen thousand.' As for others, there is no count of them.

    1. Refers to letters No. 407, 411 and 412.
    2. This letter was written from New York, where Jawaharlal Nehru attended the
special session of the United Nations General Assembly on Peace and Disarmament.

The journey from Delhi–Bombay to New York was a good one and fairly comfortable. Altogether it was about twenty-four hours. I was a little tired, of course, at the end of the journey, but not nearly as much as I had expected. The Boeing flies smoothly and its take-off and landing are both easy and without jerks. We stopped at Cairo, Paris and London.

To my surprise, I found New York unusually warm, almost as warm as Delhi now. In fact, all our rooms in the hotel are being cooled by air-conditioners. This hotel – The Carlyle – is a relatively quiet place. I thought that it was fairly small also. But, though smaller than the Waldorf Astoria and some others, it is still fairly big. Indeed, our rooms, which are right at the top, are on the thirty-fourth and thirty-fifth floors. We occupy some kind of a self-contained flat. On the lower floor, that is the thirty-fourth, there is a sitting room, a dining room and one or two small rooms. Above it, on the thirty-fifth floor, is a bedroom which I occupy, and another sitting room which is hardly used. There is also a balcony. The views from our windows and the balcony of New York City are probably the best I have seen. When we stopped at the Waldorf Astoria, we were higher than this, but, on the whole, I think our present views are better. There is a kitchenette attached to our rooms also. Altogether, it is a comfortable place and much more suited to me than the Waldorf Astoria with all its noise and bustle. This flat at the top is, I believe, called a penthouse.

Much of my time is spent in the General Assembly meeting of the U.N. and for the rest I meet people in my rooms or in their hotels. There have been many enquiries about you, both from Americans and others who have come here from the ends of the earth. In the Assembly, we do the listening while others speak in the general debate. Probably I shall have my say on Monday next, the 3rd October. The atmosphere here is thick with the Cold War. Khrushchev is in a state of high irritation, which of course is bad. The speeches delivered by some people have irritated him greatly. Today, while Macmillan was speaking, Khrushchev could not restrain himself at all and got up and interrupted him two or three times. As the interruption was in Russian, none of us could understand what it was till we found out much later. When Macmillan said something he did not like, he thumped the table with vigour – an unusual procedure in the U.N. Khrushchev has had some reason for his irritation here because of the attitude of the U.S. Government.

I went to call on Fidel Castro who was staying in a third-class Harlem hotel. We met, with a crowd of his companions, in a small double-bedded room. He has an attractive personality, full of life and confidence and full also of extreme dislike and distrust of the Americans, to which he gives frequent expression. His speech in the General Assembly lasted four and a half hours. I listened to it for about two and a half hours, but then had to keep another engagement. He enquired from me about your going to Cuba.

Sukarno[1] arrived yesterday with an entourage of forty-one persons. Many others, including Castro, had brought a large number of persons with them.

Last night, I went to see the premiere of a new film called *Sunrise at Campobello*. This is based on a play of the same name which perhaps you might have seen. It deals with Franklin Roosevelt's early life and shows how he battled with his infantile paralysis and largely overcame it by his determination and perseverance. It is a good film and I liked it. I am told that the actual play was better still. The whole Roosevelt family was present at this first showing.

Day after tomorrow, I am going to dinner and theatre with Dorothy Norman[2] and, two days later, John D. Rockefeller[3] is taking me to some play. I had at first hesitated to go to these plays because it is a great nuisance to go about New York with two red-lighted police cars screeching all the way and a third police car behind. All this fuss gets on my nerves. It has one use, however, as it clears the traffic. Otherwise, it is hardly possible to move in New York now. Most of the roads have been reserved for one way traffic. This has helped a little. As there are a large number of foreign dignitaries in New York now, you can well imagine the state of the roads with these police processions passing up and down.

Two days ago, I gave a dinner at my hotel to about fifty or sixty Heads of Delegations, etc. Each one was accompanied by a troupe of security men. I was rather alarmed when I saw these crowds of security men who seemed to fill the place.

Ajit and Amrita[4] came to breakfast with me this morning. They looked well.

I am not sure when I shall go back. Much depends on developments here. I have engagements up to the 5th October. Possibly I might start on my return journey on the 7th or 8th. But if anything important turns up, I might stay for another day or two. I do not intend stopping in London unless Puphi is there.

I am keeping excellent health and am congratulated on it by many people. I am informing you of this, so that you may be in full possession of the facts and not worry about me.

1. Achmed Sukarno: first President of independent Indonesia, 1945–67.

2. Dorothy Norman: American author, photographer and a friend of the Nehru family; among her books is *Nehru: The First Sixty Years*.

3. John D. Rockefeller, jun.: oil magnate and philanthropist.

4. Ajit Hutheesing, son of Krishna Hutheesing (see Kinship Circle); Amrita is his wife.

I do not intend going to any place outside New York.
I hope you are keeping well.

Love,<br>Papu

---

416.

Hotel Del Prado,<br>Mexico,<br>27th October, 1960

Darling Papu,
The Mexicans are a warm-hearted people & have a great deal of good-will for India. They feel that we are the only two peoples who have a distinct personality – others are copying America or Europe! They are hurt about our not having an Ambassador here.

I was most impressed yesterday by the University City – 59,000 students – a most charming & intelligent Rector. He is an atom scientist & friend of Homi Bhabha. Dr Radhakrishnan stayed with him.

The social security system is very interesting – it covers all aspects of the workers' lives. I am seeing more of it today.

Tomorrow we start our travelling.

I am eating far too much. This morning I had something called 'Egg rancheros' – it turned out to be two fried eggs on two *phulkas*! [1]

Indu

---

417.

Hotel Merida,<br>Mexico,<br>31st October, 1960

Darling Papu,
Two days out of our short stay in Mexico have been lost; one, due to bad weather near the volcanoes – all plane services suspended – & now we are stuck because of a strike for better pay by the ground staff of the airport.

The Belgian Prince Albert & his new bride Paola are travelling around these regions & our guide, philosopher & friend from the protocol division (a charming young girl of twenty-four) is trying to arrange for us to be picked up by the Belgian special plane.

The hotel is full of disgruntled passengers whose schedule have been upset by the strike.

---

1. A thin circular unleavened bread which forms part of the daily diet in India.

This is the land of the Mayas and for the last two days we have been visiting the ruins of their ancient civilisation – mostly temples & wells where sacrifices (human) were made and some palaces & a nunnery. The architecture is quite unlike anything else but in modern life the Mayas seem akin to our Lushais. They are short, flat-faced but very pleasant-looking, gay and musical and their looms and weaving designs remind one of the hill tribes of Assam.

By the way, the Professor of Archaeology who is taking us around says that the Mayas invented the zero about the same time as the 'shunya'[1] was discovered in India.

Love,<br>Indu

P.S.
The Belgians sent word that their plane is overloaded because of purchases! Govt is sending another plane for us.

---

418. Prime Minister's House,<br>New Delhi,<br>4th November, 1960

Indu darling,
This afternoon I received your letter from Mexico[2] of the 27th October. I was happy to have a few lines from you. Thus far I have had only scrappy news from the newspapers from time to time. I suppose that your Mexican tour is now over and you are somewhere in New Mexico.

Dr Heuss, former President of West Germany, has been here for three days. He is, as you know, a delightful old man. He often asked about you and he has sent a rather lovely bowl for you. Also two little packets for Rajiv and Sanjay which I have not opened or seen yet. He is leaving Delhi tomorrow for Agra and then for a long tour in other parts of India.

This letter will go to New York and may reach you just round about Election day.[3] Perhaps after that day there will be some peace and the noise and shouting of election time will end.

Here we live our more or less normal lives. There was a major interlude when I went to Raipur for the A.I.C.C. meeting. This was a big

1. Zero.
2. Refers to letter No. 416.
3. The American presidential elections were to take place on 8th November, the candidates being John F. Kennedy (Democrat) and Richard Nixon (Republican).

affair and far more members came to it than is usual. No doubt they came there not because of important world or national issues but the internal squabbles of the Congress brought them. They imagined probably that we would discuss them there, which we did not, that is, not in the A.I.C.C. session. There were of course private talks. We passed two major resolutions – one about the third Five-Year Plan and the other about international affairs. They were good resolutions. But there is little room for a good debate in a resolution with which most people agree and so newspapers say that it was a dull meeting. There was some excitement, however, about various changes in the Congress Constitution, about the elective element in the Working Committee, and the elections to the Central Election Committee.

Raipur was full of vast crowds and if that is a test of Congress popularity, this was very much in evidence. Raipur is a city of about 125,000 persons. Actually, at a public meeting I addressed, there were nearly 300,000 persons present. A large number of these were Adivasis from the surrounding areas, including Bastar. Some of these Adivasis presented me [with] various things, such as their type of headgear, etc, and a baby peacock which I have brought here and put in the cage of the pandas.

The U.P. affairs drag on. They are likely to be decided in the course of the next few days or, at any rate, a major decision is going to be taken about Sampurnanand's resignation. Sampurnanand intends to stick to his resolve to resign. I do not think it is feasible to get Sri Prakasa or anyone from outside there. So the choice will have to be made locally and the choice is pretty limited.

I am going to Bhopal for a day for the big electric plant there. Soon after our Parliament session begins on my birthday and I suppose I shall be kept rather heavily occupied.

Padmaja will be coming here [the] day after tomorrow for the Governors' Conference. She will stay on for the various birthdays.

A few days ago I wrote to Rajiv and Sanjay. I shall send Rajiv another letter on the eve of his examination.

Look after yourself and keep well.

Love,<br>
Papu

419.

The Bishop's Lodge,
Santa Fe,
New Mexico,
6th November, 1960

Darling Papu,
This is the quietest place I have seen in a long time. It is a desert area
[of] vast spaces but not flat – there are hills covered with scrub and in
the distance snow-capped mountains. Not far off is the Rio Grande
gorge. The colour of the trees has to be seen to be believed – like
dazzling golden sunlight – but we are told we are a little late & that it
was even more magnificent some time ago. This is Spanish & American
Indian country. We visited one of the reservations & were rather disappointed. The hunting season has just begun & all the men were out.
The people we saw seemed rather slow-witted! Tomorrow we go to
New York & the day after is Election day. Texas which we passed
through the day before seems solidly for Nixon although in some states
the Kennedy–Johnson team is leading.

I have not had any news of India since I left Delhi. It is quite worrying.

I am still feeling very low – I wish I could find something to do which
would absorb all my attention & thinking.

Love,
Indu

420.

The Westbury,
New York City,
10th November, 1960

Darling Papu,
This is just a line to send my love for your birthday & for always.

I am so very *tired* – I feel I cannot even stand. However that too is
part of life.

We had a terrible night of ups & downs & contradictions in the figures
but finally Kennedy has won. He is better for India & Asia but most of
the vote was anti-Nixon rather than pro-K[ennedy]. Shall write more
coherently later.

Love,
Indu

421.                                                Fieldwood Farm,
                                                   Briarcliff Manor,
                                                        New York,
                                             12th November, 1960

Darling Papu,
I came to New Haven by train from New York yesterday & spent the
day or rather, half the day & night, at the President's (of Yale University)
house. The speech & prize-giving was in the evening. I also unveiled
the portrait of old Elihu Yale [1] which you had presented to President
Eisenhower. Everything went off very well. I'm not at all sure what to
do with the $1500 which I have received. I shall consult Bijju Bhai. [2]
   I came here this noon to stay overnight with the Rockefellers. What
very lovely grounds they have. This is the end of autumn, so the air is
crisp & cold, the trees bare.
   Throughout the Mexican trip & again in New Mexico, U.S.A., I was
wishing I had not come as I seemed to be enveloped in a black cloud
of misery. From the 9th, whether it is the time element of a lecture from
Fory I do not know, but I feel much lighter & see things in a better
perspective.
   I am well but terribly tired.
                                             Much love,
                                             Indu

---

422.                                           Prime Minister's House,
                                                        New Delhi,
                                             14th November, 1960

Indu darling,
I have had a long day today. U Nu [3] and Madame Nu are here – they
stayed on an extra day because of my birthday. I could not go out of
Delhi, as I did last year, as Parliament started its session today and there
were other engagements. In the morning there was an International
Cooperation Conference, in the afternoon a party to U Nu given by

---

   1. Elihu Yale (1648–1721): chief benefactor of New Haven Collegiate School,
renamed (1718) Yale College, now Yale University. He had worked for the British East
India Company and was Governor of Madras.
   2. At this time B. K. Nehru was Commissioner General for Economic Affairs,
Washington (1958–61), and Member of the Indian Delegation to the U.N. General
Assembly.
   3. U Nu: Prime Minister of Burma, 1947–58 and 1960–2.

M.P.s and later a children's show organised (of all people) by the Family Planning Dept!

We did not invite any outsider to meals, but we have Shridhara[1] & Raj staying with us and Tara and of course Padmaja. Also U Nu's party, five of them including A.D.C.s. After dinner we invited the staff to coffee, birthday cake, etc, and there was quite a concert for over an hour. There were songs in Urdu, Hindi, Bengali, Burmese and Russian (by Shridhara!) and recitations. Mehra[2] sang very well in Urdu and Bose[3] of course also sang well.

I have missed you very much and my thoughts have been constantly with you. I received your letter[4] today written after Election night in New York.

You must have reached Paris and I hope you are staying in a hotel. I made this clear to V.P. [Vice-President] and Shrimali. I hope your stay in Paris will be restful and not too tiring.

Soon there will be your birthday and you will be in my mind thus even more than usual. Darling, you have all my love.

And now I am retiring, ignoring for the moment the work that awaits me. Boshi Sen is coming within a few minutes to massage me.

Love,
Papu

---

423.

UNESCO,
Paris,
15th November, 1960

Darling Papu,

I sent you the briefest of telegrams[5] yesterday but it brought all my love.

I am getting more & more worried about this UNESCO business. As you know Dr Radhakrishnan had said I could leave Paris by the end of the month. Now it seems that if I get elected to the Executive Board[6] (it isn't certain by any means!) I must attend the first meeting which starts on the 14th Dec. Our V.P. says that it might be possible for me to return to India around the 26th or 27th Nov. & then come back by Dec. 14th, if the UNESCO Secretariat is willing to

---

1. Shri Shridhara Nehru: see Kinship Circle.

2. and 3. B. N. Mehra and K. P. Bose were members of the staff at Teen Murti House.

4. Refers to letter No. 420.

5. Telegram not published.

6. Indira Gandhi was elected a member of the UNESCO Executive Board on 18th November, 1960.

pay! But if the membership is going to involve so much time *twice* a year, I don't see how I can manage it without cutting adrift from every other activity.

About staying at the Embassy – I am afraid it will be extremely difficult to move now without offending the Raghavans.[1] I have spoken with Shrimali.

Paris is very dismal after New York – this is partly due to the weather which is cloudy.

Love,
Indu

---

424.                                                             Paris,
                                                  16th November, 1960

Darling Papu,

I am in a fix. The V.P.'s bright idea cannot be followed up because the UNESCO rules are very clear on the point that travelling expenses will be paid only for the second meeting of the Executive Board. Shall I stay on until the 19th Dec., so as to be able to attend at least the first session of the Ex. Board? It seems a terribly long time. Rajiv & Sanjay will be home on the 20th Dec., so I must be there then. Dr Radhakrishnan thinks this will be all right but I do not know what view the UNESCO people will take. Otherwise of course I come away as previously planned on the 30th Nov. & do not attend the Executive at all. Dr Radhakrishnan will be back by the 27th Nov. in Delhi.

Hansaben[2] is not taking my nomination at all well – I hate being pushed into such positions when someone else has to be dislodged.

*18th November, 1960*

I could not finish this on the 16th nor yesterday, which was a dreadful day. I did not wake up until ten fifteen a.m.! & therefore had to rush all day to catch up. Dr Radhakrishnan left yesterday & I felt quite forlorn!

Everyone is now insisting that I stay on until the end of the Conference – the Executive meets for only one day on the 13th or 14th Dec. & I could go home then. Isn't it a bore?

We have quite long days – not in comparison with Indian schedules – starting at around nine a.m. until seven p.m. Then we have to go

---

1. N. Raghavan: Indian Ambassador to France, 1959–60.
2. For Hansa Mehta see p. 364 n.1, letter No. 189.

straight on to several receptions which because of traffic congestion take at least a couple of hours. Lunches are also out.

After the bubbling-over friendship of the American people, the French seem rather distant, unconcerned & even grumpy. In America, anybody one met, whether the cloakroom girls, the hairdressers, the lift boy, etc, asked about India, you, Gandhi & all kinds of things. One person – a Hungarian refugee who massaged my face – had heard of the Gita & of Shri Ramakrishna! Thanks to Dorothy Norman, I was constantly meeting people active in different spheres & intensely interested in India.

Staying on here is not going to be great fun! I am also worried about your being all alone for so long. I believe Tara & Bebee will both be going away soon.

Much love,<br>Indu

7 p.m.

I was sitting in the Programme Committee with Hansaben while the voting for the Executive Board was going on in the General Committee. Dr Shrimali says there was much excitement. The Japanese candidate got 88 votes out of a total of 91 and I was second with 86 votes. Raghavan is terribly excited.

---

425.

Prime Minister's House,<br>New Delhi,<br>23rd November, 1960

Indu darling,
I am dictating a few lines in haste. Today, I received two letters from you, one dated November 12th [1] from the Rockefellers' country home, the other dated Paris, 16th November. [2]

I was very happy to read your letter from the Rockefellers' house and to know that you were feeling better. In Paris, I suppose, work at the UNESCO meeting will keep you busy. In your letter from Paris you mention your difficulty about returning here as you had first intended. I cannot advise. This is a matter which you will no doubt decide as you think best. The children, as you know, will be coming here about the 20th of December. Perhaps Rajiv may come for two or three days

---

1. Refers to letter No. 421.
2. Refers to letter No. 424.

before that, and then return to the School for some final functions. His examination is going on still. I sent him a message.

Padmaja left this morning for Calcutta. And so I am by myself in this house. That really does not make much difference as I am spending practically the entire day in Parliament House or my Ministry. Yesterday and today, we had a debate on foreign affairs, and I could not even come back for lunch.

Soon, [the] Crown Prince and Princess of Japan will be here.

I am keeping well, even though the problems that face us appear to increase. Just at present, I am a little worried and irritated at the happenings in the Congo. [1]

On December 3rd, we are having our usual lunch on the President's birthday.

Love,<br>
Papu

---

426.                                                        UNESCO,
                                                            Paris,
                                          24th November, 1960

Darling Papu,

I wanted to send this in the diplomatic bag & am suddenly told that it must go at once.

I have been receiving so many invitations from Germany that I thought I would go over for a couple of days. I go on the 5th to Bonn – stay the 6th or 7th & on the 8th to Berlin for a day. Din Tyabji [2] has made the arrangements.

Paris is depressing as ever. The Conference is deadly dull. Everything seems so second-rate. They are spending a lot of money on a voluminous publication on the History of Civilisation. It seems to me to be rather superficial. Panikkar [3] was on the board of editors but has made scathing remarks about the bits about India.

The French brought in rather an interesting farseeing resolution: 'The conquest of outer space must be put to peaceful ends since it is already discernible how artificial satellites or machines positioned nearer

---

1. On 14th September a military coup was staged by Colonel Mobutu against the Lumumba regime and Lumumba was arrested. By November Mobutu's authority had waned and he lost control of his troops, leading to further unrest and the deaths of some members of the U.N. peace-keeping force.

2. Badr-ud-din Tyabji: diplomat and author.

3. K. M. Panikkar: well-known scholar and diplomat.

to the earth could enable educational programmes covering vast areas to be disseminated.'

Lots of love,
Indu

___

427.

UNESCO,
Paris,
26th November, 1960

Darling Papu,
I wrote to you yesterday [1] but as that has gone by bag, it may not reach you until later. Life here continues as usual – yesterday there was a big dinner given by the Director-General, followed by the usual platitudinous speeches.

I heard a story. The member of the Executive Board from New Zealand is called Beeby. He is a scientist & a friend of Homi Bhabha. Once they were together at a meeting in Vienna. There was a dinner & the Austrian scientist Krast (or some such name) sat between them. When Mrs Krast asked her husband how the dinner had gone, he said, 'I sat between Baba & Beeby.' 'You're drunk,' replied the wife!

The Raghavans' heavy luggage goes off by freighter on the 29th or 30th so they are terribly busy with the packing.

With much love,
Indu

___

428.

Prime Minister's House,
New Delhi,
27th November, 1960

Darling Indu,
We have not heard from you about your return. I imagine that you will now stay on in Paris till the meeting of the Governing Body about the middle of December.

Rajiv is not coming here now during this interim period after his examination. The Doon School is celebrating its Silver Jubilee and apparently they want these elder boys to remain there to help. I am told that both Rajiv and Sanjay will return on the 20th December.

I shall be going to Santiniketan for the convocation of the Visva-Bharati University. I intend leaving Delhi in the early afternoon of the

___

1. Possibly refers to letter No. 426.

22nd December so as to reach there in the evening. The convocation is the next day. Probably I shall stay in Santiniketan on the 23rd and 24th December. On the 25th I want to visit the steel plant in Durgapur and also the Mayurakshi-Canada Dam. Both these places are not far from Santiniketan. If possible, I shall go there by helicopter, first to Mayurakshi in the morning and then to Durgapur. I might spend the night at Durgapur. On the 26th December morning I propose to go to Allahabad and stay there for two or possibly three days. I have not quite finalised my programme yet.

At first I thought that you might like to visit Santiniketan and take the children there also. But I am not at all sure if this would be convenient to you soon after your return.

Lado Chachi has sold her house in Allahabad and is making arrangements to live in Dehra Dun. But she says that there is a gap period of a month or so and therefore she would like to stay in Anand Bhawan for that month. I have told her that she can do so, occupying rooms on the ground floor. I hope you agree.

It is now fairly cold in Delhi, the nights are specially getting colder. The morning is very pleasant and so is generally the whole day.

I hope you are keeping well.

Love,<br>Papu

I have just heard that the V.P. is reaching Palam this morning. Probably he will bring news of you.

---

429.                                              UNESCO,
                                                  Paris,
                                        1st December, 1960

Darling Papu,
I am taking advantage of the bag to send you a line.

The Conference is going so very slowly that now the Executive Board will not meet until the 16th Dec. However, this date is now final. So I can only leave on the 17th.

I had not expected Martyn[1] to allow Rajiv to come home earlier, so it was no surprise.

1. J. A. K. Martyn: Principal, Doon School, Dehra Dun.

My cold is much better but I am rather run down & feel tired all the time.

Love,<br>Indu

---

430. UNESCO,<br>Paris,<br>4th December, 1960

Darling Papu,

Tomorrow I am going to West Germany, returning on the 8th evening.

In his speech to the Plenary Session of the UNESCO, Sir David Eccles, the British Minister for Education & leader of the British delegation to UNESCO, strongly criticised Bijju by name for his speeches regarding loans to India's Five-Year Plans. Now he is proposing a draft resolution, the operative part of which runs as follows: the General Assembly of UNESCO '*Decides* to convey both to the Secretary-General of the U.N. and the appropriate financial organisation of the U.N. the considered view of this Organisation that assistance to educational projects should form a large proportion of all aid offered to the less developed countries.'

He had the cheek to ask me to second it. Unfortunately I shall not be here but have given points to Hansaben (anyhow she is now the leader of our delegation). It is a hit at our plans for industrial development. Why should UNESCO interfere with other agencies – surely they are competent enough to judge priorities? The British are being quite obnoxious here. Another member of this delegation, Papper or Pappes, made an extremely stupid speech on Congo's admission to UNESCO, urging 'tolerance and understanding' & claiming smugly that Britain had nothing to be ashamed of in its colonial policy. [1]

There is very definite hardening of the British attitude – Macmillan has given the brief himself. I wish we hadn't agreed to the Queen's visit. [2] They think they can get away with anything. If Malcolm MacDonald [3] had still been in India I would have written to him.

My seat has finally been booked on the Air India service leaving Paris

---

1. On 2nd December UNESCO passed a resolution condemning colonialism and calling for the accession of all colonial countries to independence. The U.K., along with France and Canada, abstained.

2. During the Commonwealth Prime Ministers' Conference in May 1960 the Queen was invited to visit India, Pakistan and Malaya. The visit to India took place in 1961.

3. Malcolm MacDonald, the son of Ramsay MacDonald, was High Commissioner in India from 1955 to mid-1960.

on 17th afternoon and reaching Delhi on the 18th forenoon, I think it
is.

Lots of love,
Indu

---

431.                                    Prime Minister's House,
                                                      New Delhi,
                                          5th December, 1960

Indu darling,

I have received your letter of the 24th November[1] and another brief
one[2] also. I find from the newspapers that you have been in Bonn and
other places in Germany. I suppose this letter will reach you just after
your return from Germany. Here, we have our usual crop of troubles.
It is quite extraordinary how they pile up, one after the other. There is
the U.P. Sampurnanand has ultimately resigned. He had himself stated
that he would resign if Gupta was elected President of the P.C.C. But,
subsequently, he was wobbling and wanted to change his mind. I felt
that would not be proper and, because of some pressure from some of
us here, he resigned. I am afraid he is rather angry with me as also with
Pantji and partly Lal Bahadur.

Although he resigned, things did not work out as we had intended,
and the Party groupings continue. Gupta is likely to be sworn in as Chief
Minister day after tomorrow. On the whole he has behaved well during
these days. He is, of course, in a difficult position because in the U.P.
Assembly there is a very strong group against him. All we can hope for
is things will take a new turn.

Then, we have the Punjab with its continuing Akali agitation. This
particular agitation is fading out. Because of that, now there is talk of a
hunger strike by a noted Sikh leader, Sant Fateh Singh, who is generally
respected and has not taken part in politics. This will be a troublesome
affair.

The Assam Hill people are clamouring for a separate State because
they are fed up with Assam. I saw a deputation of them and told them
that a separate State will be very harmful to them politically and econ-
omically. And I am quite sure that they will fall out among themselves.
But, short of that, I went very far in giving them all kinds of autonomy
and making them completely responsible for their development, language, etc. They are not satisfied, though I still have some hope that we

1. Refers to letter No. 426.
2. Refers to letter No. 427.

might ultimately get their agreement. They take up such extreme attitudes in public that later they find it difficult to withdraw from them.

The Bengali refugees from Assam are mostly still there, though matters have cooled down for the present. In Bengal, a mighty agitation is being built up about the transfer of half of Berubari Union to Pakistan which we agreed to two years ago.

These are some of the odd difficulties we face. There are, of course, others. I went yesterday to Rajpura where Amtus Salam[1] is functioning. I was much surprised and pleased to find how this place has developed as a rural industry centre. Of course, the Central Government and the Punjab Government have helped them.

The Akalis had made a dead set at this visit of mine to Rajpura. But in spite of their efforts, they failed completely. I must say Partap Singh Kairon[2] has shown great courage and ability in dealing with this agitation.

The Crown Prince and Princess of Japan have been here. Everyone was charmed by the Princess who is both rather lovely and very bright.

You will be here I suppose in another eleven days' time. It will be good to have you here after this rather long interval.

Love,<br>Papu

---

432.                               Bristol Hotel Kempinski,
Berlin,<br>7th December, 1960

Darling Papu,

We have just arrived in Berlin – it is a dark foggy day – we had a very formal reception. Willy Brandt[3] is not here but has sent a most beautiful bouquet of red & white carnations (the Berlin colours) & a charming letter. In a little while we shall go out to see the reconstruction work on the Western side & then across to the Eastern Sector. As we do not wish to be conspicuous we are going in a Volkswagen bus! On the way from the airport we saw quite a few bombed houses.

*Later*

We have had our little tour, complete with three motor-cycle pilots.

---

1. Amtus Salam: adopted daughter and disciple of Mahatma Gandhi; organised rehabilitation work at Borkamta in Bengal, 1944–6, and in Noakhali, 1946–8; established Kasturba Kendras, homes for destitute women, in Punjab.

2. Partap Singh Kairon: a Congress leader and Chief Minister of Punjab, 1956–64.

3. Leader of the German Social Democratic Party, later Chancellor of the Federal Republic of Germany.

Then I met the acting mayor & at an impressive ceremony, at which the local diplomats were present, signed the Golden Book of Berlin & made a little speech. I have been presented an enormous vase. I shall have to send a present too. Then there was a lunch & after that I had a private talk with Dr Hertz. It was suggested that Berlin might help with some technical training programme. Another person there mentioned the possibility of Berlin City doing something for Calcutta City – perhaps the training centre could cater specifically for the Bengali refugees.

Love,
Indu

P.S.
I forgot to mention that Dr Hertz said something about the W. German Govt wishing to negotiate with the East German Govt through a 'neutral' intermediary. Perhaps they mean India – however this matter will be taken up with our Ambassador in Bonn. I shall also mention it to Tyabji.

---

433.

Prime Minister's House,
New Delhi,
9th December, 1960

Darling Indu,
I have received two letters from you, of December 1 and 4.[1] We have also been reading about your visit to West Germany, Bonn and Berlin. Evidently you had good receptions wherever you went and I hope you have enjoyed your visit.

On the 17th December, that is a day before you arrive here, Anita Bose, the daughter of Subhas Bose, is coming to Delhi and will be staying with me. She will be reaching Calcutta day after tomorrow, and after spending a few days there, will come here. I do not know how long she will stay here, but she knows that I am leaving on the 22nd. So, I suppose she will be here for four or five days at the most.

Later in the month, probably on the 30th, the Prime Minister of Ceylon, Mrs Bandaranaike,[2] is coming with her children, two girls and a boy. She is really on a pilgrimage to the various Buddhist places in India. That part of her visit is more or less private. But she wants the

1. Refers to letters Nos 429 and 430.
2. S. R. D. Bandaranaike: Prime Minister of Sri Lanka, 1960–5 and 1970–7; the first woman to be elected Prime Minister.

Delhi visit to be treated as a State visit. I have invited her to stay in our house. Some members of her party will be staying in a hotel, but she and her children will, of course, be together here. I suppose there will have to be some public functions for her – a banquet, etc.

I was much interested to read in your letter [1] of the speech delivered by Sir David Eccles at the Plenary Session of the UNESCO, in which he criticised Bijju and our planning. The U.K. Government is not overflowing with affection for us at the present moment. They dislike our attitude in regard to the Congo as well as generally about colonialism. Then there is, of course, South Africa hanging in the air. In spite of all this, I suppose the Queen will get a good welcome here from the public.

Love,<br>
Papu

---

434.

Prime Minister's House,<br>
New Delhi,<br>
10th December, 1960

Darling Indu,

Yesterday, I wrote [2] to you. Previously I had sent you my programme for going to Santiniketan and round about and then to Allahabad. Even while I wrote all this, there was a lingering doubt in my mind about this programme. Our Parliament will not end till the 23rd December and probably the 24th. I was not quite sure if I would be able to get away during the last two days.

The last days of Parliament are always rather busy and anything might happen. But this time, there is the Constitution Amendment Bill relating to some exchange of territories with Pakistan in accordance with the agreement arrived at more than two years ago. The matter was referred to the Supreme Court for their decision as to the method of implementing it. This took a full year. There has been a big agitation in Bengal especially over this matter. We tried informally to make some change in the agreement, again by agreement with Pakistan. But President Ayub Khan [3] was not only rigid about it, but objectionably so. Obviously, we cannot go back on our formal agreement. And so, we are proceeding with the Bill in Parliament before this session ends. I have, therefore, been compelled to give up the idea of going to Santiniketan. I am still

---

1. Refers to letter No. 430.
2. Refers to letter No. 433.
3. Mohammed Ayub Khan (1907–74): President of Pakistan, 1958–69.

thinking, however, of going to Allahabad on the 26th of December for two or three days.

Love,<br>
Papu

---

435.                                         Prime Minister's House,
                                                    New Delhi,
                                              9th March, 1961

Darling Papu,
When the news about Pantji[1] reached me in Bombay, I was surrounded by the women whose function was the main purpose of my Bombay visit. For a few moments I was undecided as to what to do. But I thought it would be improper to attend a song and dance performance, so I made every effort to get back to Delhi.

Unfortunately, we could not contact the crew of the I.A.F. plane and finally Dhebarbhai, Chavan and I came by the afternoon service, arriving here just after the funeral was over. However, we went straight to the *ghat*[2] where Raja, Lal Bahadurji and Morarjibhai and some others were waiting. I sat about an hour and then went to Pantji's house to sit with the womenfolk.

Rajiv had gone to Pantji's house in the morning all by himself. He came to the airport to fetch me and accompanied us to the *ghat*. After a while I saw his face crumpling up and sent him home on the excuse that it was getting chilly. When I came home about two hours later, I found he had been crying and vomiting and had a severe headache. I do not know if I told you that throughout Pantji's illness he had been most concerned. Probably, this has reminded him of Feroze. He was thoroughly upset and just could not get to sleep. I sat up with him at night and decided that it would be a good thing for us both to get away from here.

As I have anyhow to go to Bombay to fulfil the engagements which were postponed, I thought I would take advantage of this to have a bit of a change and to take Rajiv to Ajanta and Ellora, which neither of us have seen. We are leaving tomorrow morning by train and shall be staying at Raj Bhavan. We shall probably go to Ajanta and Ellora by car on the 16th, returning to Bombay on the 19th and taking the train as soon as possible after that back to Delhi.

1. Refers to the death of Govind Ballabh Pant, the Home Minister. He died on 7th March, 1961. Jawaharlal Nehru was on a visit to the United Kingdom at this time.
2. The word here means cremation ground. It is also used for the bank of a river.

The Supreme Court was about the only place that remained open the day of Pantji's death. I believe, the explanation they gave was that the Government had not ordered a holiday when Chief Justice Kania [1] died so they saw no reason why they should close on this occasion.

*Later*

Shastriji and others insist that I should stay on in Delhi for at least a day to meet Guptaji and to discuss some other problems. So now we go on the 11th. Guptaji is coming tomorrow.

Love,
Indu

---

436.                 9 Kensington Palace Gardens,
London W.8
13th March, 1961

Darling Indu,
Your letter of March 9th [2] has just reached me. I am sorry I have not written to you since I came here.

We heard of Pantji's death on arriving at Geneva. It was almost expected.

I am glad of your decision to go with Rajiv to Ajanta and Ellora.

Apart from our Conference meetings I have practically accepted no engagement – no parties and no entertainment. The result is that I have had a quieter time and a little more leisure. Day before yesterday, Saturday, Puphi and I went to Broadlands. Yesterday I went from there to Chequers and this morning I came back to London. Last week I paid a visit to Oxford. I reached there in the evening at seven thirty and went straight to the Union. After dinner with the Union people I attended the Union debate and spoke. Coming back by car from Oxford to London, we had a very thick fog or mist almost throughout the journey. We reached our house here at two fifteen a.m.

I have now decided to leave London on my journey back on Sunday, 19th March. On the 17th I am going to Edinburgh, returning on the 18th. As President Nasser had been pressing me to stop in Cairo, I am doing so for a day. In order to be able to do so I have had to get Air India International to agree to make a slight change in their flight schedules. The plane I am taking ought normally [to] have to go to Beirut, but now they have diverted it to Cairo.

---

1. Harilal Jekisondass Kania was Chief Justice of India from 1947 to 1951.
2. Refers to letter No. 435.

This means that I shall reach Bombay on the 21st morning. If it suits you, you can remain in Bombay till then and we can go back to Delhi together. As soon as my programme is finalised, I shall send you a telegram, probably in a day or two.

Love to you and Rajiv,

Your loving,
Papu

---

437.                                        Prime Minister's House,
                                                       New Delhi,
                                                  4th April, 1961

Darling Papu,
You were in such a rush, with Lal Bahadurji hovering about that I was unable to talk. The more I think about Rajiv's going abroad, the less I like it. It would not be an auspicious start to his career to be featured in *Current*[1] or *Blitz*.[2] Mrs Crishna[3] was telling me about some woman who is absolutely wild because she is not allowed to send her son although his uncle is earning abroad!

Rajiv will be disappointed & the Harrow Headmasters annoyed but those are minor compared with the feeling of a whole country that Rajiv was getting special favours.

I hope your programme is not too rushed.

Much love,
Indu

---

438.                                    9 Kensington Palace Gardens,
                                                         London,
                                                  29th May, 1961

Darling Papu,
Kirpal[4] thought it might be better for me to come to London now rather than later, so Rajiv & I left Paris Saturday morning. Rajiv is staying on but I return to Paris early tomorrow. Rozario & Tikki[5] both

1. *Current*: an English news magazine started by D. F. Karaka in Bombay in 1949.
2. *Blitz*: an English weekly started by R. K. Karanjia in Bombay in 1941.
3. Amie Crishna: Personal Secretary to Indira Gandhi.
4. P. N. Kirpal was Secretary, Ministry of Education, Government of India.
5. T. N. Kaul was Deputy and Acting High Commissioner in London in 1961. Later became Indian Ambassador in Moscow and Washington, and Foreign Secretary of India.

say that by going to St Stephen's College in Delhi, Rajiv will lose a whole year – he will not be able to join Cambridge until 1963. If he is allowed to stay here & take tuition he will probably be able to take the qualifying exam by June 1962 & if he passes, or even if he takes it again in Sept. 1962, he can join Cambridge the same year. Anyhow Rozario is going up to talk to the masters of Trinity.

Col. Sheorey[1] will be writing to you about my talk with Lord Evans[2] regarding diet & treatment. His advice seems much more practical & sensible.

Love,
Indu

Puphi is much better.

---

439.                                    Paris,
31st May, 1961

Darling Papu,

This letter will be rather out of date by the time you get it as you would have probably already heard about the Moscow side from K.P.S. [Menon] and about London from Col. Sheorey and Puphi.[3] However, I am repeating these things so that you have the background.

The Moscow visit was very satisfactory and I had interesting talks both with Furtseva[4] and Khrushchev. Khrushchev confirmed my own impression that nothing much could come out of the Vienna meeting. He used a phrase which startled K.P.S.: 'I miss Dulles very much.' His point of view, as usual, was practical and down-to-earth. He felt that Dulles for all his anti-Communism knew his own mind and his stand was well-known to others. He was therefore in a position to give in occasionally. Kennedy is in a weak position at home and is considered by many as inexperienced and far too liberal. Therefore if he agrees to any point raised by Russia he will immediately be accused of pro-Communism. The Russian attitude on Germany and Berlin seems to have hardened considerably.

I met Mrs Khrushchev for the first time. She is a nice homely person. She has also had a kidney operation. Most of our talk concerned our insides. She told me that she had also been given a very strict diet sheet by her doctor, but later on this was changed and she was told that it was

1. Col. Sheorey: medical consultant.
2. Lord Evans: Harley Street specialist.
3. Vijaya Lakshmi Pandit was High Commissioner in London at that time.
4. Mme Furtseva: Soviet Minister for Culture.

unnecessary in view of the medical advancement. This was the reason which prompted me to discuss the matter with Puphi and, on her advice, with Lord Evans. Lord Evans felt that such a long list of items to be avoided was ridiculous and said that it is enough if you avoid strawberries (also rhubarb), spinach and chocolate. He stressed the need for greater consumption of liquids and also felt that a tablet of Alka Seltzer in the morning would be helpful. I have arranged for these to be sent to you from London as it may not be available in India. Please do take it at home as well as when you go on tour. It is so much less complicated than having to send diet lists all over the place.

Now about Rajiv. L. K. Jha [1] was in London and at my request Tikki Kaul had a talk with him. Dr Rozario and Tikki are very firm in their opinion that if Rajiv goes to St Stephen's as we had planned, he cannot join Cambridge until 1963 and even then they are not sure whether he would get the requisite grounding at mathematics at St Stephen's. Rozario feels that good arrangements for tuition in London could enable Rajiv to take the qualifying exam in June 1962. If he fails, he can take the exam again in Sept. 1962. He would thus be able to join a college in Cambridge in October 1962. This saves a whole year & I am told that this qualifying exam is an exceedingly difficult one. It is not concerned with superficial knowledge or cramming but with a deep and fundamental knowledge of mathematics. Rozario said that some students who came from India with good academic records have failed in this exam, while others who have not done well at home passed here. They feel, therefore, the tuition arrangements in India are not adequate.

L.K. Jha told Tikki that the whole confusion about foreign exchange had arisen because of the high level at which this matter had been taken up. He advised me that I should write direct to the Reserve Bank. Tikki drafted the letter which I have signed and which must have been sent off from London. I had asked Puphi to send you a copy and I do hope you do not disapprove.

If this matter is satisfactorily solved, it means that Rajiv will remain in London when I return to India. Puphi is trying to see whether we can find a good family with whom he could live. He is far too young to be on his own in lodgings.

I took Rajiv to his first play – *The Mouse Trap* by Agatha Christie. He thoroughly enjoyed the experience. He was a little unhappy at my leaving London but I am sure that this will be helpful to him to live independently later on.

As you will have gathered, I went off to London almost as soon as I

---

1. L. K. Jha was Secretary to the Prime Minister, 1964–7, and Governor of the Reserve Bank of India, 1967–70.

reached Paris as we had a couple of days' holidays at the UNESCO I found Puphi much better and just beginning to go out. In fact, we went to a matinee together and on another day she went to see Margot Fonteyn dance. The Armstrong-Joneses [1] were also present at the show and for the dinner afterwards. An American friend of Puphi's was staying there. Puphi is greatly looking forward to Bebee's visit but is a little bit anxious too because of Bebee's health.

I hope you are keeping well and that arrangements for Manali have been finalised. Do try and take a few more days off. A week or ten days is hardly adequate.

I shall be in Paris until the 14th or 15th & will then go to London again.

Much love,
Indu

P.S.
I am staying at Hotel Windsor, Etoile, 14 Rui Beaujon, Paris-8.

---

440.

Hotel Windsor, Etoile,
14 Rui Beaujon,
Paris,
2nd June, 1961

Darling Papu,
I am so happy to have your letter [2] yesterday, but I am naturally upset that you should be getting more and more tired. When one gets so tired, a short holiday does not help at all as one needs many days' rest.

This morning I had a phone call from Puphi and Rajiv. Rajiv went up to Cambridge yesterday in pouring rain and met the Master of Trinity. He was told that he would be exempted from the advanced level exam as well as the college entrance exam, but would have to secure over 60 per cent marks in the qualifying exam, which is required of all students wanting to take the Mechanical Sciences Tripos. I think it is only fair to Rajiv that he should be given this chance. If he cannot make the grade then it is better to give up the question of a Cambridge education and we should try to put him in some technical training straight away.

Puphi wanted me to make up my mind immediately but I am awaiting Dr Rozario's letter giving more detailed information.

1. Princess Margaret married Anthony Armstrong-Jones in 1960.
2. Letter not published.

*3rd June*

Tikki Kaul telephoned this morning. It seems that the Reserve Bank has issued instructions & I may have to write again. All this is just for your information – you don't have to do anything about it.

Much love,<br>
Indu

---

441.

Prime Minister's House,<br>
New Delhi,<br>
5th June, 1961

Darling Indu,

I have today received two letters from you, one dated 31st May and the other 2nd June. [1]

I entirely agree with you that, in the circumstances you have mentioned, Rajiv should stay on in London and prepare for his Cambridge examination. I do not quite understand what the position is about foreign exchange. If this can be arranged satisfactorily, of course there can be no objection.

Sanjay came here from school this morning. He is looking well. We shall go to Manali on the 8th morning. At present, I intend staying there for ten days. If nothing special happens, I might extend my stay there by another two days. More I cannot do, because of engagements here.

You had told me that on our return from Manali, Sanjay can be sent to Simla. But, as you will be returning soon after, I think it will be better for Sanjay to stay on here and meet you. I am sure he would like to do that.

We are taking the two dogs with us to Manali – Pepi and Putli.

Fatehsingh, Maharaja of Baroda, has asked me for the two tiger cubs. He wants to send them to the London Zoo to keep a promise which he made to them some time ago. I propose to let him have them.

Lal Bahadur is still in Assam. [2] He is expected to return tomorrow night. He has worked very hard there and I hope that something will come out of his visit. The situation, as you know, is an extraordinarily complex one. But still I am not giving up hope of dealing with it adequately.

Delhi has been as hot as usual in this time of the year. Several of our Ministers are out of Delhi, so is the President, and work is at a low ebb. This is welcome because it has enabled me to deal with some arrears

1. Refers to letters Nos 439 and 440.
2. Lal Bahadur Shastri, the Home Minister, had gone to Assam in connection with the linguistic agitation in that state.

of it. I am taking a trunk full of old letters and papers with me to Manali, apart from many other books and papers.

Papu

---

442.                                                    [Paris],
                                                       [1961]

Darling Papu,
This is a brief & hurried note – written while the Russian delegate is talking on a resolution on colonialism, of which India is a co-sponsor along with Brazil, Sweden, Morocco, Madagascar, Poland & the U.S.S.R.

There seems to be some confusion about the various circulars from the Reserve Bank, so I have decided to go to London for the weekend, leaving tonight. Bebee is already there & I am looking forward to seeing her.

I hope you will have a restful holiday & that Sanjay & the dogs will not be a bother.

Lots of love,<br>Indu

12th June

Sorry this didn't go in the bag as intended.

Rozario thought it would be a good idea for me to come to London to talk about Rajiv & although it meant spending out of my very meagre cash in hand I am glad I came. It has been useful. Tonight I go back to Paris & return & London on the 15th until the 19th.

Love,<br>Indu

---

443.                                          Forest Rest House,
                                                      Manali,
                                              14th June, 1961

Darling Indu,
I have been here for five days now. They have been quiet and very restful days although I have done a good deal of work also. I have now to think of going back to Delhi. The air route is a doubtful one and depends on the weather. Probably, I shall be back in Delhi by the 20th. If I go by road, then I shall have to start from here on the 19th.

Bhadri[1] came here this evening and is trying to induce me to go by road and stop for a while at Jogindernagar. From there he wants me to go by rail trolley to a place called Barot. This is an ascent of 5000 feet from Jogindernagar and takes about three hours. I gather from Sanjay that you have been there. This will be decided by tomorrow as to which route to take.

Sanjay has been keeping well. I am a poor companion for him but, fortunately, he has better companions – three dogs who keep him busy all day. We go out for little walks morning and afternoon. Col. Bhatia usually accompanies us.

Bhatia has induced me to take B-12 injections. Whether it is B-12 or the rest here, I certainly have been feeling better.

This morning we had the sad news of Dr Krishnan's (of N.P.L.)[2] death. He was a very fine and able man and undoubtedly a first-class scientist. His death is a great loss to us and I feel sad. Some two or three years ago he had a heart attack and it took him some months to recover from it. I suppose he had another attack on this occasion from which he could not recover.

I have had no news about you since I came here. I hope you are keeping well.

There is a good deal of talk, chiefly in American newspapers, about my going to the United States to meet Kennedy. S. K. Patil,[3] who is in the United States, has also added his voice to this. I have no desire at all to go out of India in the near future but there is always a possibility of circumstances being too strong for me.

Love,
Papu

---

444.                                    9 Kensington Palace Gardens,
                                                        London,
                                              18th June, 1961

Darling Papu,
Thank you for your letters. I came to London on Thursday 15th night. Went up to Cambridge the next day to meet the Senior Tutor of Trinity & have been here since.

1. Raja Bajrang Bahadur Singh of Bhadri who was Lieut-Governor of Himachal Pradesh.
2. N.P.L.: National Physical Laboratory in New Delhi. Dr K. S. Krishnan, F.R.S. was its founder director.
3. S. K. Patil: Congress leader from Bombay, at that time Minister for Food and Agriculture.

The Reserve Bank has agreed to my request for foreign exchange for Rajiv, so he will remain here at K.P.G. until Puphi leaves & after that with Tikki Kaul until we can make other arrangements.

I am going to Geneva tomorrow evening – shall be staying with the Bertolis. As you know, he is the agent for Air India International. I take the plane for India on the 23rd afternoon & reach Delhi, via Bombay on the 24th morning.

I am not feeling too well & am dreading the heat & the strain of Delhi. I have not had the opportunity of relaxing or having a holiday during this long stay in Europe.

Tikki Kaul's maid from Spain is called Manali![1]

Love,<br>Indu

---

445.                               Commission for India,<br>Nairobi,[2]<br>24th August, 1961

Darling Papu,

I do hope this will reach you before you leave Delhi. We don't have much news of you here but the summary of the Rajya Sabha speech came through.

Nairobi is rather a lovely city. It is such a relief to the eyes to be able to look so far distant up to the horizon. In India everything seems so overcrowded, people, buildings falling one on top of the other. We went to the Game Park yesterday & saw various animals & a small family of lions who had just had their breakfast. They looked very smug & replete!

We have also met Kenyatta.[3] He is a most warm-hearted person & reminds one strongly of Paul Robeson. Crowds of people are still thronging from far & wide to see him. He took me around & introduced me. I said a few words. I was rather astonished to find the women's songs very similar in tune & rhythm to some of our folk songs.

Some people have come, so I shall stop.

Lots of love & good wishes for your trip to Belgrade. It will not be

---

1. Manali is also the name of a hill resort in Northern India.

2. Indira Gandhi was sent by Jawaharlal Nehru to Kenya as his emissary to establish contact with Jomo Kenyatta. The latter had recently been released from prison.

3. Jomo Kenyatta: the distinguished leader of the struggle for independence in Kenya. Imprisoned by the colonial government for nine years, he was released in 1961 and became leader of the Opposition. He became the first President of his country after its liberation, serving from 1964 to 1978.

an easy situation. Give my greetings to the Titos, the Khrushchevs & all the others.[1]

Love,
Indu

---

446.
Commission for India,
Nairobi,
25th August, 1961

Darling Papu,

You will, of course, have received the news long before my letter reaches you. There is tremendous excitement in Nairobi. The two quarrelling political parties – K.A.N.U. & K.A.D.U.[2] – have come to an understanding together with Jomo Kenyatta that there should be a coalition Govt. with J. Kenyatta as P.M. The Governor has hinted his approval but the hitch is Macleod.[3]

The position of Indians is indeed a difficult one. They may have sinned in the past but the future cannot bring them anything but insecurity, no matter how friendly they now are with the Africans. Peter Koinange[4] is back from exile. He seems the most balanced person we have met & everyone feels he will pull his weight towards sanity & unity & fair play for all communities.

We returned this morning from the Amboseli National Park. Drought conditions are prevailing & there is famine in several parts. Carcasses of dead cows were strewn all over the place. But from the point of view of wild life, what a perfectly entrancing place it is. It was fun to drive around & come across herds of that comic, supercilious creature the giraffe, the prosperous & plump zebra, fleet-footed gazelles of different kinds & the lordly & kindly (looking at least,) lion & his family. But the best part was the unexpected frolic that took place right in front of my hut in the pale hours of dawn – elephants, giraffes, zebras, gazelles were thoroughly enjoying themselves. Earlier we had seen a most captivating lion family: two lionesses & four cubs. Just a short distance away was the lion with his latest & most favourite wife . . . [incomplete]

---

1. Jawaharlal Nehru was due to proceed to Belgrade for the Non-Aligned Conference in the first week of September. After the Conference, he planned to return from Belgrade through Moscow in response to an earlier invitation by Nikita Khrushchev.
2. K.A.N.U.: Kenyan African National Union; K.A.D.U.: Kenyan African Democratic Union.
3. Iain Macleod (1913–70): at this time Secretary of State for the Colonies.
4. Peter Koinange: one of the rebel associates of Jomo Kenyatta.

447.                                       Prime Minister's House,
New Delhi,
6th September, 1961

Darling Papu,
I received your cable in Dar-es-salaam (the Haven of Peace). This has been a worthwhile tour &, I think, has done some good. The situation is so fluid in Uganda & Kenya that it is difficult to say what will happen or who will come on top besides Kenyatta but it certainly was exciting to be there.

Nyerere[1] sent his greetings to you. He might come for the Seminar on Portuguese Colonies, which you have promised to inaugurate in Delhi.

Chhoti Puphi is worried because you have not sent a message of condolence after her mother-in-law's death. I only heard today & telegraphed immediately.

Love,
Indu

---

448.                                  The Davenport Western Hotel
Spokane,
Washington,
28th March, 1962

Darling Papu,
Just to say that all is well so far. Rajiv has landed in New York and will join me in Seattle tomorrow. We all felt the trip would be good education for him. My lecture agents had agreed to pay the inland fares for a secretary and they did not mind Rajiv going instead. So I pay only for our hotel rooms & meals. It seemed too good an opportunity for him to miss. He will see a lot of the country & meet a lot of the young people, since I am speaking almost entirely in colleges & junior colleges.

In Seattle are the Boeing works which should interest Rajiv.

Krishna Menon, neutralism & Goa – that is all anybody is interested in.[2] But they have such closed minds that whatever one says does not seem to make much difference.

---

1. Julius Nyerere: President of Tanganyika, 1962–4, and of Tanzania, 1964–85.

2. Opinion in Washington at this point was generally critical of India with regard to the integration of the Portuguese colony of Goa in the Indian Union, and the press disliked V. K. Krishna Menon.

My thoughts are very much with you & India.
Love,
Indu

*Seattle, 30th March*

Forgot to post this. Seattle is a very beautiful city. Lakes & snow-covered mountains, rock gardens & sloping farms. The spring flowers are out & the cherry blossoms too.

On Monday we go to Los Angeles. Rajiv is a big hit with the women of all ages!

---

449.                     In flight, Los Angeles–Sacramento,
                                   4th April, 1962

Darling Papu,

One feels so terribly cut off, the other side of the globe from India. There has been no news from home except Seshan's cable giving Col. Rao's [1] report. It was good to have that as I was very worried & anxious. I hope you are better.

Sunil Roy, our Consul General, telephoned from New York & I asked him to write to Shastriji for news from India, as my own letters from the West Coast will take an age to reach Delhi.

This is a strange country – there is much that is stimulating but alongside there seems to be growing rigidity too. California is most extraordinarily rightist, they are anti-UNESCO because it 'smacks of one-worldism'. They refused help from the Ford Foundation on the same grounds.

Congressional election will take place in Nov. & much of Kennedy's domestic policy will depend on the results. The main stumbling block to progress seems to be the solid group of Democrats from the South who combine with the Republicans on all issues.

You must have heard that Kennedy met me – it was an informal half-hour visit. He was extremely nice, even warned me of the questions that would be asked & hinted at the answers I might give! Speaking is rather a bore because of the lack of knowledge; one has to say the same thing over & over & to say it in words of one syllable.

Do try to prolong the rest, if you possibly can.
Love,
Indu

---

1. Col. M. S. Rao: personal physician to Jawaharlal Nehru.

450.                                                    Chicago,
                                                  15th April, 1962

Darling Papu,
I know you are well looked after & that there is nothing extra I could
have done and yet it has been most frustrating for me to be here, on
the other side of the globe while you needed me most of all to see that
all the wheels of the house run smoothly, so as to allow you the maximum
of quiet, rest & perhaps some recreation too. My own trip is going all
right, but I am quite tired & longing to be home. Your cable amused us
all. Rajiv may go off to London in a week's time. I shall probably be
home in the first week of May.
                              Lots of love,
                                  Indu

---

451.                                                  New York,
                                                  23rd April, 1962

Darling Papu,
We came here for a two days' respite over the Easter weekend. Last
night Rajiv left for London ... I think this tour has been of value
to him & a worthwhile experience. For me it was a great joy to have
him along & he was a good ambassador for India amongst the younger
set.
    I met Tara yesterday – she seemed well. She had just been in the
Easter Parade, which, from all accounts, is the most amazing &, to me,
rather revolting exhibitionism. Hundreds of thousands of New Yorkers
& out-of-town people parade up & down Fifth Avenue dressed in astonishing clothes, designed to attract attention to themselves. The temperature was 86° & from the pictures that have appeared in the papers this
morning, everybody was walking shoulder to shoulder!
    I hope you have got over the after-effects of illness & medication.
What about a holiday? Can we all go together to some quiet place?
                              Love,
                                  Indu

---

452.                                                  New York,
                                                  29th April, 1962

Darling Papu,
My last lecture was on the night of the 26th but I had made other

engagements such as lunches, dinner with Mrs Roosevelt & a reception at Dorothy [Norman's] for the following two days. Tonight I leave for London & then Delhi.

I am terribly worried about the Kashmir debate.[1] This whole country, & I believe many U.N. people of other countries too, are suffering from a K.M. phobia. The current President is or is going to be Chinese.

I hope the Dehra Dun stay was restful. It is terribly warm here – 91°. . .

Love,
Indu

---

1. Pakistan formally requested the U.N. to consider the question of Kashmir. India asked the Council to refuse the request. In the Security Council debate which followed Krishna Menon, the Indian delegate, described Pakistan as the aggressor, since Kashmir was part of India.

# POSTSCRIPT

The last letter in this volume of correspondence is dated April 1962. The events of the next two years brought father and daughter even closer to each other than before. Jawaharlal Nehru faced a difficult winter in 1962, because of serious conflict with China. Not long afterwards his health became a cause for concern to Indira Gandhi, and indeed to the nation as a whole.

Jawaharlal Nehru died on 27th May, 1964. The passing of a leader who had struggled so selflessly for the freedom of India and its subsequent transformation into a modern nation left a void which was difficult to fill. Yet after a brief interregnum Indira Gandhi stepped into the high office held earlier by her father and occupied it with distinction. Perhaps her letters to Jawaharlal Nehru reveal, more than anything else, the rare quality of the individual who was Prime Minister of India from 1966 to 1984, with a brief break in the late 1970s.

Indeed, the correspondence between Indira Gandhi and Jawaharlal Nehru, over the years, illustrates several things. At the outset, it highlights the bonds of affection between the father and the daughter. Next, it shows how Jawaharlal Nehru provided a liberal and broad-based education for his daughter. Last but not least, it reveals that by the late 1930s, Indira Nehru had acquired a sensitive understanding of politics in India as well as in the world community. Such an expansion and ripening of the mind stood her in good stead later, when she bore the responsibilities of high political office.

As is well known, Jawaharlal was succeeded by Lal Bahadur Shastri, who was a trusted colleague for a number of years. Shastri persuaded Indira Gandhi to join his Cabinet as Minister for Information & Broadcasting. She had already been President of the Congress Party and a member of its Central Parliamentary Board. Lal Bahadur Shastri was fated to hold the office of Prime Minister for only a year and a half. His death in January 1966 threw the question of succession to the most powerful position in India once again in the open.

At this critical point, the Congress Party and the nation as a whole turned to Indira Gandhi for leadership. The compassion and firmness with which she acted as Prime Minister for nearly two decades constitutes a part of the recent history of our country. This is not the place to say anything about the distinction with which Indira Gandhi served India, or the leading position she came to occupy in the world community. It is sufficient to point out that the letters exchanged between

Indira Gandhi and Jawaharlal Nehru give a glimpse of the indomitable courage, the inner strength, the high idealism and the sensitivity to the needs of the people which sustained her during the long years she presided over the destiny of India.

# INDEX

Abbottabad, 64, 167, 169, 171
Abdullah, Sheikh Muhammad, xxv,
    13, 140, 324, 330, 391, 485, 499,
    501, 503, 514, 516–17, 551–3,
    555–7, 577; entertains IG and
    Feroze, 135, 138, 139; at Anand
    Bhawan, 323; eye injury, 520,
    521; arrest and trial of, 530n,
    531n, 534, 596; political crises,
    554–5, 594, 596
Abhayanand, Swami, 264, 267, 429
Aden, IG visits, 578–9
Aga Khan Palace (Poona), 368, 369,
    499
Agarwal, Kishorilal, 567
Agarwal, Radhakrishan, 567
Agarwal, Rai Amarnath, 406
Agarwal, Mrs Raj Narayan, 129, 130
Ahmadnagar, climate of, 193, 358,
    362, 366, 375, 502
Ahmadnagar Fort Prison: JN in,
    141–468; censorship at, 199,
    213, 273, 466; conditions in,
    423–4, 444, 448; JN revisits,
    580, 583
Akali Dal (movement), 632–3, 656,
    657
Akbar (Moghul Emperor), 159, 174n,
    314, 387
Alexander, A. V., 529n
Alexander, Horace, 200, 384, 526
Alfassa, Mirra ('the Mother'), 605n
Ali, Aruna Asaf (née Ganguli), xxx,
    182, 593
Ali, Asaf, xxix, xxxi, 140, 149, 351,
    367, 532, 533
Ali, Mohammad, 585, 597
Ali, Sadiq, 290, 625
Ali, Mrs Shareefah Hamid, 9
All India Science Congress (1944), 152
All India Women's Conference
    (A.I.W.C.), 9, 11, 12, 220n, 326,
    364

Allahabad: JN arrested in, 77;
    A.I.C.C. at, 133n; Culture
    Centre, 451, 458; R.S.S. rally in,
    548; 1954 Kumbha Melá in, 599;
    hospital, see Kamala Nehru
    Memorial Hospital
Almora, 29, 42, 43; JN's memories of,
    25–6, 438–40, 443
Almora Prison: JN in, 201, 439,
    504–7; compared with Bareilly
    Prison, 506
Amery, Leopold, 199
'Amma' see Kaul, Rajpati
Amrit Kaur, Rajkumari, xxv, 10, 125;
    visits JN in prison, 123
Amrita Bazar Patrika (newspaper), 319,
    357n, 423, 424, 430, 447, 468
Amritsar, JN in, 4–5, 9
Anand Bhawan (Nehru family home),
    xxii–xxiii, 11, 17, 47, 78–9, 90,
    93, 142, 203, 280, 329, 654;
    garden, 151, 232, 235, 264, 271,
    279, 306–7, 311; JN's memories
    of, 180, 317; without JN, 280,
    289; renovation of, 298–9, 301,
    303–4, 317, 454; use of, during
    family wedding, 329, 331; Lin
    Yu-tang stays at, 352–3;
    mangoes from, 502, 507
Andheri, Planning Committee in,
    58–9, 60
Andrews, Charles F., 51
Aristarchi, Princess F. E. ('Efy'), 13, 67
Armstrong, Martin, 111–12
Armstrong-Jones, Anthony, 665
Arundale, G. S., 443
Aryanayakam, E. W., 385, 387, 392
Ashvaghosa (poet/philosopher),
    293–4
Asia (magazine), 211, 218, 237, 387
Assam, 114, 645, 656–7, 666
Atal, Ganga (née Raina), 22n, 24, 25,
    280

Atal, Brig. Hiralal, 542
Atal, Jai Kumar ('Makkhi'), 22, 24, 25, 280
Atal, Madan ('Madan Bhai'; IG's cousin), xx, 73, 218, 222; attends JN's trial, 77; visits JN in prison, 96, 97, 99, 105–6; and IG's illness, 96, 97, 99; and IG's convalescence, 105, 107, 108, 109, 110, 113, 114, 120; arrest of, 227, 326, 372; father's death, 227, 232; ill health of, 415, 441
Atal, Motilal (IG's great-great-grandfather), xix, 314
Ataullah, Qazi, 522
Attlee, Clement, 37, 529n, 589
Aundh, JN visits, 69
Ayyangar, M. Ananthasayanam, 616
Azad, Maulana Abul Kalam, xvii, xxv, xxix, 129, 134, 137, 185, 371, 391, 474, 530, 576; as Congress President, 35, 39, 40, 48, 424n; JN's views on, 35–6; in prison with JN, 149, 152–3, 196, 292, 437, 474n; scholarship of, 152–3, 166, 171, 175, 200–1; wife's death, 175, 184, 186; and naming of Rajiv, 414, 419; at Simla Conference, 511, 512

Badminton School, Bristol, 190n, 228, 245
Bahadurji, D. N., 240
Bajaj, Jamnalal, xxv, 17n, 129
Bajaj, Jankibai, 132
Bajaj, Kamalnayan, 129
Bajpai, G. S., 564, 565
Baker, Beatrice May, xxx, 190–1
Bakhshi, Ghulam Muhammad, 327, 551, 596, 632, 633, 634, 635–6, 637, 638, 639
Bakshi, Rashid, 6, 634
Bal Bhawan scheme, 602
Balasarasvati, T., 606
'Ballo' see Nehru, Balwant Kumar
Bandaranaike, Mrs S. R. D., 658–9
Banerji, Purnima (née Ganguli; 'Nora'), 111, 200; in prison, 147, 170, 171, 175, 177, 192, 205, 211, 212, 235; poor health of, 235–6, 242, 317; divorce of, 501
Banerji, Pyarelal, 214

'Bappi' see Kathju, Swarup
'Bapu' see Gandhi, Mahatma
Barcelona: JN visits, 74, 92; IG visits, 85
Bareilly Central Prison, 189, 469; JN in, 193, 210, 458, 459, 470–504, 505; compared with Ahmadnagar Prison, 471, 506, and Almora Prison, 506; weather at, 193, 496, 502
Batlivala, Bee see Mansell, Mrs Bee
Beaton, Cecil, 360
'Bebee' see Naidu, Padmaja
Beethoven, Ludwig van, 108, 109, 177, 250
Beg, Mirza Mohamad Afzal, 503, 520, 521
Behari, Dr Jairaj (Allahabad), 295, 300
Belgium, in 1940, 59, 60
Benares: JN visits, 11–12, 70; IG visits 261–2; floods in, 275
Bengal, 133, 294, 331; famine in, 263, 273; and relief work for, 263–4, 267, 271, 323; JN gives financial aid to, 323, 325; rioting in, 540n; and Pakistan, 657, 659
Benton, William, 413, 420, 465–6, 475
Berlin, IG visits, 652, 657–8
Besant, Mrs Annie, 443
Betty see Hutheesing, Krishna
Bevin, Ernest, 564
Bex (Switzerland), IG in, 49, 72, 75, 79, 88, 358, 362
Bhabha, Homi, 436, 644, 653
Bhagwandas, Dr, 262
Bhandari, Kamini, 245, 370–1, 375
Bhandari, Dr P. C., xxx, 67, 94, 607, 678; and IG's illness, 3, 29, 34, 41–2, 46, 48, 55, 57, 58, 60, 61–2, 79, 89; illness of, 327; IG and children stay with, 584, 587
Bharati see Sarabhai, Bharati
Bharucha, Dr (Bombay), 217, 219, 221, 227, 488
Bhatia, Prem Narain, 668
Bhopal, JN visits, 601–2, 646
Bibi Amma, xix, 495
Bihar, 540, 541
'Bijju' see Nehru, Braj Kumar
'Bijju Chachi' see Nehru, Rameshwari

'Birju Bhai' *see* Nehru, Brijlal
Blackwell's (Oxford booksellers), 27, 28, 43
Blaine, Anita, 132
Bombay: JN in, 17, 53–4, 56; Planning Committee in, 50, 53, 66, 71; IG in, 217–20, 252–3, 363–4, 398, 402–23, 563; harbour explosions (1944), 363 and *n*
Bonn, IG visits, 652, 656, 658
Bose, Anita, 658
Bose, K. P., 649
Bose, Subhas Chandra, xxv, 528*n*
Brailsford, Evamaria, 524
Brailsford, H. N., 524
Brandt, Willy, 657
Brewster, Achsah Barlow, 43–4, 441
Brewster, Earl H., 441
Britain: in WWII, 31, 32, 37; National Government of, 32, 37; IG visits, 89, 118, 584–9, 597; Cripps Mission, 131*n*; JN visits, 559, 560, 564, 585, 608–9; Cabinet Mission (1946), 529–32, 535
British Broadcasting Corporation (BBC), 57
Broadlands, Hampshire, 559, 561, 564, 585, 587, 588, 608, 622, 661
Bromfield, Louis, 163, 182
Buddhism, 278, 337, 418, 496
'Bul' *see* Naoroji, Khurshedben
Bulgaria, in WWII, 461–2
Burma: Dobama Thakin (party), 47; JN visits, 527
Butler, R. A., 609

Cabinet Mission (1946), 529–32, 535
Calcutta, IG in, 112, 113–15, 118–20
Cambridge University: JN awarded Hon. LL.D by, 590; Rajiv prepares for entrance to, 663, 664, 665, 666; *see also* Trinity College
Campbell, Roy, 111
Capek, Karel, 21
Captain, Goshiben ('Psyche'), xxx, 54, 56, 227, 228, 296; with IG in Panchgani, 217, 219, 229, 234, 239, 245; with IG in Poona, 223,

224; and spinning, 225, 246, 247, 293, 297, 339, 377, 430; sends books to JN, 238, 304, 308; advises IG, 252, 303; and Kamala Nehru Memorial Hospital, 275, 279, 285, 288; and Mahatma Gandhi's release, 368
Captain, Homi, 372–3
Captain, Maneckji Sorabji ('Mac'), 219, 224, 373
Captain, Nargis ('Nurie'), 223, 229, 288, 372, 373, 377, 378, 381, 382, 384
Captain, Perin, xxx, 279, 387
Caroe, Sir Olaf, 555
Carroll, Lewis, 167
Castro, Fidel, JN meets, 642–3
Cawnpore: JN visits, 70; Legal Aid Committee in, 275; hand-made paper from, 297, 314; R.S.S. rally in, 548
Central Election Committee, 646
Central Legislative Assembly, 448, 522, 657
Central Parliamentary Board, 683
Central Public Works Department (C.P.W.D.), 615
Ceylon, 314, 496
Chakrata, IG in, 571–2
Chakravarty, Amiya C., xxx, 352, 616
Chaman Lall, Diwan, xxv, 517, 532, 533, 535; wife of, 517
Chamberlain, Neville, 32, 37, 59*n*
Chamoun, Camille, 624
Chamson, André, 178–9
'Chand' *see* Mehta, Chandralekha
Chand, Dr Khazan (Khali), 438
Chandra Bhal, 262
Chaplin, Ralph, 192*n*
Chattopadhyaya, Kamaladevi, xxv–xxvi, 578
Chaudhri, Kumar, 319, 323, 330
Chequers, JN at, 622, 661
Chew, Mrs (Chinese governess), 141, 143, 149, 169, 211
'Chhoti Puphi' *see* Hutheesing, Krishna
Chiang Kai-shek, Mme, 89, 90, 130, 297
China: JN visits, 21, 276; culture of, 90; JN compares India with, 90, 117, 286–7, 309; in WWII, 482

Chitale, Venu, 524
Chitnis, S. L., 374
'Chitti' *see* Hutheesing, Krishna
Chopra, S. P., 211
Chopra, Shyama Mohini (*née* Zutshi; IG's cousin), xxii, 211, 483–4
Choudhry, Nabakrushna, 614
Chungking, 74, 89, 265–6, 483
Churchill, Sir Winston, 59n, 561, 564, 585, 586, 589, 590, 608, 609
Citrine, Sir Walter, 33
Civil Disobedience movement, 54, 55, 71, 101, 227n
Coelho, Dr, 420–1
Cold War, 642
Committee for Economic Development (USA), 466
Commonwealth Prime Ministers' Conference: (1948), 559n; (1949) 563n; (1953) 580n, 585, 590; (1955) 608; (1957) 619n, 622; (1960) 655n; (1961) 661
Communist Party of Great Britain, 564, 626
Communist Party of India, 396n, 499, 566n, 605, 626; sends books to JN, 456, 460
Congo, 652, 655, 659
Congress, Indian *see* Indian National Congress
Constituent Assembly of India, 374, 538, 547
Constitution Amendment Bill (1960), 646, 659
Copenhagen, JN visits, 620
Cripps, Dame Isobel, 530, 581
Cripps, Sir Stafford, 131, 529n
Crishna, Amie (IG's Personal Secretary), 662
Croce, Benedetto: *History as the Story of Liberty*, 401
Curie, Eve, 382, 387, 400

Dalai Lama, 62
Dar, Avtar Krishna, xxi, 580
Dar, Kishan Bhai, 330
Dar, Krishan Prasad, 240, 242
Dar, Maharaj Kishan, 535
Dar, Rita (*née* Pandit; IG's cousin), xxi, 6, 217, 352, 628; love of dogs, 6, 149, 164, 224, 290; at Anand Bhawan, 11, 90, 141–2,

350; education of, 83, 139, 211, 478; family moves from Anand Bhawan, 289, 290; birthday, 291; IG spends Christmas with, 323; and father's illness/death, 326–7, 333; appendectomy, 403, 406, 409, 410, 414; and Rajiv's birth, 416; malaria, 422; in USA, 478, 480; in Srinagar, 553; accompanies JN on Indian tour, 554; engagement of, 580
Darbyshire, Helen, xxx, 279
Darling, Sir Malcolm, 56–7
Dartington Hall, Devon (school), 378
Das, Seth Govind, 617
Datadin (Anand Bhawan gardener), 213–14, 258, 264, 271, 274, 300, 306
Dayal, Mr and Mrs Bhagwat, 129
Dayal, Harishwar, 543
Dayal, Rajeshwar, 624
de la Mare, Walter, 390–1, 396
Defence of India Rules (D.I.R.), 365
Defence of Kashmir Rules, 533
Dehra Dun: climate of, 97, 444; hand-made paper from, 267, 275, 297; Rajiv and Sanjay at school in, 604, 608
Dehra Dun Prison: JN in, 83–129, 149, 151, 196, 292, 443; censorship at, 101–2
Delhi, 200; Prime Minister's residence in, 549n
Deo, Swami Sant, 495
Desai, Dhirubhai, 539, 559
Desai, Khandubhai, 615
Desai, Madhuri, 559
Desai, Mahadev, 369
Desai, Morarji J., xxvi, 563
Deshmukh, C. D., 614
Deva, Acharya Narendra, xxix, xxxii, 166, 183, 195, 241, 276, 418, 419, 422, 473
Dhawan, S. S., 458
Dhebar, U. N., 613, 615, 625, 626, 660
Diefenbaker, Mrs, 622
*Diwali* (festival of light), 294, 297, 457
'Dol Amma' *see* Nehru, Swarup Rani
Doulatram, Jairamdas, xxvi, 578
Drummond, Lindsay, 90
Dube, Mrs Bhagwandin, 57

Dublin, JN visits, 564
Dulles, John Foster, 561, 663
Dutt, Chandra, 469
Dutt, Vidyavati (*née* Nehru; JN's
    niece), xxii, 139, 214, 328, 333,
    444, 446

Eccles, Sir David, 655, 659
Eddy, Sherwood, 67
Eden, Anthony, 608, 609
Eden, Clarissa, 609
Edib, Halide, 481
Edinburgh, Philip, Duke of, 622
Education Bill, Indian (1959), 626
Eliot, T. S., 602
Elizabeth II, Queen: JN and IG at
    coronation of, 578n, 580n, 584;
    visit to India (1961), 655, 659
Encyclopaedists, French, 36, 153
Evans, Lord (medical specialist), 663,
    664
Everest, Mount, 592
Executive Council (Wavell), 359n,
    365n, 514, 530, 540

Fa Hien, 45
Faizabad Jail, 147, 161, 175, 209–10
Faridkot, 530
Finland: in WWII, 31, 32, 33, 37; JN
    visits, 620, 621
Fischer, Louis, 134, 212
'Fory' *see* Nehru, Shobha
France, in WWII, 37, 59, 67, 74, 88
France, Anatole, 383
Francklin, W.: *History of the Reign of
    Shah Alum*, 201–2
Franklin, Benjamin: *Autobiography*,
    158
Fraser, Rev. A. G., 356, 361
Fraser, Alex Campbell, 22
Furtseva, Mme, 663

Gandhi, Chhaganlal, 503
Gandhi, Feroze (IG's husband), xi,
    17n, 84, 93, 97, 333, 342, 470,
    592; sends picture of IG to JN,
    17, 22; marriage, 131n, 173n; in
    Kashmir with IG, 134–9, and
    family, 638, 640, 641; in prison,
    147, 155, 161, 168–9, 171, 175,
    190, 214, 244; ill health, 147,
    216; foot problem, 161, 218, 520;
    JN recommends electric shaver
    for, 156, 254, 247, 252; prison
    communications with JN, 168–9,
    191, 308, 311, 315–16; IG visits
    in prison, 169, 203, 204, 209,
    216, 218; release of, 239, 241; at
    Anand Bhawan, 264, 281, 290,
    306–7, 317; acquitted in appeal,
    265; working activities of, 279,
    300, 323, 411, 552–3, 638; and
    IG's first pregnancy, 346, 350,
    407, 410, 416, 418; and release
    of Mahatma Gandhi, 368; JN's
    financial support for relief work
    of, 411, 420; Rajiv resembles,
    435; takes photos of Rajiv,
    500–1, 531; sends mangoes to
    JN, 502; Lucknow house of, 547;
    joins Board of *National Herald*,
    547n, 567; inertia, 635; death of,
    641, 660
Gandhi, Indira: convalescence in
    Switzerland, 3–53; depression of,
    14, 18, 246, 253; on Finland,
    Russia and the war, 31–3, 37–8;
    and German advance in Europe,
    59, 61; and fall of Paris, 67;
    efforts to leave Switzerland,
    79–80; in Lisbon, 84–8; in
    London (1941), 88; en route to
    India, 94–5; in Mussoorie,
    107–8, 110–13; and JN's advice,
    112; medical treatment in
    Calcutta, 118–20; wedding
    preparations, 129–31; Tagore
    Town house of, 131n, 168, 177,
    194; in Kashmir (1942), 134–40;
    in Gulmarg, 139, 519–22; and
    Quit India Resolution, 141, 147;
    in Naini Prison (1942), 147,
    154n, 160–92; health in prison,
    154, 168, 214; on prison food,
    171–2, 177–8, 213; release of,
    203n; 'service bob' haircut of,
    212; continuing health problems,
    217; in Bombay, 217–20, 252–3;
    sends books to JN, 223, 230,
    267, 366, 390, 402, 406, 450; in
    Poona, 223–4, 226–30; in
    Panchgani, 234–6, 239–40,
    243–6, 248; and Nora Banerji,
    235–6; visit to Benares, 261–2;

Gandhi, Indira – *contd*
and Bengal relief work, 263–4,
267; renovates Anand Bhawan,
298–9, 303–4; visits Jaipur,
313–14; and death of Ranjit
Pandit, 332–4; first pregnancy of,
346, 384–5; and Lin Yu-tang,
352–3; in Matheran, 353–5,
357–61; and Bombay explosion
(1941), 363–4; and Mahatma
Gandhi's release, 368–9; in
Mahabaleshwar, 370–4; and
Krishna Hutheesing, 410, 456,
522; birth of Rajiv, 414*n*;
motherhood, 420–2, 426, 455,
464, 465, 492, 497; on JN's
birthday, 428; and Kamala Nehru
Memorial Hospital, 437, 447,
450–1; fund-raising, 458; on
seeing JN outside Naini Prison,
469; in Srinagar (1945),
484–504; in Naini Tal, 529–30;
second pregnancy of, 536*n*; birth
of Sanjay, 544; Rajiv's third
birthday, 547; life in Lucknow,
547–9; on growth of R.S.S.,
548–9; and situation in Kashmir,
551–2, 554–5, 556; and refugee
relief work, 558; and
Sanskritisation of India, 565; and
*National Herald*, 566–8, 569; and
prospects of border war, 575,
577; in London (1953), 583–4,
586–9; in Russia (1953), 590–1,
592–4; in Zurich (1953), 596–7;
1953 electioneering tour, 598–9;
and Social Welfare Board,
603–4; and Orissa, 613; and
States of the Indian Union,
614–15; and works of art for
public buildings, 615–16; 1957
tours of, 616–18; and use of
mobile medical units, 618; and
Government hospitality, 619;
advises JN, 623, 626, 629–30;
and unrest in Lebanon (1958),
624; elected President of Indian
National Congress, 624;
reluctance to continue as
President, 627–8; and problems
in Turkey, 629, 630; in Srinagar
(1960), 633–41; death of Feroze,
641; in Mexico (1960), 644–5,
647; and 1960 US elections, 647;
and UNESCO work, 649–51,
652–3, 654–6; in Berlin (1960),
657–8; and death of G. B. Pant,
660–1; and Rajiv's education,
662–3, 664, 665–6, 668–9; in
London (1961), 662–3, 664–5;
and Mrs Khrushchev, 663–4; in
Paris (1961), 665–6; in Nairobi
(1961), 669–71; in USA (1962),
671–4; becomes Prime Minister,
675

reading of: 27–8, 43, 52–3, 110,
163–4, 170, 176, 178–9, 183,
184–5, 187, 199, 248, 383; on
her arrest, 498–9; on
bird-watching, 188–9, 235, 240,
268, 272, 291, 360, 492; on diets,
244; on flowers, 38–9, 43–4; on
gardening, 162–3, 235, 264, 268,
271, 279–80, 306–7; on
happiness, 381–2; on mothering
and childrearing, 187–8, 373,
381; on old age, 394; on
technological inventions, 16,
29–31

Gandhi, Kasturba ('Ba'), 369
Gandhi, Mohandas Karamchand
(Mahatma, 'Bapu', 'Bapuji',
'Gandhiji'), 15*n*, 39, 40, 90, 133,
406; declares Civil Disobedience,
55, 71; JN visits, 60, 76, 134,
140; and opening of Kamala
Nehru Memorial Hospital, 93;
birthday, 127*n*; tires easily, 140,
381, 421; prison fast of, 157, 186;
illness of, 363, 370, 371; release
of, 368–9, 370, 499; lack of
privacy of, 370; methods of
treatment, 382, 386; clear
thinking of, 394; receives gifts,
408–9; anthologies in
appreciation of, 409, 411–12,
427, 430; and Rajiv, 421; ability
to sleep of, 539–40; assassination
of, 550, 552*n*
Gandhi, Rajiv (IG's first son): birth of
(1944), 414*n*; concern about
health of, 418–19, 427, 459, 488,
497, 512, 516, 523; early
development, 422, 426, 430, 431,

434, 446, 464, 465, 474, 492–3,
497, 501, 504, 505; naming of,
414, 417–18, 422, 492, 497;
horoscope of, 421–2; IG sends
photos to JN, 429, 435, 497,
500–1, 505, 531; ear and throat
infection, 455–6; first summer in
Srinagar, 483, 493, 500, 504,
484–516; first birthday, 520;
relationship with JN, 538, 547,
549, 574, 586, 646; third
birthday, 547; swimming, 563,
577; Hindi improves, 574;
education of, 576, 600, 604, 608,
610, 625, 638, 650, 651–2, 653,
662, 663; riding, 577; in England
(1953), 584, 595, 597; IG's pride
in, 587; skating, 607; arm in
plaster, 611–12; and father's
death, 660; prepares for
university entrance, 663, 664,
665, 666, 669, 673; accompanies
IG on US tour, 671–3;
popularity with women, 672
Gandhi, Sanjay (IG's second son):
birth of (1946), 536n, 544;
swimming, 563, 612, 633, 635,
640; amusing remarks of, 572;
riding, 577; in England (1953),
584, 595, 597; independent
nature of, 587, 589; skating, 607;
education of, 608, 610, 625, 653;
waterskiing, 641; spends holiday
with JN, 666, 667–8
Gandhi Seva Sadan (social service
institution), 225, 430
Ganges, river, 124–5
Garhwal, JN in, 124
Geissler, Eva, 49, 523
Geissler, Louise ('Lu'), xxxii, 49, 79,
499, 527
Geneva: Ecole International, 362;
Indo-China peace conference in,
601n, 610–11
Germany, Nazi, 59, 74, 357, 482–3,
484, 548
Germany, West, IG visits, 652, 656,
658
Ghalib, Asadullah Khan (Urdu poet),
quoted: 171, 190, 196–7, 202,
205–6, 209–10, 211, 234, 238,
242–3, 246, 274, 277, 284, 302

Ghose, Tushar Kanti, 357
Ghosh, Dr Prafulla Chandra, xxix,
444
Gilani, Beltie Shah, 484
Gilder, Dr (heart specialist), 368
Gogoi, N. N., 355, 374
von der Goltz, Gen. Rudiger, 32
Golwalkar, Madhav Sadashivaro
('Guruji'), 548
Gopal, S.: *Jawaharlal Nehru: A
Biography*, 563n
Gorakhpur, 7; JN's arrest and
imprisonment in, 76, 77–83, 305,
324
Goray, N. G., 354
Gulmarg, IG in, 139, 519–22
Gunther, Frances, 3, 10, 90, 246, 253,
262, 466
Gunther, John, 3, 10
Gupta, Chandra Bhan, xxvi, 567, 618,
656, 661
Gurtu, Ram Narain, 328, 352
Gurudev *see* Tagore, Rabindranath
Guzdar, Nadir, 377, 538
Gwalior, 359, 377, 385, 389, 390,
410, 422

Haksar, P. N., xxvi, 93
Hālī, Altaf Hussain (Urdu poet), 222
and n, 228; quoted, 222, 251–2,
287–8
Handoo, Chandra Kumari (IG's
cousin), 93
Handoo, Krishna, xiii, 93
Hansen, Hans Christian, 617, 620
Hari (valet), xxxii, 47, 128, 138, 190,
281, 303, 515, 533, 543, 559;
family of, 210, 358
*Harijan* (English weekly magazine),
15, 21
Harrison, Agatha, xxxii, 3, 90, 588,
589; sends books to IG, 21, 22,
28; and IG's illness, 79; JN sends
money for IG, 87, 93; and
gardening, 189, 245, 251, 268
Harrow School, 316, 367, 629, 662
Hartland, Barbara (nurse), 392,
396
Hasan, Lady Wazir, 319
Havel, E. B., 122, 308, 320
Heath, Carl, 90
Helsinki, JN visits, 620, 621

Hemmerlin, Mlle Lydia, xxxii, 56, 298; sends books to IG, 10, 14–15, 22, 43, 170; visits IG in hospital, 33, 38; school, 49n; and IG's wartime visit to Switzerland, 49, 75, 79, 88

Henderson, Mrs, 44

Hertz, Dr, 658

Heuss, Dr, 645

Hewitt, John, 271–2

Hindi: JN's interest in, 121, 171, 175; history of, 255

*Hindu, The* (Madras), 357, 468, 566, 595

Hinduism, 599n

Hiuen, Tsang, 45

Hogben: *Science for the Citizen*, 152, 158

*Holi* (spring festival), 47, 455, 457

Holland, in WWII, 59, 60

Holland, Sir Sidney George, 594, 609

Holtby, Winifred, 43

Housman, A. E., 47

Husain, Syed Akbar, 222

Husain, Tajammul, 533

Husain, Dr Zakir, xxii, 121

Hutheesing, Ajit (son of G. P. and Krishna), xvii, 5; at Anand Bhawan, 58; at school, 359, 362, 377, 389, 390, 395, 398–9, 410–11, 422–3; in London, 608; in New York, 643

Hutheesing, Amrita, 643

Hutheesing, G. P. (husband of Krishna; 'Raja'; 'Rajabhai'; 'Pupha'), xxi, 5–6, 133, 327, 333; Planning Committee, 46; visits JN in prison, 90; health, 126, 127, 208, 217, 253, 302, 346, 364, 377, 386, 389, 393, 406; in prison, 142 and n, 175, 210, 377n; in Matheran with IG, 354, 356, 358, 361; and Mahatma Gandhi, 368, 385, 386, 389; fails to make will, 372; official release of, 377; superstitious beliefs of, 395, 398; birth/naming of Rajiv, 414, 421–2; in Kashmir with IG, 485–501, 503, 504

Hutheesing, Harsha (son of G.P. and Krishna), xxi, 5; at Anand Bhawan, 58; health, 123; at

school, 358–9, 362, 377, 385, 389, 390, 395, 398–9, 410–11, 422–3; in hospital, 581, 584, 589, 590; in London, 608

Hutheesing, Krishna (née Nehru; JN's sister; 'Betty'; 'Puphi'; 'Chhoti Puphi'; 'Chitti'), xxi, 5–6, 57, 61, 81, 84, 87, 191, 413, 622; and IG's illness, 19, 28, 39, 49; wedding, 25; Bombay home of, 29, 49, 54, 94, 110, 111; at Ramgarh Congress, 39, 46; social life of, 46, 49, 54, 191, 358; at Anand Bhawan, 57, 75, 76, 178, 334, 432, 446, 447; at JN's trial, 77; prison visits of, 90, 123, 424, 445; JN's memories of, 104, 362, 440, 445; in Kashmir with IG, 123, 450, 451, 452, 454, 479, 484–501, 512, 514; and JN's prison requests/needs, 147, 156, 169, 183, 197, 211, 231, 236–7, 275, 278, 298, 335, 340, 436, 475, 502, 522; sends presents to JN, 148, 155, 249, 257, 301, 305, 308, 311, 339, 365, 393, 431, 454, 471; husband's illness, 208, 302; IG stays with, 217–18, 252–3, 363, 398, 402–23; and Ranjit Pandit's illness/death, 327, 333; author of *With No Regrets*, 344, 356, 360, 410, 417; and birth/naming of Rajiv, 346, 384, 385, 416, 417–8, 419; in Matheran with IG, 354, 358, 361; superstitious beliefs of, 354, 395, 398, 404, 416–17; and Mahatma Gandhi's release, 368, 371, 383; and childrearing, 373, 378, 381; misses children, 395; IG annoyed with, 456, 522; in London, 628; JN upsets, 671

Hutheesing, Narottam, 494

Huxley, Aldous, 225, 230, 433–4, 477

Ibarruri, Dolores ('La Pasionaria'), 15n, 593

Iftikharuddin, Ismet, 242, 302, 484, 519

Iftikharuddin, Mian ('Ifti'), 5, 484, 517, 518, 519, 520

India: in WWII, xiii, 37, 130, 131, 133; JN on understanding, 46, 121–2, 320–1, 344; China compared with, 90, 117, 286–7, 309; history and culture of, 121–3, 166, 255–6, 325, 340; countryside of, 124–5, 216; theatre in, 293; education in, 375–6; Soviet Union compared with, 480; USA compared with, 480; travelling conditions in, 486–7; and membership of Commonwealth, 563*n*; *see also* Indian National Congress

India House (London), 585, 588, 589, 590, 608

Indian Air Force, 592

Indian National Army, 528, 539*n*, 580–1

Indian National Congress: relations with the British, xii, 507, 529; resolutions, xiii, 26, 40, 141, 646; Working Committee, 9, 24, 26–7, 37, 66, 70, 71, 72, 535, 614, 646; National Planning Committee, 17, 23, 46, 50, 53, 58–9, 60, 66, 69, 71, 295, 374; Provincial Congress Committee (P.C.C.), 17, 613, 656; All India Congress Committee (A.I.C.C.), 70, 132–3, 171, 514, 515, 542, 646; and Cripps Mission, 131*n*; Legal Aid Committee, 275, 289; Provincial Assembly, 522; and British Cabinet Mission, 529, 535; Constitution of India, (1950) 577*n*, (1960) 646; and Five-Year Plans, 614, 646, 655; Parliamentary Committee, 616; IG's Presidency of, 624, 627–8, 683; *Sessions*: Ramgarh (1940) 23, 26, 27, 35*n*, 38, 39–40, 44–5; Madras (1955) 606; Raipur (1960) 645–6

Indo-China, 601*n*, 610

International Cooperation Conference (1960), 648

Iraq, 624

Ironside, Lady, 32

Italy, in WWII, 37, 61

Jain sect, 46*n*, 314

Jaipur, IG in, 311, 313–14, 318, 320

Jan-e-Janan, Mazhar (medieval Urdu poet), 256

Janaki Amma, V. A., 301*n*

Jansen, G. H., 624

Jha, Amarnath, 390

Jha, L. K. (JN's secretary), 664

Jinarajadasa, C., 437, 443, 445, 446, 448–9, 460, 468

Jinnah, Mohamed Ali, xxvi, 519, 522

Joshi, Puran Chand, 396, 403

Juhu, 54, 56, 86, 350, 372, 394

Jumna, river, 17*n*, 51, 214, 470, 550*n*

Kabir, Humayun, 604

Kachru, Dwarka Nath, 553, 554

Kairon, Partap Singh, 657

Kak, Jainath (Allahabad surgeon), 295, 455

Kak, Ramchandra, 535

Kalhana, *The Rajatarangini* (narrative poem), 122

Kamala Nehru Memorial Hospital (Allahabad), 212, 272, 352–3, 405; building of, 11; opening of, 93; Committee, 275, 279, 285, 288, 319, 324, 430, 436, 450; ambulance service for, 283, 289; IG's involvement with, 437, 447, 450–1, 458; proposed statue of founder, 447; fund-raising for, 450–1, 452, 458; mobile health van, 618

Kamaraj, K., 614

Kania, Harilal Jekisondass, 661

Kanungo, Nityanand, 613

Karachi, JN visits, 542–3

Karaka, D. F., 375, 400–1, 662*n*

Kashmir, 38, 200, 279; JN's liking for, 13–14, 50, 82, 224, 342, 473, 489; JN in, 62, 63–5, 532–5; JN's articles on, 68–9; IG and Feroze in, 134–40; IG takes Rajiv to, 450, 452, 459, 466, 477–8, 484–504; political crises in, 530–5, 554–5, 592, 594, 596; JN's detention in, 533–5; Pakistan invasion of, 552, 556, 558; Rajiv's love of, 623

Kasturba Kendras scheme (for homeless women), 599, 657*n*

Kathju, Kanwarlal ('Nikku'; JN's cousin), xxii, 136, 486, 488, 495, 501, 633

Kathju, Moti (JN's cousin), xxii, 203–4, 206, 210–11, 400

Kathju, Naresh, xx, 314, 608, 636

Kathju, Om, 265, 288, 426

Kathju, Pyarelal N. ('Mausaji'; IG's uncle), xvi, 204, 206, 220, 252, 315, 353, 410, 429, 636

Kathju, Shiv Nath, 598

Kathju, Siddhartha, 488

Kathju, Swarup (née Kaul; 'Bappi'; 'Masi'; IG's aunt), xx; illness of, 70, 93; moves to Jaipur, 204, 220, 288–9; IG stays with, 307, 315, 321; and IG's first pregnancy, 383, 388, 403, 407–8, 410; and Rajiv's destiny, 421; at Anand Bhawan, 426

Katju, Dr Kailas Nath, xxvi, 430, 450–1

Kaul, Gen. B. M. ('Bijji Kaul'), 606

Kaul, Gautam, xx, 264, 273, 279, 409

Kaul, Kailas Nath ('Mamu'; IG's uncle), xx, 204, 273; in London, 95, 167, 261, 264, 265, 273–4, 406, 409; JN finances return of, 269, 274; son resembles, 279; back in India, 425, 426, 429, 435

Kaul, Prakash, 593

Kaul, Rajpati ('Amma'; 'Nani'; IG's grandmother), xv, 29, 627; IG plans to visit, 70, 90, 139–40, 220, 224, 242, 251, 253, 483; visits JN in prison, 127, 128, 129, 424; JN's prison communications with, 191, 198, 232, 259, 265, 269, 273, 477; eye trouble of, 204, 206–7, 211, 248, 254, 257; sends food/medicine to JN, 282, 291–2; and IG's first pregnancy, 383, 403, 407–8, 416; at Anand Bhawan, 426

Kaul, Sheila ('Mami'), xvi, 167, 265, 269, 273, 279, 409, 425, 429, 434; first child, 95, 264; second child, 314; IG offers holiday, 432, 434, 447

Kaul, T. N. ('Tikki'), xxxii, 662, 664, 666, 669

Kaul, Pandit Upendranath, 634, 636

Kennedy, John F., 647, 663, 668, 672

Kenya, IG visits, 669–71

Kenyatta, Jomo, 669, 670, 671

Khali: IG's internment in, 204–5; JN's liking for, 342, 431–2; IG plans trip to, 431, 434, 437–8, 447, 450, 451

Khaliq (servant), 213, 303, 358, 372

Khan, Abdul Ghaffar ('Frontier Gandhi', 'Badshah Khan'), xxvi, 5n, 63, 135, 140, 484, 517

Khan, Abdul Qayyum, 519, 521, 522

Khan, Abdul Wali, 484

Khan, President Ayub, 659

Khan, Kabir, 307

Khan, Liaquat Ali, 575

Khan Saheb, Dr, xxvi–xxvii, 484, 515

Khan, Sami, 410

Khan, Shah Nawaz, 537, 538, 539

Khan, Shyam Kumari ('Shammie Didda'; JN's niece), xxi, 307, 333, 398, 410, 446, 599

Khan, Sikandar Hyat, 517

Khan, Yahya, 409

Khanan, Abdul Rahim Khan (Hindi poet), 255

Kher, B. G., 566, 580, 584, 587, 588, 589, 597

Khosla, Justice Gopal Das, 607

Khrushchev, Mrs, 663–4

Khrushchev, Nikita, 642, 663

Kidwai, Rafi Ahmed, xxvii, 210, 386, 398, 404, 415, 449, 456, 459, 567

Kidwai, Shafi Ahmed, 329

Kirpal, P. N., 662

Kisan march, 506

Kishtwar, JN plans to visit, 631, 632, 633, 634, 636, 637, 639

Kitabistan (Allahabad publisher), 20, 21, 271, 305, 318, 413, 441, 442

Koestler, Arthur: Darkness at Noon, 125

Koinange, Peter, 670

Kolahoi glacier, 65, 135, 137, 138, 501

Koul, Chand Bahadur ('Mamu'; IG's uncle), xix, 140, 211, 261, 479, 485, 517, 553, 600; children of, xx, 261, 485

Koul, Rup, xix, 261n, 388, 416, 480

Kripalani, J. B., xxiii, xxv, 133, 158, 168, 301
Kripalani, Krishna Ramchand, xxviii, 6n, 365, 382
Kripalani, Nandita, 6, 183, 364–5, 382
Kripalani, Sucheta, xxvii, 158, 168, 183, 450
Khrishnamurti, Y. G.: *Jawaharlal Nehru, Betrayal of Freedom*, 338
Krishnan, Dr K. S., 465, 474, 478, 668
Kulkarni, Sumitra (*née* Gandhi), 550
Kumaramangalam, Surendra Mohan, 128, 456
Kumarappa, J. C., 503
Kumari, Chandra *see* Handoo, Chandra
Kunzru, Hriday Nath, 214

Ladakh, JN in, 631, 632
'Ladlibhai', 'Ladli Chacha' *see* Zutshi, Ladli Prasad
'Lado Chachi' *see* Zutshi, Lado Rani
Lahore, JN in, 5, 488, 517–18; Women's Prison, 182
Lal, K. B., 579
Lawrence, D. H., 53, 253
Lea, Homer: *The Day of the Saxon*, 158
*Leader, The* (Indian newspaper), 241–2, 319, 330, 424, 473
League of Nations, 33, 245
Lebanon, 624
Legal Aid Committee, 275, 289
Leningrad: IG in, 593–4; Hermitage Museum, 594
Leopardi, Giacoma (Italian poet), 379
Levi, Sylvain (French orientalist): *Le Théâtre Indien*, 238, 241, 293, 297
Lewis, C. S.: 'Epitaph', 266
Leysin (Switzerland), IG convalesces in, 3–71
Li Po (Chinese poet), 380
*Life* magazine, 238, 450; articles on JN in, 3, 10, 15, 243
Lin Yu-tang, 90, 148, 157–8, 164, 186, 352–3, 381–2
Lisbon, IG in, 86–7, 91
Lloyd, Selwyn, 589
Lokanathan, Dr P. S., 456

London: IG in, (1941) 88, 118, (1953), 583–9, 597; JN in, (1935) 221, (1948) 559, 560, (1949) 564, (1953) 585, 590, (1955) 608–9, (1957) 622, (1961) 662–3, 664–5
Lorenzini, Maria, 502
Lucknow: JN in, 7–8, 12; All India Science Congress in, 152; Legal Aid Committee in, 275; IG visits, 330, 547–9; R.S.S. rally in, 548

MacDonald, Malcolm, 655
Macleod, Iain, 670
Macmillan, Harold, 642, 655
MacNeice, Louis, 79n
'Madan Bhai' *see* Atal, Madan
Madan, Kalavati (*née* Nehru), 215
Madgavkar, Sir Govind, 372, 377–8, 383
Madgavkar, Usha, 372, 378
Madrid, 80
Mahabaleshwar: IG in, 359, 361, 366, 368–77; honey from, 393, 394–5, 404, 408–9
Mahajan, Justice Mehrchand, 555
Mahan, Alfred Thayer, 117, 119
Maharashtra, 614; JN's tour of, 581–2
Maharashtra Provincial Congress Committee, 614
Mahmud, Hamidah, 240, 279, 302, 307, 382, 386
Mahmud, Said-ur-Rahman, 382, 386, 387
Mahmud, Dr Syed, xxvi, 219, 382, 426, 484; sons of, 26–7; visits JN in prison, 128, 148, 172, 175, 194, 195; poor sight of, 225, 244, 246, 259, 301; JN gives books to, 225, 251, 259, 335; release of, 423, 444
Maillart, Ella, 611
Malabar, relief work for, 364
Malaviya, Kapildev, xxvii, 262, 451
Malaviya, Keshav Deva, xxvii, 210, 329
Malaviya, Pandit Madan Mohan, xxvii, 261–2, 352
Malaviya, Mukund, 262
Malaya, JN visits, 525, 529
'Mamu' *see* Kaul, Kailas Nath

Mannerheim, Baron Karl Gustav Emil von, 32
Mannin, Ethel: *Commonsense and the Child*, 373, 380, 381
'Manno Didda' *see* Sahgal, Man Mohini
Mansell, Mrs Bee (*née* Batlivala), 118, 589
Marc, Franz, 111
Margaret, Princess, 665
Martyn, J. A. K., 654
Masani, Minoo R., 374
'Masi' *see* Kathju, Swarup
Mathai, M. O., 533, 537, 538, 540, 541, 550, 576, 582, 584, 585
Mathai, Mrs, 619
Matheran, IG visits, 353–5, 357–61
Maulana *see* Azad, Maulana Abul Kalam
'Mausaji' *see* Kathju, Pyarelal
Maxwell, Reginald Maitland, 359
Mayakovski, Vladimir Vladimirovich, 38
Mehr Taj, 150, 409, 484
Mehra, B. N., 649
Mehrotra, Lalji, 543
Mehta, Chandralekha (*née* Pandit; 'Chand'), xxi, 6, 83, 90, 141, 152, 430, 445; in prison, 147, 155, 161, 162, 163, 172, 178, 184, 186; release of, 161, 169, 170, 175, 192; prison communications with JN, 165, 179, 187, 198, 274, 332, 334, 464, 477; plans to study in USA, 191, 198, 204; departure, 205, 211; JN's admiration for, 233, 480; in USA, 274, 278, 310, 480; graduation, 490; JN sent picture of, 388; in London with JN, 560
Mehta, Dinshaw, 382
Mehta, Hansaben, 363–4, 372, 650, 651, 655
Mehta, Dr Jivraj N., xxvii, 431; and IG's illness, 48, 55, 56; and Kamala Nehru Memorial Hospital, 93, 434; prison release, 372, 378; and IG's first pregnancy, 384, 385, 415, 419, 420, 421, 431; and birth of Rajiv, 421

Mehta, Krishna, xxxiii, 557–8, 631, 632, 637
Mehta, Urmila, 364
Mendès-France, Pierre, 610
Menon, K. P. S., xxvii, 591, 593, 663
Menon, V. K. Krishna, xxviii; and IG's illness, 3, 49; acts for JN, 22, 90, 91, 95, 118, 128, 137, 227, 237, 243, 263, 274, 409, 412, 622; writes to JN, 24, 25, 37; personality of, 25, 37; health, 245, 251; family circumstances, 301n, 307; in India, 533, 538, 554, 596, 635; as High Commissioner in London, 559, 588, 589; and IG's 1953 visit to London, 584, 587, 597; needs tactful handling, 585–6, 588; and UN, 589, 594, 595, 601n, 674n; as Defence Minister, 671
Menon, V. P., xxviii, 577
Menzies, Robert, 609
Mexico, IG visits, 644–7, 648
Mir, Mir Taqi (Urdu poet), 205, 269
Mohanmarg, 139
Molotov, Vyacheslav Mikhailovich, 31
Mookerjee, Syama Prasad, 591–2
Morarji, Sumatiben, 371, 614, 660
Morgan, Charles L.: *Sparkenbroke*, 304
Morin, Jean-Jacques, 57, 88, 92, 191
Morin, Louise, xxxiii, 119; sends books to IG, 23, and JN, 304; visits IG in Switzerland, 67, 72, 191; in occupied France, 74, 88, 92
Moscow: IG visits, 590–1, 663; JN visits, 670
Mountbatten, Edwina, Countess, 554, 559, 560, 578, 585, 588, 609, 611
Mountbatten, Lady Pamela, 554, 559, 561
Mountbatten of Burma, Louis, 1st Earl, 527n, 547, 554, 559, 561, 585, 609
Mridula *see* Sarabhai, Mridula
Mudie, Sir Robert Francis, 448
Mukherjee, Sharda, 333
Mukherjee, Air Marshal Subroto, 333, 631, 637, 639, 640
Mukherji, Dhan Gopal, 269

Munshi, K. M., 368, 503
Munshi, Lilavati, 368, 503, 599
Munzenburg, Willie, 356–7
Murray, Gilbert, 109, 114, 158, 376, 380
Muslim League, 519*n*, 521, 522
Mussoorie, 320, 443, 547; IG in, 107–8, 110–13, 127; after independence, 552
Myers, L. H., 387–8

Naidu, Leilamani ('Papi'), xxxiii, 10, 579, 609, 618
Naidu, Padmaja ('Bebee'), xxxiii, 132, 142, 333, 355, 395, 526, 652; at Anand Bhawan, 10, 90; health, 232, 371, 665; and Beverley Nichols, 360; and Mahatma Gandhi's release, 368, 371; wedding of, 473, 477; in Srinagar, 503; at A.I.C.C., Meerut, 542; and Rajiv, 547; travels with JN, 579–80, 582, 586, 590, 592; stays with JN, 595, 610, 646, 649, 651; in London, 665, 667
Naidu, Sarojini, xxviii, 10, 186, 308, 333, 378, 458, 526; in prison, 142 and *n*, 172; and Mahatma Gandhi's release, 368, 371; writing gift, 426; and Rajiv, 430, 431; at A.I.C.C., Meerut, 542
Naini Prison, 181, 213, 218, 449, 458, 470; IG in, 147–203, 207, 209, 220, 469–91; conditions in, 154; JN in, 182, 194; censorship at, 187; JN's release from, 203
Naini Tal: IG in, 529–30; after independence, 552
Nairobi, IG visits, 669–70
Nambiar, A. C. N. ('Nanu'), xxxiii, 83, 428, 499; financial problems of, 33, 67, 75, 79, 88, 92, 93; fate of, 523
'Nan' *see* Pandit, Vijaya Lakshmi
Nanavati, Mr and Mrs, 3, 4, 15, 19, 28, 29, 31
Nanga Parbat, 139, 494, 521
'Nani' *see* Kaul, Rajpati
'Nanu' *see* Nambiar, A. C. N.
Naoroji, Khurshedben ('Bul'), 218, 229, 289, 390, 397, 406, 426, 524

Narayan, Krishna, 432, 434
Narielwala, P. A. ('Pan'), 275, 285, 387, 615
Nasser, President, 661
*National Herald*, 409*n*; sent to IG, 6, 10, 12, 19, 21, 28; article by JN in, 31; JN's association with, 239*n*, 568–9; dispute over sale of equipment, 239–40, 242; Feroze Gandhi joins Board of, 547*n*; IG's evaluation of, 566; threat to impartiality of, 567–9
*Nauroz* (Kashmiri New Year Day), 52, 170, 174, 186, 353, 463, 465
Nayar, Sushila, 369, 499
Nehru, Anand Kumar ('Anand Bhai'; IG's cousin), xx, 307, 358, 380, 389
Nehru, Arun, 389
Nehru, Balwant Kumar ('Ballo'; son of Brijlal Nehru), xx, 134, 291, 329, 331, 339, 346
Nehru, Braj Kumar ('Bijju'; 'Bijju Bhai'; son of Brijlal Nehru), xx, 93, 131, 483, 513, 648, 655, 659
Nehru, Brijlal ('Bijju Chacha'; 'Birju Chacha'; 'Birju Bhai'; Motilal Nehru's nephew), xx, 8, 100, 136, 200, 242, 367, 485, 494, 496, 497, 501, 503, 516, 535
Nehru, Jawaharlal: accident in Amritsar, 4–5, 9, 22; tours U.P., 6–8; and All India Women's Congress, 9, 11; feelings of purposelessness of, 10, 12; and Kamala Nehru Memorial Hospital, 11, 93, 283–4; in Bombay, 17, 53–4, 56–7; sends books to IG, 21, 24, 125, 159–60, 173, 193, 216, 338; health of, 23, 207, 209–10, 444, 448, 505–6; and independence resolution, 26; plans to start writing, 26, 113, 116, 348, 375; and separation from IG, 34–5, 74; and Maulana, 35–6, 149, 152–3, 166, 175, 184, 196; at Ramgarh Congress, 39–41, 44–5, 46; tours India, 45–5, 522–6, 581–3; at camp, 48, 50–1; and IG's convalescence, 48–50, 55–6, 82, 99; liking for

Nehru, Jawaharlal – *contd*
    mangoes, 54, 230–1, 502; and
    German advance in Europe, 60,
    62, 65; and Mahatma Gandhi,
    60, 134, 370; in Kashmir (1940)
    62, 63–5; and Aundh, 69; and
    Civil Disobedience, 71, 101; and
    bombing of Chungking, 74, 89;
    in Dehra Dun Prison (1940–1),
    81–129, release, 129n; and
    China, 90, 149, 265–6, 286–7,
    308–9; advises IG, 97–9, 100,
    105–6, 438–40; and prison
    interviews, 99, 121, 125–6, 424,
    453; and censorship restrictions,
    101, 147, 153, 187, 199, 265,
    273, 285; and life with Kamala
    Nehru, 103, 104, and Motilal
    Nehru, 103–4, 287; and IG's
    health, 113, 154, 168, 207, 209,
    215, 220–1, 295, 334, 342–4;
    spinning, 126, 224–5, 229, 292;
    and IG's wedding, 129–30; and
    Quit India Resolution, 141; in
    Ahmadnagar Prison (1942–4),
    141–468; on prison life, 149–50,
    166, 207, 221–2, 247–8, 266,
    341, 407, 453–4; and Urdu
    poetry, 152, 225, 256, 270;
    concern about IG in Naini
    Prison, 154–5, 168; on prison
    food, 194; magazine
    subscriptions for, 237, 387,
    463–4; and Bengal relief, 323,
    325–6; and death of Ranjit
    Pandit, 331, 334; and IG's first
    pregnancy, 349–50, 385–6, 392,
    407; and Eve Curie, 387, 400;
    absentmindedness of, 392–3; and
    birth of first grandson, 415–19;
    concern for Rajiv, 427, 431–2,
    437–8, 459, 474, 488, 497, 574;
    and Frank Thompson, 427–8,
    460–2; and Kamala Nehru
    Scholarship, 435–6; and prison
    transfer, 452–3, 467–8, 470–1,
    472–3; in Bareilly Prison (1945),
    470–503; and end of WWII,
    482–3; in Almora Prison (1945),
    504–7; release of, 507; at Simla
    Conference, 511–16; in Lahore,
    517–18; in Penang, 527–8; and

    British Cabinet Mission, 530–2;
    in Kashmir (1946), 532–5; and
    Bihar riots, 540–1; in Cairo, 543;
    becomes India's first Prime
    Minister, 547; residence of,
    549n; at Commonwealth
    Conference, London (1948),
    559–60; in Paris, 560–1; at
    Commonwealth Conference,
    London (1949), 563n, 564; and
    *National Herald*, 569; and
    prospects of border war, 576; on
    military exercises, 580–1; and
    Sheikh Saheb, 594, 596; and
    Ramakrishna, 601–2; at
    Commonwealth Conference,
    London (1955), 608–9; and
    Orissa, 613–14; and IG's
    electioneering, 616–17; on tour
    of Europe (1957), 620–1; at
    Commonwealth Conference,
    London (1957), 621–2; in
    London (1960), 628; and
    proposed visit to Ladakh, 631–3;
    at UN General Assembly (1960),
    641–4; and inter-State agitation,
    656–7; at Commonwealth
    Conference, London (1961),
    661–2; declining health of,
    667–8, 672–3; death of, 675
    reading of: 22, 24, 90, 109–10, 117,
    122, 125, 148, 152, 157–60, 167,
    173, 183, 187, 199, 206, 216,
    254, 261, 265, 293, 296, 304–5,
    312, 339–40, 350–1, 344,
    399–401, 433–4, 449, 475, 477,
    481; on Begam Samroo, 200–2;
    on birdwatching, 200, 232–3,
    276–7, 351; on censorship,
    101–2; on childrearing, 378–80;
    on depression, 249–50, 260; on
    drama, 293–4; on education,
    375–6; on gaining weight, 21–2,
    233; on gardening, 151, 155–6,
    182–3, 208, 232, 265, 335–6,
    397, 401–2; on harmonious
    living, 286–7; on illness, 9; on
    Indian countryside, 124–5, 216;
    on Indian culture, 121–3, 166,
    256, 325; on Indian history,
    255–6, 340; on Kashmir, 13–14,
    50, 62, 65, 82, 224, 342, 452,

489, 496; on *khadi*, 127–8, 276, 339; on language, 347; on letterwriting, 100–1, 457; on pain, 195; on public meetings, 518; on the *Samvat* Calendar, 173–5, 183–4; on science, 58; on shoes and *chappals*, 236; on solar eclipses, 396–7, 404; on sorrow, 336–8; on time, 324–5; on travelling in India, 486–7; on writing, 102–3, 116; on Yogic exercises, 151–2, 367

WORKS: *Autobiography*, 102–3, 220, 295, 412; US edition, 70, 412; truthfulness of, 102; Marathi edition, 348, 354, 361; Malayalam edition, 355, 374; Hebrew edition, 403, 413, 419–20; extracts reprinted from, 409, 411–12

*The Discovery of India*, 46n, 526n, 531

*Glimpses of World History*, 15, 18, 21, 22, 103, 294, 413, 436; Urdu translation of, 97; US edition, 175, 196; Tamil edition, 300, 309, 319; Urdu edition, 322; Marathi edition, 348, 354–5, 361, 365, 374n; Malayalam edition, 355, 374; extract reprinted from, 436

*India and the World*, 430, 431

*Letters from a Father to his Daughter*: Assamese edition, 319, 321–2, 355, 374; Urdu and Hindi translations of, 322; scholarship fund from sales of, 322, 403; Malayalam edition, 355; sole agency of, 441–2

*The Unity of India*, 90, 118, 128, 225, 240, 241; US edition, 237, 315

Nehru, Kamala (*née* Kaul; 'Mummie'; JN's wife and IG's mother), xix, 314, 348, 447; political activities of, 17n; JN's memories of, 64, 103–4, 105, 156, 362, 439; JN requests photographs of, 228, 231, 257, 269; Scholarship Endowment Trust Fund, 435–6; proposed statue of, 446; *see also* Kamala Nehru Memorial Hospital

Nehru, Kishenlal ('Kishen Chacha'; IG's uncle), 214, 327–8, 477, 504

Nehru, Manoharlal, 446, 458

Nehru, Mohanlal (JN's cousin), 239, 242, 330, 446

Nehru, Motilal ('Dadu'; JN's father), xix, 277, 352, 358, 362, 451, 481, 495; JN's memories of, 64, 336, 439; death of, 97, 103, 104, 352; health, 181; care of servants, 282; and *National Herald*, 283n; influence on JN, 287; portrait of, 616; influence on IG, 627

Nehru, R. K., 528

Nehru, Raj Dulari ('Raj Chachi'), xxi, 333

Nehru, Rajan (Ratan Kumar Nehru's wife), xxi, 134, 226, 231, 328, 330, 333, 367, 390, 530, 628

Nehru, Rameshwari ('Bijju Chachi'; Brijlal Nehru's wife), xx, 220, 329, 331, 346, 446, 456, 500, 513

Nehru, Shivrajvati ('Shona Chachi'; Kishenlal Nehru's wife), xxii, 189, 214, 227

Nehru, Shobha ('Fory'; Braj Kumar Nehru's wife), xx, 93, 483, 494, 648

Nehru, Shri Shridhara ('Shridhar Chacha'; JN's cousin), xvii, 189, 649

Nehru, Swarup (*née* Razdan), 291, 414, 500

Nehru, Swarup Rani ('Dol Amma'; JN's mother), xix, 103–4, 488, 419, 457, 495, 534

Nehru, Uma, xxi, 302, 307, 333

Neill, A. S., 373, 381

Neogi, Nagendra Nath, 319, 322

New Mexico, IG visits, 647, 648

*New Statesman*, 128, 237

New York: JN visits, 641–4; IG visits, 647–8

Nichols, Beverley, 360, 475

Nikhilanandji, Swami, 441

'Nikku Bhai' *see* Kathju, Kanwarlal

Nilima (writer/publisher), 445–6, 526

Niloufer, Princess, 519

Nishtar, Sardar Abdur Rab, 541

Noakhali, 540

'Nora' *see* Banerji, Purnima

Norman, Dorothy, 643, 674

North West Frontier Province, 135, 521
Norway: in WWII, 59, 217, 600; IG's
    liking for, 595
'Nurie' *see* Captain, Nargis
Nyerere, Julius, 671

Oberoi, Vimala, 280
O'Neill, Eugene, 345
Orissa, 613
Ornsholt, Anna (governess), 96, 271,
    289, 290, 300, 323; and IG's first
    pregnancy, 392, 402, 466; helps
    with Rajiv, 422, 462; in Kashmir
    with IG and Rajiv, 466, 485, 491,
    494; IG leaves Rajiv with, 512,
    516; in Gulmarg, 519, 521
Oslo, JN visits, 620, 621
Oxford: University Union, JN visits,
    661; *see also* Somerville College

'Padmaja' *see* Naidu, Padmaja
Pahalgam, 65, 137, 496; IG visits,
    500, 503–4, 514, 517, 575, 576
Pakistan: and Kashmir, 552, 556, 558,
    674; and Bengal, 657, 659
'Pan' *see* Narielwala, P. N.
Panchgani, IG visits, 219, 234,
    239–40, 243, 245
Pande, Badri Dat, 440
Pandit, Pratap, 297, 327, 330, 333
Pandit, Ranjit Sitaram ('Pupha'; Vijaya
    Lakshmi Pandit's husband), xxi,
    46, 51, 83, 582; at Ramgarh
    Congress, 46; in prison, 94, 96,
    97, 106, 122–3, 155, 156, 161,
    162, 189, 210; works translated
    by, 94, 122, 123, 290, 295;
    gardening expertise of, 155, 162,
    276; health, 161, 223, 230, 237,
    290, 294, 304, 310, 317, 318;
    seriously ill, 326–7, 330, 383;
    death, 331, 333; JN's sorrow at
    loss of, 333–4
Pandit, Saraswati Bai, 297
Pandit, Vijaya Lakshmi (*née* Sarup
    Nehru; 'Nan'; 'Puphi'; 'Bari
    Puphi'; JN's sister), xx–xxi, 6, 83,
    110, 136, 141, 224, 246, 327;
    ageing of, 9; wedding, 25; at
    Ramgarh Congress, 46; at JN's
    trial, 77; arrest of, 87; prison
    visits of, 96, 97, 126, 424; JN's

memories of, 104; at Anand
    Bhawan, 136, 166, 167, 172, 175,
    203; in prison, 147, 155, 161,
    163, 184, 187, 192, 207, 210,
    211, 212, 213; prison
    communications with JN, 167–9,
    172–3, 175, 198, 204, 231, 237,
    294, 299, 392, 424; on parole,
    171, 175; prison release, 203n,
    204; in Poona, 224, 368, 383;
    birthday presents from JN, 247,
    252, 253, 396, 404, 410; in
    Calcutta, 267, 270, 290; family
    moves from Anand Bhawan,
    280–1, 285–6, 289, 290, 291,
    395; husband's final illness and
    death, 326, 330, 331, 333; and
    Mahatma Gandhi's release, 368,
    369, 371, 383; JN receives gifts
    from, 397, 407, 430, 477; and
    daughter Rita's appendectomy,
    403, 406, 409; and Rajiv, 414,
    416, 417, 418, 493; visits USA,
    424, 428, 429, 443, 456, 457,
    463, 477, 478, 480, 490; author
    of *Prison Days*, 498, 506; as
    government minister, 524n, 529,
    549, 550, 559, 595; health, 577,
    665; and Rita's engagement, 580;
    as High Commissioner in
    London, 661, 663, 664, 665
Pandit, Saraswatibai, 327, 330, 333
Panikkar, K. M., 652
Pant, Apasaheb, 69n, 368
Pant, Balasaheb, 69
Pant, Govind Ballabh ('Pantji'), xxviii,
    xxix, 137, 438, 440, 443, 450; in
    prison with JN, 175, 405, 415,
    444, 469, 627; health, 452, 613,
    625, 632; release of, 471, 476; at
    Simla Conference, 512; as Chief
    Minister, U.P., 566, 567, 618,
    627, 656; death of, 660, 661
Pant, Pitamber, 524
'Papi' *see* Naidu, Leilamani
Paris: fall of, 67, 74; JN visits, 238n,
    560–1, 610; IG visits, 605–6,
    649–53
Parliament, Indian, 586, 629, 648,
    659; Public Accounts Committee
    (PAC), 638
Parmar, Dr Chandravati, 573

Parmar, Dr Y. S., 601, 604
Pasha, Ismail Sidqi, 543
Pasha, Mustafa Nahas, 543
Patel, Dahyabhai V., 567
Patel, Sardar Vallabhbhai, xvii, xxviii, xxix, 134, 555
Pathak, Radhey Shyam, 474
Pathshala, Kayastha, 129
Patil, S. K., 668
Patna, Working Committee in, 24, 26-7
Peattie, I. D. C.: *Flowering Earth*, 53, 57
Penang, JN visits, 527-8
Peshawar, 63, 135
Peston, Kuverji, 519
Pétain, Henri Philippe, 68
Pethick-Lawrence, Lord, 529n
Pillai, M. Krishna, 355
Pillai, N. R., 629
Plato, 109, 148, 153, 158, 259, 344
Poland, in WWII, 483
Pondicherry, 601, 605-6
Poona: Pupils' Own School, 34, 56n; A.I.C.C. in, 70; IG visits, 223-4, 226-30, 390, 394; International Book Company, 350, 388, 409
Pooviah, Rohini (Kathak dancer), 272
Portugal, 68, 80
Prabhavati Devi, 218
Prague, 266
Praja Socialist Party (P.S.P.), 617
Prasad, Dwarka, 432
Prasad, Rajendra, xxviii, 405, 406
Pratima Devi, 385
Proust, Marcel, 148
Provisional Nationalist Government *see* Executive Council
'Psyche' *see* Captain, Goshiben
Punjab: crowd behaviour, 4; standard of living in, 7; IG electioneering in, 616; Akali agitation in, 656
Purandare, Dr N. A. (Bombay), 346, 350, 372, 384, 385, 386, 392

Quit India movement, xiii-xiv, xxv, 136n, 143n, 157n, 212n, 369n; Resolution adopted, 141, 147
Qureshi, Shuaib, 130-1

Radhakrishnan, Dr S., 352, 538, 629, 644, 649, 650
'Rafi' *see* Kidwai, Rafi Ahmed

Raghavan, N., 650, 653
Rai, Lala Lajpat, 615
Raina, Ganga *see* Atal, Ganga
Raina, Raja Narendranath, 22n
Raipur, 1960 Congress at, 60
'Raja' *see* Hutheesing, G. P.
'Rajan Didda' *see* Nehru, Rajan
Rajputana, 320
Rajputs, 314, 340
Rajwade, Rani G. Laxmibai, 10
Rallia Ram, Lajwanti *see* Yunus, Lajwanti Rallia Ram
Ram Lall, Diwan, 242, 451, 452, 484, 491
Ramakrishna, Dr, 601-2, 604
Ramgarh, xiii; A.I.C.C. at, 23, 27, 35n, 38, 39-40, 44, 45, 47
Rana, Maharaja Juddha Shamsher Jang Bahadur, 571
Rao, Kitty Shiva, 191, 328, 485, 519, 520
Rao, Col. M. S., 672
Rashtriya Swayamsewak Sangh (R.S.S.), 548-9, 552n
Rau, M. Chalapathi, 409, 411-12
Razdan, Swarup *see* Nehru, Swarup
*Reader's Digest*, 211, 387; article on JN in, 15
Republican Union Party (R.U.P.), 15
Rita *see* Dar, Rita
Robeson, Essie, 282, 289, 445, 446
Robeson, Paul, 282n, 669
Roche, Dr Hilary (Montana), 14, 44, 50
Rockefeller, John D., 643, 648
Rohatgi, Dr Jawaharlal, 519
Rolland, Madeleine, 314
Rollier, Dr Auguste: and IG's illness, 3, 4, 8, 15-16, 18, 19, 21, 29, 42, 48, 49, 52, 55, 56, 61, 68, 79, 118; theories of, 11, 38
Roosevelt, Eleanor, 674
Roosevelt, Franklin D., 643
Roy, Dr Bidhan Chandra (Calcutta), xxiv: and IG's convalescence, 113, 114, 115, 117, 118, 119, 132, 526, 527; JN praises, 342
Rozario, Dr, 662, 663, 664, 665, 667
Rural Uplift (rural improvement programme), 549
Russell, Bertrand, 379
Russo-German Pact, 31

St Laurent, Louis Stephen, 585, 609
Sachar, Bhimsen, 604
Sachdev, M. R., 620
Saha, Prof. Meghnad, 322, 456
Sahai, Raghupati, 129
Sahgal, Man Mohini (*née* Zutshi; 'Manno Didda'; IG's cousin), xxii, 211, 218
Sahgal, Nayantara (*née* Pandit; 'Tara'), xxi, 6; at Anand Bhawan, 11, 25, 90, 141–2; at school, 83; JN writes to, 155, 332, 334, 477; plans to study in USA, 191–2, 198, 204; departure, 205, 211; in USA, 274, 278, 480, 673; JN sent photo of, 388; with JN in New Delhi, 550, 649, 651; with JN in London, 560
Saiyidain, K. G., 570, 604
Salam, Amtus, 657
Samant, Dr Vatsala, xxxiii, 217, 227, 330; gives medical advice to IG, 203, 210, 219, 220, 295, 326, 346; as Medical Superintendent of Kamala Nehru Memorial Hospital, 272, 297, 319, 434, 437, 450; engagement of, 319; wedding of, 323; has baby, 405, 420
Sampurnanand, U. P., 536, 646, 656
Samroo, Begam, 185, 200, 201–2, 213
*Samvat* era, 173–4, 183, 463
Sanskrit, 116, 325; JN's interest in, 166, 175, 183
Santiniketan, 34; Visva-Bharati University, 653–4, 659
Sapru, Anand, 318, 319, 324, 328
Sapru, Savitri, 329, 346, 520
Sapru, Sir Tej Bahadur, 263, 264, 268, 319, 328, 352, 447, 496, 562
Sarabhai, Bharati, xxxiv, 218, 248, 254–5, 261, 267, 273, 485, 497, 507
Sarabhai, Mridula, xxiii, 355, 366, 391, 437, 468, 538, 600; at Anand Bhawan, 10; visits JN in prison, 115, 123, 126; JN praises, 232; health, 289, 318, 343, 391, 397; relief work of, 363–4; and birthday anthology for Mahatma

Gandhi, 409, 411–12, 413; social work of, 591, 603–4
Sarabhai, Mrinalini, xxxiv, 364, 485
Sarabhai, Saralaben, xxxiii, 289, 485
Sarabhai, Vikram, xxxiv, 364, 485
Sarala (prison baby), 161, 179, 187, 188, 215
Saran, Raghunandan ('Nandan'), xxxiv, 108, 483, 500; visits JN in prison, 123, 125, 126; illness of, 386, 391–2, 456
Saran, Raksha, xxxiv, 123, 456, 483, 500
Saran, Ram, 108, 127
Saraswati (goddess of learning), 103
Sardar, the *see* Patel, Sardar Vallabhbhai
Schmidt, Dr (Les Frênes), 3
Sen, Boshi, 440, 578, 649
Sen, Gertrude Emerson, 440
Sen, Hannah, 485
Senanayake, Dudley (Shelton), 585
Seshan, N. K., 630
Setalvad, Motilal, 503
Seth, Padma (*née* Nehru; IG's second cousin), xxii, 328
Sethna, Janaki, 301n
Sevagram, 76; Mahatma Gandhi's ashram at, 162n
Shah, K. T., 128
Shah, R. D., 355, 365
'Shammie Didda' *see* Khan, Shyam Kumari
Shastri, Lal Bahadur, xxviii, 617, 656, 660, 662, 672, 675
Shaw, Bernard, 176, 182, 184–5, 195
Sheikh Saheb *see* Abdullah, Sheikh Muhammad
Shen Shih-hua, Mr and Mrs, 398, 403
Sheorey, Col. (medical consultant), 663
Shergil, Amrita (Indian painter), 305–6
Shih Nai-an: *All Men are Brothers*, 152
Shirodkar, Dr V. N. (Bombay), 385, 386, 392, 395
'Shona Chachi' *see* Nehru, Shivrajavati
Shrimali, Dr Kalu Lal, 626, 649, 650, 651
Shrinivasrao, Bhavanrao *see* Pant, Balasaheb

Shukla, Chandrashanker, 430, 436
Shurga, Janki Nath, xxii, 575
Simla, 320, 443; Conference (1945),
    511–16; after independence,
    552; IG and family in, 607
Sinclair, Upton, 199
Sing Sing Prison (New York), 182
Singh, Raja Bajrang Bahadur, 668
Singh, C. P. N., 500, 612
Singh, Chandra, 227, 235, 432
Singh, Dalip, 533
Singh, Maharaja Hari, 495, 534, 535,
    555
Singh, Dr Karan, xxxii, 549n, 639
Singh, Lady Maharaj, 42, 43, 44, 494
Singh, Maharaja Pratap, 495
Singh, Choudhari Ranbir, 616
Singh, Sant Fateh, 656
Singh, Sardar Swaran, 615
Singh, Maj.-Gen. Yadunath, 619
Sino-Japanese war, 74n
Smith, Vincent: Early History of India,
    122
Somerville College, Oxford, IG at, xi,
    43, 44, 49, 279
Sorensen, Lord Reginald William,
    371
Soviet Union: Russo-German Pact,
    31; in WWII, 31–2, 37; JN's
    interest in, 308–9; JN compares
    India with, 480; IG visits, 590–4;
    JN visits, 670
Spain, 15, 32, 80
Spanish Civil War, 15n, 74n
Spender, Stephen, 28
Sri Prakasa, xxxiv, 262, 409, 413, 646
Srinagar: JN visits, 64, 65, 574; IG
    and Feroze visit, 134, 135–6,
    139; climate of, 479; IG takes
    Rajiv to, 484–504, 551–8,
    574–5, 633–41; refugee camps
    in, 558
Srinagesh, Gen. S. M. and Mrs,
    571–2
Stalin, Joseph, 37, 458, 552n, 626
States of the Indian Union, 614n
States' Peoples' Conference, 17, 539
Stimpson, Kay, 77
Stinnes, Mr and Mrs, 19–20, 25, 193
Subbaroyan, Dr P., 128, 129
Sufi mystics, 277
Suhrawardy, H. S., 74, 622

Sukarno, Achmad, 643
Sun Yat-sen, Mme, 90, 352
Sundaram, C. R. ('Chinnibhai'), 402,
    423
Suyin, Han: Autobiography, 265–6
Swaraj Bhawan (Freedom House),
    xxiii, 13, 283, 290, 299, 311, 354,
    419, 426
Sweden, JN visits, 621
Switzerland: IG convalesces in, 3–79;
    IG plans to leave, 79–84

Taba Tabai, Haider Ali Nazm (Urdu
    poet), 190, 206
Tagore, Rabindranath ('Gurudev'),
    xxviii–xxix, 51, 90, 162, 178, 364,
    385, 481, 525, 616
Tagore, Soumyendranath, 430
Tagore Town house, 168, 177, 191,
    194
Tai Hsu, Abbot, 12
Tandon, Purushottam Das, 244,
    565n, 567
Tankha, Pushkar Nath, 107
'Tara' see Sahgal, Nayantara
Tarachand, Dr, 352
Taraporevalas (Bombay booksellers),
    318
Tendulkar, D. G., 218, 222, 227, 230,
    409, 411–12, 413
Tenzing, Sherpa, 592
Thadani, A. B., 578
Thimayya, Gen. K. S., 553, 640
Thompson, Edward, xxxiv, 90, 92,
    128; sends books to JN, 158, 289,
    316–17, 427; The Making of the
    Indian Princes, 310, 316; illness
    and recovery of, 427, 499–500,
    507; birthday tribute to JN, 428
Thompson, Frank, 427, 460–2
Thurber, James, 10, 14
Thussu, Ammaji, 111
Tibet, 625; JN visits, 631, 632
'Tikki' see Kaul, T. N.
Time magazine, 10, 100, 450, 475
Times Book Club, 237, 262–3, 274
Tod, Col. James: Annals and
    Antiquities of Rajasthan, 339–40
Toller, Ernst, 110, 267, 273, 356
Travancore, 595
Trinity College, Cambridge, 664, 665,
    668

Tulsi Das (medieval Hindi poet), 255
Turkey, 629, 630
Twain, Mark, 231
Tyabji, Badr-ud-din, xxxiv, 652, 658
Tyabji, Raihana, 369

Uday Shankar Company (dance group), 8n, 139
U Nu (Burmese Prime Minister), 648, 649
UNESCO, 602, 672; IG elected to Executive Board, 649–50, 651, 652, 654, 665, 672; Plenary Session (1960), 655, 659
United Nations (UN), 560, 561, 589, 594, 595, 655, 674; General Assembly on Peace and Disarmament (1960), 641–4
United Provinces (U.P.): JN tours, 6–7; political situation in, 71; prison regulations in, 154, 165, 168–9, 171, 173, 191, 198, 214; hand-made paper from, 297; Education Department of, 322, 403; Legislative Assembly, 598n
USA (United States of America): JN's interest in, 308–9; Committee for Economic Development, 466; JN compares India with, 480; JN visits, 641–4; Presidential election (1960), 645, 647; IG visits, 647–8, 651
Upadhyaya, Martand, 368
Upadhyaya, Mrs, 406
Upadhyaya, S. D. (JN's Personal Secretary), xxxiv, 56, 77, 83, 100, 126, 128, 177, 412, 413, 432, 440, 449, 471, 476, 478, 539, 541; and IG's convalescence, 107, 110, 111, 113; family of, 119, 127, 235, 276, 406; in prison, 227, 290, 372; following release, 426
Urdu language: JN's interest in, 121, 125, 149, 152, 159, 166, 171, 225, 231–2, 270; history of, 255–6
Usmani, Hammad, 617

Vaisakhi Purnima (Buddhist New Year's Day), 496

Vakil, Coonverbai, xxxiv, 56, 136, 138–9, 219, 234, 273, 354, 358, 359, 422, 426, 429, 600
Vakil, Ira, 364
Vakil, Jehangir Jivaji, xxxiv, 56, 136, 138–9, 219, 273, 358, 368, 426
Van Passen, Pierre, 22
Vanchoo, Rup (née Nehru), 330
Vasanta Panchami (spring festival), 13, 91, 93, 186, 332, 443–4, 457
Vatal, Hira, 329
Verma, Vimla, 147, 184, 192, 194
Vesugar, Pilloo, 228
'Vidya' see Dutt, Vidyavati
Village Service Organisation (India), 598
Vira, Dharam, 584, 589
Vishakadatta: Mudrarakshasa, 123 and n
Vivekananda, Swami: Lectures and Letters, 481
Voltaire, 299, 499
Vyas, Brij Mohan, 319, 329
Vyshinsky, Andrei, 561

Wadia, Sophia, 409
Wall, W. G. P., 435, 446
Walsh, Richard (US publisher), 222, 236–7, 243, 315, 372, 387, 412, 464
Wang, Shelley, 271, 276
Wardha: Working Committee at, 9, 11, 66, 70, 71, 72; A.I.C.C. at, 132
Watal, Avtar Krishna, 484, 490, 491, 500, 501, 503
Watal, Shama, 501
Wavell, Lady, 515
Wavell, Lord (formerly Sir Archibald), 312, 530, 540, 547
Wazir, Khwaja Mohammed, 225–6
Webb, Beatrice and Sydney, 195; Soviet Communism, 206
Welles, Sumner, 246
Wells, H. G., 156, 196, 318, 376
Wilde, Oscar, 413
Willingdon, Lady, 135, 367
Willkie, Wendell: One World, 351
Windsor Castle, 622
Woodstock School (Mussoorie), 83, 191, 430
Woolf, Virginia, 194, 261, 267

World War II, 31; build-up to, 37, 54; German advance in Europe, 58, 59, 60, 65, 67–8; reaches India, 130, 131; ends in Europe, 482–3, 484

Yale, Elihu, 648
Yeats, W. B., 260, 335, 350
Yeravada Prison, 175, 346
Yunus, Lajwanti Rallia Ram, 429, 458, 484, 485, 490, 491, 493, 503
Yunus, Mohammad, xxxiv; JN stays with, 63; TB and recovery from, 167, 169, 177, 261; detention of, 171, 198, 261, 458, 463, 533; engagement of, 429, 458; wedding of, 477, 479, 484; in

Kashmir, 139, 485, 490, 493, 500, 503, 504, 507, 516; political activities of, 513, 521–2, 532

Zauq, Muhammad Ibrahim, 344–5
Zoshchenko, Mikhail, 95
Zurich, IG visits, 596–7
Zutshi, Janak, 90, 333
Zutshi, Ladli Prasad ('Ladlibhai'; 'Ladli Chacha'; IG's uncle), xxii, 218–19, 258, 333, 447; acts as family adviser, 97, 98, 149, 214, 232, 264, 271, 279, 283, 299, 372, 458
Zutshi, Lado Rani ('Lado Bhabhi'; 'Lado Chachi'), 70, 211, 213, 458, 654